On Arbitration

At the International Arbitration Institute (IAI)
Forum in Dijon, September 2008

On Arbitration

V. V. Veeder QC, Selected Writings and Contributions to the Development of Law

Edited by
SAM WORDSWORTH KC
MARIE VEEDER

Great Clarendon Street, Oxford, OX2 6DP,
United Kingdom

Oxford University Press is a department of the University of Oxford.
It furthers the University's objective of excellence in research, scholarship,
and education by publishing worldwide. Oxford is a registered trade mark of
Oxford University Press in the UK and in certain other countries

© Oxford University Press 2023

The moral rights of the authors have been asserted

First Edition published in 2023

All rights reserved. No part of this publication may be reproduced, stored in
a retrieval system, or transmitted, in any form or by any means, without the
prior permission in writing of Oxford University Press, or as expressly permitted
by law, by licence or under terms agreed with the appropriate reprographics
rights organization. Enquiries concerning reproduction outside the scope of the
above should be sent to the Rights Department, Oxford University Press, at the
address above

You must not circulate this work in any other form
and you must impose this same condition on any acquirer

Public sector information reproduced under Open Government Licence v3.0
(http://www.nationalarchives.gov.uk/doc/open-government-licence/open-government-licence.htm)

Published in the United States of America by Oxford University Press
198 Madison Avenue, New York, NY 10016, United States of America

British Library Cataloguing in Publication Data
Data available

Library of Congress Control Number: 2023932539

ISBN 978-0-19-286913-5

DOI: 10.1093/oso/9780192869135.001.0001

Printed and bound by
CPI Group (UK) Ltd, Croydon, CR0 4YY

Links to third party websites are provided by Oxford in good faith and
for information only. Oxford disclaims any responsibility for the materials
contained in any third party website referenced in this work.

To Anne

Contents

List of Illustrations	xi
Table of Cases	xiii
Table of Treaties, Legislation and Rules	xxv
Introduction	xxxv
Judge Stephen M. Schwebel	

I. LEARNING FROM THE PAST

Introduction to Part I	1

1. The Historical Keystone to International Arbitration: The Party-Appointed Arbitrator—from Miami to Geneva, *Proceedings of the ASIL Annual Meeting*, Volume 107   7

2. Investor–State Disputes and the Development of International Law: Arbitral Lessons from the Private Correspondence of Queen Victoria and Lenin, 98 *Proceedings of the ASIL Annual Meeting*   33

3. Inter-State Arbitration, *Oxford Handbook on International Arbitration*, eds. Schultz and Ortino   39

4. 1922: The Birth of the ICC Arbitration Clause and the Demise of the Anglo-Soviet Urquhart Concession, *Commerce and Dispute Resolution: Liber Amicorum in Honour of Robert Briner*, eds. Aksen and Briner   56

5. The 1921–1923 North Sakhalin Concession Agreement: The 1925 Court Decisions between the US Company Sinclair Exploration and the Soviet Government, *Arbitration International*, Volume 18, Issue 2   74

6. Lloyd George, Lenin and Cannibals: The Harriman Arbitration, *Arbitration Insights: Twenty Years of the Annual Lecture of the School of International Arbitration*, eds. Lew and Mistelis   96

7. The *Lena Goldfields* Arbitration: The Historical Roots of Three Ideas, 47 *International and Comparative Law Quarterly*, Volume 47, Issue 7   123

8. The Tetiuhe Mining Concession 1924–1932: A Swiss–Russian Story (Where the Arbitral Dog Did Not Bark), *Liber Amicorum Claude Reymond—Autour de l'arbitrage*   167

viii   CONTENTS

9. Two Arbitral Butterflies: Bramwell and David, *The Internationalization of International Arbitration: The LCIA Centenary Conference*, eds. Hunter, Marriott and Veeder   186

II. THE INTERNATIONAL ARBITRAL PROCESS

Introduction to Part II   197

10. The 'Y2K Problem' and Arbitration: The Answer to the Myth, *Arbitration International*, Volume 16, Issue 1   203

11. The 2001 Goff Lecture: The Lawyer's Duty to Arbitrate in Good Faith, *Arbitration and Oral Evidence*, eds. Lévy and Veeder   204

12. The Natural Limits to the Truncated Tribunal: The German Case of the Soviet Eggs and the Dutch Abduction of the Indonesian Arbitrator, *Law of International Business and Dispute Settlement in the 21st Century: Liber Amicorum Karl-Heinz Bockstiegel*   226

13. Issue Estoppel, Reasons for Awards and Transnational Arbitration, *Complex Arbitrations (ICC Pub. No. 688E)*   238

14. The Need for Cross-border Enforcement of Interim Measures Ordered by a State Court in Support of the International Arbitral Process, *New Horizons in International Commercial Arbitration and Beyond* , ed. Van den Berg   247

15. The Transparency of International Arbitration: Process and Substance, *Pervasive Problems in International Arbitration*, eds. Mistelis and Lew   278

16. Free Spirits—the Search for "International" Arbitration, *Liber Amicorum en l'honneur de Serge Lazareff*, eds. Lévy and Derains   290

17. The Role of Users, *Players Interaction in International Arbitration*, ed. Hanotiau and Mourre   299

18. From Florence to London via Moscow and New Delhi: How and Why Arbitral Ideas Migrate, *Journal of International Dispute Settlement*, Volume 4, Issue 1   306

19. Jurisdiction, Admissibility and Choice of Law in International Arbitration, *Jurisdiction, Admissibility and Choice of Law in International Arbitration: Liber Amicorum Michael Pryles*, eds. Kaplan and Moser   327

CONTENTS ix

III. KEY QUESTIONS FOR ALL USERS OF INTERNATIONAL ARBITRATION

Introduction to Part III	339

20. Whose Arbitration Is It Anyway—The Parties' or the Arbitration Tribunal's? *The Leading Arbitrators' Guide to International Arbitration*, eds. Newman and Hill — 345

21. Is There Any Need for a Code of Ethics for International Commercial Arbitrators? *Les Arbitres Internationaux, Colloque du 4 février 2005* — 360

22. Still More on Arbitral Deliberations: An English Perspective, *Mélanges en l'honneur de François Knoepfler* — 366

23. Why Bother and Why It Matters? Presented to the Institute for Transnational Arbitration—Dallas June 2006, *World Arbitration & Mediation Review*, Volume 7, Issue 1 — 380

24. The Importance of a Party Treating as Independent Its Independent Arbitrator, *Investor-State Arbitration—Lessons for Asia*, ed. Moser — 387

25. Is there a Need to Revise the New York Convention?, 1 *Journal of International Dispute Settlement*, Volume 1, Issue 2 — 394

26. Who Are the Arbitrators?, *Legitimacy: Myths, Realities, Challenges*, ed. Van den Berg — 402

27. Arbitrators and Arbitral Institutions: Legal Risks for Product Liability?, *American University Business Law Review*, Volume 5, Issue 3 — 412

28. The Alexander Lecture 2015, London 26 November 2015: 'What Matters—about Arbitration', *Arbitration: The International Journal of Arbitration, Mediation and Dispute Management*, ed. O'Reilly — 430

29. Lessons for the Future from the Past: Individual Hedgehogs and Institutional Foxes (Tenth Kaplan Lecture, 23 November 2016), *International Arbitration: Issues, Perspectives and Practice: Liber Amicorum Neil Kaplan* — 442

Postscript: Johnny Veeder as Teacher, Mentor, Colleague, and Friend — 455

Appendix I: Selected Extracts from Certain Key Arbitral Awards (in Cases Where Johnny Veeder Was the Presiding Arbitrator) — 465

Appendix II: Excerpts from Lectures given by Johnny Veeder to LLM Students at King's College London (in the Period 2017–2019)[1] — 485

Index — 507

---

[1] Johnny Veeder, Visiting Professor on Investment Arbitration at King's College London for almost twenty years, gave a series of ten two-hour lectures to the LLM class on investor–State arbitration.

List of Illustrations

At the International Arbitration Institute (IAI) Forum in Dijon, September 2008

V. V. Veeder interviewing V. I. Lenin about the reasons for rejection of Urquhart's concession, Gorki, USSR, September 1922 (private archive). Donated to V. V. Veeder by an arbitral colleague, 2003

Before Mass Grave Number 1 at the Donskoy Cemetery in Moscow, 1996. The following text is carved on the stone: *Here lie buried the remains of the innocent tortured and executed victims of the political repression of 1930–1942. May they never be forgotten*

At Jesus College, Cambridge, 2016

Seeking a view of Mount Everest from Dhulikhel, Nepal before an extended visit to Tibet, 1995

V. V. Veeder pictured at the 2005 Chambers Bar Awards

Addressing the International Arbitration Institute Forum, Château du Clos de Vougeot, Dijon, France, 2008

With his beloved daughter, Anne, 2001

At Château de Millemont, France, 2009

Relaxing at his summer home in Manchester-by-the-Sea, 2013

Onboard *Hurricane*, 2012

Table of Cases

INTERNATIONAL AND REGIONAL COURTS AND TRIBUNALS

Court of Justice of the European Union

Allianz SpA (formerly Riunione Adriatica di Sicurta SpA) v West Tankers Inc
(C-185/07) ECLI:EU:C:2009:69, [2009] 1 AC 1138 . . . . 291, 293, 295–96, 297
Antonissen v Council of the European Union (C-393/96 P (R))
ECLI:EU:C:1997:42, [1997] ECR I-441 256
Asteris AE v Commission of the European Communities (C-97/86)
ECLI:EU:C:1988:199 478
CETA Investment Court System (Belgium), Re (Opinion 1/17) ECLI:EU:C:2019:341 . . .496
Commission of the European Communities v BASF (C-137/92 P)
ECLI:EU:C:1994:247 478
Commission of the European Communities v Ireland (C-459/03)
ECLI:EU:C:2006:345 . . . . .470, 495
Denilauler v SNC Couchet Frères (125/79) ECLI:EU:C:1980:130,
[1980] ECR 1553. . . . . 253–54, 259–60
Draft Agreement on the European and Community Patents Court, Re
(Opinion 1/09) ECLI:EU:C:2011:123 471
Eco Swiss China Time Ltd v Benetton International NV (C-126/97)
ECLI:EU:C:1999:269 . . . . .471, 496
Marc Rich & Co AG v Societa Italiana Impianti SpA (C-190/89)
19 February 1991 (AGO). 251–52
Marc Rich & Co AG v Societa Italiana Impianti SpA (C-190/89)
ECLI:EU:C:1991:319, [1991] ECR I-3855. 251–52
Mietz v Intership Yachting Sneek BV (C-99/96) ECLI:EU:C:1999:202,
[1999] ECR I-2277 . . . . .252, 259
Moldova v Komstroy LLC (C-741/19) ECLI:EU:C:2021:655 .496–97
Mox Plant case. *See* Commission of the European Communities v Ireland (C-459/03)
Opinion 1/09. *See* Draft Agreement on the European and Community Patents
Court, Re (Opinion 1/09)
Opinion 1/17. *See* CETA Investment Court System (Belgium), Re (Opinion 1/17)
Reichert v Dresdner Bank (C-261/90) ECLI:EU:C:1992:149,
[1992] ECR I-2149 . . . . 252, 253–54
Slovak Republic v Achmea BV (C-284/16) ECLI:EU:C:2018:158 . . . . 460, 469, 495–97
Textilwerke Deggendorg GmbH (TWD) v Commission of the European
Communities (C-355/95 P) ECLI:EU:C:1997:241. 478
Van Uden Maritime BV (t/a Van Uden Africa Line) v Kommanditgesellschaft in
Firma Deco-Line (C-391/95) [1998] ECR I 7105 (AGO) 252
Van Uden Maritime BV (t/a Van Uden Africa Line) v Kommanditgesellschaft
in Firma Deco-Line (C-391/95) ECLI:EU:C:1998:543,
[1998] ECR I-7091 . . . . .251–52, 253, 254–60, 276–77
West Tankers case. *See* Allianz SpA (formerly Riunione Adriatica di Sicurta SpA) v
West Tankers Inc (C-185/07)

xiv TABLE OF CASES

European Commission of Human Rights

Axen v Germany (B.57) 14 December 1981 279

European Court of Human Rights

Werner v Austria (21835/93) (1998) 26 EHRR 310 279

International Arbitration Cases

AAPL v Sri Lanka. *See* Asian Agricultural Products Ltd v Sri Lanka

Abaclat and others v Argentina, ICSID Case No ARB/07/5, Decision on
  Jurisdiction and Admissibility, 4 August 2011 493–94

Achmea BV (formerly Eureko BV) v Slovak Republic, UNCITRAL, PCA Case
  No 2008-13, Award on Jurisdiction, Arbitrability and Suspension,
  26 October 2010 .... 340, 456, 459–60, 469

Achmea BV (formerly Eureko BV) v Slovak Republic, UNCITRAL, PCA Case
  No 2008-13, Award, 7 December 2012 495–96

Alabama Claims Arbitration (United States v Great Britain), Declaration on
  Indirect Claims, 19 June 1872................................. 24–25, 29–30, 36

Alabama Claims Arbitration (United States v Great Britain), Award,
  14 September 1872.........xxxv, 12–14, 29, 34–35, 40, 377–78, 387, 389, 390–91, 392

Alaska Boundary case (Great Britain v United States), Award, 20 October 1903......12–13

Alemanni and others v Argentina, ICSID Case No ARB/07/8, Decision on
  Jurisdiction and Admissibility, 17 November 2014 494

Ambiente Ufficio SpA and others v Argentina, ICSID Case No ARB/08/9,
  Decision on Jurisdiction and Admissibility, 8 February 2013.................493–94

Apotex Holdings Inc and Apotex Inc v United States, ICSID Case No ARB(AF)/12/1,
  Award, 25 August 2014 ....xliv–xlv, 476–80

Arctic Sunrise Arbitration (Netherlands v Russia), PCA Case No 2014-02, Award,
  14 August 2015 51–52

Arif v Moldova, ICSID Case No ARB/11/23, Award, 8 April 2013...................482

Asian Agricultural Products Ltd v Sri Lanka, ICSID Case No ARB/87/3,
  Final Award, 27 June 1990...................................... 53, 387, 435–36

Azinian v Mexico, ICSID Case No ARB (AF)/97/2, Award, 1 November 1999 481

Azurix Corp v Argentina, ICSID Case No ARB/01/12, Award, 14 July 2006 473–74

Barbados v Trinidad and Tobago, PCA Case No 2004-02, Award, 11 April 2006......51–52

Bay of Bengal Maritime Boundary Arbitration (Bangladesh v India),
  PCA Case No 2010-16, Award, 7 July 2014....................................51–52

Betsey, The, Decision of Jay Treaty Commission, 1796 127–28

Chagos Marine Protected Area Arbitration (Mauritius v United Kingdom),
  PCA Case No 2011-03, Award, 18 March 2015................................51–52

Chevron Corp and Texaco Petroleum Corp v Ecuador (II), UNCITRAL,
  Decision on Track 1B, 12 March 2015 481

Chevron Corp and Texaco Petroleum Corp v Ecuador (II), UNCITRAL,
  Second Partial Award on Track II, 30 August 2018 ....xxxv, 340, 456, 481–83

Chlebprodukt v Internationale Warenaustausch AG, Award,
  29 April 1927...xliii–xliv, 231, 232–33

Claimants v Crédit Lyonnais and Société de Banque Occidentale, Award, 7 July 2008 438–39

CME Czech Republic BV v Czech Republic, UNCITRAL, Partial Award,
  13 September 2001...xlvii, 198, 473–74

Corn Products v Mexico, ICSID Case No ARB(AF)/04/01, Decision on
  Responsibility, 15 January 2008 54

TABLE OF CASES   XV

Croatia v Slovenia, PCA Case No 2012-04, Final Award, 29 June 2017 51
Delimitation of Maritime Boundary (Guyana v Suriname), PCA Case No 2004-04,
  Award, 17 September 2007 51–52
Delimitation of Maritime Boundary in the Bay of Bengal (Bangladesh v Myanmar),
  Award, 14 March 2012 51–52
Dispute Concerning Coastal State Rights in the Black Sea, Sea of Azov, and
  Kerch Strait (Ukraine v Russia), PCA Case No 2017-06, Award,
  21 February 2020 51–52
Duzgit Integrity Arbitration (Malta v São Tomé and Príncipe), PCA Case
  No 2014-07, Award, 5 September 2016 51–52
Electrabel SA v Hungary, ICSID Case No ARB/07/19, Decision on Jurisdiction,
  Applicable Law and Liability, 30 November 2012 . . . . 469–76, 495–96
Electrabel SA v Hungary, ICSID Case No ARB/07/19, Award,
  25 November 2015 . . . . .340, 456, 460
Elf Aquitaine Iran v National Iranian Oil Co, Award, 14 January 1982 127–28
Enrica Lexie Incident (Italy v India), PCA Case No 2015-28, Award, 21 May 2020 51–52
Enron Corp and Ponderosa Assets LP v Argentina, ICSID Case No ARB/01/3,
  Award, 22 May 2007 8
Eureko BV v Slovak Republic. See Achmea BV (formerly Eureko BV) v
  Slovak Republic
GEA Group Aktiengesellschaft v Ukraine, ICSID Case No ARB/08/16, Award,
  31 March 2011 482
Glamis Gold Ltd v United States, Award, 8 June 2009 499
Grynberg v Grenada. See RSM Production Corp and others v Grenada
Harriman Arbitration (Harriman v Union of Soviet Socialist Republics),
  Settlement Agreement, 14 September 1928 . . . . .xxxix, 99, 116–18, 168–69
Himpurna California Energy Ltd and Patuha Power Ltd v Indonesia,
  Interim Award, 26 September 1999 . . . . 113, 235–36
Himpurna California Energy Ltd and Patuha Power Ltd v Indonesia,
  Final Award, 16 October 1999 . . . . .xliv, 369–70
Himpurna California Energy Ltd and Patuha Power Ltd v PT (Persero)
  Perusahaan Listruik Negara, Final Award, 4 May 1999 . . . . .xliv, 233–34
ICC Case No 5082, Partial Award, 1989 376–77
ICC Case No 5514, Award, 1990 (1992) 110 JDI 1022 358–59
Indus Waters Kishenganga Arbitration (Pakistan v India), PCA Case No 2011-01,
  Award, 20 December 2013 31–32
Jay Treaty cases. See Betsey, The
JOC Oil Ltd v Sojuznefteexport, Award, 9 July 1984 .126–27, 160–61,
                                                              281, 320–22, 323–24
Joy Mining Machinery Ltd v Egypt, ICSID Case No ARB/03/11, Award on
  Jurisdiction, 6 August 2004 387
La Brea y Pariñas Arbitration (United Kingdom v Peru), Award, April 1922 . . . 381, 455–56
Lauder v Czech Republic, UNCITRAL, Final Award, 3 September 2001 . . . . xlvii, 198, 473–74
Lena Goldfields Co Ltd v Union of Soviet Socialist Republics, Award,
  2 September 1930 . . . . xxxviii–xli, 3, 99, 102, 123–31, 141–43, 145,
                                          146, 154, 159, 161–64, 168–69, 183, 233–34, 487
LG&E Energy Corp, LG&E Capital Corp, and LG&E International Inc v
  Argentina, ICSID Case No ARB/02/1, Decision on Liability, 3 October 2006 8
LIAMCO v Libya, Award, 12 April 1977, (1982) 62 ILR 140 127–28
Loewen Group Inc and Loewen v United States, ICSID Case No ARB(AF)/98/3,
  Award, 26 June 2003 . . . . .9, 11–13, 53–54, 439–40, 481, 482, 490–91

xvi TABLE OF CASES

Malaysian Historical Salvors Sdn Bhd v Malaysia, ICSID Case No ARB/05/10,
Award on Jurisdiction, 17 May 2007 387
Mamidoil Jetoil Greek Petroleum Products Societe SA v Albania, ICSID
Case No ARB/11/24, Award, 30 March 2015 482
Metalclad Corp v Mexico, ICSID Case No ARB(AF)/97/1, Award,
30 August 2000 .... 472, 473–74
Methanex Corp v United States, UNCITRAL, Partial Award,
7 August 2002 .... 340, 456, 465–67
Mondev v United States, ICSID Case No ARB(AF)/99/2, Award,
11 October 2002 ....54, 481, 482
MOX Plant case (Ireland v United Kingdom), PCA Case No 2002-01,
Final Award, 6 June 2008... 238–39, 241
National Grid Plc v Argentina, UNCITRAL, Decision on Jurisdiction,
20 June 2006 387
Oostergetel v Slovak Republic, UNCITRAL, Final Award, 23 April 2012..............481
Orinoco Steamship Co case (United States v Venezuela), PCA Case No 1909-02,
Award, 25 October 1910 477
Owners of M/S Parthenia (Messrs Houlder Bros and Co) v Executors of the late
Ralph Firbank, Award, 27 October 1883...................................356
Pac Rim Cayman LLC v El Salvador, ICSID Case No ARB/09/12, Decision on the
Respondent's Jurisdictional Objections, 1 June 2012.......................468–69
Parkerings-Compagniet AS v Lithuania, ICSID Case No ARB/05/8, Award,
11 September 2007...473–74
PepsiCo Arbitration, SCC Arbitration Institute, Final Award, 26 January 2005......384–85
PepsiCo Arbitration, SCC Arbitration Institute, Final Award, 7 July 2005 384–85
Philip Morris Asia Ltd v Australia, PCA Case No 2012-12, Award on Jurisdiction
and Admissibility, 17 December 2015 439–40
Philip Morris Brand Sàrl (Switzerland), Philip Morris Products SA (Switzerland)
and Abal Hermanos SA (Uruguay) v Uruguay, ICSID Case No ARB/10/7,
Decision on Jurisdiction, 2 July 2013.....................................439–40
Pious Fund of the Californias (United States v Mexico), PCA Case No 1902-01,
Award, 14 October 1902 .... 47–48, 476, 478
Plama Consortium Ltd v Bulgaria, ICSID Case No ARB/03/24, Decision on
Jurisdiction, 8 February 2005 459
Plama Consortium Ltd v Bulgaria, ICSID Case No ARB/03/24, Award,
27 August 2008 474
Poštová banka as and Istrokapital SE v Greece, ICSID Case No ARB/13/8, Award,
9 April 2015..493–94
Poštová banka as and Istrokapital SE v Greece, ICSID Case No ARB/13/8,
Decision on Annulment, 29 September 2016...............................494
Radio Corp of America v China, PCA Case No 1934-01, Award, 13 April 1935 52–53
Rebagliati v International Olympic Committee, Final Award of the CAS-TAS
Ad hoc Division, 12 February 1998 129
RSM Production Corp and others v Grenada, ICSID Case No ARB/10/6, Award,
10 December 2010 ....477, 480
Russian Claim for Interest on Indemnities (Russia v Turkey), PCA Case No 1910-02,
Award, 11 November 1912 47–48
Sempra Energy International v Argentina, ICSID Case No ARB/02/16, Award,
28 September 2007...473–74
SGS Société Générale de Surveillance SA v Pakistan, ICSID Case No ARB/01/13,
Decision on Jurisdiction, 6 August 2003 238–39
SNE v Joc Oil. *See* JOC Oil Ltd v Sojuznefteexport

TABLE OF CASES   xvii

South China Sea Arbitration (Philippines v China), PCA Case No 2013-19,
Award, 12 July 2016 51–52
Spyridon Roussalis v Romania, ICSID Case No ARB/06/1, Declaration,
28 November 2011 502
Starrett Housing Corp v Iran, IUSCT Case No 24, Interlocutory Award,
19 December 1983 473
Strabag SE, Raiffeisen Centrobank AG and Syrena Immobilien Holding AG v Poland,
ICSID Case No ADHOC/15/1, Partial Award on Jurisdiction, 4 March 2020 460
Suez, Sociedad General de Aguas de Barcelona SA and Vivendi Universal SA v
Argentina, ICSID Case No ARB/03/19, Decision on Jurisdiction, 3 August 2006 . . .387
Tapie case. *See* Claimants v Crédit Lyonnais and Société de Banque Occidentale
Técnicas Medioambientales Tecmed SA v Mexico, ICSID Case No ARB (AF)/00/2,
Award, 29 May 2003. . . . . 472, 473–74
Telenor Mobile Communications AS v Hungary, ICSID Case No ARB/04/15,
Award, 13 September 2006 473–74
Texaco Overseas Petroleum Co v Libya, Preliminary Award,
(1979) 53 ILR 389 . . . . 126, 127–28
Tippetts, Abbett, McCarthy, Stratton v TAMS-AFFA Consulting Engineers
of Iran, IUSCT Case No 7, Award, 29 June 1984. 473
TOPCO v Libya. *See* Texaco Overseas Petroleum Co v Libya
Turriff Construction (Sudan) Ltd v Sudan, Award, 23 April 1970 52–53
Venezuela Preferential case (Germany, Great Britain, Italy v Venezuela),
PCA Case No 1903-01, Award, 22 February 1904 47–48
Wena Hotels Ltd v Egypt, ICSID Case No ARB/98/4, Award, 8 December 2000 387
White Industries Australia Ltd v India, UNCITRAL, Final Award,
20 November 2011 317–18

International Court of Justice

Anglo-Iranian Oil Co (United Kingdom v Iran) [1952] ICJ Rep 2 . . . . xlvi, 127–28, 144
Asylum case (Colombia v Peru) [1950] ICJ Rep 266 478
Case Concerning Ahmadou Sadio Diallo (Guinea v Democratic Republic
of the Congo) [2010] ICJ Rep 664. 481
Corfu Channel (United Kingdom v Albania) (Merits) [1949] ICJ Rep 4. 478
Effect of Awards of Compensation Made by the United Nations Administrative
Tribunal (Advisory Opinion) 13 July 1954 476
Elettronica Sicula SpA (ELSI) (United States v Italy) 20 July 1989 482
Guinea-Bissau v Senegal [1991] ICJ Rep 53 51
Honduras v Nicaragua [1960] ICJ Rep 192 51
Interpretation of Peace Treaties with Bulgaria, Hungary and Romania
(Second Phase) 18 July 1950 127–28

Permanent Court of International Justice

Case Concerning the Factory at Chorzów (Germany v Poland) 16 December 1927 478
Case Concerning the Factory at Chorzów (Claim for Indemnity) (Germany v Poland)
(1928) PCIJ Ser A No 17 126–27

NATIONAL COURTS

Aden Colony

Anglo Iranian Oil Co Ltd v Jaffrate (The Rose Mary) [1953] 1 WLR 246 (SC) 144

xviii TABLE OF CASES

Australia

Barlin-Scott Air Conditioning v Robert Salzer Constructions,
26 April 1979 (SC (Vic)) 356–57
Commonwealth v Cockatoo Dockyard Pty Ltd (1995) 36 NSWLR 662 (CA (NSW))....129
Esso Australia Resources Ltd and others v Plowman and others
(1995) 128 ALR 391 (HC) 278
Resort Condominiums International Inc v Bolwell [1993] QSC 351..................249

Bermuda

Sojuznefteexport v Joc Oil Ltd, 7 July 1989 (CA) 281, 321–22, 323–24

France

Aita v Oijeh, 18 February 1986 (Paris C d'A).....................................280
Avax v Tecnimont, 2 November 2011 (Reims C d'A) 300
Case No 89-18.708 (Dutco Construction v BKMI Industrienlagen GmbH and
Siemens AG) 7 January 1992 (Cass)................................. 369–70, 408
Claimants v Crédit Lyonnais and Société de Banque Occidentale,
17 February 2015 (Paris C d'A) 439
Claimants v Crédit Lyonnais and Société de Banque Occidentale,
3 December 2015 (Paris C d'A) 439
FFIRC case. See Société Filature Française de Mohair v Fédération Françaises
des Industries Lainières et Cotonnières
General National Maritime Transport Co v Götaverken, 1980 Rev arb
107 (Paris C d'A) 294
Gosset v Carapelli, 7 May 1963 (Cass) 289, 323–24
Hilmarton Ltd v Omnium de Traitement et de Valorisation SA, 23 March 1994 (Cass)...... 292
Industrija Motora Rakovica v Lynx Machinery, 1981 (Cass) 374
Navimpex Centrala Navala v Seetransport Wiking Trader, 1990..................323–24
SNF SAS v Chambre de Commerce Internationale, 2009 (Paris C d'A)........ 415–16, 426
Société Atlantic Triton v République Populaire Révolutionnaire de Guinée
et société Soguipêche, 18 November 1986, (Cass, 1 civ) 274–75
Société Balenciaga v Société Allieri et Giovanozzi, 29 November 1989 (Cass, 1 civ).....275–76
Société Cubic Defense Systems Inc v Chambre de Commerce Internationale,
20 February 2001 (Cass, 1 civ) 424–25
Société d'exploitation du cinema REX v Rex, 3 June 1979 (Cass, 3 civ) 274–75
Société Filature Française de Mohair v Fédération Françaises des Industries
Lainières et Cotonnières, 2006 (Paris C d'A)................................414
Société Filature Française de Mohair v Fédération Françaises des Industries
Lainières et Cotonnières, 2010 (TGI Nanterre) 414–16
Société Horera v Société Sitas, 6 March 1990 (Cass, 1 civ).....................275–76
Société International Contractors Group v X, 10 July 1992 (Paris C d'A) 205
Société PT Putrabali Adyamulia v Société Rena Holding et Société Moguntia Est
Epices, 29 June 2007 (Cass)...292
Terex v Banexi, 12 December 1990 (Paris C d'A) 274–75
VSK Electronics v Sainrapt et Brice International SBI, 20 January 1988 (Paris C d'A) 275

Germany

Bundesgerichtshof (VII ZR 68/68(2)) 27 February 1970............. 289, 321–22, 323–24
Bundesgerichtshof (KG 2 129) (A-A Werke Gmbh v W) 1930 378–79
Bundesgerichtshof (ZZP 427) 22 May 1957 268–69

TABLE OF CASES xix

Kammergericht (Berlin) (22.W.9132.27/13) (Chlebprodukt v Internationale
Warenaustausch AG) 28 February 1928 . . . . xliv–xlv, 231–33

Hong Kong

China Nanhai Oil Joint Services Corp v Gee Tai Holdings Ltd, 13 July 1994 (HC) . . .213–14

India

Bharat Aluminium Co v Kaiser Aluminium Technical Services,
6 September 2012 (SC) 306, 312–13, 317–18
Bhatia International v Bulk Trading SA (2002) 4 SCC 105 (SC) 317–18
Citation Infowares Ltd v Equinox Corp (2009) 5 UJ 2066 (SC) 317
Indtel Technical Services Pvt Ltd v WS Atkins Plc (2008) 10 SCC 308 (SC) 317
National Thermal Power Corp v Singer, AIR 1993 SC 998 316
Oil and Natural Gas Commission v Western Company of North America,
AIR 1987 SC 674 (SC) 316
Venture Global Engineering v Satyam Computer Services Ltd and another
(2008) 4 SCC 190 (SC) 317–18

Indonesia

PT Pertamina v Himpurna California Energy Ltd and Patuha Power Ltd,
22 July 1999 (Jakarta Central DC) . . . . xliv, 234

Luxembourg

Ruckert v Karmann, Case No 12898, 26 November 1991 (CA (7th Chamber)) 254–55

Netherlands

Himpurna California Energy Ltd and Patuha Power Ltd v Indonesia,
21 September 1999 (Hague DC) 227
Telekom Malaysia Berhad v Ghana, 18 October 2004 (Hague DC) 361–62
Telekom Malaysia Berhad v Ghana, 5 November 2004 (Hague DC) 361–62

New Zealand

Chamberlains v Lai [2006] NZSC 70 421
Television New Zealand Ltd v Langley Productions Ltd [2000] 2 NZLR 250 (HC) 281

Pakistan

Hitachi Ltd v Rupali Polyester and others, 1998 SCMR 1618 (SC) 314, 315
Hubco Power Co v Water & Power Development Authority
[2000] 19 Arb Int 439 (SC) 314–15
Taisei Corp v AM Construction Co (Pvt) Ltd, 27 April 2012 (Lahore HC) 315
Tethyan Copper Co Pty Ltd v Balochistan, 7 February 2012 (SC) 315

Russian Soviet Federative Socialist Republic

Chlebprodukt v Internationale Warenaustausch AG, 1927 (SC) . . . . xliii–xliv, 230–31
Criminal Proceedings Against Kolyasnikov and others, 8 May 1930
(SC Criminal Collegium) 149–51
Supreme Council for National Economy v Sinclair Exploration Co,
24 March 1925 (Moscow Guberniya Ct) 75–87

xx   TABLE OF CASES

Supreme Council for National Economy v Sinclair Exploration Co,
22 May 1925 (SC) 75–76, 88–91

Singapore

Turner (East Asia) Pte Ltd v Turner (East Asia) Pte Ltd and another [1988] SGHC 47 301–2

Sweden

AB Nörrkopings Trikafabrik v AB Per Persson, 1936 (SC) 323–24
Bulgarian Foreign Trade Bank Ltd v AI Trade Finance Inc, 27 October 2000 (SC) 278
Czech Republic v CME Czech Republic BV, 15 May 2003 (Svea CA) .... xliv–xlv, xlvii,
238–39, 242, 243–44, 245–46, 366–67, 375–77, 378–79

Switzerland

Séfri SA v Komgrap (BGE 111 Ia 336) 1985 (Fed Trib) 374–75, 376–77
Tobler v Blaser (BGE 59 I 177) 7 October 1933 (Fed SC)................ 289, 323–24, 326

United Kingdom

AEGIS v European Re. *See* Associated Electric & Gas Insurance Services Ltd v
European Reinsurance Co of Zurich
AG der Manufacturen IA Woronin Leutschig v Frederick Huth & Co
(1946) 79 Ll L Rep 262 (KBD)... 132–33
Ali Shipping Corp v Shipyard Trogir [1999] 1 WLR 314 (CA (Civ Div)) 129, 244–45
AM Luther Co v James Sagor & Co [1921] 3 KB 532 (CA) 99, 137–38
Anton Piller KG v Manufacturing Processes Ltd [1976] Ch 55 (CA (Civ Div)) 248–49
Aquarius Financial Enterprises Inc v Lloyd's Underwriters (The Delphine)
[2001] 2 Lloyd's Rep 542 (QBD (Comm)......................... 219–21, 223–24
Arenson v Arenson [1977] AC 405 (HL).......................... 413–14, 418–19, 420
Arnold v National Westminster Bank Plc (No 1) [1991] 2 AC 93 (HL)................ 241
Arthur JS Hall & Co v Simons [2002] 1 AC 615 (HL)............................... 421
Associated Electric & Gas Insurance Services Ltd v European Reinsurance Co
of Zurich [2003] 1 WLR 1041 (PC (Ber)) .... xliv–xlv, 238–39, 240–41,
242–43, 246, 278, 282–83, 287
Badger, In re (1819) 106 ER 517 (KB).. 355–57
Bain v Cooper (1841) 8 M & W 751 (Ex Ct) 244
Bank Mellat v GAA Development Construction Co Ltd [1988] 2 Lloyd's Rep 44
(QBD (Comm)) 237, 373
Bankers Trust case. *See* Department of Economic Policy and Development of the
City of Moscow v Bankers Trust Co
Barry D Trentham Ltd v Lawfield Investments Ltd, 2002 SLT 1094 (OH).............. 265
Bragoseo Ltd v J Sagor & Co (1921) 8 Ll L Rep 388 (KBD) 99
Bremer Vulkan Schiffbau und Maschinenfabrik v South India Shipping Corp Ltd
[1981] AC 909 (HL)... 295
C v D [2007] EWCA Civ 1282... 335–36
Cantiere San Rocco SA (Shipbuilding Co) v Clyde Shipbuilding &
Engineering Co Ltd [1924] AC 226 (HL) 126–27
Cargill International SA Antigua (Geneva Branch) v Sociedad Iberica de
Molturacion SA [1998] 1 Lloyd's Rep 489 (CA (Civ Div)).................... 372–73
Carl Zeiss Stiftung v Rayner & Keeler Ltd [1967] AC 853 (HL) 242
Cassidy v Ministry of Health [1951] 2 KB 343 (CA)............................ 279–80
Chandris v Isbrandtsen-Moller Co Inc [1951] 1 KB 240 (CA) 356–57

TABLE OF CASES xxi

Channel Tunnel Group Ltd v Balfour Beatty Construction Ltd [1993] AC 334 (HL) 126
Christopher Brown Ltd v Genossenschaft Oesterreichischer Waldbesitzer
    Holzwirtschaftsbetriebe GessmbH [1954] 1 QB 8 (QBD)....................127–28
Clough v Tameside and Glossop HA [1998] 1 WLR 1478 (QBD) 218
Commerce & Industry Insurance Co (Canada) v Lloyd's Underwriters
    [2002] 1 Lloyd's Rep 219 (QBD (Comm))................................220–21
Czarnikow Ltd v Roth Schmidt & Co [1922] 2 KB 478 (CA) 126
David Taylor & Son v Barnett Trading Co [1953] 1 Lloyd's Rep 181 (CA) 322
De Havilland v Bowerbank (1807) 170 ER 872 (Assizes)...........................352
Department of Economic Policy and Development of the City of Moscow v
    Bankers Trust Co [2004] EWCA Civ 314 282–89
Deutsche Schachtbau- und Tiefbohrgesellschaft mbH v Ras Al-Khaimah
    National Oil Co [1987] 2 Lloyd's Rep 246 (CA (Civ Div)).......................126
Doleman & Sons v Ossett Corp [1912] 23 KB 257 (CA) 293
Donoghue v Stevenson [1932] AC 562 (HL)...............................xlviii, 413
DST v RAKOIL. *See* Deutsche Schachtbau- und Tiefbohrgesellschaft mbH v
    Ras Al-Khaimah National Oil Co
Dyson Appliances Ltd v Hoover Ltd (Costs: Interim Payment) [2004] 1 WLR 1264
    (Ch D (Patents Ct)) 255–56
Eastern Saga case. *See* Oxford Shipping Co Ltd v Nippon Yusen Kaisha
    (The Eastern Saga) (No 2)
Ecuador v Occidental Exploration & Production Co [2005] EWCA Civ 1116........54–55
Enka Insaat Ve Sanayi AS v OOO Insurance Company Chubb [2020] UKSC 38........198
Esso Petroleum Co Ltd v Milton [1997] 1 WLR 938 (CA (Civ Div)) 502
European Grain and Shipping Ltd v Johnston [1983] QB 520 (CA (Civ Div)) 371–72
Fidelitas Shipping Co Ltd v V/O Exportchleb [1966] 1 QB 630 (CA) 240–41
Finix, The. *See* Nea Tyhi Maritime Co of Piraeus v Compagnie Graniere SA
    of Zurich
Fiona Trust & Holding Corp v Privalov [2007] UKHL 40...........................323–25
Gleeson v J Wippell & Co Ltd [1977] 1 WLR 510 (Ch D) 244
Gold v Essex CC [1942] 2 KB 293 (CA)...280
Gouriet v Union of Post Office Workers [1978] AC 435 (HL).......................250
Gregg v Raytheon [1980] 1 Lloyd's Rep 255 (CA (Civ Div)) 295
Hadley v Baxendale (1854) 156 ER 145 (Ex Ct) 353
Hamlyn & Co v Talisker Distillery [1894] AC 202 (HL) 310–11
Hanak v Green [1958] 2 QB 9 (CA) 502
Harbour Assurance Co (UK) Ltd v Kansa General International Insurance
    Co Ltd [1993] QB 701 (CA (Civ Div)) 159, 281, 322–24
Henderson v Henderson (1843) 3 Hare 100 (Ct of Ch) 240–41
Heyman v Darwins Ltd [1942] AC 356 (HL) 159, 319, 323–24
Hodgson v Imperial Tobacco Ltd (No 1) [1998] 1 WLR 1056 (CA (Civ Div)) 285
House of Spring Gardens Ltd v Waite (No 2) [1991] 1 QB 241 (CA (Civ Div)).........242
Ikarian Reefer, The (No 1). *See* National Justice Compania Naviera SA v
    Prudential Assurance Co Ltd (The Ikarian Reefer)
International Bulk Shipping and Services Ltd v Minerals and Metals Trading Corp
    of India [1996] 2 Lloyd's Rep 474 (CA (Civ Div))...........................162–64
James Miller & Partners Ltd v Whitworth Street Estates (Manchester) Ltd.
    See Whitworth Street Estates (Manchester) Ltd v James Miller & Partners Ltd
Jivraj v Hashwani [2009] EWHC 1364 (Comm)........................407, 408, 410
Jivraj v Hashwani [2010] EWCA Civ 712...............................407–8, 410
Jivraj v Hashwani [2011] UKSC 40........................ 406–7, 408, 409, 410, 411
Johnson v Gore Wood & Co [2002] 2 AC 1 (HL) 240–41

xxii TABLE OF CASES

Karl Construction Ltd v Palisade Properties Plc, 2002 SLT 312 (OH) 265
Kastner v Jason [2004] EWHC 592 (Ch) 262–63
Kelly v Northern Ireland Housing Executive [1999] 1 AC 428 (HL) 410
Kuwait Airways Corp v Kuwait Insurance Co (No 3) [2000] Lloyd's Rep IR 678 (QBD) 353
Kuwait Prison case. *See* Ministry of Public Works of Kuwait v Gruppo International
    Contracting Co
Lesotho Highlands Development Authority v Impregilo SpA
    [2006] AC 221 (HL) 295, 331–32, 333–38
London, Chatham and Dover Railway Co v South Eastern Railway Co
    [1893] AC 429 (HL) 353
London Explorer, The. *See* Timber Shipping Co SA v London and
    Overseas Freighters
Mareva Compania Naviera SA v International Bulk Carriers SA (The Mareva)
    [1975] 2 Lloyd's Rep 509 (CA (Civ Div)) 247–48
Marshall v Grinbaum (1921) 8 Ll L Rep 342 (Ch D) 143, 176–77
Mills v Cooper [1967] 2 QB 459 (DC) 241
Ministry of Public Works of Kuwait v Gruppo International Contracting Co,
    17 May 1971 (QBD (Comm)) 294
National Bank of Greece SA v Pinios Shipping Co No 1 [1990] 1 AC 637 (HL) 357–58
National Justice Compania Naviera SA v Prudential Assurance Co Ltd
    (The Ikarian Reefer) (No 1) [1995] 1 Lloyd's Rep 455 (CA (Civ Div)) 218, 221–22
Naviera Amazonica Peruana SA v Compania Internacional de Seguros de Peru
    [1988] 1 Lloyd's Rep 116 (CA (Civ Div)) 295–96
Naylor v Preston AHA [1987] 1 WLR 958 (CA (Civ Div)) 218
Nea Tyhi Maritime Co of Piraeus v Compagnie Graniere SA of Zurich
    [1978] 1 Lloyd's Rep 16 (CA (Civ Div)) 356–57
Nippon Yusen Kaisha v Karageorgis [1975] 2 Lloyd's Rep 137 (CA (Civ Div)).......247–48
Occidental Exploration & Production Co v Ecuador. *See* Ecuador v Occidental
    Exploration & Production Co
Occidental Worldwide Investment Corp v Skibs A/S Avanti (The Siboen and
    The Sibotre) [1976] 1 Lloyd's Rep 293 (QBD (Comm)).........................107
Odyssey Re (London) Ltd (formerly Sphere Drake Insurance Plc) v OIC Run Off Ltd
    (formerly Orion Insurance Co Plc) [2001] Lloyd's Rep IR 1 (CA (Civ Div)) 220
Orion Compania Espanola de Seguros v Belfort Maatschappij voor Algemene
    Verzekgringeen [1962] 2 Lloyd's Rep 257 (QBD (Comm)).................126, 295
Oswald v Earl Grey (1855) 23 LJQB 69 369–70
Oxford Shipping Co Ltd v Nippon Yusen Kaisha (The Eastern Saga) (No 2)
    [1984] 2 Lloyd's Rep 373 (QBD (Comm)) 287
Percy v Church of Scotland Board of National Mission [2006] 2 AC 28 (HL)..........410
Philip Alexander Securities & Futures Ltd v Bamberger [1996] CLC 1757
    (CA (Civ Div)) 329–30
Podar Trading Co v François Tagher [1949] 2 KB 277 (KBD).....................356–57
Practice Note (Arbitration: New Procedure) [1997] 1 WLR 391 (QBD (Comm)).......286
President of India v La Pintada Cia Navigacion SA ("La Pintada") [1985] AC 104 (HL)...... 353
Profilati Italia SRL v Paine Webber Inc [2001] 1 Lloyd's Rep 715 (QBD (Comm)) 216–17
R. v M'Naghten (1843) 10 Cl & F 200 (HL) 19–20
Ranger v Great Western Railway (1854) 5 HL Cas 72 (QB).........................301
Rasu Maritima SA v Perusahaan Pertambangan Minyak Dan Gas Bumi Negara
    (Pertamina) [1978] 1 QB 644 (CA (Civ Div)).............................247–48
Refco Capital Markets Ltd v Credit Suisse First Boston Ltd
    [2001] EWCA Civ 1733 220–21
Rondel v Worsley [1969] 1 AC 191 (HL) 421

Russian Commercial & Industrial Bank v Comptoir d'Escompte de Mulhouse
[1925] AC 112 (HL) 143–44
Russian Gold case. *See* Marshall v Grinbaum
Russian Volunteer Fleet v King, The (1923) 15 Ll L Rep 74 (KBD)................137–38
Salomon v Salomon & Co Ltd [1897] AC 22 (HL) 244–45
Scott v Scott [1913] AC 417 (HL) 285, 287
Soleimany v Soleimany [1999] QB 785 (CA (Civ Div)) 126
Spinney's (1948) Ltd v Royal Insurance Co Ltd [1980] 1 Lloyd's Rep 406
(QBD (Comm)) 282–83
Spurrier v La Cloche [1902] AC 446 (PC (Jer)).................................311–12
Sulamerica Cia Nacional de Seguros SA v Enesa Engenharia SA
[2012] EWCA Civ 638 310–11
Sutcliffe v Thackrah [1974] AC 727 (HL)............................ 413–14, 418–19
Swaps case, The. *See* Westdeutsche Landesbank Girozentrale v Islington LBC
Sybray v White (1836) 1 M & W 435 (Ex Ct).....................................239
Thoday v Thoday [1964] P 181 (CA) 241
Thrasyvoulou v Secretary of State for the Environment [1990] 2 AC 273 (HL) 241
Three Rivers DC v Bank of England (No 3) [2000] 2 WLR 1220 (HL).................213
Three Rivers DC v Bank of England (No 3) [2001] 2 All ER 513 (HL).................213
Timber Shipping Co SA v London and Overseas Freighters [1972] AC 1 (HL) 129
United Kingdom Mutual Steamship Assurance Association v Houston & Co
[1896] 1 QB 567 (QBD)..127–28
UR Power GmbH v Kuok Oils & Grains PTE Ltd [2009] EWHC 1940 (Comm) 323–24
Vernon v Bosley (No 1) [1997] 1 All ER 577 (CA (Civ Div)).........................209
Vernon v Bosley (No 2) [1999] QB 18 (CA (Civ Div)).............................209–11
Wadsworth v Lydall [1981] 1 WLR 598 (CA (Civ Div))...........................353
Walford v Miles [1992] 2 AC 128 (HL) 213
Walneff (t/a Walneff Bros) v All-Russian Cooperative Society
(1921) 9 Ll L Rep 527 (CA) 99
Westdeutsche Landesbank Girozentrale v Islington LBC [1996] AC 669 (HL) 352, 357–58
Whitehouse v Jordan [1981] 1 WLR 246 (HL) 217–18
Whitworth Street Estates (Manchester) Ltd v James Miller & Partners Ltd
[1970] AC 583 (HL)...294
Wright v Paton Farrell, 2006 SC 404 (IH (1 Div))................................421

United States

FFM v Chemical Carriers, 751 F Supp 467 (SDNY 1990) 378–79
Gideon v Wainwright, 372 US 335 (1963) 208–9
Loewen v United States, 31 October 2005 (DDC) 10–11
McCreary Tire & Rubber Co v Ceat SpA, 501 F 2d 1032 (3d Cir 1974) 268
Prima Paint Corp v Flood & Conklin Manufacturing Co,
388 US 395 (1967) 321–22, 323–24
Publicis Communication v True North Communications, 206 F 3d 725 (7th Cir 2000) 249
Weilamann v Chase Manhattan Bank, 192 NYS 2d 469 (1959) (SC) 162–64

Table of Treaties, Legislation and Rules

INTERNATIONAL INSTRUMENTS

Algiers Declaration 1981 53
Agreement between the United
    Kingdom and the Union of Soviet
    Socialist Republics concerning the
    Settlement of Mutual Financial
    and Property Claims 1968. 162–64
    Art 2 162–64
    Art 4 162–64
Agreement between the United
    Kingdom and the Union of
    Soviet Socialist Republics for
    the Promotion and Reciprocal
    Protection of Investments 1989 . . . 164
American Arbitration Association-
    International Centre for Dispute
    Resolution (AAA-ICDR)
    Arbitration Rules 2006. 348–49
Anglo-Soviet Temporary Commercial
    Agreement 1930 162–64
Anglo-Soviet Trade Agreement 1921 99,
    101–2, 104–5, 106–43, 162, 176–77
Anglo-Soviet Trade Agreement
    1934 162–64
Australia-Hong Kong Bilateral
    Investment Treaty 1993 439–40
Australia-India Bilateral Investment
    Treaty 1999 317–18
Canada-European Union Comprehensive
    Economic and Trade Agreement
    2016 (CETA) 435–36, 437, 496
    Ch 8 437
Central America-Dominican Republic
    Free Trade Agreement 2004
    (CAFTA-DR) 53, 435–36
Convention between Great Britain and
    the United States of America for
    the Adjustment of the Boundary
    between the Dominion of Canada
    and the Territory of Alaska 1903 . . . 12–13
Convention for the Pacific Settlement
    of International Disputes 1899
    (1899 Hague Convention). 41–42,
        45–48, 50
    Art 15 47
    Art 16 47

Art 54 50
Art 55 49–50
Convention for the Pacific Settlement
    of International Disputes 1907
    (1907 Hague Convention). 46–48,
        52–53
    Art 37 47
    Art 38 47
    Art 39 47
    Art 40 47
    Art 54 31–32
    Art 81 50
    Art 82 50
    Art 83 50
Convention on Jurisdiction and the
    Enforcement of Judgments in
    Civil and Commercial Matters
    1968 (Brussels Convention) 250–52,
        253–55, 256, 259–61, 276–77
    Title III. .256, 259
    Art 1(4) 251
    Arts 2–18 256
    Art 24 . . . . . 251–52, 253–60, 269–70, 277
Convention on Jurisdiction and the
    Enforcement of Judgments in
    Civil and Commercial Matters
    1988 (Lugano Convention). . . .250, 251,
        259–60, 261, 276–77, 400–1
    Art 1(4) 251
    Art 24 . . . . .272, 273, 277
Convention on the Execution of
    Foreign Arbitral Awards
    1927 . . . . xlvi, 56, 74, 100, 103, 162,
        187–88, 189–90, 191, 194–95,
        293–94, 310–12, 313–15, 444–45
Convention on the Recognition
    and Enforcement of Foreign
    Arbitral Awards 1958 (New York
    Convention) . . . . xlvi, 55, 56, 70–71, 100,
    126–27, 160–61, 164, 167–68, 189, 192,
    194–95, 208, 213–14, 215–16, 248–50,
    262–63, 265, 268, 276–77, 281, 293–94,
    296, 297, 310–11, 313–18, 320, 323,
    331, 339, 364–65, 370–71, 394–97,
    398–401, 422–23, 431, 437,
    444–46, 447, 467, 471, 488
    Art I 313–14

Arts I–VII(1)....................394
Art II...............322, 394, 397, 467
Art II(1)........................467
Art II(2)........................397
Art II(3)........................268
Art V 315, 394
Art V(1)(d) 329–30
Art V(2)(b) 215–16, 398–99
Art VII................292, 394, 400
Art VII(1) 400–1
Art VII(2) 310–11
Convention on the Settlement of
    Investment Disputes between
    States and Nationals of Other States
    1965 (ICSID Convention)....... 30–31,
        50–51, 52–53, 55, 70–71, 167–68,
        314–15, 321–22, 381–82, 383, 385,
        395, 410, 422–23, 431, 435–36, 437,
        439, 455, 470–72, 487–88, 492, 501
    Art 21.......xxv–xxvi, 365, 385, 422–23
    Art 22...........................365
    Art 25.......................493–94
    Art 25(1) 493
    Art 26(1) 53
    Art 52........................50–51
    Art 64...........................51
Council of Bars and Law Societies
    of Europe (CCBE) Code of
    Conduct for European
    Lawyers 1988...........205, 206, 363
Council of Bars and Law Societies
    of Europe (CCBE) Code of
    Conduct for European
    Lawyers 1998...........205, 206, 363
    Pt 4..........................205–6
    Art 1.5 205
    Art 4.1 205–6
    Arts 4.1–4.4...................205–6
    Art 4.2 ....206, 363
    Arts 4.2–4.4....................206
    Art 4.3 ....206, 363
    Art 4.4 ....206, 363
    Art 4.5 205–6
Cyprus-Greece Bilateral Investment
    Treaty 1992 493–94
Czechoslovakia-Netherlands Bilateral
    Investment Treaty 1991..........495
Energy Charter Treaty 1991 (ECT) ... 37–38,
        53, 459, 469, 471, 472, 474, 496–97
    Art 13(1) 473
European Convention on Human
    Rights and Fundamental
    Freedoms 1950 (ECHR) 265

Art 6......... 208, 259–60, 279, 369–70
Art 6(1) 279
Art 14..........................408
Protocol 12 408
European Convention on
    International Commercial
    Arbitration 1961.........160–61, 164
    Art V(3).....................160–61
European Convention providing a
    Uniform Law on Arbitration
    1966.......................194–95
Foreign Trade Arbitration
    Commission (FTAC) Rules of
    Procedure 1975
    Art 1(3) 160–61
Franco-Danish Treaty 1911
    Art 1..........................47–48
    Art 2..........................47–48
General Treaty for the Renunciation
    of War as an Instrument of
    National Policy 1928
    (Kellogg-Briand Pact) 433
German-Soviet Provisional
    Treaty 1921 .... 62–63, 99, 226–27
    Art 13..........................227
German-Soviet Treaty 1925.... xliii–xliv, 99,
        226, 227–28, 230, 231–33, 433, 447–48
    Ch VI: Agreement Concerning
        Commercial Courts of
        Arbitration .... xliii–xliv, 226, 227
    Art 3..........................228
    Art 3(1)(1).....................228
    Art 3(1)(2).....................228
    Art 3(1)(3).....................228
    Art 3(1)(b).....................231
    Art 3(2) 228
    Art 4............ xliii–xliv, 228, 231
    Art 4(5) 228
    Arts 4–6.......................228
German-Soviet Treaty 1935...........226
German-Soviet Treaty 1939...........226
Germany-Pakistan Bilateral
    Investment Treaty 1959 53
Germany-Switzerland Arbitration
    Treaty 1921 ....433, 498
Grain and Feed Trade Association
    (GAFTA) Arbitration
    Rules No 125 372–73
Greece-Slovakia Bilateral Investment
    Treaty 1991 493–94
Helsinki Final Act 1975 ....164, 189
Indus Waters Treaty between India
    and Pakistan 1960............31–32

TABLE OF TREATIES, LEGISLATION AND RULES   xxvii

International Bar Association (IBA)
Guidelines on Conflicts of Interest in
International Arbitration 2004. . . .360–62
International Bar Association (IBA)
Rules of Ethics for International
Arbitrators 1987 . . . . .223, 360
International Bar Association (IBA)
Rules on the Taking of Evidence
in International Commercial
Arbitration 1999. . . . . . . 214, 217, 218,
223–24, 348–49
Art 3 .214, 362–63
Art 4 .214, 362–63
Art 5 214
Art 5(3) 214–15
International Bar Association (IBA)
Supplementary Rules Governing
the Presentation and Reception
of Evidence in International
Commercial Arbitration 1983 214
International Centre for Dispute
Resolution (ICDR) Arbitration
Rules. 302
International Centre for Settlement
of Investment Disputes (ICSID)
Arbitration (Additional Facility)
Rules 2006 435–36
International Centre for Settlement
of Investment Disputes
(ICSID) Rules of Procedure for
Arbitration Proceedings 2003. 416
r 9(10). 416
International Chamber of Commerce
(ICC) Arbitration Rules 1922 56,
189–90
International Chamber of Commerce
(ICC) Arbitration Rules 1988 205
Art 13 . . . . 156–57, 358–59
Art 16 156–57
International Chamber of Commerce
(ICC) Arbitration Rules 1998 147,
156–57, 205–6, 236, 238–39,
246, 364–65, 425–26
Art 12(5) 113, 147–48, 236
Art 19 156–57
Art 23 266
Art 25(2) 238–39, 246
Art 28(6) 238–39, 246
Art 34 . . . . 415–16, 425–26
International Chamber of Commerce
(ICC) Arbitration Rules 2012 199,
302, 305, 348–49, 426–27
Art 40 . . . . 415–16, 426–27

International Criminal Tribunal for the
former Yugoslavia-Association of
Defence Counsel (ICTY-ADC)
Code of Conduct 363
International Law Commission (ILC)
Draft Articles on Diplomatic
Protection 2006
Art 5(1) 12–13
Art 5(4) 12–13
International Law Commission (ILC)
Draft Articles on the Responsibility
of States for Internationally
Wrongful Acts 2001 . . . . .474, 475
Art 4 474
Art 8 474–75
International Law Commission
(ILC) Model Rules on Arbitral
Procedure 1958. . . . . 31–32, 50–51
Art 3(3) 31–32
Art 35 50–51
Art 36(1) 51
Johnson-Clarendon Treaty 1869. 16–17
Art 1 16–17
Locarno Pact 1925 . . . . .433, 498
London Court of International
Arbitration (LCIA) Arbitration
Rules 1981 . . . . .419, 424, 451
Art 14(1) 424
London Court of International
Arbitration (LCIA) Arbitration
Rules 1985 .302
Art 5.1 .348–49
Art 19.1 424
London Court of International
Arbitration (LCIA) Arbitration
Rules 1998 . . . . . . 147, 205–6, 236, 302,
348–49, 364–65, 497
Art 12 . . . . 113, 147–48, 236
Art 14.1 302
Art 25.1(c) 262
Art 26.1 238–39
Art 26.6 . . . . .353, 358–59
Art 26.9 .238–39
Art 30 279
Art 31 424
London Court of International
Arbitration (LCIA) Arbitration
Rules 2014 . . . . . . 327–28, 337–38, 424
Art 26.4 337–38
Art 31.1 424
Art 31.2 424
Netherlands-Slovakia Bilateral
Investment Treaty 1991 495

xxviii TABLE OF TREATIES, LEGISLATION AND RULES

North American Free Trade Agreement
1992 (NAFTA) . . . . .xliv–xlv, 9–13,
30–31, 33, 37–38, 53, 54, 435–36, 437,
439–40, 465, 466–67, 476, 489–91
Ch 11 . . . . 10–11, 53, 437, 465,
466, 467, 480, 482
Art 1101. 465
Art 1101(1) 466–67
Art 1105. 54
Art 1110. 54
Art 1116. 479
Art 1120. 437
Art 1122(1) 467
Art 1124(4) 437
Art 1131. 476
Art 1131(1) 479
Art 1139. 479, 480
Art 1139(g) 480
Art 1139(h) 480
Art 1222. 467
Peace of Münster between the
Netherlands and Spain 1648 39–40
Peace of Westphalia 1648. 39–40
Permanent Court of Arbitration (PCA)
Arbitration Rules 2012. 52–53
Permanent Court of Arbitration
(PCA) Optional Rules for
Arbitrating Disputes between
Two Parties of Which Only One
is a State 1993 52–53
Permanent Court of Arbitration
(PCA) Optional Rules for
Arbitrating Disputes between
Two States 1992. 52–53
Permanent Court of Arbitration
(PCA) Optional Rules
for Arbitration Between
International Organizations and
Private Parties 1996 52–53
Permanent Court of Arbitration
(PCA) Optional Rules
for Arbitration Between
International Organizations and
States 1996. 52–53
Permanent Court of Arbitration
(PCA) Rules of Arbitration and
Conciliation for Settlement of
Investment Disputes between
Two Parties of Which Only One
is a State 1962 52–53
Peru-United Kingdom Arbitration
Treaty 1921 381

Protocol on Arbitration Clauses 1923 . . .56, 74,
100–1, 103, 134–35, 162, 187–88,
190, 191, 194–95, 227, 293–94,
310–11, 314–15, 431–32, 444–45
Romania-Sweden Bilateral
Investment Treaty 2002 439
Rules and Procedures of the
International Court of Justice 1978
Art 67 51
Singapore International Arbitration
Centre (SIAC) Arbitration Rules
2007 302
Singapore International Arbitration Centre
(SIAC) Arbitration Rules 2016. . . .327–28
Soviet-Japanese Basic Convention
1925 . . . . xxxix, 75
Statute of the International Court
of Justice 1945
Art 36. 51
Art 36(2) 48
Statute of the Permanent Court of
International Justice 1920 xl
Art 36. 48
Art 38. 144
Art 38(1)(c) 126
Stockholm Chamber of Commerce
(SCC) Arbitration Rules 302, 384
Switzerland-Uruguay Bilateral
Investment Treaty 1988 439–40
Trans-Pacific Partnership Agreement
2016 (TPP) 435–36, 439–40
Ch 9, s B, Art 9.18 435–36
Treaty Banning Nuclear Weapon Tests
in the Atmosphere, in Outer
Space and Under Water 1963 97
Treaty concerning the formation of a
General Postal Union 1874
Art 16. 43
Treaty of Amity, Commerce, and
Navigation, Between His Britannic
Majesty and the United States of
America 1794 (Jay Treaty) 13, 39–40
Treaty of Arbitration between
Argentina and Italy 1898
Art 1 42–43
Treaty of Brest-Litovsk 1918 . . . . .226, 433, 498
Treaty of Non-Aggression between
Germany and the Union of Soviet
Socialist Republics 1939
(Nazi-Soviet Pact) . . .432–34, 447, 498–99
Art 5 . . . . 433–34, 498–99
Additional Protocol 433–34

TABLE OF TREATIES, LEGISLATION AND RULES   xxix

Treaty of Paris 1783 39–40
Treaty of Peace between the Allied
   and Associated Powers and
   Germany, and Protocol 1919
   (Treaty of Versailles) 101–2, 226,
                  433, 498
Treaty of Rapallo 1922 134–76,
              226, 227, 433
Treaty of Washington 1871 ..... xxxvii, 13,
       14–16, 17, 23–24, 25–26, 27,
      28–30, 35–36, 37, 40–41, 387, 389
United Nations Commission on
   International Trade Law
   (UNCITRAL) Arbitration Rules
   1976 .... xliv, 30–31, 160–61,
     164, 228, 233, 234, 282, 284–85,
     287, 361, 364–65, 375–76, 387
  Art 25(4) 279
  Art 26........................ 249–50
  Art 32(3) 238–39
  Art 32(5) 279
United Nations Commission on
   International Trade Law
   (UNCITRAL) Arbitration
   Rules 2010 ... 30–31, 302, 395, 422–23
  Art 16........................... 423
United Nations Commission on
   International Trade Law
   (UNCITRAL) Arbitration Rules
   2013 .... 327–28, 348–49, 435–36, 479
United Nations Commission on
   International Trade Law
   (UNCITRAL) Model Law on
   International Commercial
   Arbitration 1985... xlii, 30–31, 70–71,
     164, 167–68, 189, 191, 192, 194–95,
     208, 227, 228, 240–41, 242, 264,
     265–66, 270–71, 280–81, 293–94,
     304, 316–17, 329–30, 348, 349,
     355–56, 366, 395, 422–23,
     431–32, 445, 449–50, 498
  Art 5........................ 293, 348
  Art 9............... 249–50, 265, 267
  Art 9(1) 265
  Art 11(1) 409
  Art 16........................ 160–61
  Art 16(1) 319
  Art 17..... 249–50, 253–54, 264, 265–66
  Art 17(2) 265
  Art 19........................ 329–30
  Art 19(1) 348
  Art 19(2) 348

  Art 28.................... 147, 329–30
  Art 29........................... 371
  Art 31(2) 238–39
United Nations Commission on
   International Trade Law
   (UNCITRAL) Model Law on
   International Commercial
   Arbitration 2006........... 331, 447
  Art 36(1)(a)(iv)............... 329–30
United Nations Convention on the Law
   of the Sea 1982 (UNCLOS) xxxviii
  Art 298....................... 51–52
  Annex V, s 2................... 51–52
  Annex VII 51–52
  Annex VII, Art 3(a) 31–32
United Nations General Assembly
   Resolution 56/83 (2001) 474
Vienna Convention on the Law of
   Treaties 1969................... 396
  Art 31........................... 493
  Art 31(1) 466
World Intellectual Property Organization
   (WIPO) Arbitration Rules
  Arts 73–76...................... 279

EU LEGISLATION

Treaties

Charter of Fundamental Rights of the
   European Union [2000]
   OJ C364/1
  Art 21........................... 406
Treaty establishing the European
   Community (EC Treaty) [2002]
   OJ C325/33
  Art 6............................ 410
  Art 12........................... 406
  Art 23........................... 410
  Art 226.......................... 472
  Art 228.......................... 472
  Art 234..................... 470, 471
  Art 292....................... 469–71
Treaty establishing the European
   Economic Community 1957
   (Treaty of Rome)
  Art 220.......................... 251
Treaty of Lisbon amending the Treaty
   on European Union and the
   Treaty establishing the
   European Community
   [2007] OJ C306/1 .... 395, 400–1

Treaty on the Functioning of the
  European Union (TFEU)
  [2012] OJ C326/47
  Art 10.............................406
  Art 18.............................410
  Art 19.............................410
  Art 218(11).......................471
  Art 258.....................407, 472
  Art 260.....................407, 472
  Art 267.............. 407, 470, 495–96
  Art 344.............. 469–71, 495–96

Regulations

Regulation (EC) No 44/2001 of
  22 December 2000 on
  jurisdiction and the recognition
  and enforcement of judgments
  in civil and commercial matters
  (Brussels Regulation)
  [2001] OJ L12/1 .... 250, 251, 261,
            295–96, 297, 400–1
  Art 31............................251

Directives

Directive 93/13/EEC of 5 April 1993
  on unfair terms in consumer
  contracts [1993] OJ L95/29 417–18
Directive 98/5/EC of the European
  Parliament and of the Council
  of 16 February 1998 to facilitate
  practice of the profession of lawyer
  on a permanent basis in a Member
  State other than that in which the
  qualification was obtained
  [1998] OJ L77/36 205
  Art 6............................205
Directive 2000/43/EC of 29 June 2000
  implementing the principle of
  equal treatment between persons
  irrespective of racial or ethnic
  origin [2000] OJ L180/22........406
  Art 3(2).........................406
Directive 2000/78/EC of 27 November
  2000 establishing a general
  framework for equal treatment
  in employment and occupation
  [2000] OJ L303/16 ....406, 407, 408
Directive 2008/52/EC of the
  European Parliament and of
  the Council of 21 May 2008 on
  certain aspects of mediation in
  civil and commercial matters
  [2008] OJ L136/3 297

NATIONAL LEGISLATION

Argentina

Code of Civil Procedure
  Art 753.......................261–62

Belgium

Law of 19 May 1998 on Arbitration
  Art 1709bis 112

Bermuda

Bermuda International Conciliation
    and Arbitration Act 1993..... 240–41,
          242, 280–81, 288–89, 498
  s 31..........................355–56
  s 45..........................280–81
  s 46..........................280–81
Constitution of Bermuda..........280–81

France

Civil Code 100–1
Code of Civil Procedure
  Art 809(2) 275
  Art 873(2) 275
  Art 1028(3) 374

Germany

Arbitration Law 1998.............265–66
Civil Code 100–1, 126–27
  Art 139......................321–22
Code of Civil Procedure (ZPO) 228,
            265–66, 267
  s 916.......................266, 267
  s 1025(1) 269
  s 1025(2)–(4)....................269
  ss 1031–1033.....................228
  s 1033 .... 267–68, 269–70
  s 1033(2) 268
  s 1039.......................261–62
  s 1040.......................261–62
  s 1041 .... 265–68, 269, 270
  s 1041(1) 265–66
  s 1041(2) 265–66, 268–69
  s 1041(2)(2).....................266
  s 1041(3) 265–66, 268–69
  s 1041(4) 265–66
  s 1042.......................261–62
  s 1042(1) 266–67
  s 1062...........................267
  s 1062(2) 269–70

TABLE OF TREATIES, LEGISLATION AND RULES xxxi

s 1062(3) 270
s 1063(3) 266–67
Code of Civil Procedure 1933
    (Nazi ZPO) 447–49, 453
    Art 1032(2) 409
    Art 1032(3) 447–48, 453
Constitution of Germany
    Art 103.....................266–67
    Art 103(1) 266–67
Law of 7 April 1933 for the
    Restoration of the Professional
    Civil Service 453

India

Arbitration Act 1940 311
Arbitration and Conciliation
    Act 1996...................316–17
    Pt 1 316–18
    s 2(2).......................316–17
    s 2(7).......................316–17
Arbitration (Protocol and Convention)
    Act 1937...................xlvi, 311
    s 9(b)........... 311, 312–13, 314, 316
Foreign Awards (Recognition and
    Enforcement) Act 1961
    s 9(b).......................316–17

Italy

Code of Civil Procedure
    Art 818.....................261–62

New Zealand

Arbitration Act 1996
    s 14 281

Pakistan

Arbitration Act 1940 315
Arbitration (Protocol and
    Convention) Act 1937
    s 9(b).......................314–15
Recognition and Enforcement
    (Arbitration Agreements and
    Foreign Arbitral Awards) Act 2011 ... 315
    s 7 315
    s 8 315

Russia

PRE-SOVIET RUSSIA
Decree of 16 March 1915 172–73
Decree of 1 July 1915 172–73
Decree of 8 February 1917........172–74

RUSSIAN SOVIET FEDERATIVE
SOCIALIST REPUBLIC
Civil Code 1922.......100–1, 103, 142–43,
                145–46, 325, 446, 453
    Art 37........................321–22
    Art 118......................84, 87
    Art 141........................87
Civil Code 1964.............320–21, 325
    Art 48.......................320–21
    Art 60.......................321–22
    Art 473......................320–21
Civil Procedural Code 1923 ....103, 134–35,
                444, 445–46
    Art 4........................89, 91
    Art 5..........................87
    Art 23.......................79, 87
    Art 24.......................79, 87
    Art 47.........................87
    Art 67.........................87
    Art 69.........................87
    Art 119........................87
    Art 166....................81, 87, 89
    Art 237........................89

RUSSIAN FEDERATION
Civil Code 446
Code of Civil Procedure 2002
    Art 209(2) 239–40

Scotland

Articles of Regulation 1695
    Art 25..........................264

Sweden

Arbitration Act 1999 ....375–76, 384
    s 21 375–76
    s 30 375–76
    s 30(1)......................375–76

Switzerland

Code of Civil Procedure (Zurich)
    s 306 273
Concordat on Arbitration 1969
    Art 26.......................261–62
    Art 31(1) 374–75
Federal Act on Private International
    Law 1987 ....270, 374–75
    Art 10........................272
    Art 183.............. 261–62, 271–72
    Art 183(1) 270–71
    Art 183(2) 270–73
    Art 183(3) 270–72

xxxii TABLE OF TREATIES, LEGISLATION AND RULES

Art 183(7) 271
Art 189 374–75
Art 190 374–75
Federal Code of Obligations
Art 20 321–22
Penal Code
Art 292 271–72

Union of Soviet Socialist Republics

Constitution of the Union of Soviet
Socialist Republics 81, 89–90
Art 1(3) 89–90
Art 1(h) 81, 87
Annex 2: Statute of the Council of
People's Commissars
Art 3(f). 81, 87
Decree of 28 June 1918. 176
Decree of 23 December 1920 on the
General Economic and Legal
Conditions for Concessions 135–36,
141–42
Decree of 3 May 1923 176–77
Decree No 1 of 24 November 1917
on Courts. 134–35
Decree No 2499/428 of
3 November 1934 162–64
Labour Code 137

United Kingdom

STATUTES
Administration of Justice
Act 1982 (c 53) 356–57
Arbitration Act 1889 (c 49) .... xli, 74,
124–25, 186–88, 293, 311–13,
328–29, 356, 431–32
s 19 125
Arbitration Act 1934 (c 14) 124–25,
311, 328–29, 356
s 4 .... 127–28, 371
s 11 .... 129, 356
s 12(1). 328–29
Arbitration Act 1950 (c 27) 186–87,
285–86, 294, 310–11, 373, 413–14, 449
Pt II. 310–11
s 9 127–28
s 9(1). 371
s 18(3). 328–30
s 19A. 356–57
s 20 .... 129, 356
s 21 294
s 40(b) 310–11

Arbitration Act 1975 (c 3) .... xlvi, 293–94,
310–11, 313–14, 315, 459
s 1 322
s 2 310–11
Arbitration Act 1979 (c 42) ... 285–86, 294,
368, 373, 432, 449, 451
Arbitration Act 1996 (c 23) .... xlvi, 127–28,
198, 211–12, 262, 283–87, 288, 291,
292–95, 296, 297, 300, 310–11,
313–14, 319, 322, 327–38, 348–49,
373, 378–79, 395–96, 397–98,
410, 420, 421, 424, 431–32,
440–41, 449, 450
Pt I 208, 327–30, 332,
334–35, 348–49
Pt II. 329–30
s 1 348
s 1(a). 208
s 1(b). 338
s 1(c). 293
s 2(1). 327–28
s 2(3). 264
s 3 327–28
s 3(a). 327–28
s 4 332–33
s 4(1). 328, 348–49
s 4(2). 332–33
s 4(3). 337–38, 348–49
s 4(4). 348–49
s 4(5). 198, 332–33, 334–37, 338
s 5 .... 327–28, 331–32, 333,
334–37, 346–47
s 5(1). 336, 346–47
s 5(4). 330–31
s 6 397
s 7 .... 159, 281, 306,
318–19, 323–24, 326
ss 9–11 348–49
ss 12–13 348–49
s 13 348–49
s 20(3). 371
s 22 371
s 22(2). 127–28
s 24 348–49
s 25 419
s 26(1). 348–49
ss 28–29 348–49
s 29 .... 213, 419
s 30 127–28
ss 31–33 348–49
s 33 .... 282, 346–47, 348
s 34 346–47

TABLE OF TREATIES, LEGISLATION AND RULES xxxiii

s 34(1)....................346–47, 348
s 37(2).........................348–49
s 38 ....262, 264
s 38(3).........................262
s 38(4).........................262
s 38(6).........................262
s 39 ....262, 264
s 39(1).......................262–63
s 39(2)(a) 262–63
s 39(4).........................262
s 40 .... 346–47, 348–49
s 41(5).........................264
s 42 264
s 43 348–49
s 44 263–64
s 44(3).......................263–64
s 44(5).......................263–64
s 44(6).......................263–64
s 46 .... 295, 296–97, 333, 337
s 46(1)(a) 332
s 46(1)(b) 126, 147
s 46(2).........................332
s 48 ....331, 334–35
s 48(1).........................337
s 48(5)(b) 337
s 49 ....331, 332–33, 334–37,
338, 353–55, 356–57
s 49(1)............... 332–33, 337, 353
s 49(2)............... 333–34, 337, 353
s 49(2)–(6)....................332–33
s 49(3)........... 332–34, 337, 354–55
s 49(3)(a) 354
s 49(3)(b) 354
s 49(3)–(4)....................129
s 49(4).........................354
s 49(5).........................354
s 49(6).........................354
s 52(3).........................373
s 56 348–49
s 59 328
s 60 .... 328–31, 348–49
s 63 304
s 65 304
ss 66–68 348–49
s 67 330–31
s 68 ....215–16, 282–84, 288,
330–31, 333–34, 336
s 68(2)(g) 211–12, 215–16
s 69 288
ss 70–71 348–49
ss 72–75 348–49
s 73 348–49

s 74 .... 415–16, 421, 422
s 78 419
ss 85–87 329–30
Sch 1 .... 328, 332–33, 348–49
Arbitration (Foreign Awards)
    Act 1930 (c 15) 310–12
    Pt I 310–11
    s 6(b).........................310–14
Civil Procedure Act 1997 (c 12) 285
Equal Pay Act 1970 (c 41) 410
Equality Act 2010 (c 15).............406
    s 83 410
Foreign Compensation Act
    1969 (c 20).................162–64
Foreign Limitation Periods
    Act 1984 (c 16) 348–49
Human Rights Act 1998 (c 42) 208
Judgments Act 1838 (c 110)...........353
Late Payment of Commercial Debts
    (Interest) Act 1998 (c 20).........353
Law Reform (Miscellaneous Provisions)
    Act 1934 (c 41)
    s 3 356–57
Law Reform (Miscellaneous Provisions)
    (Scotland) Act 1990 (c 40).......264
Limitation Act 1980 (c 58).........348–49
Senior Courts Act 1981 (c 54)
    (Supreme Court Act)
    s 35A.........................353
    s 37 247–48
Sex Disqualification (Removal)
    Act 1919 (c 71) 404
Unfair Contract Terms Act
    1977 (c 50).................417–18
Union with Scotland Act 1706 (c 11) ...211

STATUTORY INSTRUMENTS
Civil Procedure Rules 1998
    (SI 1998/3132)......... 284–85, 286,
287, 288, 411
    Pt 25 255–56
    Pt 32 221–22
    r 32.5(2) 220
    PD 32 paras 17–25 221–22
    Pt 35 221–22
    r 35.3(1) 221–22
    r 35.3(2) 221–22
    PD 35 221–22
    r 62.10.......................283–84
    r 62.10(1) 283–84
    r 62.10(3) 283–84, 288
    r 62.10(3)(b) 285

xxxiv TABLE OF TREATIES, LEGISLATION AND RULES

Employment Equality (Religion or
 Belief) Regulations 2003
 (SI 2003/1660)............406–7, 408
 reg 6(1)........................407–8
Rules of the Supreme Court
 (Revision) 1965
 (SI 1965/1776)
 Ord 73 285–86

Unfair Terms in Consumer
 Contracts Regulations 1999
 (SI 1999/2083)...............417–18

United States

New York Civil Practice Law and Rules ... 333
 s 5001(a).........................332
 ss 5001(b)–5004 332

Introduction

Stephen M. Schwebel*

For a quarter of a century, Van Vechten Veeder—universally known as 'Johnny'—was a towering figure in the worlds of international commercial arbitration and arbitration between States and foreign investors. He was towering literally for he was taller than most anybody else. He was towering figuratively because he was unsurpassed as an arbitrator; tribunal chairman, and expositor, analyst, and historian of international arbitration. Excerpts from some of the many arbitral awards to which he contributed as tribunal president are contained in Appendix I to this book. The last and longest such award, in *Chevron and Texaco v. Ecuador (II)*, illustrates his exceptional powers as an expositor of the factual and legal arguments of the parties, as an analyst and judge of the positions of the parties, and as an impartial and wise jurist sensitive to the public interest and the international interest.

Johnny happily did not confine his writings to arbitral awards. He was a riveting public speaker of flair and wit, who entertained his students and his professional audiences with his analyses of significant arbitrations and arbitral issues. This book reproduces his leading essays in this sphere.

The volume is divided into three main parts: (I) Learning from the Past, (II) the International Arbitration Process, and (III) Key Questions for All Users of International Arbitration. In each essay, the reader will at once recognize Johnny's extraordinary intelligence and acuity as well as his wit. For, however erudite, there is nothing dry in Johnny's way of approaching the evolution of international arbitration and its current successes and problems. Who else, for example, would give a leading lecture entitled 'Lessons for the Future from the Past: Individual Hedgehogs and Institutional Foxes'? Yet, such a title is entirely typical for Johnny as it reflects two of his firm beliefs.

First, Johnny believed—and convinced whoever was in his audience—that the cases and institutional developments in a period from the late nineteenth century to the 1930s could teach contemporary practitioners a very great deal about contemporary issues and not just by way of putting such issues into their proper historical perspective. And, of course, in this he was correct, and it has been an incomparable pleasure in drafting this Introduction to see, again, how much there is to be learnt from cases like the *Alabama Claims Arbitration* of 1872 and the Soviet concession cases of the 1920s and 1930s that were of high import to the contemporaneous political leaders such as Lenin, Trotsky, and Stalin. Indeed, in using the past

---

* Former Judge and President of the International Court of Justice.

On Arbitration. Edited by: Sam Wordsworth KC and Marie Veeder, Oxford University Press. © Oxford University Press 2023.
DOI: 10.1093/oso/9780192869135.001.0001

to explain lessons for the present and the future, Johnny was more free to express his originality and the depth of his thinking and could be less concerned about expressing views that might incorrectly be thought relevant to whichever particular difficult issue of contract or treaty arbitration he was then having to decide.

Second, Johnny believed—or, at least, this came entirely naturally to him—that it was vital to generate reflection and amusement on the part of his audience as well as to pass on his thoughts. Hence, to speak of 'Individual Hedgehogs and Institutional Foxes' as a means of conveying his views on the competing value in each member of the current generation of international arbitration practitioners acting as an individual, as opposed to an indivisible part of any given institution or organization, was, for Johnny, all very much par for the course. And this is all the more so as the views are communicated via a description of the nature and importance of the contribution to the development of international arbitration of figures as diverse as F. F. Martens (a key figure behind The Hague Peace Conferences of 1899 and 1907 and the establishment of the Permanent Court of Arbitration), Dr Friedrich Gaus (the drafter of several arbitration treaties for Germany, who was one of the very few senior figures in the German Foreign Office who were not to join the National Socialist Party, voluntarily or otherwise), and Bertie Vigrass (Director General of the Institute of Arbitrators and subsequently of the London Court of International Arbitration).

In each part of this volume, the reader will see like examples of Johnny's customary vivacity.

Part I: Learning from the Past

Part I of the volume begins with the first of two pieces on the seminal international arbitration between States of the past two centuries, the *Alabama Claims Arbitration* of 1872. Its process and product settled a grave dispute that threatened to generate a catastrophic war between the United States and the British Empire. It demonstrated to an attentive world the value and potential of arbitration in the settlement of important international disputes. While States previously had established specific claims commissions between them, the success of the *Alabama Claims Arbitration* provided an instructive and unmatched stimulus to the peace movement of the nineteenth century and beyond.

In his essay, 'The Historical Keystone to International Arbitration: The Party-Appointed Arbitrator—from Miami to Geneva', Johnny persuasively maintains that the history of the case also shows that the party appointment of arbitrators is crucial for the parties to have trust in the decision-making process. That lesson—in the view of the author of this Introduction, and, I believe, in Johnny's view—appears to have been lost by the European Union, which proposes to replace investor–State arbitration by an international investment court whose members would be chosen solely by States.

If and when that court is established and functions, it will remain to be seen whether in practice it will render judgments sounder and more effective than those that have been rendered in the course of investor–State arbitration. If one compares the balance and implementation of the arbitral awards authored under the presidency of Johnny working with party-appointed arbitrators with the soundness of awards in State-to-State judgments concerning foreign investment, there may be room to question the validity of the criticism of a Commissioner of the European Union, who acidly described investor–State arbitration as evidencing 'the rule of lawyers' rather than the rule of law.

Johnny's essay imaginatively entitled 'Investor–State Disputes and the Development of International Law: Arbitral Lessons from the Private Correspondence of Queen Victoria and Lenin' also reverts to the *Alabama Claims Arbitration*. In negotiating the Washington Treaty referring their dispute to arbitration, Great Britain's negotiators understood that the arbitration tribunal was to assess the legal basis and dimension of US claims for the depredations of Confederate cruisers such as the *Alabama*, whereas the United States claimed that, in addition to such direct damages, the tribunal was also entitled to assess indirect damages for the prolongation of the Civil War. The difference in the enormity of the resultant claims was immense. Johnny's essay colourfully recounts how the arbitral tribunal itself was able to sidestep the US claims for indirect damages. It made an award in favour of the United States, promptly paid by the United Kingdom, in a sum then the largest in arbitral history. It was not otherwise approached in size until the award of some 50 billion US dollars against the Russian Federation in the *Yukos* cases, an award being challenged in Dutch courts.

Johnny's essay on 'Inter-State Arbitration' addresses—with his customary meticulous scholarship and vivid portrayal of leading personalities involved— arbitration between States as facilitated by The Hague Conferences of 1899 and 1907. Those conferences produced the Permanent Court of Arbitration ('PCA'), which actually is not a court, permanent or impermanent, but a standing facility for the creation of specific arbitral tribunals. Its tribunals produced a small number of awards before the First World War and another small number between the two World Wars, several of considerable importance. For decades thereafter, the PCA went into hibernation. It was reawakened in 1981 by facilitating the establishment in The Hague of the Iran–United States Claims Tribunal, which, over the past forty years, has successfully addressed hundreds of disputes between the United States and the Islamic Republic of Iran, largely arising out of actions taken by the latter's revolutionary Government against US investments. At issue also are massive Iranian claims against the US Government for armaments ordered and paid for by the Imperial Government of Iran, delivery of which was interdicted by the United

xxxviii INTRODUCTION

States because of Iran's imprisonment of US diplomats. The Tribunal's awards by now comprise some forty volumes.

During these years, a cascade of other arbitral awards has flowed from other tribunals as well. There have been many hundreds of awards by tribunals addressing claims by foreign investors against States in the implementation of bilateral investment treaties (BITs), which themselves have numbered a few thousand. A great many of these cases have been ably administered by the World Bank's International Centre for Settlement of Investment Disputes (ICSID). Other such arbitral proceedings have been administered by other centres including the International Chamber of Commerce, the Stockholm Chamber of Commerce, the London Court of International Arbitration, and the American Arbitration Association.

The Third United Nations Convention on the Law of the Sea has also been the source of arbitral proceedings between Convention Parties involving the interpretation or application of that great, comprehensive Convention. In all, today, there are many more international arbitration proceedings between States, and between States and other parties, than in the previous history of international law.

The essay entitled '1922: The Birth of the ICC Arbitration Clause and the Demise of the Anglo-Soviet Urquhart Concession' is a fascinating, deeply researched account of efforts to restore negotiated contractual coverage and operations for vast British mining investments of Czarist days. These efforts ultimately foundered because, in the 1922 negotiations between the British mining magnate Leslie Urquhart and the Soviet Commissar for International Trade, Leonid Krasin, Urquhart insisted on neutral arbitration of disputes. Soviet leadership was divided. One element was willing to accept neutral arbitration of concession disputes because much-needed foreign capital would not flow without it. Moreover, as explained by Krasin in a letter to Stalin of 26 August 1926, accepting arbitration in the sphere of private relations was perceived as risking nothing, 'especially because the entire enterprise, the capital invested by the concessionaire, the equipment, etc.—all remain on our territory; and, if we want, we can always take any measures against the concessionaire'. As the *Lena Goldfields* experience was to demonstrate, Veeder observes, 'This latter argument was, of course, brutally correct.'

The extended negotiations between Urquhart and Krasin did result in a provisional concession agreement containing an international arbitration clause 'For the settlement of disputes which may arise between the Government and the Concessionaire on questions of interpretation or fulfilment of the present Concession Agreement'. Each party was to nominate two arbitrators who were to elect the tribunal president. If they were unable to do so, they would choose a president from among six candidates chosen by the Government 'of worldwide or European fame, lawyers, engineers or public men'. Urquhart was unwilling to sign the provisionally negotiated Agreement without such an arbitration clause, whereas Lenin (and Trotsky, who chaired the Soviet concessions committee) proved unwilling to ratify the Agreement with it. The deleterious effects on budding relationships between the Soviet Government and Great Britain, and on prospects for foreign investment in the USSR, were significant.

The essay on 'The 1921–1923 North Sakhalin Concession Agreement: The 1925 Court Decisions between the US Company Sinclair Exploration and the Soviet Government' recounts the nullification by Soviet courts of a thirty-six-year concession agreement made in 1922 between Sinclair and the effective agent of government of the USSR. Because of the then occupation of North Sakhalin by Japanese troops, Sinclair's effort to launch development of the concession in 1924 was frustrated by the Japanese arrest of the members of Sinclair's expedition on arrival in North Sakhalin. Subsequently, pursuant to a Soviet–Japanese Treaty of 1925, Japanese troops withdrew from North Sakhalin and Japan recognized the USSR and received economic concessions in North Sakhalin bearing upon Sinclair's position. USSR courts cancelled Sinclair's concession on the ground of its non-fulfilment by Sinclair. Sinclair pleaded *force majeure*. USSR courts, whose translated judgments are attached to the essay, rejected the plea of *force majeure*, essentially on the ground that the parties were aware of the presence of Japanese troops when they concluded the concession agreement.

The point Johnny makes is that, for a short period from 1925 (Lenin having died in 1924), the USSR was willing to learn from the very negative foreign reaction to the judgments against Sinclair and to agree to ad hoc arbitration clauses in concessions so as to attract desperately needed foreign investment, that being a lesson that retains a contemporary relevance. As Johnny concludes, 'Those who forget history are condemned to remember.'

The chapter 'Lloyd George, Lenin and Cannibals: The Harriman Arbitration' is another expansively entitled essay which reflects Johnny's gifts for characterization and the penetration of his research. In 1925, Averell Harriman negotiated a concession for recovery and renewed production of manganese, of which Georgia was a prime source. It remarkably provided for a three-man arbitration tribunal, each party naming an arbitrator and the chairman to be a neutral drawn from the faculty of the Universities of Paris or Oslo. Remarkably, it also provided for a truncated tribunal to proceed in case of a failure of an arbitrator to act. The enterprise was a commercial failure; the concession agreement and the arbitral provision were terminated on agreed terms, which included payment to Harriman of modest compensation, whose final instalments were still being paid to Harriman in 1941 when he arrived in Moscow as Roosevelt's personal envoy to Stalin. Harriman subsequently served with great distinction as US Ambassador to the USSR. The prescient and groundbreaking terms for arbitration that he negotiated in 1925 were a foretaste of his performance as a statesman that was appreciated even by the Soviet leadership.

The essay on 'The *Lena Goldfields* Arbitration: The Historical Roots of Three Ideas' is especially rewarding. The fate of the Lena Goldfields investment is a 'baleful monument to the absolute power of a State by force alone to thwart the

xl INTRODUCTION

consensual process of international arbitration.' Johnny so concludes because the United Kingdom found itself the ultimate paymaster for four successive grievances: expropriation of a British company without compensation (1918), repudiation of the subsequently revised concession agreement (1929), failure to honour the arbitration award (1930), and repudiation of the settlement agreement between the United Kingdom and the USSR (1940). Johnny, however, concludes that:

> Juridically, over the last 65 years, its direct beneficiary has been the modern system of international commercial arbitration to which the *Lena* Tribunal applied three innovative and hugely important ideas: (i) the application of a non-national system of law to the merits of a private law dispute, namely, 'general principles of law'; (ii) the power of the majority of an arbitration tribunal to continue the proceedings in the absence of the minority; and (iii) [...] the legal autonomy or 'separability' of an [...] arbitration clause [...] In the broadest sense, the *Lena* case represents the development of modern commercial arbitration.

The *Lena* award was a majority award made by a tribunal chaired by Dr Otto Stutzer, professor at the Freiburg School of Mines, jointly appointed by the parties after Lena declined to accept the Russian proposal to appoint Dr Albert Einstein as chairman. Lena appointed Sir Leslie Scott, a British arbitrator. The Russian-appointed arbitrator refused to attend the hearing on orders involving Stalin and Molotov. Nonetheless, the tribunal met in London. The tribunal dissolved the most important concession granted by the USSR and required it to pay a sum for unjust enrichment of £13 million, plus interest, equivalent nowadays to about £350 million, a very large sum but much less than Lena's actual loss.

The *Lena* award is apparently the first by a private arbitration tribunal applying a general principle of law recognized by civilized nations by reference to the sources of law set out in the Statute of the Permanent Court of International Justice. The *Lena* award led directly to the governing law clause of the 1933 concession agreement between Persia and the Anglo-Persian Oil Company, which has influenced the drafting of concession agreements and many other international contracts ever since.

That coincidence apparently arises from the fact that a counsel of Lena in its arbitration and a counsel to the Anglo-Persian Oil Company in the drafting of its 1933 concession agreement was the same man, namely, Dr V. R. Idelson. Dr Idelson, a Russian lawyer practising in St Petersburg, fled the Red Terror in 1918, arriving in England in 1920. He practised as an émigré lawyer, mainly as an expert witness on Russian law. He was naturalized, read for the Bar, was called to Gray's Inn, took silk, and by 1947 was admitted as a Bencher of Gray's Inn. Johnny's remarkable research extends not only to official Russian archives and legal works in Russian and German but also to the grandchildren of Dr Idelson.

INTRODUCTION xli

Another groundbreaking element of the *Lena* concession agreement was the specification that, if one party did not send its appointed arbitrator to the hearing, the chairman and the other party-appointed arbitrator could proceed to decide the dispute. Johnny persuasively credits Dr Idelson with the drafting of this prescient provision, which the tribunal applied.

Russia is perceived as contending in the *Lena* proceedings that an arbitration agreement loses its force if one of the parties rescinds the underlying contract. Johnny finds that the *Lena* Tribunal did not pass upon the accepted doctrine of the separability of the arbitration clause but that the USSR accepts it in any event.

'The Tetiuhe Mining Concession 1924–1932: A Swiss–Russian Story (Where the Arbitral Dog Did Not Bark)' recounts the founding and operation of a successful zinc, lead, and silver mining company north of Vladivostok before the First World War. Its operations suffered badly from the war and the Bolshevik Revolution. Its mines were resuscitated during the years of the New Economic Policy by British investments, this being one of the three largest foreign concessions granted by the USSR at the time (alongside the Harriman and *Lena Goldfields* concessions). But when the Great Depression hit, the concession became unprofitable and then became unworkable in the winter of 1930–1931 due to the impacts of Stalin's first Five-Year Plan. The mines and their improvements were, however, sold to the Russian Government at a fair price.

Johnny explains the importance of the role played by the agreement to arbitrate in this settlement. In typically vivacious language, Johnny invokes Sherlock Holmes's famous watchdog—'international commercial arbitration is significant because it does "nothing in the night-time"'. Wary of the USSR's failure to engage in the arbitral process in the *Lena* case, but also aware of the acute damage that this failure had caused to the USSR's commercial and diplomatic reputation, the concession-holders (principally, the Bryner family) threatened but pulled back from arbitration in March 1931, securing a successful settlement later in that year. Johnny delights in the characters and the complex, high-level politics involved in reaching the settlement; but the ultimate focus is on 'the arbitral dog', which even though not unleashed, promoted an amicable settlement.

The final essay in Part I, 'Two Arbitral Butterflies: Bramwell and David' recalls the Arbitration Code of 1883 drawn up by Lord Bramwell, which was quickly displaced by the English Arbitration Act 1889. However, as Johnny explains, the latter drew upon an important feature of the Bramwell Code, making consensual arbitration pre-eminent and placing it within the law of contract. The importance of this, as Johnny explains, is that only contractual arbitration could ever become truly international:

With arbitration rooted in contractual consensus, there was then no logical reason to limit the effect of an arbitration agreement or an award between parties of different nationalities to the territory of any particular State. And there was

xlii INTRODUCTION

thus no logical reason to limit the enforcement in different States of arbitration agreements and awards between parties of different nationalities.

The second fleeting proposal was the International Institute for the Unification of Private Law (UNIDROIT) Rome Draft 1936, which, however, indirectly led to the 1985 United Nations Commission on International Trade Law (UNCITRAL) Model Law. The arbitral butterfly here is Professor René David, who played a major role in the drafting and commentary to the Rome Draft, a uniform law consisting of forty articles that was approved by the International Chamber of Commerce (ICC) Congress in 1937, subject, however, to criticisms expressed by four national committees (Australia, Japan, the United Kingdom, and the United States), which ultimately led to the demise of the Draft.

Part II: The International Arbitration Process

Johnny had a particular interest in the international arbitral process. He expressed that interest not only by his analyses of and commentaries upon existing processes, but also by playing a leading part in proposing—and negotiating—improvements in those processes.

Part II of the volume gathers together a number of essays and short pieces written by Johnny that focus on different aspects of process in international arbitration.[3] The pieces are presented in the order that they were written, beginning with the paper of seminal importance of March 2000 entitled 'The "Y2K Problem" and Arbitration: The Answer to the Myth'. No doubt, given the sensitivity of the topic, the paper was published under the name of Professor Dr Ylts, a Veeder pseudonym that will be instantly recognized by any regular subscriber of *Arbitration International* (of which Johnny was a one-time editor and then general editor).

Part II continues on a more serious note with the 2001 Goff Lecture in Hong Kong addressing 'The Lawyer's Duty to Arbitrate in Good Faith'. Consistent with a theme underlying many of the essays of Part I introduced above, Johnny writes that 'without world trade, there can be no world peace; international arbitration is the oil which lubricates the machinery of world trade'; but he continues, 'and the mechanics, the international arbitration practitioners, now deserve better practical guidance as to how to apply that oil'. He asks the question as to 'what is procedural unfairness' and identifies how this can, in turn, raise acute questions of legal, professional, and cultural diversity which are now of immense importance in the practice of international arbitration by parties and, particularly, by their lawyers.

---

[3] The reader is also referred to the contributions of Johnny Veeder collected by the International Congress and Convention Association (ICCA) in *V. V. Veeder QC Congress Series Memorial Volume: An ICCA Congress Series Tribute to Johnny Veeder (1948–2020)*.

Veeder thus explains that the issues raised in ensuring procedural fairness in international arbitration are more complex than before national courts, in part because the representatives of the parties are diverse and often do not share the same legal culture. Further, unlike most national court systems, there is no appeal on the merits from an arbitration award. There is a lack of transparency in international arbitration, 'the whole activity takes place in a cloud of privacy without the same public scrutiny directed at state courts'. While good faith in the performance civil procedural obligations is assumed by civilian lawyers, 'English law on good faith says nothing about the activities of a party's representatives in an international arbitration.' What is needed, Veeder writes, is practical guidance on good faith for the legal representatives of parties.

The focus is then on the solutions that have been proffered, including through the various sets of rules published by the International Bar Association (IBA). In his conclusions, Johnny makes some 'modest suggestions', including with respect to factual and witness evidence. In international arbitration, a party and not the tribunal leads its own factual and expert witnesses. The witnesses reduce into writing in advance what would be their own evidence-in-chief. That prevents 'ambush' and saves time and money. The problem, however, is that the evidence tends to be written not by the witness but by his or her counsel, even if approved by the witness. This practice diminishes the statement's probative value and increases the need for cross-examination. Johnny approves requiring an attachment to witness statements by the counsel who procured them, specifying in explicit detail how and by whom the statement was prepared.

The next essay, 'The Natural Limits to the Truncated Tribunal: The German Case of the Soviet Eggs and the Dutch Abduction of the Indonesian Arbitrator', examines two episodes in the history of arbitral tribunals that acted in the absence of a party-appointed arbitrator.

The first episode is used to illustrate the difference between a refusal to act and a mere failure to act, which may not in any way be obstructive of the arbitral process. The 1925 German–Soviet Treaty contained an Agreement concerning Commercial Courts of Arbitration. It provided at Article 4 that should an arbitrator die or be unable to act or refuse to fulfil his duties, the appointing party must appoint another. A German company, IWA, concluded an agreement with Soviet authorities to market, as sole European distributor, eggs exported from Russia. A dispute arose. The Soviet supplier appointed a Soviet arbitrator; IWA appointed a German arbitrator. These arbitrators appointed a Soviet chairman. The Soviet chairman called a hearing in Moscow in four days, but the German arbitrator replied that he had a prior business engagement on that day. The chairman fixed a second date, but the German arbitrator replied that he had an engagement that day as well. The chairman then applied to the president of the Russian Soviet Federative Socialist Republic (RSFSR) Supreme Court for an order removing the German arbitrator and replacing him with a substitute, a Russian national. It was granted. The three

xliv INTRODUCTION

Soviet arbitrators eventually made a unanimous award in Moscow in favour of the Soviet exporter. When enforcement was sought, two German courts refused to enforce the award on the ground that the German arbitrator had not refused to fulfil his duties.

The second case was more dramatic. In 1994, two Bermudan companies owned by US investors made power purchase agreements for the development and operation of electricity-generating facilities in Java. In 1998, the Bermudan companies began arbitrations against a government-owned company, Pertamina, and the Indonesian Government. These resulted in two large awards against Pertamina, which it refused to pay. The claimants proceeded with other claims against the Indonesian Government. Pertamina then obtained injunctions from a Jakarta court enjoining the enforcement of the awards and imposing a penalty of US $1 million a day on any party (apparently including the arbitrators) continuing with the arbitrations. The tribunal removed the place of the next hearing to the Peace Palace in The Hague, as it was entitled to do under the UNCITRAL Rules and its Terms of Appointment.

The Republic of Indonesia then applied to the District Court in The Hague for an injunction against the arbitrators approaching the Peace Palace. The application failed. The flight of the Indonesian-appointed arbitrator from Indonesia to The Hague was interrupted by an agent of the Indonesian Government, who joined him at Dulles Airport, flew with him to Amsterdam, and prevented him from joining his colleagues. He was obliged to fly back to Indonesia. The dolorous details are set out in Johnny's essay. The remaining two arbitrators, informed of the reasons for the absence of their colleague, proceeded as a truncated tribunal to make awards on the merits. It appears that the Bermudan companies were substantially indemnified by their political risk insurers.

As Johnny notes, the problem in finding a solution to such a scandalous case is how and where to strike the balance. The principal lesson that he draws is that there is a danger of overreacting to such outrages, which, after all, are very rare, while ultimately the case is to be taken as proving only that international arbitration works.

The next three essays concentrate on issues that have come to the fore in more recent cases. In 'Issue Estoppel, Reasons for Awards and Transnational Arbitration', Veeder considers whether it would not be absurd for parties to relitigate issues in a different arbitration where those same issues have already been decided in the reasons for an earlier award between the same parties. Johnny is sympathetic to the application of issue estoppel where the facts support it. He analyses two contemporary international arbitrations—the *Aegis* and *CME* cases—in which issue estoppel was at issue. It succeeded in neither. In one of those cases, the three arbitrators testified before the Svea Court of Appeal, which distinguished the two awards and upheld the latter, challenged award which was handed down days after the earlier award. While noting the existence of a waiver and the very particular facts of the *CME* case (where there was a refusal of an offer to consolidate), Johnny raises the question of principle, which remains topical today: 'where the parties are the same (or very similar) and capable of being bound by successive awards in different arbitration proceedings, how are these parties to protect themselves against the risk of inconsistent decisions from the different tribunals on similar issues of fact or law?' In answer to this question, Johnny highlights the potential importance of the concept of issue estoppel, a concept that he returned to as part of the tribunal deciding the North American Free Trade Agreement (NAFTA) case *Apotex Holdings Inc. and Apotex Inc. v. USA* in 2014.

The chapter, 'The Need for Cross-border Enforcement of Interim Measures Ordered by a State Court in Support of the International Arbitral Process', addresses the difficulties of developing effective cross-border interim measures despite the need for them. Johnny identifies the absence of a universal regime for cross-border enforcement as a 'curious gap in the modern system of international commercial arbitration' and incisively examines this complex problem with his characteristic legal and linguistic learning.

The chapter entitled 'The Transparency of International Arbitration: Process and Substance' perceptively examines the limitations on the confidentiality of the arbitral process, and of arbitral awards once they are challenged in court proceedings, and also highlights the need for a spectrum that recognizes that different arbitrations may give rise to quite different demands in terms of confidentiality.

The essay 'Free Spirits – the Search for "International" Arbitration' sees Johnny writing in a more humorous and less pragmatic mode, addressing the 'philosophical question [...] frequently asked by many: which came first—the arbitral chicken or the arbitral egg?'. In fact, this is another critical essay intelligible to readers steeped in arbitral theory, practice, and controversy. A comparison is drawn between the French and English approaches to (or concepts of) arbitration. The enormous significance of France to the development of international commercial arbitration is recognized and the suggestion made that there is much to be learnt from the French school of arbitral philosophy.

Johnny's short chapter 'The Role of Users' identifies the rather more prosaic point that 'users are a necessary fact to every international arbitration: it is their arbitration' and notes how it is incorrect to assume that the users' interests are exactly the same as lawyers' interests. He asks questions that might well be asked by the parties to arbitral proceedings but, in practice, are not asked. The heavy costs and long delays of document production—discovery—are notorious. Why do none of the most used arbitration rules provide the option of excluding discovery? The cost of oral hearings is very high. Why is it so rare to exclude oral hearings, or, at least, the hearing of witnesses? Why should not costs be capped at the outset of an arbitration? Johnny suggests ways of doing so.

The next essay, another expansively entitled lecture, 'From Florence to London via Moscow and New Delhi: How and Why Arbitral Ideas Migrate', reveals Johnny in far more discursive mode and is a good example of Johnny at his finest and most unique. Who else would introduce an essay on international arbitration with a discussion of the sixteenth-century saint, Maxim the Greek, 'the only known arbitrator to be a saint'? He is offered as an example of how one man, armed only with ideas, could migrate from Italy to Moscow to influence the course of Russian history; and he acts as a springboard to show how arbitral ideas—one bad, one good— have migrated across the globe.

Veeder initially examines an error that occurred in 1930 when England enacted the 1927 Geneva Convention on Arbitral Awards. Parliament added: 'nothing in Part I of the Act on the recognition and enforcement of Convention awards shall "apply to any award made on an arbitration agreement governed by the law of England"'. This extra-territorial provision was abandoned by the English Arbitration Act 1975. However, it had migrated to the law of India in its 1937 Act and was acted upon by courts of India (and later by courts of Pakistan). The result was that foreign awards made outside of India and Pakistan could be reviewed by their courts as domestic awards—and were. The English colonial error that migrated to India/Pakistan was, however, corrected in Pakistan by the 2011 enactment of the New York Convention. The position in India remains more complex and deleterious. It has seriously detracted from foreign investment in India, so much so as to have been a cause of significant electricity shortages.

This essay then addresses a foundational principle of international arbitration: the doctrine of separability. This is the second and good 'idea', which is depicted as migrating eventually to London. The invalidity or rescission of the main contract containing the arbitration clause does not entail the invalidity or rescission of the arbitration clause, an accepted principle ignored by the counsel of Iran in its pleadings before the International Court of Justice in the *Anglo-Iranian Oil Company Case*.

In the final essay in this part, 'Jurisdiction, Admissibility and Choice of Law in International Arbitration', Johnny examines what he characterizes as two quixotic limitations on party autonomy under the United Kingdom's Arbitration Act 1996. One relates to costs of arbitration, the other to pre-award interest. The first is portrayed as a real problem, the second as a myth.

Part III: Key Questions for All Users of International Arbitration

Part III brings together a number of Johnny's pieces (arranged in chronological order) that either expressly ask or address overarching questions relevant to international arbitration. The first such piece is entitled, and asks, the critical question: 'Whose Arbitration Is It Anyway—The Parties' or the Arbitration Tribunal's?'. In answering this question, Johnny considers three complications concerning (i) the problem of arbitrators seeking to second-guess the interests of the parties, (ii) the difference between an arbitral tribunal and a court, and (iii) the scope for being diverted by theoretical issues. Johnny explains why the arbitration is the parties' arbitration. But the arbitrator is the master of the award. Johnny traces the arbitral history of awarding interest, simple and compound. He observes that commercial arbitration has awarded compound interest before national courts have done so.

The next four essays in Part III focus on the decision-makers and the institutions that support an arbitration. The first of these asks and addresses the question, 'Is There Any Need for a Code of Ethics for International Commercial Arbitrators?' and sets out Johnny's doubts. Although he does advise arbitrators to carry professional indemnity insurance cover, the conclusion is 'if it ain't broke, don't fix it: and so please, unlike Oliver Twist, no more ethical porridge'.

In 'Still More on Arbitral Deliberations: An English Perspective', Johnny reviews the nature of deliberation among the members of a modern international arbitral tribunal. The key point is that the chairman shall ensure that all the members of the tribunal are equally heard; but, if the tribunal is not unanimous, the dissenting arbitrator may not be permitted to require unending deliberations, nor may they be entitled to participate in the drafting of the majority award. Johnny rightly cites the judgment of the Svea Court of Appeal in the case of *CME v. The Czech Republic* in support of these conclusions (also considered in Johnny's essay in Part II, 'Issue Estoppel, Reasons for Awards, and Transnational Arbitration'). It was a case in which two arbitrations addressed much the same events concurrently, although the nominal parties and the bilateral investment treaties differed. The seat of the earlier launched arbitration was London; of the later, Stockholm. The London arbitration rendered its award five days before the Stockholm tribunal issued its award. The Stockholm award has been criticized for reaching conclusions on concordant facts and law opposed to those of the London award. In the view of the writer of this Introduction, that criticism is unfounded, as amply demonstrated by the testimony of the arbitrators before the Svea Court of Appeal. Not only was the Stockholm award drafted before sight of the London award, but the London award was also issued first because of unreasonable delay on the part of the dissenting arbitrator that slowed the issuance of the Stockholm award.

The essay 'Why Bother and Why It Matters?' is concerned with how legal institutions may suddenly crumble, with the focus being ICSID and whether it will retain support. It is a question that, as Johnny puts it, 'has begun to bother many of us and it matters to all of us'. In typical Johnny style, the question of why it matters is addressed by reference to an example from history, the fate of the 1908 La Brea concession in Peru. In 1921, Great Britain and Peru had been able to agree to a one-off arbitration treaty and the then dispute was resolved. No such remedy could be agreed or was available in 1963, when a further and acrimonious dispute developed, which ultimately led to scandal and to a military coup, followed in turn by economic ruin. Hence why investment arbitration matters, and ICSID too. As another example of why ICSID matters, Johnny points to Article 21 ICSID Convention and the immunity for arbitrators established by that provision. As to

xlviii INTRODUCTION

the threat to ICSID, Johnny focuses on factors including the sudden loss of its two most senior officers and threats to its budget. The precise nature of the threats may have changed, but the pertinence of this short essay does not.

'The Importance of a Party Treating as Independent Its Independent Arbitrator' leads Johnny to revisit what he terms 'the catastrophic appointment' of the then Lord Chief Justice Sir Alexander Cockburn as arbitrator in the *Alabama Claims Arbitration*. He was openly partisan and discourteous. Johnny observes that the appointment of a partisan arbitrator is counterproductive because he loses influence with the presiding arbitrator. A party-appointed arbitrator should ensure that all the arguments of his party get a thorough and fair hearing; while, importantly: 'A party's appointment of an independent arbitrator carries with it an obligation to respect that arbitrator's independence.'

The essay entitled 'Is there a Need to Revise the New York Convention?' is a witty demolition of any such proposal which is incapable of pedestrian summary. In his short essay on 'Who Are the Arbitrators?', Johnny then considers, with his customary vivacity, that diversity as regards gender and race in the appointment of arbitrators and counsel has a long way to go but, in recent decades, has begun to move significantly in a progressive direction.

The final three pieces of this volume comprise two prestigious lectures given by Johnny in 2015–2016 and an important essay on the current practical problems facing arbitral institutions and arbitrators regarding potential legal liability to disappointed users. The latter, entitled 'Arbitrators and Arbitral Institutions: Legal Risks For Product Liability?' takes as its starting point an analogy to the infamous tort case, *Donaghue v. Stephenson* and asks us to recall that not only will 50 per cent of arbitration customers (the losing parties) be dissatisfied but also that even the winning party may find 'that our particular bottle contains not only a decomposed snail, which can make the drinking experience less than satisfactory, but worse, that the bottle contains no ginger beer at all. In the ginger beer trade, technically that is called "annulled ginger beer".' Adding to this the contractual nexus which did not exist in *Donaghue v. Stephenson*, and the notable cost of arbitration, Johnny records a developing trend in arbitrators and/or arbitral institutions being pursued by disappointed parties and concludes with a practical solution.

In 'The Alexander Lecture 2015, London 26 November 2015: "What Matters—about Arbitration"', Johnny was one of the few leading international arbitrators to speak up publicly in defence of investor–State arbitration, which has been an object of professional and unprofessional criticism in recent years. He cogently questions the proposals of the European Community to replace investor–State arbitration with a standing international investment court. At the same time, with typical self-effacement, Johnny questions whether he is well placed to ask the relevant questions:

Arbitrators, arbitration practitioners and, dare I say it, even arbitral institutions are not the most persuasive advocates for arbitration. We are, of course, thoroughly objective and fair-minded people; but what we say in defence of arbitration can often seem to others as self-interested. Rather like Ms Rice-Davies famously during the Profumo inquiry, 'they would say that, wouldn't they'.

The concluding essay is based on the Kaplan Lecture of 2016, 'Lessons for the Future from the Past: Individual Hedgehogs and Institutional Foxes', as already discussed at the beginning of this Introduction. It recalls The Hague Peace Conferences of 1899 and 1907 and the 'intellectual energy of the Russian representative, F.F. Martens, who was largely responsible for this remarkable achievement', the establishment of the Permanent Court of Arbitration. In the 1920s, international commercial arbitration could be agreed between Soviet authorities and foreign traders but was abandoned, as were concessions themselves, with the demise of the New Economic Policy. However, in June 1946, Soviet arbitration specialists took part in the conference convened by the International Chamber of Commerce. That conference eventually led to the 1958 New York Convention. The essay sketches the careers and contributions of diverse arbitration specialists, some noted, others forgotten, but, as was ever typical with Johnny, all leading to a conclusion with contemporary and enduring significance. In this respect, Johnny's concern in this essay is with the way arbitral institutions develop:

> This arbitral oak-tree has deep historical roots. In reforming and re-legitimising arbitration, there are ways to apply lessons from the past, without having to plant a new sapling every time or to re-invent an existing wheel. That is why, I suggest, these four and many other individuals from the past should remain important for us. Unlike most institutions, they each kept their minds as individuals on one big thing, without even knowing that it was to become so big.

This volume concludes with a short Postscript that seeks to testify to Johnny's exceptional qualities as a teacher, a mentor, a colleague, and a friend.[4] In the appendices, the reader will find selected extracts from some of the seminal arbitral awards to which Johnny contributed (Appendix I) and excerpts from Johnny's lectures to students at King's College London (Appendix II).

The reader of Johnny's essays and other contributions will profit by his extraordinary legal learning and insight and by the breadth and depth of his devotion to the arbitral process. Johnny's lucid writings give a sense of his humanity, of his warmth and wit. His mentoring of many juniors and assistants illustrated his limitless generosity. To know Johnny was to know one of the greater minds and finer characters of our time.

---

[4] The reader is also referred to the tributes to Johnny in the special issue of *Arbitration International*, Volume 37, Issue 2 (June 2021).

PART I
LEARNING FROM THE PAST

Introduction to Part I*

Even if, in Coleridge's words, 'the light which experience gives is a lantern on the stern, which shines only on the waves behind us'; then those waves come from storms which lie ahead.

Judge Schwebel has already provided a review of the essays contained within this Part I, and the purpose of this more specific Introduction is to offer a further insight into Johnny Veeder's very particular interest in the history of international arbitration and his pleasure in discovering and conveying how much there is to learn from the past. A very important starting point is a legal figure from Johnny's own personal history.

In 1967, Johnny went up to Cambridge to read modern languages. After a rather unhappy first year at Jesus College, Johnny approached the Director of Legal Studies to discuss a switch to law. Although Johnny thought this would only be a formality, he was immediately turned down. Believing there was no possibility of dissuading the Director, Johnny got up to leave the room when he suddenly heard the voice behind him say, 'Wait—what did you say your name was...?' Judge Veeder, Johnny's namesake, was a noted legal practitioner and judge. He was also a well-known legal historian. He was a contributor to the *Columbia* and *Harvard Law Reviews* and was the author of *Legal Masterpieces: Specimens of Argumentation and Exposition by Eminent Lawyers* as well as numerous articles on the English judicature that were published in *The Green Bag*. The Director of Studies knew Johnny's grandfather's historical sketches and so he took a chance on the young Veeder and Johnny's change to law was confirmed.

A legal lifetime later, one of the greatest joys of Johnny's life was attending the 150th anniversary celebration of the establishment of the Federal District Court Eastern District of New York held in 2015. The Court was created upon the passage of a bill signed in 1865 by the then President Abraham Lincoln. Johnny's participation at the event was set in motion late in 2014 when he answered a telephone call from the United States. A woman with a distinct New York accent asked, 'Are you Mr Van Vechten Veeder QC and, if so, are you any relation to Judge Van Vechten Veeder?' The answer could only have been 'Yes'. Appointed by President Taft in 1911, Johnny's American grandfather had indeed been a Federal Judge of the Eastern District. A current member of the court was familiar with Johnny's legal articles and thought it would be wonderful if he could attend.

Johnny was profoundly moved by the welcome he received when he arrived at the Court on 16 March 2015. He was formally presented and graciously introduced to the distinguished audience that consisted of no less than two Supreme Court Justices and many distinguished jurists of the State of New York. Indeed, at the luncheon, he had the pleasure of sitting and conversing with Supreme Court Justice Sonia Sotomayor. He was also introduced to Justice Ruth Bader Ginsburg. Being recognized on that day as his grandfather's flag bearer in many ways completed the circle of his life. Although Judge Veeder died in 1942, six years before Johnny was born, the judge certainly had an impact on his grandson's life.[1] Without him, Johnny might never have become a lawyer.

As Johnny's own legal practice developed and broadened, he became an adept commentator on contemporary legal issues. As his career became more focused on international arbitration, he often chose to address issues related to this field by examining and drawing lessons from the past. And he was never a lazy historian: he knew the value of original source materials. Archival visits were interspersed throughout holiday travel or arbitration hearings. A holiday trip to Russia for him became a trans-Siberian train journey to Vladivostok followed by an extremely uncomfortable seven-hour car journey to the Lena Goldfields. When he arrived unannounced, the officials were deeply suspicious of him. However, when Johnny travelled to the country of Georgia to attend the wedding of his beloved nephew, he added a day trip to Chiatura, the centre of the Manganese Mining Concession awarded to W. Averell Harriman during Lenin's New Economic Policy. Such was Johnny's curiosity and charm, the more hospitable Georgians immediately allowed him to visit the site and the well-preserved Harriman office, and he was shown the utmost courtesy.

Many young students who applied to spend a week or two learning about the law would find that Johnny had arranged days in court, introductions to distinguished colleagues, and trips round the Temple. They would often also be sent off

---

[1] Judge Veeder's obituary records that he was 'a member of the Harvard research group on International law, the International Maritime Commission and from 1930 to 1936 was president of the Maritime Law Association of the United States'. He was a partner of the firm Burlingham, Veeder, Clark & Hupper: he was also a committed historian and retained memberships in the American Historical Association, the New York State Historical Association, the Medieval Academy of America, the St Nicholas Society of New York, and the Holland Society. He only sat as a Federal Judge for six years; perhaps, like Johnny, he found a wide-ranging international practice more to his liking.

to various archives in search of his latest research subject. I too spent two weeks in the National archives at Kew hunting for Foreign Office papers linked to the *Lena Goldfields* Concession. Whenever I accompanied him to Washington, I was certain to spend a day or two examining the Harriman archives in the Library of Congress. There were particularly important Harriman papers deposited there; there were more at Harvard University, close to our summer home. The British Library outpost at Colindale was also a stop where outdated microfiche rolls held other secrets. When based in Moscow, I was sent to Sergiyev Posad (Zagorsk) to find and photograph the grave of Maxim the Greek (who else?).

Perhaps the most important research Johnny undertook was achieved with the assistance of a Russian-speaking Fellow at Jesus College. In the 1990s, when Johnny became aware that Russian archives, including the State Archives, were to be opened, researchers based in Moscow were found and directed to comb the shelves for Soviet-era legal documents that had never previously been made public. Much was copied and sent to him here in England before those archives once again were made off limits, and much of this material is reflected within the pieces of this Part I.

On a trip to Moscow in the 1990s, Johnny led us to the Donskoy Monastery and the adjoining cemetery where the crematorium operated by the NKVD dealt with victims of the Great Terror. There, the ashes of Dr S. B. Chlenov, arbitrator in the *Lena Goldfields* case, were deposited in a mass grave that came to be called Grave No. 1. We crossed Moscow to pay tribute to a man who was 'guilty only of living in the worst of times'. Johnny was a powerful writer and historian because, though he sought the big picture, he cared about details and he cared about the individuals swept up in these historical tempests.

In the *Lena Goldfields* piece included here, Johnny quoted Coleridge to explain that 'the light which experience gives is a lantern on the stern, which shines only on the waves behind us'. Johnny enhanced it with his view that these waves could also inform of an impending storm ahead. Johnny worked tirelessly to guide the legal world away from storms. His writings and lectures were his efforts to place navigational aids and hazard warnings at the disposal of current and future practitioners. That his scholarship was recognized during his lifetime pleased him. That he was able to teach at King's College London alongside my fellow editor, Sam Wordsworth, particularly delighted him. That his name would live on in the many ways individuals and institutions have sought to pay homage to his memory would have astonished him.

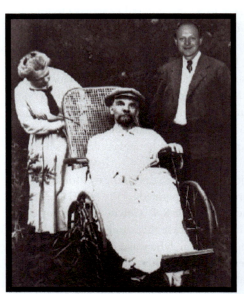

V.V. Veeder interviewing V.I. Lenin about
the reasons for rejection of Urquhart's concession.
Gorki, USSR, September 1922
(Private archive)

V. V. Veeder interviewing V. I. Lenin about the reasons for rejection of Urquhart's concession, Gorki, USSR, September 1922 (private archive). Donated to V. V. Veeder by an arbitral colleague, 2003

Before Mass Grave Number 1 at the Donskoy Cemetery in Moscow, 1996. The following text is carved on the stone: *Here lie buried the remains of the innocent tortured and executed victims of the political repression of 1930–1942. May they never be forgotten*

At Jesus College, Cambridge, 2016

1

The Historical Keystone to International Arbitration

The Party-Appointed Arbitrator—from Miami to Geneva[*]

A. Introduction

There is a new attack on the system of party-appointed arbitrators in both commercial arbitration but, more particularly, investor-state arbitration. This is not the usual criticism of partisan arbitrators, infected with actual bias or rank prejudice, who will always vote mechanically for their appointing parties come hell or high water, but rather an objection in principle directed at the legitimacy of the traditional system of impartial arbitrators appointed by each disputing party, as opposed to arbitrators all appointed by a neutral appointing authority. We start with Miami, before turning to Geneva.

Four years ago, Professor Jan Paulsson delivered his inaugural lecture at the University of Miami School of Law, entitled 'Moral Hazard in International Dispute Resolution'.[1] It had been preceded by Professor Albert Jan van den Berg's supportive article, 'Dissenting Opinions by Party-Appointed Arbitrators in Investment Arbitration'.[2] This article contained a striking statistical schedule showing that no known case exists, in the field of investment arbitration, in which a party-appointed arbitrator has ever dissented against the interests of his or her appointing party. Earlier studies in the field of international commercial arbitration

---

[*] The author acknowledges, with many thanks, the generous assistance of Ms Lesley Whitelaw, the Archivist of the Middle Temple Library, Professor Ladislas Mysyrowicz, formerly of the University of Geneva, the Cantonal Archive Department of the City of Geneva, the Public Record Office (London), Professor Jan Paulsson, Professor Albert Jan van den Berg, M Jérôme Bürgisser, Mr James Gastello, Mr Bart Legum, and Mr Sam Wordsworth QC. Nevertheless, all errors and views here expressed are those of the author alone. This contribution is adapted from the publication in 107 ASIL Proc 387 (2013) of the Inaugural Charles N Brower Lecture on International Dispute Resolution delivered on 5 April 2013 at the Annual Meeting of the American Society of International Law.

[1] Jan Paulsson, 'Moral Hazard in International Dispute Resolution' (2010) 25 ICSID Rev—FILJ 339.

[2] Albert Jan van den Berg, 'Dissenting Opinions by Party-Appointed Arbitrators in Investment Arbitration' in Mahnoush H Arsanjani, Jacob Katz Cogan, Robert D Sloane, and Siegfried Wiessner (eds), *Looking to the Future: Essays on International Law in Honor of W Michael Reisman* (Brill 2010) 821.

On Arbitration. Edited by: Sam Wordsworth KC and Marie Veeder, Oxford University Press. © Oxford University Press 2023.
DOI: 10.1093/oso/9780192869135.003.0001

8 ON ARBITRATION

had suggested that almost all dissenting opinions—said to exceed 95% of all such dissents—were written by the arbitrator appointed by the losing party.[3]

In brief, these two distinguished scholars then both teaching at Miami, collectively sharing a unique experience in the modern practice of arbitration, and, significantly, great advocates for and not against arbitration, severely criticised the current system of party-appointed arbitrators on the grounds of legitimacy. Professor Paulsson proposed, as the only decent solution, that all arbitrators should be appointed jointly by the disputing parties or appointed by a neutral body.[4] Professor van den Berg proposed that investment arbitration would function better and more credibly if party-appointed arbitrators observed the principle of *nemine dissentiente*.[5] These views influenced many (including this author). Yet, the road to Damascus, with the angel of history, is instructive, and we must wonder now whether the proposed solutions are not worse than the ailment, if it be an ailment at all.

First, as Professor Paulsson recognized, the genie—a party's traditional right to appoint an arbitrator—cannot easily be put back into the bottle.[6] Second, the Anglo-Saxon legal tradition greatly values a judge's right to dissent from a collegiate decision as a significant aspect of judicial independence imposing an important intellectual discipline on the full tribunal, with dissenting judgments not invariably illuminating future legal thinking. The same is almost true of arbitrators, particularly for investment disputes and disputes between states. Moreover, dissents are not that common in the field of international commercial arbitration. While becoming more frequent in the field of investment arbitration, their known number does not yet reach the statistics available for dissenting judgments in Anglo-Saxon judicial systems.[7] Third, as Professor Paulsson also recognized, only a few arbitral institutions can make credible claims to legitimacy. It would be invidious here to name these singular exceptions (nor did he), but it is a fact that, for one reason or other, most arbitral institutions cannot be trusted with arbitral appointments. And even worse, as he rightly concluded, this important arbitral task could never be entrusted to the institutional equivalent of Ali Baba and the Forty Thieves.

---

[3] Paulsson (n 1) 348, referring to Alan Redfern, 'Dissenting Opinions in International Commercial Arbitration: The Good, the Bad and the Ugly—2003 Freshfields Lecture' (2004) 20 Arb Int'l 223 and Eduardo Silva Romero, 'Brèves observations sur l'opinion dissidente' in Les Arbitres Internationaux, Colloque du 4 février 2005, 8 Centre Français de Droit Compare 179 (Société de Législation Comparée 2005).

[4] Ibid 352.

[5] van den Berg (n 2) 834. This arbitrator practises what he preaches: contrast his non-dissenting decisions in *LG&E Energy Corpn, LG&E Capital Corpn and LG&E International Inc v The Argentine Republic*, ICSID Case No ARB/02/1, Decision on Liability (3 October 2006) and *Enron Corpn and Ponderosa Assets LP v The Argentine Republic*, ICSID Case No ARB/01/3, Award (22 May 2007).

[6] Paulsson (n 1) 352.

[7] See V V Veeder, 'Still More on Arbitral Deliberations: An English Perspective' in Pierre Wesner and François Bohnet (eds), *Mélanges en l'Honneur de François Knoepfler* (Helbing Lichtenhahn 2005) 269; Neal Geach and Christopher Monaghan (eds), *Dissenting Judgments in the Law* (Wildy, Simmonds & Hill 2012); Frederic Reynold, *Disagreement and Dissent in Judicial Decision-Making* (Wildy, Simmonds & Hill 2013).

THE HISTORICAL KEYSTONE TO INTERNATIONAL ARBITRATION   9

Yet, both Professors Paulsson and van den Berg raised serious questions about the present system of international arbitration, echoed by others. Their analyses do not deserve to be left as 'voices in the desert', as they feared; and their criticisms require answers to enhance the essential legitimacy of international arbitration, which is increasingly under threat from special interest groups pressing for a new system of permanent international courts.[8] Others have and will have their own analyses, and no complete answer is here proposed, but we can take the first few steps with two well-known arbitrations, by way of illustrating both the suggested problem and, if it be a problem, its possible solutions.

B. The *Loewen* Arbitration

The first was cited by Professor Paulsson in support of his thesis: it is the *Loewen* arbitration finally decided by the tribunal in August 2004, following an award made in June 2003. In this NAFTA dispute between two Canadian investors and the United States, the investors complained of unlawful treatment by the state courts of Mississippi. The corporate investor had been held liable by a local jury for US$500 million, which included US$400 million as punitive damages. It was unable to appeal from that verdict because the local law required the posting of a supersedeas bond equal to 125% of the judgment, an impossible burden for a small foreign corporation facing imminent bankruptcy. The award of the NAFTA tribunal and its subsequent clarification were made unanimously by the three arbitrators, two of whom had been appointed by the parties. The Canadian investors thereby lost the NAFTA arbitration, for reasons that were and remain much discussed academically, but these need not concern us here.[9]

After the NAFTA arbitration, in December 2004, the American arbitrator took part in an academic symposium in New York where he spoke publicly about his experience as an arbitrator appointed by the United States in the *Loewen* case. Professor Paulsson said this in his lecture:

The symposium happened to be recorded, and the tenor of his remarks was notably made public in a law review in 2009, in a footnote that could easily be traced

---

[8] See, e.g., Corporate Europe Observatory and the Transnational Institute, 'Profiting from Injustice—How Law Firms, Arbitrators and Financiers are Fuelling an Investment Arbitration Boom' (November 2012) <http://www.tni.org/sites/www.tni.org/files/download/profitingfrominjustice.pdf> accessed 27 August 2014.

[9] See generally Noah Rubins, 'Loewen v United States: The Burial of an Investor-State Arbitration Claim' (2005) 21(1) Arb Int'l 1; see also Barton Legum, 'Does the Loewen Award Endanger the Credibility of the NAFTA Dispute Settlement Mechanism?' (2005) 6 J World Inv & Trade 89, 92; Emmanuel Gaillard, 'Chronique des sentences arbitrates CIRDI' (2004) 131 J Droit Int'l 213, 232; Jan Paulsson, 'Continuous Nationality in Loewen' (2004) 20(2) Arb Int'l 213, 214, later re-stated in Jan Paulsson, *Denial of Justice in International Law* (Cambridge University Press 2005) 183 et seq.

back to retrieve astonishing verbatim remarks. This included the revelation that the arbitrator had met with officials of the U.S. Department of Justice prior to accepting the appointment, and that they had told him: 'You know, judge, if we lose this case we could lose NAFTA.' He remembered his answer as having been: 'Well, if you want to put pressure on me, then that does it.'[10]

The American arbitrator, Judge Abner Mikva, was a senior legal figure with extensive experience in the judicial, legislative, and executive branches of the United States. Professor Paulsson castigated this arbitrator's conduct and, still more so, the officials from the US Department of Justice who sought during this interview to pressure him, as an arbitrator appointed by the United States, into supporting a favourable decision for the United States in the NAFTA arbitration.

Leaving aside the wisdom of any arbitrator ever disclosing at a public symposium the unknown workings of a recent arbitration (particularly here when ancillary legal proceedings were shortly to begin to vacate the award),[11] does this incident in fact support the criticism levelled at the system of party-appointed arbitrators? We know that pre-appointment arbitral interviews do take place between a party's lawyers and a putative arbitrator. This procedure is not new: for decades, it has been informally regulated by the well-known 'Aksen Rules',[12] and also for some more recently by the guidelines established by the Chartered Institute of Arbitrators.[13] It is a procedure practised by many users in international commercial arbitration; and there is no reason to treat differently state parties to an investment arbitration. Professor Paulsson did not suggest that the American arbitrator, after his appointment, had any improper discussion with the Department of Justice, and Professor Paulsson did not cite it as a case of an illicit ex parte communication between one party and one member of an arbitration tribunal in regard to the tribunal's award. As for the content of the interview, was the putative American arbitrator improperly subjected to pressure by his appointing party? Many of us not remotely involved in the *Loewen* case knew at the time that this arbitration was a significant case for the United States and for Chapter 11 of the

---

[10] Paulsson (n 1) 346. A similar account appears in Jan Paulsson, *The Idea of Arbitration* (Oxford University Press 2013) 160–1.

[11] This was here particularly unwise because, albeit unknown to the American arbitrator, the parties' dispute revived on 13 December 2004 when the individual investor petitioned the US District Court for the District of Columbia for an order vacating and remanding the tribunal's award, which was eventually rejected on procedural grounds on 31 October 2005.

[12] See Gerald Aksen, 'The Tribunal's Appointment' in Lawrence W Newman and Richard D Hill (eds), *The Leading Arbitrators' Guide to International Arbitration* (2nd edn, Juris Publishing 2008) 35.

[13] 'Practice Guideline 16: The Interviewing of Prospective Arbitrators' (2011) 77 Int'l J Arb Mediation Dispute Mgmt 447; see also Noah Rubins and Bernhard Lauterburg, 'Independence, Impartiality and Duty of Disclosure in Investment Arbitration' in Christina Knahr, Christian Koller, Walter Rechberger, and August Reinisch (eds), *Investment and Commercial Arbitration—Similarities and Divergences* (Eleven International Publishing 2010) 170.

NAFTA, and, simply from reading newspapers, we knew also that this same perception was shared by many legislators on Capitol Hill and not a few journalists. It may therefore be doubted that the American arbitrator was told anything that he could not already have learned as an informed member of the general public. As for the American arbitrator's quoted response: 'Well, if you want to put pressure on me, then that does it', that statement, by itself, seems insufficient to impute a commitment by that arbitrator to make improper decisions in favour of the United States as his appointing party. As cited, Professor Paulsson took his brief quotation from an article published in 2010 by Professor Schneiderman. In its full context, taken from the audio tape-recording of the symposium, there was clearly no such commitment.[14]

With hindsight, of course, it would have been wiser for the American arbitrator and the Department of Justice to disclose the fact of this pre-arbitral interview to his co-arbitrators and to the Canadian investors, but at the time such interviews were not regarded as matters requiring formal disclosure. Even now, the ethical position remains unclear. Of course, it should not be so—but it was. It is therefore unfortunate that this incident is now entering the mythology of arbitration, being cited by even distinguished scholars as an example of gross misconduct by a party-appointed arbitrator and his appointing party to the detriment of investment arbitration generally.[15] We must remember that the decisions in this

[14] As cited, Professor Paulsson took his quotation from David Schneiderman, 'Judicial Politics and International Investment Arbitration: Seeking an Explanation for Conflicting Outcomes' (2010) 30 Northwestern J Int'l Law & Bus 383, 405; see Paulsson (n 1) 346 n 18. However, as appears from the audiotape, Judge Mikva's words were spoken in a different context: 'I was called by the Department of Justice and asked whether I'd be interested in this arbitration which involved a dispute between a Canadian investor and the United States under NAFTA, and I said "Yes, that sounds interesting", and I met with the Department of Justice lawyers. Under the arbitration procedures, you're allowed to meet with the parties up until the time that the panel is constituted and at that point everyone is supposed to act as a neutral and avoid *ex parte* contacts. This was before the panel was constituted, and I met with the Justice Department lawyers and one of them said to me, "You know, judge, if we lose this case, we could lose NAFTA", and I said "Well, if you want to put pressure on me that does it, but why is this so important?", and he said "Well, they're seeking US$400 million damages or US$300 million damages under a provision that I'll bet you didn't know was in NAFTA when you voted for it", and I said, "You're talking about an arbitration procedure", and he said "Yes", and I said, "You're right. Not only didn't I know about it but I would venture that most of the Members of Congress who voted for NAFTA had no idea that there was an arbitration procedure in it or how far that arbitration procedure extended". The fights that were going on about NAFTA were whether we were maintaining a free and level playing field for our workers, whether we were preserving environmental conditions, whether the pact was going to lead to the exporting of jobs to Mexico and perhaps to Canada, and whether in fact this was an appropriate treaty for three countries that have different levels of economic activity. Those were the debates. No one ever talked about arbitrations, no one ever talked about investor disputes. I had heard of bilateral investment treaties before, but I never even conceived that NAFTA had provisions that paralleled some of those BITs' specific provisions. Well, I agreed to do it, and the panel was duly constituted ..', Pace Law School, New York Symposium (6–8 December 2004), 'The Judiciary and Environmental Law—Trade, the Environment and Provincial/State Courts' (transcribed from the audio tape at 26:31 to 28:35).

[15] See, e.g., Tai-Heng Cheng, *When International Law Works—Realistic Idealism after 9/11 and the Global Recession* (Oxford University Press 2012) 187–92, strongly deprecating 'ex parte' communications with an appointed arbitrator, n 59 (noting, also erroneously, that 'the transcripts and audio

12   ON ARBITRATION

NAFTA arbitration were made unanimously by the *Loewen* tribunal. It is utterly inconceivable that the two other arbitrators—former senior appellate judges from Australia and England—could have been pressured in turn by the American arbitrator into agreeing to that which they were not minded to agree. We might also remember that all three arbitrators were former senior judges of their respective states, who may have found more difficulty with international law providing an effective personal remedy to the Canadian investor under NAFTA, which was absent on well-settled principles long accepted within a national legal system based on common-law principles.[16]

Far from treating the *Loewen* case as a bad precedent for party-appointed arbitrators, it falls into the classic example of a party appointing a well-known senior legal figure who can be relied upon to exercise a strong-minded, informed, and independent judgment. This is not always solely motivated by that party's desire to win the case. It can also include a measure of self-protection for the person making the appointment in the event that the case is lost, whether it be an officer of a state or an officer of a corporation. In the *Loewen* case, what better example to show Capitol Hill and news media hostile to NAFTA, if the case had been decided against the United States, that the American arbitrator, as a publicly known legal and political figure, had jointly agreed on that adverse award with his two foreign arbitral colleagues?[17] As with most awards, we can never know exactly why the *Loewen* tribunal decided that case in the way it did: to some, its reasons in the award and subsequent clarification raise questions which could only be answered by breaching the secrecy of its deliberations.[18] Fortunately, we have an older case—in Geneva. It

tapes of Judge Mikva's remarks at the conference are no longer publicly available, and the accuracy of Schneiderman's claims is difficult to assess').

[16] *The Loewen Group Inc & Raymond L Loewen v The United States of America*, ICSID Case No ARB(AF)/93/3, Award (26 June 2003) paras 233 et seq.

[17] That happened in another case cited by Jan Paulsson: the *Alaskan Boundary Case* between Great Britain and the United States over a disputed strip of land on Canada's west coast (adjoining Alaska) referred to a mixed commission (not an arbitration) appointed by the United States and Great Britain under their 1903 treaty. The decision was made in favour of the United States by four of the six commissioners, the three American commissioners being joined by Lord Alverstone, England's Lord Chief Justice, with the two other (Canadian) commissioners dissenting. Any decision adjusting land boundaries is controversial; but the fact that Lord Alverstone agreed with the US commissioners made the result less unpalatable, at least to Great Britain. And that fact depended in turn on his appointment by Great Britain: it would not have been so if he had been a 'neutral' stranger appointed by an arbitral institution. See Paulsson (n 1) 341–3.

[18] As regards the most often expressed criticism regarding the jurisdictional decision on continuous nationality, the *Loewen* tribunal appears to have been vindicated with time. After the presentation of its claim under NAFTA but before the tribunal's award, the corporate claimant effectively changed its Canadian nationality to US nationality following its bankruptcy and reorganization; and accordingly the *Loewen* tribunal decided that it had no jurisdiction to decide its claim for want of a continuous Canadian nationality: 'there must be continuous material identity from the date of the events giving rise to the claim ... through to the date of the resolution of the claim', *Loewen* (n 16) para 225. Later, as regards the continuous nationality of a natural person with a claim against a respondent state, Art 5(1) of the 2006 ILC Articles on Diplomatic Protection was to provide: 'A State is entitled to exercise diplomatic protection in respect of a person who was a national of that State continuously from the date of injury to the date of the official presentation of the claim'; and Art 5(4): 'A State is no longer entitled to exercise

was also an international arbitration in which the two appointed arbitrators, both senior legal figures, dealt directly with their appointing parties (ostensibly with the parties' consent); where the arbitral deliberations were not secret, being attended by the parties' legal representatives; and where, fortunately for us, several of those representatives later wrote their memoirs.[19]

C. The Alabama Arbitration

The Alabama Claims Arbitration took place in Geneva in 1872 under the Treaty of Washington of 1871 between the United States and Great Britain. The difficulty with saying anything about the Alabama Arbitration, as the late Lord Bingham noted almost ten years ago, is that, like Hamlet, everyone knows the story and its ending.[20] It was, however, an unusual case, still rich in materials from many different perspectives. The award was made in September 1872 by an international tribunal, the first international tribunal of its kind in modern times and the basic model for international arbitration today, with the two disputing parties each appointing one arbitrator as a minority of the tribunal.[21] By that award, the Alabama tribunal decided that Great Britain had failed to use due diligence in the performance of its neutral obligations during the American Civil War, in permitting the CSS Alabama and certain of her fellow raiders to be built in England and delivered to the Confederacy for warlike operations; and, as compensation, the tribunal ordered Great Britain to pay the sum of US$15.5 million in gold to the United States, with simple interest—equivalent, in today's money (taking into account relative British GDPs) to about US$225 billion dollars.[22]

diplomatic protection in respect of a person who acquires the nationality of the State against which the claim is brought after the date of the official presentation of the claim.' Although these provisions are directed at natural persons, the ILC Commentary applied the same provisions to the Loewen case without any material criticism of the award on the ground that the Loewen claimant's new nationality was that of the respondent state and hence its claim could not require the United States to pay compensation to its own national. See International Law Commission, Report on the work of its fifty-eighth session (1 May to 9 June and 3 July to 11 August 2006), GA Official Records, Sixty-first session, Supp No 10 (A/61/10), 37–8, 40, Art 5 paras 5 and 13 <http://legal.un.org/ilc/reports/2006/2006report.htm> accessed 9 September 2014.

[19] No memoirs of the Alabama Arbitration were published by any of the five arbitrators. However, Count Sclopis (the Italian arbitrator) left papers which have become publicly available; see P C Baldelli, Power Politics, Diplomacy and Avoidance of Hostilities between England and the United States in the Wake of the Civil War (EMP Publishing 1998, translated from 'Arbitrati e politica di Potenza'). For a detailed account of the events leading to the Alabama Arbitration, see Amanda Foreman, A World on Fire: Britain's Crucial Role in the American Civil War (Penguin 2010) and J T DeKay, The Rebel Raiders (Pimlico 2004).

[20] Lord Bingham, 'The Alabama Claims Arbitration' (2005) 54 ICLQ 1; see also Gillis Wetter, The International Arbitral Process, vol 1 (Oceana Publications 1979) 13 et seq; V V Veeder, 'Arbitral Lessons from the Private Correspondence of Queen Victoria and Lenin' (2004) 98 ASIL Proceedings 33.

[21] Under the Jay Treaty of 1794 between the United States and Great Britain, there were joint commissions, but not arbitrations.

[22] Figures extrapolated from Roy Jenkins, Gladstone: A Biography (Pan Books 2002) 359.

14   ON ARBITRATION

By the Alabama Arbitration, an imminent war was averted between Great Britain and the United States, with untold consequences for both nations, particularly for Canada and other British territories from Bermuda to the Caribbean which faced possible invasion and annexation by the United States, with its large army and powerful navy tempered by the Civil War. For present purposes, the ending of the arbitration is, however, irrelevant. Although the British party-appointed arbitrator strongly dissented from part of the award and issued a lengthy dissenting opinion, including the amount of compensation (for which he has been much criticised, but ultimately proven right),[23] he nevertheless agreed on Great Britain's legal liability for the CSS *Alabama,* by far the worst of the Confederate raiders; and, despite strong language elsewhere, his dissenting opinion ended with a courteous encouragement to his own countrymen, as well as the citizens of the United States, to accept the adverse award;

> [W]hile the award of the tribunal appears to me to be open to these exceptions, I trust that, by the British people, it will be accepted with the submission and respect which is due to the decision of a tribunal by whose award it has freely consented to abide. The United States, on the other hand, having had the claims of their citizens for losses sustained considerably weighed, and compensation awarded in respect of them, will see, I trust, in the consent of Great Britain to submit these claims to peaceful arbitration, an honest desire on her part to atone for any past errors or omissions, which an impartial judgment might find to have existed—and will feel that all just cause of grievance is now removed—so that, in the time to come, no sense of past wrong remaining unredressed will stand in the way of the friendly and harmonious relations which should subsist between two great and kindred nations.[24]

We can leave the award there, because it is the middle of the arbitration, three months earlier in June 1872, which illustrates the important role played by the party-appointed arbitrators in the Alabama Arbitration. At that time, the arbitration almost broke down over the United States' so-called 'indirect claims' advanced as national losses then calculated at US$2 billion, equivalent in today's money (again adjusted) to about US$30 trillion. These were unprecedented claims by one nation against another undefeated by war.

There were five individual arbitrators in the Alabama tribunal. The first three were Brazilian, Swiss, and Italian, appointed respectively by the Emperor of Brazil, the President of the Swiss Confederation, and the King of Italy.[25] None of these

---

[23]   Having eventually paid all its citizens' direct claims, the United States was left with a significant surplus from the proceeds of the Alabama award.

[24]   London Gazette Supplement, 24 September 1872.

[25]   Marcos Antonio de Araujo, Baron d'Itayubá (the Brazilian Minister at Paris), Jakob Stämpfli (the former President of the Swiss Confederation), and Count Federico Sclopis (of Italy).

three arbitrators spoke English; none followed the oral submissions made in English by the parties' counsel at the arbitration's hearings; all three worked from the French translations of the parties' written pleadings; the arbitral deliberations were conducted in French; and the arbitrators drafted the operative award and individual assenting opinions in French,[26] with only the award issued in English, as translated jointly by the American and British arbitrators (with the tribunal's English-speaking Swiss secretary).[27] These remaining two arbitrators, American and British, were appointed by each of the two parties: Charles Francis Adams by the United States, the grandson and son of the second and sixth Presidents of the United States and the former American Minister in London; and Sir Alexander Cockburn by Great Britain, then Chief Justice of the Queen's Bench Division. Both Adams and Cockburn spoke French fluently, as a first language, but that was not their principal contribution to the Alabama Arbitration. It was the fact that they were party-appointed arbitrators. Without the right to party-appointed arbitrators, albeit as a minority of the five-member tribunal, there would have been no Treaty of Washington, no Alabama Arbitration, and, most certainly, no Alabama Award.

The Treaty of Washington, with its provision for arbitration, emerged after almost eight years of difficult diplomatic negotiations. By letter dated 23 October 1863, during the Civil War, the American Minister in London (the same Charles Francis Adams) had indicated to Lord Russell, the British Foreign Secretary, that the United States was ready to agree to any fair and equitable form of arbitration to settle the Alabama Claims. This idea found no favour with the British Government because, among other factors, the Alabama Claims impugned the honour, if not also the integrity, of the law officers and senior ministers in the British Government, including Russell, Gladstone, and Palmerston.[28] By letter dated 30 August 1865, Lord Russell finally rejected any idea of arbitration and instead proposed the appointment of a joint commission. It was an undiplomatic rebuff that the British Government was later much to regret. After the end of the Civil War, the unresolved dispute over the Alabama Claims increasingly soured relations between the United States and Great Britain.

The suggestion of arbitration as means of resolving the Alabama Claims had also been raised by a private American lawyer in Paris, the historian Thomas Balch, who had witnessed the sinking of the CSS *Alabama* off Cherbourg in June 1864 by the US Navy.[29] In November 1864, Mr Balch took his idea of an 'ad hoc international court of arbitration' to President Lincoln during a visit to Washington. President

---

[26] Their own reasons were drafted in French and Italian.

[27] M Alexandre Favot from Bern.

[28] Clive Parry, 'Rétrospective séculaire sur l'arbitrage de l'Alabama' in *Arbitrage de l'Alabama Genève 1872–1972* (Hotel de Ville 1972) 49 et seq. (This article, with others cited below, was a contribution to the publication marking the centenary celebrations organized by the City of Geneva, with the support of the United States and the United Kingdom.)

[29] Thomas Willing Balch, *The Alabama Arbitration* (Allen, Lane & Scott 1900).

16 ON ARBITRATION

Lincoln said that he thought arbitration was 'a very amiable idea but not possible just now, as the millennium is still a long way off'. But, less discouragingly, Lincoln added: 'Start your idea. It may make its way in time, as it is a good one.' Mr Balch then formalized his proposal in a letter to the *New York Times*, published on 31 March 1865.[30] Paragraph IV of his proposal provided for each party's appointment of two competent jurists as arbitrators, with these two appointing a third arbitrator to form an international arbitration tribunal to decide the Alabama Claims. Mr Balch discounted the traditional idea of a third sovereign appointing a sole arbitrator or tribunal as anti-republican and undemocratic in modern times. His ideas were developed by the German-American military jurist and war veteran, Francis Lieber, in an open letter to William H Seward, the US Secretary of State, published in the *New York Times* on 22 September 1865.[31] Like Mr Balch, Mr Lieber rejected the appointment of a sovereign as an arbitrator or appointing authority. Instead, he proposed as a tribunal, not private individuals, but the law faculty of a foreign university appointed jointly by the parties, such as the law faculties at the Universities of Berlin, Heidelberg, and Leyden. This achieved nothing at the time, because on 17 October 1865, the United States formally withdrew its long-standing offer of arbitration to Great Britain; and on 21 November 1865, the United States also rejected Lord Russell's suggestion of a joint commission. Nonetheless, several later political commentators found the origin of the Treaty of Washington's arbitration provision in the campaigning work of Thomas Balch and Francis Lieber.

In 1866, there was a change of government in London, with a new Foreign Secretary (Lord Stanley) and a new Prime Minister (Lord Derby). This British Government was now much concerned to find an amicable solution to the increasingly troubled relations with the United States over the Alabama Claims (together with other disputes). In January 1867, in its turn, the British Government proposed arbitration, provided that a fitting arbitrator could be agreed upon and agreement also reached on the points to be decided by that arbitrator. Inevitably perhaps, by letter of 12 January 1867, the US Secretary of State, Mr Seward, summarily rejected the British suggestion of arbitration. To cut short this awkward diplomatic story, the two governments, subject to ratification, eventually agreed on a form of arbitration for their respective claims in the Johnson-Clarendon Treaty of 14 January 1869.[32] This treaty was never ratified by the United States. It provided first for a joint commission of four members, two appointed by each party, with any disagreement to be referred to a sole arbitrator to be jointly appointed by the four commissioners, or, in default of such appointment, by one of two nominees appointed by each party and then chosen by lot. In April 1869, the Johnson-Clarendon Treaty was rejected by the US Senate, with strong opposition

---

[30] Thomas Balch, *International Courts of Arbitration* (Allen, Lane & Scott 1874, republished 1896).
[31] Lieber had fought at Waterloo in 1825 and later in the Greek War of Independence.
[32] Johnson-Clarendon Treaty (signed on 14 January 1869) Art 1.

from Senator Sumner, then the powerful Chairman of the Senate's Committee on Foreign Affairs, especially in regard to the Alabama Claims. During his speech, Senator Sumner also advanced a powerful case, in strident and uncompromising terms, for 'indirect claims' also to be made by the United States against Great Britain, with the strong inference that an appropriate remedy, in default of full compensation, would be the seizure by the United States of British territories in the New World, from Canada to South America. These suggestions horrified the British Government, it then being erroneously considered that Senator Sumner, from his senior position in the Senate, was also speaking for the new President, Ulysses S Grant, and the new Secretary of State, Hamilton Fish. In passing, Senator Sumner also attacked the treaty's provisions for the appointment of the sole arbitrator, particularly the use of a lottery inconsistent (he said) with the solemnity which belonged to the Alabama Claims.

In May 1869, Thomas Balch was back in Washington, pressing his idea of an arbitration tribunal of jurists in meetings with President Grant, Secretary Fish, and Senator Sumner. At the same time, the idea of an international arbitration before a legal tribunal to decide the Alabama Claims was being promoted by the Swiss lawyers, Johann K Blüntschli and Gustave Moynier (the former later founding the Institute of International Law and the latter a co-founder and president of what became the International Committee of the Red Cross).[33] The case for arbitration as a means of addressing the Alabama Claims was by now becoming irresistible. From the summer of 1869 onwards, confidential initiatives from both governments led eventually to the meeting of their joint negotiating commission in Washington in February 1871, leading in turn to the Treaty of Washington of 8 May 1871, which was approved by the Senate (including support from Senator Sumner), with a significantly new provision for arbitration.[34] As regards the Alabama Claims, as we have seen, that treaty provided for a tribunal of five arbitrators to be appointed as to the first three by three Italian, Swiss, and Brazilian sovereigns, with a fourth sovereign, the King of Sweden and Norway, as a default appointing authority. For the first time in an international arbitration, each of the two disputing parties appointed its own arbitrator to an international tribunal comprised of a majority of jurists having other 'neutral' nationalities. Thus was the concept of party-appointed arbitrators introduced into the modern world of international arbitration to decide a dispute which touched the vital interests of two nations on the brink of armed conflict, with the last war (the War of 1812) still a living memory.

---

[33] Ladislas Mysrowicz, 'L'affaire de l'Alabama' in *Arbitrage de l'Alabama Genève 1872–1972* (Hotel de Ville 1972) 22, 48. See also Francis Stephen Ruddy, 'La portée de l'arbitrage de l'Alabama' in ibid 53.

[34] For the Treaty of Washington of 8 May 1871, see Wetter (n 20) 44. Its negotiations were not without difficulties—see the exchange of diplomatic correspondence dated 23 September and 6 November 1869 passing between Hamilton Fish and Lord Clarendon, in Wetter (n 20) 28–43; and also the account in John Chandler Bancroft Davis, *Mr Fish and the Alabama Claims: A Chapter in Diplomatic History* (Houghton Mifflin 1893).

18   ON ARBITRATION

So who were these two party-appointed arbitrators? Charles Francis Adams was said to be a cold fish, with the room temperature dropping ten degrees whenever he made an entrance. He was a lawyer by training, although he never practised law. More significantly, as we have seen, he had been the American Minister in London for most of the period of the Civil War at issue for the Alabama Claims, not only well acquainted with the facts, but also well informed as a personal witness, if not also an interested actor, in the dealings (or non-dealings) of the British Government in regard to the Confederate cruisers. Mr Adams was, by any account, a highly successful minister in dealing forcefully with the British Government in London, particularly Lord Russell; he was to become the undoubted hero of the Alabama Arbitration; and he maintained throughout good personal relations with his British counterparts, even visiting Lord Russell in England after the Alabama Arbitration. He is the subject of many memoirs, including those written by his sons, Henry Adams and Charles Francis Adams, Jr, and so we need not spend time here on his many attributes, save two.[35] First, as already mentioned, Charles Adams spoke French fluently, having learned it when he lived as a young child in St Petersburg where his father, John Quincy Adams, was then the American Minister to Russia. Second, as to the strongest and weakest characteristics of his nature, Adams' obituary, published in the *New York Times* on 21 November 1886, concludes with this passage:

> Independent and self-reliant to the last degree, no fear of partisan criticism and no considerations of propriety would moderate the expression of a view which he had once formed. At the same time his temper, not unlike that of his paternal grandfather, caused him to couch his opinion in the most offensive terms and to announce it with scornful indifference to the feelings which it might wound in others. Throughout his career there are to be seen frequent examples of these traits which render his undoubted success in diplomacy, the art of all others requiring most self-restraint—the more remarkable.[36]

In Geneva, Mr Adams kept his bad temper, even under the most trying of circumstances; and he also put his fluent French to good diplomatic use towards his francophone co-arbitrators. Regrettably, his arbitral colleague from London did not, expressing by the end of the arbitration angry and open contempt for both parties' counsel (he was not in the least partisan in his disaffections) and all but one of his co-arbitrators—that exception being Mr Adams, whom he held to the end in high regard.

---

[35] Charles Francis Adams Jr, *Charles Francis Adams* (Houghton Mifflin 1900, republished 1980); Henry Adams, *The Education of Henry Adams* (Oxford University Press 1907, republished 1918); Worthington Chauncey Ford (ed), *Letters of Henry Adams: 1858–1891* (Houghton Mifflin 1930).
[36] 'Charles Francis Adams: The Aged Statesman Gone to His Rest', *New York Times* (21 November 1886).

THE HISTORICAL KEYSTONE TO INTERNATIONAL ARBITRATION   19

Sir Alexander James Edmund Cockburn was certainly no Adams, but they had much in common. Like Charles Adams, Cockburn was the son of a diplomat living abroad, and before becoming a judge, Cockburn had gained experience in both the legislative and executive branches of the British Government. He was born in 1802 in Hungary to a British envoy and his French wife, who was the daughter of a former French aristocrat, the Vicomte de Vignier. Cockburn's paternal uncle was Sir Geoffrey Cockburn, one of Nelson's youngest captains, who later, as an English admiral, took part during the War of 1812 in the punitive attack on Washington, DC, which resulted in the burning of the White House in August 1814.[37] Cockburn was educated on the European continent and spoke French, German, Italian, and Spanish. After attending Cambridge University and teaching law as a Fellow at Trinity Hall, he was called to the English Bar in 1829. From all reports, Cockburn was a man of great accomplishments outside the law—a linguist, musician, and sailor, and, it is said, of exceptional literary and social acquirements, a friend of Charles Dickens and a great raconteur. It is also said that he had an 'ardent temperament' with feelings 'quick and excitable', which was probably a kind way of saying that he had a hot temper which was easily lost. This was not the best character trait for any judge, but it was particularly unfortunate for an international arbitrator in Geneva, with the arbitral deliberations open to the parties and their memoirs.[38]

After a slow beginning at the English Bar, Cockburn had made his legal reputation as a master of difficult cases with factual and expert complications, including his successful defence of the assassin McNaughten on the ground of insanity in 1843, thereby establishing the 'McNaughten rules'. Politically, he was a liberal reformer and entered Parliament in 1847, later becoming successively Solicitor-General and Attorney-General. In 1856, he was appointed Chief Justice of the Common Pleas; in 1859, the Chief Justice of the Queen's Bench; and after the judicature reforms in 1875 (which he opposed), the first Lord Chief Justice of England and Wales, where he presided until his death in 1880. There is no biography of Sir Alexander Cockburn, and he never wrote his own memoirs of the Alabama Arbitration. There is a sympathetic article on his judicial accomplishments written in 1900 by an American legal historian, then a US federal judge in New York, published in the *Harvard Law Review*. That author, my grandfather, never met Cockburn personally, but later he probably met Cockburn's colleagues in England, and he may have had access to papers not now publicly available. This article starts apologetically; 'The large measure of public attention which Sir Alexander Cockburn commanded during his lifetime probably led to an undue estimate of

---

[37] Admiral Sir Geoffrey Cockburn (1771–1853). He served as one of Nelson's captains and conveyed Napoleon as a prisoner to St Helena. As the flag-officer in 1812, he launched the punitive expedition against the United States from Bermuda, then a British colony with a major naval base.

[38] Frank W Hackett, *Reminiscences of the Geneva Tribunal* (Houghton Mifflin 1911) 222.

20   ON ARBITRATION

the permanent value of his judicial services.'[39] Unfortunately, for present purposes, the article does not address further his conduct in the Alabama Arbitration. More unfortunately, Sir Alexander Cockburn's reputation, not good to begin with even in England, also weathered badly at the hands of the American counsel writing their memoirs of the Alabama Arbitration, in particular the writings of General Cushing who was described, even by his countrymen, as an Anglophobe. Regrettably, these contemporary materials have influenced later historians: even Gladstone's distinguished British biographer, Lord Jenkins, described Cockburn less than fairly 'as a natural illiberal British chauvinist'.[40] It is time to redress the balance—to the extent possible.[41]

Sir Alexander Cockburn was certainly no Victorian. He was born into the moral standards of an earlier time. A notorious ladies' man, he later lived openly with one mistress and with one or possibly two of their children, along with his paramour's mother and sister.[42] Cockburn also lived well, apparently beyond his means. There is a story of the young Cockburn escaping through the window of the barristers' robing room at Rougemont Castle at Exeter in Devon, to evade his creditors' bailiffs awaiting him outside court.[43] Alexander Cockburn was knighted upon his first political appointment as Solicitor-General, and he later became a baronet, an inherited family title of Scottish origin. However, most unusually for a Lord Chief Justice, he was never elevated to the peerage or granted any other honour in the gift of the Crown. Some say he refused such honours; but others say Queen Victoria flatly refused to honour a man she regarded (with others) as morally despicable.

Sir Alexander Cockburn had written a dark and morally troubled novel in his early days at the English Bar, some time between 1827 and 1831, when his legal practice was almost non-existent. The novel was never published; it bears no title; and it is never mentioned in any public account of his life. It is now to be found in nineteen bound notebooks written in his own handwriting, in the archives of the Middle Temple in London.[44] The manuscript seems untouched, save for one-and-a-half readers over the last 150 years. The novel is supposedly a personal memoir

---

[39] Van Vechten Veeder, 'Sir Alexander Cockburn' (1900) 14 Harv L Rev 79. See also his descriptions of Cockburn both as judge and counsel in, respectively, 'A Century of English Judicature 1800–1900' in *Select Essays in Anglo-American Legal History* (Little, Brown, and Co 1907, republished in 1968); and *Legal Masterpieces*, vol 1 (Callaghan and Co 1903) 587 et seq on Cockburn's 'Argument in Defense of Daniel NcNaughten'.

[40] Jenkins (n 22) 359.

[41] There is a sympathetic portrait of Cockburn at Trinity Hall, Cambridge University by George Frederic Watts as Lord Chief Justice painted in 1875; see 'Sir Alexander Cockburn' (BBC) <http://www.bbc.co.uk/arts/yourpaintings/paintings/sir-alexander-cockburn-18021880-lld-lord-chief-justice-of15027/print/ info> accessed 27 August 2014.

[42] The first child was a daughter; and the second, a boy, bearing his name (Alexander Cockburn), was the major beneficiary under Sir Alexander Cockburn's will. Both died childless.

[43] Bingham (n 20) 17 n 83.

[44] The manuscript is to be found in the 'Ledgers relating to legal practice and MSS novel' of Sir Alexander Cockburn in the Middle Temple Archives under Record Reference GD.4, Catalogue Reference NRA 32552.

THE HISTORICAL KEYSTONE TO INTERNATIONAL ARBITRATION   21

found in a trunk in Germany and translated into English from the original French. It starts with this passage:

> During an excursion in France in the summer of 1801, it was the good fortune of the publisher of the following memoirs to become acquainted with the younger brother of Count S ... a German nobleman whose talents in character were as distinguished as his family was rich and his properties extensive ...

It continues with a complicated love story, entangled relationships, and multiple betrayals amid the horrors of French autocracy, the French Revolution, and Napoleon, as told by an old man, Monsieur Auguste de Morbière, now a refugee living with the German nobleman. The novel finishes with a flourish featuring the much-younger Auguste:

> On a sudden [the] door of [the] boudoir flew open. Féicie, whose visage had just before been refreshed in my heart by the portrait of her mother, rose blushing from her seat, at the foot of which stood [the] cradle of my son. Overpowered by a thousand emotions I rushed towards her, and falling at her feet embraced her knees. I thought I felt her lips touch my brow—I know not if it was so, for my senses reeled with the excess of my joy ...

And, so magnificently reunited after so many vicissitudes, the couple were then happily married, in accordance with a deathbed wish made by their mutual friend, Adèle.

Who was the departed Adèle, who was the blushing Félicie, who was the mother of the baby son, and what happened to Auguste in the middle of this novel? I regret that I cannot tell you myself—because Cockburn's handwriting became increasingly unreadable, and I had to stop halfway. The only person known to have read every page is the late novelist and social historian, Siân Busby,[45] and I have permission to reproduce part of her wonderful summary:

> The (untitled) novel is fairly typical of the gothic romances popular in the late Regency period—the sort of work Jane Austen mocks in 'Northanger Abbey', with nuns, wicked stepmothers, thwarted lovers, ghosts, intrigue and dungeons. It is epistolary in structure. It tells the story of Auguste de Morbière, a young man living in France in the last year of Louis XV's reign. He tells the story in flashback from the vantage point of 1801, having read an unflattering version of his story

---

[45] Siân Elizabeth Busby, the novelist, broadcaster, and historian (1961–2012), wrote inter alia the novel *McNaughten* (Short Books 2009) and, as transcribed by her husband after her death, *A Commonplace Killing* (Short Books 2013). In *McNaughten,* the near-fictional Cockburn appears prominently, with much credit, as the accused's Counsel.

22   ON ARBITRATION

in a book by someone else. He falls in love with the ward of his profligate father, Félicie, who he fears for much of the early part of the book might be his sister, and then his father's mistress. He is wrongfully imprisoned when taken at the house of a revolutionary (a scene written with a great deal of radical fervor—Cockburn was a lifelong reforming liberal Whig). A ghost appears to him in his dungeon pointing him to a series of letters concealed in the bricks of the cell wall. These point to the true identity of Félicie, and also imply an intrigue against her parents and the King which turns out to have been instigated by Auguste's father's mistress, the scheming Madame de Mainville. There are many twists and turns in the convoluted plot, which eventually leads to Auguste witnessing what he believes to be his father's marriage to Félicie (always described as 'pale and trembling'), and Auguste's own love affair with Adèle, another victim of Madame de Mainville's intriguing. We also learn that the scheming Madame de Mainville has been a mistress of the King, and has something to do with his poisoning at the hands of Madame du Barry ... Eventually Auguste ends up in another dungeon, but his lover Adèle sacrifices herself by agreeing to enter a convent so that he might go free. This satisfies the intriguers who want to get their hands on the orphan's family's estates. While in the convent Adèle gives birth to Auguste's natural son and dies, but not before she has made the acquaintance of Félicie, who has also entered the convent, and tells her the whole story. Auguste is recovering from one of those deliriums that heroes of this kind of novel invariably fall into—mentally and physically exhausted and also confused about which of the two women he loves most—is introduced to his baby son without realising who the child is, and then learns the entire story (again in a series of letters, this time written by Adèle before her death). He is eventually reunited with Félicie and restored to his father (who it seems was an unwitting instrument of the evil Madame de Mainville) and acknowledges Adèle's son as his own. As he and Félicie prepare to marry she hands him a final letter from Adèle: 'If you have ever loved me let your unceasing study be the happiness of Félicie. She, I know, will not fail to make you happy'. With that the novel concludes with Auguste de Morbière, back in 1801, announcing: 'This is the true history of my youth. My tale is done!' The novel does not have a great deal of literary merit, but it is written with a certain degree of verve and consistent in tone and style. It offers a fascinating insight into Cockburn for any future biographers ... It is the novel of a young man with a bit of time on his hands, and with a young man's romantic notions of sex, love and women. There is nothing especially learned about the book, either in its style or content; not much sense of the historical setting, and very little maturity of insight into characters and their motivations. Apart from one passionately written passage denouncing 'Universal Corruption' and predicting the blood-letting to come in the French Revolution ('Tyrants will tremble in their palaces, long and bloody will be the struggle, but it will not be doubtful!'), there is very little social or political commentary. But it is well-paced and a good, light read.

At the very least, this novel shows Sir Alexander Cockburn to have been a warm-blooded human being and therefore a useful complement to his fellow party-appointed arbitrator, the cold-blooded Charles Francis Adams, in regard to the crisis confronting the Alabama Arbitration in June 1872 threatening its imminent demise.[46]

That crisis arose from the wording of the Washington Treaty. It had effectively fixed, with its three rules on neutrality, the liability of Great Britain retrospectively for certain of the 'direct claims' made by the United States; but it did not expressly address any 'indirect claims'. The direct claims arose from the destruction of vessels and cargoes by the CSS *Alabama* and her fellow cruisers, causing loss to American citizens in relatively modest sums. The United States' indirect claims had been pleaded in the written *Case of the United States* submitted in December 1871 in the Alabama Arbitration, without prior notice to Great Britain (thereby preventing any adequate written response under the arbitration's procedural timetable).[47] These indirect claims were advanced as a national claim for the increased costs of marine insurance, for losses in the transfer of US tonnage to the British and other flags, and, most controversially of all, for the full costs incurred by the United States from the prolongation of the Civil War by two years, from the battle of Gettysburg in 1863 to the end of hostilities in 1865, in a total amount (with interest) that would have bankrupted Great Britain at that time. It was these indirect claims which had been and were still being pressed by Senator Sumner (from whom they had origin-ated), with strong popular support in the United States.

The case pleaded by the United States raised an immediate diplomatic storm in England because the British Commissioners negotiating the Treaty of Washington had been left with the firm impression that no such indirect claims claim would be made by the United States and that the treaty conferred no jurisdiction on the Alabama tribunal to decide any indirect claims. There was also a general sense in England that the British Commissioners had somehow been duped by the American Commissioners during the treaty's negotiations, and that both the Secretary of State (Hamilton Fish) and President Grant were guilty at least of shabby and ungentlemanly conduct.[48] Accordingly, the British Government expressed the firm opinion that the Alabama tribunal could enjoy no jurisdiction to receive any of these indirect claims. Secretary Fish, supported by President Grant, expressed a diametrically opposite opinion, and it was firmly contended, not entirely without

---

[46] It may be that an entrepreneurial syndicate could be formed to transcribe and publish this novel; but its commercial success is perhaps not entirely assured, even with the Alabama's Arbitration's 150th anniversary less than a decade away.

[47] Not suspecting any surprises from the United States, Great Britain had agreed a short procedural timetable following the exchange of the parties' written cases, with no adequate opportunity for a full written response.

[48] See Veeder (n 20).

24 ON ARBITRATION

justification, that the wording of the Washington Treaty supported the position of the United States.

Over the next six months, the two governments exchanged lengthy and learned memoranda advancing jurisdictional and other arguments, to no effect. The jurisdictional issue was thus entirely unresolved diplomatically when the tribunal opened its first hearing in Geneva on Saturday, 15 June 1872. At this point, the British Government was ready to walk away from the arbitration if the tribunal assumed jurisdiction to decide the indirect claims, but the government also knew that the United States would insist that the tribunal should continue its work in the absence of Great Britain (as it could). Nonetheless, at this hearing the British Government's Agent, Lord Tenderden, refused to present Great Britain's final written argument and requested from the tribunal an adjournment of eight months to enable a supplementary treaty to be negotiated and concluded between the two parties. There was then a great stillness in the room, according to the participants present, because everyone there knew that if the arbitration adjourned for eight months, not only would there be no supplementary treaty, but the arbitration would never resume, with the inevitable prospect of war between the United States and Great Britain. To this request, the American Agent, Mr Bancroft Davis, calmly replied that he was unable to state the response of the US Government to Lord Tenderden's request and asked in turn for a short adjournment to receive instructions from the State Department, until the following Monday afternoon, 17 June 1872, a delay which was granted by the tribunal (it was later extended to Wednesday, 19 June).

These five days were crucial for the history of international arbitration. When the hearing resumed on the fifth day, the tribunal declared as regards the indirect claims, in the words recorded in the official English protocol after the necessary recitals:

> The Arbitrators think it right to state that, after the most careful perusal of all that has been urged on the part of the Government of the United States in respect of these claims, they have arrived, individually and collectively, at the conclusion that these claims do not constitute, upon the principles of international law applicable to such cases, good foundation for an award of compensation or computation of damages between nations, and should upon such principles, be wholly excluded from the consideration of the tribunal in making its award, even if there were no disagreement between the two Governments as to the competence of the tribunal to decide thereon ... [49]

---

[49] Hackett (n 38) App III, 393.

THE HISTORICAL KEYSTONE TO INTERNATIONAL ARBITRATION   25

This was not an arbitration order or award: it was ostensibly a spontaneous 'declaration' issued unanimously by the tribunal within the Alabama Arbitration, without any hearing, and with no argument or request from any of the parties' counsel. What happened during those five days? The story is told by Mr Davis, the American Agent, by Mr Hackett, the private secretary to General Cushing (one of the three counsel to the United States), and by Sir Roundell Palmer (later Lord Selbourne), the English Attorney-General and the senior Counsel for Great Britain, supplemented by other contemporary materials.[50]

(1) The First Day

On this first day, Saturday, Mr Davis privately suggested to Mr Adams after the hearing that the tribunal should address the direct claims before addressing the indirect claims; Mr Adams responded that the same idea had occurred to him. Mr Adams said that he would ask Mr Evarts, the senior American Counsel, to speak to Sir Roundell Palmer, the English Attorney-General.[51] (Mr Evarts had acted as Adams' legal adviser in London on the Alabama Claims and was later US Secretary of State and subsequently a US Senator for New York.)[52] Later that same day, Mr Davis wrote accordingly to the Secretary of State, Hamilton Fish:

> [Mr Adams] told me that he had no doubt himself that the indirect claims were within the scope of the Treaty; and that he had thought of the same way as cutting the knot, and letting the arbitration go on. It would be a way most unpalatable to England, but if there is pluck enough in the tribunal, it might be done. I have not much faith that it will be . . .

That afternoon, after meeting with the American Counsel, Mr Davis visited Mr Adams at his villa outside Geneva, where he was staying with his wife and family. Mr Adams, who had already spoken to Mr Evarts, requested that Mr Davis now visit Lord Tenderden (the British Agent), which Mr Davis did that same evening. Mr Davis then told Lord Tenderden what Mr Adams had told him, namely that the indirect claims should be put aside by the tribunal pending further discussions between the two governments so as to allow the tribunal to continue its work on

---

[50] Davis (n 34) 98 et seq; Hackett (n 38) 235 et seq; see also Adrian Cook, *The Alabama Claims: American Politics and Anglo-American Relations 1865–1872* (Cornell University Press 1975) 235 et seq; A C Cushing, *The Treaty of Washington* (1873); Alan Nevins, *Hamilton Fish: The Inner History of the Grant Administration,* vol 2 (Dodd, Mead & Co 1936, Frederick Ungar Publishing Co 1957); and Roundell, Earl of Selbourne, *Memorials: Family and Personal* (Macmillan 1896).

[51] Hackett (n 38) 238, 240.

[52] William M Evarts had earlier acted as Adams' legal adviser in London on the Alabama Claims, assigned in 1863 by Secretary of State Seward; see Walter Stahr, *Seward: Lincoln's Indispensable Man* (Simon & Schuster 2012) 373.

26   ON ARBITRATION

the direct claims, without the lengthy adjournment requested by Great Britain. Mr Davis also said that he had come at the request of Mr Adams, but not officially. Lord Tenderden, after necessary diplomatic equivocations, replied that Mr Adams would have to go much further, by having the tribunal decide now to reject the indirect claims as beyond its jurisdiction. This was, of course, an unacceptable proposal for the United States: it had always considered that the indirect claims were covered by the Treaty of Washington and accordingly had been properly referred to the tribunal. However, there was a good relationship between Mr Davis and Lord Tenderden; they had become friends during the negotiations for the Treaty of Washington, and they trusted each other. There was therefore a conversation between the two in an effort to find a possible compromise. That same evening, Mr Davis discussed the matter with the American Counsel, Mr Waite (later Chief Justice of the US Supreme Court) and Mr Evarts. (General Cushing had already gone to bed.) Later that night at about midnight, Lord Tenderden knocked on Mr Davis' bedroom door at his hotel in Geneva. (The American Agent and Counsel were then staying at the Hotel Beau Rivage, before moving to an elegant villa outside Geneva for the remainder of the arbitration, with the British all staying throughout at the nearby Hotel des Bergues, including Sir Alexander Cockburn.) After his earlier meeting with Mr Davis, Lord Tenderden had discussed the matter with the English Attorney-General, Sir Roundell Palmer, just as he was preparing to leave Geneva for London, believing the arbitration to be adjourned indefinitely. The Attorney-General had in turn discussed the matter with Sir Alexander Cockburn. Subsequently, the Attorney-General had listed three points for Lord Tenderden, which Lord Tenderden now dictated to Mr Davis at this midnight meeting.

The first point was to preclude the tribunal from giving any judgment on the indirect claims, as not having been submitted by the parties to the tribunal. The second point was to preclude Sir Alexander Cockburn, as the arbitrator appointed by Great Britain, from taking any part, directly or indirectly, in any expression of opinion on the indirect claims. (This was readily agreeable to the American Counsel, who had already formed an adverse opinion of Cockburn, and the British Counsel were by now probably aware of Cockburn's intense distaste for the Treaty of Washington.) The third point was to preclude the tribunal from making any expression of opinion on the indirect claims binding on the parties, without the assent of both parties. During this midnight meeting, an idea emerged between Mr Davis and Lord Tenderden that the tribunal might make, with the assent of both parties, an extra-judicial expression of opinion on the indirect claims, short of an actual award.

(2) The Second Day

On Sunday, Mr Davis submitted Sir Roundell Palmer's three points to the American Counsel, who decided that negotiations should continue between Mr Evarts and

THE HISTORICAL KEYSTONE TO INTERNATIONAL ARBITRATION   27

Sir Roundell Palmer. Mr Evarts and Sir Roundell Palmer met that evening, and they confirmed that the principal obstacle concerned the third point: What kind of extrajudicial expression on the indirect claims could be made by the tribunal, by consent of the parties, as regards jurisdiction and the merits? In the meantime, during the afternoon, Mr Evarts and Mr Davis went to see Mr Adams, reporting to him in full the events of the previous twenty-four hours. Here, it is best to record the actual words used by Mr Davis in his contemporary memorandum for the State Department, recording Mr Adams' response:

> He [Mr. Adams] said that he had had some conversation with Mr. Fish, before leaving Washington, in which Mr. Fish had told him that he was willing to have the indirect claims decided adversely, and that he had said to Mr. Fish that in his judgment they ought to be so disposed of—that Mr. Fish had felt so much interest in the matter that he had sent a special message to him in Boston, by Mr. Boutwell [Mr. Boutwell had been Governor of Massachusetts and was now US Secretary of the Treasury], to see Sir Alexander Cockburn in London and endeavour to arrange some way to have it done; that he [Mr. Adams] had seen some influential persons in London on the subject, but had not seen Sir Alexander, because he did not think him the best person to see for that purpose ...[53]

Despite their demerits, Mr Adams also repeated his opinion to Messrs Evarts and Davis that the indirect claims lay within the tribunal's jurisdiction.

Later that afternoon, after seeing Count Sclopis (the tribunal's Italian president), Mr Adams delivered to Mr Davis a draft declaration which might be made by the tribunal, together with an expression of the tribunal's view that it was inadvisable for the arbitration to be adjourned. This draft was to the effect that the arbitrators must decline to assume any jurisdiction over the indirect claims but, if jurisdiction were assumed, that the indirect claims would not succeed under recognized rules of international law.[54] Mr Davis carried the draft to the American Counsel. They decided that the draft was unacceptable given its statement that the indirect claims fell outside the scope of the Treaty of Washington and beyond the tribunal's jurisdiction.

(3) The Third Day

On Monday, the American Counsel re-drafted Mr Adams' draft declaration and asked Mr Evarts and Mr Davis to deliver this revised draft to Mr Adams. It was to the same effect that the indirect claims would fail as a matter of international

---

[53] Hackett (n 38) 246.
[54] Ibid 247–8.

28 ON ARBITRATION

law; but, significantly, that the tribunal would not decide upon its jurisdiction to decide such claims, one way or the other. When Mr Evarts and Mr Davis arrived at Mr Adams' villa, they found him with M Stämpfli (the Swiss arbitrator). Mr Adams indicated that he had already spoken to Baron d'Itayubá (the Brazilian arbitrator) and was soon to speak again with Count Sclopis (the Italian presiding arbitrator) at the tribunal's private meeting fixed for that afternoon, before the resumed hearing with the parties. Mr Adams later called on Mr Davis, with a further revised draft, as to which Mr Davis expressed his disappointment, again because it stated that the tribunal considered that the indirect claims fell outside its jurisdiction.

At the resumed hearing that day, Mr Davis explained to the tribunal that he had not yet received instructions from his government responding to Lord Tenderden's application to adjourn the arbitration for eight months, requesting further time to Wednesday, 19 June. This was, of course, a half-truth which deceived no one. When the president turned to Lord Tenderden for his response, Lord Tenderden said, doubtless with a straight face: '*Je ne puis faire aucune objection*'. Later that same Monday afternoon, in a private meeting, the tribunal decided unanimously not to adjourn the arbitration, but to dispose of the indirect claims by an extra-judicial declaration, at the joint suggestion of Sir Alexander Cockburn and Mr Adams, with the precise form of that wording still to be settled.

(4) The Fourth Day

On Tuesday morning, Sir Roundell Palmer delivered to the American Counsel his own revised draft of the American re-draft which had been submitted by the American Counsel to Mr Adams the previous day (Monday). That American re-draft had come to Sir Roundell Palmer from Sir Alexander Cockburn, via Mr Adams, and it had provided the basis for Sir Roundell Palmer's revised draft intended as a compromise acceptable to both parties. Although Sir Alexander Cockburn left no personal account of his own, he described these events to Sir Roundell Palmer, as recorded in the latter's memoirs:

> During the pause afforded by these adjournments, Sir Alexander Cockburn told me that the idea of getting rid of the difficulty by a spontaneous declaration of the Arbitrators against the indirect claims had been suggested by Mr Adams, and that the rest of the Arbitrators were inclined to entertain it; and he desired me to consider in what form it could be done, so as to leave the position assumed by our Government untouched, without shutting the door against its acceptance on the other side. Accordingly I drew up a form of declaration, which I thought might be accepted on both sides, unless the United States preferred the failure of the

Treaty to the abandonment of those claims; and this being communicated by Sir Alexander Cockburn to the other Arbitrators, was adopted by them.[55]

This compromise draft was indeed agreeable to the American Counsel; and it was submitted to the full tribunal by Sir Alexander Cockburn with Mr Adams' approval that same day. At this private meeting of the tribunal in the house occupied by Count Sclopis in Geneva, the tribunal unanimously approved the revised draft declaration to which the parties' counsel had assented, with the joint support of Mr Adams and Sir Alexander Cockburn.

(5) The Fifth Day

Accordingly, when the arbitration resumed the following day, Wednesday 19 June, the tribunal made its extra-judicial declaration in a form of words which had been quietly agreed by counsel for both parties, with the active intermediation of Mr Adams and Sir Alexander Cockburn as party-appointed arbitrators. It was not an award, order, or any form of judgment, and it remained ostensibly subject to the assent of both parties.[56] Subject to formalities as to each government's instructions and further negotiations over the precise wording of these two assents, both parties accepted the declaration as binding upon them and determinative of the indirect claims, the United States on 25 June and Great Britain on 27 June.[57] The British Counsel then filed their final written argument; Count Sclopis delivered an opening address in the tribunal's name; the arbitration continued un-adjourned with the direct claims only; the tribunal issued its award on 14 September;[58] and Great Britain promptly paid in full the compensation thereby awarded to the United States.[59] The rest is history.

The tribunal's declaration in June had cleverly preserved the essential positions of both parties; neither had compromised what, politically, they could never compromise, particularly with presidential elections imminent in the United States and a likely change of government in London. Great Britain had finally rid itself of the indirect claims; the United States had won the acknowledgment by the tribunal within the arbitration, albeit extra-judicially, that the indirect claims were

---

[55] Ibid 253.

[56] For the text of the declaration, see Wetter (n 20) 163.

[57] For the protocols of these two hearings, see ibid 165, 167.

[58] The Alabama award was published in the *London Gazette Supplement*, 14 September 1872 (it is reproduced in Wetter (n 20) 48). Sir Alexander Cockburn's dissenting opinion was published in the *London Gazette Supplement*, 24 September 1872 (the 'Conclusion' is re-printed in Wetter (n 20) 55). Separate opinions issued by the three neutral arbitrators were published in the *London Gazette Supplement*, 30 September 1872.

[59] For the form of payment, see Balch (n 30); but see also Bingham (n 20) for overpayment. (Cockburn was perhaps right to dissent on quantum.)

30 ON ARBITRATION

not necessarily outside the scope of the Treaty of Washington but were in any event devoid of any substance on the merits, contrary to populist sentiments; and, for all practical purposes, the arbitration was saved by the active intervention of the two party-appointed arbitrators. Although both saw themselves as representatives of their two countries, neither in fact represented his country's case in the Alabama Arbitration.[60] Charles Francis Adams was always opposed to the United States' indirect claims (albeit on the merits and not on jurisdiction), and Sir Alexander Cockburn could not hide his contempt for the retrospective effect of the Treaty of Washington's three rules on neutrality, to the dismay and increasing irritation of the British Government. Indeed, in response to the publication of Cockburn's dissenting opinion, the Chancellor of the Exchequer, a senior member of the British Cabinet, attacked Cockburn publicly for not 'simply signing the award with the other arbitrators'.[61]

D. Conclusion

It may be said that the Alabama Arbitration is only a story from olden times, that it could never happen now, and that it should therefore be discounted as completely inapt to the new demands for dispute settlement in modern times. The first and second statements may be true, but as to the third, I suggest otherwise, for several reasons.

First, the Alabama Arbitration is the origin of what international arbitration is today, with the system of party-appointed arbitrators recognized by many arbitration rules and treaties, including the ICSID Convention, NAFTA, the UNCITRAL Model Law, and the UNCITRAL Arbitration Rules (1976 and 2010). The system worked successfully then, in untried but testing conditions, and for the most part it does still. We should be wary of abandoning a well-established tradition without good cause. Arbitral reform remains desirable, after reflection and consensus, but it is certainly not a necessary solution to switch now to a new, untested, controversial, and radically different system where all arbitrators are appointed by institutions, in default of the parties' joint agreement. If it were, then why not establish a permanent international court for investment disputes and even abandon international arbitration altogether? This question answers itself. For good reasons, the parties to the Alabama Arbitration chose international arbitration and rejected the idea of a sole arbitrator appointed by a sovereign or other institution, and for most

---

[60] The Geneva archives contain two photographs of both arbitrators posing with the parties' respective Counsel, wives, and staff in Geneva, as if to record two opposing football teams with their skippers. No such photographs would be taken today.

[61] The speech of the Chancellor of the Exchequer (Mr Lowe) was reported in the *Pall Mall Gazette* (27 September 1872).

THE HISTORICAL KEYSTONE TO INTERNATIONAL ARBITRATION   31

users those same reasons hold true today. As Shakespeare (almost) said, 'Put not your trust in princes—nor arbitral institutions as appointing authorities'.

Second, the right of each party to appoint an arbitrator makes the arbitration the *parties'* arbitration, deciding *their* dispute with *their* tribunal. The preference by users for arbitration over litigation has many explanations, but one manifest reason is the sense of ownership by a party over the arbitral process because it has participated in the formation of the tribunal as to which all parties have consented. This also explains why, despite the risk of increased costs and delays, users still prefer an international tribunal comprising three or more arbitrators and not a sole arbitrator appointed by an appointing authority. This is much more than a 'genie', but a deeply ingrained reality in the settled practice of international arbitration.

Third, let us not be too 'Victorian' over party-appointed arbitrators and their dissenting opinions: arbitrators should not all be men or women regimented in grey suits. There is room and indeed a need for characters, just as 'Rumpole of the Bailey' is not entirely a work of fiction for English barristers or trial lawyers everywhere. The Alabama Arbitration probably benefited overall from Sir Alexander Cockburn, a most unusual but colourful, if not also choleric, Chief Justice. It undoubtedly benefited from Charles Francis Adams, as a cold and calculating diplomat. So too the current system of international arbitration usually benefits from a wider, not smaller, pool of arbitrators. Myths should not diminish this arbitral pool. Moreover, dissenting opinions by party-appointed arbitrators remain a modest issue. Adopting Alan Redfern's famous triage,[62] arbitration can benefit from 'good' dissenting opinions, which almost inevitably will be made by a party-appointed arbitrator. Such dissents are more often (if rationally and courteously expressed) a sign of healthy intellectual vigour within arbitral deliberations, rather than evidence of any fatal malady in the system of party-appointed arbitrators. For all that, the other relatively few 'bad' or 'ugly' dissenting opinions are a small price to pay.

Fourth, what may be wrong today, if anything, is not the principle of party-appointed arbitrators, but rather their appointment in some cases to a three-arbitrator tribunal, potentially ensuring an undue significance in their relations with the presiding arbitrator, particularly in highly controversial disputes involving one or more states. That factor would be absent if there were not three but five arbitrators with the majority not appointed by the parties, as took place in the Alabama Arbitration. Historically, that greater number has often been agreed in arbitrations involving states.[63] In the ILC's 1958 Model Rules on Arbitral Procedure, the default number of arbitrators was codified as 'preferably five', a provision apparently so uncontroversial that it there required no commentary or published travaux (Article 3.3). In the pending arbitration between Mauritius and the United Kingdom, part of the acrimonious dispute over the Chagos Archipelago in the Indian Ocean, the

---

[62] Redfern (n 3).
[63] See, e.g., the 1907 Convention for the Pacific Settlement of International Disputes, Art 54.

tribunal is composed of five arbitrators under Article 3(a) of Annex VII of the 1982 United Nations Convention on the Law of the Sea, requiring 'five members': the claimant and the respondent each appointed one arbitrator, with the other three arbitrators being appointed by the President of ITLOS. Similarly, the Indus Waters Treaty between Pakistan and India required the Indus Waters tribunal to be comprised of seven members, two appointed by each of the parties and the other three (including the presiding arbitrator) to be named by the UN Secretary-General, the Lord Chief Justice of England, and the Rector of Imperial College, London University. Its decisions were unanimous, culminating in its award of 20 December 2013. For complex arbitrations between states, there remain good reasons for preferring more than three arbitrators, and, since there must be an uneven figure, five or seven (not one) is the obvious solution. Particularly with a five-arbitrator tribunal, any possible disadvantages in having party-appointed arbitrators are diminished, without losing any of their actual advantages.

Lastly, let us apply in our minds the following litmus-paper test to a long-standing dispute almost as potentially troubling as the Alabama Claims: the ancient claim by Argentina against the United Kingdom over the sovereignty of the Falkland Islands or Las Malvinas, which has already led to warlike operations between the two countries.[64] Put yourself in the position of these two states and assume (which we cannot yet) that both states jointly wished in good faith to have that claim and its consequences determined finally by international arbitration. Would either of these two parties agree to an arbitration tribunal composed of one or more arbitrators *all* appointed by an arbitral institution, or would they follow the model established by the Alabama Arbitration, with the right of each to appoint an arbitrator of its own choice to the tribunal? We can be certain that it would not be the former, but rather that arbitral history would repeat itself—for good reasons.

All this suggests that the traditional system of party-appointed arbitrators remains today the robust keystone to international arbitration, without which arbitration would inevitably assume a significantly different form adverse to the interests of its users. Moreover, if international arbitration were to fail as a legitimate procedure for dispute resolution in the twenty-first century (as it may, particularly for investment arbitration), the effective cause will be quite other than the system of party-appointed arbitrators, with or without their dissenting opinions.

---

[64] This controversy is not one-sided: see W Michael Reisman, 'The Struggle for The Falklands' (1983) 93 Yale L J 287; contrast the account in Sir Lawrence Freedman, *The Official History of the Falklands Campaign* (Routledge 2005).

2

Investor–State Disputes and the Development of International Law

Arbitral Lessons from the Private Correspondence of Queen Victoria and Lenin

In these depressing times, there are many arbitral nightmares: forgetting to deal with one claimant's claim in a milestone arbitration under the North American Free Trade Agreement (NAFTA); or arriving at a decision under one bilateral investment treaty (BIT) that is exactly opposite another tribunal's on identical factual and legal issues under a different BIT; and making an error in the application of international law, only to be corrected publicly by a local state judge. In the field of investment arbitrations, these are all, of course, nightmares most unlikely to happen in real life, so for practical purposes, we can set them entirely aside.

My own nightmare is to wake up in Northern Sakhalin in the Russian Far East, where Western and Russian oil companies are investing billions of U.S. dollars to extract oil and gas for export to Japan, and there to be asked without prior notice, unaided, to draft with extreme urgency for unforgiving investors and local and national governments dispute resolution mechanisms for each of the different BITs, concession agreements, and commercial contracts. This is a task which would probably challenge the sanity and courage of any legal adviser, whether advising the investor, or more particularly the host state, given the fast-moving juridical developments in the field of investment arbitration. What can be done to assuage these and like nightmares in both developed and developing nations, save to derive comforting historical lessons from the private correspondence of Queen Victoria and Lenin?

On January 31, 1872, at her house at Osbourne on the Isle of Wight, Queen Victoria opened a letter from the British Prime Minister, William Gladstone. It read:

10 Downing Street, 30th January 1872: Mr. Gladstone presents his humble duty to your Majesty, and reports that the Cabinet this day considered the proper order of business to be pursued in the House of Commons at the commencement of

---

On Arbitration. Edited by: Sam Wordsworth KC and Marie Veeder, Oxford University Press. © Oxford University Press 2023.
DOI: 10.1093/oso/9780192869135.003.0002

34 ON ARBITRATION

the Session .... The chief and most anxious subject of their deliberations was the case which has been prepared and presented by the American Government on the subject of the Alabama claims. Your Majesty's advisers cannot conceal from themselves that this document contains a mass of matter which is at once irrelevant and exasperating, and advances claims and pretensions such as it is wholly incompatible with national honour to admit, or to plead to before a Tribunal of Arbitration. The Cabinet have requested the aid of the Law Officers, and they will maturely consider the whole of this undoubtedly very grave and anxious matter before tendering any advice to your Majesty.

Queen Victoria was not at all amused by these troubles emanating from what was then, of course, a developing country; her letter in reply to the prime minister was immediate and direct. It read as follows:

Dear Mr. Gladstone, I am commanded by the Queen to assure you that her Majesty fully participates in the anxiety which you have informed the Queen is felt by the Cabinet with respect to the Alabama claims. The Queen hopes that, on reference to the Law Officers, it will be found that the legal advisers of the British Commissioners have not been in error, but her Majesty can well understand that the Commissioners thought they were treating with gentlemen actuated by honourable feelings, and did not suspect that a trap was being laid for them. Her Majesty thinks it may be useful that you should know that, during an interview with Lord Derby [of Her Majesty's Opposition], he said of his own accord to the Queen that he was indignant at the conduct of the Americans, and considered the matter so serious that he would endeavour to do his best to help the Government on this question.

As we now know, the Alabama Claims Arbitration at Geneva did eventually take place later that year, beginning on June 27, 1872, having been dangerously delayed from June 15. It eventually resulted in the famous award of September 14, 1872, in favor of the United States and against the United Kingdom.

The award was made by a collegiate international tribunal comprised of five arbitrators, the first international tribunal of its kind in modern times and the basic model for investment arbitration today. By that award, decided by a majority with the British arbitrator (the Lord Chief Justice Sir Alexander Cockburn) strongly dissenting, the arbitration tribunal held that the United Kingdom had failed to use due diligence in the performance of its neutral obligations during the American Civil War, principally in permitting the Alabama and her fellow cruisers to be built in England and delivered to the Confederacy; and as compensation, the tribunal ordered the United Kingdom to pay the sum of $15.5 million in gold to the United States. By that award an imminent war was averted, with untold consequences for both nations, particularly in relation to Canada, which faced invasion and possible annexation by the United States.

For present purposes, although it was hardly an investor-state dispute, the Alabama Claims Arbitration is interesting because of the near-fatal ambiguity in the Washington Treaty of May 8, 1871, that created the arbitration tribunal and defined its jurisdiction. This treaty was the product of lengthy negotiations, both public and private, in London and Washington, extending over three years; it was much debated in both the U.S. Congress and the British Parliament. The treaty included an elaborate and carefully drafted agreement on three rules applicable to the United Kingdom as a neutral.

These rules ensured that the United Kingdom would be held liable by the Geneva tribunal, even though the rules imposed higher duties than those previously accepted under international law. It was a particular pleasure enjoyed by the U.S. Commissioners that the United Kingdom, long preaching as a gamekeeper the elevated duties to be imposed on poachers, had now to swallow its own medicine as the poacher—a reversal of roles not entirely unknown to foreign investment today.

In that sense, the Alabama award was fixed in advance; but the Washington Treaty most certainly did not fix the full extent of the United Kingdom's liability or the quantum of any compensation, particularly in respect of the new claims of the United States for so-called indirect damages, advanced in the amount of $9.1 billion. These "indirect" claims had first been pleaded, belatedly but with deliberate intent, in the written Case of the United States submitted in December 1871 for the arbitration. They were there advanced in equity rather than at law, but the distinction brought no comfort to the United Kingdom, and, as we have seen, it aroused Queen Victoria's ire. The claim for direct damages arose from the destruction of U.S. vessels and cargoes by the Alabama and her fellow-cruisers, causing loss to American citizens in the relatively modest sum of about $14 million, over which there was no equivalent controversy.

The new claim for indirect damages was advanced as a national claim for the increased costs of marine insurance; losses in the transfer of U.S. tonnage to the British flag; and, most controversially of all, the costs incurred from the prolongation of the Civil War after the battle of Gettysburg, from July 4, 1863, to the end of the hostilities two years later, all together with interest at 7 percent per annum from July 1, 1863, to the date of the award. With these indirect claims, the United Kingdom faced a potential liability in excess of $10 billion in gold—a massive sum by any contemporary standards for both developed and developing countries.

The case pleaded by the United States raised an immediate diplomatic storm, because the British Commissioners had been left with the firm impression that no such claim would be made; that any such claim had been waived during their long and detailed negotiations; and that the Washington Treaty conferred no jurisdiction on the arbitration tribunal to hear indirect claims. Queen Victoria's sense of outrage was matched by strong public feeling in England; there was a general sense that the British Commissioners had somehow been tricked by the U.S. Commissioners; and that the U.S. secretary of state and president were guilty at least of shabby and ungentlemanly conduct. Accordingly, the British government expressed the firm opinion that the arbitration tribunal at Geneva could enjoy no jurisdiction to decide upon any of these claims for indirect losses. The U.S. Secretary of State, Hamilton Fish, supported by the U.S. President, Ulysses S. Grant, expressed a diametrically opposite opinion; it was firmly contended, not entirely without justification, that the wording of the Washington Treaty supported the contention of the United States.

Over the next six months, there was much heated debate in the House of Commons and the House of Lords as to the conduct of the British and American Commissioners. The two governments exchanged lengthy and learned memoranda advancing jurisdictional arguments. The jurisdictional issue was entirely unresolved when the arbitration tribunal opened hearings in Geneva on June 15, 1872. At that point, the British government was minded to walk away from the arbitration if the tribunal assumed jurisdiction over the indirect claims of the U.S., but the British government also knew privately that the United States and the American arbitrator would then insist that the truncated tribunal should continue its work in the absence of the United Kingdom and its arbitrator. Instead, the British government's counsel asked for an adjournment, which was granted.

There then took place a wonderful act of arbitral imagination. The American arbitrator, Charles Francis Adams, brokered a compromise by which the tribunal would declare, but not formally decide, that it would not assume jurisdiction over the indirect claims. When the hearing resumed on June 19, 1872, the arbitration tribunal declared, in the words recorded in the official protocol:

> The Arbitrators think it right to state that, after the most careful perusal of all that has been urged on the part of the Government of the United States in respect of these claims, they have arrived, individually and collectively, at the conclusion that these claims do not constitute, upon the principles of international law applicable to such cases, good foundation for an award of compensation or computation of damages between nations, and should upon such principles, be wholly excluded from the consideration of the Tribunal in making its award, even if there were no disagreement between the two Governments as to the Competency of the Tribunal to decide thereon.

At the next hearing on June 25th, the United States expressed its assent at the tribunal's declaration; and at the hearing on June 27th, the United Kingdom likewise expressed its acceptance and withdrew its application for a general adjournment of the arbitration proceedings. The arbitration tribunal then commenced its work on the merits of the remaining claims.

INVESTOR–STATE DISPUTES AND THE DEVELOPMENT   37

This happy news reached Boston on June 27, 1872, where the secretary of state read the telegram to President Grant from the United States' agent at Geneva: "British argument filed. Arbitration goes on." It is said that tears of relief moistened the old warrior's eyes. The same immense relief was felt in England by Gladstone and Lord Glanville, the foreign secretary. A terrible war was thus averted by an arbitral whisker; and the cause of peace and the peaceful settlement of disputes were much advanced, to our lasting and enormous benefit even today.

What is the particular lesson we can draw for present purposes, in Sakhalin and elsewhere? There was, it seems, no actual subterfuge or negligence by any of the American and British commissioners in the negotiation and drafting of the Washington Convention. All were skilled and experienced statesmen, well used to the legal niceties of the English language in both developed and developing nations. The explanation was more simple, as recited by Professor Mountague Bernard of Oxford University, one of the British Commissioners, in *A Historical Account of the Neutrality of Great Britain during the American Civil War:*

A Treaty is an instrument which you cannot send to be settled in a conveyancer's chambers, nor commit to a knot of wrangling attorneys; no, not even to the family solicitor. It is an instrument in the framing of which the sensitive and punctilious self-respect of governments and nations has to be consulted, and discussion must never be suffered to degenerate into altercation; in which it is often necessary for the sake of agreement to accept a less finished or even less accurate expression instead of a more finished or more accurate one, and which must be construed liberally and reasonably, according to what appears to be the true intention of the contracting parties. In all this, there is no excuse for equivocal expression, and no defense of such ambiguities can be founded on it; but of apparent faults of expression it has often been, and often will be the unavoidable cause.

Had the United States pressed its indirect claims before the Washington Treaty, the United Kingdom would never have agreed to the treaty. Conversely, if pressed by the United Kingdom, the United States could never have expressly abandoned its indirect claims, even at the cost of the treaty itself. Both governments chose to see only what they wanted to see, because the alternative was much worse: a terrible modern war between friendly nations who could then have become permanent enemies.

To those who criticize negotiated treaties (whether BITs, NAFTA, the World Trade Organization, or Energy Charter Treaty (ECT)) or concessions or commercial contracts, the lesson from the Alabama Claims Arbitration is equally straightforward, for both investor and developing country: Why not trust the arbitral process? This is not an original or radical idea. We may find, however low our expectation of international investment arbitration and however much international arbitration remains susceptible to improvement, that the arbitral system can work and that it can spring a surprising and fair result in apparently the worst of times, as Charles Francis Adams did at Geneva. In any event, as for the U.S. and British governments in the Alabama Claims Arbitration, there is still no equivalent practical alternative to arbitration for investor-state disputes; or any system which is not much, much worse, even short of war.

As for Lenin, space sadly precludes further consideration of his later arbitral correspondence; and it must therefore be left for another time. Yet already it can be said, although (so far as is known) Lenin and Queen Victoria never exchanged correspondence about international arbitration for investor-state disputes, that if they ever did, after the Alabama Claims Award, Queen Victoria was surely, almost certainly, less unamused.

3

Inter-State Arbitration

Inter-state arbitration is largely influenced by two different traditions, drawn from diplomacy and commerce under public and private international law respectively. At a time when the legitimacy of many forms of arbitration is encountering increasing difficulties (both substantive and procedural),[1] the historical path taken to reach the present practice of arbitration by states may explain the growing hostility towards arbitration shared across the political spectrum, particularly where a bilateral or multilateral treaty imposes an obligation on states to agree to arbitration in advance of a dispute: i.e. 'obligatory' arbitration and not a form of *compromis*.[2]

As to this first diplomatic tradition, from the earliest times of nation-states, princes, potentates, and popes have resorted, upon request or at their own initiative, to different forms of arbitration to settle peacefully existing disputes between states, including a home state's espousal of its national's claim against a host state. The alternative of conflict between disputing states was regarded generally as unpalatable, if a diplomatic settlement could resolve the particular dispute. For example, in 1493, Pope Alexander IV decided the geographical dispute between Spain and Portugal over the division of their colonial empires. In modern times, the origin of inter-state arbitration has been attributed to the Jay Treaty of 1796 between the USA and Britain, which provided for arbitration as a quasi-judicial means to end myriad differences outstanding from the American Revolution and the Treaty of Paris of 1783. Its commissions produced more than 500 decisions over five years. These were, however, mixed claims commissions composed of the two states' representatives, not swayed by the appointment of independent arbitrators,

---

[1] The USA's blocking of new members to hear disputes by the WTO's Appellate Body, thereby compromising the WTO system as a whole, derives from a contempt for 'unaccountable international tribunals' as recently expressed by the President of the USA to the UN General Assembly (see *Financial Times*, 2 October 2016, 1). Since 2014, similar political views have been repeatedly expressed by the European Commission. E.g. the European Trade Commissioner (Dr Cecilia Malmström) in 2015 rejected investor–state arbitration (ISDS) for the EU's new free trade agreements: 'there is a fundamental and widespread lack of trust in the fairness and impartiality of the old ISDS model'; and, under the EU's proposal for a new international investment court and appellate body, 'It will be judges, not arbitrators, who sit on these cases'. See also Sophie Lemaire, 'Arbitrage d'investissement et Union Européenne', Rev. arb. 1029 (2016), 1034 'elle [EU] propose une révolution du modèle contentieux qui le caractérise.'

[2] The phrase 'obligatory arbitration' is here borrowed from the first Hague Peace Conference, where it signified an agreement by states to arbitrate in advance of any dispute, as distinct from a *compromis* agreed after the outbreak of a dispute.

On Arbitration. Edited by: Sam Wordsworth KC and Marie Veeder, Oxford University Press. © Oxford University Press 2023. DOI: 10.1093/oso/9780192869135.003.0003

40 ON ARBITRATION

a neutral appointing authority, or the use of an established arbitral procedure. It followed an earlier precedent under the Treaty of Münster of 1648 between the Netherland and Spain (as part of the Peace of Westphalia). Moreover, consistent with the historical role of arbitration, the Jay Treaty addressed existing disputes and did not cover future disputes between the two states. If it was arbitration at all, by today's standards, it was arbitration by arbitrators in name only.[3]

The second commercial tradition is older. Transnational arbitration between merchants, before an impartial tribunal of the parties' choosing, under an established procedure, pre-dates the emergence of nation-states. In the nineteenth and twentieth centuries, the increasing use of concession contracts and investment agreements between a host state and a foreign national made use of this commercial tradition in the form of arbitration clauses contractually agreed between the foreigner and the state.[4] Later, when host states established, in their place, nationalized companies or wholly owned foreign trade corporations to contract with foreign nationals (as in the USSR, an example followed by most 'socialist' countries in Europe and China), their arbitration clauses conformed to this second commercial tradition.

The major changes began during the last part of the nineteenth century. The Washington Convention of 1871 between the USA and Britain introduced a significant change to the diplomatic tradition. That treaty primarily addressed existing claims by the USA (for itself and also espousing its nationals' claims) arising from Britain's misconduct as a neutral state during the American Civil War. The USA and Britain there agreed an arbitration tribunal comprising a majority of impartial arbitrators (three), together with the parties' respective representatives (two). It gave rise to the *Alabama Arbitration* in Geneva and its majority award of 1872, thereby precluding a real risk of a third war between these two states. Drawing upon both diplomatic and commercial traditions, the parties and the arbitration tribunal also firmly established the general principle of consensual arbitration as the preferred alternative to armed conflict, even for a major dispute involving matters of honour for both parties.

However, the Washington Convention addressed only existing disputes. By the end of the nineteenth century it was becoming necessary to introduce an arbitration mechanism for future disputes between states, as existed for commercial arbitrations between merchants. Such an obligatory arbitration, agreed by states in advance of a dispute, was addressed at length by the Hague Peace Conferences of

---

[3] As concluded by J. G. Merrills in regard to the Jay Treaty and its progeny: 'These early Anglo-American commissions were not judicial tribunals in the modern sense, but were supposed to blend juridical with diplomatic considerations to produce (in effect) a negotiated settlement.' See *International Dispute Settlement*, 6th edn (Cambridge University Press, 2017), 89.

[4] See Jean Ho, *State Responsibility for Breaches of Investment Contracts* (Cambridge University Press, 2018).

1899 and 1907. These two conferences established both the high- and low-water marks for the peaceful settlement by arbitration of disputes between states.

The 1899 Peace Conference was convened by the Russian Empire on 12 August 1898 in a note (or 'rescript') by the Russian Minister of Foreign Affairs addressed to foreign ambassadors in St Petersburg. It called for an international conference between states to ensure a true and stable peace and, above all, to put an end to the progressive development of modern armaments. It was thus to be primarily a peace conference at a time when several European states maintained standing forces measured in millions of soldiers and sailors, absorbing 25 per cent or more of state revenues. For such states, including Russia, these ruinous and ever-increasing costs threatened national security almost as much as armed conflict. The 1899 Conference was also to take place within living memory of Germany's victory in the Franco-Prussian War 1870–71, with France's lost territories in Alsace and Lorraine still unrecovered, the conflict between Chile and Peru in 1882, the Sino-Japanese War of 1894, the war between Greece and Turkey in 1897, the Spanish–American War of 1898 and, as regards incipient armed conflict, the 'Fashoda incident' between France and Britain also in 1898.

The Russian Note came as a surprise to many, not least to the Russian Minister for War and also its principal international jurist, F. F. Martens, acting as legal adviser to the Russian Ministry of Foreign Affairs (but then away from St Petersburg on holiday).[5] The Russian proposal nonetheless proved immediately popular in many countries; as a result, it could not be ignored by the Great Powers notwithstanding deep suspicions in many places as to Russia's true motives. Later, these were partially dispelled by Russia's proposed programme for the Conference, prepared by Martens for the Russian Ministry of Foreign Affairs. His memoranda of 11 October 1898 and 1 March 1899 proposed a universal conference, open to all 'civilised nations', to be held in St Petersburg (later changed to The Hague as a compromise between Paris, Brussels, Bern, and Copenhagen).[6] His memoranda

---

[5] Fedor Fedorovich Martens (1845–1909), born in what is now Estonia and also known as Friedrich Fromhold von Martens or Frédéric de Martens (in German and French), had been an arbitrator in the *Bering Sea Arbitration* between Britain and the USA over pelagic seal fishing by Canada (1892–3); the sole arbitrator in the *Costa Rica Packet Arbitration* between Great Britain and the Netherlands (1895–7); and the presiding arbitrator (or 'umpire') in the *Anglo-Venezuelan (Guiana) Arbitration* (1897–9) held in the Quai d'Orsay in Paris (sitting with Lord Justice Russell and Lord Collins, appointed by Britain, and Justices Fuller and Brewer of the U.S. Supreme Court, appointed by Venezuela). Martens spoke fluent German, French, and English (in addition to, of course, Russian). Martens was later appointed as the first Russian representative to the PCA and an arbitrator in the first two arbitrations brought before the PCA under the 1899 Hague Convention: the *Pious Fund Arbitration* (1902) and the *Venezuela Preferential Claims Arbitration* (1904). He helped to negotiate for Russia the arbitration submission between the USA v Russia in 1900 (the '*Asser Arbitration*'). In 1905, he attended the Portsmouth Peace Conference convoked by President Theodore Roosevelt to bring a peaceful end to the Russo-Japanese War.

[6] Although Martens recorded that the choice of The Hague surprised many, he strongly supported that choice given the Netherlands' historically good relations with Imperial Russia and its status as the home of Hugo Grotius (Huig de Groot): see Frédéric Martens, 'La Conférence de la Paix à la Haye' (Arthur Rousseau, 1900), 10.

42   ON ARBITRATION

primarily addressed issues of peace and disarmament; but he also proposed the creation of a permanent mechanism for international arbitration for the peaceful settlement of disputes between states. Perceptively, as a practical realist, Martens warned against the creation of an international court binding upon states 'always and in all instances'. That was, in his view, 'utopian'. His proposal excluded compulsory arbitration to prevent a future war or to terminate an existing war, but it included obligatory arbitration for limited categories of future disputes between states.[7]

The first Hague Conference was opened on 6 May 1899, attended by 27 states represented by many well-known international jurists.[8] Its sessions were private, excluding the general public. The conference was closed on 17 July 1899, to broad acclaim as regards its conventions on the laws and customs of war, commissions of inquiry and arbitration.[9] Martens, albeit not the head of the Russian delegation, was regarded as the 'soul' of the conference with his extensive legal, diplomatic and linguistic abilities. For the conference, Martens had submitted a draft outline for a convention on obligatory arbitration of certain categories of dispute 'so far as they do not concern the vital interests nor national honor of the contracting states' (Art. 8 of the Russian proposal). These latter exceptions were explained in an accompanying note: 'no Government would consent in advance to adhere to a decision of an arbitral tribunal which might arise within the international domain, if

---

[7] For Martens' comprehensive biography, see Vladimir Pustogarov, *Our Martens*, trans. W. Butler (Kluwer Law International, 1993, 2000); see also 'Frederic de Martens' (Editorial Comment), 3 American Journal of International Law 983 (1909); Thomas Holland, 'Frederic de Martens', 10 Journal of the Society of Comparative Legislation 10 (1909); Hans Wehberg, 'Friedrich v. Martens und die Haager Friedenskonferenzen', 20 Zeitschrift für Internationales Recht 343 (1910); Lauri Mälksoo, 'Friedrich Fromhold von Martens (Fyodor Fydorovich Martens) (1845–1909)' in Bardo Fassbender and Anne Peters (eds), *Oxford Handbook of the History of International Law* (Oxford University Press, 2012); Rein Müllerson, 'F. F. Martens—Man of the Enlightenment: Drawing Parallels between Martens' Times and Today's Problems', 25 European Journal of International Law 831 (2014). Having been forgotten or spurned for so long, even in Russia, Martens is now the subject of many legal histories, of which only a selection are listed here. Very belatedly and dwarfed by the over-large portrait of Tsar Nicholas II, a bust of Martens is now displayed in the Peace Palace's Small Arbitration Room.

[8] Austria-Hungary, Belgium, Bulgaria, China, Denmark, France, Germany, Britain, Greece, Italy, Japan, Luxemburg, Mexico, Montenegro, The Netherlands, Persia, Portugal, Romania, Russia, Serbia, Siam, Spain, Sweden (with Norway), Switzerland, Turkey and the USA. Korea attempted to attend the Conference but was refused admission, being treated as part of Japan. Apart from Mexico, no Latin American state attended the conference, although many were supporters of general arbitration treaties: see e.g. Art. 4 of the Plan of Arbitration agreed by the Pan-American Congress of 1890 (by 16 of 19 American states), and Art. 1 of the Treaty of Arbitration between Argentina and Italy of 23 July 1898. The majority of states taking part in the 1899 Hague Conference were European.

[9] For a full account of the Hague Conferences, see Shabtai Rosenne (ed.), *The Hague Peace Conferences of 1899 and 1907 and International Arbitration: Reports and Documents* (Asser Press, 2001); Arthur Eyffinger, *The 1899 Hague Peace Conference: The Parliament of Man, the Federation of the World* (Kluwer Law International, 1999); Jean Allain, *A Century of International Adjudication: The Rule of Law and its Limits* (Asser Press, 2000); Hersch Lauterpacht, *The Function of Law in the International Community* (Oxford University Press, 1933), 27, 184; Hans von Mangoldt, 'Development of Arbitration and Conciliation Treaties and Arbitration and Conciliation Practice since The Hague Conferences of 1899 and 1907', in J. Gills Wetter (ed.), *The International Arbitral Process: Public and Private* (Oceana, 1979), 243.

it concerned the national honour of a state, or its highest interests, or its inalienable possessions.'[10]

This left disputes for obligatory arbitration as to two broad classes: (i) pecuniary damages suffered by a state or its nationals as a consequence of international wrongs on the part of another state or its nationals; and (ii) disagreements as to the interpretation or application of treaties between states in four defined fields. The latter comprised: (a) treaties relating to posts and telegraphs,[11] railroads, submarine telegraph cables, regulations preventing collisions between vessels on the high seas, and navigation of international rivers and inter-oceanic canals; (b) treaties concerning the protection of intellectual, literary, and artistic property, money and measures, sanitation, veterinary surgery, and phylloxera; (c) treaties relating to inheritance, exchange of prisoners and reciprocal assistance in the administration of justice; and (d) treaties for marking boundaries, so far as they concerned purely technical and political questions (Art. 10 of the Russian proposal).[12]

In the accompanying note, Martens also explained the necessity for obligatory arbitration, without the need for a *compromis* to be agreed by the parties after their particular dispute had arisen:

> The recognition of the obligatory character of arbitration, were it only within the most restricted limits, would strengthen legal principles in relations between nations, would guarantee them against infractions and encroachments; it would neutralize, so to speak, more or less, large fields of international law. For the states obligatory arbitration would be a convenient means of avoiding the misunderstandings, so numerous, so troublesome, although of little importance, which sometimes fetter diplomatic relations without any reason therefor. Thanks to obligatory arbitration, states could more easily maintain their legitimate claims, and what is more important still, could more easily escape from unjustified demands. Obligatory arbitration would be of invaluable service to the cause of universal peace. It is very evident that the questions of the second class, to which alone this method is applicable, very rarely form a basis for war. Nevertheless, frequent disputes between states, even though with regard only to questions of the second class, while not forming a direct menace to the maintenance of peace, nevertheless disturb the friendly relations between states and create an atmosphere of distrust and hostility in which some incident or other, like a chance spark, may more easily cause war to burst forth. Obligatory arbitration, resulting in absolving the interested states from all responsibility for any solution of the difference existing

---

[10] Allain (n. 9), 23; Rosenne (n. 9), 97.

[11] Martens invoked, as the earliest example of obligatory arbitration, Art. 16 of the multilateral Postal Union of 1874, providing for the settlement by arbitration of all disputes between contracting states arising from the interpretation and application of that treaty. This obligation extended to future disputes.

[12] Eyffinger (n. 9), 'The Work of The Third Commission'; Allain (n. 9), 22–3.

44 ON ARBITRATION

between them, seems to be fitted to contribute to the maintenance of friendly relations, and in that way to facilitate the peaceful settlement of the most serious conflicts which may arise within the field of their most important interests.[13]

The Russian proposal was referred to the conference's third commission, chaired by the French delegate, Léon Bourgeois. It was partly opposed by the USA as regards the inclusion of treaties concerning rivers and canals; but most of all by Germany with its general objections to any form of obligatory arbitration, supported at different times by Austria, Italy, Turkey, and Romania. Their opposition to obligatory arbitration almost wrecked the work of the third commission. During the third commission's second meeting on 26 May 1899, addressing (inter alia) arbitration, Britain's delegate, Sir Julian Pauncefote, adopted Martens' proposal and took it further (with Martens' support):[14]

> If we want to make a step in advance, I believe it is absolutely necessary to organise a permanent international tribunal which can assemble instantly at the request of contesting nations. This idea being established, I believe that we shall not have very much difficulty in coming to an understanding upon the details. The necessity for such a tribunal and the advantages which it would offer, as well as the encouragement and even impetus which it would give to the cause of arbitration have been set forth with vigour and clearness—and equal eloquence—by our distinguished colleague, Mr Descamps, in his interesting 'Essay on Arbitration' ...[15]

This British proposal was subsequently reduced to writing, in the form of seven draft articles. Art. 1 provided for the organization of a private tribunal, governed by a code to be agreed at the Conference; Art. 2 provided for a permanent office and secretariat; Art. 3 required each contracting state to nominate two of its respectable jurists as members of the tribunal; Art. 4 provided for the role of the secretariat in receiving notices from disputing parties and transmitting names for the parties' selections as arbitrators (not limited to names submitted by contracting states); and Art. 5 offered recourse to the tribunal to all states, whether or not contracting states. The remaining articles established a 'Permanent Council of Administration'

---

[13] Rosenne (n. 9), 97.

[14] Sir Julian Pauncefote (1828–1902), later Lord Pauncefote, had been a member of the English and Hong Kong Bars. After a distinguished career in the British Colonial and Foreign Services (including stints as Attorney-General of Hong Kong), he was appointed in 1889 the UK's ambassador to the USA. In that capacity, Pauncefote negotiated in 1897 the 'Olney–Pauncefote' treaty between Britain and the USA providing for general arbitration, subject to exceptions (albeit never ratified by the USA) and the USA–UK treaty leading to the Bering Sea Arbitration over Canadian pelagic sealing rights. As a practising lawyer and senior diplomat, Pauncefote was undoubtedly familiar with both state–state and private commercial arbitration. There is no biography of Lord Pauncefote; but see his obituary in *The London Times*, 26 May 1902.

[15] Baron Descamps was the Belgian representative and a member of the third commission.

to control the office and addressed the allocation of expenses between the contracting states and disputing parties.

The 'Essay on Arbitration' cited by Pauncefote included a compilation by Baron Descamps of arbitration clauses in treaties concluded by states attending the Hague Conference. Paradoxically, Descamps opposed Martens' proposal; but he now suggested, perhaps mollified by Pauncefote's diplomatic flattery, that the third commission establish a *comité d'examen* to consider the British and Russian proposals, soon joined by a third proposal by the USA providing (inter alia) for a right of appeal from an award for 'a substantial error of fact or law'. This committee was to comprise an extraordinary group of international jurists: T. M. C. Asser (Netherlands), Baron d'Etournelles (France), F. W. Holls (USA), H. Lammasch (Austria-Hungary), F. F. Martens (Russia), E. Odier (Switzerland), and P. Zorn (Germany), with Baron Descamps (Belgium) as president.[16] Notably, Pauncefote was missing; apart from Holls, all represented European states. The committee met on seventeen occasions; and the third commission considered its work on nine occasions during May to July 1899. [17]

The third commission's committee laboriously addressed the establishment of a permanent court of arbitration and the binding obligation on states, by treaty, to refer to this new arbitral body certain (but not all) categories of dispute, always excluding disputes touching upon a state's dignity and vitally important interests. These proposals were supported by Russia, the USA, and Britain, but, again, strongly opposed by Germany.[18] Germany eventually moderated its position under the influence of its delegate (Zorn), supported by the USA's delegate (Holls) on their joint consultative visit to Berlin. The committee also considered Martens' proposal for a code of arbitration procedure.

The eventual result was a consensus in the form of The Hague Convention on the Peaceful Settlement of International Disputes, which entered into force on 19 September 1900 (the 1899 Hague Convention). It created the Permanent Court of Arbitration (PCA), which was neither a court nor an arbitration tribunal, still less a permanent court or arbitration tribunal. It was nonetheless a permanent mechanism comprising a secretariat, a registry, and a chamber of senior jurists appointed by the contracting states as potential arbitrators. Its name and functions were, inevitably, a compromise to achieve unanimity. As to the PCA's name, Germany had proposed 'Permanent Organisation for Arbitration', or 'Permanent List of Arbitrators', or 'Permanent Court of Arbitrators' (but not 'Arbitral Court');

---

[16] In addition to Martens and Descamps, these comprised T. M. C. Asser of The Netherlands (1838–1913), Baron d'Estournelles of France, F. W. Holls of the USA, H. Lammasch of Austria-Hungary (1853–1920), E. Odier of Switzerland (formerly IDRC secretary), and P. Zorn of Germany.

[17] See Eyffinger (n. 9) for a detailed account.

[18] See the critical account of Germany's conduct in Sabine Konrad, 'The Asser Arbitration', in Ulf Franke, Annette Magnusson, and Joel Dahlquist (eds), *Arbitrating for Peace* (Wolters Kluwer, 2016), 41–4.

46 ON ARBITRATION

when these were all opposed, it proposed 'Permanent Court of Arbitration', which was accepted. This was the high-water mark. As to the PCA's function, Germany (Zorn) adamantly refused to accept any form of obligatory arbitration, supported by Italy (Nigra). Martens, Descamps, and Pauncefote intervened to no avail. As explained by Zorn: 'To hasten this evolution too greatly would be to compromise the very principle of arbitration, towards which we are all sympathetic.' This was, after so much effort by Martens and such an expenditure of goodwill by other states, the low-water mark.

The results of the second 1907 Hague Peace Conference were somewhat disappointing as regards obligatory arbitration. The original proposal for this second conference on peace, the rules of war, and disarmament had come from the USA's President Theodore Roosevelt prior to the Russo-Japanese War in 1905. However, after the Portsmouth Peace Conference putting an end to that war, the USA diplomatically left the formal invitation to Russia and the Netherlands. The groundwork was again prepared by F. F. Martens, at the request of the Russian Ministry of Foreign Affairs. Martens proposed (inter alia) improving the provisions for inter-state arbitration in the 1899 Hague Convention. After an audience with Tsar Nicholas II, Martens (with B. E. Nolde, a former student, as his secretary)[19] visited Berlin (twice), Paris, London, Rome, Vienna, and The Hague for preparatory consultations. In a mark of the respect accorded to him personally, Martens was received by the German Emperor Wilhelm II, the French President (Armand Falkier), King Edward VII and the British Prime Minister and Foreign Secretary (Sir Henry Campbell-Bannerman and Sir Edward Grey), the Queen of the Netherlands, King Victor Emmanuel III (with the Italian Prime Minister), Emperor Franz Josef (with the Austro-Hungarian Minister of Foreign Affairs); and then again by the German Emperor on his return to Russia for a further audience with Nicholas II. For an international jurist and arbitrator (particularly a commoner from a modest background with no aristocratic status in Russia), these consultations were unprecedented.

The second Peace Conference was opened at The Hague on 15 June 1907, attended by 44 states and 232 delegates. It now included several Latin American states. The Conference's work was concluded on 18 October 1907. Its achievements were limited by new rivalries between Britain, France, and Russia on the one side and, on the other, Germany and Austria-Hungary. The Conference led to the replacement of the 1899 Convention with the 1907 Convention for the Pacific

---

[19] Baron B. E. Nolde (1876–1948) was a jurist, diplomat and Baltic German (born in what is now Latvia). He became in 1914 the legal adviser to the Russian Ministry of Foreign Affairs and was appointed to membership of the PCA by Russia in 1914. In 1921, after the October 1917 Revolution, Nolde and his immediate family escaped from Soviet Russia to settle as permanent exiles in Paris. In 1930, Nolde was a co-arbitrator in the second *Harriman Arbitration* in Paris under the US company's concession agreement agreed with the USSR in 1925: see V. V. Veeder, 'Looking for Professor B. E. Nolde', in A. I. Muranov et al. (eds), *In Memoriam: V. A. Kabatov and S. N. Lebedev* (Moscow, 2017), 401, revised (in English) in *Jus Gentium* 3(1) (2018), 255.

Settlement of International Disputes (the 1907 Hague Convention). The issue of obligatory arbitration was again raised by the delegations from the USA and Portugal supported by Martens (Russia) and Léon Bourgeois (France). It was again strongly opposed by Germany. There was to be no permanent international court and no obligatory arbitration.

The Conference nonetheless confirmed the role of inter-state arbitration under Art. 37 of the 1907 Convention, as first recorded in Art. 15 of the 1899 Convention: 'International arbitration has for its object the settlement of disputes between states by judges of their own choice and on the basis of respect for law.' Art. 38 of the 1907 Convention, restating Art. 16 of the 1899 Convention, provided:

In questions of a legal nature, and especially in the interpretation or application of international Conventions, arbitration is recognised by the Signatory Powers as the most effective, and at the same time the most equitable means of settling disputes which diplomacy has failed to settle.

The Conference also maintained, in theory but certainly not in practice, the principle of obligatory inter-state arbitration on the unilateral demand of one state for questions 'which may arise eventually' (i.e. future disputes), subject to the disputing parties' agreement (Art. 39 and 40 of the 1907 Convention). As the German representative commented: 'It is difficult to say less in more words.'[20] The delegates agreed to hold a third Hague Peace Conference in 1915. By the end of this second Conference, Martens was exhausted and seriously ill. As he noted in his diary: 'The Second Peace Conference has ended, and in all likelihood I will not be at the Third.'[21] Martens died in 1909. With the outbreak of the World War in August 1914, there was to be no third Hague Conference in 1915.

The PCA was first housed at Prinsengracht 71, The Hague from 1901 to 1913 and thereafter to the present day at the Peace Palace. Its existence for more than a century marks the development of modern inter-state arbitration.[22] Its work began almost immediately. The first arbitrations under the 1899 Convention were the *Pious Fund Arbitration* (1902) and the *Venezuela Preferential Arbitration* (1904).[23] The first commission of inquiry addressed the dispute between Great Britain and

---

[20] Baron Marschall von Bieberstein, cited in Lauterpacht (n. 9), 193 (fn. 3).

[21] Pustogarov (n. 7), 327.

[22] See the summaries of arbitration awards under the 1899 and 1907 Hague Conventions in P Hamilton et al. (eds), *The Permanent Court of Arbitration: International Arbitration and Dispute Resolution—Summaries of Awards, Settlement Agreements and Reports* (Kluwer Law International, 1999). See also International Bureau of the Permanent Court of Arbitration, *Analyses des sentences* (PCA, 1934).

[23] *The Pious Fund Arbitration* (USA v Mexico), Award, 14 October 1902 (H. Matzen, E. Fry, F. de Martens, T. M. C. Asser, A. P. de S. Lohman), UNRIAA, 14 October 1902, Vol. IX; *Venezuela Preferential Arbitration* (Germany, Great Britain, Italy v Venezuela), Award, 22 February 1904 (N. V. Mouraviev, H. Lammasch, F. de Martens), UNRIAA, 22 February 1904, Vol IX, 107–10; Hamilton (n. 22), 31–5.

48 ON ARBITRATION

Russia over the *Doggerbank Incident* (1904).[24] The selection of arbitrators was not limited to the individual members of the PCA, as shown by the composition of the tribunal in *Russian Claim for Indemnities*.[25] Between 1899 and 1914, under the 1899 and 1907 Hague Conventions, there were eight references to arbitration before the PCA, together with two commissions of inquiry. There was also a change in the practice of several states agreeing bilateral treaties providing for obligatory arbitration in conformity with the Russian proposal at the first Hague Conference. For example, Art. 1 of the 1911 Franco-Danish treaty provided that future differences of a juridical character shall be submitted to arbitration provided that 'they do not affect the vital interests, independence or honour of either of the contracting parties nor the interests of third Powers'; and Art. 2 of the treaty excluded from this proviso disputes over pecuniary claims, contractual debts due to nationals of the other party, the interpretation and application of commercial and navigation treaties, and all conventions relating to industrial (intellectual) property, copyrights, posts and telegraphs, etc.

After the 1914–18 World War, there was still no third Hague Conference. There were, however, indirect results from the Hague Conferences: the creation of the Permanent Court of International Justice (1925) and, after the Second World War, the International Court of Justice (1946), with their jurisdictions capable of agreement prior to a dispute under Art. 36 and 36(2) respectively. Although such legal proceedings before the PCIJ and ICJ were not arbitrations, as observed by Professor P. J. Baker in regard to the PCIJ, it was on the doctrine embodied in the Russian proposal at the Hague Conferences 'that all subsequent development, both of theory and practice, was based'.[26] In 1928, the League of Nations sought to establish a universal treaty for inter-state arbitration, the 'Geneva General Act', but it came to nothing, despite attempts by the UN General Assembly to revive it in 1947–1949.[27]

These developments included the continued rejection by states of appellate appeals from the merits of an award, the eventual agreement of many states to different forms of obligatory arbitration, and the participation of non-state actors in arbitrations against states. As to the first, the finality of arbitration awards was an important issue at the first and second Hague Conferences. As already noted, the USA's delegate at the first Hague Conference (Holls) proposed a right of appeal

---

[24] The Doggerbank Incident (1904) brought Britain and Russia to the brink of war when the Russian fleet, on its voyage from the Baltic to the Sea of Japan during the Russo-Japanese War (1904–5) mistook British unarmed fishing-boats for Japanese warships in the North Sea. It was the first Inquiry under the 1899 Hague Convention: see The Dogger Bank Report, 26 February 1905 (Spaun, Fournier, Dombassoff, L. Beaumont, Ch. H. Davise); Hamilton (n. 22), 297.

[25] *Russian Claim for Indemnities* (Russia v Turkey), Award, 11 November 1912 (Ch. E. Lardy, M. de Taube, A. Mandelstam, A. Arbro Bey, A. Réchid Bey); Hamilton (n. 22), 81–7. André Mandelstam was not a member of the PCA.

[26] P. J. Baker, 'The Obligatory Jurisdiction of the Permanent Court of International Justice', 6 BYIL 68 (1925), 84.

[27] See von Mangoldt (n. 9), 247–50.

from an adverse award, exercisable within three months, for a substantial error of fact or law (Art. 7 of the USA proposal). The committee rejected this proposal. The Dutch delegate (Asser) proposed a limited form of revision for an award. In a modified form (if agreed by the disputing parties), the committee adopted the latter proposal for revision by a bare majority.

Martens strongly opposed both proposals, particularly the USA's proposal. His address merits citing at length because it remains relevant today:[28]

> ... in what does the importance of this question consist? Is it true that a re-hearing of a judicial award based upon error or upon considerations not sufficiently founded is not desirable? Ought we not, on the contrary, to wish to have an error corrected by new documents or new facts which may be discovered after the close of the arbitration? No, gentlemen, it would be most unsatisfactory and unfortunate to have an arbitral award, duly pronounced by an international tribunal, subject to reversal by a new judgment. It would be profoundly regrettable if the arbitral award did not terminate, finally and forever, the dispute between the litigating nations, but should provoke new discussions, inflame the passions anew, and menace once more the peace of the world. A rehearing of the arbitral award, as provided for in Article 55, must necessarily have a disastrous effect. There should not be left the slightest doubt on this point. The litigating Power against which the arbitral award has been pronounced will not execute it, certainly not during the three months, and it will make every effort imaginable to find new facts or documents. The litigation will not have been ended, but it will be left in suspense for three months with the serious aggravation that the Government and the nation which have been found guilty will be drawn still more into recrimination and dangerous reciprocal accusation. That is the explanation of the significant fact that in the committee of examination Article 54 [sic] was adopted by only five votes to four. The end of arbitration is to terminate the controversy absolutely. The great utility of arbitration is in the fact that from the moment when the arbitral judgment is duly pronounced everything is finished, and nothing but bad faith can attack it. Never can an objection be raised against the execution of an arbitral award. Now, if we accept the principle of a hearing, what will be the role of the arbitrators before and after the award? At the present time they are able to end forever an international dispute, and experience has shown that as soon as the award has been rendered, newspapers, legislative chambers, public opinion, all bow in silence to the decision of the arbitrators. If, on the contrary, it is known that the award is suspended for three months, the state against which judgment has been given will do its utmost to find a new document or fact. In the meantime the judgment will be delivered over to the wrangling of public opinion.

---

[28] Eyffinger (n. 9), 'To the Rescue of Arbitration'.

It will not settle or put an end to the matter. On the contrary, it will raise a storm in the press and parliament. Everything will be attacked—the arbitrators, the hostile Government, and above all the home Government. They will be accused of having held back documents and concealed new facts. For three months the discussion upon the judgment will be open. Never can a judgment given under such conditions have a moral binding force which is the very essence of arbitration ...

The USA's proposal for an appeal on the merits was also rejected by the third commission. As a result, the 1899 Hague Convention precluded any appeal from an award.[29] Conversely, the commission accepted the committee's draft on revision, resulting in Art. 55 of the 1899 Hague Convention.[30] The second Hague Conference likewise rejected any appeal from an award.[31] However, it introduced the possibility of referring back to the arbitration tribunal any dispute as to the award's interpretation or execution, as well as re-stating the earlier provision on revision.[32] There is a significant practical difference between an appeal on legal and factual merits from an award and other attacks on the finality of an award, whether in the form of interpretation, revision, remission, or even annulment for want of jurisdiction or other significant defect in the arbitral procedure.

The Hague Conferences accepted this difference, as did the International Court of Justice. The court has no general or inherent jurisdiction to adjudicate upon the validity of an arbitral award between states, still less between a state and a non-state party. As regards states, when the PCIJ was being established, a proposal was made to empower it as a court of review for claims of nullity of awards between states on the basis that the PCIJ was to be considered as a higher authority and the guarantor of impartial decisions.[33] In 1929, the Assembly of the League of Nations adopted a resolution inviting the Council to consider the procedure whereby states could refer to the PCIJ a complaint that an international arbitral tribunal had exceeded its jurisdiction.[34] In 1958, a limited jurisdiction to review awards (but not by way of appeal on the merits) was considered in the ILC's Model Rules on Arbitral Procedure.[35] Art. 35 of these Model Rules provided: 'The validity of an award may

---

[29] Art. 54 of the 1899 Hague Convention provided: 'The award, duly pronounced and notified to the agents of the parties at variance, puts an end to the dispute definitively and without appeal.' (Art. 81 of the 1907 Hague Convention provided: 'The award, duly pronounced and notified to the agents of the parties, settles the dispute definitively and without appeal.')

[30] Art. 55 of the 1899 Hague Convention provided: 'The parties can reserve in the compromise the right to demand the revision of the award ... It can only be made on the ground of the discovery of some new fact calculated to exercise a decisive influence on the award, and which, at the time the discussion was closed, was unknown to the Tribunal and the party demanding the revision ...'

[31] Art. 81 of the 1907 Hague Convention restated, in different wording, Art. 54 of the 1899 Hague Convention (see n. 29).

[32] Arts. 82 and 83 of the 1907 Hague Convention.

[33] Karin Oellers-Frahm, 'Judicial and Arbitral Decisions, Validity and Nullity', *Max Planck Encyclopaedia of Public International Law*, §20.

[34] Lauterpacht (n. 9), 206 (fn. 2).

[35] ILC Report, A/3859, 83ff.

be challenged by either party on one or more of the following grounds: (a) That the tribunal has exceeded its powers; (b) That there was corruption on the part of a member of the tribunal; (c) That there has been a failure to state the reasons for the award or a serious departure from a fundamental rule of procedure; (d) That the undertaking to arbitrate or the compromis is a nullity.' Seven years later, its terms influenced the drafting of Art. 52 of the ICSID Convention 1965 on the grounds for annulment of an ICSID award under the ICSID Convention.

Art. 36(1) of the ILC's Model Rules also provided: 'If, within three months of the date on which the validity of the award is contested, the parties have not agreed on another tribunal, the International Court of Justice shall be competent to declare the total or partial nullity of the award on the application of either party.' The rationale for this proposal was explained by the Special Rapporteur, Professor George Scale, in his Third Report: 'In our view, intervention by the International Court of Justice must be maintained in this case as the only acceptable solution, since the Court's prestige, as also the exceptional nature of the proceedings, is likely to prove reassuring.'[36]

The Special Rapporteur's Fourth Report proposed that the ICJ should act as a court of cassation: 'Among the precedents for this we may mention a resolution adopted by the Institute of International Law at its session in 1929 held at New York; more particularly, the discussions held in the Council and Assembly of the League of Nations under the chairmanship of Rundstein, the eminent Polish jurist, between 1928 and 1931; and lastly, Art. 67 of the rules of the International Court of Justice.'[37] That proposal also went nowhere, save as regards arbitration awards referred for annulment to the ICJ by the disputing parties' ad hoc consent, as in *Guinea-Bissau v Senegal* (1989) and *Honduras v Nicaragua* (1960).[38] Accordingly, the ICJ's jurisdiction over disputed arbitration awards must still be established ad hoc, by special agreement or submission, or, possibly, through declarations made under Art. 36 of the ICJ's Statute. In short, the disputing state parties must by some means or another consent to the ICJ's reviewing the award.[39] What remains significant is that there was no support in the ILC, PCIJ, ICJ, or ICSID for any appeal on the merits of an award, be it for errors of law or errors of fact.

As to the eventual agreement of many states to different forms of obligatory arbitration, between 1899 and 1999, 33 disputes were referred to the PCA and, from

---

[36] A/CN.4/109 and Corr. 1, §76.

[37] A/CN.4/113, §26.

[38] *Guinea-Bissau v Senegal*, Award, 31 July 1989, Judgment, [1991] ICJ Reports 53; *Honduras v Nicaragua*, Award, 23 December 1960, Judgment, [1960] ICJ Reports 192. (Art. 64 of the 1965 ICSID Convention provides that any dispute between contracting states concerning the interpretation or application of the convention (but not the finality of an ICSID award) shall be referred to the ICJ unless the concerned states agree otherwise. To date, there has been no such reference.) See, generally, W. Michael Reisman, *Nullity and Revision* (Yale University Press, 1971).

[39] In the absence of any mechanism for the review of an award, the dispute over the award may compound that of the original dispute: see the unresolved controversy over the Final Award of 29 June 2017 in *Arbitration between Croatia and Slovenia* (where the PCA acted as the registry).

52   ON ARBITRATION

1999 to 2016, a further 180 disputes. These included many obligatory arbitrations. Even where there exists a permanent international court as an alternative forum, several states have preferred inter-state arbitration under Annex VII of UNCLOS administered by the PCA, to inter-state litigation before ITLOS in Hamburg.[40] The PCA's membership has increased from 71 contracting states in 1970 to 121 contracting states in 2017.

As to disputes involving a state and a foreign national, as already indicated, Martens had proposed at the first Hague Conference obligatory arbitration for future disputes between states relating to 'pecuniary damages suffered by a state or its nationals as a consequence of international wrongs on the part of another state or its nationals'. At first, the PCA would not accept for arbitration a dispute between state and non-state. It did so gradually, beginning in 1935 with *Radio Corporation v China*.[41] In 1962, the PCA changed its arbitration rules, expressly permitting the reference of such disputes under the 1907 Hague Convention.[42] In 1970, the first PCA arbitration between a state and a foreign national took place between Sudan and the English construction company, Turiff, under a *compromis* applying to a dispute arising from their construction contract. It led eventually to an award in Turiff's favor.[43] In 1993, the PCA introduced its 'Optional Rules for Arbitrating Disputes Between Two Parties of Which Only One Is a State'.[44] By this date, many states had acceded to the 1965 ICSID Convention providing for the obligatory

---

[40] E.g., as to obligatory arbitration, *The Barbados v Trinidad and Tobago Arbitration* (2004), *The Guyana v Surinam Arbitration* (2007), *The Bangladesh v India Arbitrations* (2009, 2014), *The Bangladesh v Myanmar Arbitration* (2014), *The Chagos Arbitration between the United Kingdom and Mauritius* (2015), *The Philippines v China Arbitration* (2016), *The Duzgit Integrity Arbitration (Malta v São Tomé and Príncipe)* (2016); *The Ukraine v Russia Arbitration* (2017), and, pending, *The Arctic Sunrise Arbitration (Netherlands v Russia)*, and *The 'Enrica Lexie' Incident (Italy v India)*. As to obligatory conciliation, on 11 April 2016, pursuant to Art. 298 and Section 2 of Annex V of UNCLOS, Timor-Leste initiated compulsory conciliation proceedings against Australia (pending).

[41] *Radio Corporation of America v China*, Award, 13 April 1935 (J.A. van Hammel, A. Hubert, R. Farrer), under an arbitration clause in the parties' agreement. Hamilton (n. 22), 145.

[42] The PCA's 1982 'Rules of Arbitration and Conciliation for Settlement of Investment Disputes between Two Parties of Which Only One is a State'; see Wetter (n. 9), 53; Antonio Parra, *The History of ICSID* (Oxford University Press, 2012), 17.

[43] *Turiff Construction (Sudan) Limited v Sudan*, Award, 23 April 1970, decided under the law of Sudan; Erades, 17 *N.T.I.R.* 200 (1970); Hamilton (n. 22), 164. The eventual tribunal comprised L. Erades (President), R. J. Parker and K. Bentsi Enchill, respectively a judge from the Netherlands, a QC from England (later a judge in the Court of Appeal of England and Wales), and, as appointed by the President of the ICJ in default of appointment by Sudan, a Ghanaian jurist. The Parties' Counsel included many English specialists in international commercial arbitration, including R. A. MacCrindle QC and (as they became later) Sir Michael Kerr, Lord Mustill, and Lord Saville, with Messrs Redfern, Hunter, and (Geoffrey) Lewis. It was not the first PCA arbitration between a foreign national and a host state: see *Radio Corporation v China* (1935).

[44] The PCA has now several sets of Optional Rules: The most recent, the PCA Arbitration Rules 2012, is a consolidation of four sets of PCA procedural rules which separately remain extant: the Optional Rules for Arbitrating Disputes between Two States (1992); the Optional Rules for Arbitrating Disputes between Two Parties of Which Only One is a State (1993); the Optional Rules for Arbitration Between International Organizations and States (1996); and the Optional Rules for Arbitration Between International Organizations and Private Parties (1996) (see 'PCA Model Clauses and Submission Agreements', available on the PCA's website: <pca-cpa.org>).

arbitration of investor-state disputes agreed by states.[45] Collectively, these were massive developments.

The 1965 ICSID Convention did not expressly address treaty-based disputes between investors and contracting states. Such a category of disputes was entirely missing from the Executive Directors' Report on the Convention.[46] The first bilateral investment treaty made between the Federal Republic of Germany and Pakistan in 1959 contained a provision for inter-state arbitration, but no provision for investor–state arbitration. Such an inter-state arbitration provision allowed the home state to espouse against the host state the investor's claim as its national, but the investor was not a party to that inter-state arbitration.

From about 1962 onwards, under bilateral investment treaties and later the ICSID Convention, the investor could initiate an arbitration under the treaty in its own name, thereby suspending diplomatic protection by the home state (as provided by Art. 26(1) of the ICSID Convention). The first investor–state dispute under a bilateral investment treaty was referred to ICSID arbitration in 1987: *AAPL v Sri Lanka*.[47] UNCTAD has since identified more than 600 treaty-based disputes referred to investor–state arbitration, producing 405 final awards (up to 2015).[48] Inter-state arbitration reached its apogee with the Iran–US Claims Tribunal, established in 1981 under the Algiers Declaration of 19 January 1981. Its work began at the Peace Palace in the PCA's Japanese Room and Small Arbitration Room; and it remains incomplete after more than 35 years. The principal change, however, has come from the practice of states since 1965 in agreeing bilateral and multilateral investment treaties providing for obligatory investor–state arbitration, including the Energy Charter Treaty, NAFTA, CAFTA, and more than 3,000 bilateral investment treaties.

Such a form of arbitration does not fit easily into the traditional forms of inter-state arbitration or international commercial arbitration. In the *Loewen* award (2003), under NAFTA's Chapter 11, the NAFTA tribunal characterized the right of the investor under a treaty to refer its claim to arbitration against the host state in its own name as deriving from the right of its home state against the host state:

---

[45] The ICSID Convention introduced investor–state arbitration by ICSID to replace an informal role performed by the World Bank in diplomatically resolving investment disputes between states involving one state's national: see Parra (n. 42), 21.

[46] Thus, para 23 of the Executive Directors' Report refers to domestic 'investment promotion legislation', 'compromis', and an 'investment agreement' between the disputing parties providing for the submission to the Centre of future disputes arising out of that agreement. There is no reference to any bilateral or multilateral investment treaty.

[47] *Asian Agricultural Products Limited v Sri Lanka*; Award, 27 June 1990 (El-Kosheri, Asante and Goldman), ICSID Case No ARB/87/3, 4 ICSID Rep 250; see also Franke et al. (n. 18), 191. (The respondent host state did not contest the ICSID tribunal's jurisdiction.)

[48] UNCTAD, 'World Investment Report 2015: Reforming International Investment Regime', (2015), Ch. IV.

54   ON ARBITRATION

There is no warrant for transferring rules derived from private law into a field of international law where claimants are permitted *for convenience* to enforce what are in origin the rights of Party states.[49]

Other arbitration tribunals have adopted different analyses. In *Mondev* (2002), the NAFTA tribunal rejected the USA's objection *ratione temporis*:

Nor do Articles 1105 or 1110 of NAFTA effect a remedial resurrection of claims a Canadian investor might have had for breaches of customary international law occurring before NAFTA entered into force. It is true that both Articles 1105 and 1110 have analogues in customary international law. But there is still a significant difference, substantive and procedural, between a NAFTA claim and a diplomatic protection claim for conduct contrary to customary international law (a claim which Canada has never espoused).[50]

In *Corn Products*, the NAFTA tribunal decided:

... when a State claimed for a wrong done to its national it was in reality acting on behalf of that national, rather than asserting a right of its own. The pretence that it was asserting a claim of its own was necessary, because the State alone enjoyed access to international dispute settlement and claims machinery. However, there is no need to continue that fiction in a case in which the individual is vested with the right to bring claims of its own. In such a case there is no question of the investor claiming on behalf of the State. The State of nationality of the Claimant does not control the conduct of the case. No compensation which is recovered will be paid to the State. The individual may even advance a claim of which the State disapproves or base its case upon a proposition of law with which the State disagrees.[51]

Whichever of these views are correct, it is manifest that investor–state arbitration under a treaty is a form of both inter-state arbitration and international commercial arbitration that is subject to public international law.[52] By and large, that form

---

[49] *Loewen Group and Loewen v USA*, ICSID Case No. ARB(AF)/98/3, Award, 26 June 2003 (Mason, Mustill, Mikva), para. 233 (emphasis added). State courts have taken different views, e.g. the Court of Appeal of England and Wales: 'The award on this point in Loewen is controversial' in *Occidental v Ecuador* 2005 EWCA (Civil) 116; [2006] QB 432, para 22, dismissing Occidental's appeal from the Commercial Court (Aikens J) (2005) EWHC 774 (Comm).

[50] *Mondev v USA* (N. Stephen, J. Crawford, S. Schwebel), Award, 11 October 2002, ICSID Case No. ARB(AF)/99/2, para. 74.

[51] *Corn Products v Mexico* (C. Greenwood, A. Lowenfeld, J. Alfonso Serrano de la Vega), Decision on Responsibility, 15 January 2008, ICSID Case No. ARB(AF)/04/01, para. 173.

[52] In *Occidental v Ecuador*, the Court of Appeal acknowledged that 'under English private international law, an agreement to arbitrate may itself be subject to international law rather than the law of a municipal legal system' (paras. 33–4). See also Zachary Douglas, 'The Hybrid Foundations of Investment Treaty Arbitration', 74 BYIL 151 (2003); José Alvarez, 'Are Corporations 'Subjects' of International Law?', 9 Santa Clara Journal of International Law 1 (2011); Johnathan Bonnitcha, Lauge

has worked well for its users. Over the last 20 years, whether fish or fowl or neither of these, investor–state arbitration has been widely supported by many states. As Judge Schwebel has observed, 'What is clear is that investor/State arbitration has proved to be a significant and successful substitute for the gunboat diplomacy of the past. It represents one of the most progressive developments of international law in the whole history of international law.'[53]

In conclusion, the recent history of state–state and also, in part, of investor–state arbitration is the history of the PCA. As intended by the two Hague Conferences more than a century ago, arbitrations under treaties are still marked by the necessity for the parties' consent (including a state's limitation as to the categories of dispute referable to arbitration), a neutral appointing or administering authority, a settled procedure subject to party autonomy, the parties' involvement in the appointment of the tribunal, and the absence of any appeal from an award for an error of law or fact. For inter-state arbitration and (notwithstanding the ICSID and New York Conventions) investor–state arbitration also, the recognition of the award by the losing party is usually made voluntarily. It is the parties' arbitration, the award is the product of their consent, and, accordingly, the award has a moral binding force for the parties often absent from non-consensual mechanisms. So far, Martens would readily recognize today's practice of arbitration by states. It is also probable that he and his colleagues at both Hague Conferences would not be surprised by the current opposition to international mechanisms for the obligatory resolution of disputes. In 1999, Judge Shi Jiuyong (later President of the ICJ), wrote: 'Today, the International Court of Justice and the Permanent Court of Arbitration are complimentary institutions within the community of nations, each having its own unique role to play in the global network of mechanism of third party dispute resolution.'[54] Almost twenty years later, for that role to continue as regards the legitimacy of obligatory arbitration, there is probably a need for a Third Hague Conference on Arbitration attended by states who resort to arbitration in its different forms (whether by themselves or by their nationals), guided by F. F. Martens' historical sense of practical realism.

Poulsen, and Michael Waibel, *The Political Economy of the Investment Treaty Regime* (Oxford University Press, 2017), 65–6; Anthea Roberts, 'Triangular Treaties: The Extent and Limits of Investment Treaty Rights', 56 Harvard International Law Journal 353 (2015).

[53] Stephen Schwebel, 'Introduction', in Franke et al. (n. 18), 6.
[54] Hamilton (n. 22), xii.

4

1922

The Birth of the ICC Arbitration Clause and the Demise of the Anglo-Soviet Urquhart Concession

Four years after the end of the war to end all wars, which had brought down four empires, impoverished a whole continent and enfeebled the world, the road to peace now lay through transnational trade; and foreign traders, both in the established capitals and the new, needed the security and confidence, derived from legal predictability and enforceable agreements, that only international commercial arbitration could provide to their transactions. To that end, from the Versailles Peace Conference onwards, via the 1922 Genoa and Hague Economic Conferences, the private vehicle for the reform of domestic arbitration laws was the International Chamber of Commerce in Paris. It led in August 1922 to the first draft of what became the League of Nations' 1923 Geneva Protocol on Arbitration Clauses, leading in turn to the 1927 Geneva Convention and eventually the 1958 New York Convention. It led also in July 1922 to the creation of ICC arbitration, with the first publication of ICC's institutional arbitration and conciliation rules. If international commercial arbitration has a birthday, its year was undoubtedly 1922. In practice, the most significant advance was the standard form ICC arbitration clause incorporating by reference ICC arbitration rules as a near-comprehensive transnational procedural code. In a few short phrases, as an alternative to national procedures, foreign traders could readily apply the fuller wording of the ICC rules without the need to re-invent the wheel or, still worse, develop a new form of pathological arbitration clause. As has long been well-known, negotiations on dispute resolution clauses tend to come at the end of the parties' commercial negotiations; and that is usually not the time, if there is any time, to introduce any elaborate drafting exercise.

This is the story of just such an untimely and awkward exercise taking place during the late summer of 1922, involving on one side the highest officers of Soviet Russia, including Lenin, Stalin and Krasin, and on the other, a Scottish mining engineer and financier, Leslie Urquhart of the Russo-Asiatic Consolidated Company. Soviet Russia was not then a member of the League of

On Arbitration. Edited by: Sam Wordsworth KC and Marie Veeder, Oxford University Press. © Oxford University Press 2023. DOI: 10.1093/oso/9780192869135.003.0004

Nations; nor were any of its organs affiliated to ICC. Although the Urquhart concession agreement can stand as a model of how a State should not negotiate an arbitration clause, it also demonstrates that transnational arbitration provides, then as now, the only practical method of resolving certain contractual disputes. An arbitration agreement, like any contract, has to be agreed by both parties; and wherever one party advances an alternative procedure advantageous for itself but disadvantageous for its counterparty, it will usually not be agreed by that counterparty.

By the summer of 1922, Lenin was already ill, having suffered his first stroke on 25 May; but during that autumn, he personally determined Soviet Russia's refusal to confirm the concession agreement made with Urquhart's English company. This agreement had been signed in Berlin on 9 September 1922 by Urquhart and Leonid Krasin, the Soviet Commissar for Foreign Trade, subject to confirmation within one month by the Council of People s Commissars. Had that 'super-concession' been confirmed and implemented then, during Lenin's New Economic Policy and Soviet Russia's continuing penury, the consequences could have been hugely significant, not only for inward foreign investment in the form of numerous other 'super-concessions' and Soviet access to large foreign loans, but also for their indirect overall effect on Soviet Russia's national economy. Those lost economic and financial opportunities confirmed the political failures of the 1922 Economic Conferences at Genoa and The Hague. The rest is history.

Negotiations with Urquhart had started in July 1921 in London and Moscow, with Lenin's active support and participation. Urquhart was a Scot, a mining engineer who had spent more than twenty-five years working in Czarist Russia, first in Baku, then in the Urals, the Altai and Eastern Siberia. He spoke fluent Russian and was familiar with the industrial and economic situation in Russia, having visited Moscow twice after the October Revolution. He had served on the boards of many Russian companies in Czarist times, including the Siberian Trade Bank; and he had worked closely with Kolchak's White regime in Siberia, until its demise in 1919 towards the end of the Civil War. The proposed Soviet concession would have restored to Urquhart many of the mines and other properties which had been the subject of his Czarist concessions in Siberia, extending over 3.5 million acres, twelve mining enterprises (with modem smelters, mills and refineries), four complete mining towns (with railway and river fleet) and offices in Petrograd, Moscow, Ekaterinburg, Omsk, Pavlodar and Semipalatinsk. These properties had been looted or sabotaged during the Civil War and, where undamaged, confiscated without compensation by the new Soviet regime. In return for the concession agreement, Urquhart was to abandon his companies' claims against Soviet Russia for the unlawful expropriation of their Czarist properties. By 1920, these claims amounted to £56 million (now equivalent to more than US$ 4 billion), being the largest single claim by a British company against Soviet Russia and about one third of the total for all such claims by all British companies.

From the outset, one of the principal questions which caused serious disagreement was Urquhart's insistence upon 'neutral' arbitration for disputes arising from the proposed concession. In October 1921, together with other commercial factors, it had led to the breakdown in negotiations, confirmed by Urquhart's publication of his private letter to Krasin recording the Soviet Government's many (in his eyes) unreasonable demands. These had included successively, in place of neutral arbitration, first Urquhart's submission to the jurisdiction of the Soviet revolutionary tribunals and second 'arbitration' in Moscow with a guaranteed majority of Soviet Russian arbitrators. Krasin was stunned by Urquhart's public breach of trust; and Lenin was outraged, damning Urquhart as a blackmailer. However, Soviet Russia needed Urquhart; and by early 1922, informal contact was resumed.

As Krasin recorded in his later reports to the Politburo in August and September 1922, it had become 'crystal clear' by the time of the Genoa Conference in April–May 1922 that a concession agreement with Urquhart was an absolute necessity for Soviet Russia. Accordingly, even before the subsequent Hague Conference in June–July 1922, the issue of the Urquhart concession was discussed by the Central Committee. On Krasin's advice, the Central Committee decided in principle that a concession agreement should be agreed with Urquhart; and a corresponding instruction was sent to the head of the Soviet delegation gathering at The Hague, M.M. Litvinov (Deputy Commissar for Foreign Affairs). The Soviet Government's subsequent failure to reach any economic agreement with other Governments at The Hague made a concession agreement with Urquhart even more important, especially with the exceptional role that Urquhart played in the British delegation and at the Hague Conference in general. As recounted by Krasin, all the Soviet delegates to the Hague and Genoa Conferences, without exception, shared the same opinion that an Urquhart concession might be the easiest and fastest way of lifting the Entente's economic and financial blockade against Soviet Russia and that every effort should be made to buy this 'leading ram'. (These delegates had included Chicherin (Commissar for Foreign Affairs), Litvinov, G.M. Krzhizhanovsky (chairman of the State Planning Commission) and K.G. Rakovsky (member of the Central Committee) and Krasin himself). At Genoa, Soviet Russia had publicly rejected arbitration for inter-State disputes but accepted the principle of arbitration for concession agreements and other foreign commercial transactions. For Krasin as Soviet Commissar for Foreign Trade, the Urquhart concession had been for over one year, in his words, 'the central issue in our international policy'; but a second public failure to conclude and ratify the concession agreement would now bring 'political suicide', with Litvinov also warning the Central Committee that failure would gravely damage relations with both England and the USA, both of which had still to recognise Soviet Russia *de jure*.

On 20 August, Litvinov and B.S. Stomonyakov (the Soviet trade representative to Germany) sent a message to the Central Committee from The Hague to the effect that Urquhart was ready to resume negotiations with the Soviet Government. In fact, Urquhart had made contact with Litvinov and Krasin at The Hague on 15 July; and at Krasin's request, at the end of the conference in August, Urquhart travelled to Berlin to meet Chicherin, Stomonyakov and N.N. Krestinsky (the Soviet ambassador to Germany). Krasin was required to return urgently, via London, to Moscow. On 24 August, the Politburo met to discuss the proposed Urquhart concession, attended by Krasin and L.M. Karakhan (Deputy Commissar for Foreign Affairs). Lenin was absent, still convalescing at Gorki.

In Krasin's account of this Politburo meeting, there was not a single vote against the proposed concession agreement. On the contrary, all participants unanimously recognised the necessity of concluding the agreement even at the cost of significant material sacrifices and compromises by the Soviet Government. Krasin indicated the principal terms to be agreed without which it was pointless to resume negotiations, namely: the scope of the concession (all Urquhart's former enterprises); the duration (ninety-nine years); the profit share due to the Soviet Government (7.5 per cent); reduction in taxes and railway tariffs; duty free import and export by the concessionaire; an advance payment partly in cash and partly in State bonds in a total amount equal to actual losses incurred by Urquhart's enterprises 'as a result of actions of the Soviet Government' during and after the Civil War; exemption from local taxes; guarantees against confiscation and requisition; and arbitration to settle 'private law' disputes between the concessionaire and the Soviet Government.

The Politburo did not consider that the duration of the concession was an insuperable obstacle because, with a ninety-nine year period, not only the concession 'but also capitalism itself will probably be gone without a trace'. The profit share was also acceptable; and the only matter that raised debate was the proposal for arbitration. It was strongly opposed by Trotsky who considered any arbitration agreement to be injurious to the State sovereignty of Soviet Russia. A curious compromise was reached whereby the Politburo decided, in Krasin's words, 'not to make any concessions or exceptions on public-law disputes but to be open to the concessionaire's requests for material concessions, to buy him'. The Politburo agreed to offer a cash sum to Urquhart of up to two million gold roubles and also to compensate him for losses to his properties caused by the actions of the Soviet Government during and after the Civil War, in an amount to be determined by an arbitration tribunal. The principle of arbitration as a method of assessing such compensation was treated as an issue distinct from and less contentious than the proposed arbitration clause in the concession agreement. The Politburo had already received a report from its Mikhailov commission concluding that damage to Urquhart's properties had been caused by Kolchak's White Armies and Urquhart's own engineers before the Red Army's arrival in mid-1919; any dispute over such compensation would relate to

60   ON ARBITRATION

past and not future events; and any claim would be decided by nonneutral arbitration in Moscow.

A Politburo commission was to be formed (comprising Krasin himself, with A.A. Andreev and I.T. Smilga, respectively a Central Committee member and a senior member of the Supreme Council of National Economy, 'VSNKh') to finalise the terms of the proposed concession agreement; Krasin was personally authorised 'to continue further negotiations with Urquhart and conclude a preliminary agreement'; and the Politburo was to review the finalised version of the agreement which was also to be submitted to the Central Committee. In other words, Krasin was entrusted by the Politburo not only to conduct negotiations with Urquhart for the proposed concession agreement but also to sign that agreement, subject only to subsequent ratification by the Politburo and the Central Committee. However, arbitration remained a controversial issue; and Krasin sought clearer instructions from the Politburo before his departure for Berlin.

As to the proposed arbitration clause, on 24 August the Politburo commission concluded in its report to the Central Committee, as drafted by Krasin, that: 'if the concessionaire agrees to have final decisions on possible disputes between him and the Government made by the Russian Court, then, of course, that procedure would be preferable to arbitration. However, because the concessionaire and the Government are the two parties to the agreement, it is not likely that the concessionaire will agree to that. Experience of all negotiations concerning concessions show that entrepreneurs never abandon the requirement for arbitration. A number of different concession and trade agreements entered into by the Soviet Government allow for arbitration, and the concessionaire can refer to the large number of precedents where the Soviet Government has accepted arbitration. The commission believes that since this concession is important, it is necessary to agree to arbitration, and the mode of selecting a super-arbitrator [i.e. the presiding arbitrator] should be the same as agreed last year during the negotiations with the same concessionaire [i.e. rejecting Soviet revolutionary tribunals but without addressing the issue of a Soviet majority on the arbitration tribunal, a proposal already vehemently rejected by Urquhart in 1921]'.

By letter dated 26 August to Stalin (for the Politburo), Krasin again pursued the broader question of an agreement to arbitrate future disputes arising from the proposed concession agreement: 'There is a large number of agreements going back to 1920 which contain articles on arbitration ... The entire policy of our Main Concession Committee would collapse and the Committee itself would have to be closed as a useless organisation if arbitration clauses in agreements with foreigners are categorically rejected. Rejecting the arbitration clause in negotiations for this concession agreement would be interpreted abroad as a radical change of the Soviet Government's position and a refusal to enter into any business agreements with foreigners.... The decision of the Central Committee [i.e. its Politburo] of 24 August accepts arbitration in order to determine the amount of compensation for damage. However, besides the amount of such compensation, the agreement will include a number of issues which may require resolution not by the unilateral act of one of the parties but by an intermediary agency. For example, the issue of periodical and mandatory (for the concessionaire) review of the production program. Last year the concessionaire categorically rejected such review. This year there is a hope that he might concede this matter. However, he will never agree to accept a situation when norms of production are decided by the other party. He will accept this condition only if the minimum norm is decided by an arbitration commission. There are dozens of other instances where a dispute over various articles of the agreement can be resolved only through arbitration. In the area of private law, arbitration is a common practice in all capitalist countries; and it does not present any threat to State sovereignty. Having studied the concessionaire's views and the way he operates for more than a year, I categorically declare that completely refusing arbitration or limiting it only to the issue of compensation will turn these negotiations into a waste of time and will produce conflict which will be more severe than the termination of October 1921. I believe that if we limit arbitration to the area of private relations, we would risk nothing— especially because the entire enterprise, the capital invested by the concessionaire, the equipment, etc. all remain on our territory; and, if we want, we can always take any measures against the concessionaire.' This latter argument was, of course, brutally correct, as was later proved in 1929–1930 by the Soviet Government's conduct towards Lena Goldfields' concession: its assets were seized, its senior personnel arrested and imprisoned, and even with diplomatic pressure from the United Kingdom it was not possible for Lena Goldfields to enforce its arbitration award against the USSR.

Krasin was personally reluctant to resume negotiations with Urquhart; and he requested Stalin to replace him with Stomonyakov; but Stalin refused. It is apparent from Krasin's private correspondence at the time that he was tired— if not already ill—and that he suspected also that his authority was not as complete as it seemed. Before his departure for Berlin, Krasin continued to express the view that an arbitration clause in the concession agreement was unavoidable; and A.I. Rykov (acting chairman of the Council of People's Commissars) informed Krasin that he would send him later in Berlin clear instructions on the concession's arbitration clause.

Krasin left Moscow in the morning of 28 August and arrived in Berlin on 29 August, having flown from Moscow to Königsberg (now Kaliningrad) and then taken the train to Berlin. He there learnt that Urquhart had left for London in the absence of any news from Moscow that negotiations were to be resumed; and Stomonyakov in Berlin had received no instructions from Moscow to keep Urquhart in Berlin. Krasin persuaded Urquhart to return to Berlin, where he arrived on 30 August; and whilst thereafter their negotiations progressed swiftly, Krasin's dealings with Moscow did not. Within a day of their resuming negotiations, on 31 August, the Politburo decided to instruct Krasin to continue his

62   ON ARBITRATION

negotiations with Urquhart 'but in no case to become entangled in the clause about arbitration prior to receiving the results of the work of the commission established by the Politburo'. This was the same Politburo commission whose members included Krasin, but it was now to be chaired by Rykov with the addition of D.I. Kursky (Commissar for Justice); and it was required to study not only the appropriateness of the proposed arbitration clause, including its scope and the tribunal's formation, but also to study 'all necessary legal materials on the practice of arbitration in other countries, the possibility of replacing arbitration with forms of guarantees and with special tribunals where representatives of concessionaires take part, similar to *tribunaux de commerce*'. The Politburo ordered the results of these studies to be completed by Tuesday, 5 September 1922. It was a late and impossible task.

On 4 September 1922, in Berlin, Krasin received a telegram from Rykov, informing him that, 'in accordance with the decision of the Central Committee, the commission again reviewed the issue of arbitration. It was decided to accept arbitration, determining as precisely as possible all issues which would be referred to the decision of the arbitration tribunal. We shall complete this work by Monday night [i.e. that same day] and let you know the results as soon as possible. The telegram also requested Krasin to collect together and forward to Moscow all legal materials on the organisation and practice of arbitration tribunals. There is no record that Krasin received in Berlin any further instructions on arbitration from Rykov at any time prior to the conclusion of the negotiations with Urquhart and the signing of the concession agreement on 9 September. More significantly, also on 4 September, Stalin received a short note from Lenin, still in Gorki, which was drafted as a directive to the Politburo: 'To grant concession to Urquhart only on condition of granting us a large loan. All Politburo members must review the report of the Mikhailov commission which inspected the enterprises to be affected by the Urquhart concession. Enemies expect that our transport and industry is totally ruined. It is critical to raise capital in order to restore these assets by taxing all commodities, imposing maximum taxes on such commodities as sugar and beer. Consider mandatory domestic bonds and income tax.' Lenin was turning against the Urquhart concession, before seeing the final text of the agreement; but for the time being nothing more was said to Krasin in Berlin.

In a letter dated 6 September 1922 to the Politburo, sent by airmail to Moscow three days before signing the agreement, Krasin described the state of his negotiations with Urquhart in regard to the concession agreement's arbitration clause: 'There was no chance to avoid the issue of arbitration during the very first meeting with the concessionaire. The concessionaire has always put this issue on the top of his priorities and to avoid discussing it would be interpreted as a lack of serious commitment to reach agreement in a speedy manner. This is why even before receiving the Politburo's decision of 31 August we had to formulate the relevant article of the agreement. The jurisdiction of the arbitration tribunal covers exclusively the interpretation and implementation of the concession agreement. Since there are no provisions having the character of public law in the agreement itself, the arbitration tribunal will consider only private-law issues in the relationship between the concessionaire and the Government. All cases where the concessionaire does not comply with general decrees of the State or local government or has a dispute with a third party would fall within the jurisdiction of the [Soviet] general judicial bodies. The place of the arbitration tribunal will be Moscow and can be moved abroad only by decision of the president. The most difficult question as to the president can be solved in the following manner: the Soviet Government will present the concessionaire with a list of several candidates of its choice (six to ten) selected from public figures recognised in Europe: jurists, technical specialists and administrators, and the concessionaire will select one of them as a superarbitrator [president and third arbitrator]. Thus, the main challenge will be to search the entire globe to find ten persons whom we could trust to chair the tribunal. The parties make their own choice of the two arbitrators; and they are allowed to bring in experts and jurists. In this way, the interests of the RSFSR are protected in the best possible way. The concessionaire will in no way agree to abandon arbitration under current conditions. We had to accept arbitration under conditions much less favourable to us in a dozen cases and we cannot enter into any serious contract abroad without an article about arbitration. The Treaty with Germany of 6 May 1921 makes arbitration obligatory for the Soviet Government. All my intelligence is insufficient to convince the concessionaire that arbitration is not acceptable in this particular case when it is being accepted in many similar cases and is validated by the Soviet-German Treaty....

I repeat, rejecting arbitration in this case meant rejecting the negotiations; and I have every reason to believe that this is how it would have been interpreted by the concessionaire.' (Krasin later insisted his letter was sent on 5 September; but it clearly bears the later date: it is possible that he was then anxious to show that the Politburo had more than ample time to instruct him *not* to sign the agreement on 9 September but had chosen not to do so).

On 7 September 1922, the Politburo decided 'to charge Comrade Krasin with responsibility to procrastinate over the issue of arbitration during his negotiations with Urquhart'. The Politburo had received materials from Rykov's commission but declared them 'inadequate'; and it now required further studies into the use of arbitration by Western countries specifically in concession agreements granted by a sovereign State and public-law issues raised by the granting of such State concessions. The Politburo also charged the Main Concessions Committee to consider the organisation of 'commercial tribunals in Russia which would allow for internal resolution of issues arising from concession contracts'. This was a still more untimely and impossible task, given the negotiating position already taken by Krasin.

Moreover, the Politburo's instruction was belatedly received by Krasin in Berlin on 11 September, two days after he and Urquhart had signed the concession

64   ON ARBITRATION

agreement. Krasin later justified his signature on the basis of his earlier instructions from Moscow: 'Following precisely the instructions from Rykov of 4 September that arbitration should be accepted, provided that the exact jurisdiction [of the arbitration tribunal] is determined, I made a request and managed to receive Urquhart's consent for the following formula: "Issues outside the area of private law between the Government and the Concessionaire are not subject to the jurisdiction of the arbitration tribunal." According to the opinion of all jurists whom I consulted, this formula absolutely removes any danger of subjecting to arbitration any public-law issues which are within the jurisdiction of the people's courts and revolutionary tribunals, as well as of any civil law claims and disputes between the concessionaire and third parties and even between the concessionaire and the Government, with the exception only of those civil law disputes which involve the concession agreement itself where the Government acts not as a Government but as a party, that is like any owner of leased property [i.e. not in the exercise of *puissance publique*]. If you add to this the fact that I managed to have the concessionaire agree that the super-arbitrator [president] is to be selected from six candidates nominated by the Soviet Government, it will appear that this is the limit of any conceivable compromise [by Urquhart] in our favour in the area of arbitration.' Krasin's important qualification on the scope of disputes referable to arbitration subsequently took the form of an agreed note to the arbitration clause's first paragraph (see the appendix below).

As Krasin wrote on 7 September to his wife, then on holiday in Italy with their three daughters: 'All these days I have been persistently continuing these difficult negotiations with the help of Stomonyakov, while Moscow brings one or another stupid surprise every day, which clearly does not make it easier, Nevertheless, there is some hope of signing an agreement shortly. To complete this business which is probably the most important matter among today's foreign affairs, I will have to take all materials to Moscow and to stay there seven to ten days to make sure that the same thing does not happen [to this agreement] as it did to the Italian trade agreement. Therefore, I will be back in Berlin on or about 20 September and only then will be able to start my vacation.... I would like to spend it in the South, to catch some sun and do some swimming but by now you must have become sick and tired of Italy. The Lido will be even more boring than Genoa; there is nothing there except sand and sea. I will leave for Moscow perhaps as soon as next Monday [11 September], it depends on the signing of the agreement.'

The concession agreement was finalised and signed on 9 September by Urquhart and Krasin in Berlin. Its duration was ninety-nine years over much of Urquhart's former properties, on conditions not materially more onerous for Soviet Russia than those briefly described by Krasin to the Politburo on 24 August. The news, seen as a unique and major development in trade between Soviet Russia and a Western company, went around the world. As for neutral arbitration, so desired by Urquhart, clause 22 provided for the arbitration of private-law disputes arising from the concession agreement before four party-appointed arbitrators and a president of 'world-wide or European fame' as a learned man, lawyer, engineer or public figure, together with the explanatory note sought by Krasin excluding public-law disputes (see the full arbitration clause set out in the appendix below). By clause 4, this arbitration clause was also to apply to Urquhart's claim for compensation, which was limited to 20 million gold roubles with an advance of £150,000 payable in cash within two months of the agreement's ratification. By clause 30, fatally, the agreement was signed subject to ratification within one month by Soviet Russia's Council of People's Commissars, i.e. by 8 October.

Urquhart was highly satisfied with the agreement as a commercial transaction and also with Krasin's conduct of the negotiations. As he later reported to his company's shareholders in October (after the agreement's non-ratification), the concession agreement gave the company everything it could hope for; and he had not a word of criticism for the steps which Krasin had taken to meet him halfway: they were business people trying to work out a business contract, without politics. In private discussions with the British Foreign Office, Urquhart estimated that his company's liability to the Soviet Government for royalties and taxation would be about £100,000 per annum, whereas payments to the Czarist Government had amounted to something like £360,000 per annum; and the agreement's minimum production norms were set at only one-tenth of the properties' pre-war output. Krasin, despite his outward show of confidence to Urquhart, knew now that ratification in Moscow had become problematic. On 12 September, Krasin left Berlin, taking the train to Königsberg and then the plane to Moscow, via Smolensk. As he wrote to his wife from a small shack at the Smolensk aerodrome on 13 September, surrounded by German pilots, he left Berlin 'feeling pretty low. After difficult negotiations with Urquhart I signed the agreement, but it still needs to be approved by Moscow and for this essentially useless, albeit unavoidable, procedure under our regulations, I am going to Moscow; and only after I complete this important matter will I be able to think of a vacation.' Krasin still hoped the procedure would be completed in time for his family holiday in Italy. He was utterly mistaken.

By this time, Lenin had received the text of the signed concession agreement, and it confirmed his growing hostility to the proposed concession, as expressed in his letter to Stalin of 12 September 1922 (with his own emphases): 'Comrade Stalin, Having read the agreement signed by Krasin with Urquhart, I am expressing my opinion against its ratification. Promising us profits in two or three years, Urquhart makes us pay now. It is absolutely unacceptable. Mikhailov, the chairman of the commission, made a special trip to the location to examine Urquhart's concession and concluded that it is not we who are responsible for destruction but *the foreigners*. And now we have to pay. Allegedly we will receive some relief after x number of years, but we have to pay now. I propose the *rejection* of this concession. It is slavery and robbery. I would like to remind you of the conclusion of Mikhailov's

66   ON ARBITRATION

commission. He was against this concession. There is not a single serious argument for it which has been added since then. We must reject it. I would like to ask you to make this known to the members of the Politburo.... [PS] It is a treacherous trick that this concession allegedly would not serve as a precedent. It certainly *will* become a precedent. *In reality*, it will inevitably happen, regardless of any words and assurances. And in general, *nothing* that was uncovered by Mikhailov's commission has been taken into account. There is a whole number of arguments against such concession.' In a letter dated 19 September to G.E. Zinoviev (a Politburo member), although indicating that his opinion had temporarily wavered, Lenin strongly criticised the concession's vast size and long duration and, more ominously, blamed Krasin for exceeding the Politburo's instructions. In a further letter to Zinoviev dated 4 October, Lenin again described having second thoughts; but having seen Mikhailov, he was now again against the Urquhart concession.

On arriving in Moscow on 14 September, Krasin was not yet aware of Lenin's growing, if vacillating, opposition to ratification. In his letter of 17 September to his wife, he still attributed such opposition to 'a lot of clever persons who, sometimes from ignorance and sometimes, perhaps, from a Christian desire to play a dirty trick on their neighbour, are hatching up something, wincing and generally turning their noses away'. He knew, however, that his Italian holiday was now substantially at risk: 'My vacation has already been approved, but it's hard to tell when I will go because of the Urquhart matter. I brilliantly concluded the agreement in Berlin, but it still needs to be ratified by Sovnarkom [the Council of People's Commissars]... I shall have to wait for two or three decisive meetings and wage the final battle. I believe nevertheless that on 20–23 September I will be able to leave and join you not later than 10 October. If you are in a hurry to go to England, it means that I will not have much time in Italy; and once back in London it will not be much of a vacation, they won't let me rest there. However, if I differ here with our people about Urquhart's agreement, then it very well may happen that I will have a very long vacation, up to my complete resignation. Well, we'll see ...' Over the next few days the position grew worse; and on 21 September, Krasin wrote despairingly to his wife and daughters: 'I have signed an agreement which, according to the world's press, exceeds in importance all the agreements signed hitherto, including even Genoa and The Hague; but the local wise men here, who on 24 August insisted on my rushing to Berlin and back by aeroplane, are now turning their snouts away. The situation is so serious that I am contemplating giving up this job altogether. So gross is the leadership's ignorance and so unbusinesslike are their methods that I am losing all hope... I have firmly resolved to resign from the Government if I do not succeed in carrying this business through, but so long as I do not lose all the points on the agreement, I must stick it out to the end ...'

Lenin remained in Gorki, absent from the Politburo meetings of 14, 21 and 28 September in Moscow. On 14 September, the Politburo decided to request Lenin's assessment of the agreement, to commission advice from the Commissariat for

Foreign Affairs and the Commissariat for Justice and also—attentive to Lenin's instructions—to suggest that all Politburo members familiarise themselves with the report of the Mikhailov commission. On 21 September, the Politburo decided to postpone for one week any further consideration but to appoint a new Politburo commission (comprising L.B. Kamenev, Andreev and Bogdanov) to prepare a draft statement in the event that a decision was made rejecting the agreement's ratification. On 28 September, the Politburo decided to refer the whole matter to the plenum meeting of the Central Committee, instructing Krasin, Bogdanov and Karakhan to prepare and distribute the materials to the members of the Central Committee. The issue of ratification was therefore left entirely unresolved until the Central Committee's meeting on 5 October, which was to be attended by Lenin. Outside the Politburo, however, the debate continued, with the most senior officers directly responsible for Soviet Russia's foreign trade, foreign affairs and economic planning expressing strong approval for the concession agreement's ratification, notwithstanding the 'neutral' arbitration clause.

In a letter dated 20 September to Stalin, as instructed by the Politburo, L.M. Karakhan (Deputy Commissar for Foreign Affairs) summarised, *inter alia*, the issue over the arbitration clause: 'By the Politburo's decision of 24 August arbitration was allowed for the purpose of determining the amount of damage suffered by Urquhart from the actions of the Soviet Government. However, in the agreement the jurisdiction of the arbitration tribunal is broadened to all disputes arising from the interpretation and implementation of the agreement. Arbitration is objectionable in principle because it expresses the concessionaire's mistrust of the Russian Court; and it validates that mistrust. In a practical sense, however, the creation of this arbitration tribunal does not present any danger to us; and if we do not make any hopeless formal mistakes, it will produce an arbitration tribunal with our majority or the transfer of the dispute to our [Soviet] Court. During the current domestic and international situation agreeing to arbitration is objectionable in general. However, there is no danger that based on the principle of preferential status it would spread to others, because this agreement grants this benefit to Urquhart individually and not to all British citizens in general.' Karakhan concluded his report: 'the political significance of the agreement with Urquhart and its role in resuming economic relations with Europe is colossal. Even now, before its ratification by the Soviet Government, this agreement has caused much excitement among financial and industrial leaders in Europe. This agreement means that "friendly" relations with the City of London are restored. Urquhart has already given several interviews in which he spoke with almost love and admiration for Soviet Russia and the charms of Soviet power ...' This was true. On his return to London, Urquhart had also spoken privately to Klyshko, Krasin's deputy at the Soviet Trade Delegation. As reported to Krasin on 14 September, clutching a pile of congratulatory telegrams and letters on the successful conclusion of his negotiations, Urquhart had said that he was confident that the concession agreement

68 ON ARBITRATION

would change European public opinion favourably towards the Soviet Government and that, not being motivated by monetary considerations, he was 'happy and proud to be a pioneer for the rebirth of Russian industry: I love the Russian people and developing Russian industry is my life's mission. And now I am pursuing one goal only, to help my Russian motherland. I trust the Soviet Government fully and believe that it will give me an opportunity to do productive work . . .' This language was not wholly typical of the Scots financier; and perhaps Krasin's deputy found it difficult to avoid all embellishments helpful to Krasin's cause in Moscow.

Also on 20 September, as instructed by the Politburo, the Deputy Commissar for Justice (N.V. Krylenko) reported to Stalin on legal aspects arising from the concession agreement, particularly as to whether 'the sovereignty of the Government's rights was protected'. He objected, *inter alia*, to the principle of arbitration, both for the purpose of assessing compensation for Urquhart's losses during and after the Civil War and for disputes arising from the concession agreement. The arbitrators would be 'private persons', deciding upon the actions of the Soviet Government; and in the case of the Soviet Government's default under the arbitration clause, the English High Court would exercise jurisdiction over Soviet Russia, 'which is inadmissible for ideological reasons and because it made no sense since the London Court could hardly force the Government to comply with its orders'. Krylenko concluded his advice, with a masterful lack of timing not unusual even in legal advisers today, by recommending that the wording of the concession agreement should now be carefully reviewed, excluding all provisions that 'do not follow from the agreement but infringe upon the Government's rights as a public legal authority'. Whilst no recommendation for the agreement's ratification, it was a lukewarm condemnation of the principle of neutral arbitration.

On 21 September, the new Politburo commission reported its conclusions on the ratification of the Urquhart concession agreement. In a short document, Kamenev and Andreev recommended rejecting it on economic grounds; whilst Bogdanov advised in favour. Neither majority nor minority commented on the arbitration clause. On 3 October, the further report of the Mikhailov commission noted the arbitration clause without adverse comment, advising only that the arbitration tribunal was to be organised 'in the usual manner'. This commission included Professor V.N. Shreter, who was a well-known legal specialist on Soviet concession agreements, including arbitration. Whatever Mikhailov's opposition to the Urquhart concession, it was not based on the concession agreement's arbitration clause.

Lenin's opposition was based on broader grounds. The diplomatic Chicherin, the Soviet Commissar for Foreign Affairs, in his handwritten letter dated 23 September 1922 to Stalin, intended for Lenin, expressed his opinion that rejection of the concession would be a 'catastrophe for Soviet Russia. It would stop the inflow of foreign capital. Signing the agreement would mean that a major businessman works with us; rejecting the agreement would mean that it is premature to work with Russia. Urquhart has close ties with English and French capital; Hoover [later the US President Hoover] is one of his shareholders and he himself is a shareholder in major German companies. He has great influence on both the English and German Governments. If he comes, others will follow. If he does not, only small traders will come. Our position will be weakened and our enemies will have their hands untied. We not only will be thrown back for several years, but an active hostile atmosphere against us will prevail.... It would be the greatest disaster ...' Stalin noted its receipt without comment and forwarded it to Lenin on the same day. Krasin also wrote personally to Lenin on 26 September, enclosing a long memorandum on the political importance of the Urquhart agreement which also traced the difficult history of the lengthy negotiations beginning in July 1921, followed by the breakdown in October 1921 and their formal resumption in August 1922, all in conformity with instructions from the Politburo. Krasin was here not only advocating ratification of the agreement but also defending himself as the Soviet negotiator who had finalised and signed that agreement, indicating that he could not continue as a member of the Soviet Government if the agreement was now rejected by the Central Committee.

Those favouring ratification of the Urquhart concession now tried once more collectively to support Krasin. In a letter to Stalin dated 26 September, all the economic arguments were vigorously re-stated by senior officers from VSNKh, the Main Concessions Committee, the State Planning Commission and the Commissariat for Foreign Affairs (Bogdanov, M.I. Frumkin, G.Y. Sokolnikov, Karakhan, Smirnov and Professor I. Gubkin). After warning of the grave consequences to Soviet diplomatic and economic policies if the concession agreement were not ratified, the letter finished: 'Based on these considerations we come to the conclusion that ratification of Urquhart's concession is an absolute necessity for us. It goes without saying that having ratified the concluded agreement the Council of People's Commissars can commission its representative to clarify certain clauses of the agreement and make certain amendments to it that will be acceptable to the concessionaire.' From the Soviet embassy in Berlin, by letter dated 28 September, Krestinsky wrote to the Politburo imploring it to ratify the Urquhart concession, warning of the grave diplomatic repercussions of disavowing Krasin and concluding: 'even if the agreement were poor and disadvantageous, ratification would cause less damage to us than refusal to approve the already signed agreement'.

On 2 October, Lenin returned from Gorki to the Kremlin, and over the next few days he attended the meetings of the Central Committee and Council of People's Commissars. At its plenum meeting on 5 October, at Lenin's insistence, the Central Committee rejected the Urquhart concession; and on 6 October, in Lenin's presence as chairman, the Council of People's Commissars officially declined to ratify it, thereby confirming its legal demise. The vote was almost unanimous, with only Bogdanov abstaining and Krasin voting for ratification. The Soviet press announced the concession's rejection on 7 October. The adverse reaction from abroad was as dire as Chicherin, Litvinov, Krasin and Krestinsky had predicted. Publicly, as the London *Times* reported from a Russian source, Lenin had championed ratification against the scruples of his Soviet colleagues; but privately the decision was widely attributed to Lenin's personal veto; and it was said that Lenin had changed his mind at least three times. At the Central Committee meeting, Lenin's opposition was apparently rooted in economic grounds only: the concession would grant to Urquhart a monopoly in non-ferrous metals in Siberia; and how many roubles would the Soviet Government be required to pay Urquhart for current expenditure compared to how many pounds sterling actually invested by him as capital from abroad? There was also the issue of local opposition from the regional authorities, as originally addressed by the Mikhailov commission, arising from loss of control of major economic assets to a foreign concessionaire, who could also pay higher wages than local Soviet enterprises. There was, it seems, no overt objection based on the concession agreement's arbitration clause. Although it was to form a pretext later, there was nothing also about Britain's failure to invite Soviet Russia to the Lausanne peace conference on Turkey. These extraneous political motives were invented to avoid further public humiliation for Krasin; and although Soviet Russia was later invited to attend the Lausanne Conference in November 1922, it did not change Lenin's position on the Urquhart concession.

Lenin's decision shocked Krasin profoundly, as it did many within the Soviet Government, and the rejection of the concession left him bitterly disappointed. He sought to resign his post as Foreign Trade Commissar; but Lenin refused his request. As he wrote from Moscow on 8 October 1922 to his wife in London: 'Once again all my work, energy, efforts and ability have been wasted, and a small group of mules and imbeciles have undone all my work, just as a boy might destroy the thin web of a spider with one blow.' His wife, in her later memoirs of these events, quoted the French politician, Waldeck-Rousseau: '*le succès n'est après tout qu 'une question de date*'. In Krasin's case, within the thirty days prescribed by the concession agreement, he had been transformed from super-hero to near-traitor.

For present purposes, what lessons can be derived from Lenin's refusal to confirm the Urquhart concession on its merits, regardless of the arbitration clause? First, Lenin's intransigence proved fatal to the economic success of the Soviet policy on 'super-concessions' even before the termination of the New Economic Policy; and although there were eventually to be three major foreign concessions agreed after Lenin's death (Lena Goldfields, Harriman and Tetiuhe in 1925), none were on the scale of the Urquhart concession, with each eventually foundering under Stalin's First Five-Year Plan; and of course there were to be no large foreign loans to the USSR until much, much later.

The lesson is starkly obvious: a nation seeking foreign trade and investment can ratify the New York and Washington Conventions; it can enact the UNCITRAL Model Law; and it can sign on every presidential State visit numerous bilateral investment treaties with provisions for investor-State arbitration; but without firm evidence of a strong and consistent political will favourable to inward investment and foreign trade, foreign investors and traders will shy or be shooed away. At this point, arbitration is irrelevant; and by itself the arbitral process cannot generate any significant foreign trade and private inward investment. Conversely, where there is such a will, foreign trade and investment will be severely stunted without the transnational process of neutral arbitration. Even more than in 1922, it is now an uncompromising pre-condition for investors and foreign traders; and developing countries that deliberately thwart the arbitral process pay inevitably a very high price. For the host State, it also requires an understanding that the price of a lost arbitration or 'bad' award may be relatively small when measured against the corresponding benefit of inward capital investment over a longer period.

Second, that understanding is not easily acquired, even by States able urgently to commission large studies into the comparative law and practice of arbitration. It requires the international arbitral process to be properly accepted by government officers, State judges and regulators on a continuous basis. There needs to be confidence that neutral arbitration can produce fairness and justice for both sides, without State or judicial interference, and an awareness that there is in fact no better alternative for the final resolution of transnational commercial private-law disputes. Here, ICC has profoundly influenced the development of international commercial arbitration over the last eighty years. The ICC arbitration clause and ICC's itinerant preachers have encircled the earth; and as the Chairman of the ICC International Court of Arbitration can prove with his multi-stamped passport, the task of persuasion requires many miles to be travelled to all points of the compass, including Moscow. But the last and most important lesson from 1922 is that it is perhaps better for a party, after negotiating, agreeing and signing a contract, not then to re-think or re-draft its arbitration clause.

Appendix: the Urquhart Concession's Arbitration Clause 22

'For the settlement of disputes which may arise between the Government and the Concessionaire on questions of interpretation or fulfilment of the present Concession Agreement and of any additions or further agreements hereto, a special arbitration tribunal shall be formed.

Note: Issues outside the area of private-law between the Government and the Concessionaire are not subject to the jurisdiction of the arbitration tribunal.

1. The arbitration tribunal shall consist of five arbitrators. Within one month of the receipt of written notice from one of the parties, both parties shall appoint two arbitrators who must give their acceptance in writing. Within the same period their representatives shall mutually communicate to one another the names, professions and addresses of the arbitrators appointed by them. Within one month more, the four appointed arbitrators shall elect, by mutual consent, a fifth arbitrator who will act as president of the arbitration tribunal. If during this month no agreement be come to between the parties as to the election of a president, the nomination of the president shall be made as follows:- The

72 ON ARBITRATION

Government shall communicate to the Concessionaire the names of six candidates of worldwide or European fame as learned men, lawyers, engineers or public men from whom the Concessionaire has the right to select at its discretion a candidate who will be acknowledged by both parties as president of the arbitration tribunal.

2. In the event of death of one of the arbitrators, or of continued illness preventing him from fulfilling his duties, or of resignation, such arbitrator shall be replaced by another elected as provided above.

3. The arbitration tribunal shall have two secretaries, one appointed by each side. In the event of one resigning he shall be replaced by another secretary appointed in the same way. The arbitration tribunal may appoint its other personnel on terms at its discretion.

4. The arbitration tribunal shall sit at Moscow, but by decision of the president meetings in case of necessity may be held elsewhere, including abroad. The arbitration tribunal shall fix the time of its meetings.

5. The side which wishes to refer any question for decision to the arbitration tribunal must give written notice to the other side, after which a session of the arbitration tribunal is called. The notice of complaint together with all documents and papers and also an exposition of all other evidence which the side considers necessary for supporting its demands, shall be sent, with certified copies of the notice and all documents in duplicate for the other side, to the secretariat of the arbitration tribunal. Within one month from the receipt of the copy notice of complaint, the other side must present to the arbitration tribunal a reply to the complaint, together with all documents and papers and all other evidence which that side considers necessary for refuting the complaint, together with certified copies thereof and of all documents in duplicate for the other side.

6. On the expiry of a fortnight from the date of receipt of the reply, the arbitration tribunal shall fix a date for hearing, sending both parties notice thereof.

7. The decisions of the arbitration tribunal are obligatory and must be fulfilled immediately.

8. If the Concessionaire, on receiving a request from the Government to form an arbitration tribunal within the period provided, refuses to do so or if the parties do not agree on a president and the Concessionaire refuses to appoint a president from the six candidates submitted by the Government, the Government has the right to refer the question in dispute to the People's Court in Moscow, to whose jurisdiction the Concessionaire shall in such case submit. In the same way, if the Government for its part refuses to form an arbitration tribunal, or does not present a list of candidates for the selection of a president, the Concessionaire has the right to refer the question in dispute to the London Courts, to whose jurisdiction the Government shall in such case submit.

Note: Reference to a national court on a certain matter in the event of refusal to form the arbitration tribunal does not relieve the parties from the obligation to form an arbitration tribunal in accordance with this agreement and to submit to its jurisdiction.'

Selected Bibliography

Soviet Archives held by RGASPI (the Russian State Archive of Social Political History, formerly the Central Party Archive), 5/O1/D2954, 5/O2/D23, 5/O2/D4 & 5/O2/D452 (here translated from Russian into English, for which I am much indebted to my colleague, Dr Ylts).

K.H. Kennedy, *Mining Tsar: The Life and Times of Leslie Urquhart* (Sydney, 1986).

T.S. Martin. 'The Urquhart Concession and Anglo-Soviet Relations 1921–1922' (1972) 20 *Jahrbücher für Geschichte Osteuropas* 551.

V.A. Shishkin, *Sovietskoe Gosudartsvo i Strany Zapada 1917–1923* [The Soviet State and Western Countries 1917–1923] (Leningrad, 1969).

Lubov Krassin, *Leonid Krassin: His Life and Work* (London, 1929).

Yu. G. Felshtinsky, G.I. Chernyavskii & F. Markiz, eds., *L.B. Krasin, Letters to His Wife and Children 1917–1926* (2003), held by the International Institute of Social History in Amsterdam and available at <www.iisg.nl/enquiries.html>.

Private Papers of Leslie Urquhart.

5

The 1921–1923 North Sakhalin Concession Agreement

The 1925 Court Decisions between the US Company Sinclair Exploration and the Soviet Government

A. Introduction

As permanent arbitration institutions, the Maritime Arbitration Commission (MAC) and the Foreign Trade Arbitration Commission (FTAC) were founded in Moscow in 1930 and 1932 respectively; and hence FTAC, now the International Commercial Arbitration Court of the Russian Federation, celebrates its 70th birthday this year. MAC was founded to decide salvage and other maritime cases; and its procedures were modelled on Lloyd's salvage arbitrations heard in London under English procedural law. Accordingly, proceedings in MAC were heard by two arbitrators and not the usual three in Russian '*ad hoc*' arbitration proceedings; and only if the two arbitrators disagreed was a third 'superarbitrator' appointed, all which then corresponded to the English arbitration practice of appointing two arbitrators and an umpire. More striking was the parties' right to appeal from a MAC arbitration award to the USSR Supreme Court, which then also corresponded to the right of a party under the English Arbitration Act 1889 to request an award in the form of a special case stated for the English High Court on a question of law. Two years later, this right of appeal was not repeated when FTAC was founded, operating with a three-arbitrator tribunal making a final award, not subject to any judicial review by the Soviet courts. Later, this Soviet system of arbitration influenced the development of international commercial arbitration in China and other socialist countries; but historically, it was not a Soviet system, being rooted in the development of transnational arbitration in Europe from the early 1920s, including the formation of the ICC Court of Arbitration, the 1923 Geneva Protocol and the 1927 Geneva Convention.

The early history of MAC and FTAC has still to be told in full; but it is possible to see its beginning in the decisions of the Soviet Courts in the case in 1925 brought

---

On Arbitration. Edited by: Sam Wordsworth KC and Marie Veeder, Oxford University Press. © Oxford University Press 2023.
DOI: 10.1093/oso/9780192869135.003.0005

by the Soviet Government against the Sinclair Exploration Company of Delaware and New York. It concerned the nullification of a 36-year concession agreement made on 7 January 1922 between Sinclair and the Government of the Far Eastern Republic in Siberia for the exploitation of oil, gas and asphalt deposits in North Sakhalin. (It had been preceded by a preliminary agreement dated 14 May 1921.) Albeit controlled by Soviet Russia, the Far Eastern Republic was then nominally an independent state; and so treated by the USA. Later, in November 1922, the Far Eastern Republic was formally absorbed into the Russian Soviet Federated Socialist Republic (RSFSR) immediately following the departure of Japanese troops from Vladivostock (US and other Allied troops had left by April 1920, at the end of the Siberian 'intervention'). On 16 August 1923, the concession agreement was novated with the USSR and/or the RSFSR (being a jurisdictional issue later addressed by the Soviet Courts[1]); and in September 1923 Sinclair despatched a preliminary expedition to the concession's properties in North Sakhalin, which still remained under Japanese military occupation.

It was a brave but hopeless exercise, lasting almost six months. On arrival in North Sakhalin, the Japanese army arrested and detained the expedition's three members, eventually deporting them to China via Japan. It was plainly impossible for Sinclair to work its concession under Japanese occupation; but there was no adverse diplomatic reaction towards Japan from the USA – as the Soviet Government had intended in first granting and then maintaining the concession to a US company. Instead, the Soviet Government recovered North Sakhalin by means of the Soviet–Japanese Treaty of 20 January 1925: Japan was to remove its troops from Russian territory, recognizing the USSR *de jure*; but in return Japan was to receive valuable oil, coal and timber concessions in North Sakhalin – rendering the Sinclair concession immediately unnecessary and potentially embarrassing to the Soviet Government.

On 20 January 1925, the USSR Council of People's Commissars (Sovnarkom) decided to take immediate steps to cancel the Sinclair concession; and on 27 January 1925, the USSR Supreme Council for National Economy (VSNKh) filed a petition with the Moscow Guberniya Court seeking its annulment on the ground of Sinclair's non-fulfilment of its contractual obligations.[2] By its judgment dated

---

[1] In December 1922, the USSR was formed as a federation of Soviet Republics, including the RSFSR (itself now including the territory of the former Far Eastern Republic).

[2] There was a limited arbitration clause in Art. 38 of the 1922 Concession Agreement: it seems that neither party thought it relevant, being dependent on Sinclair's exercise of a right to terminate the concession under specified conditions. There were two jurisdiction clauses: Art. 41 provided (originally) for the jurisdiction of 'the proper court of the Far Eastern Republic' over the agreement's disputed nullity; and Art. 59 provided (originally) for 'all legal disputes and claims arising in connection with the Company's enterprise in Russian Sakhalin between the Company and the Government [of the Far Eastern Republic] or between the Company and private individuals or institutions to be settled in the courts of the Far Eastern Republic' (as translated from the Russian original version). The appropriate

76   ON ARBITRATION

24 March 1925, the Moscow Guberniya Court ruled that the agreement be declared null and that the application for retention by VSNKh of a bond furnished by Sinclair in the sum of 200,000 roubles be refused: (see Document 1 below). Sinclair lodged an appeal with the RSFSR Supreme Court; and on 22 May 1925, the Supreme Court's Board of Appeal for Civil Cases dismissed the appeal: (see Document 2 below). Both judgments relied on the testimony of Mr J.P. McCullough, the leader of Sinclair's failed expedition to North Sakhalin: (see Document 3 below). Thus, the Sakhalin concession granted to Sinclair came to an end, just as Japanese troops were to leave North Sakhalin and Japanese concessionaires were making preparations to arrive, including the Japanese North Sakhalin Petroleum Company.

The *Sinclair case* was a famous dispute at the time. The texts of the Soviet Court decisions were not widely known; they can still be found in the former Soviet archives in Moscow, along with other materials; and they have not been published previously in English translation. The decisions are interesting for two contrasting reasons. First, the judicial reasoning is careful and impressive, particularly on the doctrine of *force majeure*. Even in such turbulent times, it ought not to be forgotten that many of the senior Russian lawyers involved in the case had long been trained in comparative law;[3] and with the 1922 New Economic Policy, methods of traditional European jurisprudence were applied by Soviet jurists. Second, the court judgments were perceived as unconvincing outside the USSR, as the product of a conveniently amenable legal system for the Soviet Government. It can be therefore no accident that from 1925, the Soviet Government's new concessions with foreign parties were to contain elaborate arbitration clauses, effectively providing for independent 'ad hoc' arbitration tribunals sitting outside the USSR. In 1930, the USSR sought to turn away from these 'ad hoc' clauses in favour of new permanent arbitration institutions in Moscow, namely MAC and later FTAC. Man learns from experience; and by that man usually means bad experience. If the 1925 *Sinclair case* was such an experience; and if it progressed the advance of international commercial arbitration leading to the 70th birthday celebrations this year in Moscow and elsewhere; and if such lessons are still being learnt, so be it. Those who forget history are condemned to remember.

---

court of the Far Eastern Republic was the Vladivostock Regional Court – but legally, as such, that court no longer existed in 1925, hence the importance of the novation with the RSFSR/USSR in 1923.

[3] The Soviet Government's case was presented by Professor V.N. Shreter (a legal specialist on foreign concessions) and M.A. Stepukhovich (Head of Glavkoncesskom's Legal Department, the USSR Main Concessions Committee within VSNKh); and Sinclair's case by Professors Worms and Muravyev.

Document 1

DECISION OF THE MOSCOW GUBERNIYA COURT DATED 24th MARCH 1925[4]

CASE No 6340-1925: IN THE NAME OF THE RUSSIAN SOCIALIST FEDERATED SOVIET REPUBLIC, the Civil Court Division of Moscow Guberniya Court sat in session on 21st, 23rd and 24th May 1925 before the Presiding Judge Wolfson, Assistant Judges Kalikson and Kulikov and Secretary Vladimirsky, to hear a petition filed by the USSR Supreme Council of National Economy (VSNKh) against the American company Sinclair Exploration Company seeking annulment of the Agreement dated 7th January 1922, together with a Supplementary Agreement thereto of the same date and a Supplementary Agreement thereto dated 16th August 1923, and seeking retention of the sum of 200,000 roubles.

B. Circumstances of the Case

On 7th January 1922, an Agreement was signed between the Government of the Far Eastern Republic (FER) and the American Company 'Sinclair Exploration Company', whereunder the FER Government granted to the Company a 36-year concession in an area of land situated in the territory of Russian Sakhalin north of the 51st parallel, for the purposes of extraction of oil, natural gases and mineral resins. On that date, namely 7th January 1922, the same parties also entered into a 'Supplementary Agreement' having the object of setting forth the circumstances in which the FER Government had the right to terminate the aforementioned Agreement.

Pursuant to the declaration of the Far Eastern Province as an inseparable part of the RSFSR, by Decree of the All-Russian Central Executive Committee (VTsIK) dated 15th November 1922, these agreements were approved and ratified by the Government of the RSFSR by order of the RSFSR Council of People's Commissars dated 23rd January 1923; and on 16th August 1923 under a supplementary agreement signed on behalf of the Government of the USSR by VSNKh Presidium Member Dolgov[5] and People's Commissar for Foreign Affairs Chicherin[6] and with the authority of Sinclair Exploration Company by Templeton,[7] amendments were

---

[4] GARF 8350/3/108/190 (Russian).

[5] A.N. Dolgov, Member of VSNKh's Collegium, to which the USSR Main Concessions Committee (Glavkoncesskom) was administratively subordinate. In 1924, as an expert member of the Soviet delegation, he attended the Anglo-Soviet Conference in London, at which (*inter alia*) a bilateral Anglo-Soviet arbitration treaty was considered, to no avail.

[6] G.V. Chicherin, USSR Commissar for Foreign Affairs.

[7] E.C. Templeton, of New York, an officer of Sinclair Exploration.

78   ON ARBITRATION

made to the text of the agreement as required to reflect the changes which had taken place in the political status of the Far Eastern Province.

On 28th January 1925, the Moscow Guberniya Court received a petition from the USSR Supreme Council of National Economy (VSNKh) wherein it was stated that Sinclair Exploration Company was in breach of the Agreement dated 7th January 1922. The substance of this breach being that the Company had failed to carry out specified work within the period stipulated in the Agreement. The petitioner averred that, according to Article 2 of the Agreement dated 7th January 1922 and Article 2 of the Supplementary Agreement, the Company was required to proceed with exploration work during the period between 7th January 1923 and 7th January 1924.

According to Article 2 of the Agreement, the Company was required within 60 days after 7th January 1924 to submit a map or maps of the exploration areas. The maps presented to the Government by the Company were not maps reflecting the exploration work carried out. In light of the Company's breach of the Agreement, under Article 41 of the Agreement the Government granted the Company a further six months grace period in which to remedy the deficiency.[8] During these six months the Company failed to carry out the work. On the basis that, under Article 41 of the Agreement, the Government was entitled in this case to seek annulment of the agreement through the courts, the USSR Supreme Council of National Economy (VSNKh) requested the Moscow Guberniya Court to make an order declaring the Agreement of 7th January 1922, the Supplementary Agreement thereto of the same date and the Supplementary Agreement between the RSFSR Government and the Company dated 16th August 1923 nullified through the fault of the Company, and to declare as the property of the USSR the sum of 200,000 roubles paid by the Company by way of performance bond, and to revoke the letter of guarantee in the sum of 800,000 roubles furnished by the Company under Article 37 of the Agreement.

This case was scheduled for hearing on 11th March 1925. Under Article 41 of the Agreement, the notice of hearing together with a statement of petition and attached documents were sent to Sinclair Exploration Company at 45 Nassau Street, New York. According to a telegram sent by the USSR Political Representation in Berlin, presented as an exhibit in this case, it is evident that the notice and accompanying documents were served on the Respondent on 18th February [1925].

On 11th March 1925, the hearing on the substance of the case was postponed for ten days by reason of illness of one of the defence attorneys on the Respondent's side. At the session of 11th March, discussions took place concerning the legal objection raised by the Respondent claiming jurisdictional non-competence of the

---

[8] This formal notice of default under Art. 41 was dated 21 May 1924 and signed by VSNKh's Chairman (Felix Dzerzhinsky) for the USSR.

THE 1921–1923 NORTH SAKHALIN CONCESSION AGREEMENT 79

Guberniya Court and seeking referral of the case to the Supreme Court of the Republic.

In a separate ruling, citing Articles 23 and 24 of the Code of Civil Procedure, the Guberniya Court declared itself competent to rule in this case.

In response to the statement of petition, the attorneys for Sinclair Exploration Company, Members of the Panel of Defenders, Worms and Muravyev, submitted a written rebuttal, setting forth the following arguments on the substance of the case:

(1) The petition was filed by the wrong claimant. The Agreement was made in the name of the RSFSR, whereas the petition was filed by the USSR Supreme Council of National Economy (VSNKh) representing USSR Sovnarkom. In the Respondent's opinion, the petition ought to have been filed in the name of the RSFSR.

(2) In the Respondent's opinion, the performance of exploration work during the first year, i.e. during the period between 7th January 1923 and 7th January 1924 was, according to the literal meaning of Article 2 of the Agreement, the right rather than the obligation of the Sinclair Exploration Company. This is confirmed by the perusal of Article 2 of the Agreement, wherein it is stated that the Company shall have the right within the first five years to carry out exploration work; but it does not state that the Company is under an obligation to do so.

(3) Regardless of whether the Company was obliged to carry out exploration work in the first year, or whether this was simply its right, non-performance of the exploration work should not have brought about the termination of the Agreement inasmuch as the work was not carried out owing to circumstances of *force majeure*, namely that the territory of Russian Sakhalin was occupied by the Japanese and that this posed an insurmountable obstacle preventing the work from being carried out. According to Article 35 of the Agreement, the occurrence of *force majeure* gives rise to an extension of the period for fulfilment of obligations under the Agreement by a period commensurate with the effective duration of *force majeure*.

(4) It is further argued that the Company was not given an opportunity to exercise freely the rights granted to it under the Agreement, which meant that the strenuous efforts made by the Company to proceed with the exploration work were [word missing: thwarted?].

Based on part 3 of Article 35 of the Agreement, the Respondent contends that the resulting postponement of the work ought to be regarded as the consequence of circumstances beyond its control. In confirmation of the fact that the Company made strenuous efforts to proceed with the work, the written rebuttal is accompanied by the transcript of a deposition made by J.P. McCullough to the Secretary of the United States Mission Merritt Swift on 8th May 1924 [in Peking: see Document

(3) below]. In this statement, it is established that the first expeditionary party from the Sinclair Exploration Company set out from New York for North Sakhalin on 27th September 1923. On 29th October, the group arrived in Peking. The authorized representative of the USSR Karakhan[9] issued McCullough and his fellow traveller MacLoughlin with visas to travel to Siberia together with papers which, according to the witness deposition, facilitated their journey through Siberia.

On 5th February 1924, the party left Nikolayevsk and crossed the Tatarsky Gulf on the ice, arriving on 7th February at Pogibi on the coast of Sakhalin, where a Japanese garrison was stationed. When the party presented itself to the Japanese military authorities, its members were detained; and following discussions with the supreme Japanese military command, which refused to allow the group to proceed with the exploration work, the entire party under the supervision of the Japanese secret police were forced to leave Sakhalin and return to Peking.

To clarify the foregoing arguments and objections, the parties gave detailed statements which are entered in the record of the court sessions.

In considering the circumstances of the case and in examining the arguments presented by the parties, the Guberniya Court considers that a judgment has to be made on the following questions:

I Was the petition lodged by the proper claimant?
II Does the performance of exploratory work during the period 7th January 1923 to 7th January 1924 constitute an obligation of Sinclair Exploration Company or its right; and if it constitutes its obligation, should the nonperformance thereof be regarded as a substantive breach of the agreement or as non-substantive default?
III Under what conditions is the Concessionaire entitled to a postponement of performance of the work?
IV Does the occupation of Russian Sakhalin by Japan constitute a circumstance of which the effects equate to force majeure?
V Does the Concessionaire have the right to a postponement of the performance of work under the terms of part 3 of Article 35 of the Agreement?
VI If the Concessionaire failed to carry out exploration work and the Agreement was to be declared null as a consequence of this, should the performance bond of 200,000 roubles be liable to retention by the USSR Treasury and should the letter of guarantee in the sum of 800,000 roubles be cancelled?

---

[9] L.M. Karakhan, Deputy Commissar for Foreign Affairs, then working in China, and from 1924, Soviet Ambassador in Peking.

THE 1921–1923 NORTH SAKHALIN CONCESSION AGREEMENT   81

I

In stating that the petition was brought by the improper claimant, counsel for the Respondent contends that the Agreement was entered into in the name of the Far Eastern Republic, although the Agreement of 16th August 1923 was signed by representatives of the USSR Government, throughout the text of the Agreement it is stated that the party thereto is the RSFSR. Article 1 paragraph (h) of the USSR Constitution states that concession agreements are made both in the name of the Union of Republics [*i.e.* the USSR] and in the name of the Union Republics [*e.g.* the RSFSR]. By construing this statement in a formalistic manner and arguing that the petition was not filed in the name of the RSFSR is not pertinent to a ruling on the substance of this case, even though pursuant to Article 166 of the Civil [Procedural] Code the Court may substitute an improper claimant by a proper claimant, the Respondent presumes that the Court must resolve this question from the standpoint of compliance with the basic principles of the Soviet Constitution.

Having considered this statement, the Guberniya Court finds:

(a) According to Article 1 paragraph (h) of the USSR Constitution, the negotiation of concession agreements both in the name of the Union and of the Union Republics is within the scope of the Union of Soviet Socialist Republics represented by its Supreme bodies;

(b) According to Article 3 paragraph (f) of the Statute of the USSR Council of People's Commissars (Sovnarkom) (Annex 2 to the USSR Constitution), the [word missing: conclusion?] and ratification of concession agreements is within the scope of USSR Sovnarkom;

(c) The object of this petition being the annulment of a concession agreement;

(d) The right to seek annulment of a concession agreement may belong only to the party making the agreement; and as a concession agreement may be made only by the USSR Government, the request for annulment of the agreement must originate from the USSR Government.

In view of this, the Guberniya Court considers that the petition was filed by the proper claimant under Article 166 of the Civil Procedural Code; and that no substitution is warranted.

II

Does the performance of exploration work during the first year of the Agreement constitute a right or obligation of the Sinclair Exploration Company?

The Respondent presents the following arguments on this point: the text of Article 2 of the Agreement states: 'in the course of the first five years of the present concession the Company is not bound to start the extraction of the minerals mentioned in this agreement, but it has the right ... to proceed with explorations concerning the aforesaid minerals ...'. Furthermore, nowhere in the Agreement is it expressly stated that the performance of exploration work is an obligation of the Company. Therefore, there is no basis for considering the performance of exploration work to be an obligation imposed on the Company, the nonperformance of which should constitute grounds for annulment of the Agreement.

In rebuttal of these arguments, the Claimant made a number of points of which the following merit attention in the Court's opinion:

(1) The question of the significance of undertaking exploration work in the first year of the Agreement must be considered closely in the precise context of the conditions under which the Agreement was made.
(2) This question should be decided moreover in the context of a range of other substantive stipulations contained in other articles of the Agreement.

Referring to the precise conditions under which the concession agreement was made, the Claimant points out that in 1922 Sakhalin was occupied by the Japanese. The occupation took place not in connection with acts of war, as Japan was not in a state of war with the FER and the RSFSR. But the fact of the occupation placed the property of the State in a position of effective ownerlessness. The interest of the Government as diligent owner lay in the fact that, if not the State itself, another party acting directly on its behalf should exercise its – that is the State's – rights of ownership. Actual performance of the exploration work was construed as the exercise of these ownership rights.

The Government did not construe the exercise of this serious interest other than as the actual performance of the work in the territory of Sakhalin by the concessionaire. The conclusion must be drawn, therefore, that performance of the exploration work was a serious interest for the State which granted the concession. This being so, the Agreement contains a number of obligations in connection with the performance of exploration. These include the obligation set forth in Article 48 of the Agreement to present to the Government representative not later than 1st December of each current year a technical estimate for the coming year, and not later than 1st May, a statement of operations and exploration work completed in the current year. It is evident from Article 48 of the Agreement that the performance of exploration work constitutes an obligation on the concessionaire and not only its right, insofar as it would be inconceivable to stipulate the obligation to submit estimates for outstanding work without being under the obligation to carry out the work itself.

The Respondent offers the following interpretation of Article 48: The concessionaire was under an obligation to submit statements for work completed in the previous year where such work was carried out; but if the work was not carried out, it would be obliged to submit estimates. This interpretation is contrary to the clear meaning of Article 48 which states: 'not later than 1st December of every year the Company pledges itself to submit ... [a technical estimate for the following year]' and further 'undertakes to submit ... every year not later than on May 1st a statistical report with estimates of the work of exploitation and exploration completed during the preceding year.'

There is no stipulation here to the effect that it is permissible not to carry out the work; no distinction is made here between exploration and exploitation work; no exception is made here for the first year of the concession. Analysis of Article 48 of the Agreement thus leads inevitably to the conclusion that the performance of exploration work in the first year of the concession constituted an obligation on the concessionaire. A number of other articles of the Agreement also contain words to the effect that the performance of exploration work was an essential condition for entering into the Agreement. In this connection, reference is made to Article 1 of the Supplementary Agreement of 7th May 1922 and the beginning of Article 36, where provision is made for the payment of a surety in the sum of 200,000 roubles in the first year of the concession, with the following stipulation: 'but prior to the beginning of exploration activities'. It is clear from this that exploration work was to have been carried out in the first year.

To support the argument that the performance of exploration work during the first year of the concession was part of the Concessionaire's obligations and that the Respondent understood precisely the meaning of these actions, the Claimant also cites the contents of the sworn deposition made by McCullough wherein the latter states that 'the purpose of this expedition ... was to commence exploration work and make preparations for more extensive operations in the following year, in order to fulfil the conditions of the agreement ...'.

Without dwelling on other considerations supporting the argument that the performance of exploration work during the first year of the concession was an obligation of the Company, the Guberniya Court considers that the foregoing constitutes compelling proof that the performance of exploration work in the first year of the concession was an essential obligation of Sinclair Exploration Company.

III

Under what conditions is the concessionaire entitled to a postponement of performance of the work?

The conditions under which the concessionaire has the right to postponement are set forth in Article 35 of the Agreement. The first part of this Article deals with circumstances customarily referred to as circumstances of *force majeure*, such as acts of war, plague, etc. The second and third parts concern themselves with circumstances considered by the parties to equate to circumstances of *force majeure*.

84 ON ARBITRATION

Thus, the general sense of Article 35 is that the concessionaire is granted a post-ponement only in the event of *force majeure*. Other than in these circumstances (normally designated and equated by the parties to the Agreement as *force majeure*), the concessionaire is not entitled to a postponement.

When the liability of any person under an agreement or under the law extends to the limits of *force majeure*, this means that the risk lies with the obligated person irrespective of its fault. This construction of Article 35 clarifies the mutual relations of the parties in the event of failure to carry out the work on time.

Failure to carry out the work on time nullifies the Agreement, irrespective of the culpability of the concessionaire. The Guberniya Court finds that these arguments are entirely consistent with the meaning of Article 35 of the Agreement. As the circumstances referred to in the second and third parts of Article 35 and circumstances equating to *force majeure* are based on conditions of occupation, the Guberniya Court considers that, apart from this, this understanding is wholly consistent with the general meaning of the Agreement as referred to above. The meaning of the Agreement entailed the performance of work on Sakhalin during the occupation. Non-performance of the work during the occupation nullified the basic meaning of the Agreement. It is clear therefore that, in construing the fact of non-performance of the work, the Government could not place the consequences of this fact in direct relation to the culpability or non-culpability of the concessionaire insofar as this is a circumstance of a subjective nature, and could only relate these consequences to objective facts such as circumstances of *force majeure*. The Guberniya Court considers that this formulation of the liability of the obligated person 'up to the limits of force majeure' is consistent with Article 118 of the Civil Code, which stipulates that the liability of a debtor for non-fulfilment of an obligation may also be established under the agreement in the particular case where the obligation is not fulfilled as a consequence of circumstances which the debtor could not prevent.

IV

Should the fact of the occupation of Sakhalin by Japan be regarded as an insurmountable obstacle to fulfilment of the Agreement?

In answering this question, the Guberniya Court notes that, according to the Claimant's assertion, shared also by the Respondent, the parties were aware during negotiation of the Agreement of the fact that Russian Sakhalin was occupied by the Japanese. The Supplementary Agreement dated 7th January 1922, and in particular paragraph 1 of that Agreement, was dictated by the need to take account of circumstances connected with the occupation of Sakhalin. The occupation itself was not regarded by the parties as a circumstance of which the consequences equated to *force majeure*. This is also evident from Article 46 of the Agreement. The beginning of the second part of Article 46 states: 'Prior to the commencement of the exploration work as well as during such time thereafter as the representatives of the Government and of the Company, owing to some insurmountable obstacles, will not be in a position to reside in Russian Sakhalin . . . '

It is clear from this paragraph that the parties envisaged the performance of exploration work during a period when, by virtue of the occupation, there would be an insurmountable obstacle for representatives of the Government and representatives of the Company to be present on Russian Sakhalin. Thus, the parties considered the occupation as a circumstance constituting an insurmountable obstacle to the performance of certain acts and not as such for the performance of other acts, in particular for the performance of exploration work. The occupation itself is not regarded as an insurmountable obstacle. Therefore, solely by virtue of the fact of occupation the concessionaire does not have the right to postponement of fulfilment of the Agreement under the first part of Article 35 of the Agreement.

V

Is the concessionaire entitled to a postponement of the performance of work on the basis of the third part of Article 35 of the Agreement? The answer to this question is related to a determination of the extent of obligations which the Government took upon itself under the second part of Article 35. The second part of Article 35 is worded as follows: 'The Government consents, within the limits of the possibilities at its disposal, to offer legitimate assistance to the representatives and employees of the Company in their operations provided for by this agreement, and to grant to the Company the possibility freely to avail itself of the rights and privileges granted by this agreement'.

The Respondent argues that the 'grant' referred to in the second part of the above paragraph entails the creation for the other party of conditions for free use of the Agreement's object, and since such conditions were not created by the Government, the consequences provided in the third part of Article 35 of the Agreement are invoked, namely that the concessionaire is entitled to a postponement. The Guberniya Court contends that the second part of Article 35 of the Agreement cannot in any way be construed as meaning that the Government undertook the obligation to make the object of the Agreement available to the concessionaire in a freely usable condition.

First, this is clearly evident from the text which refers to the freedom of use of rights and not of the object of the Agreement; secondly the interpretation offered by the Respondent can mean nothing other than an obligation of the Government vis-à-vis the concessionaire to liberate Russian Sakhalin from occupation, the implication of enjoying freedom of use of the object of the Agreement being that this would only be fully possible once the occupation had been removed.

Such a circumstance, to say nothing of its fundamental inconceivability in an agreement with a private entity, would contradict the previously established essential meaning of the Agreement, would effectively defer its fulfilment until the occupation was removed, and would have equated the fact of occupation to a circumstance regarded by the parties as *force majeure*, which as is apparent from the foregoing, the parties did not envisage.

As the concessionaire's obligations in respect of the performance of exploration work extended up to *force majeure*, it could have made a case for postponement if it proved that the Government was culpable in failing to carry out those acts which it was obliged to carry out under the Agreement or culpable in circumstances impeding its attempts to carry out the work. The concessionaire makes no such allegation, and from the documents available to the Court it is apparent that the Government took all possible steps to render assistance to the Company in the exercise of its rights. This is supported by the following documents originating from the Respondent. In the sworn deposition by McCullough, it is stated that Government representative Karakhan assisted the expedition by issuing travel visas and also provided papers which greatly facilitated their passage through the country. A letter by the representative of the Sinclair Company representative Templeton dated 6th March 1924 also contains a reference to the fact that Comrade Karakhan rendered all possible assistance to the expedition.

Hearing of the obstacles placed by the Japanese authorities in the way of representatives of the Company arriving to carry out work on Sakhalin, the USSR People's Commissariat for Foreign Affairs ['Narkomindel'] sent a note of protest to the Japanese Minister of Foreign Affairs, Baron Matsut, on 20th May 1924. The Guberniya Court contends that these and similar actions are the reflection of an undertaking to 'grant [to the concessionaire] the possibility freely to avail itself of the rights and privileges granted by the concession agreement' as provided in part 2 of Article 35 of the Agreement. These actions were taken by the Government. Therefore, no case can be made for the Government's culpability entitling the concessionaire to a postponement.

Based on the foregoing, the Guberniya Court concludes that the Sinclair Exploration Company is not entitled to a postponement of the work under Article 35 of the Agreement, and that non-performance by the Respondent of the work provided in Article 2 of the Agreement and the obligations under Article 48 confer upon the Claimant the right to terminate the Agreement in accordance with Article 41 of the Agreement.

VI

Is the sum of 200,000 roubles paid by the Company by way of surety for the Agreement subject to retention by the USSR Treasury?

THE 1921–1923 NORTH SAKHALIN CONCESSION AGREEMENT   87

The Guberniya Court considers the payment of 200,000 roubles as the imposition of a penalty in accordance with Article 141 of the Civil Code. The term 'penalty' has a dual meaning: a fine for non-fulfilment of an agreement or a means of compensating losses. The Claimant has not stated to the Court that it claims the two hundred thousand roubles as compensation for losses resulting from non-fulfilment of the Agreement; it has not indicated the extent of its losses, but it has stated that it reserves the right to claim compensation by separate petition. Therefore, within the terms of this petition, no order will be made for the payment of a penalty by way of compensation.

At the same time, the Guberniya Court, in accordance with the aforementioned grounds for annulment of the Agreement (in which the element of the concessionaire's culpability for non-fulfilment was not considered insofar as the Agreement was declared subject to annulment irrespective of the establishment of the concessionaire's culpability) and in view of the fact that the Agreement establishes the liability of the concessionaire up to the limits of *force majeure*, has no basis for imposing a penalty by way of a fine. Therefore, the Guberniya Court finds that the sum of 200,000 roubles paid by the concessionaire is not subject to retention by the USSR Treasury. As to the letter of guarantee in the sum of 800,000 roubles, this document is null and void.

In consideration whereof, on the basis of Articles 118 and 141 of the Civil Code, Articles 5, 23, 24, 47, 67, 69, 119 and 166 of the Civil Procedural Code, Article 1 paragraph (h) of the USSR Constitution, and Article 3 paragraph (f) of the Statute of the USSR Council of People's Commissars (Sovnarkom), the Moscow Guberniya Court hereby Orders:

The Agreement made by the Government of the Far Eastern Republic with the Sinclair Exploration Company dated 7th January 1922, the Supplementary Agreement thereto of the same date and the Supplementary Agreement between the Government of the RSFSR and the aforenamed Company dated 16th August 1923 have ceased to have effect and are hereby annulled.

Similarly, the letter of guarantee in the sum of eight hundred thousand roubles (800,000 roubles) furnished by the Sinclair Exploration Company has ceased to have effect.

The sum of 200,000 roubles (two hundred thousand roubles) paid by the Sinclair Exploration Company by way of surety for the fulfilment of the Agreement is not subject to retention by the USSR Treasury.

On the matter of the award of court costs and legal expenses, a separate order shall be made following determination of the cost of the petition for annulment of the Agreement.

This order is final – with possibility of appeal to the Supreme Court within one month.

88   ON ARBITRATION

Document 2

APPELLATE JUDGMENT OF 22ND MAY 1925[10]

DECISION

IN THE NAME OF THE RUSSIAN SOCIALIST FEDERATED SOVIET REPUBLIC ON 22nd MAY 1925 THE SUPREME COURT

THE BOARD OF APPEAL FOR CIVIL CASES

Comprising: Presiding Judge S.M. Prushitsky
Members: A.A. Kramer-Ageyev and F.I. Prokofyev
in the presence of the Public Prosecutor B.M. Brodsky

In open court session, heard the case concerning the petition filed by the USSR Supreme Council of National Economy (VSNKh) against the Sinclair Exploration Company for annulment of an agreement, the appeal lodged by the Sinclair Exploration Company against a ruling made by Moscow Guberniya Court on 21st, 23rd and 24th March 19225 wherein it is ordered:

'The Agreement made by the Government of the Far Eastern Republic with the Sinclair Exploration Company dated 7th January 1922, the Supplementary Agreement thereto of the same date and the Supplementary Agreement between the Government of the RSFSR and the aforenamed Company dated 16th August 1923 have ceased to have effect and are hereby annulled. Similarly, the letter of guarantee in the sum of 800,000 (eight hundred thousand) roubles furnished by Sinclair Exploration Company has ceased to have effect. The sum of 200,000 (two hundred thousand) roubles paid by the Sinclair Exploration Company by way of surety for the fulfilment of the Agreement is not subject to retention by the USSR Treasury.

On the matter of the award of court costs and legal expenses, a separate order shall be made following determination of the cost of the petition for annulment of the Agreement'.

On 6th April 1925 an additional order was made: 'The Guberniya Court finds that the cost of the petition in the sum of 400,000 roubles is fair. In view of the refusal to

---

[10]   GARF 83.50/3/108/198 (Russian).

satisfy the petition in equal parts, the Guberniya Court finds that court costs and legal expenses are not liable to be awarded in favour of either one of the litigant parties.'

Having examined the appeal, having heard submissions by representatives for the Claimant and Respondent and the Public Prosecutor's report, the Civil Appeals Board finds, first of all, that the question raised by the appeal as to whether a concession agreement is law, and at the same time can a breach of a concession agreement be regarded as a breach of the law, and consequently be subject to judgment in a court of appeal, and constitute grounds to overturn a court order, in accordance with Articles 4 and 237 of the Civil Procedural Code, is not pertinent to this case insofar as, according to practice established in the Civil Appeals Board, a court of appeal is permitted to interpret agreements on aspects concerning the clarification of points of general law raised by the agreement. The appeal by the Sinclair Exploration Company may be considered within these terms of reference.

The statement by the Appellant that the petition was filed by an improper claimant, even if it was correct in this assertion, could not constitute grounds to overturn the court order, as the Civil Appeals Board can take no cognizance of formal objections unrelated to the real interests of the litigants. For the Respondent in this case, as acknowledged by its representative at the Civil Appeals Board hearing, it is of no essential significance whether the Claimant is the USSR Supreme Council of National Economy (VSNKh) or the RSFSR; and given that the Guberniya Court, having considered the question of the proper claimant in accordance with Article 166 of the Civil Procedural Code the purpose of which is to eliminate formal objections and delays in court proceedings associated therewith, found no basis for substitution of the original Claimant by another person, the decision of the Guberniya Court, once it came into effect, would guarantee the Respondent against any adverse consequences.

Aside from its purely formal character, this assertion is essentially incorrect. The Appellant based its interpretation on Article 1 paragraph 3 of the USSR Constitution. But in order to arrive at a correct determination, the disputed matter must not be confined solely to the USSR Constitution. Referring to the Constitution of the RSFSR in its latest wording designed to bring it into line with changes brought about by the accession of the RSFSR into the Union, we find therein no stipulations concerning the independent right to enter into concession agreements. The Sovnarkom Decree dated 21st August 1923 on the establishment of the Main Concessions Committee ['Glavkoncesskom'] for the centralisation of concession activities within Union institutions, provides only for the existence in the Union Republics of concession committees subordinated to Glavkoncesskom and having the right to sign only preliminary draft agreements with the authorisation of Glavkoncesskom. Thus, the conclusion reached by the Appellant to the effect that Union institutions have no rights to terminate agreements in their own name and allowing the filing of suits only at the direction of Union Republics, in this case the RSFSR, is not supported in current legislation.

On the question of the determination made by the Moscow Guberniya Court on the interpretation of the Agreement between the Soviet Government and Sinclair Exploration Company, the Civil Appeals Board finds no contradiction in the Court's findings relating to the Respondent's obligation to commence exploration work in the first year of the concession, inasmuch as the Moscow Guberniya Court based its finding upon Articles 2, 36 and 48 of the Concession Agreement and upon their aggregate meaning. The reference made by the Moscow Guberniya Court to the acknowledgement of this obligation on the part of the witness McCullough, whose sworn deposition was presented to the Moscow Guberniya Court by the Respondent, does not require examination in these appeal proceedings.

Similarly, the Civil Appeals Board perceives no inaccuracy in the Moscow Guberniya Court's determination on the interpretation of Article 35 of the Agreement. The inevitable logical conclusion from the interpretation of Article 35 of the Agreement by the Respondent's representatives is a situation wherein the concessionaire merely has to observe certain formalities in order for the initial period of the Agreement to be extended until such time that, as a result of the activity of the other contracting party (the Soviet Government) it was able to proceed with the exercise of its rights under the Agreement. The incorrect interpretation of Article 35 of the Agreement stems from the incorrect interpretation of the term 'force majeure'. An impediment preventing the fulfilment of an obligation becomes force majeure not by virtue of its internal inherent properties. As shown in the Civil Appeals Board judgment in the case of 'Omsk Otmestkhoz' versus the Siberian Railways Board (Ref. N 28-24), even a natural occurrence such as a fire should not invariably be equated with the notion of force majeure and release from liability. An impediment to the fulfilment of an obligation becomes force majeure depending on the interplay of a whole range of conditions and circumstances. Something that is easily surmountable in one place in one set of circumstances may become insurmountable in another. Something that one contracting party is able to overcome may be impossible for the other. Determination of whether or not a set of conditions and circumstances constituting force majeure actually existed is a matter of substance and is not subject to challenge by an appellate procedure. However, precisely because of the relative nature of the concept of force majeure itself, no merit whatsoever can be found in the Appellant's argument that the occupation of North Sakhalin by Japanese forces is covered by this concept. An agreement cannot be made while recognising that conditions exist that are insurmountable for the contracting parties at the same time as the agreement is being negotiated. Therefore, the Moscow Guberniya Court is quite correct in finding that the fact of occupation does not fall within the terms of Article 35 of the Agreement and regarding the relations between the parties on the basis that, in entering into Agreement, the parties constructed their rights and obligations with respect to each other on the fact of the occupation of the object of the agreement by Japanese forces.

It is impossible to ignore a serious contradiction in the Appellant's arguments. At the beginning of the appeal, the Respondent's representatives developed the thought that a concession agreement is not an ordinary type of agreement, that it falls within the ambit of Article 4 of the Civil Procedural Code, *i.e.* it must be interpreted in accordance with the general principles of Soviet Law and the general policy of the Workers' and Peasants' Government. However, in oral submissions on the question of interpretation itself, the Appellant emphasizes that the question of the guiding purpose of each party in entering into the Agreement is not pertinent and Article 35 of the Concession Agreement ought to be interpreted as one of the clauses in any agreement, *i.e.* applying the general principles of the law of obligations. This contradiction leads the Appellant to conclude its argument with the proposition that the grant of rights stipulated under the Agreement is inseparable from the grant of the object of the Agreement. There is no basis for denial of the possibility of entering into transactions in respect of property held in foreign and, from the standpoint of the contracting parties or one of them, unlawful possession, insofar as both parties took account of and stipulated this obligation during negotiation of the Agreement.

If the Appellant's proposition were logically followed through to its conclusion, it would be necessary to cast doubt on the validity of the Agreement from the very outset, in that under Article 1 of the Supplementary Agreement of 7th January [1922], the Agreement may be terminated in the event that the Government of the North American United States fails to render assistance to the Concessionaire. However, the Respondent cannot be responsible for the actions of the Government of the North American United States. Nevertheless, the Concessionaire accepted this condition, and the possibility of predicting the actions or declarations of the Government of the North American United States during the year is no different from predicting the actions of occupying forces in Sakhalin. And the entire centre of gravity of the dispute was correctly found by the Moscow Guberniya Court not in the question of whether it was possible to predict the nature of the actions of occupying forces, but in the question of the significance to the parties in negotiating the agreement of the fact of occupation and, following on from this, the question of the limits of the concessionaire's liability, and the question of increased liability stipulated in Article 35 of the Agreement.

In consideration of the foregoing, and finding no breach of the law in the order delivered by the Moscow Guberniya Court, the Civil Appeals Board hereby rules: that the appeal lodged by representatives of the Sinclair Exploration Company is not upheld.

92 ON ARBITRATION

Document 3

DEPOSITION OF MR JOSEPH PAUL MCCULLOUGH OF 8th MAY 1924[11]

Republic of China
City of Peking
Notarized

Before me, Merritt Swift, Second Secretary to the United States Mission in Peking, being duly authorized and qualified for the purposes hereunder, did appear in person one J.P. McCullough who, having been duly sworn, made the following representation and statement under oath:

My name is Joseph Paul McCullough. The following is an official and true report of the First Expedition of Sinclair Exploration Company to North Sakhalin:

Following the approval in Moscow on 28th August 1923 [sic] of a Concession Agreement between the Union of Soviet Socialist Republics and Sinclair Exploration Company for the development of lands in the territory of Sakhalin Island north of the 51st parallel, for the extraction of oil, natural gases and mineral resins, the Company sent a preliminary exploration party to the island.

The purpose of this expedition, comprising myself, D.T. MacLoughlin and a Russian assistant and interpreter, was to commence exploration work and make preparations for more extensive operations in the following year, in order to fulfil the conditions of the agreement. To achieve this purpose, we took with us technical documents, engineering equipment and other supplies sufficient for an extended stay on the island.

The party left New York on 27th September 1923 and travelled through Canada to the west coast, from where we departed for Shanghai on 5th October 1923. We arrived in Peking on 29th October 1923. I presented my credentials to the delegated representative of the Union of Soviet Socialist Republics in Peking, Mr. Karakhan, who issued Mr. MacLoughlin and myself with visas to enter Siberia, and gave us papers which greatly facilitated the party's journey through Siberia. Our Russian, Mr. Lopukhin, who did not have full citizenship of any country, was refused entry into Russian territory and, as the party could not wait for papers granting him citizenship to arrive from Moscow, he was sent back to America.

---

[11] GARF 8350/1/944/39 (Russian: the original version in English was translated into Russian for the legal proceedings in Moscow, as certified by the First Moscow State Notarial Office on 9th March 1925 (Register No. 5573); that original version has not been found in the Moscow Archives; and this English text has been translated back into English from the Russian translation).

THE 1921–1923 NORTH SAKHALIN CONCESSION AGREEMENT   93

I travelled to Vladivostok by rail, where I was later joined by Mr. MacLoughlin who had arrived with the baggage by steamer from Shanghai. In Vladivostok, we took on I.M. Yaroslavtsev as interpreter to make up the party. Here we also purchased furs, provisions and certain necessary equipment and, to take advantage of the opportunity to travel down the Amur, the party left Vladivostok on 11th January 1923 by rail for Khabarovsk.

In Khabarovsk we obtained horses and sleds, and the party set out for Nikolayevsk on 17th January 1924. Thirteen days were spent on the road and we arrived in Nikolayevsk on 30th January 1924. A Russian driver and assistant, who were making a private journey to Sakhalin, were hired to escort the party to Aleksandrovsk and, having obtained permission from the authorities to travel to Sakhalin, we left Nikolayevsk on 5th February 1924.

Travelling down the Amur from Nikolayevsk to the mouth of the river, then south along the mainland coast, we passed through the last Russian staging post on the morning of 6th February 1924 and stopped for the night in the Gilyatsky village of Yarka. Early the next morning we crossed the Tatarsky Gulf on the ice and arrived at the coast of Sakhalin Island some 15 versts north of Pogibi, where a Japanese garrison was stationed. The party entered Pogibi at 1.15pm on 7th February 1924.

Individual permits to travel to Sakhalin had been issued by the Nikolayevsk authorities to all members of the party, including the driver; Mr MacLoughlin and I held United States passports properly stamped by the Russian authorities, and Mr Yaroslavtsev held a Russian passport. These passports were shown at the request of the Japanese who inquired as to the purpose of our visit to Sakhalin. We did not attempt to hide anything. I requested permission to travel on to Aleksandrovsk, stating that we were in Sakhalin on behalf of the Sinclair Exploration Company in connection with a concession agreement between the Union of Soviet Socialist Republics and the Company, and I presented a letter of authority from the Sinclair Company.

The post commander indicated that this information would be transmitted by telephone to the military governor in Aleksandrovsk and, until instructions were received from him, we would be required to remain in Pogibi. We were put in a poorly-heated draughty room, where it was very difficult to wash and prepare food and which was made to feel very uncomfortable by the presence of people and animals seeking shelter from the snowstorm. Our request for permission to move to more comfortable accommodations in the nearby village of Vangi was ignored. At this time we were asked to hand over all our papers which were carefully copied, and a garrison officer tried several times to obtain information from Mr. Yaroslavtsev about expedition members and conditions in Siberia.

Colonel Sato, Chief of Staff Lieutenant-General Inuwe, and the Commander in Chief of the Japanese Expeditionary Army in Sakhalin arrived in Pogibi on the

94 ON ARBITRATION

evening of 7th February 1924 and departed on 9th February 1924, having seen none of the members of our party, but leaving behind an accompanying staff interpreter.

In the afternoon of 9th February 1924, all our verbal protests having been ignored, I wrote a message to the garrison commander pointing out the discomfort our party was suffering and requesting, as an American citizen, an immediate reply to my previous request for permission to travel to Aleksandrovsk or sufficient reason for our detainment, in more comfortable accommodations. Early that evening, General Inuwe sent instructions to the garrison commander to provide for the comforts of the 'gentleman agents of Sinclair'. Before nightfall we were given a more suitable room in the officers' quarters.

In a message to General Inuwe, I reiterated my request to travel to Aleksandrovsk, stating that in my opinion it was not possible to reach a clear mutual understanding of a situation having more than a passing significance at such a distance, through interpreters. On 13th February 1924, General Inuwe replied that exploration was not allowed in this area and that the party was not permitted to enter the territory of Sakhalin Island. To my request to provide a fuller explanation, General Inuwe replied that mining and excavation operations could only be carried out by those who had started their work before the occupation, and that no new companies would be allowed: 'Therefore you are not allowed'.

I then requested permission for the party to leave Sakhalin as private citizens via the southern post of Otomari. I was told that we would encounter cold, smallpox and numerous other dangers on the road. I repeated my request in answer to this. General Inuwe then offered to arrange passage from Aleksandrovsk to Otaru aboard a navy ice-breaker which was due in port in a few days. This offer was accepted and we left Pogibi for Aleksandrovsk on 16th February 1924 accompanied by Japanese staff interpreter, Mr. Honda.

The journey to Aleksandrovsk was made in four days, and the party arrived there in the afternoon of 19th February 1924. On the way we stayed in Japanese military posts. No deviation from the direct route was permitted and Mr. Honda was present at all times.

General Inuwe invited the members of our party to dinner in the evening of the day of our arrival in Aleksandrovsk. He spoke excellent English and this resulted in a much more satisfactory conversation. He explained that neither Japan nor the United States recognized the Russian Government now in existence, that Japan could not therefore recognize any agreements made by that Government, and that the matter must be settled between Tokyo and Washington.

The next morning we were escorted to the ice-breaker, and on 1st March 1924 we arrived in Otaru [in Hokkaido]. From there we set off for Kobe, under the constant supervision of the Japanese secret police. From Kobe, I returned to Peking by

THE 1921–1923 NORTH SAKHALIN CONCESSION AGREEMENT   95

rail, Mr. MacLoughlin followed on with the baggage by steamer to Tian-Shin, and Mr. Yaroslavtsev returned to Vladivostok via Churugu.

(signed) J.P. McCullough   Notarized and sworn in my presence, on this day

Preliminary Exploration   8th May 1924, Merritt Swift
Team Leader   Second Secretary to the United States Mission.
[Stamp]

6

Lloyd George, Lenin and Cannibals

The Harriman Arbitration[*]

A. Introduction

Over 35 years ago, on a warm summer's evening on 26 July 1963, two elderly men walked across the Kremlin Square towards the Terem Palace. The shorter man was the First Secretary of the Central Committee of the Communist Party and the Chairman of the USSR Council of Ministers, Nikita Khrushchev. The second man was tall, looking like the millionaire son of a millionaire, which was what he was. He had served as the American ambassador to Moscow and London; and he had worked as a personal adviser to Presidents Roosevelt, Truman and now, President Kennedy. He had also been elected Governor of New York and had been a candidate for his party's nomination for President. An Anglophile, he had been a supporter and friend of Winston Churchill in London during the darkest days of the Second World War, a good friend of his son Randolph; and as it proved, an even closer friend of his daughter-in-law, Pamela (who later, much later became his wife). This man was William Averell Harriman.

No two men could have been more different in background, outlook and character than Krushchev and Harriman; or so it might have seemed. As they approached the far side of the Kremlin near the Palace of Congresses, people waiting to enter this concert-hall applauded Khrushchev; and he began to shake hands with the crowd. At some point, as recorded by journalists present, Khrushchev

---

This is a revised version of the author's 1999 School of International Arbitration Freshfields Arbitration Lecture delivered on 24 November 1999. The editors acknowledge with thanks permission to publish this contribution granted by Freshfields and the School of International Arbitration, Centre for Commercial Law Studies, Queen Mary and Westfield College, London University

---

[*] For access to the unpublished papers of Leslie Urquhart, I am much indebted to his grandson, Neil Foster, and his biographer, Professor Kett Kennedy, Mining Tsar: The Life and Times of Leslie Urquhart (Sydney, 1986). I am also grateful for help in researching the American, British and Russian archives (and other materials) from Naomi Benson, Micheline Decker, Artemis Kassi, Nudrat Majeed, David Mortlock, Tatyana Nazarenko, Sebastian Veeder, Sam Wordsworth and Ikko Yoshida. Of course, any errors are mine alone.

On Arbitration. Edited by: Sam Wordsworth KC and Marie Veeder, Oxford University Press. © Oxford University Press 2023. DOI: 10.1093/oso/9780192869135.003.0006

turned to introduce Harriman, addressing him as a friend and colleague, a fine fellow (in Russian '*molodiets*'): 'This is Mr Harriman. He has just signed a test-ban agreement with us and now I am taking him to dinner. Do you think he has earned his dinner?' And the crowd cheered both men.[1] This was the occasion of the 1963 Moscow Treaty between the United States, the USSR and the United Kingdom, banning nuclear tests in the atmosphere, space and ocean. There were several significant moments between 1945 and 1989 where the Cold War took a decisive turn away from nuclear conflict; and this occasion was certainly one of them – barely nine months after the Cuban missile crisis and only 15 months before Khrushchev's fall from power.[2]

B. The Harriman Concession (1925)

Now what was the reason for this open cordiality between Khrushchev and Harriman? It did not exist with the British negotiator, Lord Hailsham. As recorded in his memoirs, Lord Hailsham regarded Khrushchev as a 'very remarkable human being whose coarseness of language and anecdote absolutely beggared description'; and as for Harriman, Lord Hailsham strongly deprecated (in his judgement) Harriman's unnecessary toughness in negotiating with the Soviet Government.[3] To Khrushchev, Harriman should have been the paradigm Soviet class and political enemy – but he was not. In his memoirs, Khrushchev warmly described Harriman as 'a highly realistic man, an experienced specialist who understood us',[4] and Khrushchev based the beginning of that special understanding on Harriman's early involvement in a Russian mining concession. In a muddled form, dictating his memoirs secretly into a tape-recorder at his dacha without access to contemporary papers long after he left power, Khrushchev recalled Harriman's concession as follows:

> It was common knowledge – I think I even read about it in the newspapers – that Harriman's family used to own some manganese mines in Georgia before the Revolution. I heard confirmation of this from Stalin's own mouth after the

---

[1] 'Life', 9 August 1963, 28ff; *see also* W. Averell Harriman, *America and Russia in a Changing World* (London, 1971), p. 99; and Isaacson and Thomas, *The Wise Men* (London, 1986), p. 633.

[2] Khrushchev had long been badgered towards this partial test-ban treaty by the father of the Soviet hydrogen bomb, Dr Andrei Sakharov: *see* A. Sakharov, *Sakharov Speaks* (London, 1974), pp. 33-34; and Khrushchev (Talbott ed. and trans.). *Krushchev Remembers – The Last Testament* (London, 1974), pp. 69-71.

[3] Hailsham, *A Sparrow's Flight* (London, 1990), pp. 340-343; G.Lewis, *Lord Hailsham* (London, 1997). pp. 204-213. Somewhat unkindly, Hailsham regarded Harriman as 'already ageing'. In return, Hailsham did not endear himself to Harriman at all: *see* W.Isaaeson and E. Thomas, *supra* n. 1, at p. 631 ('the shallow and ill-prepared Lord Hailsham').

[4] Krushchev, *supra* n. 2, at p. 382.

[1941-45] war ... Stalin mentioned in passing that it might be a good idea to compensate Harriman in some way for the loss of his mines. I don't know if anything ever came of the suggestion. I know it wasn't discussed in the leadership. Nothing was discussed in the leadership. Stalin could not stand to have his ideas questioned or deliberated. He might let you talk to him if you agreed with him.[5]

In fact, the Harriman concession had been granted *after* the Bolshevik Revolution, in 1925. At a time when the United States had firmly spurned any diplomatic or other official contact with the USSR, Harriman had been one of the first American traders to take advantage of the Soviet policy on foreign concessions, with the help of American and German capital. The Harriman concession was eventually a commercial failure; and after three years, Harriman terminated his concession on agreed terms, including compensation payable by the USSR. The Soviet Government honoured that settlement; and it was still paying off the final instalments when Harriman arrived in Moscow in late 1941 as Roosevelt's personal envoy to Stalin.

It was this early, personal experience which gave Harriman his 'special' understanding of the realities of Soviet power, to which thereafter, for the next 60 years of his life, he was always adamantly opposed as a politician and diplomat. Harriman was no appeaser; but equally, he was a realist: his toughness as a negotiator in business and diplomacy was the means to an end and never an end in itself. Harriman is recognised as one of the great statesmen of the twentieth century; and he was perhaps the greatest diplomat ever to serve the United States of America, a task he performed almost to the end of his long life in 1986, aged 94.

C. The Harriman Arbitration (1928)

All this may seem a long way from international commercial arbitration. And yet, Harriman's settlement was the direct result of arbitration proceedings brought by his company against the USSR in 1928. These proceedings secured Harriman's amicable exit from the concession with financial compensation, a feat not equally achieved by any other British or US concessionaire. Also, in taking on the Soviet Government by means of an arbitration, Harriman plainly earned its respect; or in Khrushchev's telling words: Harriman 'understood us'. The Harriman arbitration was one of the first international arbitrations to which the USSR was a party, predating even the Lena Goldfields Arbitration of 1930;[6] and it was certainly

---

[5] *Ibid.* p. 351.

[6] Under the 1921 and 1925 German-Soviet Treaties, there had been a number of non-consensual arbitrations between Soviet and German parties; but their number and extent are contested; *contrast* A. Nussbaum, 'Treaties on Commercial Arbitration – A Test of International Private-Law

LLOYD GEORGE, LENIN AND CANNIBALS   99

the first arbitration between the USSR and any American firm.[7] The proceedings were kept confidential by both parties, then and later; Harriman never spoke about the arbitration publicly; nor did the Soviet Government.[8] It is only the later release of archives in Moscow and Washington which allows us to know the story at all.[9]

D. 'Why' Is Arbitration?

The story of the Harriman arbitration addresses a question on international commercial arbitration which may need answering for the beginning of the twenty-first century, 76 years after it began with the League of Nations' Geneva Protocol on Arbitration Clauses of 1923 and 41 years after the New York Arbitration Convention of 1958. In recent Freshfields lectures, we have heard a great deal about 'what' is arbitration and 'how' is arbitration; and I can add nothing useful to those answers, so superbly given by previous Freshfields lecturers. In this lecture, I should like to address the different question, 'why'; or in short, why does international commercial arbitration exist at all?

It is now axiomatic that in the field of transnational trade all over the world, arbitration is the preferred method for resolving business disputes; but its

---

Legislation' (1942) 56 *Harv. L.Rev.* 219, 220 and E.S. Rashba, 'Settlement of Disputes in Commercial Dealings with the Soviet Union' (1945) 45 *Col. L.Rev.539* at p. 546 n. 82. (Underlying the English test cases surrounding the 1921 Anglo-Soviet Trade Agreement, there had been an arbitration clause in the timber sale contract agreed between Krassin and Sagor in August 1920; but that contract was probably collusive in order to test the position under English law in regard to third party claimants: *Luther v. Sagor (also 'Sagor')*[1921] 3 KB 532, 7 Lloyds Rep. 218, 109, 157 (Court of Appeal), reversing [1921] 1 KB 456, 5 Lloyd's Rep. 451, 287 (Roche J); *Walneff v. The All-Russian Co-Operative Society* (1921) 8 Lloyd's Rep. 338 (Bailhache J); and *Bragoseo v. Sagor* (1921) 8 Lloyd's Rep. 388 (Sankey J)).

[7] Dr Armand Hammer referred to an 'arbitration' in the summer of 1924 between Sinclair Oil and the Soviet Government, cancelling a concession over oil fields in Northern Sakhalin: *see* Hammer, *The Quest of the Romanoff Treasure* (1932), p. 141. This was a concession agreement granted in 1922 to Sinclair Exploration Company but cancelled by the Soviet Government in 1924 on the ground that the concessionaire had failed to take up its concession (because the Japanese still occupied Sakhalin and refused it entry); there was in fact no arbitration and the termination was ordered by the Moscow People's Court: see B. Landau, 'Konzessionsen in Sowjetrussland' *Ostrecht* 1926 No. 5, 478, at p. 487 (Professor Landau was a legal specialist on foreign concessions in Moscow).

[8] Harriman never referred to it in his writings or interviews; and before the Lena Goldfields Arbitration in 1930, the Soviet Government denied that any arbitration had ever taken place with any of its concessionaires.

[9] The American archives on the Harriman concession are found principally at the US National Archives, Washington DC, US State Dept Decimal File 861.637 (cited *infra* as 'US Decimal File'); and the archives of the USSR Main Concessions Committee (*Glavkoncesskom*) are kept at the State Archive of the Russian Federation in Moscow (cited *infra* as 'GARF'). I have also made extensive use of Leslie Urquhart's extensive private papers, an invaluable archive on microfilm (cited below as 'Urquhart Papers'), which was commissioned by Professor Kennedy for his outstanding biography, *supra* n. **.

100   ON ARBITRATION

increasing popularity cannot be explained solely by the relative enforceability of awards under the 1958 New York Convention, as compared with national court judgments. Its attraction preceded the New York Convention; and even then it did not depend upon the more limited effect of the 1923 Geneva Protocol or 1927 Geneva Convention. Nevertheless, its age is deceptive: international arbitration is still precocious and its existence less assured than it might seem. The number of international arbitrations is relatively small compared to the increasing volume of transnational trade; and its jurisprudence is surprisingly slight given that the wealth of the world is now predominantly made up of contractual promises. For example, its jurisprudence does not begin to compare historically with the weight of law made by (say) the English Commercial Court in London or the Federal and State Courts in New York. The efficacy of its procedures is even now being sorely tested by users and practitioners, in England and elsewhere; and it remains uncertain whether it can survive these tests in their more extreme form. And so 'why' is international arbitration is a big question; the complete answer remains elusive, at least to me; but my answer here is happily confined by the title of this lecture.

From 1920, the development of foreign trade with Soviet Russia and the USSR took place in political, economic and legal conditions utterly hostile to the development of international commercial arbitration; and yet it did develop. In the early months of Soviet Russia, before the Soviet policy on foreign concessions and Lenin's New Economic Policy, the Soviet leaders were legal nihilists deeply antipathetic to commercial law and the independent adjudication of civil law disputes. Indeed there was then no civil or commercial code in Soviet Russia; the Czarist codes and courts had been swept away; and in the words of Lenin's principal specialist on legal affairs, A.G. Goikhbarg: 'Each conscious proletarian knows ... that religion is the opiate of the people. But very seldom does anybody realise that law is a still more poisonous and intoxicating opiate for the same people'.[10] The Harriman arbitration was thus a flower which sprang from poisonous and blasted ground; and moreover this was not *terra incognita* but *terra nova*. The Harriman arbitration was nonetheless no solitary plant. It blossomed against the background of the 1923 Geneva Protocol, the creation of the ICC Court of International Arbitration in 1922; and the new world-wide interest in commercial arbitration as an alternative to state courts – because the immediate origin of all these events was essentially the same.

---

[10] See O.S. Ioffe and P.M. Maggs, *Soviet Law in Theory and Practice* (London, 1983), p. 14 (yet, Goikhbarg was also partly responsible for the 1922 RSFSR Civil Code, on which he also published a leading commentary; this code was promulgated in the autumn of 1922 as a result of the NEP and the 1922 Genoa Conference; and its terms were heavily influenced by the French and German civil codes: *see* E.H Carr, *Socialism in One Country 1924-1926* (London, 1958) p. 75ff).

E. Peace Through Trade

From the beginning of the Versailles Conference, the British Prime Minister, Lloyd George, had promoted the view that the future for peace lay with transnational trade. Even after the Versailles Treaty of 1919, at a time when much of Europe lay impoverished or in famine, with many of her workers unemployed and her factories silent, Lloyd George still promoted 'Peace through Trade'. Thwarted by the malign efforts of others, Lloyd George's policy had failed in regard to Germany, with tragic results. However, that same policy now almost succeeded with Soviet Russia. His efforts to re-establish trade and diplomatic links with Soviet Russia led the British Government in January 1920 to open negotiations with the Soviet Government in the guise of the Trade Delegation from the Russian Co-Operative Societies; in March 1921 to conclude the first Anglo-Russian Trade Agreement, with *de facto* recognition; and in 1922 to convene the Genoa Economic Conference which Soviet Russia attended, along with representatives or observers from 34 countries (whether or not members of the League of Nations or even recognised by each other). From the beginning, Lloyd George also contended that essential to trade, as trade was to peace, was a system of law and a process for deciding legal rights; and from his earliest meetings with the leader of the Soviet Trade Delegation (Krassin), Lloyd George secured agreement on the process of arbitration.[11] Lloyd George's policy towards Soviet Russia was bitterly opposed by France and by members of his own cabinet, including the Foreign Office (which played no significant part in the 1921 Trade Agreement or even the 1922 Genoa Conference). In the House of Commons on 7 June 1920, Lloyd George defended his negotiations with the Soviet Trade Delegation, in these terms:

> It is quite a new doctrine that you are responsible for the Government when you trade with its people. Were we responsible for the Czarist Government? Were we responsible for it, with its corruption, its misgovernment, its pogroms, its scores of thousands of innocent people massacred? We were not responsible for this, yet we continued our relations. Why, this country has opened up most of the cannibal

---

[11] At their first meeting on 31 May 1920, both Lloyd George and Krassin raised the question as to the legal basis on which trade could be conducted (*Documents on British Foreign Policy 1919-1939*, Vol. VIII, No. 24, p. 281 at pp. 284, 290-291); and at their meeting on 16 June 1920, when Lloyd George contended that British traders had no knowledge and therefore no confidence in Soviet Russia's judicial system, Krassin replied that he was prepared to agree to the establishment of an 'arbitration court' (partly British and partly Russian) to settle such disputes (Lloyd George MSS, House of Lords Library, Folder 3, Box 107 No F/202/3/19, pp. 8 and 11). The latter meeting was also attended by the Norwegian explorer, Dr Fridjof Nansen, who countersigned the minutes as a fair summary of the proceedings. (For reasons which remain obscure, there was no reference to arbitration in the eventual 1921 Trade Agreement).

102 ON ARBITRATION

trade of the world, whether in the South Seas or in Kumassie.[12] Have we ever declined to do it because we disapproved of the population?[13]

Later on 3 April 1922, before the Genoa Conference, Lloyd George laid out the basic principle in his new policy towards Soviet Russia: 'We have failed to restore Russia to sanity by force. I believe we can save her by trade. Commerce has a sobering influence in its operations'.[14] Again, this was 'Peace through Trade'. This double-edged reference to cannibals, however, was never popular with the Soviet Government.[15]

The Genoa Conference failed in May 1922; its follow-up conference at the Hague in June-July 1922 did not succeed; there was no Marshall Plan for economic recovery; the United States remained aloof from European affairs; and Lloyd George left office in October 1922, never to hold public office again. But Lloyd George's policy of Peace through Trade is the great lesson of the twentieth century. It is the policy which at last brought permanent peace between France, Germany and Western Europe; and the rock on which the future depends for the European continent (from Cork to Khabarovsk) – and the world. Yet the same question remains today as it did for Lloyd George: even assuming that we are not listed on the menu and the cannibals are not warming the pot, how exactly do you do business with cannibals? The Anglo-American experience with Soviet concessions in the period up from 1920 to 1929[16] shows that there is an answer: you can eat with cannibals if the spoon is long enough; and if that spoon (or one of them) is international commercial arbitration.

F. Soviet Concessions Policy

The Soviet policy on foreign concessions pre-dated Lenin's New Economic Policy; but by 1921, the two were related in the Soviet Government's conduct of foreign trade. From the beginning, this policy was a massive departure from all previous Soviet economic policies. First, in offering back as concessions industrial properties confiscated from their former foreign owners, the Soviet Government was virtually restoring those properties to the control and benefit of those former owners.

---

[12] Kumasi is now in Ghana.
[13] Hansard, Vol. 152, col. 1898 (3 April 1922).
[14] Hansard. Vol. 152, col. 1898 (3 April 1922).
[15] Gromyko and Ponomarev (ed.), *Soviet Foreign Policy 1917-1980*, Vol. 1 (1917-1945) (Moscow, 1981), p. 129. In the Lena Goldfields Case, the German and British arbitrators were attacked in Pravda on 9 September 1930 for making an award without the third Soviet arbitrator, on the otherwise curious ground (*inter alia*) that as 'bad jugglers of figures' unable even to amuse children, 'they ought to find their audience amongst the savages of the Pacific islands who do not know how to count up to three'.
[16] In 1929, the Soviet Government's foreign concession policy effectively ended when Stalin introduced the First Five-Year Plan.

Although title to such properties was retained by the Soviet Government, the long term of the concession was commercially similar to the leasehold estate held by the foreign owner on lands owned by the Czar (which had been common for Siberian mining properties). Second, the right freely to export and import granted to the foreign concessionaire was a major exception to the Soviet Government's foreign trade monopoly. Third, the concession delivered over to the foreign concessionaire rights over Soviet labour and Soviet trade unions, as an extraordinary exception to the general law. Fourth, the Soviet Government suspended many of its powers against the foreign concessionaire and its foreign employees: for example, the right to enter and leave Soviet Russia freely, exemption from oppressive taxation, immunity from requisition of labour and materials, and so on. Lastly, and most important for present purposes, the Soviet Government was prepared (eventually) to exempt the foreign concessionaire from the Soviet courts in regard to disputes over the concession. For all these reasons, a concession agreement was much more than a private law contract under Soviet law: it was also a special higher law derogating from the general law.

In fact, there was then little Soviet law on contractual and civil obligations. The Russian Civil Code came only in late 1922, partly as a result of Lloyd George's endeavours in London and Genoa; the 1923 Russian Civil Procedural Code did not permit commercial arbitration at all; and of course Soviet Russia could not ratify the 1923 Geneva Protocol or 1927 Geneva Convention. That was a strange irony: the Geneva Protocol was conceived at the Genoa Conference which had passed on the project to the League of Nations at Geneva.[17] But whilst it was possible for Soviet Russia to support arbitration at Genoa, it remained politically hostile to the League of Nations and as a non-member, it could not accede to the 1923 Protocol or 1927 Geneva Convention; and it never did so.

G. Urquhart and Hammer

The Harriman Arbitration was preceded by a number of false starts. He was preceded by two other concessionaires from the United States and the United Kingdom: Leslie Urquhart of Russo-Asiatic Consolidated Limited and Dr Armand Hammer, then of the Allied Drug and Chemical Corporation.

---

[17] Article 14 of the Resolutions of the Genoa Conference's Economic Committee, relating to the best means of safeguarding the validity of voluntary agreements for international commercial arbitration, was referred by the League's Council at its meeting on 13 May 1922, on the British Government's initiative, to a sub-committee of six experts of its Economic Committee; the chairman of this sub-committee was F.D. MacKinnon KC (soon to become Mr Justice MacKinnon); and after a drafting session on 3-4 July 1922 at the Board of Trade in London, the eventual result was the 1923 Geneva Protocol: *League of Nations Official Journal*, June 1922 (pp. 616, 618, 620); August 1922 (pp. 987, 992, 1004); and November 1922 (p.1410).

104   ON ARBITRATION

(1) The Urquhart Negotiations (1921)[18]

The first concessionaire, British or American, was to have been Leslie Urquhart. He was a Scottish mining engineer, then the chairman of Russo-Asiatic Consolidated Limited, an English company run from London which had controlled the largest copper, zinc, and iron mines in the Urals and Western Siberia before the October 1917 Revolution. Its mines had also produced silver and lead (60 per cent of Russia's total annual production), extending over a million hectares of land. Born in Russia in 1875, Urquhart had spent almost 25 years working in Russia before the October Revolution, dealing in liquorice to oil in the Caucasus as well as minerals in Siberia; he was well-informed on Russian affairs; he spoke good Russian; and his rotund appearance, in the later words of one Soviet official 'made him seem the reincarnation of an old-time Russian landowner, an enlightened nobleman of tsarist times'.[19] In every sense, Urquhart was a huge figure in Russia before and after October 1917, with enormous physical and financial courage. As Vice-Consul in Baku during the 1905 Revolution, he had been awarded the Victoria and Albert Medal for saving the lives of the British community, the equivalent today of the George Cross. After 1905, Urquhart built up his Siberian mines with English and American capital, which included the financial and engineering skills of Herbert Hoover, long before he became Secretary of Commerce and later President of the United States. After the nationalisation of his company's properties in 1918, Urquhart's company had registered claims for compensation against Soviet Russia in the massive sum of £56,000,000 (about one third of the total for such British claims); but the Soviet Government vehemently denied such claims, even if it had any money to pay such compensation (which it did not).

And so after the Anglo-Soviet Trade Agreement, in early June 1921, Urquhart attempted to obtain long leases over four of his former mining enterprises in negotiations with Krassin, the head of the Soviet Trade Delegation in London, in the form of a longterm concession. He and Krassin became friends; and the latter was frequently invited with his family to Urquhart's country home. Krassin was an unusual revolutionary: an electrical engineer, he had been a director of Siemens in St Petersburg before the First World War; and he was almost as much a practical businessman as Urquhart himself. After preliminary discussions, Krassin invited Urquhart to visit Moscow in August and September 1921; Lenin encouraged these negotiations (in which he took part personally); and a draft concession agreement

---

[18] *See generally* T.S. Martin, 'The Urquhart Concession and Anglo-Soviet Relations, 1921-1922' *Jahrbücher für Geschichte Osteuropas* 20 (1972), pp. 551-559; K.H. Kennedy, *supra* n. **, p. 162ff; Lubov Krassin, *Leonid Krassin: His Life and Work* (London, 1929), p. 184ff; and S.I. Liberman, *Building Lenin's Russia* (Chicago, 1945), p. 159ff.

[19] S.I. Liberman, *ibid*, at p. 159. (Liberman, a Soviet foreign trade specialist in timber, worked with Krassin in London before defecting from the USSR Commissariat for Foreign Trade).

was prepared. Given Urquhart's position as a major claimant, this draft agreement was intended by the Soviet Government to establish publicly its policy of the former foreign owner being offered back his confiscated property under a long-term concession agreement, on terms which included the waiver of all claims for compensation arising from nationalisation. Accordingly, the Soviet Government was not merely negotiating a contract with Urquhart: it was also seeking to establish a public precedent.

There were, however, several grave problems, one of which concerned the arbitration clause where the Soviet Government was insisting that the chairman, or umpire, must be a Russian nominated by the Russian Academy of Science. There was a meeting of the parties' joint commission on 12 September 1921 in Moscow which recorded their very different starting-points: 'Arbitration Commission: The Soviet Government representatives insisted on the candidate for the position of arbiter being a Russian subject. This the Concessionaire categorically refused to accept and insisted on the wording of his own draft clause'.[20] Back in London, on 21 September 1921, Urquhart reported the difficulty to his board and principal shareholders; and as those minutes record:

Clause 21: The Meeting strongly felt that an arbitrator must of necessity be a free and unprejudiced person whose actions are not controlled in any way by either of the contracting parties, and who is free from any restriction or restraint of any kind which might directly or indirectly tend to prejudice his findings in favour of either party. For this reason the Meeting emphasised that the President of the proposed Arbitration Committee should be a person of position and experience, unprejudiced in any way, and the Meeting decided that it could not withdraw the proposal that, failing mutual agreement, such President should be nominated by the American Society of Mining and Metallurgy.

And as the board and principal shareholders concluded:

It was the unanimous feeling of the Meeting, in view of the suppression of the [Czarist] Civil Code, the suppression of Mining and Forest Regulations and of the power previously held by the local authorities in regard to schools, hospitals, roads etc, that the Company is running very great risks in signing an Agreement of this nature without the new conditions pertaining to these or any new institutions which may be established clearly set forth in the Agreement; and it was decided that until this is done, an Arbitration Clause, giving an unprejudiced arbitrator the widest powers, is deemed a vital necessity.[21]

---

[20] Urquhart Papers, Reel 7, p. 5985 at p. 5987 (in English; but note Urquhart's use of the Scots term 'arbiter' and not 'arbitrator').
[21] Urquhart Papers, Reel 4, p. 3369 at pp. 3370 and 3371.

106   ON ARBITRATION

Urquhart then continued his negotiations with Krassin in London; but neither side would budge on the arbitration clause.[22] Urquhart and his board were adamantly insisting upon a neutral presiding arbitrator; and the Soviet Government insisted that he must be a Soviet citizen. This dispute over the arbitration clause was one of the principal reasons for the collapse of the negotiations in mid-October 1921; and Urquhart withdrew from further talks with the Soviet Government, with a strongly-worded announcement to his shareholders. This was a severe public blow to Soviet prestige, only six months after the Anglo-Soviet Trade Agreement which had promised so much but so far delivered little.

At a subsequent meeting of the Council of Labour and Defence chaired by Lenin, a Soviet foreign trade specialist (Liberman) recalls Lenin asking what had happened to the negotiations with Urquhart[23]: 'Whatever has become of our Comrade Urquhart? We do not hear of him or about him any more. And yet he was so polite and obliging when he was here on his visit. He was so full of flattery that we thought any minute now he might file an application for membership of the Communist party!' After a moment's silence, the answer came from the Vice-Commissar of Foreign Trade, Moisel Frumkin, Krassin's deputy and an old Bolshevik, in these terms:[24]

> Let me tell you a Jewish story: A Jewish woman was very sad because her husband had gone away and showed no sign of returning to her. Her friends finally advised her to go to a wise rabbi with the question, 'When will my husband come back?' But, as was usual in such minor cases, the rabbi's assistants would not let her in for a personal interview with the sage. She had to submit the question in writing ... An assistant brought back the rabbi's answer: 'Your husband will return in two weeks'. Two weeks passed, and two more, and still there was no husband. The woman went to the rabbi again, sent in the question ... for the second time, but received the same written reply: 'Your husband will come back in two weeks'. But when a month had elapsed after that, with no result whatsoever, and then a third month, the indignant woman demanded a personal meeting with the rabbi. It was granted. The rabbi listened to the woman, then said: 'Your husband won't return at all'. Heartbroken, crushed, the woman left the rabbi's study. On her way out she encountered the assistant and she halted to berate him for deceiving her with the two previous answers, allegedly given by the rabbi. But the assistant said: 'I didn't deceive you. Those first two replies were from the rabbi'. 'But why',

---

[22] The negotiations were formally terminated by Urquhart in mid-October 1921 during a visit to Krassin in London, followed by a long letter quoted in Lubov Krassin, *supra* n. 18, pp. 188-198. Urquhart did not blame Krassin personally; and his letter went through many drafts before its final version, clearly aimed at another audience in Moscow.

[23] Liberman, *supra* n. 18, at p. 162.

[24] M.I. Frumkin, shot on 29 July 1938: see R. Conquest, *The Great Terror* (Oxford, 1990), p. 120.

wailed the poor woman, 'why did he say on those first two occasions that my husband would come back to me?' 'Because the first two times he didn't see you in person!' was the assistant's explanation. 'Well, Vladimir Ilyich', Frumkin summed up, 'we should all understand why Urquhart will never return. He hadn't seen us before he came here'.

There was, however, one immediate beneficiary from the failure of Urquhart's negotiations in October 1921. After this public disappointment, the Soviet Government needed a quick propaganda victory for its foreign concession policy, preferably with an American untainted by connections with Britain. Speed and other circumstances therefore dictated a friendly co-contractor, a political pilgrim already trading in Moscow. That friendly American resident trader existed in the person of Dr Armand Hammer, then only 25 years old and still at the very beginning of his extraordinary business career, or careers.[25] Within three very short weeks, Hammer became the first American concessionaire in Soviet Russia.

(2) Hammer's First Concession (1921)[26]

In his great study on Soviet concessions, the American historian Anthony Sutton places Dr Hammer and his family firmly in the group of foreign concessionaires with non-economic links to the Bolshevik cause, their contribution being to lead the way and to instill confidence in the Soviet Government in the hope that other genuine foreign traders would follow.[27] Hammer's first concession was a concession agreement of 28 October 1921 for the Alapayesk asbestos mine near Ekaterinburg in the Urals;[28] and it was publicly announced in Moscow on 3 November 1921 as a 'victory for the concession policy of the Soviet Government'.[29] The Alapayesk mine was a small mine; it was never a successful concession; and it lost money for

---

[25] Hammer's special business skills are best illustrated in the case decided by the English Commercial Court in *Occidental Worldwide Investment Corp.* v. *Skibs A/S Avanti and others (The Siboen and Sibotre)*[1976] 1 Lloyd's Rep 293 (Kerr J).

[26] *See generally* Armand Hammer. *The Quest of the Romanoff Treasure* (1932), p. 149ff; A.C.Sutton, *Western Technology and Soviet Economic Development 1917-1930* (Stanford, 1968), pp. 108, 237, 268, 285; S. Weinberg, *Armand Hammer: The Untold Story* (London, 1989), p. 42ff; and E.J. Epstein, *Dossier: The Secret History of Armand Hammer* (New York, 1996).

[27] Sutton, *supra* n. 26, at pp. 283 and 285ff.

[28] Armand Hammer, *supra* n. 26, at p.84. It was signed in the Commissariat of Foreign Trade by Hammer and Boris O. Mishell for the Allied Drug and Chemical Corporation and P.A. Bogdanov (Chairman of VSNKh) and Maxim Litvinov (as Vice-Commissar of Foreign Affairs) for the RSFSR (GARF 8350/3/833, p.4 *see also* Urquhart Papers, Reel 4, p. 3684, for an English translation, without the addendum).

[29] Letter to Urquhart dated 16 February 1922 from the Department of Overseas Trade (Foreign Office and Board of Trade), relaying a despatch from the British Commercial Mission in Moscow with an English translation of Hammer's concession agreement, then still confidential (Urquhart Papers, Reel 4, p. 3682).

108 ON ARBITRATION

Hammer; but it was soon amicably terminated, in or before 1924, having served its immediate political purpose.

In fact, as legal document, this concession agreement was a sham. We can tell because it had a most peculiar arbitration clause, contained in a confidential addendum. In the concession agreement itself, article 19 provided that the Soviet Government could terminate the concession by decree if the concessionaire was in breach; article 21 provided that the concession agreement could also be cancelled 'in a [Soviet] court of law'; and article 30 provided for Soviet court jurisdiction over all disputes. However, Hammer had also secured an amendment to these draconian provisions; the addendum was drafted by Hammer, and as recorded by him in English, it read as follows:

> To avoid all red tape, delays and hindrances, the [Soviet] Government undertakes to appoint a committee of two persons, one from the Workers' and Peasants' Organisation and one from the 'Cheka' to whom in case of misunderstandings, we can refer as competent authority to settle all disputes without loss of time.[30]

Lenin agreed this addendum without hesitation;[31] and why not? Unlike Urquhart, Hammer was not seeking the appointment of any neutral arbitrator. And Lenin doubtless had great confidence in the Soviet worker or peasant arbitrator, particularly if he or she were guided by a Soviet co-arbitrator from the Cheka, the Soviet secret police little known for its lack of partisanship in the Soviet cause. And we should note here the absence of any third arbitrator or umpire (neutral or otherwise). With a Chekist as co-arbitrator, it would not in practice be necessary to have a third arbitrator or any other tie-breaking mechanism.

Not surprisingly, the Soviet Government never publicised Hammer's addendum containing this arbitration clause; and Lenin's *Collected Works*, as published over the years in Moscow and abroad, omitted any reference to its terms.[32] The friendly termination of this asbestos concession meant that the 'Cheka' arbitration clause was never invoked by Hammer; and indeed, how could it be? For a real arbitration clause intended to provide an effective remedy, it was necessary to await the return of Leslie Urquhart.

---

[30] Armand Hammer, *supra* n. 26, pp. 49 and 82. (The first organisation was RKI or Rabkrin, the Workers' and Peasants' Inspection (*Rabochaya i Krest'yanskaya Inspektsiya*).

[31] Hammer's version was an incomplete draft, limited to five clauses. There was a further draft (in Russian) signed in English by Hammer and Mishell on 28 October 1921; and the final version was signed by Lenin on the following day as chairman of the RSFSR Council of Peoples' Commissars, with seven clauses (GARF 8350/3/83, pp. 12 and 13; GARF 8350/1/83, p.8). Subject to a slight difference in wording, probably caused by translating Hammer's text into Russian, the 'Cheka' arbitration clause remained the same.

[32] *See*, for example, V.I. Lenin, *Collected Works* (London, 1970), Vol. 45, pp. 362, 394, 684. Yet, Hammer published his version of the addendum in 1932; but like several statements in this book, at the time maybe no-one took it too seriously.

(3) Urquhart's Concession Agreement (1922)

As Lloyd George pursued his foreign policy on Soviet Russia further into 1922 with the Genoa and Hague Conferences, the earlier breakdown in negotiations over the Urquhart concession proved only temporary. Urquhart attended both conferences, as chairman of the Association of British Creditors in Russia and as an unofficial adviser to the British Government; and so did Krassin for the Soviet Government. During the summer of 1922, shortly after the Hague Conference had dispersed, negotiations resumed between Urquhart and Krassin, on the Soviet Government's initiative. These negotiations were soon successful; and a concession agreement was signed in Berlin on 9 September 1922 by Krassin and Urquhart for a period of 99 years – subject to formal ratification by the Soviet Government within one month.

The arbitration clause was a compromise of the parties' previous positions. There would be five arbitrators, two appointed by each party and the fifth presiding arbitrator, if not agreed by the four arbitrators within one month, would be chosen by the concessionaire from a list of six candidates drawn up by the Soviet Government, who would be 'of world wide or European fame as learned men, lawyers, engineers or public men'. This form of wording did not necessarily exclude a Soviet citizen; but equally it did not necessarily mean that all six candidates would be Soviet citizens. It was a major compromise by the Soviet Government towards accepting a neutral presiding arbitrator. There was another compromise by Urquhart: the arbitration must sit in Moscow; but its decisions would be final and require immediate fulfilment. And if the concessionaire or the Soviet Government defaulted in the machinery for appointing any arbitrator, the other innocent party could then refer the dispute to the London High Court or the Moscow People's Court (as the case might be).[33]

The news of this concession agreement spread around the world: it was seen as an historic breakthrough. Krassin left immediately for Moscow to procure the Soviet Government's ratification; and that is when the trouble began. On 5 and 6 October 1922, at Lenin's insistence and in his presence, the Central Committee and the Council of People's Commissars refused to ratify the Urquhart concession. The true reasons remain unclear, partly because Lenin (already ill) changed his mind more than once. One reason given at the time by the Soviet Government was the continuing absence of diplomatic relations between Soviet Russia and Great Britain, with *de jure* recognition; and another reason was the British Government's

---

[33] The concession agreement was signed and sealed by Krassin and Urquhart, the former using the seal of the RSFSR (as authorised by its Council of Peoples' Commissars) and the latter (for want of the company's seal in London) his personal signet ring with the Urquhart clan's motto: 'mean, speak and do well' (PRO FO371/8162; Urquhart Papers, Reel 4, p. 3690; Lubov Krassin, *supra* n. 18, p. 199). The arbitration clause was contained in article 22 of the agreement.

110 ON ARBITRATION

then refusal to admit Soviet Russia to the Lausanne Conference on the Turkish Question. Maybe Lenin feared that the Urquhart concession would still bring no large foreign loans urgently needed for industrial recovery in Russia. And maybe, looking at the concession agreement, Lenin did not like it as a public precedent for other foreign concessionaires: whilst not offering any compensation for the loss of its property rights, the concession agreement nonetheless granted to the foreign concessionaire an advance of £150,000 in cash and 20 million roubles in Russian state bonds; and this concessionaire, as an active supporter of the former 'White' Kolchak regime in Siberia, had been severely criticised by the Soviet Government's Mikhailov Commission. However, whatever the reason or reasons, there is no evidence at all that Lenin's veto was based on the existence of an arbitration clause where the balance of decision-making could lie with a neutral non-Soviet presiding arbitrator.

This veto was Lenin's firm and final decision on the Urquhart concession, one of the last political decisions in his working life; and the Soviet Government made it public on 7 October 1922. Krassin was bitterly disappointed; and as he wrote from Moscow on the following day to his wife in London: 'Once again all my work, energy, efforts and ability have been wasted, and a small group of mules and imbeciles have undone all my work, just as a boy might destroy the thin web of a spider with one blow'.[34] Krassin then sought to resign from his post as Commissar for Foreign Trade; but his offer was bluntly refused by Lenin: 'We dismiss people from their posts; but we do not permit them to resign'.[35] Urquhart never received his concession; and Lloyd George's Government fell in the following week, on 19 October 1922. However, what was Soviet Russia's loss became Australia's gain. Urquhart then devoted the remaining years of his life to developing a new mine in Australia; and today Mount Isa Mines in Queensland remains a tribute to Urquhart's huge mining and financial skills.

H. The Harriman Concession Agreement

By 1923, the Soviet policy on foreign concessions appeared to have failed. There were a large number of small concessions mostly with German and Baltic firms; but there was nothing in the form of 'superconcessions', in Krassin's phrase, from either Britain or America. The position began to change with the United Kingdom's *de jure* recognition of the USSR on 1 February 1924; and in June 1924 in New York, negotiations began between Harriman and representatives of the Soviet

---

[34] Lubov Krassin, *ibid*, at p. 203.
[35] Lubov Krassin, *ibid*, at p. 204, Krassin then fell ill; he recovered and eventually died in London on 24 November 1926. His family did not return to the USSR.

Government. These negotiations were protracted, partly because Harriman was concerned to keep the support of the mines' former owners, particularly those in Germany; and the Soviet Government was coordinating its negotiations with other British and American interests concerned with mining concessions in Siberia, the Lena Goldfields Company[36] and the Tetihue Mining Corporation.[37] All three involved British and American capital; Lena Goldfields was to be the largest concession ever granted by the USSR; and Harriman's concession was to be the second largest.[38]

The Harriman concession agreement was eventually signed on 12 June 1925 in Moscow; and it included an elaborate arbitration clause in Russian and English. The concession concerned a large manganese deposit at Chiatura, to the west of Tbilisi in Georgia, an area which before the First World War had been the world's largest producer of manganese, producing almost half the world supply. The deposit had then been worked by a number of small private owners: Georgian, German, Belgian and French. Their mines had been confiscated by the Soviet Government (without compensation), after the Soviet invasion of independent Georgia in February 1921. (Harriman bought up their claims as a condition of the concession agreement in return for a share of the profits). Harriman undertook to work the whole deposit for 20 years, covering 7,000 acres, to build a modern concentration plant and a new broad-gauge railway and to import the technical services of US and British mining engineers. It was a vast project in difficult terrain, in every sense.

Harriman was also taking a calculated commercial risk: the world-wide demand for manganese in steel production was relatively stable; and accordingly the world

---

[36] Lena Goldfields was an English company; and under its concession agreement made in April and November 1925, in the Russian language only, it took over its own former mining properties in Siberia. This agreement contained an elaborate arbitration clause; and it was negotiated by the Soviet Government in tandem with the arbitration clause in the Harriman concession (which was made in both Russian and English). The two arbitration clauses are therefore very similar (but not identical); and although the Lena Goldfields clause was agreed earlier in time, it became effective later. (The history of the Lena Arbitration in 1930, two years after the Harriman Arbitration, has already been told elsewhere: see the author's article in (1998) 17 *ICLQ* 717 appending the Lena arbitration clause, with the references there cited).

[37] The Tetihue Mining Corporation Limited was also an English company incorporated on 18 May 1925 (its London Soheitors were Freshfields, Leese and Munn). Unusually, it was formed to take over an existing concession granted by the Soviet Government on 25 July 1924 to Russian citizens who had been the previous owners of these lead, silver and zinc mines 230 miles north of Vladivostock in Eastern Siberia. If a copy exists of this 1924 concession agreement, it has not been found; but as a Soviet concession, it would probably not have contained any arbitration clause. The concession was terminated under a settlement agreement made in 1932 without recourse to arbitration.

[38] For the history of the Harriman concession, *see generally* Harriman, *supra* n. 1, at pp. 2-7; W. Averell Harriman and Elie Abel, *Special Envoy to Churchill and Stalin 1941-1946* (New York, 1975); E.J. Kahn Jr, 'W. Averell Harriman Profiles Plenipotentiary – II', The New Yorker (10 May 1952), pp. 19-51; J.E. Spurr, 'Russian Manganese Concession' *Foreign Affairs* V, No. 3 (April 1927), pp. 506-507; C. Lewis, *The United States and Foreign Investment Problems* (Washington DC, 1948), p. 178; W. Isaacson and E. Thomas, *supra* n. 1, p. 99; and E.H. Carr, *Socialism in One Country*, Vol. 3, Pt I (London, 1964), pp. 183-185. (None of these memoirs, interviews or histories records the Harriman Arbitration).

112   ON ARBITRATION

price of manganese was highly sensitive to over-production. Harriman thought that he had bought control of all Soviet manganese exports; but he was to be proven wrong. In addition to competition from new manganese mines in other parts of the world, the Soviet Government (with German technical assistance), soon decided to break his *de facto* Soviet monopoly by opening itself a new manganese mine in the Ukraine; and there were to be other grave difficulties for Harriman in operating the concession. To avoid financial disaster, Harriman soon resorted to the concession agreement's arbitration clause.

I. The Harriman Arbitration Clause

At a time when there were no institutional arbitration rules acceptable to the Soviet Government, it is not surprising that the Harriman arbitration clause was a long clause providing detailed rules on the composition of the arbitration tribunal, the conduct of the arbitration and the enforcement of its decisions.[39] The clause consisted of 17 distinct provisions, only a few of which are here relevant: the full English version is appended below.[40]

The first paragraph was an attempt to ensure that all disputes between the Soviet Government and a concessionaire including its interpretation, execution, performance and breach should be referred to and determined by an arbitration tribunal. The second paragraph was crucial: the Soviet Government there agreed that there would be three arbitrators, two designated by the parties, but the third, the presiding arbitrator, was to be designated either by mutual agreement of the parties or by a special procedure ensuring that he would not be a Soviet arbitrator. This was a significant first step for any state at that time, but particularly for the Soviet Government. It ensured that in the event of a dispute, it would be determined not by the Soviet Government or its nominee, but by an independent neutral third arbitrator as chairman of the arbitration tribunal. This model is today standard form for international arbitration, except that all three arbitrators (not just the chairman) are required to be impartial and independent of the parties.

Paragraph 3 set out the procedure if there was to be no mutual agreement between the parties on the appointment of the presiding arbitrator. If within 30 days, there had been no agreement by the parties, then the Soviet Government was within two weeks to name six candidates from professors of the University of Paris (the Sorbonne) or from professors of the University of Oslo; and it was from those

---

[39] As to enforcement of its decisions by (*inter alia*) a system of prescribed fines (paragraph 14), the arbitration tribunal's powers long foreshadowed the apparently innovative and controversial article 1709bis of the New Belgian Arbitration Law of 19 May 1998, which provides: 'the arbitrators may impose a fine on a party for non-compliance'; *see* (1999) *Arb Int* 101 at p. 102.

[40] The concession agreement was published by the USSR in or shortly after 1927 (GARF 8350/4/105, p.1). For the Lena Goldfields arbitration clause, *see* (1998) 17 *ICLQ* 717 at p. 790.

French and Norwegian professors that Harriman would be required to choose, again within a two week period, the one professor who would be the chairman and third arbitrator. Paragraphs 4 and 5 dealt with a situation where one or other party failed to comply with its obligations of nomination or choice of these several professors; and the result of these provisions is that neither party could take unfair advantage from a failure to nominate or choose. In that event the clause gave both the choice and designation of the presiding arbitrator to the non-defaulting party. This was also significant: the arbitration clause thus contained its own self-help provisions in the event of default which did not require an application to any state court for the appointment of the presiding arbitrator.

Paragraph 6 again was significant in the context of what we know today as the 'truncated tribunal'. It provided that if upon receipt of a summons from the presiding arbitrator, fixing the date and place of the first meeting, an arbitrator could not attend, or refused to participate in the arbitral award, then the disputed matter at that hearing could at the request of the other party, be decided by the chairman and the other arbitrator. It was a similar provision in the Lena Goldfields Arbitration which in 1930 allowed the German chairman and the British arbitrator to hold the hearings and make an award even though the Soviet Government had deliberately withdrawn its arbitrator in order to frustrate those proceedings. Today, where a state party can prevent an arbitrator from attending a hearing, as recent events have confirmed, this kind of provision is still needed for international commercial arbitration.[41]

Paragraph 7 protected the two arbitrators and the parties in the fixing of dates and places. Both the chairman and the arbitration tribunal as a whole were required to take into consideration the time reasonably necessary for each one of the parties to prepare for the journey, arrive in time at the destination, and also the accessibility to either party of the appointed place within the time fixed. By omission, it is plain here that Moscow was not fixed as the legal place (or seat) of the arbitration. That place would be fixed first by the neutral chairman and secondly by all three arbitrators (see Paragraphs 11 and 12); and it would thus be likely that a neutral place would be fixed, such as Oslo or Paris. Indeed, the Soviet Government's advisers then generally assumed that the place of the arbitration would be the place of the chairman's residence. Again, this was an important development which is now standard form. As with footballers in the European Cup, no-one likes playing in the other team's home stadium; and for arbitration users, almost invariably, a neutral place is the preferred solution.

In short, this arbitration clause (like the arbitration clause in Lena Goldfields' concession agreement) was a giant leap forward for international commercial arbitration. As regards the Soviet Government, it established, by contractual

---

[41] For example, *see* article 12(5) of the ICC Rules and article 12 of the LCIA Rules, see also *Himpurnia v. Indonesia*, Interim Award of 26 September 1999, Mealey's Int. Arb. Rep. 15, 1, A-1 (2000).

114 ON ARBITRATION

negotiation and not by treaty, the essential principle of neutral arbitration, with a neutral chairman at a neutral place.

J. The Harriman Versus USSR Dispute

At first, the Chiatura mines were successfully worked; and their exports represented a large percentage of world production. But by 1926, Harriman was experiencing difficulties with the Soviet Government, particularly over the latter's development of its large new mine at Nikopol, north of Odessa, which inevitably depressed the world price for manganese ore;[42] and unwisely in his concession agreement, Harriman had agreed to pay a minimum royalty on a guaranteed minimum production, regardless of actual sales or prices. There were also difficulties with the Soviet Georgian Government, technical difficulties in building the new broad gauge railway; labour troubles with the local miners' union; and a looming problem over the new official exchange rate required to buy roubles for local expenditure (which doubled Harriman's local costs).

In Berlin, on 4 December 1926, Harriman met Chicherin, the Soviet Commissar for Foreign Affairs; and these negotiations were sufficiently promising for Harriman to travel to Moscow to negotiate with the chairman of the Main Concession Committee, Trotsky. This was Trotsky's last official post within the Soviet Government, from which he was dismissed less than a year later, shortly before his internal exile to Alma Ata. With Chicherin's assurance that an adjustment satisfactory to all parties could be found, Harriman (as he records in his memoirs) spent four hours in detailed discussions with Trotsky on 28 December 1926:[43]

> We went over the concession agreement in detail, paragraph by paragraph. His mind was like a steel trap; he understood rapidly what I was talking about but in no way revealed his own attitude on what I had said ... At the end of each point he asked me politely whether I had anything to say, and when I replied in the negative he proceeded to the next one. After we had concluded the analysis of our concession he asked me if I had anything further to add. When I indicated I had concluded, he got up and shook hands with me ... turned on his heels and walked toward the door through which he had entered.[44]

---

[42] Hammer also identified the sharp fall in the world price for manganese as the cause of the Harriman's concession's failure: see Hammer, *supra* n. 7, at p. 121.

[43] Trotsky was dismissed on 17 November 1927; and he was exiled to Alma Ata on 16 January 1928; *see* D. Volkogonov, *Trotsky* (London, 1996), pp. 303 and 306. (He was succeeded as head of the Concessions Committee by V.N. Ksandrov, and later, L.B. Kamenev, both of whom were to deal with Harriman).

[44] Harriman, *supra* n. 1, at pp. 3 and 4.

LLOYD GEORGE, LENIN AND CANNIBALS 115

Harriman believed that Trotsky's conduct was caused by a justifiable concern that their conversation was being recorded and its possible effect on his precarious political position; and this impression was later confirmed by Trotsky's own interpreter whom Harriman met again during the war, in Moscow.[45] In the Moscow archives, there is indeed an apparently verbatim account of the meeting between Harriman and Trotsky. It records a short meeting, lasting less than 30 minutes and far short of the four hours recalled by Harriman in his memoirs. Moreover, Trotsky intervened on numerous occasions; and many of his points were extremely sharp. This document concludes with the following exchange:[46]

> Trotsky: What should I advise the Government? During the last year and a half production has frozen and the number of workers reduced. At the same time the concessionaire demands: first, instead of a wide-gauge railway, construction of which would cost not less than 6-7 million dollars and which was the concessionaire's obligation to build, according to the concession agreement, – to spend 2 million dollars for improving the narrow-gauge railway; second, to lower the minimum quantity for export; and third, to lower the royalty per ton. We have no right to interfere with the production and technical operations of the concession, but at the same time a sliding scale puts us in a position of risk, connected with the concession's trading operations. And finally, nothing gives us a warranty that the concessionaire will not one day turn from an ally into an enemy.
>
> Harriman: We do not do things like that.
>
> Trotsky: But in history we have many examples of that. Italy prior to 1914 was an ally with Germany and Austro-Hungary, but that did not prevent it during the war from going over to the Entente [the Allies]. And the United States did not consider that a crime. I raise such sensitive questions because I am being asked the same questions. I believe that openness should be the basis of business relations, as well as personal relations.

And on that sour note, the meeting apparently ended. After Moscow, Harriman visited Georgia and the Chiatura mines, where he concluded that there was no future in the concession. His discussions with Trotsky had not succeeded;

---

[45] Trotsky's interpreter was George Andreychin, a Bulgarian and former American resident who was arrested in 1935 during the Great Terror but later released, meeting Harriman again in Moscow and Paris during and after the war (*see* Harriman and Abel, *supra* n. 38, at pp. 49 and 556). In Maxim Litvinov's (assumed) *Notes for a Journal* (New York, 1955), Trotsky is recorded as complaining to Litvinov about his post in 1926, suspecting that Stalin appointed him head of the Concessions Committee 'purposely to compromise him in the eyes of young communists ... It's already being said that I'm on Averell Harriman's pay-roll' (p. 23).

[46] GARF 8350/1/802, p. 198ff (translated into English).

116   ON ARBITRATION

there were still problems with 'the government and railroad bureaucracies'; and Harriman had also now gathered that Stalin was opposed to foreign concessions. More significantly, Harriman had become convinced that the Bolshevik Revolution was, in his words, a 'reactionary revolution' and a 'tragic step backward in human development'.[47] There was nonetheless, on 7 July 1927, an amendment agreed to the concession agreement; but it only postponed the inevitable rupture.[48]

On 6 March 1928, Harriman commenced arbitration proceedings under the concession agreement. He appointed James Richardson Glass as his arbitrator. Glass lived in London; but he may have been an American. By telegram of 17 March 1928, the USSR appointed as its arbitrator, Dr S.B. Chlenov, a lawyer working at the Soviet Trade Delegation in Paris, a friend of Ilya Erenburg and a schoolfriend of Nikolai Bukharin. (This same Dr Chlenov was later to be appointed arbitrator in the 1930 Lena Goldfields Arbitration). It also gave notice of a defence and counterclaim in the same telegram, followed by letter of 23 March 1928. By consent, the parties extended the time for the appointment of the third presiding arbitrator; and the USSR began to draw up its list of six names as required by the arbitration clause, which included the Norwegian explorer and representative of the International Red Cross, Dr Nansen.[49] Significantly, each of the Soviet Government's six nominees was a serious candidate as a neutral presiding arbitrator.

Before the Soviet Government was required to submit its list to Harriman for his choice under the arbitration clause, the parties' negotiations in Berlin and Paris were successful in resolving their disputes; and a settlement agreement was signed in Moscow on 28 August 1928. Both sides took a realistic view of their respective prospects of success in the arbitration; and indeed neither claim nor counterclaim could succeed in full. The Soviet Government was advised that requiring Harriman to conduct all foreign exchange through the USSR State Bank (at highly disadvantageous exchange rates) could be seen as a measure

---

[47] Harriman, *supra* n. 1, at p. 7. (Harriman only returned to Russia in late 1941 as President Roosevelt's special envoy; and again in 1943 as the US Ambassador to the USSR).

[48] The 1927 amendment also confirmed a novation between W.A.Harriman & Co Inc and the Georgian Manganese Company Lunited, both of Delaware, USA and controlled by Harriman (as permitted by article 66 of the concession agreement).

[49] Article 65(3) of the concession agreement: *see* Appendix *infra*. The six were Professor Halvdan Koot (Vice-President of the Norwegian Academy of Sciences and a member of the Nobel Committee), Av. Professor Edv Bull (former Norwegian Foreign Affairs Minister, VicePresident of the Norwegian Labour Party and a historian on Marxism and the October Revolution); Dr Nansen (who had attended one of the meetings between Lloyd George and Krassin in 1920: *see supra* n. 11), Professor Stand (former rector of Oslo University and member of the Nobel Committee), Professor Killnau (an economist) and Professor Knoph (a professor of jurisprudence) (GARF 8350/1/811, p. 103 and GARF 8350/1/823, p. 11). These names had been selected by the Soviet Ambassador to Norway and Sweden, Mme Alexandra Kollontai. (In the 1930 Lena Goldfields Arbitration, the USSR's first choice as presiding arbitrator was to be Professor Albert Einstein of Berlin, another serious candidate regrettably rejected by the English company).

LLOYD GEORGE, LENIN AND CANNIBALS   117

amounting to partial expropriation;[50] but in so far as Harriman's case rested on a monopoly of Soviet manganese exports, it would fail on the terms of the concession agreement itself (which granted no such monopoly). He had taken a commercial risk; and things had just not worked out for him on the world market for manganese ore.

There was therefore no arbitration award in the Harriman Arbitration; and the settlement was recorded in a formal order terminating the arbitration proceedings, signed by the two arbitrators in Paris on 14 September 1928.[51] The compensation agreed by the USSR was US$3.45 million, to be paid over 15 years by interest-bearing state notes with a face value of US$4.45 million. The compensation was not sufficient to recover Harriman's investment; but certainly he left the Soviet Union without the heavy losses suffered later by other foreign concessionaires, including Lena Goldfields and Tetihue Mining. As Harriman also recognised, his concession's withdrawal from Chiatura left their local employees, particularly the young women interpreters and secretaries of educated or 'bourgeois' background, exposed to recriminations from the Soviet Government. As he recalled in his memoirs: 'We tried to keep in touch with them and their families and assist them financially, but one of the tragedies of the operation was the unhappiness that came to these intelligent and decent people'.[52] It was more than unhappiness; and the Soviet employees of Lena Goldfields were also to suffer savage treatment in 1930.

The figures immediately troubled the US State Department when it learnt of the settlement: if the Soviet Government agreed to settle at US$3.45 million, why did it agree to pay US$4.45 million, with interest? The answer came soon from the Chase National Bank, which under the USSR state notes was the paying agent in New York for the USSR State Bank.[53] It transpired that the greater sum also included a separate loan of US$1 million at 7 per cent interest made by another Harriman company to the USSR as an inducement to agree the

---

[50] This advice came privately from the Soviet arbitrator, Chlenov, who was 'generally pessimistic' regarding the Soviet Government's case, although he did not agree with all Harriman's arguments (GARF 8350/1/823, p. 118). Other Soviet officials expressed the view that by virtue of circumstances over which neither party had any control (the development of world manganese production), Harriman was guilty of a breach of the concession agreement; and the compensation paid to him was 'a matter of pure expediency; not as the payment of anything that is legally due' – attributed to a high Soviet metallurgical authority from Moscow by the US Embassy in Berlin, possibly V.I. Mezhlank, vice-president of VSNKh and responsible for the Soviet iron ore and manganese industry (US Decimal File 861.637-Harriman/14: D.C. Poole's letter of 19 November 1928).

[51] GARF 8350/1/815, pp. 145 and 140.

[52] Harriman, *supra* n. 1, at p. 6. The US Commercial Attache in Prague later reported that a number of Harriman's Soviet employees had been imprisoned without trial after the settlement and that two stenographers had been sent to Siberia on 10-year sentences (US Decimal File 861.637-Harriman/27: K.L. Rankin's letter dated 17 July 1929 to the Department of Commerce based upon an interview with B. Rascovitch, one of Harriman's former consulting engineers in Georgia).

[53] Letter dated 24 October 1928 from the Chase National Bank, New York (Reeve Schley) to the US State Department (US Decimal File 861/637-Harriman/18).

118   ON ARBITRATION

settlement.[54] This was the first commercial loan ever granted by any American financial institution to the Soviet Government, an important precedent then and now.[55]

Significantly, the settlement agreement also contained an arbitration clause, almost identical to the arbitration clause in the original concession agreement. It dropped the reference to Oslo University as a choice for the presiding arbitrator, limiting that choice to the Sorbonne in Paris. It was needed. In 1930, there were minor difficulties over the implementation of the settlement; and this time the arbitration clause was invoked by the Soviet Government, again appointing Dr Chlenov as its arbitrator. Harriman responded with a defence and counterclaim, appointing as arbitrator Professor Nolde and proposing a list of three candidates as neutral chairman.[56] All three were rejected by the Soviet Government; and Harriman in return rejected its proposed candidate as chairman (significantly, again a serious candidate as a neutral presiding arbitrator).[57] As before, however, it appears the parties amicably resolved their disputes without ever appointing a chairman or proceeding to an award.

Notwithstanding these disputes over the settlement agreement, the USSR eventually paid in full its state notes, principal and interest.[58] So Harriman was lucky; but he was a lucky man with two effective arbitration clauses. Without those remedies, luck might not have been sufficient for Harriman. In 1928 and 1930, Harriman was merely a private investor without any home state protection: the United States was not to recognise the USSR until 1933.

[54] The lender was the Russian Finance and Construction Corporation, a Harriman company formed in Delaware, USA (GARF 8350/1/814, p. 236).

[55] As well as sweetening the Soviet Government's financial obligations under the settlement, the loan also secured for Harriman the release of a guaranty bond in the sum of US$1 million, which had been issued on his behalf by the National Surety Company of New York in favour of the Soviet Government under article 67 of the concession agreement.

[56] Harriman proposed Professor Max Huber (of Switzerland), Professor Walter Shuking (of Kiel University), or Marcel Plezan (a French Senator from Paris). The Soviet Government was compiling its list of six Sorbonne professors (none lawyers because, as it complained, the Sorbonne then had no law school); but it was looking at other candidates for agreement with Harriman, including Professor Nussbaum, then of Berlin University, (GARF 8350/1/823). Its eventual nominee (but rejected by Harriman) was Dr Kringe, formerly head of the legal department of the German Ministry of Foreign Affairs.

[57] In his later commentary on the practice of international arbitration in Soviet foreign trade, Dr Chlenov stressed the need for Soviet draftsmen to formulate an arbitration clause in such a way that it guaranteed for the Soviet party unbiassed arbitrators: 'The Arbitration Clause in Contracts with Foreign Firms' *Vneshnyaya Torgoviya* 1935. No. 13, p. 3. (It is often important to remember that both sides can have legitimate concerns over the impartiality and independence of an arbitrator).

[58] For the form of USSR state note denominated in US$1,000, see GARF 8350/1/814, p. 232. (Full payment was not the case with the later modest settlements agreed between the USSR, Lena Goldfields and Tetihue, in 1932 and 1934. But these were British companies; and in 1928, after the diplomatic breach in relations with the United Kingdom following the Arcos affair in 1927, the USSR was and remained concerned to obtain diplomatic recognition from the United States).

K. Conclusion

If we answer the question honestly: 'is international commercial arbitration important?', the answer is obvious. By itself, the answer is plainly 'no'. There is no Nobel Prize for International Commercial Arbitrators; and whilst we may recall that in 1977, Lord Clark was much criticised for not discussing at all the rule of law in his famous BBC lectures on 'Civilisation', no-one thought to complain that he omitted any reference to international commercial arbitration. But if we change the question: 'is arbitration completely unimportant?', the answer is also plainly 'no'; and the Harriman Arbitration suggests two reasons why this is so.

First, arbitration has much to do with the rule of law; and the rule of law has everything to do with confidence in transnational trade. When rights and remedies can be frustrated with complete impunity, then trade inevitably suffers. And today, for transnational trade there is no equivalent and effective alternative remedy to international commercial arbitration. The existence of an arbitration clause with (at least) a neutral presiding arbitrator in a neutral place provides elements of fairness, certainty and predictability which are all essential to transnational trade. In 1922, two former practising lawyers, albeit very different and who never met each other, understood just that for Anglo-Russian trade; the former Welsh Solicitor, Lloyd George and the former St Petersburg Attorney, Lenin. Since 1922, we have seen how countries which have attacked international arbitration have soon lost foreign investment, like India and Pakistan. Whilst India appears now to have abandoned its aversion to international arbitration, other countries in Asia have sadly taken her place.

Second, Lloyd George was right: commerce does have a sobering influence in its operations; and so does international commercial arbitration. Commerce imposes its own discipline; and as for arbitration, it is part of the human instinct, in the depths of the darkest dispute, to find a means to resolve that dispute. With happily few exceptions, if there is a way, most human beings prefer to avoid disputes and not to exacerbate them, or to find reconciliation rather than enmity. Traders generally prefer to trade; and statesmen generally prefer peace to war. Increasingly, transnational trade and peace are linked; both are now indispensable to global prosperity and freedom; and international commercial arbitration is inextricably intertwined with transnational trade.[59]

And so returning to that summer's evening in the Kremlin in July 1963, it is perhaps not surprising that it was Harriman who brought those negotiations to a successful conclusion. The skills of the trader in 1928 who settled his arbitration were the same skills of the diplomat 35 years later. The world is a safer place where such skills can be deployed successfully; and as we live still through our own uneasy

---

[59] As Professor Pipes contends, property is an indispensable ingredient of freedom; and arbitration has of course much to do with property (see Pipes, *Property and Freedom* (London, 1999)).

120　ON ARBITRATION

Genoa Conference since 1989 (for Europe and elsewhere), we should remember those who laboured successfully in much more troubled, dangerous and difficult times, as manifested by the Harriman Arbitration: namely, Lloyd George, Lenin and (of course) the Cannibals.

L. Appendix

The Harriman Arbitration Clause (Section 65 of The Concession Agreement Dated 12 June 1925, English Version)
Board of Arbitration – Section 65

1. Should the Government and the Concessionaire differ with respect to the proper interpretation of, or the proper execution and performance of, or breach of any provisions of this agreement, or of any annex or supplementary agreement thereto, such difference shall on notice from either party, be referred to and determined by an Arbitral Board.
2. The Arbitration Board shall be composed of three members, one to be designated by the Government, one by the Concessionaire and the third, the Super-Arbiter, shall be designated by the parties by mutual agreement.
3. Should such an agreement not be attained within thirty days from the day on which the defending party receives a summons in writing to appear before the Arbitral Board, accompanied by a statement concerning the matter in dispute and designating the plaintiff's member of the Board, the Government shall within two weeks time name six candidates from among professors of the University of Paris (Sorbonne), or from among professors of the University of Oslo (det Kongelige Frederiks Universitet i Oslo), of whom the Concessionaire shall choose within the following two weeks, one who shall be the Super-Arbiter.
4. Should the Concessionaire, unless prevented from doing so by insurmountable obstacles, fail to select a Super-Arbiter, within said two weeks time the Government shall have the right to request the Governing Body of any one of the said educational institutions to appoint a Super-Arbiter from amongst six candidates chosen by the Government as above.
5. Should the Government, unless prevented from doing so by insurmountable obstacles, fall to select six candidates for Super-Arbiter within the above mentioned two weeks, then the Concessionaire shall have the right to request the Governing Body of any one of the above mentioned educational institutions to designate such six candidates, and thereupon the Concessionaire shall select from amongst them, the Super-Arbiter as above indicated.

6. If, on receipt of a summons from the Super-Arbiter fixing the date and place of the first meeting, either party shall fail to send its arbiter, or refuses to participate in the Arbitral Board, then the disputed matter, at the request of the other part shall be decided by the Super-Arbiter and the other member of the Board, provided that the decision is rendered unanimously.

7. The Super-Arbiter, as well as the Arbitral Board, when fixing the date and place of the meeting of the Board shall take into consideration: (1) the time reasonably necessary for each one of the parties to prepare for the journey and arrive in time at the place of destination, and (2) the accessibility to either party of the appointed place within the time fixed.

8. At the same time, the party which might encounter an insurmountable obstacle in despatching, for the appointed place, its member of the Board or its representative must take all measures to advise in time the Super-Arbiter and the Arbitral Board accordingly.

9. In all events, the Super-Arbiter or the Arbitral Board when deciding on the opening of the sitting in the absence of one of the parties must pass a ruling to such effect and give its reasons therefor.

10. The Board of Arbitration shall appoint a permanent Secretary who shall keep a record of all its proceedings. The compensation of the Chairman and the Secretary of the Board and the expenses therefor shall be borne equally by the parties, and each of the parties shall bear the compensation and expense of its member of the Board of Arbitration, as well as all expenses incurred by it in connection with any Arbitration proceeding.

11. Questions for determination by the Board of Arbitration shall be submitted in writing to the Chairman of the Board of Arbitration, and the party submitting any question for determination shall furnish the other party with a copy thereof. The Super-Arbiter shall fix the place and time of the first sitting of the Arbitral Board.

12. Thereafter the Board of Arbitration shall have full power to determine the places and times of its sittings, as well as its methods and order of procedure. Each party shall furnish the Board, in the manner and within the time prescribed by the latter, all information necessary in the case which they are able to produce, with due regard, however, to considerations of State importance.

13. The decisions of the Board shall in all cases be in writing, and a copy of each decision shall be promptly furnished to the parties. Every decision of the Board concurred in by a majority of the members therefor shall be final and binding upon the parties, and shall be promptly complied with.

14. When rendering a decision requiring one of the parties to perform a certain act, or to refrain therefrom, the Arbitral Board shall, at the same time, determine and communicate to the interested party the consequences of non-compliance with such decision, namely, it shall prescribe in such

contingency the payment to the other party of a certain fine, or it shall grant to the other party the right to repair the omission of the party at fault for the latter's account, or it shall prescribe the cancellation of the agreement.

15. In the event of failure of either party to comply with any decision of the Board of Arbitration, the other party shall have the right to bring suit for the enforcement of said decision in courts of any country. Notice of suit in such case shall be served on the representative of the other party then resident in that country, and the parties hereby declare that they will not question the jurisdiction of the court of said country to try and to execute a decision of the Board of Arbitration, provided said court shall recognise that the Arbitral decision had been rendered in due form.

16. In case of necessity, as provided in the preceding paragraph, of bringing suit for the enforcement of an Arbitral Board decision, the parties agree that either party shall have the right, to assign claims arising from such decision of the Arbitral Board to any third party, in whom shall be vested all right as to the enforcement of claims granted to the parties under this Section.

17. The parties agree that the time of limitation for the bringing of disputes before the Arbitral Board provided or under this agreement shall be one and one half years.

7

The *Lena Goldfields* Arbitration

The Historical Roots of Three Ideas*

A. Introduction

On 12 February 1930 a near-insolvent English company began arbitration proceedings against a large and hostile foreign State under an *ad hoc* arbitration clause contained in a written concession agreement signed by both parties. This concession had been granted by the Soviet Union in 1925 in respect of gold mining and other properties previously operated by the English company's Russian subsidiaries until their dispossession by the Soviet Russian government in 1918, following the October 1917 Revolution. In May 1930, after three months, the Soviet Union abruptly withdrew from the arbitration proceedings, abandoning both its defence and counterclaim and instructing its appointed arbitrator to take no further part in the proceedings. Four months later, on 2 September 1930, the English company obtained a massive monetary award in its favour, signed in London by two arbitrators only. Yet the financial result of *Lena Goldfields Limited* v. *USSR* was to benefit David little and cost Goliath less. The Soviet Union never recognised the *Lena* award despite protracted diplomatic negotiations between the Soviet Union and the United Kingdom. Later, the Soviet Union paid a modest amount under a long-term settlement finally agreed in 1935 which it repudiated in 1940. Eventually, by a twist of fate over 50 years later in 1992, the United Kingdom found itself the ultimate paymaster for the Soviet Union's residual obligations arising from Lena Goldfields' four successive grievances: nationalisation without compensation (1918), repudiation of the concession (1929), failure to honour the arbitration award (1930) and repudiation of the settlement agreement (1940). In short, Goliath won.

---

* This was a paper originally delivered to the International Law Association's Edinburgh meeting on 11 May 1996, based upon English archival and other materials collected over several years. It has been substantially rewritten to take account of archives which became available subsequently in Moscow and Berlin for which I express my thanks to Dr Jana Howlett, Oleg V. Khlevniuk and Dr Jürgen Luh. I also record my gratitude for the help and interest extended towards this research by HE Judge Stephen Schwebel, Professor S.N. Lebedev and Professor Sir Eli Lauterpacht CBE QC, together with many others regrettably too numerous to mention here. Of course, all errors are mine alone.

On Arbitration. Edited by: Sam Wordsworth KC and Marie Veeder, Oxford University Press. © Oxford University Press 2023.
DOI: 10.1093/oso/9780192869135.003.0007

124 ON ARBITRATION

Historically, the *Lena* case remains a baleful monument to the absolute power of a State able by force alone to thwart the consensual process of international arbitration, a threat to transnational trade still present in many parts of the world. Juridically, over the last 65 years, its direct beneficiary has been the modern system of international commercial arbitration to which the *Lena* tribunal applied several innovative and hugely important ideas. This article considers three: (i) the application of a non-national system of law to the merits of a private law dispute, namely "general principles of law"; (ii) the power of the majority of an arbitration tribunal to continue the proceedings in the absence of the minority; and (iii) the related jurisdictional concepts of "*Kompetenz-Kompetenz*", the legal autonomy or "separability" of an arbitration clause and the scope of the reference of a specific dispute to a particular arbitration tribunal. In the broadest sense, the *Lena* case represents the development of modern commercial arbitration; and its context is the economic and political history of Europe during the middle part of the twentieth century, including years of unparalleled horror in the Soviet Union. It also remains a story with practical lessons for many in commercial arbitration and transnational trade involving States and State agencies, not limited to Europe. Even if, in Coleridge's words, "the light which experience gives is a lantern on the stern, which shines only on the waves behind us", then those waves come from storms which lie ahead.

B. The *Lena* Award

The *Lena* award was a majority award made in German at the Royal Courts of Justice in London by Dr Otto Stutzer, Professor in Fuel Geology at the Freiberg School of Mines (the German chairman jointly appointed by the parties) and Sir Leslie Scott (the British arbitrator appointed by Lena Goldfields). The *Lena* tribunal also read out an English translation of the award to invited journalists which was partly reproduced in the London *Times* of 3 September 1930.[1] By its award, the *Lena* tribunal dissolved the most important foreign concession granted by the Soviet Union; and it ordered the Soviet Union to pay almost £13 million (plus interest), an enormous sum now equivalent to about £350 million. It was payable as compensation for unjust enrichment resulting from the Soviet Union's breach of the parties' concession agreement itself consequent upon the implementation of Stalin's First Five-Year Plan in 1929, which had eventually made the concession inoperable by Lena Goldfields. The award was unusual by any prevailing standards;

---

[1] The original *Lena* award is filed in the Moscow archives, bearing the signatures of Stutzer and Scott (GARF 8350/4/54). It includes the appendices and seven pages from paras. 1-4, 26 and 27 of the *Lena* award missing from the English version published by the London *Times* of 3 Sept. 1930, as later reproduced by Nussbaum's 1950 article (see *infra* n.24) and summarised by H. Lauterpacht (1929–1930) 5 Annual Digest *Cases Nos.1 and 258*, pp.3 and 426. It is possible that there was an English original version of the *Lena* award; but if so it has not been found.

it remains the only arbitration award to which the Soviet Union was a party; and as an award made in London, it was remarkably untainted by defects in the contemporary law and practice of English commercial arbitration.[2] On the merits the result was also somewhat unexpected: the Soviet Union could have won the arbitration both in its own estimation and in the original opinions expressed by Lena Goldfields' advisers; and yet the quantum of the award was much less than the English company's actual loss.

(1) An English Award

It is important to note from the outset that the *Lena* award was an English award made in London as the place appointed by the *Lena* tribunal under the parties' arbitration agreement; that accordingly English law was the *lex loci arbitri*; and also that the arbitration was a private arbitration between a State and an English legal person. The parties' concession agreement was not a treaty; and the *Lena* arbitration was not an arbitration between States subject to public international law. In 1935 Sir Hersch Lauterpacht only reluctantly noted the *Lena* award in his *Annual Digest*, querying the exact nature of the *Lena* and like tribunals: "in a sense they stand half-way between international and municipal arbitrations"; later both Sir Gerald Fitzmaurice and Dr Mann treated the *Lena* arbitrators as a private tribunal making its award under a municipal legal system[3]; and as Dr Mann submitted, "the *lex arbitri*...was clearly English, so that the English Arbitration Act [1889], English procedure and English private international law applied; and the arbitration was not subject to public international law. It may well be that the law which the arbitrators were instructed, or decided, to apply was, at any rate, public international law. But this is the effect of the English conflict of laws which applied on account of the *lex arbitri* being English..."[4] And yet, the *Lena* arbitration was never treated by the parties or its arbitrators as a purely English arbitration; and, over the years, legal commentators have treated the case as having a broader significance in both private and public international law.

---

[2] In 1930 English arbitration was still governed by the Arbitration Act 1889; and although the 1927 McKinnon Committee on the Law of Arbitration had published its report on necessary statutory reforms (Cmnd 2817), the Arbitration Act 1934 still lay in the future.

[3] See Lauterpacht, *op. cit. supra* n.1 (1935), note at p.428; Fitzmaurice (1957) B.Y.I.L. 246, n.2; Mann (1959) B.Y.I.L. 34, 56, n.2; and likewise Mann, *Studies in International Law* (1973), pp.264–265 (see also next footnote).

[4] Mann (1967) B.Y.I.L. 1, 8. In his 1950 article (*infra* n.24) Nussbaum mistakenly dismissed the question of the English courts' jurisdiction under the 1889 Act as "too academic to warrant discussion" (see n.27, at p.41). It was potentially most significant, if only because of the Special Case procedure under s.19 of the 1889 Act whereby the English court could require an arbitration tribunal at any stage of the proceedings "to state in the form of a special case for the opinion of the Court any question of law arising in the course of the reference".

126 ON ARBITRATION

(2) General Principles of Law

The *Lena* award is now cited as an early example, if not the first, of a private arbitration tribunal applying a general principle of law recognised by civilised nations by reference to Article 38(1)(c) of the Statute of the Permanent Court of International Justice, namely compensation for unjust enrichment.[5] As such, Professor Dupuy relied upon the *Lena* award in his Preliminary Award in the *Texaco* v. *Libyan Arab Republic* arbitration (1979); but, much earlier, the *Lena* arbitration had led directly to Articles 21 and 22 of the 1933 concession convention between the Persian government and the Anglo-Persian Oil Company, which have influenced the drafting of concession agreements ever since.[6] However, in the *Lena* arbitration the parties had not agreed on the application of public international law or general principles of law; and indeed there was no express provision on applicable law in their concession agreement. In such circumstances, for an English arbitration tribunal to choose to apply nonnational rules of law to a private party's civil law relationship was then unique.[7] Indeed, it is only in recent years that the English courts have countenanced that possibility even where the parties have so agreed expressly. [8]

(3) Expropriation Compensation

The *Lena* award has also been identified as a source of law relevant to compensation for nationalisation;[9] and it has been cited in the Iran–US Claims Tribunal on

[5] Lauterpacht, *op. cit. supra* n.1 (1935), at p.3; Jessup, *A Modern Law of Nations* (1949), p.33; McNair (1957) B.Y.I.L., 1, 8–12; Fitzmaurice (1957) B.Y.I.L., 203, 246, 249; Schwarzenberger *International Law* (1957), Vol.1, pp. 43, 146, 578–579; Mann (1959) B.Y.I.L. 35, 55; Mann (1967) B.Y.I.L. 1, 7–8; Mann, *Studies in International Law* (1973), pp. 2 29 , 238, 264, 475; Lew, *Applicable Law in International Commercial Arbitration* (1978), pp.11 4, 124, 506; J. Kuusi, *The Host State and the Transnational Corporation* (1979), p. 70; Oppetit, "Les états et l'arbitrage international" (1985) Rev. arb. 493, 498; Schwebel, *International Arbitration: Three Salient Problems* (1987), p.138; Brownlie, *Principles of Public International Law* (4th edn; 1990), p.17; Jennings and Watts (Eds), *Oppenheim's International Law* (9th edn), Vol.1, p.39; Horacio Grigera Naón, *Choice-of-law Problems in International Commercial Arbitration* (1992), p. 120 and Dicey and Morris, *Conflict of Laws* (12 edn, Collins (Ed.)), Vol.2, p.1219 (n.86). (The *Lena* award also exists as a spurious footnote, possibly humorous, on "frozen law" in Redfern and Hunter's *International Commercial Arbitration* (2nd edn, 1991), p.104, n.12.)

[6] *Texaco* v. *Libyan Arab Republic Arbitration* (1979) 53 I.L.R. 389, 453; McNair, *idem*, p.7; and Schwebel, *idem*, pp.76 *et seq.* Mann believed Arts.21 and 22 to be the first of such clauses: Mann (1959) B.Y.I.L. 34, 51. (As to the drafting of the 1933 concession convention, see *infra*.)

[7] See *Czarnikow* v. *Roth, Schmidt & Co.* [1922] 2 K.B. 478,488, especially Scrutton LU's *dictum*: "There must be no Alsatia in England where the King's writ does not run"; see also Megaw J in *Orion* v. *Belfort Maats* [1962] 2 Lloyd's Rep. 257, 264.

[8] See *DST* v. *RAKOIL* [1987] 2 Lloyd's Rep. 246 and *The Channel Tunnel Case* [1993] A.C. 334, 368 under the 1958 New York Arbitration Convention; and for an arbitration agreement made in England applying "Jewish religious law" see *Suleimany* v. *Suleimany* (C.A., 13 Mar. 1995 and 30 Jan. 1998, unrep.); see also Kerr (1993) 2 Am. Rev Int.Arb. 377, Boyd (1990) 6 Arb.Int. 122 and s.46(1)(b) of the Arbitration Act 1996.

[9] W. Friedmann, *The Changing Structure of International Law* (1964), pp.146, 207 (where it is mischaracterised as a mixed claims commission after the First World War); F. Francioni, "Compensation for Nationalisation of Foreign Property: The Borderland between Law and Equity"

THE *LENA GOLDFIELDS* ARBITRATION   127

the "discounted-cash flow method" of assessing compensation for expropriation.[10] In assessing compensation for the value of Lena Goldfields' property by which the Soviet Union had become enriched without legal right, the *Lena* tribunal measured "the present value, if paid in cash now, of future profits which the company would have made and which the [Soviet] Government now can make—on the assumption of good commercial management and the best technical skill and up-to-date development... The problem is, therefore, similar to that of ascertaining a fair purchase price for a going concern..." [11] As a concessionaire not owning its mining properties, Lena Goldfields could not measure its loss on an asset-based valuation. Paradoxically, the *Lena* tribunal invoked (*inter alia*) Scots law on restitution for unjust enrichment because English law did not then fully recognise such a general principle; but the *Lena* tribunal did not invoke any public international law precedent on unjust enrichment.[12]

(4) Procedural Rules

As to procedural matters, the *Lena* award is often cited to illustrate the legal doctrine of the separability of the arbitration clause whereby it survived the termination or alleged termination of the concession agreement,[13] together with the

---

(1975) 24 I.C.L.Q. 255, 276; C. F. Amerasinghe, "Issues of Compensation for the Takings of Alien Property in the Light of Recent Cases and Practice" (1992) 41 I.C.L.Q. 22, 37; K. M. Meesen, "Domestic Law Concepts in International Expropriation Law", in R. Lillich (Ed.), *The Valuation of Nationalized Property in International Law* (1987), Vol.IV pp.157, 163; K. P. Berger, Formalisierte oder "schleichende" Kodifizierung des transnationalen Witschaftsechts (1996), p.223; but see C. H. Schreuer, "Unjustified Enrichment in International Law" (1974) 22 A.J.Comp.L. 281, 289 ("This case, although frequently quoted in support of a 'principle against unjust enrichment' in international law, has probably contributed nothing but a great deal of confusion.").

[10] B. M. Clagett, "Just Compensation in International Law: The Issues Before the Iran–United States Claims Tribunal", in Lillich, *idem*, pp.31, 63; W. C. Lieblich, "Determinations by International Tribunals of the Economic Value of Expropriated Enterprises" (1990) 7 J.Int.Arb. 37, 41; and W. Mapp, *The Iran–United States Claims Tribunal: The First Ten Years 1981–1991* (1993), pp.166, 211.

[11] The *Lena* award, para.26. In paras.26 and 27 (not reproduced in *The Times* of 3 Sept. 1930), the *Lena* tribunal calculated the "present value" by multiplying the probable annual income from different parts of the concession by the relevant number of years remaining under the concession agreement. It did not award in full the compensation claimed by Lena Goldfields in para.15 of its Statement of Claim dated 27 May 1930 (see *infra* n.56); and Lena Goldfields made no claim in damages for separate breaches of the concession agreement: see *The Times*, 27 Aug. 1930.

[12] The *Lena* tribunal did not refer to The *Chorzów Factory Case* (1928) PCIJ Ser.A No.17. It derived the general principle from the German Civil Code, French, Soviet and Scots law (as considered by the House of Lords in *Cantiare San Rocco SA* v. *Clyde Shipbuilding and Engineering Company Limited* [1924] A.C. 226, reversing 1922 S.C. 723; LIX S.L.T. 520: see para.23 of the *Lena* award. In *SNE* v. *Joc Oil* (1984) the FTAC arbitration tribunal in Moscow (Professors Posdnyakov, Bratus and Naryshkina) applied restitution for unjust enrichment under Soviet law without any reference to the *Lena* award: see (1993) XVIII I.C.C.A. Yearbook 92, 101–105 and (1990) XV I.C.C.A. Yearbook 384 for the foreign enforcement proceedings under the 1958 New York Arbitration Convention.

[13] Schwebel, *op. cit. supra* n.5, at pp.35–37; Schwebel, (1990) I.C.C.A. Congress Series No.5 227 and 316; S.J . Toope, *Mixed International Arbitration* (1990), pp.64, 70; K. P. Berger, *International Economic*

128 ON ARBITRATION

related doctrine of "*Kompetenz-Kompetenz*", i.e. the ability of an arbitration tribunal to address the question of its own jurisdiction without suspending the arbitral process on one party's jurisdictional challenge.[14] As such, the *Lena* case was a lengthy footnote in the United Kingdom's Memorial in the *Anglo-Iranian Oil Company Case* (1951); it was cited by Professor Dupuy in *Topco* v. *Libya* (1975) and by Professor Gomard in the *Elf Aquitaine* case, on *pacta sunt servanda* (1982).[15] The *Lena* award is also cited as an example of a binding award made *ex parte* in the absence of a recalcitrant party refusing to take part in the arbitration proceedings; and further as an example of a "truncated tribunal" making a majority award notwithstanding that one of the arbitrators has refused to attend the arbitration hearings, to take part in the arbitrators' deliberations and to sign the award.[16] As such, the *Lena* award was cited by the United States and the United Kingdom in their respective arguments in the *Peace Treaties* case (1950).[17] However, in 1930 the English common law required unanimity and signature from all three arbitrators, otherwise the award was a nullity.[18] Yet, albeit controversial at the time, all that was done by the *Lena* tribunal in regard to these procedural matters would be permitted today under the English Arbitration Act 1996.

Arbitration (1993), p.121 (see also pp.530, 545); and Schwebel, *Justice in International Law* (1994), pp.200, 206.

[14] The ability of an arbitration tribunal to rule on its own competence after challenge by a respondent was a principle of public international law recognised in England from 1796 (Lord Loughborough LC in the *Jay Treaty* cases); but the English common law rule was only fully stated by Devlin J. in *Brown* v. *Genossenschaft* [1954] 1 Q.B. 8. In 1982 Professor Schmitthof argued for a new English statutory rule allowing an "arbitrator" to decide on his own jurisdiction: "The Jurisdiction of the Arbitrator" in Schulz and van den Berg (Eds), *The Art of Arbitration* (1982), pp.285, 293; and see now s.30 of the Arbitration Act 1996.

[15] *TOPCO* v. *Libya*, para.16 of the Preliminary Award (1979) 53 I.L.R. 389, 408–412; see also *LIAMCO* v. *Libya* (1982) 62 I.L.R. 140, 203 and (1981) 20 I.L.M. 69; *Elf Aquitaine Iran* v. *NIOC* (1986) XI I.C.C.A. Yearbook 97, 101, ann. Fouchard Rev.arb. 1984.333; and the *Anglo-Iranian Oil Company Case: Memorial of the United Kingdom of 10.x.1951; ICJ Pleadings* (1952), p.119, where the UK argued that the unilateral termination of the 1933 concession convention by Iran (for the purpose of nationalisation) could not render ineffective its arbitration clause, whereby compensation payable to the Anglo-Iranian Company would be assessed by the arbitration tribunal and not by the Iranian Parliament (see also *infra*).

[16] See Lauterpacht, *op. cit. supra* n.1 (1935), at pp.1, 25; Mann (1967) B.Y.I.L. 1, 25; and Schwebel, *op. cit. supra* n.5, at pp.211 *et seq.*, 161. Judge Schwebel recognised that the authority of the *Lena* award on the problem of "truncated tribunals" is diminished on the ground that the arbitration clause there expressly authorised two of the three arbitrators to render a decision where the third defaulted; concluding nonetheless that, as a matter of intention, it supported the case that a truncated international tribunal is entitled to proceed and render a valid award (see pp.214, 216); see also Schwebel (1990) *loc. cit. supra* n.13; (1994), *op. cit. supra* n.13, at p.206; and I.C.C. Bull., Nov. 1995, p. 19 .

[17] *Interpretation of Peace Treaties with Bulgaria, Hungary and Romania (Second Phase) ICJ Pleadings, Oral Arguments, Documents*, pp.231 *et seq.*, 356–360 and 189–190, 369–379; see also the dissenting opinion of Judge Read, I.C.J.Rep. 1950, 242; see also Schwebel, *op. cit. supra* n.5, at pp.226–235.

[18] See *UK Mutual Steamship Assurance Association* v. *Houston* [1896] 1 Q.B. 567. On the recommendation of the 1927 McKinnon Committee (*supra* n.2, at para.21), English law was later changed to allow the award of any two of three arbitrators to be binding on the parties: s.4 of the Arbitration Act 1934, re-enacted as s.9 of the Arbitration Act 1950; and see now s.22(2) of the Arbitration Act 1996.

(5) Other Features

The *Lena* arbitration has other interesting legal features by today's standards. These include the extraordinary speed of the arbitration from dispute to award in a difficult and complicated case, less than seven months from notice of arbitration to final award (these were olden times, in Lord Mustill's famous phrase, before the invention of "slow-track" arbitration);[19] the desperate absence of any interim measures available from the *Lena* tribunal or any State court immediately after the commencement of the arbitration, without which the loss of Lena Goldfields' concession was inevitable (what Lena Goldfields called at the time a "*modus vivendi*"); the procedural flexibility of factual evidence adduced in writing by affidavit and orally, at a time when English court trials were an oral event; the application of a "second-best evidence rule" to allow Lena Goldfields to overcome the enforced absence of its Russian witnesses and the loss of its documents in Russia confiscated by Soviet authorities, long before that practice emerged from the Iran–US Claims Tribunal;[20] the conduct of Lena Goldfields' case in English and German by an émigré Russian lawyer, Dr Idelson (who had just qualified as a member of the English Bar); the fact that Soviet, German, French and other foreign laws were debated at the hearings without resorting to the orthodox English method of proving all foreign law as fact by expert legal witnesses; the awarding of post-award contractual interest at a time when interest generally bristled with difficulties under English law;[21] and lastly, in opening the arbitration hearings to the press and publishing much of the award in the London *Times*, the *Lena* tribunal established an important exception to the legal principle of privacy and confidentiality in commercial arbitration where transparency is required in the public interest, a decision now probably at odds with English authorities but consistent with the recent approach of the New South Wales Court of Appeal.[22]

---

[19] It is often forgotten that the first ICC arbitration in 1923 took, from reference to final award, no more than 3 hours; but speed remains attainable in sports arbitration: the FIA/FISA Contract Recognition Board in Geneva will make a final award within eight days of a dispute between driver and F1 teams; and at the Nagano 1998 Winter Olympic Games, the Canadian snow-board giant slalom gold-medallist received back his gold medal by an arbitration award made within 12 hours of his appeal: *Rebagliati* v. *IOC, Final Award of 12 February 1998 of the CAS-TAS Ad hoc Division* (Young, Paulsson and Zuchowicz) (1998) 13#6 Mealey's International Arbitration Report 12 and B1.

[20] See the *Lena* award, para.15; and M. Kazazi, *Burden of Proof and Related Issues* (1996), pp.357–359.

[21] See the *Lena* award, para.31. At English law, there was no power to order contractual interest after the date of the award. In *The London Explorer* [1972] A.C. 1, the House of Lords held that s.20 of the 1950 Act (previously s.11 of the 1934 Act) gave to an English arbitrator power only to determine whether or not the award should carry interest at the statutory rate for an English judgment debt; but prior to 1934, even this limited power did not exist. (Under s.49(3)–(4) of the Arbitration Act 1996, an English arbitrator now has power to award simple or compound interest up to and after the date of the award until payment.)

[22] In *Commonwealth of Australia* v. *Cockatoo Dockyard Pty Ltd* (1995) 36 N.S.W.L.R. 662, it was held that where one of the parties to the arbitration is a governmental agency, the arbitrator had no power to make procedural orders imposing an obligation of confidentiality concerning its own documents so as to limit the executive's duty to pursue the public interest. This exception was expressly left undecided in the most recent of the English cases on confidentiality: *Ali Shipping Corporation* v. *Shipyard "Trogir"*

130   ON ARBITRATION

C. The *Lena* Case

After more than 65 years of legal references, the accounts published in *The Times* of the *Lena* arbitration and award remain the only immediate source for what happened in the dispute between Lena Goldfields and the Soviet Union.[23] There was a full transcript taken of the main hearing in August 1930; and together with the papers, exhibits and photographs used in the arbitration proceedings, these materials were deposited in a safe place at the end of the arbitration by the *Lena* tribunal's secretary. It has not been possible to locate their whereabouts; and they must now be presumed lost. If deposited in the City of London, the records may have been destroyed in 1940 during the Blitz; and if in Freiberg, the ravages of war and occupation may have ensured their disappearance. In the United States the fullest account of the *Lena* arbitration was set out in Professor Nussbaum's 1950 article on the *Lena* award, to which he attached a copy of that part of the award published in the London *Times*.[24] Nussbaum there criticised Dr Rashba's 1945 article which had appeared to introduce new unpublished material in support of the Soviet Union's case in the *Lena* arbitration, with the implicit but mistaken accusation that Rashba was a Soviet apologist.[25] In his own article, Rashba was referring only to a contemporaneous document which had not been seen by Nussbaum: a 1930 publication prepared by the Soviet Union's Main Concessions Committee: *Documents concerning the Competence of the Arbitration Court set up in connection with the Questions outstanding between the Lena Goldfields Company Limited and the USSR.* This publication was intended by the Politburo to defend the Soviet Union in the diplomatic controversy following the *Lena* award with the United Kingdom and Germany.[26] It reproduced much of the correspondence between the parties and the *Lena* tribunal from January to May 1930; and it included two legal commentaries by the Soviet

---

[1998] 1 Lloyd's Rep. 643, 655; and see the UK's Departmental Advisory Committee's 1996 Report on the Arbitration Bill, para.16 (1997) 13 Arb.Int. 278, citing the *Lena* award.

[23] In addition to the report of the *Lena* award on 3 Sept. 1930, *The Times* reported the argument and evidence on 7, 8, 9, 12, 13, 14, 15, 20, 21, 22, 27 and 28 Aug. 1930.

[24] A. Nussbaum, "The Arbitration between the Lena Goldfields, Ltd. and the Soviet Government" (1950–1951) Cornell L.Q. 31, 42 (appendix). Earlier in Berlin, Nussbaum had contributed a case-note on the *Lena* award in (1931) 3 Internationales Jahrbuch für Schiedgerichtswesen 429 (of which he was the editor). See also Sutton, *Western Technology and Soviet Economic Development 1917 to 1930* (1968), pp.95–100 and *ibid.* 1930 to 1945 (1971), pp.23–27.

[25] *Idem*, pp.38–41; E. S. Rashba, "Settlement of Disputes in Commercial Dealings with the Soviet Union" (1945), 45 Col.L.Rev. 530, 539–540. Dr Evsey Rashba was then a Special Fellow in Law in Columbia University: he had received an LL.M. degree from Columbia Law School in 1944; and he died in 1973 in Lausanne.

[26] The English version of this document was attached to the USSR's diplomatic note dated 4 Dec. 1930 to the British Foreign Office, rejecting the UK's note of 1 Nov. 1930 regarding the *Lena* award (PRO FO 371/14869). Professors Komarov and Boguslavsky in Moscow kindly supplied me with the German version; and a separate English copy was found at the British Library, along with other important materials, by my research student, Ms Ann Moore-Williams. (For convenience, this document is cited below as "*USSR Documents*", with page references to the English version.)

THE *LENA GOLDFIELDS* ARBITRATION   131

Union's legal advisers in the *Lena* arbitration, Professor V. N. Shreter (a Soviet legal specialist on foreign concessions at the Plekhanov Institute of National Economy in Moscow) and Professor M. Ya. Pergament (formerly Professor of Civil Law at St Petersburg University's Law Faculty). It is an invaluable document; and it has recently been possible to check much of its quoted correspondence against original documentation in the Moscow archives. It is to be read with another 1930 publication prepared during the arbitration proceedings, again on the Politburo's instructions: Dr S. A. Bernstein's *The Financial and Economic Results of the Working of the Lena Goldfields Company Limited* (1930).[27] This pamphlet undoubtedly drew on private Soviet materials because Bernstein was an adviser and representative of the Soviet Union in the *Lena* arbitration, taking part in settlement negotiations with Lena Goldfields. His pamphlet was sent to the *Lena* tribunal during the arbitration proceedings; and Sir Leslie Scott's copy can be found at Loughborough University Library. (This pamphlet was available to Nussbaum in 1950, who curtly dismissed Bernstein's statements for lack of any legal relevance.)[28] In addition to his contribution to *USSR Documents*, Professor Pergament also published in Russia a longer academic article on the *Lena* arbitration.[29]

Regrettably, apart from Shreter, Pergament and Bernstein, the persons immediately involved in the *Lena* arbitration left no memoirs of the case. However, the story can now be told more fully with the benefit of English, Russian and German archives on Lena Goldfields, many only recently released. The British Foreign Office archives are found in the Public Record Office, Kew; Soviet archives in the Russian Centre for the Preservation and Study of Documents of Contemporary History (Rossiiskii tsentr khraneniya i izucheniya dokumentov noveishei istorii: "RTsKhIDNI") and the State Archive of the Russian Federation (Gosudarstvennyi Arkhiv Rossiiskoi Federatsii: "GARF"), both in Moscow; and German archives in the Bundesarchiv, Reichswirtschaftsministerium ("Barch. RWM"). It is a complicated story with roots in the early economic history of

---

[27] These two publications, *USSR Documents* and Bernstein's pamphlet, were published pursuant to the decision of the Politburo's "Lena commission" in paras.5 and 6 of its protocol of 18 June 1930 (Rykov, Kamenev, Molotov and Piatakov; GARF 1446/55/1970). This Lena commission was comprised of both Politburo members and other senior Soviet officials who undertook the bulk of the USSR's work on Lena Goldfields' concession, claim and arbitration from 1923 to 1930, subject to the approval of the Politburo.

[28] Nussbaum, *op. cit. supra* n.24, at p.38 where Bernstein is described as "a Soviet economist". Lena Goldfields informed the Foreign Office that a copy of Bernstein's pamphlet had been put before the *Lena* tribunal prior its award, at the instigation of the USSR: see also the *Lena* tribunal's opening statement at the main hearing in August 1930 (*The Times*, 7 Aug. 1930). Bernstein (also transliterated as "Bernshtein") was a legal specialist on Soviet concessions, the author of *Ocherk kontsessionogo prava SSR* (*Outline of Soviet Law on Concessions* (1930); and (with B. Landau and V. Mashkevich), *Pravovyie usloviya kontsessionnoi deyatel'nosti* v. *SSSR* (*Legal Conditions of Concession Activity in the USSR*) (1931).

[29] M. Ya. Pergament (1930) 12 Mezhdunarodnaya zhizn' 43. (This is not the same work to which Professor Nussbaum refers in his 1950 article, the unseen Pergament commentary in *USSR Documents* cited by Rashba; Nussbaum's reference to A. J. Pergament also miscites Rashba's reference, possibly confusing Pergament with his daughter, who was also a law professor in Moscow.)

132 ON ARBITRATION

Soviet Russia preceding Lenin's New Economic Policy, intertwined with the United Kingdom's early diplomatic and trade relations with Soviet Russia, particularly Lloyd George's foreign policies at the 1922 Genoa and Hague Conferences. Regrettably, space does not permit the full account to be related here; and moreover the historical and diplomatic records remain incomplete.

(1) Lena Goldfields

Lena Goldfields was an English company, incorporated in 1908 for the purpose of acquiring 70 per cent of the shares of the Russian Lena Goldmining Company (also called "Lenskoye"), itself created in 1855 to develop gold mining along the river Lena and its tributaries in Siberia. Lena Goldfields' numerous shareholders could be found in England, Russia, France, Germany and the United States; and it was at first highly profitable, until the 1912 "Lena massacre" (when Czarist gendarmes killed 170 of its Lenskoye workers on strike at Bodaibo) and the outbreak of the First World War in 1914. In July 1918 the Soviet Russian government nationalised all mining properties without compensation, including Lenskoye's mines. After the final defeat of the White armies, in March 1921 Lena Goldfields lodged a formal claim against the Russian government with the Russian Claims Department of the United Kingdom's Board of Trade. In its 1925 concession agreement, Lena Goldfields agreed to waive any claims for compensation against the Soviet Union (now incorporating Soviet Russia) and also to indemnify the Soviet Union in the event of claims by its Russian subsidiaries, which had not themselves been nationalised.[30] In order to control the making of these claims and more particularly to assuage the natural concerns of dispossessed shareholders where the concession was to comprise the Russian companies' own nationalised properties, Lena Goldfields acquired all the shares of these Russian companies at a cost of £4.5 million.[31] For Lena Goldfields' financial backers this was a large investment, in addition to the substantial investments already lost upon Soviet nationalisation; and

---

[30] At least formally, these Russian companies still retained a legal existence even in 1928: see *A.G. der Manufacturen I.A. Woronin and Cheshire* v. *Frederick Huth & Co.* (1946) 79 Ll. L.R. 262, 265 (on Idelson's expert evidence of Soviet law).

[31] See the *Lena* award, para.29. These Russian companies were Lenskoye, Altai District Mining Limited, Sissert Company Limited and the Pavda Company. The acquisition of their bearer shares outside the USSR, begun in late 1923, was controversial. Many Russian shareholders were living in exile under strained financial circumstances; and much resentment was expressed over share purchases made by Lena Goldfields without first disclosing the negotiations for its concession with the USSR (which would have increased the market value of the shares); and further that shares held as custodian by the Russian and English Bank (controlled by G. O. Benenson and Herbert Guedella, Lena Goldfields' principal financial backers) had been improperly sold to Lena Goldfields without their owners' authority: see the article by Prince A. D. Galitzine in *Posledniye Novosti*, 16 July 1925 (edited in Paris) and Leslie Urquhart's contemporary views of this "shady operation", summarised in K. H. Kennedy, *Mining Tsar: The Life and Times of Leslie Urquhart* (1986), p.228; see also Bernstein for the Soviet view, *op. cit. supra* n.27, at p.12. Lena Goldfields denied at the time any impropriety.

it reflects how both English investors and the Russian exiled community still retained the hope that the Bolshevik regime would collapse or at least mutate into a more benevolent form, allowing nationalised properties to be returned to their private owners. In September 1926, after both parties had ratified the concession agreement, Lena Goldfields duly wrote to the Russian Claims Department withdrawing all its Russian claims.

(2) The Concession Agreement

The concession agreement was made in Russian and signed in Moscow on 30 April 1925 after two years' difficult negotiations;[32] and it became effective on 14 November 1925 upon its ratification by Lena Goldfields and the USSR Council of People's Commissars, the latter by its decision of 11 August 1925.[33] The concession agreement was signed by Major F. W. D. Gwynne for Lena Goldfields and by Mikhail Stipukhovich, the chief legal adviser to the USSR Main Concessions Committee, whose chairman was Trotsky. It was also countersigned by Felix Dzerzhinsky, the chairman of the USSR Supreme Economic Council (also head of the Cheka and OGPU, its successor) and the Deputy People's Commissar for Foreign Affairs, Maxim Litvinov (who was by now also Acting Commissar since Chicherin's illness). The Soviet Union thereby granted to Lena Goldfields the exclusive right to mine gold and other metals in the Urals and parts of Siberia; namely the old Lenskoye placer gold mines near Bodaibo, the Sissert and Revda copper and iron mines in the Urals and gold, silver, copper, lead and zinc works in the Altai near the Mongolian and Chinese borders (now Kazakstan)—all vast, remote and near inaccessible areas up to 4,500 miles from Moscow.

The concession period was to run in part for 30 years and in part for 50 years. With this concession, Lena Goldfields was to assume control of 30 per cent of the gold, 80 per cent of the silver and 50 per cent of the copper, lead and zinc production in the Soviet Union. It was required during the first seven years of operation to invest 22 million roubles (then £2.25 million); and it was entitled to import and export freely to and from the Soviet Union without adverse sanctions as a capitalist enterprise. Lena Goldfields' counterparty was invariably described as the Soviet Union, but it was represented by the Main Concessions Committee

---

[32] The main obstacles were the USSR's agreement to Arts.86 and 90 of the concession agreement, whereby (in Lena Goldfields' view) the USSR "waived its sovereign privilege of acting as supreme judge in disputes which might arise between it and the concessionaire" (Major Gwynne's written remarks at the Berlin settlement conference of 12 Sept. 1931, p.5, Barch. RWM 31.01 20044). The Politburo only approved of an arbitration tribunal with a neutral "super-arbitrator" on 9 Apr. 1925, to be selected from five professors in legal and mining matters from a university outside the USSR, England and the US (RTsKhIDNI 17/162/002). For the texts of Arts. 86 and 90, see respectively *infra* n.46 and Appendix.

[33] In fact, the decision to allow ratification was made by the Politburo on 7 Aug. 1925, on the proposal of the Main Concessions Committee (RTsKhIDNI 17/003/514).

134 ON ARBITRATION

("Glavkoncesskom") under the Supreme Economic Council ("VSNKh"), which was itself administratively subordinate to the Council of People's Commissars. The Supreme Economic Council was the executive organ responsible for the general direction of the Soviet Union's economic affairs; and it oversaw the management of the bulk of the country's industries, including mining and ore extraction. Later, Litvinov was to argue to the British Embassy in Moscow that his own signature to the concession agreement was merely a form of notarisation for a private legal transaction concluded between Soviet organs on the one hand (Glavkoncesskom and VSNKh) and a private firm on the other.[34] This argument was a diplomatic pretext to force the United Kingdom to deal directly with the Concessions Committee on Lena Goldfields' claim to enforce the award and not with the USSR Commissariat for Foreign Affairs. In fact, both the concession agreement and the *Lena* award bore on their face the USSR as the name of Lena Goldfields' counter-party; and yet the question arises: why did Litvinov sign the concession agreement? The answer was that it was no mere private legal transaction; it was also a Soviet legislative instrument with a significant effect on both the juridical status of the ar-bitration clause under Soviet law and the conduct of the *Lena* arbitration.

(a) The arbitration clause

Article 90 of the concession agreement provided that both parties had the right to submit all disputes and misunderstandings concerning the interpretation or per-formance of the concession agreement to a court of arbitration consisting of a nom-inee of Lena Goldfields, a nominee of the Soviet Union and a "super-arbitrator", i.e. chairman and third arbitrator, to be appointed by mutual agreement of the parties or by the procedure designated in the arbitration clause.[35] As to the phrase "court of arbitration", it was a notion then common also in England and France that a consensual arbitration tribunal or institution could be described as a "court". For all its terminology, the arbitration clause provided for the three-arbitrator tribunal in widespread use today in the field of transnational trade. In 1925, however, a pri-vate agreement to refer future disputes to arbitration was not valid under Soviet

---

[34] See Litvinov's Note to the British Embassy's Counsellor (Strang) of 5 Sept. 1932 (PRO F0371/16376). In 1930 Litvinov had become People's Commissar on Chicherin's resignation on grounds of ill-health.

[35] The full text of Art.90 is set out *infra* in the Appendix, in English translation from the Russian original text. The word "super-arbitrator" was probably a mistranslation, first into Russian and then into English, from the German word for a presiding third arbitrator: "*Obmann*" (which is similar to the Scots legal term for chairman of an arbitration tribunal "oversman"). This German wording suggests that the Soviet draftsman took the arbitration clause from the German texts of earlier concession agree-ments previously granted under the New Economic Policy, of which Germany was then the principal foreign beneficiary following the 1922 Rapallo Treaty. Within the same arbitration clause, the "super-arbitrator" is also described as a "president" (in Russian); and it is possible here to see here the hand of a second non-Soviet draftsman. The text of Art.90 in the German edition of *USSR Documents* renders this Russian phrase as "*der Obmann des Schiedsgerichts*" (p.40); and it also translates the different Russian word for "president" as "*Obmann*".

law;[36] and the Soviet Union was never party to the League of Nations' 1923 Geneva Protocol on Arbitration Clauses. On the other hand, the juridical nature of an arbitration clause contained in a concession agreement made with the Soviet State was different, as explained by Professor Dr Eugen Kelman of Kiev University in an article published in 1926, translated from the German:[37]

In Soviet law, concession agreements means such contracts as are approved by the Council of People's Commissars in a particular form which is regulated by mandatory rules and which may bestow upon a private person the right to pursue an economic activity which would not otherwise be available to such private person. It is generally accepted that this approval gives the concession agreement the effect of a special statute. If arbitration clauses are included in these concession agreements, this excludes the legal effect of the general rules applying to arbitration clauses insofar as the same are expressly regulated by the concession agreements: "*Lex specialis derogat legi generali*" (special law derogates from the general law). Accordingly, the clauses of such concession agreements which provide for the settlement of future disputes by arbitration tribunals are also valid in law although the position would be otherwise under municipal Soviet law. This result is, incidentally, connected with the nature of concession agreements which usually contain exceptions to the law which otherwise applies. In other words, it would be wrong to subject to general civil and procedural law rules an arbitration procedure made for the purpose of settling disputes arising out of a concession agreement.

These "mandatory rules" included the 1920 Decree of the Council of People's Commissars on Concessions, establishing (*inter alia*) the Soviet government's guarantee that the foreign concessionaire's property invested in the undertaking would not be liable to nationalisation, confiscation or requisition and that no unilateral changes would be made by any regulations or decrees of the government to the terms of the concession agreement.[38] Under Soviet law, both the arbitration

---

[36] The Soviet Russian Decree No.1 on Courts of 24 Nov. 1917 allowed private persons to refer to arbitration an existing claim in a civil case subject to certain formalities, excepting any dispute arising out of family or labour relations or if it fell within the special jurisdiction of any State court; and on the merits there was a high degree of judicial control over the award. In 1924 the procedure formed part of the RSFSR Civil Procedural Code; but this form of arbitration was never widely used in the USSR; and it was of course quite useless for a foreign company seeking to refer future commercial disputes to binding arbitration: see S. Kucherov, *The Organs of Soviet Administration of Justice: Their History and Operation* (1970), p.34; Rashba, *op. cit. supra* n.25, at pp.536–538; and Nussbaum, *op. cit. supra* n.24, at pp.36–37.

[37] Kelman, "Recht der Sowjet-Union" (1926) 1 Internationales Jahrbuch für Schiedsgerichtwesen 134, in German. (This English translation omits references in the German text.)

[38] Soviet Russian Decree dated 23 Dec. 1920 on the General Economic and Legal Conditions for Concessions; see Degras, *Soviet Documents on Foreign Policy* (1978) Vol.1, p.220—where it is dated 23 Nov. 1920; see also Lenin's speech on concessions of 27 Nov. 1920 at p.221. For a similar speech made on 20 Sept. 1920, strongly advocating foreign concessions, see Pipes (Ed.), *The Unknown Lenin* (1996), pp.95, 112–114.

136 ON ARBITRATION

clause and the concession agreement had the legal status of a decree of the Council of People's Commissars (thereby explaining why Litvinov as an Acting Commissar also signed the concession agreement); and neither could be repudiated or terminated by one party unilaterally as if it were a simple civil law or civil procedural law contract. This was also how Lena Goldfields understood the position, as conveyed by its chairman, Guedella, to its extraordinary general meeting on 30 July 1925: "we are advised that the concession is equivalent in law to a private Act of Parliament in this country".[39]

(3) The Lena Concession 1925–1929

Lena Goldfields began operations on its concession in October 1925. Its mining operations were an important source of foreign exchange for the Soviet Union, with air-shipments of gold bullion to London beginning in early 1926. Nonetheless, Lena Goldfields worked its concession in the Soviet Union with grave practical difficulties created by governmental agencies, including local Soviet trade unions as the monopolist supplier of labour. Lena Goldfields' concession survived the breaking-off of diplomatic relations in 1927 between the United Kingdom and the Soviet Union over the "Arcos" affair; and it overcame grave financial problems in 1928 during which it contracted heavy debts to German and Czech creditors. By early 1929, Lena Goldfields could show that it had performed its principal contractual obligations towards the Soviet Union and returned a modest profit for the first three years of £760,390 on gold production officially valued at £3.6 million (about a quarter of total Russian gold production). It had also invested £3.4 million in developing the mines, which was substantially more in shorter time than the capital investment required under the concession agreement (even at Soviet exchange rates); and it had repatriated to London only £170,000, partly as a result of Soviet obstacles. By 1929, however, the New Economic Policy was over; the First Five-Year Plan was adopted by the XVIth Party Conference in April 1929; and the chairman of the Council of People's Commissars (A. I. Rykov) declared to the Main Concessions Committee in November 1929 that the number of concessions was now falling sharply, measured "in tenths of one per cent" and that concessionaires should now be required to work with their own capital with "no squeezing [of the Soviet economy] and no business with counter-revolution".[40] There was to be no room for concession agreements with foreign capitalists. Accordingly, these

[39] See *The Times*, of 31 July 1925. (As to the probable identity of the Russian lawyer who so advised him, see *infra.*)
[40] See extracts from Rykov's speech to the Main Concessions Committee on 29 Nov. 1929 in Degras, *op. cit. supra* n.38, Vol.11 (1925–1932), at p.404.

THE *LENA GOLDFIELDS* ARBITRATION   137

foreign concessions began to disappear; by 1936, only 11 remained; and by 1938, none; but Lena Goldfields was one of the first to be attacked.[41]

From the autumn of 1929, Lena Goldfields was increasingly subjected to rough treatment, at a time when it was also suffering the economic consequences of an accident to its new dredge on the Lena and other financial mishaps. As a result, Lena Goldfields' production did not meet the planned requirements of the concession agreement; by October 1929 it had not paid royalty payments due to the Soviet Union in the sum of about 645,000 roubles (£65,000); and on 1 December 1929, in London, it defaulted on the payment due to its note-holders for want of remittances from Moscow.[42] It was Lena Goldfields which was being "squeezed", so successfully that it now risked being wound up in liquidation proceedings brought by its English and foreign creditors in the English Companies Court. On 15 December 1929 matters between Lena Goldfields and the Soviet Union came to an abrupt head, with massive raids carried out by the OGPU throughout the night on Lena Goldfields' establishments in Siberia, Moscow and Leningrad. Its papers were confiscated; and its senior officers and staff arrested. Its Moscow manager, G. F. Sampson, was released the next morning when he made a full report to the newly arrived British Ambassador, Sir Esmond Ovey. On 4 January 1930 Sampson was tried before the Moscow Labour Court on criminal charges under the USSR Labour Code for permitting late payment of wages. He was convicted, fined and sentenced to eight months of hard labour. He appealed; and later that month the British Ambassador, accompanied by Major Gwynne, intervened with Litvinov to allow Lena Goldfields to pay off with a further fine his sentence of hard labour with the right also to leave the Soviet Union. Major Gwynne's urgent visit to Moscow had also revealed how utterly precarious was now Lena Goldfields' position in the Soviet Union.

D. The Commencement of the Arbitration

By early February 1930 the effect of the Soviet Union's Official harassment meant that Lena Goldfields could not carry on the concession. All protests to the Soviet

---

[41] See Hélène Carrère d'Encausse, *A History of the Soviet Union 1917–1953*, Vol.1 (1983, trans. Ionescu), p.134 and Lewis, *The United States and Foreign Investment Problems* (1948), p.150. There is an English translation in the Foreign Office papers at the Public Record Office of an article dated 2 Feb. 1930 from the *Moskauer Rundschau*, to the debatable effect that "Liquidation of new concession businesses during the past year was carried out with full consent of both parties under conditions agreeable both to the concessionaires and the Soviet Government" (PRO FO 371/14378).

[42] *The Times*, 3 and 31 Dec. 1929 and 7 and 28 Jan. 1930; and Guedella's speech to Lena Goldfields' annual general meeting on 16 Dec. 1929 (Barch. RWM 31.02 20042). The USSR had given two notices of default for non-payment of royalties under the concession agreement, by letters dated 3 Oct. and 1 Dec. 1929 (*USSR Documents*, pp.10, 11, and GARF 8350/4/57). This was a monetary claim allowed to the USSR in the *Lena* award, para.28; see also the final speech by Lena Goldfields' counsel at the Aug. 1930 hearing, recorded in *The Times*, 28 Aug. 1930.

138   ON ARBITRATION

government had gone unheeded; all attempts to negotiate any settlement had failed; it faced utter and imminent calamity; and its Russian staff were terrified. By telegram dated 12 February 1930 from its chairman, Guedella, to the Supreme Economic Council, Lena Goldfields referred the matter to arbitration under the arbitration clause and appointed as its arbitrator Sir Leslie Scott PC, KC (1869–1950).[43] He was a senior English barrister, then 61 years old, who had practised in Liverpool until 1906, taken silk in 1909 and been elected to Parliament in 1910 as a Conservative member for Liverpool until 1929, during which he had been Solicitor-General from March to October 1922 in Lloyd George's coalition government. A less honourable man could have then become Attorney-General or even Lord Chancellor under the new Conservative government under Bonar Law; but Scott rejected the offer as an invitation to betray his political friends. At the Bar, Sir Leslie Scott was acquainted with Russian litigation, appearing for the plaintiff in *Luther* v. *Sagor* [44] and for the Soviet Russian government in *Russian Volunteer Fleet* v. *The Crown*.[45] Later in 1935, he was appointed directly to the Court of Appeal, retiring in 1946.

In its notice of arbitration, it is significant that Lena Goldfields did not call expressly for the legal termination of the concession, nor did it even refer in its list of articles at issue to article 86 of the concession agreement which (as it knew) governed exhaustively its dissolution.[46] If Lena Goldfields was making any such claim, it would have done so in this telegram; and it did not. It cannot have been an oversight; and the omission must be treated as a deliberate tactical decision. Possibly, Lena Goldfields did not then wish to disappoint the hopes of its creditors still concentrated on an amicable settlement and the concession's immediate continuation, rather than its forced dissolution under an arbitration award. Lena Goldfields' reference in its notice to the impossibility of performing its own part of the concession agreement was advanced as a defence to claims already levelled by the Soviet Union that it had failed to pay royalties and committed other breaches of the concession agreement, in the event that the Soviet Union advanced a case based upon such defaults. Indeed, the Soviet Union later described Lena Goldfields' notice of arbitration as "hasten[ing] to forestall a move by the Government against [Lena Goldfields'] failure to carry out the concession agreement";[47] and even within Lena

---

[43] A copy of the original telegram exists in the Foreign Office files (PRO FO 371/14367); and see also *USSR Documents*, p.24 and GARF 8350/4/57.

[44] [1922] 3 K.B. 532.

[45] (1923) 15 Ll. L.R. 35 and 74.

[46] Art.86 of the concession agreement provided (in English translation): "The concession shall only be terminated before its time by a decision of the arbitration court. The Government is entitled to terminate the concession before the stipulated time if, on informing the arbitration court of its intention, the latter establishes (1) that Lena was guilty of failing to make payments at the due date, in accordance with articles 50 and 61 respecting business accounts, and that the Company had failed to make such payments in full within 4 (four) months after receipt of two written reminders over a period of 2 (two) months, after the lapse of time agreed for such payments …".

[47] *USSR Documents*, p.6, and GARF 8350/4/57.

THE *LENA GOLDFIELDS* ARBITRATION   139

Goldfields there was at first only muted confidence in the success of its claim. Its own counsel had advised that the chances of winning the arbitration "were good, provided that Lena and not the Russian side were the claimant and that the arbitration take place before any liquidation proceedings were commenced".[48] One of Lena Goldfields' directors and financial advisers (Hamlett) believed that Lena would lose the arbitration, whereas other directors (Guedella, Benenson, Gwynne, Harari and Malozemov) expected only that "it will be possible to obtain at least 1.5 to 3 million pounds [sterling] from the Russians, so that all creditors and possibly part of the shareholders will be paid".[49] During his recent visit to Moscow, as recounted by the British Ambassador, "Major Gwynne indicated to me that [the] arbitration would result in the payment of a large sum of money to the Company, but at other times, and particularly after our interview [with Litvinov], he seemed less confident". [50]

(1) The USSR's Counterclaim

In Moscow Lena Goldfields' notice of arbitration was considered by the Politburo's Lena commission on 20 February 1930. It decided to advance a counterclaim based on Lena Goldfields' failures, including a request to the arbitration tribunal "to consider our right to terminate the Agreement". [51] It also selected the USSR's arbitrator, Dr S. B. Chlenov, together with a juridical commission to assist him. The Politburo on 24 February 1930 approved, with minor but significant changes, its draft answer to Lena Goldfields; and by telegram dated 25 February 1930, the chairman of the Main Concessions Committee replied to Lena Goldfields with notice of a defence and counterclaim based on a list of 31 articles of the concession, not including Article 86.[52] The chairman was now L. B. Kamenev, far from his former positions as Lenin's deputy and (on Lenin's death) a member of the troika with Stalin and

---

[48] Dr Idelson, at the meeting with Lena Goldfields' German creditors on 6 Feb. 1930, p.3 (Barch. RWM 20043). After the *Lena* award, Idelson expressed the view that Lena Goldfields' "real claim, which could fairly easily have been substantiated, was more in the neighbourhood of twenty-two millions [pounds sterling]": see Fitzmaurice's note of their meeting on 18 Oct. 1930 (PRO F0371/14868).

[49] L. Schmidt, Report of the London negotiations between Lena Goldfields and its German creditors of 23–31 Jan. 1930 (Barch.RWM 31.01 20043).

[50] Sir Esmond Ovey's letter dated 6 Feb. 1930 to the Rt Hon. Arthur Henderson MP (PRO FO 371/ 14867).

[51] RTsKhlDNI 17/162/008 (approving the Lena commission: Kamenev, Stomonyakov and Litvinov).

[52] *USSR Documents*, p.25 and GARF 8350/4/7. This cable also rejected Lena Goldfield's telegram of 21 February 1930, requesting the USSR Government to undertake necessary arrangements for the suspension of Lena's business in the USSR as its organisation was entirely dislocated, adding significantly "We do not of course surrender concession but pending arbitration award must withdraw leaving all property of Lena in trust of the Government" (*USSR Documents*, p.34 and GARF 8350/4/7). By subsequent telegram of 1 Mar. 1930 to Lena Goldfields, Kamenev added to the list of articles infringed by Lena Goldfields on which the USSR was advancing its counterclaim, again without reference to Art.86 (*USSR Documents*, p.26 and GARF 8350/4/7).

140   ON ARBITRATION

Zinoviev. At this stage, Kamenev understood that the concession agreement could only be terminated by the decision of the arbitration court under Article 86; and he also believed that the Soviet Union's case for termination without compensation rested only upon Lena Goldfields' non-payment of royalties—which had to have occurred by virtue of Lena Goldfields' own fault.[53] Kamenev had been party to the Lena commission's decision to counterclaim for the termination of the concession agreement; and earlier there had been press reports from Moscow that the Soviet Union had served notice of its intention to annul the concession on Lena Goldfields.[54] In such circumstances, the Soviet Union's omission in its answer to refer at all to Article 86 or to counterclaim for termination of the concession must also be considered a deliberate tactic, designed to keep intact Lena Goldfields' continuing obligations under the concession agreement (which it now could not perform at all) and thereby to force Lena Goldfields to abandon the concession before any decision from the arbitration tribunal. Indeed, Kamenev's cable twice expressly required Lena Goldfields to continue the performance of its obligations under the concession agreement "in the future". But this was only a tactic: on 25 February 1930 the Politburo approved a general policy for the termination of all foreign concessions by dividing them into three groups for special treatment. Lena Goldfields fell into the third, least favoured group: "These concessions should be liquidated in the more or less immediate future, at the appropriate political moment."[55]

E. General Principles of Law

There was no reference to applicable law in the concession agreement; and none was advanced in Lena Goldfields' notice of arbitration of 12 February 1930 or its statement of claim dated 27 May 1930.[56] Lena's later pleading advanced the concession agreement as a contract, referring generally to Article 89 on goodwill, good faith and the reasonable interpretation of its terms[57] and setting out the Soviet Union's breaches by specific reference in each case to other articles of the concession agreement. In asserting its later claim for the dissolution of the concession agreement, Lena Goldfields also advanced a contractual case, pleading in paragraph 10 of its statement of claim that the Soviet Union's breaches "went to the root

[53] Undated letter from Kamenev to Rykov, probably of Feb. 1930 (GARF 5446/55/1970). The opinions there expressed doubtless derived also from Kamenev's legal advisers, although Kamenev himself had studied law at Moscow University.
[54] See *The Times*, 14 Feb. 1930, where Guedella denied that Lena Goldfields had received any such notice.
[55] USSR Politburo decision of 25 Feb. 1930, appendix No.12 (RTsKhIDNI 17/162/8).
[56] For the Statement of Claim, see *The Times*, 23 June and 7 Aug. 1930 and the *Deutsche Allgemeine Zeitung*, 22 June 1930.
[57] Art.89 of the concession agreement provided, in English translation: "The basis of the present agreement on the part of both parties is one of goodwill, good faith, as well as a desire to interpret its provisions reasonably."

of the Agreement [and] created a state of things when the performance of its part of the Agreement by Lena was being rendered impossible and in fact nullified the concession".

There was also nothing relating to applicable law in the Soviet Union's correspondence during its participation in the arbitration proceedings. In awarding compensation for unjust enrichment, the *Lena* tribunal relied on the Soviet Union's breach of the concession agreement using the English legal term for a repudiatory breach of contract "going to the root of it", rejecting Lena Goldfields' alternative claim based on contractual damages because it considered that the measure of compensation would not be different in restitution or contract (paragraph 25 of the *Lena* award). In arriving at that result, the *Lena* tribunal adopted the argument on applicable law advanced by Lena Goldfields in relation to restitution for unjust enrichment.

(1) Lena Goldfields' Argument

At the main August 1930 hearing, as later recorded in the *Lena* award, Lena Goldfields' counsel argued that the tribunal should apply general principles of law to its claim for unjust enrichment as the "proper law" of the concession agreement. The argument was advanced by reference to (i) the historical fact that the 1925 concession agreement and one of 13 amendments had been signed not only on behalf of "the Executive Government of Russia but by the Acting Commissary of Foreign Affairs" (the latter being a reference to Litvinov) and (ii) "that many of the terms of the contract contemplated the application of international rather than merely national principles of law". This was doubtless a reference to Articles 86 and 90 of the concession agreement whereby the Soviet Union as a sovereign State entrusted to a private arbitration tribunal abroad the power finally to decide upon the termination of the concession (a factor which had stalled the precontractual negotiations for two years).

The motive for Lena Goldfields' argument is plain. It could have been dangerous to subject the concession agreement to Soviet law as its single applicable law when the substance of Lena Goldfields' case related, directly or indirectly, to the imposition at the highest level of the Soviet policies, laws and administrative regulations which comprised the First Five-Year Plan; and it would have been hopeless to argue for the application of English law (or any other national system of law), particularly so when English law did not then fully recognise the principle of unjust enrichment. Tactically, no doubt, it would also serve the award's eventual recognition if Lena Goldfields were to receive an award blessed by widely accepted general principles of law, particularly where no remaining member of the *Lena* tribunal was qualified in Soviet law. However, Lena Goldfields also acknowledged the application of Soviet law as the second "proper law" of the concession agreement

142   ON ARBITRATION

relevant to its contractual interpretation, performance by both parties inside the Soviet Union and "domestic matters in the USSR" (save in so far as these laws were excluded by the concession agreement).[58]

(2) The Lena Tribunal

The tribunal accepted Lena Goldfields' argument with the laconic words: "In so far as any difference of interpretation [of the concession agreement] might result, the court holds that this contention is correct."[59] What did this mean? There appears to have been no material difference of interpretation; and no explanation was given by the tribunal to justify the leap in logic from interpretation, performance and domestic matters governed by Soviet law to unjust enrichment governed by general principles of law. If Soviet law applied at all to the parties' transaction, then why not also those provisions of the 1922 RSFSR Civil Code dealing with unjust enrichment as the law characterising Lena Goldfields' cause of action or the law of the place of the enrichment or the law of the debtor? This was not a case where Soviet law lacked any appropriate remedy, as the tribunal itself recognised in its award. And if there were to be two "proper laws", then why make the split along these particular lines? On any view, the tribunal expressed itself obscurely on issues of critical importance; and like many precedents in the field of arbitration, it may be that those immediately involved at the time did not fully consider the enormity of what they were deciding. Nussbaum severely criticised this part of the Lena award: "such a splitting of applicable legal systems was not warranted; the 'proper law' of the entire contract was Soviet".[60] However, as Nussbaum also pointed out, of all the public attacks on the Lena award the Soviet Union never itself voiced this particular criticism. There is no record in the Politburo archives of this point having been considered, although the Soviet Union did not refrain from other harsh comment on

---

[58] See the Lena award, para.22, where the Lena tribunal recorded and accepted the submission of Lena Goldfields' counsel. (Unfortunately, the reports of the Aug. 1930 hearing in The Times contain no record of such submission.) As for the reference to Soviet law, both the 1920 Decree dated 23 Dec. 1920 (see supra n.38 above) and Art.76 of the concession agreement precluded the USSR from making by itself any change to the concession agreement "by disposition, decree or other unilateral acts of the state authorities"; but where the concession agreement was silent, Art.75 subjected Lena Goldfields to "the existing legal code and to future enactments and ordinances of the Government of the USSR". The Lena tribunal decided that Lena's legal position was completely protected under these provisions: see the Lena award, para.18(i). In practice, however, Lena's legal position could be changed at the USSR's will—and it was.

[59] The original German text of the Lena award reads similarly for the equivalent passage in its para.22: "Insoweit wie sich eine Meinungsverschiedenheit über die Auslegung ergibt, hält das Gericht diesen Standpunkt für richtig."

[60] Nussbaum, op. cit. supra n.24, at p.36: see also Mann (1959) B.Y.I.L. 34, 56: "It is doubtful whether any such scission which is justifiably criticised by Nussbaum was possible in law. It is still more doubtful whether in the circumstances of the case there was any warrant for it." The characterisation of claims for unjust enrichment remains difficult: see T. W. Bennett, "Choice of Law Rules in Claims of Unjust Enrichment" (1990) 39 I.C.L.Q. 136.

THE *LENA GOLDFIELDS* ARBITRATION   143

the legal merits of Lena's claim. Any further explanation of the award on the application of general principles must be found not from its terms but from the remarkable jurist who made the argument to the *Lena* tribunal, Lena Goldfields' counsel, Dr Idelson.

(3) Dr V. R. Idelson[61]

Born in Rostov on Don in 1881, Vladimir Robertovich Idelson had practised as a lawyer in St Petersburg until 1917. He was educated at the Taganrog Classical Gymnasium, near Rostov on the Sea of Azov, and at the Universities of Kharkhov (where he studied law) and Berlin (where he received his doctorate in philosophy). From 1906 he was a dozent teaching commercial law at the Imperial Peter the Great Polytechnic in St Petersburg. After the February 1917 Revolution he worked as legal adviser to the Russian Treasury under the provisional government. After the "Red Terror" broke out in Petrograd in 1918, Idelson escaped arrest and execution by fleeing to the Crimea, then controlled by the Whites, to rejoin his young wife in Yalta for eventual exile in France and England, arriving in London by January 1920. As commercial disputes and opportunities emerged from Soviet Russia's nationalisation decrees, Idelson practised as an émigré Russian lawyer in London, in particular as an expert witness on Russian law in the English courts. In July 1921 he advised the Bank of England in the *Russian Gold* test action in the English High Court which decided that Soviet gold roubles were not attachable in respect of obligations of the previous Czarist and provisional governments, thereby enabling the Anglo-Soviet Trade Agreement of March 1921 to take effect.[62] Encouraged by an English High Court judge to read for the Bar, Idelson was called to Gray's Inn in June 1926 and was a pupil to D. N. Pritt. He became a naturalised British citizen in 1930, took silk in 1943 and was admitted as a Bencher of Lincoln's Inn in 1947. He died on 20 November 1954, aged 73. Idelson is still remembered in Lincoln's Inn, in his older years after the Second World War, as a large and likeable character. Having arrived from Russia in middle age, Idelson had a most successful legal career in England as a practitioner and scholar for over 30 years. He was, it seems, the first foreign-born naturalised King's Counsel.

---

[61] I am indebted to Dr Idelson's son and granddaughter, R. F. Idelson and Tamara Idelson, for unpublished information and documents relating to his life and career. There are two obituaries of Idelson: Professor N. de Mattos Bentwich (1955) 4 I.C.L.Q. 27 and "KSC", *idem*, p.28; and see also *Who Was Who* (1951–1960). In *Russian Commercial Bank* v. *Comptoir d'Escompte de Mulhouse* [1925] A.C. 112, the printed case for the appeal to the House of Lords contains the transcript of Idelson's expert testimony which provides biographical details not available elsewhere; and the record of benchers of Lincoln's Inn Library also contains Idelson's photograph, in full-bottomed wig and owl-like glasses, probably taken in 1947.

[62] See *A. G. Marshall* v. *Mary Grinbaum and Bank of England* (1921) 8 Ll. L.R. 342 and R. H. Ullmann, *The Anglo-Soviet Accord*, ibid, p.453. (Idelson was paid 100 guineas by the Bank of England's solicitors, Freshfields & Leese: Freshfields' private letter dated 18 Aug. 1921.)

144   ON ARBITRATION

In England Idelson's work in the field of public and private international law was extensive. After the *Lena* arbitration, instructed by the British Petroleum Company, Idelson drafted much of the Anglo-Iranian concession convention of 29 April 1933, including the arbitration clause. Its Article 22 provided for an arbitration award based on the juridical principles contained in Article 38 of the Statute of the Permanent Court of International Arbitration; and its Article 21 provided for the application of "principles of mutual goodwill and good faith as well as on a reasonable interpretation of this Convention" (translated from the French).[63] Idelson's draftsmanship explains why these provisions bear remarkable similarities both to the *Lena* award and to Articles 89 and 90 of the Lena concession agreement, including several of the "default" provisions and the tribunal's choice of the arbitral seat. Ever since, Idelson's innovative drafting has much influenced later draftsmen of concessions and State contracts. Later in 1951, towards the end of his life, Idelson was closely involved in the dispute between Iran, the United Kingdom and the Anglo-Iranian Company, advising the latter in regard to both its own arbitration proceedings against Iran over the nationalisation of its assets and the United Kingdom's complaint before the International Court of Justice in the *Anglo-Iranian Oil Company* case (where the *Lena* award was cited in the United Kingdom's Memorial[64]).

Shortly after Iran's nationalisation, Eli Lauterpacht (then John Megaw's pupil) also recalls an early conference with his father and Idelson at the latter's chambers at 13 Old Square, Lincoln's Inn, where the beginnings of the legal argument were discussed which lead eventually to *The Rose Mary*,[65] where the Aden court held that the disputed oil on that vessel remained the company's property because, not being an Iranian national, the court could refuse to recognise Iran's nationalisation as amounting to expropriation without compensation contrary to international law (as argued by, *inter alios*, Megaw as junior counsel for the plaintiff).

---

[63] In 1931 Idelson advised the company with Wilfred Greene KC that the existing concession was legally binding on the Persian government; and in Jan. 1933 Idelson attended the meetings in Geneva between the British Foreign Secretary (Sir John Simon) and representatives of the Persian government aimed at an amicable settlement of the dispute, with Dr Edward Benes as the rapporteur (the Czech Republic's Foreign Secretary): see R. W. Ferrier, *The History of the British Petroleum Company*, Vol.1, p.619; and J. H. Bamberg, *The History of the British Petroleum Company*, Vol.2, pp. 39 *et seq.* Idelson had earlier advised BP on its interests in Venezuela in 1927: *idem*, pp.144 *et seq.*

[64] See *Anglo-Iranian Case Pleadings* (1952), *supra* n.15. This part of the memorial of 10 Oct. 1951 was prepared by Sir Hersch Lauterpacht KC. His first draft did not contain any reference to the *Lena* award: see E. Lauterpacht (Ed.), *International Law (being the Collected Papers of Hersch Lauterpacht QC)* (1970), Vol.4, p.23. Prior to Iran's nationalisation in May 1951, there was a joint opinion by Idelson and Lauterpacht, undated but probably from Mar. 1951, on the operation of the 1933 concession convention's arbitration clause, instructed by Linklater & Paines for BP (PRO F0371/91526). The company invoked arbitration on 8 May 1951, appointing Lord Radcliffe as its arbitrator; but Iran failed to appoint its arbitrator and eventually the President and Vice-President of the ICJ declined to perform the task of appointing the sole arbitrator assigned to the President of the PCIJ under Art.22(d) of the concession convention. The arbitration clause was thereby rendered ineffective, as Idelson and Lauterpacht had warned in their joint opinion; see also Mann (1967) B.Y.I.L. 1, 20–24.

[65] [1953] 1 W.L.R. 246.

(4) Idelson's Argument

Against this legal background, it necessarily must be assumed that Idelson's argument on applicable law was not fully recorded in the *Lena* award. It doubtless proceeded from an analysis of the legal order which the parties intended to govern their legal relationship (by inference or presumption), from an assumption that the Soviet Union could agree, at least in part, to the application of legal rules other than Soviet law, and then to the conclusion as regards the substance of the parties' transaction, that the parties cannot have intended their relationship to be governed exclusively by Soviet law, as with their arbitration agreement involving a non-Soviet *lex loci arbitri*. At this point, "general principles of law" offered a more acceptable solution than any other national system of law. There was no attempt by Idelson to apply public international law *stricto sensu*; and no reliance seems to have been placed on the "good faith" provision in the concession agreement (Article 89) as a choice of applicable legal rules. It is more difficult to explain the particular split between "proper laws" recorded by the *Lena* tribunal. However Idelson would have been acquainted with Soviet scholarly writings on foreign concessions, including the works of the Soviet Union's legal adviser in the *Lena* arbitration, Professor V. N. Shreter. In his 1924 work Shreter had analysed the dual juridical nature of a concession agreement under Soviet law: it created a unique relationship consisting of both (i) a special law in the form of a decree of the USSR Council of People's Commissars exempting the concession from the general law; and (ii) the bilateral agreement of the Soviet Union and the concessionaire. In this sense, it differed from an English or French statute granting a monopoly which was only the unilateral act of the sovereign power. This dual nature probably lay at the heart of Idelson's argument on the split between the application of Soviet law and general principles of law, as appears from the following passage in Shreter's work (translated into English):[66]

> The concession is an act of public law, but it does not mean that all the conditions of a concession agreement have necessarily the same nature. The complex nature of the concession relationship in our country, as well as in the West, combines elements of both private and public law. For example, the grant of a right to establish an enterprise and the obligation to fulfil a production programme creates a relationship in public law, as well as the grant of any privilege in the fields of taxation, foreign trade, etc. At the same time, the handing-over of nationalised plant to a concessionaire and the concessionaire's obligation to maintain such plant in order to return it at the concession agreement's expiry to the Government without compensation, this is a private law condition. The dual nature of a concession relationship does not create any specific practical problems, because the

---

[66] Shreter, Systema promyshlennogo prava SSSR (*System of Industrial Law of the USSR*) (1924), pp.80–81.

relationship is so unique that it does not fit into any norms of the [1922] Civil Code or public law. The concession agreement should provide exhaustive regulation of all conditions for the concession, referring to the general law only in those instances where the concession does not create any special rights or obligations for the parties. However, this circumstance becomes very important when it comes to the question of jurisdiction over disputes between the parties arising from the concession. Such disputes are not limited to issues of civil law and are thus not subject to jurisdiction under civil law; and according to our law such disputes should be filed as administrative complaints all the way up to the Central Executive Committee [TsIK SSSR—the Soviet Union's supreme legislative and executive organ]. Practical inconvenience caused by this dual jurisdiction for disputes arising from the same concession agreement is usually resolved by the concession agreement providing specially for reference to arbitration for the settlement of disputes arising between the Government and the concessionaire from the interpretation and performance of their agreement.

Accordingly, this Soviet legal distinction between "private law" and "public law" may explain the difference in the *Lena* award between the application of general principles of law to the private claim for unjust enrichment and the application of Soviet law as public law to the concession agreement's interpretation, internal performance and domestic matters, where there is also an echo of the French "*contrat administratif*". Given the arbitration clause as a special law, the *Lena* tribunal had jurisdiction to apply both private and public law to the parties' dispute—hence the need to identify two "proper laws" in the *Lena* award. If in this manner Idelson's approach was rooted in Soviet scholarly writings, it would also explain the absence of any Soviet complaint over the *Lena* tribunal's treatment of applicable laws.

As Lena Goldfields' counsel in the *Lena* arbitration, Idelson's internationalisation of a transnational contract was a gigantic first step for international commercial arbitration, almost equivalent to the caveman's discovery of fire. His innovation eventually spawned a mass of followers in France, Switzerland and elsewhere, not limited to State contracts or concessions. Most recently, in England, Lord Wilberforce, speaking extrajudicially in the House of Lords during the second reading of the Arbitration Bill in January 1996 said:[67]

> I would like to dwell for a moment on one point to which I personally attach some importance. I have never taken the view that arbitration is a kind of annex, appendix or poor relation to court proceedings. I have always wished to see arbitration, as far as possible, and subject to statutory guidelines no doubt, regarded as

---

[67] *HL Hansard*, 18 Jan. 1996, col.778.

a free standing system, free to settle its own procedure and free to settle its own substantive law—yes, its substantive law.

Under section 46(1)(b) of the English Arbitration Act 1996, based upon Article 28 of the UNCITRAL Model Law, an English arbitration tribunal may now decide a dispute (if the parties so agree) in accordance with considerations other than a national law, as are either agreed by the parties or determined by the tribunal; and the new 1998 LCIA Rules allow an arbitration tribunal to decide the parties' dispute applying the law(s) or rules of law which it considers appropriate, both where the parties have so chosen but also in the absence of any chosen national law (as do the ICC rules, old and new). Yet the historical roots of this original idea lie not in Paris, Geneva, Vienna or Rome but in the mind of an Anglophile Russian exile in London over 65 years ago.

F. Truncated Tribunal

Under most modern systems of international arbitration, an arbitrator appointed by one party is nonetheless an arbitrator for all parties. There can be no unilateral secret communication between a party and an arbitrator after the formation of the tribunal (still less a secret "juridical commission" to assist his work); and an appointing party cannot properly instruct an arbitrator to thwart the arbitral process. Moreover, an arbitrator cannot baldly resign his office at the demand of his appointing party in order to stall the arbitration. Over the years, for their respective conduct in the *Lena* arbitration, the Soviet Union and its appointed arbitrator, Dr Chlenov, have received severe condemnation from many legal commentators. In fact, the true position was more complicated; and it may also explain why the Soviet Union so abruptly abandoned the *Lena* arbitration in mid-journey.

(1) Article 90(F)

The parties' arbitration clause contained an important provision. If one party did not attend or send its appointed arbitrator to the arbitration hearings, then, at the request of the other party, the dispute was to be decided by the other member of the arbitration court and the chairman: see Article 90(F) below. This was a provision clearly intended to protect Lena Goldfields against any procedural recalcitrance by the Soviet Union; and (in so far as can now be known) it had not emerged in previous concession agreements with English companies.[68] There was no general

---

[68] Contrast the arbitration clause in the 1922 draft concession agreement negotiated by Urquhart's Russia-Asiatic Consolidated Ltd to retrieve its former Russian mining properties in the form of a

148   ON ARBITRATION

principle of English law allowing a majority of the tribunal to continue with the proceedings to a binding award in such circumstances; and even the phrase "truncated tribunal" had still to be invented. Even today, such a provision is controversial but nonetheless essential to the conduct of international commercial arbitration.[69] Whoever drafted this part of Article 90, it was an innovative and experienced jurist. Sadly, unlike the masters of great paintings, legal draftsmen do not sign their work. However, in the circumstances, it had to be a lawyer engaged by Lena Goldfields and not by the Soviet Union, a Russian draftsman (given the language of the concession agreement), someone by 1925 experienced in the pitfalls of Anglo-Soviet trade and, given that the arbitration clause was a sticking-point in the parties' negotiations for more than two years, a person available to Lena Goldfields outside Soviet Russia from at least 1923. It had also to be a jurist known to and trusted by Guedella and Benenson, Lena Goldfields' principal backers. There is no direct evidence of his identity, but there is only one person known to qualify as the draftsman: this part of the *Lena* arbitration clause was almost certainly drafted between 1923 and 1925 by Idelson.[70] For the *Lena* arbitration, his drafting was prescient in the extreme.

(2) Three Events

The parties' further settlement discussions began in Berlin on or soon after 4 April 1930, without immediate result. They were nonetheless continued to the extent that the original hearing date before the tribunal on 30 April 1930 was put back at the request of the Soviet Union and with Lena Goldfields' consent, with the place of the hearing also changed from Paris to Berlin.[71] The *Lena* tribunal thus fixed the first procedural hearing of the arbitration for Friday, 9 May 1930 at the Adlon Hotel, Berlin. Before that hearing took place, however, three events occurred which changed the entire conduct of the *Lena* arbitration.

---

concession agreement with Soviet Russia (PRO F0371/8162). The Urquhart arbitration clause had Moscow as the arbitral seat whereas the Lena clause had a foreign seat selected by the arbitration tribunal; and the Urquhart default procedures were limited to failures in forming the arbitration tribunal whereupon the aggrieved party could invoke the jurisdiction of the Moscow or London courts, as the case might be. Urquhart's draft, including its arbitration clause, was personally vetoed by Lenin in Oct. 1922. Urquhart's negotiations with the USSR continued until at least 1929 but his efforts were eclipsed by the Lena concession in 1925: see the Politburo's "Urquhart" and "Lena" commission decisions of 11 and 29 July 1924 (RTsKhIDNI 17/003/448 & 17/003/453): see also *infra* n.76.

[69] E.g. see Art.12 of the New 1998 LCIA Rules "Majority Power to Continue Proceedings"; and Art.12(5) of the New 1998 ICC Rules allowing the ICC Court to order proceedings to continue.
[70] His contribution to the arbitration clause is perhaps also evidenced by its use of the Russian term "president" rather than the Soviet Russian word "super-arbitrator": see Art.90(G), (H) *infra* in the Appendix and *supra* n.35.
[71] See *The Times*, 3 June 1930.

THE *LENA GOLDFIELDS* ARBITRATION   149

(a) The "Stutzer problem"

Stutzer was chosen by Lena Goldfields on 7 April 1930 from a list of six mining professors at Freiberg nominated by Kamenev on 26 March 1930, as required by the parties' arbitration agreement. Stutzer had not been the first choice of either party. Under Article 90(B) the parties could agree the chairman; and during the Moscow negotiations in March 1930, Guedella had proposed as "super-arbitrator" the Swedish lawyer Dr E. Loefgren or the Swiss Professor Eugène Borel. Kamenev declined these nominations and in turn proposed a distinguished German scientist, then the Director of the Kaiser Wilhelm Institute for Physics at Berlin University and winner of the 1921 Nobel prize: Professor Albert Einstein. Lena duly reciprocated by formally vetoing Kamenev's nomination. As almost invariably happens today, Lena Goldfields probably rejected Einstein on the ground only that he was the Soviet Union's nominee. Accordingly, under Article 90(C), the Soviet Union was now required to compile a list of six candidates from the Freiberg Mining Academy. In order to prepare this list, Kamenev sent Professor Federovskii of the Moscow Institute of Applied Mineralogy to Freiberg to check its professors; and after discussions with the USSR Trade Delegation in Berlin, Federovskii's list included Stutzer who, as he reported to Kamenev, "has made no unfriendly public statements against the USSR."[72] Trouble began on 1 April 1930 when Kamenev received other information from Berlin that Professor Stutzer had made a report "in which he spoke in sharply negative terms about the situation in the USSR and our Five-Year Plan". Kamenev immediately discussed the problem with his deputy, V. N. Ksandrov; and both concluded that there was no choice but to stand by the Soviet Union's previous list of 26 March 1930. Kamenev also reported his concerns by letter of 1 April 1930 addressed to Rykov (as chairman of the Council of People's Commissars); but from annotations on that document, it seems that Rykov reported the matter to Stalin on 4 April 1930.[73] And then, three days later, catastrophe struck: Lena Goldfields selected Professor Stutzer as chairman of the Lena tribunal from the Soviet Union's own list in strict compliance with the parties' arbitration agreement.

(b) The "Lena show-trial"

The Soviet Union's long-planned show-trial began in Moscow on 16 April 1930, intended to blacken Lena Goldfields' name and to exert pressure for an early and favourable settlement at the parties' negotiations in Berlin.[74] In *Pravda* the trial was

---

[72] Stutzer had visited the USSR in early 1929 to inspect brown coal deposits in Moscow and Tula: (see his report at Zeitschr.Deutsch.Geol.Ges. 82 (1930) 8, 5, 453–462); but I have found nothing to justify the USSR's attack on Stutzer's independence or impartiality. Lena Goldfields' German creditors had also investigated the six professors on the USSR's list; and after private enquiries, they canvassed Lena Goldfields for Stutzer's appointment after hearing the mayor of Freiberg describe him as "a patriotic, well-read and energetic gentleman" (Kandler-Schmidt report of 8 Apr. 1930: Barch. RWM 31.01 20043).

[73] Kamenev's letter dated 1 Apr. 1930 (GARF 5446/55/1970).

[74] Such a show-trial had first been proposed by the Lena commission on 20 Feb. 1930, based upon the OGPU's seizures of Lena Goldfields' papers in mid-Dec. 1929 (RTsKhIDNI 17/162/008); but on

150 ON ARBITRATION

called "Spies and Saboteurs";[75] and it received wide publicity in England. The three Russians facing criminal prosecution were Lena Goldfields' chief metallurgist (K. D. Kolyasnikov), its chief legal adviser (N. M. Muromtsev) and an engineer (Ryabov de Ribon). The fourth defendant was a simple-minded Russian worker employed as a foreman by the State-owned Ridder-Zinc foundry (A. A. Bashkirtsev). All pleaded guilty save Muromtsev. Whilst not present at the trial or even indicted, the effective defendants were senior officers and employees of Lena Goldfields, all safely outside the Soviet Union: Benenson, F. L. Ivanov, A. Malozemov, Gulyayev and G. T. Eve. Another absent accused was Leslie Urquhart of Russia-Asiatic Consolidated Limited, now attacked as a foreign predator absurdly still claiming 560 million gold roubles as compensation from the Soviet State for his lost enterprises as the foremost British entrepreneur in Czarist Russia. These had included the Ridder foundry, now State-owned but allegedly burnt down in August 1929 by Lena Goldfields' spies, saboteurs and counter-revolutionaries, at a massive loss to the Soviet Union in excess of 2,000 million roubles.[76]

The trial continued to 8 May 1930 before the USSR Supreme Court's Criminal Collegium presided over by V. P. Antonov-Saratovsky. The defendants were facing execution; and there was grave concern expressed in the English press and Parliament where both Lena Goldfields and the British Foreign Secretary (Arthur Henderson) strenuously denied all allegations of espionage. The trial was clearly modelled on the 1928 Shakhty show-trial which had implicated German engineers on similar charges; and it was doubtless also designed for both domestic and foreign consumption.[77] Of the four defendants, Kolyasnikov and Muromtsev were found guilty of espionage and economic counter-revolution and sentenced to ten years in prison, reduced to six years followed by loss of civic rights for five years; Bashkirtsev was found guilty of counter-revolutionary arson at the Ridder-Zinc foundry and sentenced to death by firing-squad, reduced to ten years in prison followed by loss of civic rights for five years; and the fourth, Ryabov de Ribon, was found guilty of a lesser charge and sentenced to one year in prison. Kolyasnikov's

20 Apr. 1930 the Politburo approved Stalin's suggestion that this trial be organised "in such a way as to illuminate sufficiently clearly the arson at the Ridder factory organised by one of Lena's managers" (RTsKhIDNI 17/162/008).

[75] See the contemporary press reports during Apr. and May 1930 in *Pravda* and *The Times* and M. M. Glazunov, "The Lena Goldfields Case" Byelleten' verkhonogo suda CCCP, 1984, No.2, 42.

[76] For the extraordinary Russian career of Leslie Urquhart (1875–1933), particularly his failed negotiations with Soviet Russia for compensation or restitution in the form of a concession, see T. S. Martin, "The Urquhart Concession and Anglo-Soviet Relations 1921–1922" (1972) 20 Jahrbücher für Geschichte Osteuropas 551; Kennedy, *op. cit. supra* n.31; and G. N. Blainey, *Mines in the Spinifex* (1960); and see *supra* n.68.

[77] As *Pravda* itself confirmed in its reports of the *Lena* trial. The Shakhty show-trial had opened on 18 May 1928, over which A. Y. Vyshinsky presided, against 5 German engineers and 48 Soviet specialists. Owing to strong diplomatic protests from the German government, the Germans were either acquitted or released without further imprisonment: see K. Rosenbaum, "The German Involvement in the Shakhty Trial" (1962) XXI Russian Review 238 (Ohio State University Press).

THE *LENA GOLDFIELDS* ARBITRATION   151

case was significant for the *Lena* arbitration. He was a graduate of the Freiberg School of Mines; he worked at Kyshtym before the October 1917 Revolution for Urquhart and Hoover;[78] after Admiral Kolchak's defeat in 1920, he escaped from Siberia to the United States and England; but in October 1925 he returned from emigration to work as Lena Goldfields' senior metallurgist, possibly because his wife had remained in Russia. Kolyasnikov had been kept in custody since the OGPU raids in mid-December 1929 despite all protests by Lena Goldfields; and at trial he pleaded guilty. His ultimate fate remains unknown, as do those of his co-defendants.

It is inevitable that the chairman of the Lena tribunal, Professor Stutzer, knew or at least knew of Kolyasnikov as a former Freiberg student. Even if Stutzer still had an open mind, it was by now most certainly not an empty mind; and the Soviet Union clearly had a problem with Stutzer. Of all the possible reasons for the Soviet Union's abrupt decision to abandon the *Lena* arbitration in early May 1930, the concern over Stutzer provides the best explanation. The confirmation comes from a note of a meeting over lunch on 18 October 1930 between Idelson and Fitzmaurice, then the Foreign Office's Third Legal Adviser:[79]

> [Dr Idelson] seemed to think that the real reason for their refusal to take part in the arbitration and for withdrawing their arbitrator, was an objection to Dr Stutzer, who had apparently only recently returned from a visit to Russia and had made certain statements in speeches, and in the German press, which were not of a very complimentary kind; that they had already suggested various other arbitrators, including amongst others Dr Einstein (!) and that they apparently really wanted to secure the constitution of a new Court of Arbitration, of which Dr Stutzer should not be the President.

This was of course not a reason which the Soviet Union could offer in public. It had, after all, nominated Professor Stutzer in its own list of six professors. In order to challenge him, it would be necessary for the Soviet Union to invent a legal pretext; and Lena Goldfields soon provided one.

(c) Lena's "abandonment"

Before the first procedural hearing in Berlin, Lena Goldfields announced to the Main Concessions Committee that it was abandoning its concession. By telegram dated 29 April 1930,[80] Lena Goldfields confirmed

---

[78] In Sept. 1911 and Oct. 1913 Herbert Hoover travelled to Kyshtim and the Ridder Mines, staying with the Urquharts: see G. H. Nash, *The Life of Herbert Hoover* (1988), Vol.1, pp.426–437, Vol.2 pp.257–275.

[79] PRO FO 371/14868. Sir Gerald Fitzmaurice (1901–1982), the Foreign Office's Third Legal Adviser (1929–1939), later judge of the ICJ (1960–1973) and judge of the European Court of Human Rights (1974–1980).

[80] *USSR Documents*, p.34; GARF 8350/4/7.

152 ON ARBITRATION

our Company has now finally decided that not only concession agreement impossible to perform under existing conditions but also that resumption of work even if certain conditions discussed by [Settlement] Commission were altered has now become entirely impossible. No one except Government can protect properties. We beg point out that any damage concession property in USSR from now cannot be our responsibility because as we already declared our undertaking in USSR cannot any more be controlled from here.

By two telegrams of 1 May 1930 to the Main Concessions Committee, Major Gwynne also complained of further actions and accusations against Lena Goldfields in Russia and demanded: "Government must henceforth pending the award be responsible for carrying on concession and we are acting accordingly."[81] In the absence of any reasonable plan from the government, Lena Goldfields intended laying the facts before the *Lena* tribunal at the forthcoming hearing in Berlin; and in the meantime it was instructing all foreign personnel to return home and cancelling all powers of attorney in Russia. As Kamenev had intended, Lena Goldfields was abandoning the concession as a matter of fact; but this was no deliberate repudiation of the concession agreement, still less its attempted unilateral dissolution. Lena Goldfields had raised during the settlement discussions both in Moscow and Berlin the need for a *modus vivendi* for the maintenance of the properties pending the *Lena* tribunal's award;[82] and in the absence of any *modus vivendi*, Lena Goldfields' decision to abandon the concession was inevitable. Nonetheless, Lena Goldfields' telegrams now created the factual basis for the Soviet Union's allegation that the *Lena* tribunal lacked any jurisdiction to decide Lena Goldfields' claim to terminate the concession agreement, thereby allowing the Soviet Union to withdraw from the *Lena* arbitration.

(3) The USSR's Withdrawal

In response to Lena Goldfields' "abandonment", the Politburo decided on 5 May 1930 to withdraw from the *Lena* arbitration, approving the Lena commission's report of 3 May 1930:[83] Chlenov was instructed not to attend the procedural hearing in Berlin; and Kamenev announced the Soviet Union's refusal to appear at that hearing by a long explanatory telegram dated 5 May 1930 to Stutzer, the chairman of the *Lena* tribunal, nonetheless offering to pay Stutzer's costs.[84] The telegram made express reference to Article 86 of the concession agreement in a passage

---

[81] *USSR Documents*, pp.22, 35; GARF 8350/4/7.
[82] See *The Times*, 3 June 1930.
[83] RTsKhIDNI 17/162/008; GARF 5446/55/1970 (Molotov, Piatakov, Kamenev and Ksandrov).
[84] *USSR Documents*, p.29 and GARF 8350/4/57: see also *The Times*, 10 May 1930.

THE *LENA GOLDFIELDS* ARBITRATION   153

inserted in the draft by the Politburo.[85] It also referred to the concession agreement now having "ceased to exist", unfortunate wording (also in the Russian text) which soon misled the *Lena* tribunal into believing that the Soviet Union was treating the concession agreement and therefore its arbitration clause as no longer extant. Stutzer replied to Kamenev's cable, by telegram dated 7 May 1930, that the Berlin hearing could be cancelled only by the wish of both parties; and he requested that Chlenov should attend the hearing. By telegram dated 8 May 1930 to Stutzer, Kamenev stood by his government's previous decision.[86]

Kamenev soon received Chlenov's response to his instructions. From the USSR Embassy in Paris, Chlenov sent this message on 9 May 1930 to Kamenev in Moscow. In English translation, it reads:[87]

> In accordance with your instructions I do not consider myself an arbitrator any more and I did not attend the session of the arbitration court. However, I consider it my duty to warn you that the position you have taken is legally very doubtful. Both parties can ask the arbitrators to recognise the arbitration as not having taken place or as having been stopped, but I have doubts that one party has the right to declare that the arbitration did not take place. It is my opinion that a party does not have the right, once the arbitration tribunal has been constituted, to call back the arbitrator it has appointed if the calling-back is legally unjustified: and the non-appearance of one of the arbitrators does give the right to the remaining two arbitrators to continue the arbitration proceedings without him. According to the newspapers, Lena Goldfields is determined to demand the continuation of the arbitration in spite of my absence. What position will you take up in that case? Chlenov.

No expert today on the truncated tribunal could have drafted a statement on the point in clearer terms. It was also a brave message. No harbinger of bad news is welcome, still less one soon proved right.

Shortly thereafter, by telegram dated 22 May 1930 to Lena Goldfields, Kamenev elaborated upon the new Soviet position:[88]

> the [Soviet] Government considers that it has proved that the concessionaire by his one-sided action infringed article 86 of the agreement actually and formally, thus refusing to carry out the concession agreement. The concessionaire has thus deprived the arbitration court, which was appointed by both parties for deciding the questions in connection with carrying out the agreement, of its raison d'être

---

[85] RTsKhIDNI 17/162/008, amending the draft prepared by its Lena commission (Rykov, Kamenev, Piatakov and Molotov).
[86] *USSR Documents*, p.31 and GARF 8350/4/57.
[87] GARF 5446/55/1970.
[88] *USSR Documents*, p.23 and GARF 8350/4/57.

154   ON ARBITRATION

... the Government is always ready to continue the negotiations in connection with the winding up of the concession and is convinced that it is possible to come to a friendly arrangement. This will, however, only be possible if you will formally renounce the arbitration court, which has now lost its validity and lawful basis, considering that it was appointed for the settlement of quite different questions.

In this cable, Kamenev's argument is clear: it was no attack on the continuing validity of the arbitration clause but rather on the limited scope of the *Lena* tribunal's jurisdiction, falling short of any new dispute relating to the termination of the concession agreement.

(4) The Procedural Hearings

At the first procedural hearing of 9 May 1930 in Berlin, the two members of the *Lena* tribunal concluded that the Soviet Union's jurisdictional challenge was based on an allegation that Lena Goldfields had cancelled the whole concession agreement and that the arbitration was thereby brought to an end. It ruled that the concession agreement could not be cancelled unilaterally by either party; by virtue of Article 86 of the concession agreement, only the court of arbitration could terminate it; and the concession agreement still being operative, its arbitration clause and the *Lena* tribunal's jurisdiction remained unaffected. Applying Article 90(F), the tribunal then continued its work notwithstanding the absence of both the Soviet Union and Chlenov; and it appointed a secretariat, ordering the parties to exchange pleadings and fixing the next hearing for 19 June 1930.[89] That order led to Lena Goldfields' statement of claim where, for the first time, it pleaded a claim under Article 86 for the termination of the concession by the tribunal. The second procedural hearing was held in London, on 19 June 1930, at the Royal Courts of Justice in the Strand.[90] The Soviet Union was again missing, as was Chlenov. By this date, as recited by Lena Goldfields' Counsel (Idelson), the Soviet Union's case had undergone three changes:[91]

First, they wanted an arbitration court, then they did not, and finally they seemed to desire a new court.... According to a well-informed newspaper correspondent in Moscow, the Soviet Government wanted a new arbitration court whose proceedings should take place in Moscow; but under the concession agreement the company had the right to ask for an arbitration court outside Russia.

---

[89] See *The Times*, 10 May 1930; but see the *Lena* award, para.11.
[90] An account of this second hearing is recited in *The Times*, 20 June 1930; see also the *Lena* award, para.14. (Until recently, it was not unusual for private arbitrations to sit in the Law Courts.)
[91] See *The Times*, 30 June 1930.

THE *LENA GOLDFIELDS* ARBITRATION   155

All this was correct; but the *Lena* tribunal still did not grasp the legal basis for the Soviet Union's jurisdictional challenge. By this time, the Soviet Union had begun publicly to justify its refusal to take part in the arbitration. It apparently sent a text to *The Times*, which the editor refused to publish.[92] It had also caused to be published in the German press various statements in its defence; and it appears also to have sent communications directly to the *Lena* tribunal, not limited to the Bernstein pamphlet.[93] All this was to no avail in the absence of the Soviet Union as a party and its appointed arbitrator within the *Lena* arbitration. Under Idelson's drafting of the arbitration clause, the *Lena* tribunal as a "truncated tribunal" could proceed to an award on the merits; and Chlenov's warning was soon proved utterly correct.

(5) Dr S. B. Chlenov

Little is publicly known of Semyon Borisovich Chlenov (1890–1937). Yet his life and its ending merit recording as one of the earliest "truncating" arbitrators in the history of modern arbitration, in stark contrast to Idelson's life in English exile. In March 1928 the Soviet Union had appointed Chlenov as its arbitrator in the arbitration commenced by Averell Harriman under their concession agreement over the manganese mines at Chiatura in Georgia; but this dispute was soon settled before any award.[94] In 1930, Chlenov was known to Lena Goldfields only as a Soviet legal adviser attached to the USSR Embassy in Paris; he was a specialist on foreign trade and international arbitration; and in October 1930, after the *Lena* arbitration, he took part in the Anglo-Soviet Debts and Claims Commission in London.[95] In late 1935 Chlenov was called back from Paris to Moscow where, in August 1936, he was arrested for "participating in a counter-revolutionary terrorist organisation". In March 1938 Bukharin at his show-trial was required to denounce his old schoolfriend; but Chlenov was safely dead, executed on 3 May 1937 after a secret hearing before the Military Collegium of the USSR Supreme Court. It is now known that Chlenov's body was taken to the Donskoi Monastery in the south of

---

[92] This was alleged in a parliamentary question to the Foreign Secretary on 30 June 1930 by the Labour MP, Edward Wise CB (1885–1933), an economic adviser on foreign trade to Tsentrosoyuz (Arcos) since 1923, previously a civil servant and a senior adviser to Lloyd George on Anglo-Russian affairs from 1918 to 1922, including the Genoa Conference. (*The Times* has not retained any such letter.)

[93] This was alleged by Dr Idelson, at the main hearing on 6 Aug. 1930 (see *The Times*, 7 Aug. 1930).

[94] The Harriman concession agreement of 12 June 1925 was "amicably" dissolved in June 1928, after Harriman's abortive negotiations with Trotsky in Moscow in 1927: see Lewis, *op. cit. supra* n.41, at pp.179–180: and W. Averell Harriman, *America and Russia in a Changing World—A Half Century of Personal Observation* (1971), pp.2–7 .

[95] Chlenov's publications include "Arbitration Clauses in Contracts with Foreign Firms", Vneshnyaya Torgoviya 1935. No.13,3; he was a friend of the writer I. G. Erenburg in whose memoirs he appears: see *Men, Years—Life* (1961, trans. Bostock and Kapp), Vol.1, pp.41–42, and Vol.4, pp.14, 100; and possibly fatally, he was also a Moscow schoolfriend of N. I. Bukharin.

156   ON ARBITRATION

Moscow. There was a new cemetery adjoining this ancient monastery in which the NKVD operated a crematorium during the Great Terror, where the bodies of its victims were secretly burnt and the ashes buried in an anonymous pit. This pit has become known as Common Grave No. 1; and surrounded by tall trees close by the old monastery wall, it is today marked by a stone plaque with the Russian inscription: "Here lie buried the remains of the innocent tortured and executed victims of the political repression 1930–1942: May they never be forgotten!". And in that pit lie now the last earthly remains of Dr Chlenov, a recalcitrant arbitrator despite himself and guilty only of living in the worst of times.[96]

G. Jurisdictional Issues: Seperability, the Scope of the Reference and "*Kompetenz-Kompetenz*"

(1) Separability and Scope

Nussbaum interpreted the Soviet Union's jurisdictional challenge to the *Lena* tribunal as an argument that "an arbitration agreement loses its force if one of the parties (as alleged was done by Lena) rescinds the underlying contract", to which he rightly took objection in common with other distinguished commentators.[97] It is, however, necessary to recall the precise legal basis for the Soviet Union's challenge. By mid-April 1930 the arbitration tribunal was constituted by both parties; it was seised of the parties' dispute; the first procedural hearing was directed to take place first in Paris and then in Berlin by joint request of the parties; and there was no hint of any protest by the Soviet Union over the *Lena* tribunal's jurisdiction to decide the parties' dispute. However, what was the parties' dispute referred for arbitration to the tribunal? At this time, it turned on the question of performance of both parties' obligations, accounting and compensation for breach of the concession agreement, whether as claim or counterclaim. Before May 1930 there was no express reference to any claim by Lena Goldfields or the Soviet Union that the concession agreement should be terminated by the tribunal; and from all the numerous references by both parties to the terms of the concession agreement, there was at that time none at all to Article 86. The scope of the parties' dispute soon became critically important for the Soviet Union. Its approach was consistent with English law then and today: an arbitration tribunal must always be careful not to

---

[96] Rasstrel'nye Spiski, (*List of Executions*), Vol.1 (1934–1940) (1993), which also contains the NKVD photograph of Chlenov on his arrest. (I am indebted to Professor Robert Conquest for this reference.) It lists 670 victims whose remains were buried in the Donskoi Cemetery between 1934 and 1940, including Soviet officials involved in the *Lena* arbitration: G. M. Arkus (1896–1936), deputy chairman of the USSR State Bank, and Y. L. Piatakov (1890–1937). Others include Isaac Babel, V. E. Meyerhold, Mikhail Koltsov and perversely the executioner's own henchman, Yezhov himself: see Shentalinsky, *Arrested Voices* (1993), p.70.

[97] Nussbaum, *op. cit. supra* n.24, at pp.37–38; see also the works listed *supra* n.13.

THE *LENA GOLDFIELDS* ARBITRATION   157

allow a party to advance a new claim which raises a dispute which is not within the scope of the original dispute in respect of which the members of that tribunal have been appointed as arbitrators, because that new dispute lies outside their jurisdiction.[98] This was the legal basis of the Soviet Union's jurisdictional challenge to the *Lena* tribunal.

It is also plain from the writings of Professors Shreter and Pergament that the Soviet Union's attack on jurisdiction was *not* based on the dissolution of the arbitration clause, but, rather, only on the original scope of the particular dispute referred to this particular tribunal. Because, the Soviet Union contended, the *Lena* tribunal addressed the termination of the concession as claimed by Lena Goldfields, it went beyond its jurisdiction. This is confirmed by the several demands made by the Soviet Union at the time for another arbitration tribunal to hear the termination dispute, to be appointed under Article 90 of the concession agreement. Those demands could hardly have been made if the Soviet Union was also contending for the dissolution of that arbitration clause, along with the concession agreement. And yet such demands were unequivocally advanced by the Soviet Union. For example, in his telegram of 5 May 1930 to Lena Goldfields and Stutzer, Kamenev had expressly referred to the prospect of the parties appointing a new arbitration court in accordance with the concession agreement, if amicable negotiations should fail to resolve the dispute over termination.[99] As Professor Pergament concluded in his 1930 article (translated from the Russian):[100]

> An examination of a case by an arbitration tribunal must be based upon a corresponding agreement or, in technical terms, a special "arbitration reference" (known in a number of linguistic variants as a "compromis"). One "arbitration reference", one "compromis" and one examination of the case by arbitration relate to one particular arbitration tribunal—while another "arbitration reference" or another "compromis"—and in consequence another examination by arbitration— relates to another arbitration tribunal ... this tribunal, chaired by a distinguished German geologist, has been entrusted by the Soviet Government with the examination of the problem of implementing the concession agreement, something quite different from the problem of the procedure to be adopted for calculating the losses resulting from termination of the concession—a task for which, very

---

[98] See Mustill and Boyd, *Commercial Arbitration* (2nd edn, 1989), pp.215, 321; and see also the historical controversy over Arts. 13 and 16 of the old ICC Rules on "Terms of Reference" in Craig, Park and Paulsson, *ICC Arbitration* (2nd edn, 1990), pp.251–268, esp. p.254. (The New 1998 ICC Rules amend these provisions and largely avoid this controversy: see Art.19.)

[99] *USSR Documents*, pp.29, 30 and GARF 8350/4/57.

[100] See (1930) 12 Mezhdunarodnaia zhizn' 43, 47. (Art.90 did not allow the USSR unilaterally to select "an accountant, economist or lawyer".) In *USSR Documents*, p.60, Pergament first acknowledged that neither party had the right or power to annul the concession agreement of its own accord; but second, returning to the Latin maxim, *Extra compromissum arbiter nihil facere potest*, he applied it to the *Lena* tribunal.

probably, the [Soviet] Government would have preferred to select a representative of another specialised profession, for example an accountant, economist or lawyer. In other words, an entirely new problem had now arisen, necessitating in consequence a new form of "compromis" or arbitration reference. The old arbitration "reference" was no longer valid; a new one was needed. It would obviously have to be worded on the basis of the same article 90 of the concession agreement; but it would still have to be a new one.

The same point was made by Professor Shreter in his separate commentary in *USSR Documents*:[101]

We assert that the arbitration court, in accordance with [Article] 90, is only competent to settle such disputes as had been submitted to it at the time of "arbitration reference", its appointment and that it is not competent to undertake the examination, without the consent of both parties, of new disagreements and disputes which have arisen as the result of the action of the one party, after its appointment, and which evidently have their origin in subsequent circumstances.

No attack was made here on the continuing legal validity of the concession agreement's arbitration clause.

All this the Foreign Office's legal advisers in London knew and understood at the time. Fitzmaurice had the parties' correspondence before him, as well as Professors Shreter and Pergament's two commentaries in *USSR Documents*. In his internal memorandum of January 1931, Fitzmaurice did not argue the doctrine of separability; nor indeed could he safely have done so on the basis of English law at that time (which did not then explicitly recognise that doctrine). Accordingly, much of the first part of his argument was intended to show that Lena Goldfields' claim for termination of the concession formed part of the parties' original dispute, i.e. that it did fall within the scope of the reference:

In the opinion of His Majesty's Government the first of the above-mentioned grounds of dispute [i.e. as to which party was responsible for the cessation of work on the concession] was already before the Court inasmuch as it had been agreed between the Company and the Government of the USSR in the telegrams of February 12th and 25th, quoted above, to submit to the decision of the Court the question whether the Government of the USSR had rendered the concession impossible of performance.

---

[101] *USSR Documents*, p.54.

THE *LENA GOLDFIELDS* ARBITRATION   159

And, because Fitzmaurice rightly regarded the Soviet Union as treating the concession agreement as intact notwithstanding Lena Goldfields' actions (including its arbitration clause), he concluded that the *Lena* tribunal had jurisdiction to decide the parties' dispute.[102]

In the *Lena* award itself (paragraph 8), the scope of the parties' dispute is first defined by reference to three telegrams: Lena's telegram dated 12 February 1930 and Kamenev's two telegrams dated 25 February and 1 March 1930. In none of these documents was there any reference to Article 86 or the dissolution of the concession agreement or even the termination of the concession, as the *Lena* tribunal itself noted. Nonetheless, the tribunal allowed the scope of the parties' dispute to be defined also by one party's later submissions during the arbitration proceedings, as follows: "subject to such further elucidation in detail as the parties might think fit or be ordered by the court to give in their written declarations under [under Article 90(H)], or in their explanations and evidence [under Article 90(K)]". Only in that manner could Lena Goldfields' later claim to have the concession terminated come within the scope of the original dispute referred to arbitration. As described above, that claim was expressly raised by Lena Goldfields for the first time at the first procedural hearing in Berlin on 9 May 1930; and it was expressly pleaded only with Lena Goldfields' Statement of Claim dated 23 May 1930. From the Soviet Union's perspective, Lena Goldfields' unilateral enlargement of the parties' dispute *after* its own notice of claim and the *Lena* tribunal's appointment rested on fragile legal ground; and in its award the tribunal did not address the Soviet Union's arguments on the limited scope of the arbitration.

In any event, it is impossible to find in the *Lena* arbitration any historical support for the doctrine of separability. The arbitration clause under Soviet law was a special law and no mere civil procedural contract capable of unilateral dissolution; the Soviet Union was not actually impugning the validity of the arbitration clause; and the tribunal's ruling of 9 May 1930 decided only that the concession agreement necessarily remained valid by virtue of Article 86, thereby avoiding any need to rule further on the separate validity of the arbitration clause. Thus, with regret, it must be concluded that the *Lena* case flies false colours on the doctrine of separability for which it is often cited. Does it matter? Of course not. The *Lena* award was a monument to practical common sense; and as the late Professor Berthold Goldman said often: in international commercial arbitration, the only reality is perception. If the *Lena Goldfields* case has been misperceived over the last 65 years, that reality has served us well.

---

[102] PO F0371/15605, p.10. (English law did not fully recognise the doctrine of separability until *Harbour* v. *Kansa* [1993] Q.B. 701, newly interpreting *Heyman* v. *Darwins* [1942] A.C. 356: see the 1994 DAC Consultation Document [1994] Arb.Int. 189, 225–228 and s.7 of the English Arbitration Act 1996.)

160   ON ARBITRATION

(2) Kompetenz-Kompetenz

The Soviet Union also criticised the *Lena* tribunal for adjudicating upon its own competence to decide the parties' dispute at the Berlin hearing on 9 May 1930; and it treated that decision as nothing more than the personal views of Stutzer and Scott with no legal consequence whatever. In other words, the tribunal should have stopped its work upon the mere jurisdictional protest of the Soviet Union. In *USSR Documents*, Pergament briefly supported the Soviet Union's position; but in his 1930 article he analysed at length the secondary legal issue of who was to decide whether the arbitration tribunal was competent to decide the parties' dispute, arriving at an answer in favour of the State court and not the arbitration tribunal—in the absence of any specific legal rule otherwise. However, Pergament's own criticism of the *Lena* tribunal was curiously muted. He recognised that views differed among international scholars, that the

> progressively, more widespread and even predominant view at the present time refused a party the right to claim that an already established arbitration tribunal had lost its jurisdiction for one reason or another. That right, according to the dominant view, is reserved exclusively for the arbitration tribunal itself ... The objection to granting one party this right is that ... the possibility cannot be excluded of arbitrary actions ... in other words of the undermining of the arbitration at the will of a partisan party.

And then, for no convincing reasons, Pergament concluded that the prevailing view should have no place in the future of Soviet law.[103]

In fact, exactly the contrary happened over the next 60 years. From 1932 the Foreign Trade Arbitration Commission in Moscow developed its own doctrine of *Kompetenz-Kompetenz*; in 1962, the Soviet Union ratified the Geneva 1961 Convention on International Commercial Arbitration, including Article V(3) on *Kompetenz-Kompetenz*; in 1975 FTAC promulgated an express procedural rule to such effect; and a FTAC tribunal later applied that rule in *SNE* v. *Joc Oil* (1984), whose award was successfully enforced abroad under the 1958 New York Arbitration Convention.[104] In 1993 the Russian Federation also enacted Article 16 of the UNCITRAL Model Law on *Kompetenz-Kompetenz*; but Soviet parties had previously made much use abroad of the UNCITRAL Arbitration Rules, together

---

[103] Pergament, *op. cit. supra* n.29. at pp.49–50. In his 1950 article Nussbaum (*op. cit. supra* n.24) accepted that an arbitration tribunal's opinion regarding its competence was not necessarily binding upon the parties and was usually subject to re-examination by a State court: but he concluded (mistakenly) that no such court remedy was available in the *Lena* arbitration: see *idem*, pp.40–41 and *supra* n.4.

[104] Art. 1(3) of FTAC's 1975 Rules of Procedure (applied in *Joc Oil, supra* n. 12) provided in English translation: "The question of competence of FTAC in a particular case shall be decided by the tribunal deciding the case": see also S. N. Lebedev, "USSR", *Int. Handbook on Comm. Arb.*, p.15.

THE *LENA GOLDFIELDS* ARBITRATION   161

with other institutional rules of arbitration outside the Soviet Union providing expressly for *Kompetenz-Kompetenz*. As Professor Lebedev concluded in his 1988 work, both Russian and foreign scholars long ago confirmed the doctrine of *Kompetenz-Kompetenz* as having a major preventive significance, without which international commercial arbitration simply could not function.[105] And the reason for this is precisely the same reason Pergament gave in his 1930 article, then so recently and clearly illustrated by the *Lena* arbitration itself. As Tass might say, it was no coincidence.

H. The End-Game

In September 1930 it was plain that the Soviet Union would refuse to honour the *Lena* award on the ground that the two arbitrators lacked any jurisdiction to make it; and in any event the Soviet Union was probably too weak financially to pay the award in full. As the hearing came to an end in London, Stalin was resting in the Crimea from where by private letter he inquired of Molotov in Moscow: "How is Lena Goldfields?".[106] After the *Lena* award's publication, at its meeting on 6 September 1930, the Politburo confirmed that all official comment on the award would be avoided; and that instead a press campaign should be initiated to ridicule the *Lena* tribunal.[107] There followed in *Pravda* a long satirical account of the *Lena* arbitration entitled "Two Zeros", comparing (adversely) the award's two authors to the "very honest and decent pig" in the Soviet circus who was trained to add up numbers correctly; and given the shortage of paper in Moscow, it recommended that the *Lena* award should be "put only to one use".[108] In England the *New Statesman* curiously defended the Soviet Union's position, rejecting the implicit accusation in the *Lena* award that "the Soviet Government had behaved all through

---

[105] S. N. Lebedev, *Mezhdunarodnoye kommercheskii arbitrazh* (*International Commercial Arbitration: The Competence of Arbitrators and the Agreement of the Parties*) (1988), pp.13–14. A. Yakovlev identifies a MAC award of 1933 (*The "San Giuseppe"*) as the first decision under Soviet law on *Kompetenz-Kompetenz*: see "International Commercial Arbitration Proceedings and Russian Courts" (1996) 13 J.Int.Arb. 37, 42; other legal scholars have pointed to the FTAC decision in *V/O Tractoroexport v. M/S Tarapore* (1974) which led directly to the 1975 FTAC Rule of Procedure 1(3) on *Kompetenz-Kompetenz* (*supra*).

[106] Stalin's letter of 24 Aug. 1930, Letter 60 in Lih, Naumov and Khlevniuk (Eds), *Stalin's Letters to Molotov 1925–1936* (1995).

[107] The Politburo confirmed the decision of the Lena commission also of 6 Sept. 1930: GARF 5446/55/1970 (Rykov, Kamenev, Molotov and Piatakov).

[108] *Pravda* of 9 Sept. 1930, signed by D. Zaslavsky. The Lena commission had recommended on 6 Sept. 1930: "Koltsov or some other sketch writer should comment on the decision of the arbitration tribunal in some kind of sketch written in absolutely mocking style. The 'verdict' and the whole affair should provide sufficient material. The text should be approved personally by Kamenev." Zaslavsky was a lampoonist, later infamous for attacking Gorky towards the end of his life: see Shentalinsky, *op. cit. supra* n.96, at p.267. (Koltsov was a well-known satirical writer on current affairs, later a journalist and friend of Ernest Hemingway during the Spanish Civil War; see *supra* n.96).

162   ON ARBITRATION

with calculated villainy"; and later an authoritative apologia was given by W. P. and Zelda Coates in their well-informed history of Anglo-Soviet relations.[109]

The *Lena* award could not be enforced in the English courts against a foreign sovereign State, still less so in Soviet courts or even in foreign courts elsewhere. The Soviet Union was not a party to the 1927 Geneva Convention on Arbitration Awards. Nor was the Soviet Union yet a member of the League of Nations.[110] There was no further legal remedy open to Lena Goldfields; and the British Foreign Office advised that there was little the United Kingdom could do to effect payment by diplomatic means. Neither the 1921 Anglo-Russian Trade Agreement nor the 1930 UK–USSR Temporary Trade Agreement contained any mechanism for the recognition of arbitration awards, unlike the equivalent treaties between the Soviet Union and Germany.[111] Nonetheless, the United Kingdom took valiant diplomatic steps from late 1930 onwards in London, Moscow and Geneva to persuade the Soviet Union to honour at least part of the monetary award, which engaged the best efforts of the Foreign Office's legal advisers (including Fitzmaurice). This difficult task was complicated by the separate, protracted negotiations between the Soviet Union and Lena Goldfields' German creditors, the latter discreetly supported by the German government. Several of Lena Goldfields' German suppliers enjoyed proprietary claims against the Soviet Union for confiscated equipment supplied to Lena Goldfields under sale contracts providing for "retention of title" until receipt of the full price.

The dispute over the *Lena* award between the United Kingdom and the Soviet Union became a major factor in their poisonous relations from 1930 to 1935.[112] Indeed diplomatic relations had only just been resumed in December 1929, after their rupture in May 1927 following the "Arcos" affair. The criminal trials in Moscow of Lena Goldfields' English and Russian personnel in January and April 1930 fore-shadowed the Metro-Vickers show trial of 1933, a much graver diplomatic incident. In 1932 the United Kingdom also denounced for Soviet violations the 1930 Temporary Commercial Agreement. Anglo-Soviet relations were partly repaired with the UK–USSR Trade Agreement of February 1934, followed by the successful visit to Moscow in March 1935 of Anthony Eden, the first British minister to visit

---

[109] *New Statesman* editorial of 6 Sept. 1930, written just before Kingsley Martin's arrival as editor. A copy of this article in the Foreign Office files bears L. Collier's annotation "That is precisely what it did do on our information" (PRO FO 371/14868). See also W. P. and Zelda Coates, *A History of Anglo-Soviet Relations* (1943), pp.467–469.

[110] The USSR, like the US, never acceded to the 1923 Geneva Protocol or the 1927 Geneva Convention on Arbitration Awards. The USSR became a member of the League in Sept. 1934.

[111] See H. J. Hilton Jr, "Commercial Arbitration in the Treaties And Agreements of the USSR" (1945) 307 US Department of State Bull. 891, reprinted in G. Ginsburgs, *The Soviet Union and International Co-operation in Legal Matters* (1988). See also Nussbaum, "Treaties on Commercial Arbitration" (1942) 56 H.L.R. 219, 220 and Rashba, *op. cit. supra* n.25, at p.541.

[112] See particularly the Government statements to the House of Commons on 13 Mar. 1933 (Baldwin), 29 Jan. 1934 (Colville) and 4 June 1934 (Colville): *HC Hansard*, cols.1595, 39; and *The Times*, 5 and 13 June 1934.

THE *LENA GOLDFIELDS* ARBITRATION 163

the Soviet Union. That diplomatic reconciliation led to the settlement agreement in March 1935 between Lena Goldfields and the Soviet Union whereby all Lena Goldfields' claims were settled, albeit in a modest amount. The Soviet Union would pay £50,000 on ratification of the settlement and £2.95 million over 20 years in the form of negotiable notes payable by the Soviet Union every six months from 1 May 1935 to 1 November 1954, without interest. This agreement made no express reference to the *Lena* award; and of course, it did not contain any arbitration clause.[113] The settlement was at first honoured by the Soviet Union; but after paying £1,067,500, it repudiated the notes in November 1940 on the pretexts, first, that the United Kingdom was unlawfully requisitioning ships from the former Baltic States annexed by the Soviet Union in June 1940[114] and later that the United Kingdom had unlawfully sequestered gold bullion "purchased" by the Soviet State Bank from the Baltic States' central banks also after annexation in 1940.[115] Much later, after a failed attempt by one US note-holder to enforce the Soviet Union's obligations in the New York courts in 1959,[116] it was only with the 1968 UK–USSR Agreement that the Soviet Union sanctioned compensation payable to its Lena note-holders.[117] Even then, however, Goliath lost nothing. The compensation was paid by the United Kingdom from the 14 tonnes of gold bullion held by the Bank of England to the account of the former Baltic States, then worth about £5.8 million.[118] In August 1991 the three Baltic States, newly independent, immediately requested from the Bank of England the return of their plundered assets; and in January 1992 the British Prime Minister confirmed that the United Kingdom would compensate Lithuania, Estonia and Latvia for the full value of their missing gold, then worth approximately

---

[113] The settlement agreement was made in Russian on 4 Nov. 1934, signed in Moscow by Arthur G. Marshall for Lena Goldfields and V. A. Trifonov of Glavkoncesskom under Decree No.2499/428 dated 3 Nov. 1934 of the USSR Council of People's Commissars. The settlement was eventually ratified by Lena Goldfields after litigation in the English High Court between Lena Goldfields and its disappointed German and Czech creditors and, after much delay, by the USSR Council of People's Commissars on 21 Mar. 1935. (The British Foreign Office translation is at Kew: PRO FO 371/18313.)

[114] *The Times*, 9 and 15 Nov. and 5 Dec. 1940; see also Coates and Coates, *op. cit. supra* n.109, at pp.644, 648.

[115] G. E. Vilkov, *Natsionalizatsiya i mezhdunarodnoye pravo* (*Nationalisation and International Law*) (1962), p.122; see also the government's statement (Whitlock) to the House of Commons on the second reading of the Foreign Compensation Bill, *HC Hansard*, 7 Nov. 1968, cols.1096 *et seq.*

[116] See *Weilamann* v. *Chase Manhattan Bank* 192 N.Y.S.2d 469, ann. (1960) 54 A.J.I.L. 410 and Vilkov, *idem*, pp.123–124.

[117] The 1968 UK–USSR Agreement concerning the Settlement of Mutual Financial and Property Claims (Cmnd 3517). Art.4 provided that the UK government "undertakes further, that, from the assets indicated in Article 2, it will make a settlement, along with other claims, of claims by the holders of unredeemed Notes issued by the Government of the Union of Socialist Republics to the British joint stock companies, the Tetiuhe Mining Corporation and Lena Goldfields Ltd of London, irrespective of the nationality of such holders". Art.2 referred (*inter alia*) to gold bullion still held by the Bank of England on deposit from the former central banks of Latvia, Lithuania and Estonia. The UK's disposal of gold belonging neither to the USSR nor the UK was politically and legally controversial during the passage through Parliament of the Foreign Compensation Act 1968; see D. A. Loeber, "The Problem of the Baltic Gold in Great Britain", in *Internationales Recht und Diplomatie* (1968), p.75 . (Tetiuhe was also a Siberian mining concession prematurely terminated in 1932 against USSR State notes.)

[118] R.J. Misiuanas and R. Taagepera, *The Baltic States—Years of Dependence 1940–1980* (1983), p.17 .

164 ON ARBITRATION

£90 million.[119] Accordingly, in the final result, the United Kingdom itself compensated the Soviet Union's unredeemed note-holders under the 1935 *Lena* settlement, both British *and* foreign. For Lena Goldfields, however, the story had ended in 1976 when the company was formally dissolved by order of the English High Court.[120]

For every action, there is an equal and opposite reaction even in the field of international commercial arbitration. After the *Lena* arbitration, transnational trade over the Soviet Union's borders was increasingly marked by the widespread use of commercial arbitration both in Moscow and abroad, particularly in London and later Stockholm, Vienna and Zurich. In December 1930 the Maritime Arbitration Commission was established in Moscow; and in June 1932 the Foreign Trade Arbitration Commission. In 1960 the Soviet Union ratified the New York Arbitration Convention, and in 1962 the Geneva Convention on International Commercial Arbitration. It agreed the arbitration provisions in the Helsinki Final Act 1975; and it supported the work of UNCITRAL in regard to both its 1976 Arbitration Rules and 1985 Model Arbitration Law. The Soviet Union also agreed a broad arbitration scheme in the 1989 USSR–UK Agreement for the Promotion and Reciprocal Protection of Investments. However, whilst the Soviet Union was constrained to accept the concept of a neutral chairman for arbitrations outside the Soviet Union, it never in practice accepted that approach for Moscow arbitrations:[121] this painful legacy from the Stutzer experience only disappeared with the Soviet Union itself.

I. Appendix: The Lena Arbitration Clause—English Translation:[122] Article 90 of the 1925 Concession Agreement

Arbitration Court: §90.

(A) All disputes and misunderstandings concerning the interpretation or performance of this agreement and all appendices thereto, on the

---

[119] *The Times*, 23 Jan. 1992; see also *HC Hansard*, 23 Jan. 1992, Vol.202, col.488 where the Prime Minister (John Major) expressed his delight that his Conservative Government had been able "to correct that smear of dishonour" created by the Labour Government in 1967–1968.

[120] Long before 1976, amongst other obstacles, Lena Goldfields' claims to enforce the award or settlement were hopelessly time-barred under both English law and Soviet law. As to the limitation periods applicable to a foreign award, see S. N. Lebedev "How Long Does a Foreign Award Stay Enforceable?", in *The Art of Arbitration (Liber Amicorum Pieter Sanders)* (1982), p.213; and under English law see *International Bulk Shipping and Services Ltd* v. *Minerals and Metals Trading* [1996] 2 Lloyd's Rep. 474.

[121] See K. Hobér, "Arbitration in Moscow" (1987) 3 Arb.Int. 119, 158.

[122] This English translation is made from the original Russian text of Art.90 of the concession agreement of 30 Apr. 1925 (to which para. letters have been added for ease of reference). This text of the concession agreement, as amended to 9 June 1927, was published in Moscow in 1928; and a copy was appended to the *Lena* award (see *supra* n.1). An earlier version of 1925 is available at the US Library of Congress and from IDC Microfiche. In minor respects, this translation differs from the incomplete translations in *USSR Documents* and the English version of the *Lena* award published in *The Times*, 3 Sept. 1930. It retains however the phrase "arbitration court" which in Russian could now be understood as "arbitration tribunal".

THE *LENA GOLDFIELDS* ARBITRATION   165

declaration of either party, shall be examined and settled by an arbitration court.

(B) The arbitration court shall consist of 3 (three) members, one of whom shall be selected by the Government, one by Lena and the third, who is to be the super-arbitrator, shall be selected by mutual agreement of the parties.

(C) If such agreement is not reached within 30 (thirty) days from the day of receipt by the defendant party of a written request to appear before the arbitration court, setting out the matters in dispute and designating the member of the arbitration court selected by the claimant party, then within 2 (two) weeks the Government shall nominate 6 (six) candidates from amongst the professors of the Freiberg Mining Academy or of the Royal High Technical School of Stockholm from whom Lena shall select one as super-arbitrator within a period of 2 (two) weeks.

(D) If Lena fails to select the super-arbitrator within the above-mentioned period of 2 (two) weeks, there being no insuperable obstacles to prevent such selection, the Government shall be entitled to request the council of one of the above-mentioned higher academic institutions to appoint a super-arbitrator from amongst the 6 (six) candidates nominated by the Government.

(E) If the Government, in the absence of insuperable obstacles, fails to nominate the 6 (six) candidates for super-arbitrator within the above-mentioned period of 2 (two) weeks, Lena shall be entitled to request the council of one of the above-mentioned higher academic institutions to nominate 6 (six) candidates and to appoint a super-arbitrator from amongst their number, as set out above.

(F) If, upon receipt of the summons from the super-arbitrator appointing the date and place of the first session, one of the parties, in the absence of insuperable obstacles, fails to send its arbitrator to the arbitration court or the arbitrator avoids participating in the arbitration court, then the matter in dispute shall, at the request of the other party, be settled by the super-arbitrator and the other member of the court, such settlement to be valid only if unanimous.

(G) The arbitration court shall appoint a permanent secretary, who shall keep records of all proceedings of the court's sessions. The remuneration of the president and the secretary of the court, as well as the latter's expenses shall be paid by both parties in equal proportions. Each of the parties shall pay its own arbitrator and his expenses, as well as the costs connected with the conduct of its case before the arbitration court.

(H) Matters to be settled by the arbitration court must be presented in written form to the president of the court, and the party bringing a claim must serve the other party with a copy of its declaration to the court. The super-arbitrator shall appoint the place and date for the first session to be held by the arbitration court.

(I) When appointing the date and place for a session of the court, both the super-arbitrator and the arbitration court shall give consideration to:

(1) the reasonable period of time required for each party to make preparations for departure and arrival on time at the appointed place and

(2) the accessibility of the place being such that each party can reach it by the date fixed.

However, if either party encounters insuperable obstacles in having its court member or its representative reach the appointed place on time, all measures must be taken by that party to inform the super-arbitrator or the arbitration court of such circumstance in a timely manner.

(J) In any case, in the event of the failure to appear by one party's court member, the super-arbitrator or the arbitration court shall, on declaring a session open, pass a special motivated resolution on this matter.

(K) The arbitration court shall have full power thereafter to fix the place and time of its sessions, as well as to settle methods and order of procedure. It shall be obligatory on each of the parties to supply to the court, at the time it requires, all necessary evidence relating to the case which it can and is able to produce, regard being had to such as may be of state importance.

(L) All decisions of the court must in each case be made in written form and a copy of each decision must immediately be notified to the parties. Every majority decision of the court shall be final and binding for both parties and shall immediately be put into execution.

(M) If the arbitration court comes to a decision requiring one of the parties to do something or to refrain from doing something, it shall at the same time decide upon and alert that party in advance of the consequences for failing to carry out its decision, namely, it shall impose in such case the payment of a certain penalty upon the other party, or it shall authorise the other party to carry out whatever was neglected at the expense of the defaulting party, or it shall declare the agreement annulled, the latter only at the request of the claimant party.

8

The Tetiuhe Mining Concession 1924–1932

A Swiss–Russian Story (Where the Arbitral Dog Did Not Bark)

A. Introduction

For disputing parties in the commercial world, the best arbitration is no arbitration; and ideally, there would be everywhere no commercial differences at all, ever. Yet merchants live in the real world; and inevitably disputes arise which require resolution one way or another. The best encouragement for the amicable resolution of such disputes is the existence of a reliable system of international commercial arbitration. Wherever arbitration is predictably effective, final and just, there is always a high proportion of commercial disputes which are settled amicably – without exhausting or even commencing the arbitral process. Moreover, even where transnational arbitration lacks these important legal features, the existence of an arbitration clause can act as a catalyst for amicable resolution. There is a spirit to international commercial arbitration which facilitates consensual settlements in a manner usually foreign to other non-consensual dispute resolution procedures. As Lord Wilberforce once wrote, "The purpose of arbitration ... is to contribute to amicable settlement. Arbitration is not meant, like litigation, to result in a judgment: its essence – and the essence of a good arbitrator – is to bring a settlement to a peaceful conclusion ..."[1]

Precise statistics to prove this thesis are of course unavailable, given the private and unregulated nature of international arbitration; but the figures speak for themselves. In 2001, Global GDP exceeded US$ 31 trillion, necessarily representing hundreds of millions of individual contracts subject to transnational arbitration agreements. Even extrapolating the ICC's 2001 figures ten thousand times (to allow for *ad hoc* and other forms of arbitration, howsoever effective),[2]

---

[1] WILBERFORCE, *The Settlement of Commercial Disputes within the Context of International Law: Arab Law Quarterly* [1986] 333, 337.

[2] For the five years ending in 2000, 2 232 requests for arbitration were filed with the ICC International Court of Arbitration; with the figures for 2001 being 566 requests, 1 058 cases pending at the year-end,

---

On Arbitration. Edited by: Sam Wordsworth KC and Marie Veeder, Oxford University Press. © Oxford University Press 2023. DOI: 10.1093/oso/9780192869135.003.0008

168   ON ARBITRATION

it seems obvious that the real success of international commercial arbitration derives from its historical existence, as opposed to its actual operation. Arbitration remains inextricably linked to the successful conduct of transnational trade in the global economy; and for international business, transnational arbitration is not only the most popular system for the resolution of disputes but, almost invariably, it is the *only* available system of choice. Nonetheless, it is remarkable how such a system works when it does not work in fact; and like Sherlock Holmes's famous watchdog, international commercial arbitration is significant because it does "nothing in the night-time".[3] Why is this so? Why does international arbitration work like preventive medicine, except that the patients do not even have to swallow the medicine? There is little legal scholarship to explain this peculiar arbitral feature; and perhaps it would take more than lawyers but rather sociologists and psychologists to explain it fully.[4] Yet this feature is hardly new. It is as old as arbitration itself, long predating the massive success of the 1958 U.N. New York Convention, the 1965 ICSID Washington Convention and the more recent 1985 UNCITRAL Model Law. In the absence of scientific research, the current explanations are usually anecdotal.

(1) Three Soviet Concessions

There exists one historical example tracing the fate of the three largest foreign concessions granted by the USSR at the time of Lenin's New Economic Policy, "the most false and ambiguous of all Soviet periods".[5] These mining concessions were all granted in 1925 and terminated by 1932 under Stalin's First Five-Year Plan. The first, Lena Goldfields, led to a malign dispute leading to a famous arbitration award in 1930, dishonoured by the USSR but eventually settled in 1935. The second, Averell Harriman's Concession, led to a confidential arbitration in March 1928 which was settled before any award in September 1928 and re-settled in 1930. Albeit less well-known, the third was the Tetiuhe

---

243 cases withdrawn and of 306 awards made, 35 were consent awards: (2002) 13/1 *ICC Bulletin* 6. (The ICC is by far the world's largest institution for international commercial arbitration, with accurate statistics).

[3] "Silver Blaze" in Arthur Conan Doyle's *Memoirs of Sherlock Holmes.*

[4] In 1992, the LCIA commissioned a study by London Business School of US "Fortune 500" corporations (unpublished); and for a more recent US study, see NAIMARK & KEER, *International Private Commercial Arbitration: Expectations and Perceptions of Attorneys and Business People* (2002) 30/5 *IBL* 203. Whilst neither quite touches upon the point here considered, both studies confirm that merchants generally treat arbitration as an extension of their business, requiring equivalent evaluations for commercial efficiency, effectiveness and proportionality.

[5] B. PASTERNAK, *Doctor Zhivago* (1957), chap. 15. (Many of the events in this novel take place in Siberia; and Lara's "saviour" at Varykino was Victor Ippolitovich Komarovsky, described as the Minister of Justice in the Far Eastern Republic, see *infra*).

Concession (containing a strong Swiss element), where the concession agreement was "amicably" terminated in 1932, without any arbitration proceedings at all. All three concession agreements contained transnational arbitration clauses; and the question arises why in similar circumstances did these similar disputes follow such different paths.[6] It is a complicated explanation.

(2) Tetiuhe Concession

The Tetiuhe Mining Corporation Limited, the foreign concessionaire, was an English company formed in 1925 to take over a mining concession granted in 1924 by the Soviet Government to Bryner & Co of Vladivostok, a Russian firm which had part-owned and operated the Russian company owning the Tetiuhe Mine before the First World War. It was a lead, silver and zinc mine with a Chinese name, the Tiu-Tie-Hé (Tetiuhe) mine in the Sikhote-Alin Mountains north of Vladivostok in Far Eastern Siberia, more than 8 500 km from Moscow. This concession was to involve some of the world's most sophisticated mining and financial entrepreneurs of their day, including in London Alfred Chester Beatty and Calouste Gulbenkian and, in Vladivostok, a mining engineer and member of a large Swiss-Russian family, Boris Bryner – now better known as the father of Yul Brynner, the famous actor. (In the USA, Yul Brynner added an extra "n" to the family name to avoid English mispronunciation.)

B. Jules Joseph Bryner (1849–1922)

The Bryner family had originated from Möriken-Wildegg, a small village near Zurich.[7] Its Siberian patriarch, Jules Joseph Bryner, was born there in 1849; but in 1865, aged only 16, he left his Swiss village for life at sea, making his first fortune as a merchant and shipowner in Yokohama, Japan. Having married a Japanese woman, Jules Bryner abandoned Japan for China and Korea, eventually settling in 1873 as a merchant in Vladivostok, there marrying for the second time a Buryat-Russian, Natalia Osipovna Kurkutova, and building a large family house

---

[6] Soviet state archives on the Tetiuhe Concession are located at RGAE (Fond 3429, op.6 d.455); English archives are held by the LSE Library as part of the Chester Beatty Archives, and by Rio Tinto plc as part of the records of Beatty's companies, the Selection Trust Limited (old and new). For the Lena and Harriman Concessions, see the author's papers: *The Lena Goldfields Arbitration: The Historical Roots of Three Ideas* (1998) 47 *ICLQ* 747 and *The 1999 Freshfields Lecture: Lloyd George, Lenin and Cannibals: The Harriman Arbitration* (2000) 16 *Arb Int* 115.

[7] See Rock BRYNNER, *Yul, The Man Who Would Be King* (1989, NY), p. 18–22. For additional details of the Bryner family's life in Vladivostok, I am most grateful for the invaluable help provided by members of the Brynner family in the USA and Canada, in particular Rock Brynner, Irena Brynner, Cyril Brynner and Zoya Brynner.

170   ON ARBITRATION

in Svetlanskaya Street and an office next-door.[8] Natalia and Jules (as a Russian, now called "Yuli Ivanovich Bryner") had six children, three girls and three boys. Boris was the middle boy, born in 1889;[9] and he trained as a mining engineer in St Petersburg and Germany with a view to working his father's mining interests at Tetiuhe.

As a successful entrepreneur in a growing cosmopolitan city and a naturalised Russian subject, Jules Bryner was well connected with the Imperial Government in St Petersburg. His firm, Bryner & Co, acted as shipping agents with branches in China, Manchuria and Korea. The firm exported Russian timber to China; it operated a shipping company; and it developed interests in coal and gold mines in the region. In 1896, with official approval, Jules Bryner secured a major timber concession with the King of Korea, who had placed himself at that time under Russian protection.[10] This concession covered an area of 1,800 sq. miles extending over the northern frontier regions of Korea; but it was much more than a commercial venture. By design, it intruded on Japan's territorial and maritime interests in Korea and Manchuria. In 1898, under a plan personally approved by Tsar Nicholas II, the Bryner concession was subsumed in Russian military attempts to control northern Korea, an event which precipitated, amongst other factors, the 1904 Russo-Japanese War.[11] By this time, however, Jules Bryner had also become interested in mineral deposits in the wilderness north of Vladivostok, which were to become the Tetiuhe Mine.

C. The Tetiuhe Mine

In early 1880s, rumours reached Vladivostok that near the river Tetiuhe, 350 kilometres to the north-west, deposits of silver-zinc ore had been found, together with traces of ancient exploitation.[12] An expedition was organised; but it foundered at sea. In 1897, Jules Bryner sponsored an expedition led by Alexander Alekseevich

---

[8] The Bryner Residence on Tiger Hill, was (and remains) a four-story building designed by the German architect G.R. Jungändel; and Bryner & Co's Offices were at 21 (now 13) Aleutskaya Street: see the photographs in Maria LEBEDKO, *Vladivostok: A Historic Walking Tour, www.wsulibs.wsu.edulvlad ivostok.*

[9] The six children were Leonid (1884–1947), Marguerite, or "Gretli" (1885–1958), Boris (1889–1948), Felix (1891–1942), Marie (1893–1969) and Nina (1895–1972), all born in Vladivostok. The family were brought up to speak French, English and Russian.

[10] A.I GIPPIUS, *0 Prichinakh Nashei Voiny s Iaponiei c Prilozheniiami (Dokumenty)*, ("On the Reasons of Our War with Japan"); St Petersburg 1905, pp. 52-55. This concession agreement contained no arbitration clause. See also SETON-WATSON, *The Russian Empire 1801-1917* (1967) at p. 588, n. 3.

[11] J.A. White, *The Diplomacy of the Russo-Japanese War* (1964, Princeton), pp. 32–49.

[12] This account is taken from several lengthy petitions in 1923, particularly the petition dated 3rd March 1923 (RGAE f.3429, op.6 d.455 p. 9), addressed by Boris Bryner to the Soviet Government (VSNKh and Glavkoncesskom), with probable contributions from his brother-in-law, A.S. Ostroumov (who was a lawyer) and possibly S.N. Pobedonostev (Bryner & Co's legal adviser in Moscow).

Maslennikov, later to become his son-in-law (upon marrying his eldest daughter). Exploration continued for another five years, with the assistance of other Russian and foreign mining specialists. In 1902, the first mining areas were allocated to Jules Bryner, and the "Upper Mine" was founded at Tetiuhe. Conditions were difficult. The deposits were spread across the mountain's precipitous slopes, then covered by impenetrable taiga, with no roads, no railway and no population, save for the occasional Siberian brigand, wolf and tiger. Communications were also difficult, the deposits lay 30 kilometres from the coast; and there were no regular shipping services north of Vladivostok. Considerable sums of money were needed to start mining operations; and still more to transport the ore to the coast for shipment to European smelters.

(1) 1907–1914

The 1904 Russo-Japanese War and the 1905 Revolution impeded all attempts to raise finance within Russia. Jules Bryner sought help abroad. In 1907, he secured financing under a long term agreement with a German firm, Aron Hirsch & Sohn of Halberstadt and Berlin, which was to sell the Tetiuhe ores to its customers in Germany and elsewhere in Western Europe. Yet more financing was required. The mine needed a narrow-gauge railway to carry the ores to Pristan on the coast; and a small port was to be built there with loading facilities for lighters, to be towed by tug to ocean-going freighters anchored in deeper waters. Accordingly, on 20th March 1909, in Halberstadt, Jules Bryner signed an agreement with Hirsch to form a Russian joint-stock company "Tetiuhe"; and on 3rd August 1909, the Russian Company's by-laws were approved by the Tsarist authorities. Its capital was one million roubles; and 4 000 bearer shares were allocated, principally to Jules Bryner and Hirsch (2 373 and 1 587 respectively). The latter assumed primary responsibility for the company's financing and sales; and Jules Bryner was charged with administering the enterprise. Jules Bryner redistributed part of his shareholding to his family and friends, including his eldest son (Leonid), his wife's relative, Y.M. Yankovsky,[13] and A.V. Dattan, an important merchant in Vladivostok.[14]

---

[13] Yury Mikhailovich Yankovsky (1879–1956) was the son of the Polish nobleman, Michael Jankovsky, who was exiled to Siberia after the 1863 Polish uprising and became well-known as a naturalist and hunter. By marriage, he was Natalia Bryner's cousin; and his family was also related to Boris Bryner's second wife (see Valery G. YANKOVSKY, *Crusades to the Gulag and Beyond*; 2001, 2nd ed, Sydney, trans. Hintze; and Donald C. CLARK, *Vanished Exiles: The Pre-War Russian Community in Korea*, ed Dae-Sook Suh, *Korean Studies: New Pacific Currents*; 1994, Hawaii; p. 41).

[14] Adolf Vasilevich Dattan (1849–1924) was a naturalised Russian subject, originally German, a Tsarist State Councillor and a partner in the Russian–German firm Kunst & Albers, which operated, inter alia, a large and opulent department store in Vladivostok (John J. STEPHAN, *The Russian Far East – A History*, 1994, Stanford, p. 85 & 215).

(2) 1914–1917

For five years, the Tetiuhe Mine prospered. It produced calamine (a high grade zinc oxide ore) and sulphide ore (containing lead, zinc and silver). Then, with the outbreak of the First World War in August 1914, disaster struck: Germany and Russia became enemies, and the market for Tetiuhe ores in Western Europe was utterly disrupted. Worse, the existence of the company's German shareholders subjected the Company to state control under special wartime legislation.[15] Under a decree of 16th March 1915, a Tsarist government official was appointed to inspect the Company; and all payments due to enemy subjects were payable to the Tsarist State Bank. Under a decree of 1st July 1915, the Council of Ministers acquired the right to liquidate joint-stock companies which had shares held by enemy aliens. Later, this decree was modified by a second decree of 8th February 1917 which substituted the liquidation of only enemy capital by cancelling shares held by enemy aliens and replacing them with new shares issued to friendly subjects or the state treasury.[16] It was self-evident that such legislation allowed intrigues by Tsarist officials; and so it proved. On 2nd February 1916, the Council of Ministers subjected the Russian Company to a "Special Board" in Petrograd. Initially, it comprised a chairman, an attorney, two generals and Jules Bryner. From the outset, the Special Board's main interest was the sale of the enterprise, to which Jules Bryner strongly objected. The Special Board therefore procured his removal and, pending the sale, it negotiated loans to the Company and sold off the Company's stockpiled ore to third parties (neither of which accrued to the Company's benefit). The Revolution of February/March 1917 and the formation of the Provisional Government did not remove this threat to the Company. In April 1917, the Special Board invited tenders for the purchase of the Mine, from which it selected a purchaser, the Piankov Brothers of Vladivostok.[17] There was however more intrigue: an Englishman named Hunter, representing the Japanese firm Suzuki, made a new bid for the Company, which in October 1917 the Board accepted in principle subject to further negotiations in Petrograd. At this point, the Bolshevik Revolution of October 1917 brought the life of the Special Board to an abrupt end, leaving the Tetiuhe Mine without any legal owner or operator. Jules Bryner, in place at Vladivostok and Tetiuhe, resumed *de*

---

[15] At the last pre-war shareholders' meeting in May 1914 in St Petersburg, 1 575 shares were held by German subjects and 2 351 shares by Russians. However, 1 754 of the Bryner family's shares were in Hirsch's custody as security for outstanding loans. Being bearer shares totalling 3 320 of the 4 000 issued shares (Hirsch later claimed a higher figure), the Germans were in thus a position to control the Russian Company.

[16] For analogous difficulties under English law in treating as enemy aliens English joint stock companies with shares held by German subjects, see FOXTON, *Corporate Personality in the Great War*, (2002) LQR 428.

[17] One of the Piankov family was a shareholder in the Russian Company. They were successful entrepreneurs in Vladivostok, the patriarch (V. Piankov) having been exiled to Siberia in the 1880s as a member of the revolutionary Narodnaya Volya ("People's Will"). For a photograph of their 1901 mansion at 43, Svetlanskaya Street, see LEBEDKO, at fn. 9 *supra*.

facto control of the Russian Company and its Mine, which was no longer being worked. The following years were tumultuous as Vladivostok was subjected to insurrection, foreign occupation and successive, if not concurrent, governments. By 1919, under the ravages of revolution, civil war and foreign intervention, the Tetiuhe Mine would be abandoned; and its railroad to the port of Pristan would lie in disrepair. By October 1922, with the USSR's "liberation" of Vladivostok, the position was different but no better. And yet, within four years the Tetiuhe Mine would be fully restored and working again, at greater capacity with foreign capital and modern technology. It was an ordeal by fire which explains much of what happened later.

(3) 1918–1922

In October 1918, after the Government of Siberia was formed in Omsk (soon to be led by the White Admiral Kolchak as "Supreme Ruler of Russia"), the Englishman Hunter renewed his efforts for Suzuki, invoking to the Omsk Minister of Trade and Industry the earlier decision of the Special Board. By this time, however, the Japanese interventionists in Far Eastern Siberia had shown themselves hostile to the Omsk Government; and Jules Bryner successfully appealed on patriotic grounds for the return of the Company to its Russian directors and shareholders. Accordingly, the Omsk Government directed the formation of a "provisional board" led by Jules Bryner and compliance with the Tsarist decree of February 1917 requiring the mandatory liquidation and transfer to the Omsk Government of shares held by enemy aliens, thereby simultaneously rejecting the Japanese bid and terminating German ownership of the Company's shares, including all shares held by Hirsch. This provisional board convened a shareholders' meeting in Vladivostok on 2nd June 1919, which elected a new board comprising (inter alios) of Jules Bryner, now aged 70. After four years of intrigue, the Russian Company was restored to its former management, albeit that the Kolchak Government held 1 575 shares. The Tetiuhe Mine however remained abandoned; the Company's financial affairs were in disarray; its goods and materials had been requisitioned for military purposes; its buildings had been looted; its port facilities at Pristan had been blockaded and shelled, with its tug-boat taken and sunk by the White Siberian Fleet;[18] and there were also new technical problems: the exhaustion of the Mine's rich upper layers required underground exploration of the lower layers and the installation of new plant. All this was aggravated by the devaluation of

---

[18] This was the "Rynda", an elderly steam-driven vessel used both for towing lighters at Pristan and as a supply-ship making the long round trip to Vladivostok. According to Boris Bryner, the vessel was taken from Pristan to Vladivostok and there sunk by the White Siberian Fleet; but the vessel had resumed service by 1925 under Captain I.N. Popov (see also YANKOVSKY, *supra*, p. 35).

174 ON ARBITRATION

successive currencies and rampant inflation. During this period, the Company was only maintained by substantial loans from Bryner & Co and a business colleague of Jules Bryner, G.A. Witt. In short, the political and economic conditions remained impossible for the resumption of mining work at Tetiuhe – but they were soon to become worse.

In November 1919, Kolchak's White regime began its disastrous retreat from Omsk eastwards, with Kolchak's capture and execution in Irkutsk completed by the Reds in January 1920. US, French, British, Czech, Canadian, Italian and other Allied troops began to leave Vladivostok, signalling the end of the interventionist period by April 1920 – but leaving Japanese troops firmly occupying Vladivostok, Northern Sakhalin and other coastal areas. The Russian Far Eastern Republic, ostensibly a non-Soviet sovereign state (albeit controlled from Moscow) was proclaimed in April 1920 as a buffer between Soviet Russia and Japan; but Vladivostok itself, still occupied by Japanese troops, was subjected to a series of local regimes, from Red to White. These included a brief anti-Japanese coalition from July to October 1920 comprised of Mensheviks, Bolsheviks and "qualified bourgeoisie", where Boris Bryner was Minister for Industry.[19] In October 1922, the last White regime collapsed with the withdrawal of Japanese troops from the Russian mainland. The subsequent arrival of the Red Army in Vladivostok on 25th October presaged the incorporation on 15th November 1922 of the Far Eastern Republic, including Vladivostok, into the USSR. These historic events took place with unimaginable suffering, including widespread atrocities inflicted upon civilians and massive damage to property.

D. Boris Yulievich Bryner (1889–1948)

In the middle of all this, the family patriarch, Jules Bryner died in March 1920. Boris Bryner succeeded him as the manager of the Tetiuhe Company and its Mine. In 1914, Boris had married Maria ("Marousia") Blagovidova. They met in St Petersburg, where both were students. Her father was a doctor in Vladivostok. Later Boris' younger brother Felix married Maria's sister, Vera (who was also a doctor). Boris and Maria had two children, Vera and Yul.[20] Felix and Vera had one child, Irena. The Bryners all settled in Vladivostok, living at the Bryner Residence on Tiger Hill. They were Russian subjects; but they also remained Swiss citizens.

---

[19] Canfield F. SMITH, *Vladivostok Under Red and White Rule: Revolution and Counterrevolution in the Russian Far East 1920–1922* (1975, University of Washington Press); p. 53 & 199.

[20] Vera (1916–1957) and Yul (1920–1985). In exile in Paris, Vera became an opera-singer and in 1939 emigrated to New York with her Russian husband, Valentin Pavlovski. After the outbreak of war Yul Brynner and his mother returned from Paris to Darien before reaching New York in 1941, where Yul was to begin his remarkable acting career.

After his death, Jules Bryner's shares in the Russian Company were redistributed amongst his children; and as a result, Boris and his two brothers held 1 745 shares personally and controlled a majority, including shares held by their youngest sister's husband (Alexander Ostroumov) and their relative in England, Louis Bryner (Jules' brother[21]). However, the family's position was precarious under Soviet rule, politically and legally. Legally, the Bryners' interest in the Tetiuhe Mine was wholly dependent upon Tsarist decrees and the decision by the White Kolchak regime whereby Bryner & Co had ousted the German shareholders and discharged its debts to Hirsch (by means of devalued currency paid to the Tsarist and Kolchak State Banks). Politically, as entrepreneurs with a foreign background, their existence was in daily jeopardy from the Soviet authorities in Vladivostok, particularly the OGPU. Boris' brother Felix had been a Tsarist officer who had also served as a French interpreter with the White Kolchak regime; and their sister Marie was married to Serge Hvitzky, a White officer in the Siberian Fleet, captured and imprisoned by the Reds. Soon there were to be personal difficulties also. In April 1924, much engaged in Moscow in efforts to retrieve the Tetiuhe Mine, Boris Bryner left his family for a well-known actress, Ekaterina Ivanovna Kornakova. She worked at the Moscow Arts Theatre with Stanislavsky and had been married to Alexei Dikoi, a famous Soviet actor.[22] Boris and his new bride returned to Vladivostok. His conduct divided the Bryner family and caused great and lasting bitterness for years to come.

There remained, however, the Tetiuhe Mine. It had proven deposits; and with new financing, its workings, railway and port could be repaired. Its ores could be sold abroad for foreign currency, which the USSR so desperately needed; and a working mine would provide work to the region's many dispossessed and unemployed. Boris Bryner knew the Mine and the Russian Company's affairs; and his immediate interests could be tailored to coincide with Soviet policies, particularly the policy on foreign concessions. The need for financing was desperate; and there were two particular difficulties. Any financing had to come from a foreign business partner; but that partner could not be Hirsch which (understandably) would no longer wish to work with Bryner & Co.

---

[21] It is uncertain whether Louis Bryner was Jules Bryner's brother: the church records at Möriken do not list a brother by that name; and he was perhaps a cousin (The Beatty Archives record him as Louis Charles Bryner, a Swiss merchant living in Redhill, Surrey; running a trading business with Jonas Blum at 36, Lime Street in the City of London; and dying in 1932).

[22] Alexei Denisovich Dikoi (1889–1955) was a well-known actor and theatre director. Arrested in 1937 during the Great Terror, he was released in 1941 and played Stalin on film, successfully. He was appointed People's Artist of the USSR in 1949.

176   ON ARBITRATION

(1) Soviet Concession Policy

The 1921 Anglo-Soviet Trade Agreement had suggested that British entrepreneurs would soon be returning to Russia as foreign concessionaires with fresh
capital, in particular the Scot Leslie Urquhart who had operated large mining
properties in Siberia before the Bolshevik Revolution. Those early hopes had faded
with the failure of the 1922 Genoa and Hague Economic Conferences, immediately
followed by Lenin's repudiation of Urquhart's draft concession agreement. Instead
the rapprochement between Germany and the USSR effected by the 1922 Rapallo
Treaty posed a new threat to Bryner & Co. As Germans suffering the effective confiscation of their shares in the Russian Company, the Soviet-German treaties could
allow Hirsch to retrieve its effective majority interest in the Company and then,
as the former owner, to take over the Tetiuhe Mine as a foreign concession from
the USSR, in its own name alone. Notwithstanding support for Hirsch from the
German Embassy in Moscow and the German Consulate in Vladivostok, the USSR
eventually declined to reinstate Hirsch on the basis that the Mine had been nationalised by the Soviet decree of 28th June 1918 expropriating all industrial enterprises
(including mines); and that the Company's shares were therefore worthless and
non-returnable. The logic of the Soviet Government's legal advisers (principally
Mikhail Stipukhovich of the Main Concessions Committee, "Glavkoncesskom")
is not now wholly self-evident; and the decision may evidence the influence of
Bryner & Co, both in Moscow and Vladivostok.

(2) Concession Agreement

By a decree of 3rd May 1923, the USSR's Council of Labour and Defence allowed
Bryner & Co, as former mining entrepreneurs residing in the USSR, to resume
within six months "on a leasing basis" the mining activities at Tetiuhe. Bryner & Co
presented timeously a draft lease, indicating yearly production of 100 000 tons. It
depended on foreign finance equivalent to 250,000 gold roubles; and Boris Bryner
assured the Soviet Government that financing was available, with loans from "one
group in England to finance the business on a large scale". That lender was identified as Arthur Grotjan Marshall of Becos.[23] In before August 1923, Marshall visited
Moscow as part of a British trade delegation and confirmed the availability of such

---

[23] The British Engineering Company of Siberia Limited ("Becos") was formed in 1913 to represent
British engineering manufacturers in Siberia, with offices in London, Vladivostok and elsewhere in
Russia. From 1918, Becos acted as supply agents for the Allied armies during the Intervention during
which it dealt with Bryner & Co in Vladivostok. Its chairman in 1923 was F.L. Baldwin (the cousin
of Stanley Baldwin, the Prime Minister); and its managing director was A.G. Marshall, who spoke
Russian and knew Siberia well, including the Bryner family. See also S. WHITE, *Britain and the Bolshevik
Revolution: A Study in the Politics of Diplomacy 1920–1924* (1979; London), p. 182–186.

THE TETIUHE MINING CONCESSION 1924–1932   177

financing to the Soviet Government, by letter of 21st August 1923; but Becos itself had none of the financial and technical resources to provide the necessary assistance. Marshall remains a mysterious figure in East-West trade, ostensibly the representative of the largest group of British creditors with Russian claims, he was also a strong and early advocate of trade with Soviet Russia.[24] After more difficulties involving counter-proposals from Hirsch, Boris Bryner finally won the right to reopen and operate the Tetiuhe Mine; and on 25th July 1924, a Concession Agreement was concluded between the USSR Government and Bryner & Co, signed in Moscow by Boris Bryner and for the USSR, by Felix Dzerzhinsky and Chicherin, as Chairman of the USSR's Supreme Council of National Economy (VSNKh) and Foreign Affairs Commissar respectively. The period of the concession was 36 years, with an option to the Government to purchase the enterprise after 25 years at an agreed valuation (art. 23); it required the Bryner firm to recommence mining operations within one year, with the help of Russian or foreign finance (addendum); and significantly it allowed the Bryner firm within three years to assign the agreement to a foreign concessionaire, subject to the Government's approval and that company's unconditional signature to the Concession Agreement (art. 32). It also contained an arbitration clause, article 33, applicable only to the future foreign concessionaire: see the appendix below. Clearly, Bryner & Co had already made advanced plans to introduce a foreign partner as concessionaire; and by July 1924, it was likely to be a partner in England, given Louis Bryner's presence in London, the involvement of A.G. Marshall and the United Kingdom's *de jure* recognition of the USSR by the Labour Government in February 1924.

E. Sir Alfred Chester Beatty (1875–1968)

Later in 1924, Boris Bryner arrived in London to seek technical and financial assistance for the Tetiuhe Mine. There he soon won the support of Alfred Chester Beatty, already a leading and influential figure in international mining, a friend of Leslie Urquhart and Herbert Hoover (the future President of the USA).[25] In August 1911, as mining engineers, Beatty and Hoover had visited Urquhart at his Kyshtim mine in Siberia;[26] and it is possible that Beatty had then met Jules Bryner in Moscow or

---

[24] In 1921, Marshall lent his name as the nominal plaintiff in the "Gold Test Case", *A.G. Marshall v Grinbaum and the Bank of England* (1921) 37 TLR 913 & (1921) 8 Ll.LR 342. This High Court judgment cleared away the last legal impediment to the 1921 Anglo-Soviet Trade Agreement, in a manner which Dr Francis Mann QC later considered, with unusual self- restraint, "remarkable": see Mann on Money (5th ed; 1992, Oxford), p. 39 & 41.

[25] See A.J. WILSON, *The Life and Times of Sir Alfred Chester Beatty* (1985, London), p. 175–184. By this date, Beatty was already embarking on the development, finance and administration of his large mining businesses in Northern Rhodesia (Zambia), West Africa and Yugoslavia. He was naturalised a British subject in 1933 and was knighted in 1954.

[26] K.H. KENNEDY, *Mining Tsar: the Life and Times of Leslie Urquhart* (1986, Allen & Unwin), p. 74; and Wilson, *ibid*, p. 130–131.

178   ON ARBITRATION

Siberia. In any event, Beatty reacted favourably to Boris Bryner's invitation. By an agreement dated 2nd January 1925 made between Bryner & Co and the Selection Trust Limited (Beatty's English company), the former granted the latter an option for the purchase of the Soviet concession. It was supplemented by an agreement dated 12th May 1925 made by the Russian Company's largest foreign creditor, G.A. Witt (succeeded by Jonas Blum, Louis Bryner's London partner); and, upon the option's subsequent exercise, an agreement dated 21st May 1925 between Bryner & Co, the Selection Trust and the newly formed English company, the Tetiuhe Mining Corporation Limited.

The entire negotiations between Beatty and Boris Bryner could scarcely have taken six months; and it is indicative of Beatty's strong management style. Within a short time of Boris Bryner's approach, Beatty had agreed to send a technical team to survey the Tetiuhe Mine; and early in 1925, three English engineers travelled by train from London *via* Berlin to Moscow and then, by the Trans-Siberian railway, to Vladivostok and onwards by sea and foot to Tetiuhe – in the depths of winter.[27] They returned to London in the spring with news that technically the development of the Tetiuhe Mine was viable, with ore reserves calculated at 430 000 tons. The decision was then taken by Beatty to form the Tetiuhe Mining Corporation as an English company, with Beatty's company as the major shareholder, along with the Bryner family and A.G. Marshall and later the Armenian oil millionaire Calouste Gulbenkian, Max Warburg and other mining and banking interests from London, New York, Australia and South Africa (including Solomon Joel). This Company was incorporated by its London solicitors, Messrs Freshfields Leese and Munns, on 18th May 1925 with an issued capital of £ 250 000 (later increased to £ 500 000); and for the sum of £ 150 000 it acquired the Soviet concession from Bryner & Co. The Soviet Government (VSNKh) subsequently confirmed the transfer in July 1925, and by later amendments to the Concession Agreement agreed on 17th August 1927, it extended the concession for the full period of 36 years.

F. The Tetiuhe Concession's Operation (1926–1931)

The Tetiuhe Mine was successfully operated by the English Company and Bryner & Co from May 1926; but it was never a commercial success.[28] The English Company rebuilt the old facilities, installed a new mill, power plant and lead smelter, greatly

---

[27] Edwin C. Bloomfield, an English mining engineer who had worked with Hoover and Leslie Urquhart before the First World War and later the Tetiuhe Concession's first general manager (1925–1927); Louis A. Wood, an English metallurgist, who became Mill Superintendent (1925–1932); and C.T. Sweet, a geologist.

[28] The concession's fascinating personal histories are related in C.A. Kidd's *History of the Tetiuhe Mine in Siberia* (1980), an unpublished typescript prepared by the Selection Trust's company secretary (Beatty Archives); see also WILSON, *ibid*, p. 182–184; and Professor K.H. Kennedy's unpublished lecture "*Beatty, Gulbenkian and Soviet Mining Concessions*".

extended the underground workings, renovated the railway and effected a large number of technical improvements using 20 or more British, German and US resident engineers (many accompanied by their wives and dependents), together with a permanent labour force of about 1 000 rising to 2 400 comprising of Chinese (from Mongolia and Manchuria), Russians and Koreans. In July 1930, the Soviet Government advanced a loan of two million roubles to match increased capital investment from London, repayable over three years; and by August 1931, the Company had expended £ 682 000. Sales of ore concentrates, other than to the Soviet Government, were conducted from London; and shipment to Europe, a voyage taking three months, was made by cargo-ships mainly of the British Glen Line. The English Company maintained long-term sales contracts for zinc concentrates with the Société Générale des Minéraux SA of Brussels; and it sold lead concentrate under separate contracts all containing London Arbitration clauses, including, perhaps inevitably, with Hirsch.

In 1927, the world price for zinc fell sharply, as freight-rates rose. In 1928, the Soviet Government exercised its right under the concession agreement to buy zinc concentrates at a market price payable in roubles, which required the English Company to agree unfavourable terms with Rudmetaltorg, the Soviet state organisation responsible for the purchase of ores and metals. In 1929, ore prices fell further. In 1930, the Soviet Government exercised its right to buy lead at a similarly discounted price, payable in roubles; but faced with this demand for over 40 % of the Mine's lead production, the Company informed the Soviet Government that, unless otherwise resolved, it was minded to commence proceedings under the Concession Agreement's arbitration clause. In the last full year of the Mine's production (1929–1930), output doubled from the previous year; but revenue was flat, given the fall in world metal prices, increased costs and rouble-denominated sales to the Soviet Government. By August 1931, the English Company had accumulated losses calculated at £222,000.

There were also growing local difficulties. The Tetiuhe Mine was regularly examined by labour and mining inspectors from Vladivostok and Khabarovsk; and as with the Harriman and Lena Goldfields Concessions, its resident general managers were arbitrarily subjected to criminal prosecution for alleged breaches of Soviet mining regulations. At the English Company's extraordinary general meeting on 10th October 1927 (as reported in *Mining World*), Beatty warned of these difficulties: "While I fully appreciate the sympathetic co-operation of the central authorities in Moscow, the interference of the local authorities and trade union officials with our staff and workmen has caused and is still causing us a great deal of trouble and cost." By 1930, petty harassment was succeeded by grave supply problems caused by Stalin's First Five-Year Plan. Coal deliveries became difficult, albeit essential to the Mine's power station and railway. Food, boots and clothing had already become scarce, particularly after rationing was introduced in 1928. In 1930, under new Soviet foreign exchange regulations, Chinese miners were forbidden

180 ON ARBITRATION

from remitting currency to their families abroad; and many began to return home. By 1931, the Mine lacked skilled and unskilled labour, with absenteeism rising to 40%; food was increasingly scarce; and coal essential to the Mine was being re-quisitioned by Soviet state industries or its sea-transport to Tetiuhe made impossible. During the winter of 1930–1931, for lack of coal, the Mine closed down; and in March 1931 the newly-built smelter was accidentally burnt down.

(1) The Settlement

In early 1931, Beatty decided to suspend mining operations and to negotiate the immediate sale of the concession to the Soviet Government. By letter dated 2nd March 1931 to the USSR Trade Delegation in London, Beatty gave notice that, if there was no satisfactory settlement in sight by 10th March 1931, Boris Bryner was instructed to start arbitration proceedings under article 33 of the Concession Agreement. At Boris Bryner's urgent protest, the decision to abandon work was itself suspended by Beatty in order to allow negotiations to continue, which had already been started by Boris Bryner in Moscow. It was wise advice: given the concessionaire's similar conduct in the Lena Goldfields concession, it is highly probable that Beatty's unilateral suspension of the Concession Agreement would have provoked the USSR's termination of the concession without any compensation. In April 1931, negotiations were successfully conducted in Moscow between M.G. Gurevitch of the USSR's Supreme Council of National Economy (VSNKh) and later L.B. Kamenev (chairman of its Main Concessions Committee) for the Soviet Government and for the Company, Colonel Ralph Micklem (its managing director), A.G. Marshall, Boris Bryner and Herman Marx (a director of Selection Trust and a partner of Cull & Co, the Company's stockbrokers). It was agreed that the Tetiuhe Concession would be sold to the Soviet Government at a price to be fixed after a joint commission had visited the Mine to provide a valuation; but there was to be no overt dispute and no arbitration proceedings. The parties concluded a provisional agreement on 2nd July 1931 and a final agreement on 2nd January 1932 signed by G.L. Piatakov (VSNKh's acting chairman) and Micklem, transferring the concession to the Soviet Government. The USSR agreed compensation of £ 932 000 (plus minor repatriation disbursements), payable in non-interest bearing USSR state notes spread over 18 years from October 1932 to October 1949, a discounted purchase price broadly related to the Company's own book value of assets and liabilities (£ 809 000). As Beatty reported to the Company's annual general meeting in London on 31st December 1931 (which approved the settlement terms): "The Government have acted very fairly during the negotiations and in carrying out all the detailed payments which were due at various times in connection with the operations of the company pending the time of actual transfer. I feel confident that the contract [ie the settlement] will be carried out fairly and honourably"; and in a

THE TETIUHE MINING CONCESSION 1924–1932   181

later letter to The "Times", Colonel Micklem expressly denied, as "totally incorrect", that the Company had been forced to abandon its concession as a direct result of pressure by the Soviet Government.[29] However politic, they did perhaps protest too much.

(2) USSR Notes

In 1933, the English Company's debenture holders exchanged their debentures for USSR state notes; and on 7th May 1936, the Company sold its remaining notes, maturing from 1939 to 1949 with a face value of £ 491 140, to Finexport of Paris at the discounted price of £ 201 000, paid in cash. In October 1936, the Company was placed in voluntary liquidation; and on the completion of the winding-up in April 1938, the shareholders received a return of 40% of their capital; £ 200 000 out of £ 500 000 (no dividend having been paid). It could have been much worse; and indeed it was for the holders of the USSR state notes. Payments were duly made, "fairly and honourably", up to October 1939; but in October 1940, the notes were dishonoured on the Soviet Government's pretext that the United Kingdom had wrongly refused to recognise the USSR's annexation of the Baltic States in June 1940. Only much later, in 1968, was modest compensation received by Tetiuhe note-holders from the United Kingdom Government, the USSR itself contributing nothing.[30]

G. The Spirit of Arbitration

There were several factors leading to the parties' amicable settlement, quite different from each other. The first concerned the Tetiuhe Concession itself. By 1930, Beatty recognised that commercially the enterprise had failed and would not now succeed given the low world prices available for its ores, for the indefinite future. Beatty also understood that there was no longer any possibility of merging the Tetiuhe Mine into a greater Siberian concession, incorporating not only Lena Goldfields but also Urquhart's former mines. Tetiuhe stood alone as a foreign concession; it would never serve as a Soviet springboard; and under Stalin's Five- Year Plan, there would be growing, if not insuperable, difficulties in conducting business in the USSR. Beatty took a realistic view of the concession's bleak future; and the English Company made no attempt to inflate the settlement price by discounting these factors. For the USSR, there was a like realism: the foreign concessionaire

---

[29] See The Times, 1st January and 17th February 1932.
[30] See The Lena Goldfields Arbitration, supra, fn. 7, at p. 789. Of course, having already disposed of the Company's notes in 1936, Beatty and Bryner & Co lost nothing.

182 ON ARBITRATION

had invested heavily in the Tetiuhe Mine and complied with its obligations under the Concession Agreement, if not in fact surpassing its requirements. Unlike Lena Goldfields, this concessionaire was not under-capitalised; it had not committed any serious breach of contract; and its poor financial results were caused primarily by the fall in world ore prices and Soviet conduct, factors similar to the Harriman Concession. This common approach meant that the settlement figure was easily negotiated between the Company and the Soviet Government in Moscow, at least by the standards of Soviet negotiations. However rational, none of this sufficiently explains the amicable settlement.

The other factors had little to do with the concession; but they were probably decisive, a characteristic feature of many amicable settlements. In 1930–32, Beatty was still a US citizen, with close links to Wall Street and Washington D.C. (including President Hoover); and as with Averell Harriman, the Soviet Government wished at that time to avoid giving unnecessary offence to US interests in order to facilitate the USSR's long-term goal of establishing diplomatic relations with the USA, soon to be achieved under President Roosevelt in November 1933. Equally, for different reasons, the presence of Marshall and Gulbenkian as interested shareholders was well-known to the Soviet Government; Gulbenkian's son-in-law (K.L. Essayan) sat on the English Company's board, as did Marshall; and Gulbenkian maintained regular dealings with Soviet trade and diplomatic representatives in Paris, including G.L. Piatakov. At that time, the continued roles of Gulbenkian and Marshall in East-West trade were considered valuable by members of the Soviet Government; and indeed, it was Marshall who later broked in Moscow the 1935 Lena settlement. Moreover, an "amicable" settlement, so acknowledged publicly and promptly by the foreign concessionaire (as indeed it was), would serve the USSR's diplomatic and commercial interests. Unlike the Lena Goldfields concessionaire, with its "Tsarist" or "White" financiers in exile and its very name synonymous with the 1912 Lena massacre, no equivalent enemies would be found amongst the English Company's directors and shareholders.

Boris Bryner's Swiss nationality counted for nothing. He was a Soviet citizen, living with his family and dependents in the USSR; and whilst he and his elder brother Leonid enjoyed relative freedom of movement into and out of the USSR from 1922–1931, most of the Bryner family were trapped in Vladivostok, including their younger brother, Felix Bryner. For the Soviet Government, Boris was a Russian-speaking Russian mining engineer, who had lived all his life in Russia; but like his father, he was also a resourceful entrepreneur who had proved many times that he could work the Soviet system (most recently with the two million rouble loan secured from the Soviet Government in July 1930, just as the Lena Goldfields' arbitration hearing was to begin in London). Time and again, for almost thirty years Bryner & Co had successfully approached Tsarist, White, Red and Soviet authorities to argue its case for the Tetiuhe Mine – on their terms. Moreover, it was not hard for Bryner & Co to pose as patriotic pioneers under pre- Soviet rule, creating and supporting the Tetiuhe Mine for the common good – because it was widely known to be true. As already described, Boris Bryner was a "qualified bourgeois". Indeed, the success of Bryner & Co under Soviet rule had provoked its commercial rivals to spread dark rumours to the US State Department that the firm was unduly favoured because one member had been active in espionage for the Bolsheviks in Vladivostok before 1922.[31] If this referred to Boris Bryner (or to any member of the family), the rumour was false; but such jealousy proved how effectively Bryner & Co operated under Soviet rule, playing according to Soviet rules.

(1) The Arbitral Dog

To the ultimate question, why did the Tetiuhe Concession settle amicably with the arbitral dog "doing nothing in the night-time", there is no single answer; but any answer must first take account of the characters of Beatty and Boris Bryner. The former was a brilliantly successful businessman, exercising decisive judgment. The latter knew better than any living person the affairs of the Tetiuhe Mine; it had been his life's work; and he swam in the Soviet sea as well as any Soviet fish. For both, however regrettable the concession's end, there was a business will to settle amicably on the best available terms; but if the Soviet Government had rejected the English Company's attempts at a reasonable settlement, as the Soviet Government understood, Beatty and Boris Bryner would have triggered the Concession Agreement's arbitration clause, knowing how best to make use of an arbitration both within and without the USSR. For the Soviet Government, the explanation is more speculative; but there was an obvious consideration. By July 1931, the Lena Goldfields Arbitration had publicly demonstrated the huge difficulties in a foreign concessionaire pursuing a claim against the USSR under an arbitration agreement; and even with strong diplomatic support from the British Government, the Lena award of September 1930 was to remain a mere piece of paper until the Soviet Government granted its modest settlement in 1935 (which was also repudiated in 1940). For the USSR's commercial and diplomatic reputation, however, the Lena Goldfields Arbitration was highly damaging: it poisoned diplomatic and trade relations with the United Kingdom; and for Soviet foreign trade organisations dealing with foreign merchants, the evident political and legal risks affected pricing and terms adversely for the USSR. Accordingly, if a reasonable settlement was available from the English Company, this was not the time for the Soviet Government to embark upon a second Lena Goldfields Arbitration. And if not that, why arbitrate at all if a reasonable, amicable settlement were possible with the concessionaire ?

---

[31] A.C. SUTTON, *Western Technology and Soviet Economic Development 1917–1930* (1968, Stanford), p. 286; see also US National Archives M316, reel 136, frame 1254.

184   ON ARBITRATION

For both sides, therefore, the Concession Agreement's arbitration clause was a relevant background factor, albeit not the decisive or the most important factor. Without it, however, it is most unlikely that the same settlement would have been reached: these were not innocent times. Even where the arbitration clause is not used, the spirit of arbitration can promote an amicable settlement – as it did here. In contrast, the prospect of litigation before a state court could never have worked in the same way: both the English Company and the USSR would have greatly distrusted Soviet and English courts, respectively. It remains a lesson not to be forgotten today, as increasingly Western lawyers address disputes elsewhere, including the Russian Far East. As Misha Gordon, Zhivago's fellow-student, ruminates at the end of Pasternak's great novel: "A thing which has been conceived in a lofty, ideal manner becomes coarse and material. Thus Rome came out of Greece and the Russian Revolution came out of the Russian enlightenment". Likewise, as Lord Wilberforce concluded long ago, international commercial arbitration was not conceived to be litigation; and all attempts to make it so will gravely imperil its unique and essential efficacy.

(2) Postscript

After the settlement negotiations in Moscow in July 1931, Boris Bryner left for London without returning to Vladivostok, the beginning of his permanent exile in Harbin.[32] With his second wife and adopted child, Boris Bryner spent the next 16 years in Manchuria, engaged on Bryner & Co's remaining business outside the USSR. In 1939, he was appointed Swiss consul to assist his brother Felix (already the Swiss and Norwegian Consul in Dairen) in protecting Swiss, British and US interests throughout Japanese-occupied Manchuria. This Swiss appointment probably saved his life. Arrested in Harbin by the invading Red Army in September 1945, Boris was eventually repatriated to Switzerland in March 1946 after strong Swiss diplomatic representations to the Soviet Government.[33] Many Russian exiles in Manchuria and Korea were killed. From Switzerland, after a visit to the USA to see Yul Brynner and his family, Boris returned to Shanghai where he died in July 1948. As for the Tetiuhe Mine, the immediate effect of the Concession's termination in 1931/32 was a loss of production and a massive loss of foreign earnings for

---

[32] In his letter dated 2nd November 1945 to the Swiss Consul-General in Shanghai (Bern Archives), Leonid Bryner stated that Boris' exile in July 1931 was prompted by news that his brother Felix had escaped from the USSR. (Felix with his wife and 13-year old daughter Irena, together with the Ostroumov family, fled from Vladivostok in a small family sailing-boat to meet on the high seas, at night, the last of the Tetiuhe Concession's British cargo-ships carrying ore from Pristan to Europe, *via* China: see Irena Brynner's memoirs, *What I remember* (2002), p. 70.)

[33] C. GEHRIG-STRAUBE, *Beziehungslose Zeiten (Das schweizerisch-sowjetische Verhältnis zwischen Abruch und Wiederaufnahme der Beziehungen (1918-1946) aufgrund schweizerischer Akten)*, (1997, Verlag Hans Rohr Zurich), p. 443–458.

the USSR. In both 1929 and 1930, the Tetiuhe Mine had shipped 18 000 tons of zinc to Europe through the Suez Canal. In 1931, the figure dropped to 6,000 tons; and it was not to recover its earlier tonnage until 1934.[34] Over the next fifty years, however, Tetiuhe became a major mining area in the USSR, developing extensive workings in feldspar, boron and zinc concentrates. In 1972, the USSR removed Chinese names from the Siberian map: the town of Tetiuhe became "Dalnegorsk", the river Tetiuhe "Rudnaya" and the port Tetiuhe-Pristan "Rudnaya Pristan". After the demise of the USSR in 1991, Vladivostok became an open city; and the Swiss connection returned: the Swiss company Glencore International SA acquired a majority interest in Dalpolymetall, the Russian joint-stock company in Dalnegorsk operating the former Tetiuhe Mine.[35] It was always a Swiss-Russian story.

Appendix: The Arbitration Clause in the Tetiuhe Concession Agreement of 25th July 1924 Between Bryner & Co and the USSR (Chester Beatty Archives, here translated into English)

"**Article 33:** All disputes and disagreements between the Government and the Concessionaire in regard to the interpretation and performance of this Agreement shall be resolved by general judicial proceedings in accordance with the laws of the USSR".[36]

"**Note:** If, in accordance with article 32 of this Agreement,[37] a foreign joint-stock company is formed, then the matters described in this paragraph shall be resolved by an Arbitration Commission formed on the basis of parity, where, in case disagreement arises, the super-arbitrator shall be appointed by the Council of the Leningrad Mining Institute".[38]

---

[34] Violet CONOLLY, *Soviet Trade from the Pacific to the Levant* (1935, Oxford), p. 7. (It is possible that some production was temporarily diverted for domestic consumption.)

[35] The shareholding has since been reduced; but Swiss-Russian commercial relations continue between Glencore and Dalpolimetall. (There is also a Swiss arbitral connection to Tetiuhe and the Bryner family: Dr Robert Briner, the current chairman of the ICC International Court of Arbitration. In olden times, Dr Briner's family name was "Bryner"; and its origins also lay in Möriken-Wildegg. The church archives date back to 1577 (when the old church burnt down), recording that the two families were related at some time between 1602 and 1759 – regrettably, the exact circumstances lie outside the scope of this contribution).

[36] As an existing Russian firm comprised of Soviet citizens, Bryner & Co itself was not granted the benefit of the arbitration agreement, that benefit being limited to the intended foreign concessionaire.

[37] Article 32 provided (as here translated): *"The Concessionaire has a right within 3 (three) years from the date when this agreement becomes effective to transfer its rights and obligations in connection with this agreement to a Russian or foreign joint-stock company specially formed for this purpose, provided however that the Government shall agree to the same terms on which this concession is granted and the newly formed company shall be obliged to sign this agreement unconditionally."*

[38] The appointment of the "super-arbitrator" by the Leningrad Mining Institute (Boris Bryner's alma mater) could have produced two Soviet arbitrators out of three, with the arbitral seat in the USSR. This imbalance favouring the USSR was not reflected in its later 1925 Concession Agreements with Lena Goldfields and Harriman (see fn. 7 *supra*, *ibid*, p. 790 & 137); nor in the earlier 1923 draft concession agreement between the USSR and Hirsch, which provided for the super-arbitrator to be agreed by the two party-appointed arbitrators and, in default of such agreement, by the concessionaire selecting one of six nominees designated by the USSR each of which "shall be a recognised authority in European science and an expert in mining industry or jurisprudence, and at least three nominated arbitrators shall be of English, Dutch or Swedish nationality". (RGAE f.3429 op.6 d.455, p. 307). In this sense, the Tetiuhe arbitration clause was materially less effective for the foreign concessionaire: it was a *small* arbitral dog.

9

Two Arbitral Butterflies

Bramwell and David

If we look back over the last 100 years to the genesis of modern international commercial arbitration, it is not from idle curiosity. We look at that past experience the better to understand the present state of international arbitration. It need not be the case, as Coleridge said that "the light which experience gives is a lantern on the stern, which shines only on the waves behind us". And we do not need the Chaos theory to see in the history of arbitration how different arbitral butterflies fluttered their wings long ago to produce some of the massive meteorological effects in today's arbitration climate. In the words of Pascal the history of the world would have been completely different if Cleopatra's nose had been longer. So also the recent history of arbitration.

And so, to this end, I would like to recall two old arbitration butterflies, themselves long gone; and I think, almost forgotten (at least) in England.

A. The Bramwell Arbitration Code 1883

The first is an English butterfly which fluttered and died during the 1880s. It was part of the draft English arbitration code prepared in the form of a digest by Lord Bramwell and his colleagues in 1883, strongly supported by the Corporation of the City of London, the newly founded London Chamber of Commerce, the Association of Chambers of Commerce and many merchants from the City of London who viewed with increasing distaste the technicalities, expense and delay of litigation in the English High Court. (This was before the creation of the English Commercial Court in 1895.)

Lord Bramwell's Code eventually fell foul of the Conservative Lord Chancellor, Lord Halsbury, and his senior civil servants, in particular Sir Courtney Peregrine Ilbert, who preferred Parliament to enact the more modest English Arbitration Act 1889. The Bramwell Code was then almost completely forgotten until Lord Mustill and Stewart Boyd QC rediscovered its existence for the first edition of their work on Commercial Arbitration in 1982.[1] Yet that 1889 Act which (re-enacted in

---

[1] Their rediscovery, together with the subsequent discovery of the text of the Bramwell Code, is related in Veeder & Dye, "Lord Bramwell's Arbitration Code" [1991] 8 *Arbitration International* p. 329.

On Arbitration. Edited by: Sam Wordsworth KC and Marie Veeder, Oxford University Press. © Oxford University Press 2023.
DOI: 10.1093/oso/9780192869135.003.0009

1950) still forms the basis of English statutory law on arbitration, drew upon an important feature of English arbitration crystallised by Lord Bramwell's Code.

This was the consensual nature of commercial arbitration – a contractual consensus rooted in the parties' private agreement under the English law of contract, rather than the general law of status, such as the common law rules relating to agents, bailees and carriers. And of the three forms of English commercial arbitration widely practised in the 19th century (i.e. statutory forms of arbitration, arbitration by order of the court and consensual arbitration), the 1889 Act like the Bramwell Code made consensual arbitration preeminent and placed such consensual arbitration firmly within the law of contract. And so we see in the 1889 Act largely taken from clause 64 of the Bramwell Code, a Schedule of contractual terms to be implied into arbitration agreements, which deal with the composition of the tribunal, the tribunal's powers and duties and the finality of the award – all as a matter of contract agreed between the parties and between the parties and the tribunal.

Even if this Bramwell butterfly knew nothing of the Chaos theory at the time, it is not hard now to see the significance of this development both for the law and practice of English "international" commercial arbitration. By definition, in the absence of contractual consensus, English statutory forms of arbitration and English court-annexed arbitration could only be *English* arbitration in England. Only contractual arbitration could ever become truly international. The freedom allowed by the English law of contract ensured that it would be; and (eventually), such an international arbitration could not be treated as a mere inferior judicial tribunal forming an intrinsic part of the English legal system.

At the time this was small step for English domestic arbitration; but it was a giant leap for the "internationalisation" of English arbitration. It meant that both an arbitration agreement and an arbitration award under such an agreement expressly emanated from the private will of the parties, quite differently from a judgment pronounced by a state court which emanated from the sovereign power of that State. With arbitration rooted in contractual consensus, there was then no logical reason to limit the effect of an arbitration agreement or award between parties of different nationalities to the territory of any particular State. And there was thus no logical reason to limit the enforcement in different States of arbitration agreements and awards between parties of different nationalities.

This feature in the Bramwell Code adopted by the Arbitration Act 1889 was thus an important stepping-stone on the long path some 40 years later leading to the 1923 Geneva Protocol on Arbitration Clauses and the 1927 Geneva Convention on Arbitration Awards.

There was another important feature of the Bramwell Code; and its effect also carried through the 1889 Act to the 1923 Protocol and 1927 Convention. The Bramwell Code was the beginning of a new close co-operation between English lawyers and merchants to promote commercial arbitration; and given the role of

188 ON ARBITRATION

the City of London as the commercial hub of the British Empire, this meant in practice transnational or "international", arbitration. In particular the Bramwell Code's failure in 1889 did not prevent its sponsors' planned next step: the creation by the Corporation of the City of London and the London Chamber of Commerce of the London Chamber of Arbitration in 1892, attended by the President of the Board of Trade (but not the Lord Chancellor): the birthday we are celebrating at the centenary conference. After the League of Nation's two treaties in 1923 and 1927, it led also to the Federation of Chambers of Commerce of the British Empire's recommendation of the London Court of Arbitration's Standard Arbitration Clause at its Cape Town conference in 1927.

Many have since regarded the 1923 Geneva Protocol and 1927 Geneva Convention as a small beginning for the "internationalisation" of arbitration. These texts were clearly not so perceived at the time in London; and without our small Bramwell butterfly in 1883, it might well have been that the UK would have throttled both these treaties at birth (or like the US would never have signed them). It now seems hard to understand that over the 1923 Geneva Protocol, both the Lord Chancellor (Lord Cave) and the Attorney-General (Douglas Hogg KC) came close to resignation in protest at the British Cabinet's decision to sign the protocol. The Law Officers and their civil servants shared a particularly English view of the role of commercial arbitration in world trade; and they viewed with particular horror any multilateral treaty where the UK could not control which other States became privy to its reciprocal rights and obligations.

The Lord Chancellor's Permanent Secretary, Sir Claud Schuster (later Lord Schuster), as recorded in his letter to Sir T. Willes Chitty of 25 October 1924 (now preserved at the Public Record Office):

> "... protested in season and out of season against any such protocol being entered into. When it had been entered into, in spite of my opposition, there was not much object in attempting to obstruct the passage of the Bill [the Arbitration Clauses (Protocol) Bill before Parliament which was to enact the 1923 Geneva Protocol].
>
> The then Lord Chancellor (Lord Cave) was also opposed to the making of the protocol. Unfortunately the whole thing took place when he was ill, and his opposition, therefore, was greatly hampered...
>
> I do not see more what we can do. I think we had better await the catastrophe which will undoubtedly follow and only hope that the officious persons who hatched this senseless document [the 1923 Geneva Protocol] will then have to bear the consequences of their misdeed."

Happily for the internationalisation of commercial arbitration this view was not shared by the Board of Trade or the Foreign Office or the British Cabinet; and it was also opposed by the users of commercial arbitration, including the London Court of Arbitration. The broad coalition of users and practitioners first formed by Lord Bramwell held the line.

If Lord Bramwell were here today, he would be much amused, and I think, relatively pleased to see the present state of international commercial arbitration. There has been no catastrophe; arbitration has become the subject of many successful multilateral treaties from the New York Convention to the Helsinki Final Act; and the Board of Trade remains the principal government department sponsoring the necessary reforms to English commercial arbitration, supporting the same broad constituency of arbitration users and practitioners.

B. The UNIDROIT Rome Draft 1936

The second butterfly fluttered and died during the 1930s; but its fluttering led indirectly, after more than 50 years, to the 1985 UNCITRAL Model Law. This was the UNIDROIT Uniform Law on Arbitration, prepared in Rome in 1936. Its origins began even earlier.

Before the First World War, different chambers of commerce in England and abroad had expressed a strong interest in promoting international commercial arbitration as a necessary consequence of their philosophy of world economic interdependence. At its Sixth Congress in June 1914 in Paris, the International Congress of Chambers of Commerce and Commercial and Industrial Associations (founded in 1905), after a long debate adopted a resolution proposing the unification of national legislation relating to commercial arbitration as one of several necessary reforms to the existing national systems of arbitration. There was to be a conference of experts to collect and consider "all the data relative to the practical application of the principle of arbitration between all citizens of different countries" for the purpose of drafting "an international convention for the unification of laws on arbitration" to be considered at a diplomatic conference organised by the French government.[2]

This proposal came to an abrupt halt some two months later with the outbreak of the First World War; and it was only revived by the First Congress of the ICC at its London meeting in June-July 1921 after the war. Amongst other reforms, this First ICC Congress called for "uniform rules of procedure for commercial arbitration".[3] At the ICC's Second Congress in March 1923 in Rome, by which time the ICC had established its own Court of Arbitration and promulgated its rules for conciliation and arbitration (in June 1922), the ICC strongly supported the draft Geneva Protocol on Arbitration Clauses then being considered within the League of Nations; it promoted a further proposal for better means for enforcing

---

[2] See Ridgeway, *Merchants of Peace*, Columbia (1938), pp. 14 and 317.
[3] See Ridgeway, *ibid.*, pp. 125ff and 319.

190 ON ARBITRATION

arbitration awards (which led eventually to the 1927 Geneva Convention); but it again passed a resolution proposing the unification of laws relating to arbitration.[4]

This was known to be difficult. In its Report of August 1922, the League of Nations' Sub-Committee of Legal Experts on the 1923 Geneva Protocol, chaired by Francis Mackinnon KC (later Lord Justice MacKinnon) had already warned of difficulties caused by the "great and perhaps curious diversity between the laws of different countries (on arbitration)".[5] For example, in France at that time an arbitration clause was ordinarily invalid; and even if the arbitration clause were valid, the French Court had an entire discretion whether or not to enforce an award.

In 1928 UNIDROIT, the International Institute for the Unification of Private Law, was founded in Rome. UNIDROIT's Council first considered international commercial arbitration in December 1929; and it requested its Secretariat to procure a report on consensual arbitration in comparative law with a view to seeing whether it was possible to promote a uniform law on arbitration and, if so, how best to achieve that goal. This task was entrusted to Professor René David, soon a young professor of law at Grenoble and the Assistant Secretary-General of UNIDROIT. He was 23 years old, at the threshold of his distinguished career.

Professor David completed his report three years later. It was a massive document of some 290 printed pages comprehensively analysing the different arbitration laws and then practices of many countries, including Germany, England, Spain, the US, France, Italy, Poland and Sweden.[6] UNIDROIT published the report in December 1932; and in April 1933 it established a special committee to prepare the draft Uniform Law envisaged by Professor David. (Professor David's report, which retains enormous historical significance, is now extremely difficult to find; and I do not believe that its existence is well known outside France. In his great work on international trade, Professor David refers to UNIDROIT's project only briefly and in modest terms.[7])

This Special Committee was chaired by UNIDROIT's President, His Excellency Mariano d'Amelio, first president of the Italian Court of Cassation; and its five members comprised Professor David, Professor H.C. Gutteridge KC from Cambridge; Professor Pagenstecher from Hamburg, Mr Simon Rundstein from Poland's Ministry of Foreign Affairs and Judge Emil Sandstroem from the Supreme Court of Sweden. The Committee was also assisted by UNIDROIT's Secretary-General (Giuseppe Righetti) and its Assistant Secretary-General (Alfred Farner).

---

[4] See Ridgeway, *ibid.*, p. 326.

[5] The Report of the Sub-Committee on Arbitration Clauses dated 24 August 1922, at p. 2 (Public Record Office, Kew). In the later Report dated 5 April 1927 on the draft 1927 Geneva Convention, the Committee of Legal Experts similarly warned of the complications caused by "the differences existing between the various systems of law, more particularly in connection with the actual scheme of arbitration, of the relationship between arbitrators and the courts...'; at p. 2 (Public Record Office, Kew).

[6] René David, "Rapport sur l'arbitrage conventionnel en droit privé – Etude de droit comparé"; Rome, 1932. UDP – Etudes III – S.d.N. 1932 – C.D. 1932. (Peace Palace Library: Y554–SS044).

[7] David, *L'arbitrage dans le commerce international*, (1982), p. 226. para. 179.

Later Professor Pagenstecher resigned from the Special Committee; and owing to pressure of work, Professor Gutteridge resigned in favour of Professor B.A. Wortley, then Reader-in-law at the University of Birmingham.

We may note three particular features in the composition of this Special Committee. First, it included no representative from the US of America. This unfortunate omission was due to the fact that the US was not a member of the League of Nations; and indeed the US had not ratified the League's two treaties on commercial arbitration (the 1923 Geneva Protocol and the 1927 Geneva Convention). Yet the US's National Committee was highly active within the ICC; and its representative, Benjamin H. Conner Esq from Paris, had sat on the League's Committee of Experts preparing the draft of the 1927 Geneva Convention. Secondly, the two successive English representatives were both distinguished academic lawyers in the field of comparative law; but neither was a practitioner or specialist in the law of English arbitration; nor were they close to the users of international commercial arbitration in the City of London. Thirdly, the Committee's composition was distinctly European; and the common law tradition was under-represented. As we shall see, these three features were perhaps significant for the eventual downfall of the draft Uniform Law at the ICC's 1937 Congress in Berlin.

The Committee met five times between 1934 and 1936. It published its preliminary draft with a draft report in June 1936;[8] and it published its final draft with a final report in September 1936.[9] Its proposed Uniform Law consisted of 40 articles, drafted in French and English. Its report (in French only) included a detailed commentary on each article. This is not the place for a detailed study of the draft Uniform Law or the Committee's report; and yet they merit further study. We can perhaps guess from their content and style that Professor David played a major part in drafting both.

The ideas expressed in both documents are the genesis of every subsequent attempt to reform the procedure of commercial arbitration at the international level even if (which is the case) these documents were soon set aside after the Second World War. In some respects the Committee made proposals which go much further than the UNCITRAL Model Law, e.g. its proposal regarding uniform interpretation of the Uniform Law: "In the Committee's opinion, it would be desirable that the Permanent Court of International Justice should assume jurisdiction to decide questions of interpretation under the Uniform Law".[10]

---

[8] The Committee of Experts met in August 1934, January and July 1935, and (after its 1936 Report) in April, August and October 1937.

[9] "Comité d'étude pour l'arbitrage en droit privé: Rapport sur le projet d'une loi uniforme sur l'arbitrage"; Rome, September 1936; S.d.N. – U.D.P. 1936 – Etudes III – Arbitrage – Doc 24 (Peace Palace Library, The Hague: S622 d5) ; and "Projet d'une loi internatinale sur l'arbitrage en droit privé"; Rome, September 1936; S.d.N. – U.D.P. 1936 – Etudes III – Arbitrage – Doc 23; (Hague Peace Palace Library, The Hague: S622 d4).

[10] See p. 53 of the Report on the Draft Uniform Law on Arbitration; September 1936 (S.d.N – UDP 1936 – Etudes III – Doc 24).

192 ON ARBITRATION

(How convenient if the New York Convention and the Model Law had contained such provisions: is in fact the "impossible dream" posed below by Judge Holtzmann and Judge Schwebel so impossible?)

In June-July 1937, the Rome draft was considered at the ICC IX Congress in Berlin. The ICC Congress gave its approval to the draft in principle, together with some comments on the wording of the draft. However, four national committees withheld such approval: those of the US, the UK, Australia and to a lesser extent, Japan. In England, criticism of the Rome Draft focused on two particular points:

First, there was a strong feeling that complete uniformity in the procedure of commercial arbitration was wholly undesirable, if not impossible. For example, in opposing the Rome Draft, the Incorporated Oil Seed Association declared itself unwilling: "to sacrifice or even to modify the Anglo-Saxon system of arbitration for the purpose of obtaining uniformity with Continental countries"; and it was also "convinced that it is quite impossible to adopt one uniform rule of arbitration for all Associations. Individual trades have their separate requirements; and it is essential that it should be open to the contractors to choose the rules of arbitration under which a contract is made".[11]

To a large extent this was possibly a misunderstanding of the Rome Draft. It allowed expressly for the parties' arbitration agreement to govern the detailed procedure of their arbitration; and to put the matter beyond doubt for institutional arbitrations, Article 40 of the Rome draft provided that: "The words 'arbitration agreement' or 'agreement of the parties' in the present law shall include the terms of any rules of arbitration which may have been incorporated in such agreement by the parties."

The second concern was substantial. It was believed that the Rome Draft enacted a form of conciliation and not arbitration where the arbitrator was bound by the relevant law applicable to the parties' contract. This concern was best expressed in a letter written to the Lord Chancellor by a young barrister and author of a recent textbook on commercial arbitration, Quintin Hogg. Mr Hogg's letter to the Lord Chancellor, Viscount Hailsham, dated 8 January 1938 merits full citation; and it reads as follows:

"Dear Father,[12]

...An attempt is being made at the instance of a body called, I understand, the Institute of Private International Law which has its headquarters at Rome

---

[11] Letter dated 4 February 1938 to the Foreign Secretary (Public Record Office).

[12] Why "father"? Not because of the traditional respect in which the Lord Chancellor is always held by every member of the English Bar; but rather because the Lord Chancellor was Viscount Hailsham, the writer's father. The writer later succeeded to the same office, twice, as Lord Hailsham; and by a happy coincidence, part of these celebrations for the LCIA's centenary were attended by the Rt Hon Douglas Hogg, the son and grandson of this letter's sender and addressee respectively. (The recent textbook was *Hogg on Arbitration*, published in 1936, for which Viscount Hailsham wrote the foreword). *Source:* Public Records Office, Kew, London.

(inappropriately enough), to introduce through Geneva a Convention which would impose as compulsory upon the Contracting Powers the foreign system of 'Conciliation' as distinct from the English system of 'Arbitration' in commercial contracts.

As you are aware, the vital distinction between these two systems, is as follows. An English Arbitrator, although chosen by the parties, is still a judge in the sense that he must administer the law. In disputes arising out of a contract (in practice, therefore, in most commercial arbitrations), his function is to give effect to the rights of the parties under the contract. He has no right to carve out a new contract for the parties, or to suggest 'reasonable' or 'equitable' courses. He is there to determine the dispute by deciding which party is right.

The Latin system of 'conciliation' is based on a totally different conception. The referee thereunder undertakes the good offices of a friend, but his decision, being under the reference, has the binding force of law. He is not limited to decide the dispute according to the rights of the parties, or even to decide who is in the right at all. His object may be equally to effect a compulsory compromise, and he may therefore by his award direct the parties to do that to which they have never agreed, and which, apart from the award, they would never have been bound to do.

Needless to say, an attempt to impose this system as compulsory in contracts made abroad is regarded with suspicion in the City, and by English lawyers interested in arbitration.

English merchants have in the past unpleasant experience of foreign 'conciliators' and have to an increasing degree inserted in their contracts clauses specifying that disputes are to be settled according to English Arbitration Law. In spite of the fact that the foreign lawyers who have to administer such clauses abroad have found some difficulty in mastering the unfamiliar system, the practice has, I understand, grown to such a degree that if the present proposed convention can be defeated it is anticipated that in a few years English Arbitration methods will be accepted abroad at least as an equally reputable method of settling disputes; and in the end will supersede 'conciliation' in commercial differences.

Already the English system or a system fundamentally in conformity therewith is practically universal in the British Empire, the U.S., the Scandinavian Countries, and I believe in S. America.

Those interested in this question recently held a luncheon at which it was decided to ask the F.O. [the Foreign Office] to oppose the proposed convention at Geneva. All the big London trade associations were I think represented and there was a strong sprinkling of lawyers. The resolution was carried unanimously.

Eden [Sir Anthony Eden, the Foreign Secretary] replied that unless he was advised to act by your dep't [the Lord Chancellor's Department] and by the Board of Trade he would not move; but he promised to send the letter to you. I gather it has not been before you personally."

194 ON ARBITRATION

Lord Hailsham's eventful and successful career has eclipsed his present recollection of these relatively minor events; and yet memories live on elsewhere. Mr Clifford Clark MC, who began his distinguished arbitral career at about this time and who attended the earlier part of these centenary celebrations, can still recall something of the controversy. He was just 20 at the time, working with Mr Vernall, a well-known commercial arbitrator in the City of London; and he can recall the controversy being discussed between Mr Vernall, his colleague Mr Brewer and one of the leading arbitrators at the English Commercial Bar, H.U. Willinck KC.

Were these English critics right in their objections to the Rome Draft? Their main concern sprang from Article 3 of the draft, which provided that: "The award shall also be set aside if the parties have expressly agreed that the arbitrators should observe the rules of law on pain of the award being set aside". From this distance in time, this text seems relatively safe for English arbitration; but UNIDROIT's own commentary suggested that without such an express agreement, the arbitrators would be *"amiables compositeurs"* because their award could not be set aside by the local court for any error of law.[13] From the English perspective at that time this seemed to be a serious objection. An English arbitrator was still an arbitrator even if his award could not be set aside for error of law by the English court, e.g. because the award bore no error of law on its face or because the parties had specifically referred that question of law to the arbitrator. He did not thereby become an *amiable compositeur* under English law. Much later, UNIDROIT saw the misunderstanding, and it added a further provision to Article 30: "Arbitrators are free from the obligation of applying the rules of law and may decide *ex aequo et bono* if the parties have expressly given them the powers of conciliators (*amiables compositeurs*)[14]." This was almost 20 years later, and far too late.

For all practical purposes the Rome Draft as a draft uniform law expired with the ICC's Berlin Congress in 1937. Yet if Professor David could be here, I think that he would be as pleased as Lord Bramwell, for different reasons. After the 1923 Protocol and the 1927 Convention, something more was needed for the "internationalisation" of international commercial arbitration. It was not satisfied by the 1958 New York Convention; and it could never be satisfied by regional conventions, such as the Strasbourg Uniform Arbitration Law of 1966 (which was directly inspired by the Rome Draft). However, it was eventually satisfied by the UNCITRAL Model Law in 1985; and by the minimum standards that the Model Law has now set for all national systems of arbitration, whether or not they adopt the text of

---

[13] "Dans le système du projet, tel qu'il résulte de l'art. 30, les arbitres sont en principe des amiable compositeurs, c'est-à-dire qu'ils doivent bien statuer conformément à la loi, mais que leur sentence ne peut être annulée si, en fait, elle n'est pas conforme à la loi: les arbitres ne cessent d'être des amiable compositeurs, dans le système du projet, que s'il existe entre les parties une stipulation expresse leur retirant ces pouvoirs et les obligeants à statuer en droit..." (p. 43; *ibid.*).

[14] The Draft of a Uniform Law on Arbitration in respect of International Relations of Private Law and Explanatory Report; UNIDROIT 1954, Rome, p. 18; see also Shifman (1987) *World Arbitration Reporter*, 121.

the Model Law. Those are truly "international" standards; and in the widest sense, Professor David's dream behind the Rome Draft is today coming true.

And so what are the lessons to be learnt today from the failure of the Rome Draft, particularly for the UK? Owing to a series of possible misunderstandings a great opportunity was lost in 1936 which could have advanced the "internationalisation" of commercial arbitration by 50 years. By 1936, the day was long past when UK merchants could impose English law and English arbitration by raw commercial strength. There was no cause in London for legal isolationism; and the enormous experience of English commercial arbitration could have been better applied to produce truly "international" commercial arbitration. There is perhaps a more basic lesson. For all the expertise and experience now accumulated in the field of international commercial arbitration, there is still something more intractable than the difficulties of comparative law. It is comparative perceptions, or misperceptions, which often lie at the heart of disagreements over international commercial arbitration. In the dramatic words of the late Professor Goldman, spoken at the LCIA's "Selsdon" conference in Nice only a few months before his final illness, "In the world of international arbitration, there is no reality – the only 'reality' is perception..."– and, of course, dreams...

PART II
THE INTERNATIONAL ARBITRAL PROCESS

Introduction to Part II*

> If, as has been said, international arbitration is the only show in town for international trade, let it at least not be a tennis game played with half the court always missing or a rugby match played by lawyers, like Sisyphus, eternally uphill.

This part brings together ten pieces by Johnny Veeder that are concerned in some way with the international arbitral process. Consistent with the almost unlimited number of issues that may arise, the individual pieces cover a wide range of topics—from the potential breadth of the lawyer's duty to arbitrate in good faith to the apparently narrower issues of issue estoppel and transparency. Yet, a number of themes run through the various pieces.

Thus, in each piece it is easy to locate both Johnny Veeder's concern with ensuring procedural fairness in the arbitral process to the end that justice be done and his keen awareness of the difficulties that may be encountered in achieving that seemingly simple objective. The two are neatly juxtaposed in the opening paragraph to the 2001 Goff Lecture (Chapter 11 below) and, although focused on commercial arbitration, would be seen by Johnny Veeder as applying in arbitration more broadly:

> For the parties to an international commercial arbitration, justice should be the paramount objective; and procedural fairness by their legal representatives is subsumed in that single objective. But the practice of international arbitration is not so simple, certainly not for the parties' professional lawyers coming from different jurisdictions to a still different place of arbitration. Lawyers are not musicians or ballet dancers: a lawyer's training, skills and ethics are still essentially rooted in a national legal system; and it is far from clear how and to what extent national professional rules apply abroad to the transnational lawyer in the international arbitral process.

---

* By Sam Wordsworth.

198   ON ARBITRATION

In three elegant sentences, one sees the progression from the overarching principle that unites the parties to an arbitration to the multiple factors that may cause division and complexity—in terms of the different laws and legal approaches that may necessarily be brought into play in the course of putting or defending the case. To equivalent effect, in writing about the importance of the concept of issue estoppel (Chapter 13), and in the light of the *CME* case,[1] Johnny Veeder identifies the unfairness that may flow from an investor being able to structure its investment so that it benefits from as many bilateral investment treaties (BITs)—and potentially BIT arbitrations—as it can, that is, enabling multiple bites at the same cherry, while the respondent State can deploy no similar device. At the same time, however, he identifies the difficulty in 'the indiscriminate use of Latin tags, particularly res judicata, which disguise under ancient clothes very different concepts in diverse national legal systems' and the absence of a uniform concept of issue estoppel.

Another important theme is that of party autonomy, examined in 'Jurisdiction, Admissibility, and Choice of Law in International Arbitration' (Chapter 19) in the context of the interaction between English law (section 4(5) of the 1996 Arbitration Act) and a choice of foreign law governing a non-mandatory issue (the award of interest). As Johnny Veeder explains:

> where non-English parties, in good faith and for good reason, have agreed in writing upon a non-English substantive law and that law specifically provides how their dispute should be resolved, it seems regrettable that it can then be said that there is an 'absence' of any agreement, not because their agreement is non-existent, invalid or fails to meet the formal requirements of the 1996 Act as the lex loci arbitri, but rather because of isolated passages in a judgment of the House of Lords. That result does not pay 'due regard' to the parties' agreement. To the contrary, it wrongly usurps the parties' arbitration agreement; and it therefore violates the fundamental principle of party autonomy in arbitration. It also works a grave disservice to the legal predictabilities and procedural certainties required for international commercial arbitration in London. Worse, it is not only a quixotic interpretation, it is simply wrong.[2]

---

[1] *CME Czech Republic B.V. v. The Czech Republic*, UNCITRAL, Partial Award (13 September 2001); cf. the different outcome of *Ronald S. Lauder v. The Czech Republic*, UNCITRAL, Final Award (13 September 2001).

[2] The analysis in this piece was approved by the UK Supreme Court in *Enka Insaat Ve Sanayi AS v. OOO Insurance Company Chubb*, [2020] UKSC 38 at para. 88:

> The interpretation contended for by Enka is also inconsistent with the legislative intent, as explained in the DAC Supplementary Report. Furthermore, as the late Mr VV Veeder QC observed, if correct, it would make a practical nonsense of the 1996 Act by requiring parties choosing a foreign law to govern an agreement for arbitration in England to analyse and identify individually in their agreement each of the 35 or so non-mandatory provisions of the 1996 Act which they wish to disapply. We agree with Mr Veeder's comment that the absurd

THE INTERNATIONAL ARBITRAL PROCESS   199

Typically, the pieces in this part point to a way forward as well as to the complexities of a given problem in the international arbitral process, but that way forward may be modest (or, at least, presented as such) or may even be a suggestion that the system is not yet ready for change. The essay on 'The Role of Users' (Chapter 17) concludes: '*As St Augustine, here the patron saint of arbitral users (almost said):* "Grant me innovation and reform in the new ICC Rules, only not yet." ' The focus on what or who really matters (here, the '*user*', i.e. the disputing party, not the institution or the lawyer) is unerring, as are the aptness and wit in the conclusion.

As in Part I, the reader will frequently see in the pieces of Part II the keen interest that Johnny Veeder had in the development of the concepts that are fundamental to the international arbitral process. Party autonomy has been touched on above, and who else would lead one to the concept of separability, taking as the starting point a sixteenth-century jurist that few have ever heard of? That jurist is Maxim the Greek, who is revealed with great playfulness (and scholarship) as an arbitrator and a saint, who can be taken as an example of how individuals can impact on legal thinking and, more broadly, history. And, as a reflection of that focus on the development of ideas, Johnny Veeder was always keen to identify and accord generous recognition to those that have influenced his thinking, whether they be household names of international arbitration or forgotten names from cases long past or the earliest origins of institutions or treaties that are now taken for granted.

Finally, the reader will also see in this part the warmth and humour for which Johnny Veeder was so well known, including most obviously in the piece that now follows on 'The "Y2K Problem" and Arbitration: The Answer to the Myth.[3]

consequences of such an interpretation speak for themselves: see Kaplan and Moser (eds), Jurisdiction, Admissibility and Choice of Law in International Arbitration: Liber Amicorum Michael Pryles (2018), Chapter 23, p. 382.

[3] For those readers fortunate enough not to recall, in the late 1990s, it was widely believed that multiple computer systems had not been programmed to a change in the year that ended other than 19xx and that this would lead to potentially catastrophic impacts on business, travel, etc. as the clock ticked on from 11.59 p.m. on 31 December 1999.

Seeking a view of Mount Everest from Dhulikhel, Nepal before an extended visit to Tibet, 1995

V. V. Veeder pictured at the 2005 Chambers Bar Awards

Addressing the International Arbitration Institute Forum, Château du Clos de Vougeot, Dijon, France, 2008

10
The 'Y2K Problem' and Arbitration
The Answer to the Myth

Professor Dr Dr Ylts*

[It is regretted that for technical reasons publication of this article was rendered impossible.]

---

* Professor Ylts is a computer specialist and an expert consultant on the Y2K Problem for several multinational organizations. He assisted the United Kingdom's DAC regarding electronic commerce and other matters for the English Arbitration Act 1996, having begun his arbitration career as secretary to the arbitration tribunal in *The Macao Sardine Case* (1986); see Sir Michael Kerr, 3 Arb Int 79.

On Arbitration. Edited by: Sam Wordsworth KC and Marie Veeder, Oxford University Press. © Oxford University Press 2023. DOI: 10.1093/oso/9780192869135.003.0010

11

The 2001 Goff Lecture

The Lawyer's Duty to Arbitrate in Good Faith*

A. Introduction

It is a great honour to be asked to deliver this Goff lecture, not only because it is a privilege to follow in the footsteps of so many distinguished lecturers but also because this lecture bears the name of one of the most respected English jurists of my professional lifetime. There are many stories of Robert Goff: he was one of the greatest advocates I ever heard; he was a creative scholar; he was the most courteous judge; he is now a distinguished arbitrator; but above all else, he was and remains the epitome of fairness and human decency. To listen to his advocate's argument even in the most contentious case provoked no sense of ill-will, just despair at the power of his legal logic; and to lose a case before him as judge left only a strong sense of his intellectual honesty. To Lord Goff, the tide of this lecture might seem so self-evident as to preclude any serious debate. Sadly, however, the debate is provoked by growing difficulties which cause the practice of transnational arbitration to fall short of his ideals.

For the parties to an international commercial arbitration, justice should be the paramount objective; and procedural fairness by their legal representatives is subsumed in that single objective. But the practice of international arbitration is not so simple, certainly not for the parties' professional lawyers coming from different jurisdictions to a still different place of arbitration. Lawyers are not musicians or ballet dancers: a lawyer's training, skills and ethics are still essentially rooted in a national legal system; and it is far from clear how and to what extent national professional rules apply abroad to the transnational lawyer in the international arbitration process.

---

* This text is a revised version of the author's 2001 Goff lecture delivered in Hong Kong on 5 December 2001 under the auspices of the City University of Hong Kong; and the editors acknowledge with thanks its permission to publish this article. The author is indebted to Mr Neil Hart for assistance in researching materials for this lecture. (The law and practice is here stated as at 1 December 2001.)

On Arbitration. Edited by: Sam Wordsworth KC and Marie Veeder, Oxford University Press. © Oxford University Press 2023. DOI: 10.1093/oso/9780192869135.003.0011

B. The European Union

For example, for a European Union lawyer practising abroad in a host Member State, Article 6 of the Directive 98/5/EC of 16 February 1998[1] which came into effect on 14 March 2000, prescribes rules of professional conduct in addition to the rules of that lawyer's home Member State: that lawyer is subject 'to the same rules of professional conduct as lawyers practising under the relevant professional title of the host Member State in respect of all the activities he pursues in that territory'. There is no further guidance in the Directive as to what professional rules of conduct apply to an English lawyer from London practising as an advocate in a Paris arbitration, except that the rules of the French avocat before a French court cannot simply be transposed to this English lawyer in an international arbitration.[2]

Of course, an English lawyer working in the European Union's other Member States must also comply with the Code of Conduct for Lawyers in the European Union adopted in 1998 by the Conseil des Barreaux de l'Union Européenne (CCBE).[3] The Code applies generally to the cross-border activities of any English lawyer working in the European Union and European Economic Area, including the great European arbitration centres of Paris, Geneva, Stockholm, Vienna, The Hague and Zurich. And the CCBE Code applies, at least in part, expressly to international arbitration.[4]

By Article 4.5, the 1998 Code provides that 'the rules governing a lawyer's relations with the courts apply also to his relations with arbitrators ...'. These particular rules are set out in Part 4 of the Code under Articles 4.1 to 4.4. Article 4.1 requires a lawyer who appears or takes part in a case before a Member States' court 'to comply with the rules of conduct applied before that court'. This rule is largely meaningless in the field of international arbitration because there are no 'rules of conduct' applied generally to lawyers before an international arbitration tribunal. The major

---

[1] Directive 98/5/EC of the European Parliament and of the Council of 16 February 1998 to facilitate practise of the profession of lawyer on a permanent basis in a Member State other than that in which the qualification was obtained. OJ L 077, 14/03/1998 0036-0043.

[2] See *Société International Contractors Group c/ Me X* (1992) *Rev. de l'Arb* 609 (where the Paris Cour d'appel decided that the prohibition against *pacta de quota litis* for a French avocat in French court proceedings was inapplicable to an avocat representing an Italian party to an international arbitration held in Paris under the ICC Rules; see commentaries by Leboulanger, *ibid* 615, and Paulsson, *infra*.

[3] Code of Conduct for Lawyers in the European Union adopted by the 18 national delegations representing the Bars and Law Societies of the European Union at the Conseil des Barreaux de l'Union Européenne (CCBE) Plenary session held in Lyons on 28 November 1998. Copies are available from the CCBE website <http://www.ccbe.org>. (The 1998 Code originated with the Perugia Declaration made by the Bars and Law Societies of the European Community on 16 September 1977. It dealt with a lawyer's social function, integrity, confidentiality, independence, professional spirit and publicity, and it updates the 1988 Code.)

[4] By Paragraph 1.5 of the CCBE Code, it applies to 'the cross-border activities of the lawyer within the EU and EEA. Cross-border activities shall mean: – (a) all professional contacts with lawyers of Member States other than their own; and (b) the professional activities of the lawyer in a Member State other than his own, whether or not the lawyer is physically present in that Member State.' Its terms are wide enough to apply to lawyer-arbitrators as well as a party's legal representative.

206   ON ARBITRATION

institutional rules of arbitration, including the ICC and LCIA Rules, are silent as to the conduct of a party's legal representative.

Articles 4.2 to 4.4 of the Code are more relevant to arbitration. Article 4.2 provides generally for the fair conduct of proceedings, excluding *ex parte* communications with the arbitrator and requiring settlement discussions not to be communicated to the arbitrator. Article 4.3 requires the lawyer to maintain due respect and courtesy towards the arbitrator; and Article 4.4 requires that 'a lawyer shall never knowingly give false or misleading information to the court'. These are valuable moral commandments; and this part of the Code is commendable for international practice. But that is the practical problem: it is such a small part that the Code provides no useful guidance on the most basic problems facing transnational practitioners of international commercial arbitration.

At best, of course, the Code applies only to regional practice for European Union lawyers in Western Europe. On a worldwide basis, what are the professional rules or guide for a lawyer seeking to discharge a duty to achieve procedural fairness in an international arbitration? The issue was raised ten years ago by a distinguished commentator, Jan Paulsson;[5] but his call went unheeded. [6] Yet the problem is real; the solution ought not to be insuperable; and the matter needs addressing by an international body because the problem applies generally to all of us, everywhere, practising as lawyers in the field of international arbitration. It applies especially in Hong Kong as a leading centre for international commercial arbitration, attracting legal practitioners from all over the world. To the question: what are the professional rules applicable to an Indian lawyer in a Hong Kong arbitration between a Bahraini claimant and a Japanese defendant represented by New York lawyers, the answer is no more obvious than it would be in London, Paris, Geneva and Stockholm. There is no clear answer; but perhaps, as we shall see, there should and could be.

C. Procedural Unfairness

In 1937, the ICC Congress met in Berlin, where its opening session was attended by the German Chancellor Hider and his colleagues Goering and Goebbels. Even then, the ICC's new president, the American Thomas J Watson of IBM, felt able to proclaim the keynote of the conference: 'world peace through world trade'.[7] Thomas Watson was right – but not as right as he would be 50 years later. The great

---

[5] Paulsson, 'Standards of Conduct for Counsel in International Arbitration' in (1992) 3 *Amer. Rev. Int. Arb.* 214, where the author analysed the earlier 1988 CCBE Code of Conduct.

[6] Indeed, many years ago, the arbitration conference in Brussels at which we were both to deliver papers on this subject was cancelled by the organizers, the Chartered Institute of Arbitrators, apparently for lack of interest.

[7] Ridgeway, *Merchants of Peace* (1938) at p. 384.

THE 2001 GOFF LECTURE   207

cause today is the same but still greater: without world trade, there can be no world peace; international arbitration is the oil which lubricates the machinery of world trade; and the mechanics, the international arbitration practitioners, now deserve better practical guidance as to how to apply that oil. International commercial arbitration cannot wait another 50 years.

Let us start with the root of the problem: what is procedural unfairness? Many decades ago, when I was at school in Bristol, in the west of England, our school rugby team played a match against a local school badly endowed with playing fields. In fact, its rugby field lay on a steep hill; and given other demands for its use (which must have included abseiling), we had time for only one half of the match, all of which we played uphill – and lost, badly. In my ears, for a long time, the phrase 'playing on a level playing field' resonated as the basic moral rule of fairness in any adversarial game. What was procedurally unfair, however, was not the pitch itself but the unfairness of playing uphill without the subsequent advantage of playing downhill. Given the range of geographic diversity, fairness is a general concept which must accommodate both flat and hilly ground.

The procedural difficulties in arbitration come from human rather than geographic diversity; and human diversity is surprisingly diverse. For example, there is a large house, beautifully built by one of our arbitration colleagues with a large circular drive leading to the main entrance, adjoining a magnificent tennis court. As many of you will know, the turning circle of a Rolls Royce is disappointingly large; and so it proved that the circular drive had to be enlarged – by taking out a large chunk of the tennis court. Tennis matches are still played at that house; the far half of the tennis court retained its full size although the near half is now severely truncated. The playing field is level, even if it is not equal; it is technically difficult serving and receiving a serve in a few feet of court; but it is not unfair if contestants take turns serving from the truncated half of the tennis court, which they apparently do. Where the tennis players are Rolls Royce owners, a turning circle is perhaps more important than a full tennis court; tennis can still be played fairly; and tennis teas can still be taken without tears. But what if not all players are Rolls Royce owners? Or if the field is not only uphill or unequal; but the other half is a cricket pitch, or a baseball diamond or a swimming pool – and there is no equivalent change at half-time? Then there can be tears; and where the game is arbitration, it can raise acute questions of legal, professional and cultural diversity which are now potentially of immense importance in the practice of international arbitration by parties and particularly by their lawyers. Such diversity can unbalance the arbitral process.

This is different from the situation where both parties equally lack recourse to documentary production or factual testimony tested by cross-examination or the use of their own party-appointed expert witnesses. There is here a level and fair playing field; and of course awards have been enforced in a state court even if the arbitration's procedure was very different from the procedures employed in that

208 ON ARBITRATION

court. We are also not dealing with deliberate dishonesty or criminal fraud here; and the international arbitral process can deal with acts of illegality,[8] which thankfully seem to be rare. And we are not addressing non-criminal misconduct which is generally regarded as morally questionable; for example, the deliberate nomination of different specialist arbitrators in multiple disputes to deprive the other parties of specialist legal advice; or the deliberate conflicting out of specialist counsel by a party to the same end; or one party's beauty-parading of arbitral candidates which looks more at partiality than beauty; or the wilful aggravation of the parties' dispute in order to put unfair pressure on the adverse party.

We are concerned here with ambiguous acts short of deliberate dishonesty which cross the line of procedural fairness because no-one really knows quite where that line is now drawn at the international level. The issue can arise on challenges to awards under national legislation before state courts, including the UNCITRAL Model Law; and the enforcement of arbitration awards under the 1958 New York Convention. Then, however, it will often be too late to put right what was at the time, perhaps inadvertently, wrong.

The common starting point is necessarily the concept of procedural fairness; and whilst no arbitration tribunal can guarantee perfection at all times in deciding substantive law or fact (because judges and arbitrators are not deities), arbitrators can reasonably be asked always to deliver procedural fairness. In England, that objective is now recognized expressly in Lord Woolf's massive reforms to civil procedure in the State courts; for arbitration tribunals, independently, it is expressed by section 1(a) of the English Arbitration Act 1996;[9] and for both courts and arbitration tribunals, directly and indirectly, by the English Human Rights Act 1998 applying Article 6 of the European Convention on Human Rights, guaranteeing a fair hearing to every person, legal and moral. But, as we all know, procedural fairness is no easy objective, and there is nothing 'natural' about natural justice.

In the Anglo-Saxon adversarial system, fairness is dependent on the standards of conduct deployed by the parties and especially the parties' legal representatives, towards each other and towards the court or arbitration tribunal. As the US Supreme Court decided long ago in the *Gideon* case,[10] a defendant's attorney at a criminal trial can be just as much an essential part of a properly constituted court as the judge or jury; and in complex civil litigation and arbitration, the same is almost invariably true. Judges just cannot do it as well or at all without the help of the parties' lawyers, and an international arbitration of

---

[8] For example, see Roth, 'False Testimony at International Arbitration Hearings Conducted in England and Switzerland – A Comparative View' in (1994) 11 *J. Int'l Arb.* 5.

[9] Section 1 (a) of the 1996 Act states as a principle on which Part I of the Act is founded: 'the object of arbitration is to obtain the fair resolution of disputes by an impartial tribunal without unnecessary delay or expense'.

[10] *Gideon* v. *Wainwright* 372 U.S. 335 (1963).

THE 2001 GOFF LECTURE   209

any size would be equally incomplete without the parties' legal representatives. This symbiotic relationship can be readily illustrated with a recent cautionary tale from England.

D. The Cautionary Tale

In *Vernon* v. *Bosley (No 2)* (1998),[11] the defendant nanny had killed by negligent driving two of the plaintiff's children and the plaintiff sued her for nervous shock. In a reserved judgment delivered long after the trial, the judge awarded damages for post-traumatic stress disorder based on expert evidence from a psychiatrist and psychologist; and the defendant then appealed to the Court of Appeal. The Court of Appeal heard this appeal and gave judgment upholding liability but reducing the amount of damages. Before the formal order was drawn up, the defendant's counsel received anonymously through the post copies of a county court judgment in different family proceedings between the plaintiff and his divorced wife relating to the custody of their remaining children and of a judgment of the Court of Appeal (differently constituted) dismissing the plaintiff's appeal from that county court judgment.

What was significant was the expert issue in these family proceedings, taking place six months after the trial in the personal injury proceedings. In stark contrast to their evidence at that earlier trial, the same psychiatrist and psychologist had given expert evidence that the mental health of the plaintiff father had dramatically improved and that he was substantially, if not fully, recovered. This was *not* a case where these experts had given false evidence or expressed opinions which were incorrect; and in this sense neither had 'changed his evidence', but rather only their prognosis as time had elapsed between the evidence in the personal injury trial and the later hearing in the family proceedings during which the plaintiff's mental health had significantly improved. As Lord Justice Stuart-Smith's judgment reports:

> It appeared to the defendant's legal advisers [this must have been somewhat of an understatement] that this evidence was materially different from the picture presented to Sedley J [the trial judge] and this court [the Court of Appeal], and in particular it might affect the judge's findings as to the plaintiffs state of health at the time of the judgment and to the prognosis for the future. This would affect the level of general damages and also elements of future loss ... (page 688D).

---

[11] *Vernon* v. *Bosley (No 2)* [1999] QB 18 (Stuart-Smith and Thorpe LJJ, Evans LJ dissenting; see *also* *Vernon* v. *Bosley (No 1)* [1997] 1 All ER 577.

210   ON ARBITRATION

The plaintiff was morally blameless; he acted on the advice of his legal advisers. He was represented by different solicitors and counsel in the two sets of proceedings; and before the trial judge delivered his reserved judgment in the personal injury proceedings, his legal advisers advised him *not* to disclose the improved prognosis to the defendant, the trial judge or even later to the Court of Appeal; and when the plaintiff learnt that his former wife might disclose these medical reports obtained in the family proceedings to the defendant's insurers, his legal advisers sought and obtained from the High Court an injunction restraining her from doing so. Factually it is a complicated case; but what is clear was the absence of any dishonesty on the part of any of the plaintiff's legal advisers. They were plainly faced with an acute problem of professional ethics where their duty to the court appeared to conflict radically with the duty to their own client.

At the resumed hearing before the Court of Appeal, the defendant submitted that by one or more of three routes, discovery or disclosure of the later medical reports or the requirements not to mislead the court, the change in prognosis should have been made known by the plaintiff and his legal advisers. As to documentary discovery, by a majority, the Court of Appeal decided that the parties' duty continued up to judgment, after the conclusion of evidence and the trial; that the notes and medical reports were not privileged; and that these materials should have been disclosed to the defendant before the trial judge delivered his reserved judgment, even though both sides had long before closed their respective cases. As to the duty not to mislead the court, Lord Justice Stuart-Smith concluded:

> I readily accept that the plaintiff's counsel did not deliberately intend to deceive the court and believed that the advice they gave [to the plaintiff) was sound. But in my judgment they made a serious error of judgment in failing to advise him on the need for disclosure. By an over-technical construction of the rules and a failure to appreciate that their previous conduct of the case would result in the court reaching an unjust result unless disclosure was made, they found themselves in an impossible position. By the time the case came to this court they should have appreciated that they could no longer seek to uphold the judge's judgment ...

The defendant's second appeal was allowed by the Court of Appeal; and damages were further reduced. However, Lord Justice Evans dissented and would have dismissed the first part of this appeal and, whereas Lord Justice Stuart-Smith decided (*obiter*) that counsel's remedy was to resign if his advice to correct testimony or disclose documentation was rejected by his client, Lord Justice Thorpe decided that counsel's duty went much further: counsel had an overriding duty to disclose the relevant material to his opponent and, unless there was agreement between the parties otherwise, to the trial judge.

For present purposes, the point is simple. Difficult as this case was for the ethics of English lawyers before an English court, what would the answer be in a like case for a party's legal representatives acting in an international arbitration? For example, what would happen if a Hong Kong solicitor or counsel acting for an Australian party in an international arbitration in Singapore discovered weeks after the final hearing and as the tribunal was writing its final award, that part of their client's case was now quite wrong? Would these lawyers advise their client that a correction must be notified to their opponent and the tribunal? And if their client said 'no', as it might and then dismissed them if they pressed their advice, would that counsel and solicitor have duty to notify their foreign opponents or the arbitration tribunal abroad? The answer should probably be 'yes'; but juridically why? It is regrettable that these questions are currently beyond any clear answer, both in Hong Kong and elsewhere.

E. Four Characteristics

International arbitration clearly raises more difficulties here than national practice before state courts; and there are four distinguishing characteristics which any solution needs to address. First, as already discussed, practitioners in the field of international commercial arbitration extend over the full rainbow colours of human diversity around the world; the legal representatives of parties do not usually share the same national legal culture or practise subject to the rules of the same professional body. In the United Kingdom, long after the Act of Union with Scotland, it was on occasion still difficult for Scots and English lawyers to work with each other,[12] but those difficulties pale into insignificance compared to the brave attempts within the European Union to subject the Member State's Bars and Law Societies to a uniform professional code of conduct, already mentioned above. Outside such legal regions, the problem is greater still. This does not mean that international practitioners are pirates sailing under no national flag; it means only that on the high seas, navigators need more than a coastal chart.

Secondly, unlike most national court systems, there is no appeal on the merits from an arbitration award. The need for finality generally outweighs justice in the particular case; and procedural mistakes can be left uncorrected even when caused by professional errors of judgement. In England, the 1996 Act has made an important difference in abolishing the English court's old power to remit an award to the arbitration tribunal on the grounds either that fresh evidence has become available after the award or that a procedural mishap has occurred short of any

---

[12] *See* D.L. Carey-Miller, 'The Advocate's Duty to Justice' in (1981) 97 *LQR* 127.

misconduct by the arbitration tribunal. These procedures can still be invoked in respect of appeals from English court judgments, but not any more in respect of English arbitration awards. A disgruntled losing party is left with the traditional but extreme remedy, if available, of challenging the award on the basis that it was obtained by fraud or contrary to public policy.[13] This quality of finality special to arbitration, but particularly so to international arbitration, means that it is even more important that an arbitration award should be the product of procedural fairness.

Thirdly, there is a lack of transparency in international arbitration. There are no useful statistics for institutional arbitration; and there is no reliable data at all for non-institutional or *ad hoc* arbitration. The whole activity takes place in a cloud of privacy without the same public scrutiny directed at state courts. In the absence of sufficient reported cases, it is not easy to learn how many arbitrations are unfairly conducted and, in particular, how fairness can be harmed by the conduct of parties' legal representatives. Yet the system of international arbitration does seem to work well. If so, like State litigation, the system must work because it is essentially self-policing – but self-policing by lawyers and arbitrators depends on practitioners having a clear idea of where the line is drawn between good and bad arbitration practices. If a lawyer advises a client that it must disclose voluntarily a relevant but harmful document or cannot plead fraud on existing materials, that client is entitled to know the reason why, and if there is no good reason, the pressures of international practice may mean that the client will find another lawyer who will do what the other has declined to do. In the field of international arbitration, like State litigation, there are many fish competing in the same sea. Clear rules and self-policing are an essential part of any solution.

Lastly, in arbitration, where the legal links between the parties usually derive from the contractual agreement to arbitrate (in whole or in part), the legal roots of a party's duty to play the game fairly must begin with that arbitration agreement, as a general contractual obligation to arbitrate in good faith. This is the most awkward characteristic: how can such a general obligation impose practical rules; and how does a contractual duty imposed on a party work itself through to rules influencing that party's legal representative? As to the former, it is obvious, even more so than in State litigation, that the rules need to be practical; and it is useless to maintain any rule at the level of supreme generality. A formulation based only on good faith could be too vague to be of practical use, and yet, in default of any other available legal principle, it is the necessary starting point. There is also a particular problem with a general principle of good faith as an English legal concept; in short, in recent history, it has not been very English at all.

---

[13] Section 68(2)(g) of the 1996 Act: *see* Mustill & Boyd's *2001 Companion* (2001) at pp. 352–354, to which we return below.

THE 2001 GOFF LECTURE   213

F. Good Faith

Good faith in the performance of civil procedural obligations is assumed by civilian lawyers. This duty of good faith is readily transposed from the duty of good faith in civil law. Professor Hanotiau, from Brussels, concluded in his work on multi-party arbitrations that it is a 'basic principle of international commercial arbitration that the parties have the duty to co-operate in good faith in the performance of their agreement as well as in the arbitral proceedings', and another distinguished commentator from Greece, Antonias Dimolitsa, identified the source of that obligation: '... the international principle of the inviolability of the arbitration agreement is actually just a special application of the principle of *pacta sunt servanda* which, together with the parallel application of good faith, is strictly applied to arbitration agreements...'.[14]

To an English lawyer, regrettably, the concept of good faith remains somewhat vague, and although the House of Lords has recently defined the term in the different context of a regulator's exemption from liability for the tort of misfeasance,[15] English law on good faith says nothing about the activities of a party's legal representatives in an international arbitration. Former students of English law may recall that Professor Sir Roy Goode QC concluded in the first edition of his great work on commercial law[16] that, surprisingly, there was no general principle of English law that requires legal remedies to be exercised in good faith, adding that it was 'at once the most remarkable and most reprehensible feature of English contract law'. That was written even before the House of Lords decided in *Walford* v. *Miles* (1992)[17] that English law could not recognize and enforce obligations to negotiate 'in good faith'.

Nonetheless the contractual duty to arbitrate in good faith is recognized in the common law outside England. It is rare in international arbitration to see this duty spelt out, but there is a useful example in Hong Kong. In *China Nanhai Oil* v. *Gee Tai Holdings* (1994),[18] the Hong Kong High Court granted leave to enforce a CIETAC award on the ground that the losing defendant was estopped from relying on the improper constitution of the arbitration tribunal, which had been formed in Beijing

---

[14] Hanotiau, 'Complex Multicontract-Multiparty Arbitration' in (1998) *Arbitration International* 369; Dimolitsa, 'Arbitration Agreements and Foreign Investments: The Greek State' in (1988) 5 *J. Int'l Arb.* 17 at p. 39.

[15] See *Three Rivers District Council* v. *Governor and Company of the Bank of England (No 3)* [2000] 2 WLR 1220 for the first judgment; and for the second judgment, see [2001] 2 All ER 513. (Section 29 of the Arbitration Act 1996 exempts, in similar terms, an arbitrator from liability save for 'bad faith').

[16] Goode, *Commercial Law* (1982, 1st ed.) at p. 117.

[17] *Walford* v. *Miles* [1992] 2 A.C. 128. This decision has generated a mass of comment, conveniently summarized in Beatson and Friedman (eds) *Good Faith and Fault in Contractual Law* (1995) at pp. 36–42. See also Brownsford *et al.* (ed), *Good Faith in Contract* (1998, Ashgate).

[18] *China Nanhai Oil Joint Services Corporation* v. *Gee Tai Holdings Limited* (1995) XX *ICCA Yearbook* 671 (reporting the decision dated 13 July 1994 of the Hong Kong High Court (Kaplan J), citing van den Berg, *The New York Convention* (1981) at p. 185).

214   ON ARBITRATION

and not Shenzhen as required by the parties' arbitration agreement. The facts need not concern us here, but Mr Justice Kaplan did not base his decision on the classic English equitable doctrine of estoppel. He cited the work on the New York Convention by the civilian Professor van den Berg, recognizing estoppel as a principle emanating from a party's general obligation to arbitrate in good faith 'enshrined in the [New York] Convention's provisions'. The learned Judge applied that duty of good faith so as to have required the defendant promptly to bring to the notice of the arbitration tribunal or CIETAC in Beijing its objections to the tribunal's formation, rather than wait two years after losing the arbitration before complaining for the first time that the arbitrators were chosen from the wrong CIETAC list of arbitrators.

What is needed is this kind of practical guidance on good faith for the legal representatives of parties. There is nothing to prevent that same approach being applied to the most contentious areas of professional practice: document production, the preparation of factual witness statements and the commissioning of independent expert reports. These procedures are now increasingly common in international arbitrations, given the widespread interest in the International Bar Association's Rules on the Taking of Evidence in International Commercial Arbitration of June 1999, and the success of this initiative may answer the second part of the problem raised above, namely: how to influence the parties' lawyers.

G. The IBA Rules

In 1983 there was a muted welcome for the first edition of these IBA Rules. Nonetheless, their quiet acceptance in practice over the next decade paved the way for the more ambitious second edition in 1999.[19] There was then criticism from some quarters over the new procedures for document production under Article 3 of the 1999 Rules – it either went too far in allowing a party to request unspecified documentation or not far enough in limiting that request to narrow and specific categories reasonably believed to exist. That criticism seems now to have died down. What was not at first controversial were Articles 4 and 5 dealing with factual witness statements and the written reports of party-appointed experts.

For international arbitration, the procedure whereby a party and not the tribunal leads its own factual and expert testimony is now well accepted by both civilian and common law practitioners and arbitrators, and it is the well-worn practice for a factual and expert witness to reduce into writing in advance what would be their evidence-in-chief or direct examination, confining their oral testimony largely to cross-examination by the adverse party and the tribunal. This procedure removes the unfair element of surprise or deliberate ambush at the main hearing; it allows

---

[19] IBA Rules on the Taking of Evidence in International Commercial Arbitration, adopted by a resolution of the IBA Council on 1 June 1999, available on <www.ibanet.org>.

expert witnesses to meet and exchange views before the hearing (a procedure now reflected in Article 5(3) of the IBA Rules); and since hearing time is money, it saves both time and money by having everyone read these materials in advance of the main hearing without the need for direct testimony to be recited aloud. That is the theory, but as experience now shows, the practice can be different, and here experience has begun to mean bad experience.

There is an increasing tendency for a factual witness statement to take the form of special pleading prepared substantially by lawyers and not the witness (albeit later formally 'approved' by that witness). This practice diminishes the statement's probative value and increases the need for oral cross-examination. There is again a similar practice whereby expert reports express less than independent expert opinions, again substantially prepared by lawyers and not the expert (albeit also 'approved' by that expert); and this practice significantly complicates the task of the arbitration tribunal. As regards document production, there is increasing evidence that such production is assessed not by any uniform professional standards, but rather by subjective, client-driven rules calculated to support the factual and witness testimony to be adduced by that client.

H. The Problem in Practice

Why does any of this matter for international arbitration? It matters first because it can easily breed procedural unfairness in the particular case, and it matters generally because it attacks the integrity of the system of international arbitration. The system of self-policing may become impossible and there may be a gradual deterioration in the standards of legal professional conduct. The international arbitral process would then be brought into disrepute and, once its good reputation was lost, it could take decades to rebuild confidence.[20] To date, for example, the English court has rejected every attempt to attack a foreign award on strictly procedural grounds under the New York Convention. Indeed, there is still no reported case of an English court refusing enforcement of any foreign award on the ground of English public policy. However, there are now cases where the English court has broadened the public policy exception for English awards in section 68 (2) (g) of the Arbitration Act 1996,[21] and there is one recent case which illustrates that the

---

[20] There is an existing analogy with the loss of professional courtesy between English arbitration practitioners, once the norm and now increasingly the exception. As Lord Mustill warned a decade ago: 'There is precious little self-discipline, comradeship or community spirit between the parties to a typical arbitration' (1992) 9 J. Int'l Arb. 5 at p. 15. There is no rational explanation for this regrettable change, which is particularly evident in correspondence, but the process now seems irreversible.

[21] Section 68 of the 1996 Act provides: '(1) A party to arbitral proceedings may ... apply to the court challenging an award in the proceedings on the ground of serious irregularity affecting the tribunal, the proceedings or the award ... (2) Serious irregularity means an irregularity of one or more of the following kinds which the court considers has caused or will cause substantial injustice to the

216   ON ARBITRATION

English court may in future look critically at serious procedural unfairness under the same public policy exception in Article V(2)(b) of the New York Convention.

(1) Document Disclosure

The case related to documentary disclosure, allegedly made deficiently in the arbitration by the successful claimant. In *Profilati Italia SRL v. Paine Webber Inc & anr* (2001),[22] the losing applicant challenged the award on the grounds that part of it had been procured by the claimant in a way which was contrary to public policy under section 68 of the Arbitration Act 1996. The substance of its argument was that the claimant had wrongly failed to disclose two material documents which would have supported the applicant's case and, having failed to do so, that the claimant allowed its counsel to make submissions to the arbitration tribunal which could not have been made in the same way or with the same force if those documents had been disclosed and, to that extent, therefore, the award was improperly procured because the tribunal was effectively misled.

The English Commercial Court (Moore-Bick J) dismissed the application on its factual merits, but the judgment makes clear that, subject to factual proof, the application could be well founded under section 68(2)(g) of the 1996 Act. The learned Judge held:

> 17. It would be unwise in my view to attempt to define the circumstances in which an award might be set aside or remitted on public policy grounds, but in the light of that comment and of the language of subsection (2)(g) as a whole I think that where the successful party is said to have procured the award in a way which is contrary to public policy it will normally be necessary to satisfy the court that some form of reprehensible or unconscionable conduct on his part has contributed in a substantial way to obtaining an award in his favour ...

And later:

> 19. Where an important document which ought to have been disclosed is deliberately withheld and as a result the party withholding it has obtained an award in his favour the court may well consider that he has procured that award in a manner contrary to public policy. After all, such conduct is not far removed from fraud ...

applicant ... (g) the award being obtained by fraud or the award or the way in which it was procured being contrary to public policy.'

[22] *Profilati Italia SRL v. Paine Webber Inc & anr* [2001] 1 Lloyd's Rep. 715.

Fraud is here actual dishonesty in the English legal sense. It is much more than a failure to disclose a document as a result of negligence or mishap or a simple error of judgment; but the Court acknowledged that something less than fraud might suffice if it qualified as 'reprehensible or unconscionable conduct' – but what is that in an international commercial arbitration? It must presumably include 'bad faith', even if that civilian term was never uttered by the English Court. If this analysis were correct, subject to further elaboration, the Court's approach could be readily imported into the IBA Rules on document production.

(2) Factual Witness Statements and Expert Reports

For witness statements and expert reports, it is here again necessary for practical guidance to turn to court decisions because of the paucity of arbitration materials. It can be found in the English cases leading to the recent Woolf reforms.

(a) Expert reports

The House of Lords held in *Whitehouse* v. *Jordan* (1987)[23] that even though some degree of consultation between experts and legal advisers was entirely proper, it was necessary that expert evidence presented to the court should be, and should be seen to be, the independent product of the expert, 'uninfluenced as to form or content by the exigencies of litigation'. In the Court of Appeal, which reversed the trial judge, Lord Denning MR had identified a number of flaws in a joint experts' report submitted by the plaintiff. Most prominent among these flaws was the intrusively editorial role played by the plaintiff's lawyers in preparing that evidence, as described by Lord Denning:

> In the first place, their joint report suffers to my mind from the way it was prepared. It was the result of long conferences between the two professors and counsel in London and it was actually 'settled' by counsel. In short, it wears the colour of special pleading rather than an impartial report. Whenever counsel 'settle' a document, we know how it goes. 'We had better put this in', 'We had better leave this out', and so forth. A striking instance is the way in which Professor Tizard's report was 'doctored'. The lawyers blacked out a couple of lines in which he agreed with Professor Strang [another expert witness] that there was no negligence.

That counsel was a distinguished senior silk, of impeccable character and now an English High Court Judge. What he did was only what we all once did; it was a professional practice not only *not* wrong under the standards then prevailing in

---

[23] *Whitehouse* v. *Jordan* [1987] 1 WLR 246.

England; but *not* to do what he did could have been widely regarded at that time as professional negligence. Lord Denning's strictures changed that practice at the English Bar, almost overnight.

This new approach to expert evidence later formed part of Cresswell J's classic summary of the duties and responsibilities of expert witnesses in *The Ikarian Reefer* (1998).[24] Foremost among those duties was the importance of the expert's autonomy from the influence of the parties to the litigation, as emphasized in *Whitehouse*. It required the expert witness to provide 'independent assistance to the Court by way of objective unbiased opinion in relation to matters within his expertise'. That expert opinion must also be complete. Where there are conflicting experts' reports, the tribunal cannot reach any satisfactory finding if the relevant materials have been partially withheld by one or more expert witnesses. As Bracewell J held in *Clough* v. *Tameside & Glossop HA* (1998):[25]

> It is not for one party to keep their cards face down on the table so that the other party does not know the full extent of information supplied. Fairness dictates that a party should not be forced to meet a case pleaded or an expert opinion on the basis of documents he cannot see. Although civil litigation is adversarial, it is not permissible to withhold relevant information, or to delete or amend the contents of a report before disclosure ...

The early identification and narrowing of expert issues is increasingly important in international commercial arbitration and, as already mentioned above, the practice of expert meetings is reflected in the IBA Rules. To make these procedures work fairly (and indeed to work at all), they must be played candidly, with open hands. As the English Court of Appeal noted in *Naylor* v. *Preston Area Health Authority* (1987),[26] the English courts:

> have moved far and fast from a procedure where tactical considerations which did not have any relation to the achievement of justice were allowed to carry any weight.... [W]hilst a party is entitled to privacy in seeking out the 'cards' for his hand, once he has put his hand together, the litigation is to be conducted with all the cards face up on the table.

All this is a sea change from the former practice of lawyers in the English courts. It has all happened within the last 15 years without primary legislation until the Woolf reforms, being driven by English judges and practitioners.

---

[24] *The Ikarian Reefer* [1993] 2 Lloyd's Rep. 68 at pp. 81–82. The Court of Appeal reversed the judgment but approved this passage intact: see [1995] 1 Lloyd's Rep. 455 at p. 496.

[25] *Clough* v. *Tameside & Glossop HA* [1998] 1 WLR 1478 at p. 1484.

[26] *Naylor* v. *Preston Area HA* [1987] 1 WLR 958 at p. 967.

(b) Factual witness statements

The practice of taking factual witness statements requires urgent reform. Increasingly, many international arbitrators pay little credence to written witness statements on any contentious issue, unless independently corroborated by other reliable evidence. It is perhaps surprising that many sophisticated practitioners have not yet understood that their massive efforts at re-shaping the testimony of their client's factual witnesses is not only ineffective but often counter-productive. Most arbitrators have been or remain practitioners; and they can usually detect the 'wood-shedding' of a witness.[27] In England, there is a recent case where wood-shedding was taken to an extreme.

In *Aquarius Financial Enterprises* v. *Lloyd's Underwriters* (2001),[28] where the English Commercial Court was concerned with a vessel allegedly destroyed deliberately by fire, Toulson J held that it was the English solicitor's duty to ensure that any factual witness was interviewed by the solicitor himself, or if that was not practicable, by a person who could be relied upon to exercise the same standard as an English solicitor. This decision was provoked by the treatment of a particular witness, Mr Schoenig, who was on board the vessel when the fire broke out; and the interviewer was Mr Ashton, a marine surveyor and investigator, previously a police officer and (more significantly) for many years a CID officer attached to the anti-terrorist squad. In cross-examination, Mr Ashton had explained his interviewing technique as follows:

Q. You resorted to intimidation to obtain the evidence you wanted?

A. I don't call it intimidation, I was forceful. I was dealing with a person that I thought was lying to me; I was not going to pussyfoot around. I knew the type of person I was dealing with. This was a very street-wise person.

Q. You had formed the conclusion that this man was not going to give you the evidence that you needed unless you bullied him, so you set about bullying him?

A. I had not formed that conclusion. I formed that conclusion at the end when he didn't give me the evidence that he could have given me. I didn't set out to bully him, I set out to talk to him in a nice manner and to deal with the matter as I would with any other witness. It was his attitude that made me become forceful and angry at times.

---

[27] In one case, where a witness had been thoroughly coached by his party's lawyers in successive dress rehearsals before a 'shadow' arbitration tribunal, the witness concluded his testimony before the actual tribunal by congratulating, inadvertently, the opposing counsel for the brevity of his cross-examination, on the ground that it was 'the shortest of all'.

[28] *Aquarius Financial Enterprises Inc & Bernard Deletirez* v. *Certain Underwriters at Lloyd's* [2001] 2 Lloyd's Rep. 542.

220   ON ARBITRATION

The learned Judge commented adversely on this style of interrogation. He said:

> 43. In English litigation, civil or criminal, there can be no proper place for trying to persuade a potential fact witness what he should say, let alone by bullying, threat or inducements.[29] Such methods are totally unacceptable. Mr Ashton's conviction that Mr Schoenig was lying is no conceivable justification. If Mr Ashton had succeeded, and if Mr Delettrez [another witness] had not been recording the conversation, the result would have been a [written witness] statement from Mr Schoenig which could have been put in evidence under the Civil Evidence Act without either the court or the opposing party knowing how it had been obtained.

The learned Judge then referred to the procedure by which witness statements ordinarily stand as witnesses evidence in chief, an integral part of practice in the English Commercial Court for some years but now prescribed under Rule 32.5(2) of the Civil Procedure Rules. He then cited Part HI.3 of the Commercial Court Guide, which provides that: 'whilst it is recognised that in commercial cases, a witness statement will usually be prepared by legal representatives, the witness statement must, so far as practicable be in the witness's own words'. His judgment continued:

> 46. It cannot be too strongly emphasised that this means the words which the witness wants to use and not the words which the person taking the statement would like him to use.

> 47. Part HI.4 of the Commercial Court Guide provides that the rules of any professional body regarding the drafting of witness statements must also be observed.

> 48. The Law Society's Guide to the Professional Conduct of Solicitors provides guidance on the taking of witness statements. It requires a high degree of skill and professional integrity. The object is to elicit that which the witness is truthfully able to say about relevant matters from his or her own knowledge or recollection, uninfluenced by what the statement taker would like him or her to say.

> 49. Counsel on both sides expressed anxiety that this is in practice not what generally happens even when statements are taken by solicitors. If it is not, the situation is worrying. In the USA pre-trial depositions of witnesses are a standard feature of civil litigation.[30] The process is costly and time-consuming. Our

---

[29] See also *Odyssey Re London Limited* v. *OIR Run-Off Limited* (unreported; *The Times* Law Report, 13 March 2000; Nourse, Brooke & Buxton LJJ, latter dissenting) a case where the perjured evidence of a director was treated as that of a company obtaining a judgment which was on that ground set aside, where Brooke LJ severely deprecated the 'charm-offensive' deployed by the company's English solicitors towards the alleged perjurer.

[30] Outside the USA, witness depositions are not usual in international commercial arbitration. Although depositions can remove much of the need for direct and cross-examination of witnesses, the procedure takes place away from the arbitration tribunal (who cannot therefore make their own

THE 2001 GOFF LECTURE 221

system is quicker and cheaper, but it depends for its proper working on witness statements being properly taken. Bad practices, like bad money, tend to drive out good. If bad practices in the taking of witness statements come to be seen as normal, so that witness statements become lawyers' artefacts rather than the witnesses' words, their use will have to be reconsidered. Central to the problem is the ignorance of the court and the other party about how any witness statement has in fact been taken. It might therefore be thought salutary that there should be a written declaration by the person who prepared the statement giving information about how, when and where it was prepared and certifying compliance with any appropriate code of practice.

50. Moreover where parties are represented in litigation by solicitors (as is almost invariably the case in the Commercial Court), I would regard it as part of their duty to ensure, so far as lies within their power, that any witness statements taken after they have been instructed are taken either by themselves or, if for some reason that is not practicable, by somebody who can be relied upon to exercise the same standard as should apply if the statements were taken by the solicitors themselves.

It would be a foolish English practitioner who did not now take heed of the strictures in this judgment.

I. The Woolf Reforms

The Woolf reforms have accelerated but did not initiate these judicial reforms in the English courts. All these reforms have undoubtedly made English practice easier by setting out more clearly the rules for English lawyers to follow, particularly in the preparation of factual witness statements and expert reports.[31] The cardinal principle requires the draft witness statement to reflect accurately the witness' evidence,[32] and the Commercial Court Guide expressly warns that: 'great care should

---

assessment of the witness); it does not always save time and expense; and the practice is regarded by the English courts as inconsistent with both court and arbitration procedures: see *Commerce and Industry Insurance Co of Canada* v. *Lloyd's Underwriters* [2002] 1 Lloyd's Rep. 219; and *Refco Capital Markets* v. *Credit Suisse (First Boston)* [2001] EWCA CIV 1733 (Court of Appeal; 21 November 2001; unreported).

[31] Part HI of the Commercial Court Guide and CPR Part 32 and 32PD, paragraphs 17 to 25. For English solicitors, there is general guidance in Chapter 21 of their Code of Conduct Rules; and as officers of the court, solicitors bear a general but wide-ranging duty not to mislead the court. The English Bar can now take and assist in taking a witness statement in civil cases; and the rules are set out in Paragraph 704-5 of the Bar's Code of Conduct and an approved guide 'Guidance on the Preparation of Witness Statements'.

[32] As to the contents of an expert report, the relevant rules are set out in Part 35 of the Civil Procedural Rules 1998 and its Practice Direction, together with section H2 and Appendix 12 of the Commercial Court Guide. There is an Expert Witness Protocol (Version 1.0) prepared by the Official Referees Solicitors Association (ORSA) for use in the Technology and Construction Court (available at <www.courtserv ice.gov.uk/notices/tcc/tcc-tecsa-ewp.htm>), and there is also a draft Code of Guidance for Experts of September 1999 awaiting approval as a Practice Direction. (These documents will be revised in 2002).

222   ON ARBITRATION

be exercised when excluding any material which is thought to be unhelpful to the party calling the witness and no material should be excluded which might render the statement anything other than the truth, the whole truth and nothing but the truth.' Expert witnesses must certify that they understand their duty to the court, as set out in Appendix 12 to the Guide (which derives substantially from Cresswell J's judgment in *The Ikarian Reefer*), and experts must address their reports to the court. It is the express duty of experts to help the court on the matters within their expertise (CPR 35.3(1)). This duty is paramount and overrides any obligation to the person from whom an expert has received instructions or by whom he or she is paid (CPR 35.3(2)).

This Appendix 12 lists specific rules:

1 Expert evidence presented to the Court should be, and should be seen to be, the independent product of the expert uninfluenced by the exigencies of litigation.
2 An expert witness should provide independent assistance to the Court by way of objective unbiased opinion in relation to matters within his expertise. An expert witness should never assume the role of an advocate.
3 An expert witness should not omit to consider material facts which could detract from his concluded opinion.
4 An expert witness should make it clear when a particular question or issue falls outside his expertise.
5 If an expert's opinion is not properly researched because he considers that insufficient data is available, then this must be stated with an indication that the opinion is no more than a provisional one.
6 In a case where an expert witness who has prepared a report could not assert that the report contained the truth, the whole truth and nothing but the truth without some qualification, that qualification should be stated in the report.
7 If, after exchange of reports, an expert witness changes his view on a material matter having read another expert's report or for any other reason, such change of view should be communicated in writing (through legal representatives) to the other side without delay, and when appropriate to the Court.

The expert witness must certify that he or she has read and understood Appendix 12 and that he or she has complied and will continue to comply with its terms at all stages of involvement in the case. The expert must also certify that the assumptions on which his or her opinion are based are not unreasonable or unlikely or that if they are, the expert has said so; the expert must certify that the facts stated in his or her report within his or her own knowledge have been identified as such and are true; the expert must certify that the opinions expressed in the report represent his or her true professional opinion; and the expert must of course sign the opinion so as to make it his or her own expert opinion. This is all very uncontroversial; it works in practice for the English Commercial Court and suitably adapted it could work equally for international commercial arbitration.

J. Possible Solutions

The question first arises whether international arbitration is susceptible to reform at all. From the English perspective, the answer is easy: if Lord Woolf could so massively reform English civil procedure, then nothing is beyond reform anywhere. For international commercial arbitration, such reforms must be possible; but equally these cannot be achieved by a mono-cultural approach, and, as indicated above, there are also certain criteria for any possible solutions. The initiative lies in the hands of international arbitrators and practitioners and, if ignored for much longer, it may pass to state or regional regulators with less affection for the arbitration process.

The general contractual duty of good faith can provide the legal umbrella for both civilian and common law lawyers, but by itself the doctrine is too general to provide an effective practical guide for parties' lawyers practising in the field of international arbitration. Also, that guide cannot be a national or regional code of conduct, crudely transplanted to apply to transnational lawyers arbitrating in that country or applied to its own national lawyers practising in another host State. Equally, it cannot be a guide designed to govern a lawyer's relations with a State court. International arbitration is different from state and national practice: it is *sui generis,* and, in its different forms, it is a much more varied and flexible procedure which requires its own guide. Nonetheless, despite its practitioners' legal and cultural differences, the practice of international arbitration is increasingly subject to harmonization. It is becoming supra-national and the solution could also be supra-national. We saw this with the 1986 IBA Code of Ethics for International Arbitrators,[33] and we see it with the 1999 IBA Rules of Evidence. Like these IBA Rules, what is needed is a voluntary solution – a guide rather than a model law or disciplinary code – and the best way to start is with micro-solutions, rather than a grand project where the usual difficulties could hinder progress for a long time, even then leading perhaps only to moralistic and impractical solutions.[34] If the first step is the hardest, however long the eventual journey, let us make it small and easy.

For witness statements under the 1999 IBA Rules, taking the suggestion proposed in the *Aquarius* case, let there be appended to the witness statement a written declaration by the parties' legal representative who procured the statement giving

---

[33] *See* Branson, 'Ethics for International Arbitrators' in (1987) 3 *Arbitration International* 72.

[34] The English Bar developed for centuries without any formal code of conduct until very recently, although a useful code was expressed informally by the Lord Chancellor in *Iolanthe* (see appendix), which speaks for itself.

his or her name and professional qualification, and giving information about how, when and where the statement was prepared, including a statement of time spent by witness and representative respectively. For expert reports under the 1999 IBA Rules, taking the success of the Woolf reforms, let there be a similar declaration by the party's legal representative, together with a statement by the expert witness acknowledging his or her independent duty along the lines of the Woolf requirements, listed above. For document production, international arbitrators should more readily complain at a party's delinquent conduct, to the extent of drawing expressly an adverse inference on the merits from procedural delinquency or making a special order on costs.

These are modest suggestions; and others will wish to add their own suggestions derived from their own experience. Once collated by the IBA or another international organization, they could make a difference in improving best practice. Bad practices, like bad money, do tend to drive out good. If bad practices in the taking of written witness statements or commissioning independent expert reports come to be seen as normal by users and by international arbitrators, their probative value will be diminished still further; and their use will have to be reconsidered. As for deficient documentary production, cynicism will breed contempt for the arbitral process. None of this is a cry of despair. On the contrary, it is a measure of the ever-increasing success of international arbitration that it must meet new challenges and provide new practical solutions on a larger scale. If, as has been said, international arbitration is the only show in town for international trade, let it at least not be a tennis game played with half the court always missing or a rugby match played by lawyers, like Sisyphus, eternally uphill.

Appendix: *An Old Ethical Code (to be adapted)*

Gilbert and Sullivan's 'Iolanthe' was first performed at the Savoy Theatre on 25 November 1882 and the libretto contains in Act One a possible starting point in the distant future for an ethical code for international arbitration practitioners, substituting international arbitration for the English Bar, etc. It is the song of the Lord Chancellor of England and Wales, who (as he sang in Arcadia) always kept his duty strictly before his eyes, and it was to that fact (he sang) that he owed advancement to his distinguished position:

> When I went to the Bar as a very young man,
> (Said I to myself, said I),
> I'll work on a new and original plan,
> (Said I to myself, said I),
> I'll never assume that a rogue or a thief
> Is a gentleman worthy of implicit belief,
> Because his attorney has sent me a brief,
> (Said I to myself, said I).
>
> Ere I go into court I will read my brief through
> (Said I to myself, said I),

And I'll never take work I'm unable to do
(Said I to myself, said I),
My learned profession I'll never disgrace
By taking a fee with a grin on my face,
When I haven't been there to attend to the case
(Said I to myself, said I).

I'll never throw dust in a juryman's eyes
(Said I to myself, said I),
Or hoodwink a judge who is not over-wise
(Said I to myself, said I),
Or assume that the witnesses summoned in force
In Exchequer, Queen's Bench, Common Pleas, or Divorce,
Have perjured themselves as a matter of course
(Said I to myself, said I).

In other professions in which men engage
(Said I to myself, said I),
The Army, the Navy, the Church, and the Stage
(Said I to myself, said I),
Professional licence, if carried too far,
Your chance of promotion will certainly mar–
And I fancy the rule might apply to the Bar
(Said I to myself, said I!).

12

The Natural Limits to the Truncated Tribunal

The German Case of the Soviet Eggs and the Dutch Abduction of the Indonesian Arbitrator

A. Introduction

It is surprising to see the European origins of modern transnational arbitration in the most unexpected texts: the Provisional Treaty made in Berlin on 6 May 1921 between Germany and Soviet Russia.[1] Although Germany had been amongst the first nations to recognise the Soviet Republic, *de jure*, under the Brest-Litovsk Treaty of March 1918, both countries had subsequently renounced that treaty and its related agreements, Soviet Russia voluntarily in November 1918 after the Armistice and Germany under compulsion from the Versailles Conference and later Versailles Treaty. Diplomatic relations between Germany and Soviet Russia were not repaired until the subsequent Rapallo Treaty of April 1922, which led eventually to the Treaty made in Moscow on 12 October 1925 between Germany and the USSR with a special chapter concerning commercial arbitration, extensively regulating the form and substance of an arbitration clause, the organisation of the arbitration tribunal and the execution of arbitral awards.[2]

---

[1] Provisional Treaty of 6 May 1921 between the German Reich and the RSFSR on the Extension of the Sphere of Activity of their Mutual Delegations Engaged in Assistance to Prisoners of War, (1921) LNTS 277. See Dr *H. Freund,* Les rapports des traités russo-allemands et l'application du droit soviétique en Allemagne, 1925 Clunet – *JDI,* 331; and Dr. *Leo Zaitseff,* The Legal position of Foreigners in Soviet Russia, (1925–26) Michigan Law Review 441, 448. (Both authors were German lawyers in Berlin).

[2] Treaty of 12 October 1925 between Germany and the USSR comprising (inter alia) an Agreement Concerning Courts of Arbitration, (1925) LNTS No 1257, 135; (1926) I Int. Jahrbuch für Schiedsgerichtswesen 216ff (ed. *Nussbaum*). See *H.J. Hilton,* Commercial Arbitration in the Treaties and Agreements of the USSR, (1945) US Dept of State Bulletin No 307, 891, reprinted in *G. Ginsburgs,* The Soviet Union and International Cooperation in Legal Matters (1988, Dordrecht), pp.3–18. The subsequent Nazi-Soviet 1935 and 1939 treaties supplementing these provisions on arbitration belong to a different legal tradition and lie outside the scope of this paper. See generally *E.H. Carr,* German-Soviet Relations between the Two World Wars 1919–1939 (London; 1952); pp. 49 ff and 85 ff.

On Arbitration. Edited by: Sam Wordsworth KC and Marie Veeder, Oxford University Press. © Oxford University Press 2023.
DOI: 10.1093/oso/9780192869135.003.0012

(1) The 1921 Treaty

The 1921 Provisional Treaty contained one of the first provisions for consensual arbitration in transnational commerce between European countries. It provided a scheme of arbitration designed to work both in Germany (where the Soviet Trade Representation in Berlin was to be active) and in Soviet Russia where German traders had remained active despite the introduction of the Soviet state monopoly of foreign trade. For Soviet Russia, it was the first such treaty on arbitration; and inevitably its concept and terms were strongly influenced by German legal scholars and arbitration practice. The text of this 1921 Treaty effectively obliged the Soviet Government to insert arbitration clauses in all foreign trade transactions made with German interests in Soviet Russia; and as regards transactions made in Germany, its organs faced a choice between consensual arbitration and the jurisdiction of the German courts applying German law to any dispute.[3]

(2) The 1925 Treaty

The 1925 German-Soviet Treaty contained in Chapter VI an Agreement Concerning Commercial Courts of Arbitration. It developed the same concept as the 1921 Treaty as supplemented by the 1922 Rapallo Treaties, with an elaborate and detailed code. Although by then clearly influenced by the 1923 Geneva Protocol on Arbitration Clauses, this text represents a much more sophisticated attempt to regulate the form of the arbitration clause (effective for both present and future disputes), the legal seat of the arbitration, the method of selecting the arbitration tribunal, the form and enforcement of the award, including state guarantees as to conditions for such enforcement. It was introduced at the apogee of the Soviet Government's New Economic Policy, including its policies on foreign concessions; and it was indeed a model convention on transnational commercial arbitration, long before the 1936 draft UNIDROIT Uniform Law on Arbitration and the 1985 UNCITRAL Model Law.

---

[3] Article 13 provided, in the English language version of the League of Nations text:

"The Russian Government undertakes to insert an arbitration clause in all legal transactions with German nationals, German firms and German corporate bodies in the territory of the RSFSR and of the States connected with it by an import and export regime established by [the Russian] Government. In respect of legal transactions concluded in Germany and their economic consequences, the Russian Government shall be subject to German law. In respect of obligations under private law it shall be subject to German jurisdiction and legal penalties, but only in so far as the obligations arise out of legal business entered into with German nationals, German firms and German corporate bodies, after the conclusion of this Agreement. The right of the Russian Government to insert arbitration clauses in legal transactions entered into in Germany remains unaffected. Moreover, property of the Russian Government in Germany shall enjoy, in Germany, protection in accordance with international law . . ."

228 ON ARBITRATION

(3) Truncated Tribunal

The 1925 Treaty also contained, in Article 4, a special provision to replace a recalcitrant arbitrator who refused to fulfil his duties as arbitrator. It was modelled on the equivalent provision in the German Civil Procedural Code, but with an important difference expressly required by the Soviet Government, as indicated below. It provided (with paragraph numbers added for ease of reference):

> "A[1] Should an arbitrator, who has not been designated in the arbitration agreement, die or be unable to act in this capacity for any other reason, or should he refuse to accept or fulfill the duties of the office of arbitrator,[4] the party who has appointed him, or on whose behalf he has been appointed in virtue of Article 3 (I), second paragraph, must at the request of the opposing party, within two weeks after the receipt of this request, appoint another arbitrator in the manner laid down in Article 3 (I), first paragraph. [2] If on the expiration of this period the arbitrator has not been appointed, he shall be designated in conformity with Article 3 (I), second paragraph. [3] Should an umpire who has not been designated in the arbitration agreement, die or be unable to act in this capacity for any other reason or should he refuse to accept or fulfill the duties of the office of arbitrator, the arbitrators must immediately by common agreement choose another umpire. [4] Should the arbitrators be unable to agree on this point, the procedure laid down in Article 3(2) shall apply by analogy. [5] The provisions of the present Article shall only apply in the absence of other agreement."

In the first and third numbered paragraphs, the Soviet Government insisted that the ground for removing and replacing a recalcitrant arbitrator or umpire should be limited to cases where he *refused* to fulfil his duties, as distinct from merely *failing* to act.[5] Notwithstanding this limitation and although the phrase *truncated tribunal* was not here used, the core concept of the truncated tribunal is readily recognisable in Article 4; and it is the historical precursor to the equivalent provisions in the 1976 UNCITRAL Arbitration Rules and 1985 UNCITRAL Model Law. (The procedure under Article 3 of the 1925 Treaty involved the state courts of Germany and the USSR, depending upon the place of arbitration).

---

[4] In the German text of the 1925 Treaty, this critical phrase is: *"[wenn ein Schiedsrichter] die Ausführung des Schiedsrichteramtes verweigert."*

[5] As the German Government's official commentary on Article 4 explained (in English translation):

> "These Articles [Articles 4–6] mainly follow the provisions of the German Civil Procedural Code, Articles 1031 to 1033. Nevertheless it was agreed that undue delay in fulfilling his duties by the arbitrator shall not be a special reason for replacing an arbitrator; this provision was not included in the Treaty at the wish of the Russian Government. But it may be possible to equate undue delay in fulfilling his duties with a refusal to fulfill the duties of an arbitrator [i.e. pursuant to Article 4[5] whereby the parties can agree otherwise: see above]," see (1926) I Int. Jahrbuch für Schiedsgerichtswesen 221.

B. The German Case of the Soviet Eggs

It has long been said that there was little or no juridical activity in Soviet-German trade regarding these successive arbitration provisions from 1921 to 1933. For all practical purposes, Professor *Nussbaum* dismissed these legal texts as having *little interest from the view point of general legal theory*; and even with his enormous specialist knowledge and arbitration experience in Berlin, he found only one case concerning the fees fixed by a German court for appointing an arbitrator. *Nussbaum*'s view was later challenged by Dr. *Rashba,* who contended that the huge arbitral activity in Soviet-German commerce, extending by the early 1930s to billions of marks and in fact constituting almost half of the USSR's imports, could not be gauged by reference to court decisions: *The dearth of German judicial data pertaining to Soviet-German arbitration may mean, of course, and in fact does mean, simply that the parties to arbitration proceedings found little or no occasion to have recourse to the courts.*[6] The debate remains open. As time passes, it is possible that Soviet archives will release details of arbitral activity which plainly remained confidential to the parties at the time – albeit that the Soviet party would ordinarily have been required to archive its papers in the Soviet Government's central archives under the Soviet system of foreign trade. It might have been thought that German court cases would be known by now; but quite by chance, the USA's National Archives contain the full record of a German Court decision made on 23 February 1928, as transmitted by the US Embassy in Berlin to the US State Department in Washington DC.[7] It concerned a protracted dispute over Soviet eggs – and a truncated tribunal.

On 3 September 1925, a German company, *Internationale Warenaustausch AG* (*IWA*) concluded an agreement with Soviet authorities to market as sole European distributor Soviet eggs exported from Soviet Russia. The agreement contained an arbitration clause providing for arbitration in Moscow; and it was to run for at least three years, ranging from 1,500 to 2,500 railway wagons each year amounting in all to over 70 million Soviet eggs. Disputes emerged over Soviet compliance with the exclusive nature of the distributorship because the Soviet authorities were allegedly supplying Soviet eggs to third parties in Western Europe (probably *Arcos* in London for resale to distributors in England). These disputes became aggravated; and the USSR Supreme Economic Council then issued an order prohibiting the Soviet supplier *Chlebprodukt* from further exporting Soviet eggs to *IWA* (this

---

[6] *Nussbaum,* Treaties on Commercial Arbitration – A Test of International Private Law Legislation, (1942) 56 Harv. L. Rev. 219,220; *Rashba,* Settlement of Disputes in Commercial Dealings With The Soviet Union, 45 Col. L. Rev. 530, 546 (1945). Dr. *Rashba* was also a German lawyer in Berlin (until 1933), having earlier emigrated from Soviet Russia.

[7] US National Archives, 861.602/224 (US State Dept Decimal File, Report No 373 of 14 July 1930 from the Berlin Embassy). See also *A. C. Sutton,* Western Technology and Soviet Economic Development 1930 to 1945 (1971; Stanford), p. 21.

230   ON ARBITRATION

supplier's name in Russian suggests that it ought to have concentrating on *bread* to the exclusion of eggs; but it may be that this order was part of a convenient defence based upon force majeure). In any event, *IWA* was accused of breaking its contractual obligations; and *Chlebprodukt* referred this dispute to Moscow arbitration under the parties' arbitration clause.[8]

The Soviet supplier appointed a Soviet arbitrator; IWA appointed a German arbitrator; and these arbitrators appointed a Soviet umpire, acting as third arbitrator and chairman, such proceedings falling squarely within the scope of the German-USSR 1925 Treaty. All three members of the tribunal had accepted their appointments; and there seems to have been no dispute over the constitution of the tribunal. So far, the story is wholly uninteresting save to historians in foreign eggs. However, what happened next is highly significant to the modern development of the truncated tribunal.

The Soviet chairman called a hearing of the arbitration in Moscow; but on receipt of this summons in Berlin, the German arbitrator (*Kogan*) already had a prior business engagement and communicated his unavailability to the chairman. The Soviet chairman had given him only four days notice of the hearing; but short notice was not *Kogan's* complaint. It is surprising how fast travelling could be before the arrival of the aeroplane. Even before the First World War, the well-known English businessman in Czarist Russia, *James "Yakov Vassileovich" Wishaw*, would frequently commute between St Petersburg and London in less than four days.[9] The Soviet chairman then called another hearing in Moscow; but again, on receipt of this summons in Berlin, *Kogan* had another prior business engagement and once more excused himself. In order to ensure that the next hearing date would be attended by three arbitrators, it appears that the Soviet party then applied to the President of the RSFSR Supreme Court[10] for an order (which the President

---

[8] The parties also concluded new agreements on 1 October 1926 whereby the Soviet supplier undertook to supply to *IWA* all unsold Soviet eggs still in transit or outside Soviet Russia, together with the balance of the original quota still to be shipped under the original 1925 agreement. Curiously, the parties agreed that disputes under these new 1926 agreements were to be referred to the German Courts, subject to German law – thereby giving rise to separate litigation in Germany. These new disputes were wide-ranging, including non-payment of the price, accounting, damaged eggs, missing eggs and fraud inducing the new agreements on the basis that the Soviet authorities had falsely stated the number of unsold Soviet eggs in England.

[9] *James Wishaw* who was born in Archangel in 1853 in a long line of Wishaw expatriates dating back to about 1770. He successfully avoided the restrictions imposed by Czarist rule on foreigners by becoming a naturalised Russian citizen. His cousin's grandson, *Sir Charles Wishaw*, also born in St. Petersburg and now celebrating his ninetieth birthday, was senior partner of Freshfields from 1965–1974: see *James Wishaw*, Memoirs of James Wishaw (London, 1935); and *Maxwell S. Leigh*, A History of the Wishaw Family (London, 1935). (Although strictly irrelevant historically, the chairman of the arbitration tribunal in the Indonesian Case, discussed below, is also a partner in Freshfields who became a naturalised French citizen – *plus ça change …*).

[10] In addition to acting as a court of first instance over civil and criminal cases of importance and as a court of cassation, the RSFSR Supreme Court then also exercised certain responsibilities in Arbitrazh: see *S. Kucherov*, The Organs of Soviet Administration of Justice: Their History and Operation (1970; Leiden), p.89.

THE NATURAL LIMITS TO THE TRUNCATED TRIBUNAL   231

granted) removing *Kogan* as arbitrator and replacing him with a substitute arbitrator, *Combarz* – who was a Soviet citizen.

The three Soviet arbitrators eventually made a unanimous award in Moscow on 29 April 1927 in favour of *Chlebprodukt*, with costs. *Chlebprodukt* then sought to enforce the award against *IWA* in the German Courts, but both the Landgericht and the Kammergericht in Berlin (sitting as a court of appeal) refused to enforce the award under the 1925 Treaty on the ground that the German arbitrator's removal by the RSFSR Supreme Court could not be justified under Article 4 of Chapter VI of the 1925 Treaty: that provision allowed his removal only in the event that he should "refuse to ... fulfill the duties of arbitrator;" and even then, he was to be replaced by a fresh nominee from the party originally appointing him; and it was only where such nomination had not been made within two weeks of the other party's request, that the other party could apply for an order from the President of the RSFSR Supreme Court.

The Kammergericht's reasoning is worth reciting, if only because the text of its judgment has lain dormant since 1930.[11] It appears that the judgment was never published in any law report or legal commentary. The Court (Judges *Kamps* and *Fabisch*) held:

> "... In this case, the Appellant [*Chlebprodukt*] considered that the arbitrator *Kogan* had refused to fulfil the duties of arbitrator; and it therefore applied for and obtained, as provided in Article 3(l)(b) [of the 1925 Treaty], the appointment of a different arbitrator by the President of the Supreme Court of the Soviet Republic responsible. However, there was no *refusal* and hence the condition precedent on which the President of the Supreme Court appointed a substitute arbitrator was not met. The Appellant itself and also the arbitration tribunal concluded that *Kogan* refused to fulfill his duties as arbitrator from the fact only that he did not attend the two hearings scheduled for 6th and 22nd November 1926. In actual fact, the arbitrator *Kogan* had excused his absence from both hearings on the ground that he was unavailable because of business engagements. It cannot be inferred therefrom that he wanted to discontinue his further contribution as an arbitrator.
>
> Be that as it may, undue default in fulfilling obligations accepted might also be regarded, where appropriate, as a refusal to carry out the office of arbitrator; but it must be borne in mind that according to the German Government's Memorandum (printed in the Reichstag Gazette 1924/25 No. 1551 pp.57 et seq., in particular p. 55) which was issued with the Treaty, the provision for *undue default* was not included in the Treaty as a special ground for appointing a substitute arbitrator at the Russian Government's express request. As a result of this, only in

---

[11] [22.W. 9132.27/13 dated 28.02.1928] US National Archives 861.602/224, ibid (enclosures to Report No 373 dated 14 July 1930 from the US Embassy in Berlin to the Secretary of State). The original text is of course in German; and the English translation was prepared for this contribution.

232   ON ARBITRATION

very exceptional circumstances can such a default be regarded as a refusal to carry out the office of arbitrator and also only when the matter is entirely free of doubt. This is entirely absent in the instant case. The arbitrator *Kogan* did not, until 2ⁿᵈ November, receive his summons to the hearing on 6ᵗʰ November 1926. It may be that there was a way of travelling to Moscow within this period, but an obligation to set out on such a journey in such a short time, disregarding all other engagements, simply to discharge the office of arbitrator, can in no way be accepted.

Be that as it may, the arbitrator *Kogan* was summonsed in time for the hearing on 22ⁿᵈ November, as he had received that summons back on 8ᵗʰ November 1925. However, the arbitrator had already pointed out previously that (because of negotiations which were to be conducted with a member of the Appellant's Board of Directors in Berlin)[12] his presence in Berlin would be necessary until the end of these negotiations. He had also already claimed that the due performance of his office as arbitrator required him, without fail, to conduct a serious study of the statement of case and other pleadings. These grounds of excuse are wholly adequate; and it was not right for the Appellant unilaterally to seek the appointment of a substitute arbitrator on the ground of the arbitrator *Kogan*'s refusal to carry out his duties as arbitrator because it did not consider the attendance of the arbitrator *Kogan* and a study of the case to be necessary. Not only is there no refusal, but there is not even undue default in the arbitrator *Kogan*'s conduct. It should be added that the quite unilateral way the umpire – without first getting in touch with the other arbitrators, and the arbitrator *Kogan* in particular – set down hearings irrespective of the latter's interests, was likely from the outset to prevent the arbitrator *Kogan*'s attendance at the hearings. Although an umpire of an arbitration tribunal is authorised alone to set down hearings, if he does not want to obtain the arbitrators' agreement, he must then have at least as much regard to the arbitrators' other interests as to ask them whether and what time would suit them and, where appropriate, to have regard to objections to the timing. This is what the umpire failed to do. Neither can the absence of the arbitrator at hearings which are set down in disregard of the latter be looked upon as default or even refusal ..."

Although perhaps the exact line is difficult to draw in legal theory, there is an important practical difference between an arbitrator's refusal to act and a mere failure to act, as illustrated by this case.[13] Accordingly, the Moscow award was not

---

[12] This passing judicial reference, without comment, to an arbitrator being somehow involved in the parties' settlement negotiations may indicate one or more contemporary factors in commercial arbitration: (i) the involvement of arbitrators as conciliators and (ii) possibly, the existence of a close and continuous link between a party and its party-appointed arbitrator.

[13] Although certain Soviet arbitration clauses in concession agreements provided for the continuation of the arbitration notwithstanding one arbitrator's *failure* to attend a hearing, that procedure could only be invoked in the absence of *insuperable obstacles* and after the umpire's fixing of a date on reasonable notice which allowed sufficient time for the arbitrators to arrive at that hearing: see the *Lena*

THE NATURAL LIMITS TO THE TRUNCATED TRIBUNAL   233

enforced or recognised in Germany; but it brought eventually no comfort to *IWA*. It survived the other litigation brought by *Chlebprodukt*; the German Courts also upheld its claim that the Soviet party was the contract-breaker; but *IWA* never recovered compensation for its severe losses. By April 1930, the *Berliner Tagesblatt* was citing its case as demonstrating "the apparent determination with which the Soviet authorities sacrifice incontestable contractual obligations towards foreign firms to other interests without being over-scrupulous in their choice of methods; their conduct in this case invites the assumption that to them the keeping of contractual obligations is merely a question of opportunism".[14] In July 1930, the US Embassy reported to the US State Department its counsellor's conversation with *IWA*'s legal adviser (Dr. *Evsey Rabinovitsch*): *IWA* had become insolvent; and its claims were now being handled in the diplomatic negotiations between Germany and the USSR in Moscow – to what eventual end the archives do not yet disclose.[15]

C. The Dutch Abduction of the Indonesian Arbitrator[16]

In 1994, *Himpurna California Energy Limited* and *Patuha Power Limited*, two Bermudian companies owned by US investors, made a number of agreements for the development and operation of electricity generating facilities in Java, in the Republic of Indonesia. One such agreement was a Power Purchase Agreement with a state-owned electrical utility, *Preusahaan Listrik Negara* (*PLN*) and another with Pertamina. These Power Purchase Agreements contained arbitration clauses providing for the resolution of disputes under the UNCITRAL Arbitration Rules.

In August 1998, the Bermudian companies began arbitrations against *PLN* and the Republic of Indonesia claiming over US $3.7 billion; and on 4 May 1999, the arbitration tribunal published awards ordering *PLN* to pay US $572 million. The awards had been made by three distinguished arbitrators: an Australian from Melbourne, an Indonesian and a French chairman.[17] PLN did not pay these awards;

Goldfields Arbitration Clause of 30 April 1925 [1998] 47 ICLQ 747, 790 and the *Harriman* Arbitration Clause of 12 June 1925 (2000) *Arb Int* 115, 137 (These preceded the 1925 German-Soviet Treaty).

[14] The *Berliner Tageblatt* of 8 April 1930.

[15] US National Archives 861.602/224 (Letter dated 14 July 1930 from *Frederic M. Sackett* to the US State Department).

[16] For the full account, as published, see the anonymous editorial, "Un Extraordinaire Cas Pathologique" in (1999) ASA Bulletin, 511; the Decision of The Hague District Court of 21 September 1999, ibid, 583; and the awards and notes cited below in Mealey's. In the last of these notes, the law firm acting for Indonesia provided its own account of the events in the Netherlands: as regards disputed matters, it does not square with these other published materials.

[17] These awards of 4 May 1999 are published in (1999) 14:12 Mealey's International Arbitration Report A-l and B-l (see also p.3). The arbitrators were Messrs. *Jan Paulsson, Setiawan S.H.* and *A. A. de Fina* who dissented on quantum. (The majority founded their decision on quantum on, *inter alia*, the arbitration award made in *The Lena Goldfields* Case of 1930, which was one of the earliest awards in Soviet foreign trade: see paras 537 and 444 respectively).

234   ON ARBITRATION

and the Indonesian Courts declined to enforce them in Indonesia. Although far short of the sums originally claimed by the Bermudian companies, this amount was nonetheless a massive sum for an economy in financial and political ruins. In June 1999, the Bermudian companies proceeded with their other claims against the Republic of Indonesia which had been stayed pending the determination of their claims against *PLN*.[18] Again, this story is so far unexceptional; but what eventually happened marks one of the darkest hours in the recent practice of international commercial arbitration.

First, the chairman of the arbitration tribunal was personally attacked for his alleged malign influence and bias. The Republic of Indonesia complained of his attempt "to further a personal crusade to establish the supremacy and independence of international tribunals of arbitration, a crusade on which he has for some years embarked [by seeking] to establish his personal views and principles as correct and his personal power as superior to any court of law." Sticks and stones may hurt arbitral bones but names will never hurt them; nor did they in this case. The personal abuse of an arbitrator may be relatively new; but it is not unique. It is a curious form of advocacy performed by professional lawyers; it is done to provoke the arbitrator into some ill-tempered indiscretion; and occasionally it works.[19] However, an arbitrator's authority is best exercised with the award: he does not need to answer in kind, still less join his assailants in the gutter. Plan A failed.

Second, on 22 July 1999, *Pertamina* obtained injunctions from the Central District Court of Jakarta enjoining the Bermudian claimants from enforcing the existing awards, enjoining the further prosecution of the arbitrations against the Republic of Indonesia and imposing a penalty of US $1 million a day on any party and (it seems) arbitrator from continuing further with the arbitrations in breach of the injunction. *Pertamina* was not a party to the arbitrations; and the Republic of Indonesia maintained that it was not responsible for Pertamina's conduct, an argument later dismissed by the two arbitrators as "incredible." *Pertamina* is, of course, wholly owned by the Republic of Indonesia which appoints its commissioners and managing directors; and significantly the Republic of Indonesia did not oppose or appeal the injunctions. Again, these forms of anti-arbitration injunctions are nothing new. They have long bedevilled international commercial arbitration in the British Commonwealth, being a procedure invented by English lawyers; and yet there are ways to circumvent these tactics. This was also the case here. The tribunal removed the place of the next hearing from Jakarta to the Peace Palace at The Hague, as it was entitled to do under the UNCITRAL Arbitration Rules and its Terms of Appointment. So Plan B failed.

---

[18] The chairman was Mr. *Paulsson*; the other arbitrators were Mr. *de Fina* from Australia and Professor *Priyatana* from Indonesia.

[19] For an extreme case in the USA, where one party set private detectives to follow and photograph an arbitrator during and after the arbitration, see "Suite Sharing: Arbitrator's Friendship With Winning Lawyer Imperils Huge Victory – Private Investigators Found the Pair in Chicago Hotel after $92 Million Award," The Wall Street Journal of 14 February 1990.

THE NATURAL LIMITS TO THE TRUNCATED TRIBUNAL   235

Third, after the tribunal fixed a hearing in the Peace Palace in the Hague for 22 September 1999, the Republic of Indonesia applied to the District Court of the Hague for an injunction to prevent the arbitrators from approaching within 200 metres of the Peace Palace (being itself UN territory). The President of the District Court declined to make such an order by a judgment delivered on 21 September 1999, the day before the arbitral hearing was due to begin. This ambitious application was of course an attempt to prevent the hearing taking place at all; but in fact, the judgment confirmed the propriety of the tribunal's conduct, in particular confirming its jurisdiction to examine its own disputed jurisdiction.[20] So Plan C failed.

This is where the mischievous final plan came into effect. The Indonesian arbitrator had flown from Washington DC to Amsterdam to meet his colleagues at the Carlton Ambassador Hotel at the Hague, close to the Peace Palace. He was intercepted by representatives of the Indonesian Government at Dulles Airport who accompanied him to Amsterdam. He was there taken to a hotel booked by the Indonesian embassy where he was prevented from communicating with his arbitral colleagues. After the Indonesian Republic's failure to obtain the injunction from the Hague District Court, the Indonesian arbitrator was conducted by officers of the embassy to Amsterdam airport where, in the words of the arbitral tribunal's chairman, *"he left for Jakarta... in circumstances that make me fear that an outrage has been perpetrated upon the personal integrity of Professor Pryatana."* There were three eyewitnesses at the airport, the Australian arbitrator, the tribunal's Dutch attorney and his chauffeur. Their three accounts were later set out in the tribunal's interim awards, and each describes a frightening atmosphere where the Indonesian arbitrator was visibly upset and at times in tears. Unequivocally, these eyewitnesses describe the unlawful abduction of an arbitrator by a party, conduct without precedent in modern international arbitration.

Nonetheless, the remaining two arbitrators were able still to hold the scheduled hearing at the Peace Palace and to make interim awards where the full facts are extensively set out;[21] and eventually this truncated tribunal made final awards on the merits. Justice was done. And on the basis of these several awards, it appears that the Bermudian companies have been substantially indemnified by their political risk insurers. No doubt, there remain awkward political consequences for the several states involved (Indonesia, the USA, the Netherlands and the United Kingdom

---

[20] Decision of The Hague District Court of 21 September 1999, (1999) ASA Bulletin, 583 (English translation). Curiously, the Dutch advocate appearing for the Republic of Indonesia has been criticised for making this application. However, it was an ingenious application; it was certainly worth the attempt; and of course it was openly lawful.
[21] These interim awards of 26 September 1999 are published in (2000) 15:1 Mealey's International Arbitration Report A-1 and B-1 (see also p. 3). The final awards of 16 October 1999 are published in (2000) 15:2 Mealey's International Arbitration Report A-1 and B-1 (see also p.3 for the Indonesian Republic's rebuttal). These awards were all made by Messrs. *Paulsson* and *A.A. de Fina*.

236 ON ARBITRATION

responsible for Bermuda's foreign affairs); but most significant of all for present purposes, the international arbitration process did not fail; and the truncated tribunal was not found wanting.

D. Conclusions

What is the solution to the kind outrage illustrated by the Indonesian Case? The problem is how and where to strike the balance. It is of course possible to over-react to the problems of the truncated tribunal. The number of abducted arbitrators as a percentage of all arbitrations is likely to remain very small; and indeed truncated tribunals also remain "exceptional," as Professor *Pieter Sanders* concluded in his recent work distilling sixty years of extensive arbitration practice.[22] Moreover, arbitration laws cannot take the place of the criminal law; arbitrators are not soldiers or policemen; and unlike the FBI and other governmental agencies, an arbitration tribunal should not be required to administer an arbitrator-protection programme. Arbitrators are only private persons; and an arbitration agreement remains essentially a private law contract. It would also serve little purpose to make a statutory rule or international convention resolving an exceptional problem, however serious, if it damaged the whole process of international arbitration. When the problem of the truncated tribunal (short of kidnapping) was discussed during the recent revisions to the ICC and LCIA Rules, there were specific provisions added to allow deliberations to be completed where an arbitrator deliberately withdrew without good cause from the work of the tribunal. But these new arbitration rules are very limited in effect: each recognises the distinction between an arbitrator's deliberate refusal to act and a mere failure to act; and neither allows the majority of the tribunal to gang up on the minority, particularly during the process preceding the tribunal's deliberations.[23]

In contrast Article 11 of the AAA International Arbitration Rules and Article 7 of the 1999 Scottish Arbitration Code both contain a much broader rule. These provide that if an arbitrator in a three person tribunal, although duly notified, fails without good cause to participate in the work of the tribunal, the two other arbitrators shall have the power in their sole discretion to continue the arbitration and to make any award, order or other decision despite the failure of the third arbitrator to participate. This makes the majority sole judge as to what constitutes the third

---

[22] *Pieter Sanders*, Quo Vadis Arbitration? (1999; The Hague), p.22.

[23] The new Article 12(5) of the 1998 ICC Rules allows the ICC Court, not the ICC tribunal, to decide after the closing of the proceedings not to replace an arbitrator and to require the remaining arbitrators to continue as a truncated tribunal. The new Article 12 of the 1998 LCIA Rules confers powers on the majority of the tribunal to continue the proceedings only if the recalcitrant arbitrator "refuses or persistently fails to participate in its deliberations," subject to the majority recording its reasoned decision in any award, order or other decision. See the interesting discussion in *Derains & Schwartz*, A Guide to the New ICC Rules of Arbitration (1998; The Hague), pp. 193–196.

arbitrator's wrongful failure to participate in their work even before the hearing starts, let alone during the tribunal's eventual deliberations. And it assumes that every recalcitrant arbitrator is here acting at the behest on one party; but as is well-known (indeed illustrated by the Indonesian Case), this is not always so. To allow the majority then to proceed is unfairly to unbalance the tribunal at the expense of an innocent party, at the instigation of the majority. This is an example of the remedy being worse than the wrong.

In the Indonesian Case, it is a fact that the unprecedented misconduct of one party, with all the powers available to a state, did not succeed in thwarting the arbitral process; and the professionalism and good sense of that truncated tribunal triumphed. In the worst of all possible worlds, it does not therefore seem necessary to amend national laws or international conventions to grant wider powers to arbitrators. Accordingly, it is suggested that UNCITRAL was right at its recent session in March 2000 not to pursue an invitation to revisit this topic with a proposed model legislative solution to be drafted in broad terms.[24] This approach also reflects the conclusions which had been reached by Judge *Schwebel* in his great work on the authority of truncated tribunals in international arbitration.[25] There is a great danger that a new international convention or national legislation, overreacting to the pathology of scandalous arbitrations, would injure the collegiality of the arbitration tribunal in general, conferring wide powers on the majority of the tribunal or its chairman which in practice would be susceptible to easy abuse. It would certainly encourage bad practices during deliberations where (even now) chairmen can occasionally act as sole arbitrators without any or any sufficient regard for their arbitral colleagues. As Lord *Steyn* held under English law in regard to an ICC arbitration: "*... the governing principle is that, after the end of the hearing, parties are entitled to an impartial and fair consideration and resolution by the arbitrators, acting together, of all the issues in the case.*"[26] Worse, it could spread these bad practices throughout the entire arbitral procedure from the outset of the arbitration where collegiality probably remains even more essential. None of this proposed reform is good or necessary. That is the historical lesson from the German Case of the Soviet Eggs; and as for the Dutch Abduction of the Indonesian Arbitrator, albeit at great personal cost to that individual, this case proves only that international arbitration works.

---

[24] UNCITRAL Note of 6 April 1999 on Possible Future Work in the Area of International Commercial Arbitration, pp.21–24.

[25] *Stephen M. Schwebel*, International Arbitration: Three Salient Problems (1987, Cambridge), p.296.

[26] *Bank Mellat v GAA Development* [1988] 2 Lloyd's Rep 44, 50 (Steyn J).

13

Issue Estoppel, Reasons for Awards and Transnational Arbitration

A. Introduction

Article 28(6) of the ICC Rules of Arbitration provides that every award 'shall be binding on the parties' and Article 25(2) that an award 'shall state the reasons upon which it [the award] is based'. The latter rule was introduced in the 1998 version of the rules, but it left unsaid whether and (if so) to what extent each individual reason forming part of an award was legally binding on the disputant parties, as distinct from the operative part – or *dispositif* – of the award itself. At first, the distinction may seem irrelevant. The primary purpose of reasons in an award is to ensure that the arbitral tribunal has given rational and adequate consideration to the parties' submissions on the particular dispute. The statement of such reasons will often facilitate the losing party's understanding of why it has lost and that understanding may help ensure its voluntary compliance with the award. Here, the legal status of the reasons plays no separate part from the binding nature of the award's operative part. However, the secondary purpose of an award is to decide the parties[1] dispute for all time, both as to the whole and as to its constituent parts. Just as it would be absurd for parties to re-litigate the same dispute time and again, like Sisyphus or the hero in 'Ground-Hog Day', would it not be equally absurd for parties to relitigate issues in a different arbitration where those same issues have already been decided in the reasons for an earlier award between the same parties? To my knowledge, no international arbitration rules expressly address this question.[2] Where an award is rooted in the legal system of the arbitral seat or the place where the award is made or enforced, it follows that the answer will be influenced by national legal rules, more often derived from the legal status accorded to the reasons for the decisions of state courts. For international commercial arbitration, the question has become

---

[1] Invitation for comments deleted. Please also note that it may be helpful to read this piece alongside the later Award in *Apotex Holdings Inc. and Apotex Inc. v. United States of America*, ICSID, Award of 25 August 2014, as to which Johnny Veeder was the presiding arbitrator. Extracts from that Award are contained in Appendix I.

[2] See Article 32(3) of the UNCITRAL Arbitration Rules, Article 26(1) and Article 26(9) of the LCIA Arbitration Rules, and Article 31(2) of the UNCITRAL Model Law on International Commercial Arbitration.

On Arbitration. Edited by: Sam Wordsworth KC and Marie Veeder, Oxford University Press. © Oxford University Press 2023. DOI: 10.1093/oso/9780192869135.003.0013

important where parties face successive but different disputes raising similar issues of law and fact in different arbitrations, as evidenced by the recent decisions of the English Privy Council in *Aegis* v. *European Re* (on appeal from Bermuda) and the Swedish Svea Court of Appeal in *The Czech Republic* v. *CME*.[3]

Let us first take a look at history, which shows that the matter is by no means new. In England it arose as long ago as 1836 in a case involving a dead horse, *Sybray* v. *White*.[4] The plaintiff's mare had fallen through the cover of an old mineshaft, but the defendant miner denied the mine was in his possession. The parties agreed to refer the dispute over the mine's ownership to a local mining tribunal – a 'barmote court' composed of a barmaster and five miners – on the defendant's separate promise to pay for the loss of the mare if the tribunal determined that the mineshaft was his. The tribunal decided, by a written decision with reasons, that the mineshaft belonged to the defendant.

The defendant refused to recognise this adverse decision and refused to pay for the lost horse. In subsequent legal proceedings brought by the plaintiff horse owner before the assize judge in Derby, the defendant sought to re-argue the issue of his possession of the mineshaft. On appeal, the court in London treated the tribunal's decision as equivalent to an arbitration award (albeit that it did not purport to be an award and therefore required no stamp duty under the Stamp Acts) and decided that the trial judge was therefore right in allowing the decision to be admitted in evidence before the Derby jury. It however added that the judge 'did not treat the verdict as conclusive, which would have been wrong, but left the question as to the possession of the shaft to the jury, on the whole of the evidence'. The plaintiff therefore won his claim for damages in the sum of 15 pounds, much to the regret of the court because it plainly did not agree that the defendant was in fact in possession of the mine-shaft.

Over the next 150 years, the conclusiveness of English court judgments and arbitration awards was much developed into a highly technical set of legal rules, of which issue estoppel is part. The laws in many countries of the British Commonwealth have been influenced by these developments. Some other legal systems do not recognise the concept of issue estoppel at all, neither for court judgments nor for domestic arbitration awards. This is the case in France and Switzerland, for instance. In certain countries the concept is recognised for court judgments while its application to arbitration awards remains unclear. The Russian Federation is a case in point.[5] In the USA, the concept of issue (collateral) estoppel

---

[3] *AEGIS* v. *European Re*, [2003] 1 W.L.R. 1041; *The Czech Republic* v. *CME*, 15 May 2003, (2003) 18:6 *Mealey's International Arbitration Report* A-1, also available at www.cetv-net.com Indeed, similar points have since arisen in *The Mox Plant Case* (between Ireland and the United Kingdom) in the Permanent Court of Arbitration and the ICSID case *SGS* v. *Pakistan*; see respectively the PCA web site at www.pca-cpa.org for Ireland's oral submissions of 13 June 2003 (p. 8 of the transcript) and the ICSID award of 6 August 2003 at pp. 15, 19, 42, 65.

[4] (1836) 1 M. & W. 435; 150 E.R. 504.

[5] Article 209(2) of the 2002 Russian Federation's code of civil procedure (which came into effect on 1 February 2003) provides expressly that the court's decision prevents the parties and other persons participating in the case (as well as their assignees) from filing a civil claim with the same cause of action

240   ON ARBITRATION

is perhaps at its broadest. However, whatever the breadth of any individual national rule, the problem remains for international commercial arbitration. In litigation or arbitration conducted in one country (where the concept of issue estoppel is recognised), the existence of an issue estoppel arising from an award made in another country may depend on whether the latter's legal system also recognises that same issue estoppel. That is the position in English law.

B.   Features of Issue Estoppel

In English law, issue estoppel is different from *res judicata* and cause of action estoppel. The term *res judicata* now refers to the general doctrine that an earlier and final adjudication by a court or arbitral tribunal is conclusive in subsequent proceedings involving the same subject matter, the same legal bases and the same parties or their 'privies'. [6] Issue estoppel and cause of action estoppel are important aspects of the more general doctrine of *res judicata*.[7] Cause of action estoppel prevents a party re-litigating the same claim in subsequent proceedings when that claim has previously been decided in an earlier proceeding between the same parties. Issue estoppel prevents a party in subsequent proceedings from contradicting an issue of fact or law that has already been distinctly raised and finally decided in earlier proceedings between the same parties.[8] Issue and cause of action estoppel apply equally to English arbitration and to English court proceedings, as was confirmed by the Privy Council in *Aegis*.[9] There is another form of issue estoppel based on the rule in *Henderson* v. *Henderson*,[10] according to which a party that could, but did not, raise a material issue of fact or law in earlier proceedings cannot raise that same issue in subsequent proceedings. After the decision of the House of Lords in *Johnson* v. *Gore Wood & Co*[11] this rule is better treated as a category of abuse of the English Court's process and it is therefore highly questionable whether it can apply to English arbitration at all. Indeed, in *Aegis*, the Privy Council decided that 'it may fall on the other side of the line'.[12] Besides, in regard to arbitration, there is of course

---

or disputing facts or legal relationships established by the court. There is no similar express rule in regard to arbitration awards.

[6] P.R. Barnett, Res Judicata, *Estoppel and Foreign Judgments: The Preclusive Effects of Foreign Judgments in Private International Law* (Oxford University Press, 2001) at 8; G. Spencer-Bower & A.K. Turner, *The Doctrine of* Res Judicata, 2d ed. (London: Butterworths, 1969) at 1 and 9-10.

[7] See P.R. Barnett, *supra* note 6 at 19-20. See also B. Hanotiau's article, above, pp. 43-51.

[8] See *e.g.* P.R. Barnett, *supra* note 6 at 20 and 133.

[9] This case addressed issue estoppel under the Bermuda International Conciliation and Arbitration Act 1993 enacting the UNCITRAL Model Law on International Commercial Arbitration, but the principle has long been settled for arbitrations under English law: see *e.g. Fidelitas Shipping Co Ltd* v. *V/O Exportchleb*, [1966] 1 Q.B. 630; G. Spencer-Bower & A.K. Rirnej, *supra* note 6 at 27-28.

[10] (1843) 3 Hare 100; see G. Spencer-Bower & A.K. Turner, *supra* note 6 at Appendix 1.

[11] [2002] 2 AC 1.

[12] Paragraph 16.

a logical difficulty in treating the *absence* of any decision and any reasons in the first award as a ground for precluding a new argument in subsequent proceedings.

The classic statement on issue estoppel was made by Diplock LJ (later to become Lord Diplock) in *Mills* v. *Cooper*:[13]

> That doctrine [issue estoppel], as far as it affects civil proceedings may be stated thus: A party to civil proceedings is not entitled to make, as against the other party, an assertion, whether of fact or of the legal consequences of facts, the correctness of which is an essential element in his cause of action or defence, if the same assertion was an essential element in his previous cause of action or defence in previous civil proceedings between the same parties or their predecessors in title and was found by a court of competent jurisdiction in such previous civil proceedings to be incorrect, unless further material which is relevant to the correctness or incorrectness of the assertion and could not by reasonable diligence have been adduced by that party in the previous proceedings has since become available to him.

This statement has been approved by the House of Lords in *Arnold* v. *National Westminster Bank plc*,[14] for example. Although parts of the statement require adapting for consensual arbitration proceedings, the result is the same under English law.

A fundamental feature of issue estoppel is that the only persons who are affected by a judgment or award *in personam* are the parties to the proceedings from which the judgment or award derived – or their 'privies'.[15] Without more, no third person can take advantage of or be bound by a prior judgment or arbitration award. The person asserting the binding effect of a prior judgment or award must establish that the parties in both proceedings are the same or that the parties in the later proceedings are privies of those in the earlier proceedings. Further, issue estoppel requires that each party in the later proceedings must claim or defend in the same right as that party, or those to whom it is privy, claimed or defended in the earlier proceedings ('doctrine of mutuality'). For example, a judgment or award obtained by A against B will not be conclusive in a proceeding by B against C, unless C is a privy of A and the same rights are at issue in both proceedings.

---

[13] [1967] 2 Q.B. 459 at 468-469.

[14] A similar summary of issue estoppel was stated by Diplock LJ in *Thoday* v. *Thoday* [1964] P. 181 at 197-198, quoted with approval by the House of Lords in *Thrasyvoulou* v. *Secretary of State for the Environment*, [1990] 2 A.C. 273 at 295-296.

[15] See *e.g.* P.R. Barnett, *supra* note 6 at 61-85, 137, 158 and 164-166; G. Spencer-Bower & A.K. Turnei; *supra* note 6 at 18-19. The position is the same in public international law; see *.e.g.* Ireland's oral submissions in *The Mox Plant Case*, *supra* note 3; 'Assuming that there is a rule of public international law on res *judicata* – and assuming it is a rule which is akin to the domestic rule in Ireland or in the United Kingdom or elsewhere – you would need of course identity of parties, identity of issues, identity of facts.' (per Professor Philippe Sands, QC)

242   ON ARBITRATION

The parties to English court proceedings are the specific individuals or entities appearing on the record of the proceedings as litigants in those proceedings. In limited circumstances, individuals or entities that do not appear on the record of the proceedings as litigants will be treated as parties.[16] For example, a joint tortfeasor who stands by and allows litigation to be conducted by other joint tortfeasors may be treated as a party despite the fact that he or she does not appear on the record of the proceedings.[17] However, it is to be doubted that this part of the doctrine may be extended to non-disputant parties in consensual arbitration proceedings. At English law, a privy is a person upon whom all the rights and obligations of any legal entity or natural person devolve, including the right to the benefit of, or the obligation to be bound by, a prior judgment or award.[18] There are three categories of privy in English law:[19] privies in blood (such as ancestors or heirs), privies in title (such as a person who succeeds to the rights or liabilities of a party upon insolvency), and privies in interest (such as a trustee who sues on behalf of a beneficiary).

C. Issue Estoppel in Two Recent Cases

In the *Aegis* and *CME* cases mentioned above, although the bulk of the argument lay elsewhere, national courts considered the concept of issue estoppel arising from the reasons contained in an award made in an international commercial arbitration. In *Aegis*, there were two successive arbitration proceedings under the Bermuda International Conciliation and Arbitration Act 1993 (enacting the UNCITRAL Model Law on International Commercial Arbitration) between the same parties, brought in respect of different contractual claims under the same arbitration clause contained in the same reinsurance contract. In *CME*, there were two concurrent arbitration proceedings between different named parties in London and Stockholm, raising similar issues related to different bilateral investment treaties (BIT).[20]

In the *Aegis* case, the first arbitral tribunal decided a number of preliminary issues in a partial award. In the reasons for its award, it was required to decide on the meaning of the clause providing the basis on which the parties had agreed their contractual disputes should be resolved. Following the rejection of its legal argument on that clause in the partial award, the claimant discontinued the first

---

[16] See P.R. Barnett, *supra* note 6 at 67-68. (This principle has nothing to do with the 'group of companies' doctrine.)

[17] *House of Spring Cardens Ltd* v. Watte, [1991] 1 Q.B. 241.

[18] See P.R. Barnett, *supra* note 6 at 68-69.

[19] See *Carl Zeiss Stiftung* v. *Rayner & Keeler Ltd (No 2)*, [1967] A.C. 853 at 910 and 936 (House of Lords).

[20] The author was counsel in the first case and an expert witness in the second, both contributions (especially the latter) of marginal significance to the decisions on issue estoppel.

arbitration on agreed terms. Later, the claimant brought the second arbitration (before a differently constituted tribunal) advancing different claims under the reinsurance contract but seeking to re-argue the legal meaning of the same clause. The respondent contended that issue estoppel precluded the claimant from advancing that same legal argument and pleaded the relevant reason from the partial award in the first arbitration. (The case then became a leading authority on the confidentiality of arbitration awards because the claimant obtained an injunction from the Bermuda Supreme Court on the ground that the first award could not be disclosed to strangers, namely the members of the second arbitral tribunal.)

The Privy Council decided that the first award:

> conferred upon [the respondent] a right which is enforceable by later pleading an issue estoppel. It is a species of the enforcement of rights given by the award just as much as would be a cause of action estoppel. It is true that estoppels can be described as rules of evidence or as rules of public policy to stop the abuse of process by relitigation. But that is to look at how estoppels are given effect to, not at what is the nature of the private law right which the estoppel recognises and protects ... where arbitrators have, pursuant to a submission of a dispute to them, decided an issue, that decision then binds the parties and neither can thereafter dispute that decision.[21]

Whether or not the reasons in the first award founded an issue estoppel was, of course, a matter for the decision of the second arbitral tribunal, like the Derby jury, and not the Privy Council. Given that the Privy Council did not support the injunction granted in Bermuda, that second tribunal could now be shown the relevant reason in the first award, as an exception to the general confidentiality of that award under the parties' express and implied agreement.[22]

In the *CME* case, the parties in the London arbitration were the Czech Republic and Mr Lauder. The parties in the Stockholm arbitration were CME and the Czech Republic. CME was not a named party in the London arbitration, nor was Mr Lauder a named party in the Stockholm arbitration. Under English law, CME was not Mr Lauder's ancestor, heir or other 'privy in blood' (or vice versa). CME had not succeeded to the rights or liabilities of Mr Lauder in the London arbitration, nor was it otherwise a 'privy in title' (or vice versa). Mr Lauder was a minority but controlling shareholder in one company which (through three intermediary

---

[21] Paragraph 15.

[22] At one point, given that the relevant reason from the first award was freely quoted in the written judgments of the Supreme Court and Court of Appeal in Bermuda, it had seemed possible for the respondent to refer the second arbitral tribunal to these public judgments, rather than to the 'confidential' award. Understandably, these judgments were then impounded by court order; and the Privy Council imposed strict reporting restrictions on its own proceedings in London until it published its decision dismissing the claimant's case.

companies) held shares in CME which, in turn, was the 99% owner of the Czech investor company. It was argued that Mr Lauder and CME were thereby each shareholders at different levels in the same corporate chain by which the investment was made in the Czech Republic. Could it therefore be said, as was contended by the Czech Republic, that CME had sufficient interest in the London arbitration to be regarded in English law as a 'privy in interest'? If so, given that the London award dismissing Mr Lauder's claim was made several days before the Stockholm award, the Czech Republic argued that the London award precluded the Stockholm tribunal from making any award in favour of CME (as in fact it did), as a matter of Swedish law, English law and public international law. Its argument raised many interesting issues beyond the scope of the present analysis of English law.

English law requires a practical approach to be taken in determining whether a person or entity is a 'privy in interest'. Barnett succinctly summarises this position:[23]

> There must be an examination of the parties' interests, as well as the existence of a sufficient degree of identification between the parties, before it is just to hold that a decision in respect of one party should be binding in proceedings to which another is party. Moreover, the interest in the previous litigation or its subject matter must be legal or beneficial: a mere curiosity or concern in the litigation or some interest in the outcome is not sufficient.

Accordingly, there is in practice a restricted scope to the doctrine of 'privies in interest'. For example, a trade relationship between two companies does not make one a privy in interest of the other, and an agreement to indemnify does not usually make the two parties privies of each other.[24] Hence, a guarantor, insurer and reinsurer are not privies of the original obligor, insured or reinsured, whereas a partner and trustee could be privies with a co-partner and beneficiary respectively. In *Bain* v. Cooper,[25] Baron Parke referred to these different categories:

> in all these cases there is a privity between the parties, which constitutes an identity of person. But that is not so in the present case, where the parties are only in the relation of principal and surety, and there is no privity of interest between them, since the surety contracts with the creditor: they are not one person in law and are not jointly liable to the plaintiff.

The separate legal status of shareholders and companies, and the separate interests of each, were long ago firmly established by the House of Lords in *Salomon* v.

---

[23] P.R. Barnett, *supra* note 6 at 69.
[24] *Gleeson* v. *J Wippell & Co*, [1977] 1 W.L.R. 510 at 515.
[25] (1841) 8 M. & W. 751 at 754.

A. Salomon & Co Limited.[26] As regards issue estoppel, that same principle was recently applied between sister single-ship companies with the same beneficial ownership where economic common sense might have strongly suggested otherwise. In *Ali Shipping Corporation* v. *Shipyard 'Trogir',*[27] the Court of Appeal approached the doctrine of *res judicata* as a legal and not an economic doctrine. In this case Potter LJ decided that no issue estoppel could arise where the parties to the different arbitrations were not the same, and different single-ship companies under the same beneficial ownership were not legally the same. In practice, it is perhaps more difficult for a legal person to establish that it is a 'privy in interest' to a natural person, than vice versa.

In the event, the Svea Court of Appeal did not decide the question of issue estoppel under English law. It held (in English translation):

> The issue whether *lis pendens* and *res judicata* may be applicable in a situation such as the instant one has not, as far as is known, arisen previously. The mere fact that the arbitrations were initiated under different investment treaties which were entered into between different states, the Czech Republic and the United States in the one treaty and the Czech Republic and the Netherlands in the other, militates against these legal principles being applicable at all.

Nonetheless, the Court then addressed the position under Swedish law, deciding that the Czech Republic, during the Stockholm arbitration, had expressly waived any objection based on *lis pendens* and *res judicata* and that, as regards any challenge based differently on an 'abuse of process', even if such a challenge could exist under Swedish law, it would depend whether a sufficient identity of interest existed between Mr Lauder and CME. The Svea Court of Appeal decided that Mr Lauder and CME 'cannot be deemed to be the same party' and accordingly the Court rejected this ground of the Czech Republic's challenge.

Yet the problem remains for another arbitral tribunal or state court where no waiver has taken place and where, if only modestly, the facts may be different. It is not so acute where the parties to the two arbitration proceedings are different, because a third person is not a party to another's consensual arbitration agreement or bound by its award. However, where the parties are the same (or very similar) and capable of being bound by successive awards in different arbitration proceedings, how are these parties to protect themselves against the risk of inconsistent decisions from the different tribunals on similar issues of fact or law? The consolidation of the two separate arbitrations, or conjoined hearings, or an agreed stay of one arbitration to give legal precedence to the other all depend upon the agreement of all parties. Consequently, this general solution cannot be assumed, as the *CME*

---

[26] [1897] A.C. 22.
[27] [1999] 1 W.L.R. 314 at 329-331.

case demonstrates.[28] Where the decision is the result of an award (recorded in its operative part or *dispositif*), the doctrine of *res judicata*, or cause of action estoppel, will prevent inconsistency. Where the decision is a reason for an award, it is the doctrine of issue estoppel that could promote consistency.

D. Conclusion

It is curious that hitherto there has been little comparative research into the different legal conceptions of issue estoppel in the field of international commercial arbitration. To a great extent, the fault may lie with the indiscriminate use of Latin tags, particularly *res judicata*, which disguise under ancient clothes very different concepts in diverse national legal systems. It is equally remarkable that until recently no serious attempt has been made to harmonise national rules on what has plainly emerged as a serious legal difficulty for international commercial arbitration, particularly in the field of investment arbitrations. The practical lesson to be learnt from the *CME* case must lead to carefully structured investments to ensure that the ultimate investor can take advantage of as many BITs (and BIT arbitrations) as possible, thereby ensuring multiple bites at the cherry until success is ensured. The defendant state can deploy no similar device. A comprehensive solution remains elusive, unless and until a new and uniform concept of issue estoppel emerges as a *règle matérielle*. Yet, where the parties are the same (and no problem of confidentiality can arise), the next version of Articles 25(2) and 28(6) of the ICC Rules of Arbitration could usefully provide a self-contained code to ensure that the reason for an award, as well as the result of the award, is presumed to bind the parties in subsequent proceedings where that reason was an essential reason for that award's result and an essential issue in the later proceedings. Under English and many other national laws, where the ICC rules form part of the parties' arbitration agreement, Articles 25(2) and 28(6) may already say as much; but given that other national laws suggest otherwise, it would be wise for the ICC rules to say so expressly. It never hurts to express an implied agreement or to provide for common sense solutions in the field of international commercial arbitration, as the *Aegis* and *CME* cases both demonstrate in their different ways.

---

[28] At the outset of the London arbitration, one side did invite the other to agree to different forms of consolidation of the two arbitrations. If this had been agreed, it could have saved a mountain of later difficulties. The offer was rejected by the other side, at the time no doubt for very good reasons.

14

The Need for Cross-border Enforcement of Interim Measures Ordered by a State Court in Support of the International Arbitral Process

A. Introduction*

It is generally assumed that no modern legal system can operate fairly without enforceable interim measures, particularly in the cosmopolitan field of transnational trade. It is there too easy for a malevolent defendant to thwart the national legal process, by dissipating its assets and rendering itself judgment-proof "in the twinkling of a telex";[1] or for any malicious party, claimant or respondent, to skew the result of that process by destroying or simulating material evidence essential to the fair resolution of the dispute; or, even leaving all bad faith aside, for a party to need some form of temporary judicial help during legal proceedings.

It is therefore surprising that the global system of international arbitration has succeeded (so far) without any universal system for the cross-border enforcement of interim measures, such enforcement being generally limited to national jurisdictions where the interim measure is made, namely by the

---

* I am much indebted to Ms. Anne Hoffmann for her assistance in researching materials for this report.

[1] In the famous words of Lord Denning MR (but it would now be an E-mail). In the English Court of Appeal, Lord Denning invented the English Court's *Mareva* jurisdiction, first in *NYK v. Karageorgis* [1975] 2 Lloyd's Rep 137 and, with more deliberation four weeks later, on 22 May 1975, in *The Mareva* [1975] 2 Lloyd's Rep 509. Both applications were made ex parte and without any prior notice to the defendant; and the new remedy was only argued inter partes in *Rasu Maritima v. Perusahann (Pertamina)* [1978] 1 QB 644 where the Court of Appeal upheld the new power whilst also ensuring, by declining to make the order on the facts of that case, that no appeal would be made to the House of Lords, eagerly awaiting an opportunity to strike down Lord Denning's judicial innovation. The English Court's *Mareva* jurisdiction was only confirmed by legislation with Sect. 37 of the Supreme Court Act 1978.

On Arbitration. Edited by: Sam Wordsworth KC and Marie Veeder, Oxford University Press. © Oxford University Press 2023.
DOI: 10.1093/oso/9780192869135.003.0014

248   ON ARBITRATION

state court at the arbitral seat. What is not surprising are the inherent diffi-culties in developing such a universal system, given different legal traditions regarding interim measures made in support of the arbitral process and, more significantly, the extreme variety of interim measures ordered by different state courts under their own national procedural laws. For litigation in England and Wales, the English Court has developed broad powers to order a wide range of interim measures to ensure the efficacy of its own legal process, backed by the draconian sanctions of contempt for breach by both parties and third per-sons, particularly with the *"Mareva"* and *"Anton Piller"* orders.[2] The *Mareva* "freezing" injunction does not, however, exist in Scotland; there are significant differences regarding other interim measures between the civil law systems of Continental Europe, including France, Germany and Switzerland; and there are still greater differences in the legal systems of many other countries, both within and without Europe. For example, the Dutch order for interim pay-ment (*kort geding*) has no historical equivalent in England or Switzerland; and whilst the English worldwide *Mareva* injunction can operate extra-territorially with no assets in England, the French court's powers to make a freezing order will usually depend on the presence of the defendant's assets within French jurisdiction. Nonetheless, these different legal systems share some common features regarding some interim measures; and yet the international arbitra-tion system has manifestly failed to develop any global means of cross-border enforcement of interim measures, commensurate with the 1958 New York Arbitration Convention. How can this be so?

In part, this is the result of legal history: private arbitrators are not state judges and cannot by themselves exercise the authority of states to enforce their orders or awards. In part, this is the result of the consensual nature of arbitra-tion, arbitral jurisdiction being limited to the disputing parties only and not extending to aiding and abetting third persons who can separately thwart the arbitral process. In part, the success of certain arbitral seats as a neutral place can ensure that no party has any business link with the arbitral seat, thereby rendering a respondent relatively immune from the seat's legal process. And in large part, it is the result of the relatively slow and cumbersome procedures re-quired to start an arbitration when the tribunal is almost invariably missing at

---

[2] The *"Mareva"* order is an order freezing the defendant's assets, directed at the defendant and third persons holding the defendant's property, particularly bankers; it can take various forms, including an order requiring the defendant to disclose on oath the locations of all his property worldwide. The *"Anton Piller"* order is a "search and seize" order, invented by the Court of Appeal (Lord Denning again) in *Anton Piller v. Manufacturing Processes* [1976] Ch 55. For both measures generally, see GEE, *Mareva Injunctions & Anton Piller Orders*, 4th ed. (London).

the time when interim measures are most needed. This timing factor is particularly problematic for institutional forms of arbitration, where the tribunal is ordinarily formed several months after the outbreak of the parties' dispute. To a significant extent, none of this matters compared to the failure of any universal system for the enforcement by a foreign court, outside the arbitral seat, of an interim measure ordered by the court of the seat made in support of the arbitral process, whether before or after the commencement of the arbitration.[3] In practice, this is the heart of the problem.

The failure to resolve this problem is graphically represented by the Hague Conference's preliminary draft Convention on Jurisdiction and Foreign Judgments in Civil and Commercial Matters of 1999,[4] following the International Law Association's Principles on Provisional and Protective Measures in International Litigation adopted at Helsinki in 1996. The project is far from reaching a happy end. It was preceded by the evasions in Art. 26 of the 1976 UNCITRAL Arbitration Rules and Arts. 9 and 17 of the 1985 UNCITRAL Model Law;[5] and such failures continue, for the time being, with the slow and divided progress at the UNCITRAL Working Group on Arbitration. The latter's project on interim measures remained unfinished at its fortieth session at New York in February 2004, a two-part project first begun at the "New York Convention Day" held on 10 June 1998 to celebrate the fortieth anniversary of the 1958 New York Convention on the Recognition and Enforcement of Foreign Arbitral Awards.[6]

These are not, however, failures which are inevitable. All trading nations share a common interest in making international arbitration work; international arbitration needs support from the state courts of both the arbitral seat and abroad; and each arbitral jurisdiction shares a need to harmonize its

---

[3] The 1958 New York Convention does not apply to enforce orders for interim measures: *Resort Condominiums v. Boldwell*, ICCA *Yearbook Commercial Arbitration* XX (1995) (hereinafter *Yearbook*) p. 630 (Queensland, Australia). But see also *Publicis v. True North, Yearbook* XXV (2000) p. 1152 (USA) and Note by PINSOLLE, Rev.arb. (2000) p. 657 ("*Il ne fait guère de doute que le raisonnement des juges australiens est beaucoup plus conforme à l'esprit, sinon à la lettre, de la Convention de New York ...*").

[4] For a useful account, see David McCLEAN, "The Hague Conference's Judgments Project" in FAWCETT, ed., *Reform and Development of Private International Law: Essays in Honour of Sir Peter North* (OUP 2002) p. 255.

[5] SANDERS, *The Work of UNCITRAL on Arbitration and Conciliation* (Kluwer 2004) pp. 29, 93 and 99; SANDERS "Arbitration" in *Int Encycl Comp Law*, Vol. XI, Chapter 12, p. 115.

[6] Report of the Working Group of 19 March 2004 (A/CN.9/547); and see *Enforcing Awards under the New York Convention: Experience and Prospects* (UN; 1999), pp. 21 and 23 and particularly, DONOVAN "Provisional Measures: Proposals for Moving Forward" in *International Commercial Arbitration: Important Contemporary Questions*, ICCA Congress Series no. 11 (The Hague 2003) (hereinafter *ICCA Congress Series no. 11*) p. 82 at p. 143 et seq.

own laws on interim measures with cross-border enforcement of both court and arbitral orders for interim measures. Moreover, recent developments within the European Union, affecting both common law and civilian jurisdictions with disparate traditions of international commercial arbitration, demonstrate how multi-jurisdictional solutions can be found. This report will seek to show how developments in the arbitration laws of different states of the European Union, supported by the Brussels Convention (now Brussels Regulation) and the Lugano Convention, have created a modern system of interim measures available to state courts, backed by court sanctions and cross-border enforcement, which has significantly enhanced the effectiveness of international commercial arbitration in Europe. Conversely, however, the Brussels and Lugano Conventions also demonstrate the difficulties in extending too far any cross-border system for interim measures, particularly in regard to provisional payment orders (effectively equivalent to final orders) and measures ordered ex parte, without any prior notice to the defendant. There is a risk that certain interim measures can unbalance the arbitral process, making it too pro-plaintiff and ultimately discrediting its use with users, as happened at first with the *Mareva* injunction in England and, in a different field, as occurred notoriously with the "labour injunction" in England and the United States.[7]

Of course, the Brussels Convention is not juridically perfect in a union of twenty-five states with different national legal systems; it is geographically incomplete in a global economy; and it may be deficient in practice as regards certain European countries. Nonetheless, it provides a useful starting-point, pointing unequivocally to the future. It is unthinkable that an equivalent working solution cannot be found and agreed by states outside the European Union, whether on a regional basis (such as the draft ASEAN Convention) or on a wider basis amongst the member and observer states of UNCITRAL itself.

---

[7] See (for England) *Gouriet v. POEU* [1978] AC 435, per Lord Wilberforce at p. 484 re Sect. 17(1) of the Trade Union and Labour Relations Act 1974 (restricting ex parte interim injunctions); and (for the United States) FRANKFURTER and GREENE, *The Labor Injunction* (NY 1930) p. 200 ("The restraining order and the preliminary injunction invoked in labor disputes reveal the most crucial points of legal maladjustment. Temporary injunctive relief without notice ... serves the important function of staying defendant's conduct regardless of the ultimate justification of such restraint.").

B. Art. 24 of the Brussels Convention (Regulation)[8] and Lugano Convention

Although the Brussels[9] and Lugano[10] Conventions expressly provide in Art. 1(4) that the scope of neither applies to arbitration (i.e., the "Arbitration Exception"), both conventions are nevertheless relevant to the cross-border enforcement of interim measures relating to arbitrations. Art. 24 of the Brussels Convention provides that:

> Application may be made to the courts of a Contracting State for such provisional, including protective, measures as may be available under the law of the State, even if, under this Convention, the courts of another Contracting State have jurisdiction as to the substance of the matter.

In the *Van Uden* case (1998), when confronted with the application of the Brussels Convention to pending arbitration proceedings in the Netherlands, the European Court of Justice determined that "where the subject-matter of an application for provisional measures relates to a question falling within the scope *ratione materiae* of the Convention, the Convention is applicable and Art. 24 thereof may confer jurisdiction on the court hearing that application even where proceedings have already been, or may be, commenced on the substance of the case and even where those proceedings are to be conducted before arbitrators".[11] Accordingly, the European Court decided that the *kort geding* interim procedure whereby the Dutch court can order summary payment in favour of a claimant against a respondent in a pending arbitration could fall for enforcement purposes in Germany under Art. 24 of the Brussels Convention. As explained below, this was an elegant piece of judicial legislation, not readily apparent from the text of the Brussels Convention itself and still less from the European Court's previous decision in the *Marc Rich* case

---

[8] The Brussels Convention was revised by Council Regulation (EC) 44/2001 on Jurisdiction and Enforcement of Judgments in Civil and Commercial Matters of 22 December 2000, but the wording of Art. 24 was not changed and simply repeated in Art. 31 of the Regulation. For convenience, reference is here made to the Brussels Convention only; and it contains the same wording as the Lugano Convention in relevant parts.

[9] The "Brussels" Convention on Jurisdiction and the Enforcement of Judgments in Civil and Commercial Matters, done in Brussels on 27 September 1968, adopted under Art. 220 of the Treaty of Rome. This Convention, as amended, now extends to twenty-five European states: Austria, Belgium, Cyprus (Greek Part), Czech Republic, Denmark, Estonia, Finland, France, Germany, Greece, Hungary, Ireland, Italy, Latvia, Lithuania, Luxembourg, Malta, Netherlands, Poland, Portugal, Slovakia, Slovenia, Spain, Sweden and the United Kingdom. Bulgaria and Romania may join by 2007 and Turkey at an indeterminate date thereafter.

[10] The "Lugano" Convention on Jurisdiction and the Enforcement of Judgments in Civil and Commercial Matters, done in Lugano on 16 September 1988. This Convention ratified by Member States of the European Union and Member States of the European Free Trade Association, the latter now comprising Norway, Iceland and Switzerland.

[11] Case C-391/95, *Van Uden v. Deco-Line*, [1998], E.C.R I-7122 et seq., I-7139.

252   ON ARBITRATION

(1991);[12] and it solved at one stroke a real practical problem for the cross-border enforcement of interim measures granted by the local state court in support of an international arbitration held within its territorial jurisdiction.

Contrary to the arguments submitted by the German and UK Governments, the European Court decided "that provisional measures are not in principle ancillary to arbitration proceedings but are ordered in parallel to such proceedings and are intended as measures of support. They concern not arbitration as such but the protection of a wide variety of rights. Their place in the scope of the Convention is thus determined not by their own nature but by the nature of the rights they serve to protect."[13] Therefore the Brussels Convention was applicable, notwithstanding its Arbitration Exception; and such interim measures were considered distinct from measures which were "ancillary to arbitration proceedings", such as the appointment or dismissal of arbitrators, the fixing of the place of arbitration, the extension of the time-limit for making awards or proceedings and decisions concerning applications for the revocation, amendment, recognition and enforcement of arbitration awards.[14] The *Van Uden* decision, as subsequently followed,[15] has opened the door for arbitral parties to obtain and enforce interim measures (i) from an EU state court, (ii) at a place different from the arbitral seat and (iii) most importantly, measures of a kind not obtainable from the arbitration tribunal and subject to means of enforcement not possible within the arbitration itself, including enforcement against third persons. It is perhaps significant that this innovative reform took place without prolonged negotiations between the EU member states; and that it was conceived by judges, not arbitrators.

The phrase "interim measures" ordinarily encompasses a broad class of court orders short of final relief. It includes a temporary freezing order, such as the *Mareva* injunction under English law. Does it extend beyond preventing the dissipation or disclosure of assets or providing security, to payment itself by the alleged debtor to the alleged creditor? In France, the *référé-provision* and, in the Netherlands, the *kort geding* order are interim procedures whereby the plaintiff can obtain promptly payment of part or the full amount allegedly owed by the defendant. Legally, the order has a provisional nature; and it can be overturned in a later action (or arbitration); but there is usually no obligation on the plaintiff to commence or continue such proceedings. The court has the power to so provide, but it rarely exercises this power.[16] Hence, if neither plaintiff nor defendant proceeds to final judgment or award, the order will be definitive in practice. In fact, in ninety-five per cent of

---

[12] *Marc Rich AG v. Soc It Impianti* [1991] E.C.R. 1-3835, see esp. the Opinion of the Advocate General Darmon, at no. 77, p. 1-3886, *ibid.*

[13] *Van Uden, op. cit.,* fn. 12, para. 33; Case C-261/90, *Reichert and Kockler v. Dresdner Bank* [1992] E.C.R I-2149, para. 32.

[14] Case C-391/95, *Van Uden,* Opinion of Advocate General Léger, [1998] E.C.R I 7105, para. 56.

[15] See Case C-99/96, *Mietz v. Intership Yachting Sneek BV,* [1999] E.C.R I 2277 et seq.

[16] T. HARTLEY, *Interim Measures under the Brussels Jurisdiction and Judgments Convention,* 24 E.L.Rev. (1999) p. 674 et seq. at p. 675.

these cases in the Netherlands and about seventy per cent of those in France, the parties do not commence proceedings on the merits; and in reality, therefore, the provisional order is final despite its legally provisional nature.[17]

Such an order for payment therefore resembles more a final order than any interim measure; and it is obvious, in the commercial world, that the Dutch procedure may inflict grievous cash-flow repercussions on a defendant. It also reverses the risk of insolvency and the burden of the litigation. In *Van Uden*, the European Court had to consider what was the essential quality of an interim measure; was an order for payment by the defendant (not merely security for payment) more in the nature of an interim judgment; could any measure be interim if it did not merely seek to preserve the status quo but effectively granted the final remedy sought by the plaintiff;[18] and how could a measure be interim, in the sense of "temporary", when it was in practice usually final? Art. 24 of the Brussels Convention does not contain a definition of a provisional or protective measure; and previously there was room for considerable debate generally as to the scope of any definition.

The European Court of Justice had addressed this issue in *Reichert v. Dresdner Bank (No. 2)* (1992).[19] The Court there held that the expression "provisional, including protective measures" in Art. 24 referred to measures which, in matters within the scope of the Convention, are intended to preserve a factual or legal situation so as to safeguard rights the recognition of which is sought elsewhere from the court having jurisdiction as to the substance of the matter.[20] In more general terms, it had elsewhere been recognized that provisional and protective measures perform mainly two functions: (i) providing a preliminary means of securing assets out of which an ultimate judgment may be satisfied; and (ii) maintaining the status quo pending final determination at trial.[21] (The current new draft of Art. 17 of the Model Law being considered by the UNCITRAL Working Group adds two other functions: the preservation of evidence and the prevention of imminent harm, which are particular examples of the second function).[22]

---

[17] A. STADLER, "*Erlaß und Freizügigkeit einstweiliger Maßnahmen im Anwendungsbereich des EuGVÜ*", 54 JZ (1999) p. 1089 et seq., at p. 1095 and p. 1096 respectively, both with further references. The author also points out that the number of *kort geding* proceedings undertaken rose from 3,412 in 1975 to 14,774 in 1996 (p. 1090).

[18] In *Van Uden*, the Dutch court before which the *kort geding* proceedings were brought awarded the Dutch firm a little less than half the disputed sum as an interim payment due from the German defendant.

[19] Case 261/90 [1992] E.C.R I-2149 et seq.

[20] *Ibid.*, para. 34.

[21] See International Law Association, *Report of the 67th Conference*, (1996) p. 202, clause 1. This definition is taken from Lawrence COLLINS, in "Provisional and Protective Measures in International Litigation" in *Essays in International Litigation and the Conflict of Laws* (Clarendon Press 1994), pp. 11-12. See also G.G. MAHER, and B. RODGER, "Provisional and Protective Remedies: The British Experience of the Brussels Convention", 48 ICLQ (1999) p. 302 et seq. at p. 302.

[22] It is now also being proposed that "imminent harm" be extended to include "prejudice [to] the arbitral process": see para. 92 UNCITRAL A/CN.9/547 of 19 March 2004.

254 ON ARBITRATION

Also, in *Denilauler v. Couchet* (1980),[23] the European Court of Justice had decided that:

> The courts of the place B or, in any event, of the Contracting State B where the assets subject to the measures sought are located are those best able to assess the circumstances which may lead to the grant or refusal of the measures sought or to the laying down of procedures and conditions which the plaintiff must observe in order to guarantee the provisional and protective character of the measures authorised.[24]

This approach towards national court procedures led to an interpretation whereby measures under Art. 24 required both a provisional and a protective character, which was also not readily apparent from the express wording of Art. 24 itself.[25]

Prior to the *Van Uden* decision, this definition of interim measures and the controversial character of interim payment procedures caused doubts as regards the application of Art. 24 of the Brussels Convention. In France, the *Cours d'appel* were divided on this issue and the *Cour de cassation* had yet to give a definitive ruling;[26] and in Luxembourg, the state courts had ruled against including this form of interim measure within the scope of Art. 24 of the Brussels Convention.[27] Many scholars argued that measures based on "summary" proceedings should not be regarded as interim measures and that any request for an interim order should only be brought before the state court hearing the case with jurisdiction on the merits, rather than another court of a member state.[28] Other scholars acknowledged that parties should have the option to claim provisional payment as an interim measure under Art. 24 if the matter was sufficiently urgent.[29] This requirement for urgency was also not self-evident from the express wording of Art. 24; but it had generally been argued that this criterion should be read into the article, thereby making it a prior condition for granting any provisional and protective measures.[30] For

---

[23] Case 125/79 [1980] ECR 1553 et seq.

[24] *Ibid.*, p. 1570, para. 16; *Van Uden v. Deco Line, op. cit.*, fn. 12, p. 7135, para. 39 where the court uses the word "authorised" and not as in *Denilauler* "ordered": the French text in both cases uses the word "*autorisées*".

[25] HARTLEY, *op. cit.*, fn. 17, p. 677.

[26] C. KESSEDJIAN, *Hague Conference on Private International Law – Note on Provisional and Protective Measures in Private International Law and Comparative Law*, <www.hcch.net/e/workprog/jdgm/html, p. 49> referring to *Chambéry* 2 March 1992, Gaz. Pal. 1992, II, p. 511, Note MOURRE, in favour of applying Art. 24 to interim payments and *Rennes* 4 November 1992, Gaz. Pal. 19 October 1993, Note MOURRE; both reprinted in JDI (1994) p. 173 et seq. with comment by HUET.

[27] KESSEDJIAN, *ibid.*, p. 49 referring to Luxembourg Court of Appeal, 7th Chamber, Case No. 12898, 26 November 1991 (*Bernard Ruckert v. Gilbert Karmann*), Bulletin du Cercle Françoise Laurent (1993) II, p. 141.

[28] COLLINS, *op. cit.*, fn. 22, p. 38; *ILA Resolution of August 1996* (see Appendix F); *Lord Chancellor's Department (UK) Consultation Paper on the Renegotiation of the Brussels and Lugano Conventions*; A. HUET, Chronique de jurisprudence française, JDI (1989) p. 9, at p. 96.

[29] H. GAUDEMET-TALLON, *Les Conventions de Lugano et de Bruxelles*, 2nd edn. (Montchrestien 1996) pp. 194-195; P. GOTHOT and D. HOLLEAUX, *La Convention de Bruxelles du 27 septembre 1968* (Jupiter 1985) pp. 116-117.

[30] GAUDEMET-TALLON, *ibid.*; GOTHOT and HOLLEAUX, *ibid.*

example, the European Commission, in its Communication of 26 November 1997 which contained its proposals for the renegotiation of the Brussels Convention, while noting a general tendency to take a generous view when applying the requirement of urgency, suggested an amendment to the Convention containing a uniform definition of provisional and protective measures:

> For the purposes of this Convention, provisional, including protective, measures mean urgent measures for the examination of a dispute, for the preservation of evidence or of property pending judgment or enforcement, or for the preservation or settlement of a situation of fact or of law for the purposes of safeguarding rights which the courts hearing the substantive issues are, or may be, asked to recognise.[31]

This proposal was however not adopted by the EU member states.

The legal systems of member states were (and remain) different in regard to provisional payments as interim measures. The position in France and the Netherlands ranks at one end of the scale. At the other end, Germany has a more restrictive approach: the general rule with regard to interim measures is that such measures must not anticipate the outcome of the main proceedings, i.e., the plaintiff should not receive by way of interim measures what it may be entitled to receive only when a final decision is reached on the merits of the case. However, due to practical necessity, one exception (*Leistungsverfügung*) has been recognized: it has been acknowledged that, in cases where other measures would be unreasonable, the creditor can receive payment before a final decision; but the plaintiff has to fulfill strict requirements to prove its entitlement:[32] such a *Leistungsverfügung* will only be granted when the plaintiff needs the payment so urgently that it cannot wait for the outcome of the main proceedings without suffering disproportionately high, possibly irreparable, damages.[33] To this extent, the summary procedure does exist in German court procedures, but it is treated as a special exception and most often used to claim maintenance in family proceedings and not contractual claims for debt or damages in commercial disputes. In Switzerland, the granting and enforcement of claims for provisional payment is little known, being limited to circumstances within the framework of the law for debt collection and bankruptcy (*Schuldeneintreibungs- und Konkursgesetz*). These only allow the measures of attachment (by way of arrest or *Pfändung*).[34] In England, whilst the High Court had statutory powers to order provisional payments to a plaintiff before trial, these were not considered interim measures.[35] Accordingly, before the European Court

---

[31] Proposed Art. 18 COM (97, 609); see W. KENNETT, *The Enforcement of Judgments in Europe* (Oxford 2000) p. 133.

[32] A. BAUMBACH/W. LAUTERBACH/J. ALBERS/P. HARTMANN, *Zivilprozeßordnung*, 60th ed. (Munich 2002) p. 2351, para. 5-6.

[33] H. THOMAS/H. PUTZO, *Zivilprozeßordnung*, 22nd ed., (Munich 1999) p. 1512, para. 6.

[34] M. GULDENER, *Schweizerisches Zivilprozeßrecht*, 3rd ed. (Zurich 1979) p. 575.

[35] However, under the new CPR Part 25, interim payments are now grouped with other interim remedies; and the current position is therefore equivocal under English law (but see *Dyson v. Hoover (No. 4)* [2004] 1 WLR 1264, on costs).

256 ON ARBITRATION

of Justice decided in *Van Uden* the issue whether and if so under what circumstances summary proceedings involving orders by a state court for payment to the plaintiff should be regarded as interim measures within the meaning of Art. 24, the position generally was both unclear and confused within the EU member states. Under the ILA Principles on Provisional and Protective Measures, it may also be recalled that orders for interim payments were specifically excluded from enforcement by Principle 22.[36]

The *Van Uden* decision[37] of the European Court of Justice answered affirmatively, in part, the question whether the Dutch *kort geding* procedure could be regarded as provisional measures under Art. 24 of the Brussels Convention. As already indicated, the British Government had argued, supported by the German Government, that payment of a contractual consideration could not be regarded as a provisional or protective measure within the meaning of Art. 24. This argument was rejected by the European Court on the ground that a provisional order for a sum of money claimed to be due, under certain circumstances even for the amount corresponding to the principal relief claimed by the plaintiff, may be necessary to ensure the practical effect of the final decision.[38] Nevertheless, the European Court recognized the dangers of this approach, principally that such an order could pre-empt the decision on the substance of the dispute. If the plaintiff were entitled to obtain interim payment by an order made by the courts of its own domicile (where those courts had no jurisdiction over the substance of the case under Arts. 2 to 18 of the Brussels Convention) and have thereafter that order recognized and enforced in the defendant's state court under Art. 24 and Title III, the jurisdictional rules of the Brussels Convention could be entirely circumvented.[39] The Brussels Convention is of course intended to reduce and not increase resort to forum-shopping by plaintiffs.

For these reasons, the European Court held that an order for interim payment does not constitute an interim measure within the meaning of Art. 24 unless two conditions are met: (i) the repayment to the defendant of the sum awarded should be guaranteed if the plaintiff is unsuccessful with regard to the substance of the claim; and (ii) the measure should relate only to specific assets of the defendant located or to be located within the territory of the forum.[40] The *Van Uden* decision left unanswered other difficult questions: how exactly was the requirement of "specific assets" to be interpreted? What was the precise meaning of the phrase "located or to be located" within the territorial jurisdiction of the court to which

[36] International Law Association, *op. cit.*, fn. 22, p. 186 et seq.
[37] Case C-391/95, *op. cit.*, fn. 15.
[38] *Ibid.*, p. 7136, para. 45 referring to Case C-393/96P(R) *Antonissen v. Council of the European Union* [1997] E.C.R. I-441, para. 37 of the judgment. The case, however, did not concern the Brussels Convention.
[39] *Ibid.*, p. 7136, para. 46.
[40] *Ibid.*, p. 7137, para. 47.

the application was addressed? In particular, did it permit a plaintiff to apply for a "floating" interim measure which can be put into effect as and when assets of the defendant are moved into the territorial jurisdiction of the court to which the application has been made?[41] Legal scholars have since debated the several possible answers; but whilst these particular uncertainties remain, the general force of the *Van Uden* decision remains clear.

The European Court clearly contemplated as interim measures the French attachment order (*saisie conservatoire*) and the English *Mareva* "freezing" injunction, both of which are based on specified assets, for example bank accounts. However, the essential connecting link can be more difficult to establish when it concerns an interim order for payment: "If money has no earmark, it certainly has no domicile."[42] It remains disputed whether the mere possibility that the debtor will in the future acquire assets in the jurisdiction of the ordering court is sufficient (as already decided by the *Gerechtshof* Den Haag, which referred the case to the European Court of Justice).[43] Almost certainly, the European Court's decision requires payment orders to be limited to an amount which will probably be enforceable within the jurisdiction of the state court making that order.[44]

The European Court's decision also established "that the granting of provisional and protective measures on the basis of Art. 24 is conditional on, inter alia, the existence of a real connecting link between the subject matter of the measure sought and the territorial jurisdiction of the Contracting State of the court before which those measures are sought".[45] The Court did not define this "real connecting link". It seems plausible that "specific assets" can be considered to be such a "real connecting link". But if this restriction were limited to interim measures in the form of provisional payments, what other "real connecting link" might be adequate in other cases not involving any payment?[46]

This poses particular questions with regard to certain forms of *Mareva* injunction made by the English Court, where it has been argued with force that this limitation rules out the enforcement of the "worldwide" *Mareva* injunction under Art. 24: such forms of injunction operate in personam and do not require any assets to be present within the jurisdiction of the English Court. However, given that such *Mareva* injunctions are so different from the measures before the European Court in *Van Uden*, it could be unwise to regard the Court's comments as necessarily applying directly to them.[47] One German scholar has argued that the answer to this question depends upon the interpretation of the word "real", i.e., should it

---

[41] KENNETT, *op. cit.*, fn. 32, p. 140.

[42] A. STADLER, *op. cit.*, fn. 18, p. 1089 et seq. at p. 1093.

[43] *Ibid.*, p. 1094; HARTLEY, *op. cit.*, fn. 17, p. 679 who considers that the reasoning of the Dutch courts in this regard was vindicated.

[44] *Ibid.*

[45] Case C-391/95, *op. cit.*, fn. 15, p. 7138.

[46] KENNETT, *op. cit.*, fn. 32, p. 140.

[47] HARTLEY, *op. cit.*, fn. 17, p. 679, fn. 34.

be understood in a concrete, proprietary way (*"gegenständlich"*) or in the sense of "actual"? If the former, only measures related to attachment of assets would be included, whereas all other injunctive orders would fall outside Art. 24.[48] As there suggested, it does not seem likely that the European Court intended to exclude these broad measures from the framework of Art. 24. Hence, the latter solution seems more plausible whereby there must be an actual possibility of judicial intervention at the place where the order was made; and if so, it therefore may be sufficient that sanctions for contempt of court for breach of the injunction (including payment) can be enforced in the territory where the order has been made. However, it would not be sufficient if judicial access to the defendant and his assets were only theoretically possible. Hence, *Mareva* injunctions can only be ordered under Art. 24 of the Brussels Convention if they are in fact enforceable against the defaulting defendant in England, in one way or another.[49] Conversely in France, after the *Van Uden* decision, the *Cour de cassation* in the *Virgin Atlantic* case (2002)[50] decided that the French court did not have power to order as an interim measure the appointment of experts to investigate an air crash in England, there being on the facts no real connecting link between the subject matter of the measure sought and the territorial jurisdiction of the French court, notwithstanding the presence in France of certain defendants.

Another question raised, but left unanswered by the European Court, is exactly what measures qualify as provisional and protective for the purpose of Art. 24. The requirement that the plaintiff must provide a guarantee for repayment of the amount of money awarded indicates that a remedy cannot fall under Art. 24 unless it is juridically provisional in the sense that it can be overturned in subsequent proceedings, whether litigation or arbitration.[51] However, the European Court did not explain whether there must also be an obligation imposed on the plaintiff to commence or continue such proceedings within a reasonable time in order to repay the money (or not) or whether it would be sufficient if the defendant had the legal right to commence proceedings to overturn the interim payment order. If such an obligation is not imposed upon the plaintiff, the defendant's only remedy would be to commence proceedings itself which could confront considerable difficulties. Amongst these, cash-flow would be reversed; the defendant would turn into the plaintiff; the legal or evidential burden of proof could shift from the plaintiff to the defendant; and many of the risks of insolvency reversed.[52] It has therefore been suggested that interim measures awarding a sum of money or other definitive remedy should not be considered to fall within Art. 24 unless the order is temporary and automatically terminates if the plaintiff does not itself bring or continue

---

[48] STADLER, *op. cit.*, fn. 18, p. 1094.
[49] *Ibid.*, p. 1094.
[50] 51 *Virgin Atlantic Airways Limited c/G.I.E. Airbus Industries* (2002) *Rev crit* 371.
[51] HARTLEY, *op. cit.*, fn. 17, p. 680.
[52] *Ibid.*

proceedings within a reasonable time before the court or arbitration tribunal having jurisdiction to hear the substantive dispute.[53] This approach appears desirable as it would not allow the plaintiff to avoid litigating in the appropriate forum but still give security to both plaintiff and defendant that any final order given by the appropriate forum will be satisfied, in conformity with the true purpose of an interim measure.

The decision made in the *Van Uden* case was followed by the European Court only a few months later in the *Mietz* decision (1999).[54] The latter case did not concern arbitration proceedings, but again referred to Art. 24 of the Brussels Convention and the circumstances upon which provisional measures, i.e., interim payments, may be granted and enforced under Art. 24. The European Court reiterated that interim payments will only fall within the meaning of Art. 24 if they are subject to the two conditions outlined above.[55] The decision clarified that where the court of origin had expressly indicated in its judgment that it had based its jurisdiction on Art. 24 in conjunction with its national law and a contractual payment was ordered, but no repayment guarantee given and no specific assets in the jurisdictional territory of the court addressed, the foreign court to which application for enforcement was made would have to conclude that the measure ordered (namely unconditional interim payment) was not an interim measure within the meaning of Art. 24 and was therefore not capable of being the subject of an enforcement order under Title III of the Brussels Convention.[56] The European Court also decided that the foreign court asked to enforce such an order must adopt a cautious approach. Hence, where the court of origin is silent as to the basis of its jurisdiction, the need to ensure that the Brussels Convention's jurisdictional rules are not circumvented requires the foreign court to presume that the court founded its jurisdiction to order interim measures on its national law governing interim measures and not on any jurisdiction derived from the Brussels Convention.[57]

There is a further special condition regarding the cross-border enforcement of interim measures under Art. 24 of the Brussels Convention, established long before the *Van Uden* decision. Under national laws of the EU member states, it is not unusual for certain interim measures to be sought and ordered by the state court ex parte, without any prior notice to the defendant, particularly where it is necessary to preserve an element of surprise. This procedure is an extraordinary exception to the otherwise fundamental rule requiring notice to the defendant, enshrined in Art. 6 of the European Convention on Human Rights. In relation to the Brussels and Lugano Conventions, it is well established, however, that such ex parte orders cannot be enforced by the state courts of other Contracting States. In *Denilauler*

---

[53] *Ibid.*; contra this approach: Advocate LÉGER at para. 136 of his opinion.
[54] Case C-99/96, [1999] E.C.R I-2277 et seq.
[55] *Ibid.*, p. 2314, para. 42.
[56] *Ibid.*, p. 2316 et seq., para. 49 et seq.
[57] *Ibid.*, p. 2318, para. 55.

v. Couchet Frères (1980),[58] the European Court of Justice concluded that ex parte orders for protective measures did not fall within the scope of the simplified procedures for recognition and enforcement set out in the Brussels Convention:[59] these procedures were predicated on the assumption that the defendant had already had an opportunity to be heard in the state court of origin; and there was no justification for their enforcement in another state's court when that precondition was not satisfied.[60] This conclusion was further supported by the existence of special rules in Art. 24 of the Convention which took account of the particular policy issues relevant to provisional and protective measures. Whilst such procedures could be found in the legal systems of member states and might be regarded, where certain conditions were fulfilled, as not infringing the "rights of the defence", the European Court emphasized that the granting of this type of measure requires particular care on the part of the national court and detailed knowledge of the actual circumstances in which the measure was to take effect.[61]

The need to reappraise this restriction has been suggested by certain scholars.[62] It is recognized that on the one hand, the legal systems of all Member States make use of protective measures and that there is a degree of similarity as to the kinds of measures made available.[63] On the other hand, there are considerable differences between States concerning their details;[64] and allowing ex parte orders to be enforced under the Brussels Convention would necessarily assume greater trust between national jurisdictions, an ingredient possibly missing amongst the Member States of the enlarged European Union. At present, there is no immediate prospect of Art. 24 being extended to interim measures made ex parte; and it is significant that the Preliminary Draft of the 1999 Hague Judgments Convention did not even seek to do so:[65] Art. 13 provides for the cross-border enforcement of provisional and protective measures; but recognition or enforcement of such an interim measure may be refused by a foreign court under Art. 28(1)(d) where "the document which instituted the proceedings or an equivalent document, including the essential elements of the claim, was not notified to the defendant in sufficient time and in such a way as to enable him to arrange for his defence".[66] Thus, this requirement will not be fulfilled by an applicant seeking to enforce an ex parte measure, obtained without prior notice to the defendant. Where angels at The Hague feared to tread, certain other angels at UNCITRAL (so it appears) do not.[67]

---

[58] Case 125/79, [1980] E.C.R. 1553 et seq.

[59] *Ibid.*, p. 1571, para. 17.

[60] *Ibid.*, p. 1569, para. 13.

[61] *Ibid.*, p. 1570, para. 15.

[62] KENNETT, *op. cit.*, fn. 32, p. 148 et seq.

[63] *Ibid.*, p. 150.

[64] *Ibid.*

[65] See <www.hcch.net/e/workprog/jdgm/html>.

[66] *Ibid.*

[67] In Europe, the topic of "ex parte" (i.e., without notice) interim measures in arbitration remains highly controversial: Hans van HOUTTE "Ten Reasons Against a Proposal for *Ex parte* Interim

C. National Overview: England, Scotland, Germany, Switzerland and France

Three of these nations (including Scotland as part of the United Kingdom) are EU member states subject to the Brussels Convention (Regulation); the fifth (Switzerland) is linked to the three by the Lugano Convention; and all five have different legal traditions in the field of transnational commercial arbitration, with Scotland and Germany as Model Law jurisdictions. This part of the report is intended to contrast the two-part requirements of a national arbitral system of interim measures: (i) orders by the arbitration tribunal; and (ii) orders by the state court in support of the arbitral process. As a working definition, interim measures are here taken to be measures "to prevent or minimize any disadvantage which may be due to the duration of the arbitral proceedings until the final settlement of the dispute and the implementation of its result".[68]

The first question is: who has the power to grant interim measures? For many years the arbitration tribunal did not usually have the power to order interim measures in many jurisdictions, or if it did, this power was extremely limited.[69] Although this is still the case in certain jurisdictions,[70] the overall approach has long changed. It is now generally acknowledged that the arbitration tribunal should have power to grant specific interim measures. Nonetheless, various national laws differ considerably as to the extent of such powers. In this regard, three different approaches can be distinguished: first, arbitration laws where the law itself vests the arbitration tribunal with a broad power to order interim relief, subject to any agreement to the contrary by the parties; second, laws which grant the power to order certain types of interim relief, but require an agreement of the parties for all other types; and third, laws where an agreement by the parties is required for the tribunal to order interim relief as no powers are implied by law.[71] This exercise

Measures of Protection in Arbitration", Arb Int. (2004) p. 85; DERAINS, "Arbitral Ex Parte Interim Relief", Dis Res Jo 61, p. 203 (also *Gaz. Pal.*2003/2 I, 14); and VAN HAERSOLTE-VANHOF, "Interim Measures of Protection – a European and Continental Perspective" in *ICCA Congress Series no. 11*, p. 150 at pp. 155 and 156; but for the United States, see contra, CASTELLO, Disp Res Jo (2003) p. 60. There is no like controversy over interim measures ordered at a hearing notified to the respondent where the latter declines to participate, also confusingly called "ex parte": see SCC Case 96/2001 in 2 Stockholm Arbitration Report (2003) p. 47 at p. 52.

[68] UNCITRAL Secretariat Report "Analytical Commentary on Draft Text of a Model Law on International Commercial Arbitration", UN Doc. A/C.N. 9/264 (25 March 1985), see H. HOLTZMAN, and J. NEUHAUS, *A Guide to the UNCITRAL Model Law On International Commercial Arbitration: Legislative History and Commentary* (Deventer 1989) p. 542.

[69] See, e.g., the old German arbitration law, where pursuant to Arts. 1039, 1040 and 1042 of the ZPO, solely final arbitral awards could be declared enforceable; and in Switzerland, see Art. 26 of the Swiss Concordat on Arbitration (replaced by PIL Art. 183 concerning international arbitration).

[70] See, e.g., Art. 818 of the Italian Code of Civil Procedure: "The arbitrators may not grant attachments or other interim measures of protection." similarly Art. 753 of the Argentine Code of Civil Procedure.

[71] See LEW, MISTELIS and KRÖLL, *Comparative International Commercial Arbitration* (The Hague 2003) p. 589 et seq.

262 ON ARBITRATION

again demonstrates that comparative laws on interim measures are complicated, including the national laws of the EU member states.[72]

(1) England

(a) Interim relief and the arbitration tribunal

The general powers of an English arbitration tribunal to order interim measures are contained in Sect. 38 of the Arbitration Act 1996, particularly Sect. 38(4) and (6) as regards the inspection, photographing, preservation, custody, detention, sampling, observation of or the conduct of experiment on certain defined property. That property must be the subject of the arbitral proceedings or property as to which any question arises in the proceedings; and it must be owned by or in the possession of a party to the proceedings. Sect. 38(3) grants the tribunal power to order security for the costs of the arbitration. These general powers do not apply if the parties have agreed otherwise; and as regards these measures, England falls within the first category described above. However, for certain other measures, England falls into the second category.

Under Sect. 39 of the Arbitration Act 1996, the parties may agree in writing to confer on the arbitration tribunal a greater power to order on a provisional basis any relief which the tribunal would have power to grant in a final award. These powers include a provisional order for the payment of money by one party to another (including payment on account of the costs of the arbitration) or the disposition of property as between the parties to the arbitral proceedings. These powers have to be conferred by the parties' written agreement, in their arbitration agreement or by arbitration rules incorporated into such agreement (such as Art. 25.1(c) of the LCIA Rules)[73] ; and it is not otherwise a power enjoyed by a tribunal in England: see Sect. 39(4) of the 1996 Act. This restriction was imposed during the consultation process after strong concerns had been expressed by users that these greater powers could be abused by arbitration tribunals. It is not considered possible for an arbitration tribunal in England, under the 1996 Act, to grant any interim measure ex parte, without prior notice to the defendant.

In a recent case, *Kastner v. Jason* (2004),[74] the English court decided that the consensual jurisdiction of the arbitration tribunal included a power by its final

---

[72] For a magnificent explanation, see NEWTON, *The Uniform Interpretation of the Brussels and Lugano Conventions* (Hart 2002) pp. 281-372. See also DICEY & MORRIS, *Conflict of Laws*, 13th ed., vol 1, p. 182 et seq.

[73] Art. 25.1(c) LCIA Rules: the Arbitral Tribunal shall have the power ...

  (c) to order on a provisional basis, subject to final determination in an award, any relief which the Arbitral Tribunal would have power to grant in an award, including a provisional order for the payment of money or the disposition of property as between any parties.

[74] *Kastner v. Jason & Sherman v. Kastner* [2004] EWHC 592 (Ch), The Times, 26 April 2004 (Lightman J.: 23 April 2004; unreported). The arbitration tribunal was the *Beth Din*; and the arbitration

award to make "freezing directions" pending satisfaction of the final award or the provision of security to that end; and accordingly, by virtue of Sect. 39(1) of the 1996 Act, the tribunal enjoyed a power by a provisional award to order the "freezing" of the respondent's only asset in England, namely his home. In circumstances where the allegations against the respondent raised issues of fraud and where he was taking steps both to dispose of his assets in England and emigrate to the United States, the tribunal prohibited him from dealing or disposing of his home without the written permission of the tribunal. The defendant nonetheless sold his home to innocent third parties and escaped to the United States with the proceeds of sale, thereby evading the enforcement in England of the eventual final award. No doubt, the final award could still be enforced against the respondent in the United States under the 1958 New York Convention, if he or his assets can be found; but neither the final nor provisional award can be enforced under English law against the third parties: a "freezing" order creates no charge, lien or other security interest in the property which is the subject matter of the order. It would have been wiser for the arbitration tribunal, with hindsight, to order the respondent to make a monetary payment by a provisional award under Sect. 39(2)(a) of the 1996 Act, which (if unpaid) could have been enforced by the English court before the final award and registered as a legal charge on the property, thereby becoming effective against third parties.

(b) The competence of the state courts

Under Sect. 44 of the 1996 Act, the English court has the same powers to make interim measures in support of the arbitral process as it enjoys for its own legal proceedings. These broad powers include the preservation of evidence, the inspection of any property at issue (even where non-parties are involved, e.g., where situated on a third person's property), the sale of goods at issue, the appointment of a receiver, *Mareva* injunctions and *Anton Piller* orders. If the case is urgent, the court may make orders ex parte for the purpose of preserving evidence or assets, including *Mareva* injunctions: Sect. 44(3). The court can make these orders before the commencement of the arbitration or appointment of the tribunal; but it should not intervene unless a tribunal or any other person with like authority has no power or is unable for the time being to act effectively: Sect. 44(5) of the Act. It may also order that when constituted a tribunal may decide, in whole or in part,

---

agreement under Jewish law included a power to grant an *ikul*, as provided in the *Shulchan Aruch*, *Chosen Mishpat* chapter 73.10:

> Where there is an outstanding debt that is not yet at term, but the lender appears before the Beth Din claiming that the borrower is running down his assets 'and I will not have from what to collect my debt' ... it is a requirement of the Beth Din to hold the funds until time for the repayment comes ... the same applies if the borrower intends to travel overseas.

that the court order should cease to have effect: Sect. 44(6) of the 1996 Act. The court has no power to order security for the costs of the arbitration, such power being reserved to the arbitration tribunal.

The court may grant these measures to assist both an English arbitration and a foreign arbitration outside England: Sect. 2(3) of the 1996 Act. In both cases, the English court may enforce its orders under its draconian powers to punish a defaulting party for contempt of court.

(c) The enforcement of interim measures

Under Sect. 42 of the 1996 Act, unless otherwise agreed by the parties, the English court may order a defaulting party to comply with a "peremptory order" for interim measures made by an arbitration tribunal in England, with the sanctions of contempt of court if the defaulting party fails to comply with the court order. A tribunal may make a peremptory order under Sect. 41(5) of the 1996 Act where a party fails or refuses to comply with any order made by the tribunal, including an order for interim measures under Sects. 38 and 39 of the 1996 Act.

(2) Scotland

(a) Interim relief and the arbitration tribunal

In Scotland, the powers of the arbitration tribunal to order interim measures of protection in an international arbitration are contained in Art. 17 of the Model Law, as enacted by the Law Reform (Miscellaneous Provisions) (Scotland) Act 1990. The range of possible measures is not statutorily defined, although the Model Law's *travaux* are thought by scholars to provide useful examples: "measures for the conservation of goods, such as their deposit with a third person, or the sale of perishable goods", "the opening of a banker's credit", "the use or maintenance of machinery or works or the continuance of a certain phase of construction if necessary to prevent irreparable harm", "securing evidence which would otherwise be unavailable at a later stage of the proceedings" and "the protection of trade secrets and proprietary information".[75] Art. 20 of the Scottish Arbitration Code (a consensual document without the force of law) provides additional examples of interim measures, with the agreed sanction for non-performance of an order barring the claim or defence, as the case may be.

---

[75] DAVIDSON, *Arbitration* (Edinburgh 2000), p. 256. (Domestic arbitrations are not governed by the 1990 Act but fall under the ancient 1695 statute, awaiting reform by the Arbitration (Scotland) Bill 2002, as yet not enacted: see DERVAIRD, et al, "Arbitration in Scotland – A New Era Dawns", 70 Arb (2004) p. 115).

(b) The competence of the state courts

By virtue of Art. 9(1), it is not incompatible with an arbitration agreement for a claimant to request or obtain interim measures from the Scots court before or during arbitration proceedings. Art. 9 confers itself no powers on the Scots court to grant interim measures, it being considered that the court will enjoy the same powers as those applicable to its own legal process and domestic Scots arbitration. These do not include the English form of *Mareva* injunction or ordering security for legal costs, although it could include the provision of security to ensure payment of any award. It is not clear whether the parties can by agreement agree to exclude the powers of the Scots court to order interim measures in support of the arbitral process.[76]

(c) The enforcement of interim measures

Art. 17(2) provides that the arbitration tribunal's decision shall take the form of an award and be enforced by the Scots court accordingly. Outside Scotland, despite its statutory nomenclature, it is questionable whether such an "award" could be enforced under the 1958 New York Convention: it would be self-evidently not a final award but a provisional order. It is also questionable whether the Scots court would enforce or recognize a decision by the arbitration tribunal made ex parte, without prior notice to the respondent party. In two recent cases, *Karl Construction v. Palisade Properties* (2002) and *Barry D Trentham v. Investments* (2002),[77] the Scots court considered the limited extent to which the provisional remedies of protective attachment under Scots law complied with the European Convention on Human Rights; and by legal analogy, the same considerations would apply to an arbitration tribunal, if not more so. It is therefore highly doubtful whether an arbitral tribunal in Scotland could ever make an interim measure ex parte, without any prior notice to the defendant.

(3) Germany

(a) Interim relief and the arbitration tribunal

Under the 1998 new arbitration law, enacting the UNCITRAL Model Law, the provision regarding interim measures is Sect. 1041 of the German Code of Civil Procedure (ZPO),[78] corresponding to Art. 17 of the Model Law. Sub-sect. 1 provides that unless the parties agree otherwise, the arbitral tribunal is entitled, at the request of a party, to grant provisional or protective measures it considers

---

[76] DAVIDSON, *ibid.*, p. 58.

[77] 2002 SLT 312; 2002 SLT 1094 (Neither were arbitration cases; and the Scots court does have a qualified power at a hearing to act ex parte, without prior notice to the defendant).

[78] All references in relation to the German law on arbitration are to the German Code of Civil Procedure (ZPO).

necessary in respect of the subject matter of the dispute. The arbitral tribunal can request adequate security from each party in relation to this measure. Sub-sect. 2 provides that each party may request the German court to permit enforcement of a measure referred to in Sub-sect. 1 unless application for a corresponding measure has already been made to the court. The court may recast such an order if necessary for the purpose of enforcing the interim measure. According to Sub-sect. 3 the court may, upon request, repeal or amend the decision referred to in Sub-sect. 2. According to Sub-sect. 4, if a measure ordered under Sub-sect. 1 proves to have been unjustified from the outset, the party which obtained its enforcement is obliged to compensate the other party for damage resulting from the enforcement of such measure or from its providing security in order to avoid enforcement. This claim may be put forward during the pending arbitral proceedings. These provisions were based on Art. 17 of the UNCITRAL Model Law.[79]

A slight restriction to the exercise of arbitral discretion may result from the requirement that it must be a measure "in respect of the subject matter of the dispute". It will be recalled that similar words were omitted from the new Art. 23 of the 1998 ICC Rules;[80] but in practice, this restriction may not be material. It nonetheless constitutes a substantive requirement with regard to the conditions for issuing interim measures by an arbitration tribunal; and as no further requirements are expressly specified, it has been argued that this is the only restriction.[81] Conversely, it has been argued that the arbitration tribunal should apply Sect. 916 et seq. ZPO which govern interim relief by German courts and provide for additional requirements, such as urgency, the likelihood that the claimant will suffer substantial harm if the relief is not granted and a good arguable case on the merits.[82] When ordering interim relief the arbitration tribunal is given the same power as state courts, including orders for attachment,[83] but it is not limited to the measures provided by Sect. 916 et seq.[84] This can be inferred from Sect. 1041(2)(2), which allows the court to recast an order made by the arbitration tribunal if necessary for proper enforcement.[85] This legal provision ensures that the arbitral order complies with the German enforcement system with its principle of strict certainty (*Bestimmtheitsgrundsatz*).

Sect. 1041 is silent on the issue whether an arbitration tribunal is entitled to order ex parte interim relief. However, Sect. 1042(1) stipulates that the parties

---

[79] The first protocol of the Reform Commission at the Federal Ministry of Justice stated that: "under no circumstances should a provision such as Art. 17 of the UNCITRAL Model Law be omitted from the New Act".

[80] See DERAINS and SCHWARZ, *A Guide to the New ICC Rules of Arbitration*, 1st ed. (Kluwer 1998) p. 274.

[81] S. BANDEL, *Einstweiliger Rechtsschutz im Schiedsverfahren* (Munich 2000) p. 32 B 34.

[82] R. A. SCHÜTZE, Schiedsgericht und Schiedsverfahren, 3rd ed. (Munich 1999) para. 237.

[83] BT-Drs 13/5274, 45.

[84] A. BAUMBACH/W. LAUTERBACH/J. ALBERS/P. HARTMANN, *op. cit.*, fn. 33, Sect. 1041, para. 2.

[85] *Ibid.*, para. 4.

have to be treated equally and have to be heard which suggests that ex parte relief would infringe this principle. However, it has been argued that this principle is only a general procedural rule and that such general rules necessarily provide for exceptions even without mentioning them expressly.[86] As an example of this relationship between rule and exception, the German constitutional guarantee of *audiatur et altera pars* is cited, which broadly corresponds to the general rule of Sect. 1042(1).[87] Art. 103(1) of the German Constitution enshrines this general guarantee without mentioning any exceptions; and it was argued before the Constitutional Court that a judge's order granted on an ex parte basis infringes the constitutional guarantee. The Constitutional Court held that, as an exception to the rule of Art. 103(1), an ex parte order does not infringe this constitutional provision if an ex parte procedure was necessary to secure interests that would otherwise be endangered, as an exception to the rule born from necessity to ensure the effectiveness of the judicial process. A similar line of argument could be developed to provide for an exception with regard to Sect. 1042(1),[88] although Art. 103 does not apply to arbitrations.[89] Conversely, ex parte provisions regarding the enforcement of interim measures exist in Sect. 1063(3), as discussed below, so that it could be argued that if the legislature had intended to allow ex parte relief to be granted by the arbitration tribunal, it would have explicitly done so. The fact that the German legislature did not do so in Sect. 1041 speaks, of course, for itself.

(b) The competence of the state courts
Although Sect. 1041 now hands to the arbitral tribunal the power to grant interim measures, the power of the state courts to grant interim measures both prior to and during the arbitral proceedings is not excluded, as provided by Sect. 1033 (corresponding to Art. 9 of the Model Law). Sect. 916 et seq. is here applicable.[90] The power given to the courts is not subsidiary, but original (*originär*, i.e., equal to the power given to the arbitral tribunal[91]) and therefore gives to parties the freedom of choice. Sect. 1033, restating the wording of Art. 9 of the UNCITRAL Model Law, limits the court to ordering interim measures relating to the subject matter of the dispute in the arbitration proceedings (this mirrors the power given to the arbitration tribunal under Sect. 1041, as discussed above). However, Sect. 1033 does not provide for the court's jurisdiction to grant interim measures: it has only a declaratory function; and the court's jurisdiction must be established under provisions of the ZPO dealing with competence for interim measures of protection (Sect. 1062).

---

[86] J. SCHAEFER, "New Solutions for Interim Measures of Protection in International Commercial Arbitration", 2 EJCL 2, p. 21.

[87] *Ibid.*

[88] *Ibid.*

[89] H. THOMAS/H. PUTZO, *op. cit.*, fn. 34, Einl. I, para. 10.

[90] *Ibid.*, Sect. 1033, para. 2.

[91] *Ibid.*, para. 4.

268 ON ARBITRATION

The principle of concurrent jurisdiction stated in Sects. 1033 and 1041 ensures that parties are entitled to apply to the German court to obtain interim measures, despite the existence of an arbitration agreement. These provisions therefore prevent the old argument that courts lacking jurisdiction to hear disputes within the scope of an arbitration agreement are thereby prevented from ordering any provisional or conservatory measures in support of the arbitral process.[92] The concurrent jurisdiction is limited as the parties are free to agree to remove certain measures from the jurisdiction of the arbitrators, an application of the more general principle of party autonomy.[93] It is also suggested that, conversely, parties can agree not to apply to the courts for provisional or protective measures during the course of the arbitration.[94] However, German scholars express the view that parties cannot opt out of Sect. 1033.[95]

(c) The enforcement of interim measures

Under the old German arbitration law, the enforcement provisions were interpreted to apply only to final awards so that its provisional character excluded any interim measure from enforcement by the German court.[96] Under the new law, the ruling regarding interim measures is classified as a decision (*"Beschluß"*); and interim measures are neither enforceable awards nor are they equated with them.[97] However, as already mentioned above, the new law contains provisions regulating the enforcement of provisional measures ordered by arbitration tribunals. Sect. 1041(2) allows a party to turn to the German court to request enforcement. The court has a certain degree of discretion: it is allowed to verify the validity of the arbitration agreement and to refuse interim measures which have a disproportionate character.[98] Sect. 1041(2) allows the court to recast an order for interim measures, if necessary, for the purpose of enforcing that measure. As indicated above, this reflects the conflict between the flexibility of interim relief available to arbitration tribunals and the limited class of measures available to German courts. Thus, even though an arbitral tribunal sitting in Germany may issue a "freezing" order, it is more than doubtful that a German court will enforce such an interim measure

---

[92] This argument was raised under the New York Convention where it has sometimes been held that by ordering a protective measure the state court contravenes Art. II(3) of the Convention: see FOUCHARD, GAILLARD and GOLDMAN, *International Commercial Arbitration* (The Hague 1999) para. 1307 (hereinafter, *Fouchard Gaillard Goldman*). See also for the United States, *Mc Creary & Tire & Rubber Co. v. CEAT S.p.A.*, 501 F.2d 1032 (3d Cir. 1974) and DONOVAN, *op. cit.*, fn. 7, p. 141.

[93] *Fouchard Gaillard Goldman, ibid.*, para. 1319.

[94] *Ibid.*

[95] BAUMBACH/LAUTERBACH/ALBERS/HARTMANN, *op. cit.*, fn. 33, Sect. 1033(2); SCHAEFER, *op. cit.*, fn. 87, p. 20.

[96] *Bundesgerichtshof, 22 May 1957*, ZZP 427 (1958), see also S. BESSON, *Arbitrage international et mesures provisoires* (Zurich 1998) para. 494 et seq.

[97] BAUMBACH/LAUTERBACH/ALBERS/HARTMANN, *op. cit.*, fn. 33, Sect. 1041(2).

[98] K.P. BERGER, *The New German Arbitration Law in International Perspective* (The Hague 2000) p. 11.

THE NEED FOR CROSS-BORDER ENFORCEMENT   269

since this kind of order is unknown in German procedural law.[99] Furthermore, the German court may, upon request by one party, in accordance with Sect. 1041(3), cancel or amend a decision on enforcement.

Sect. 1025(1) implements the territorial theory, i.e., that the new German law applies only to arbitrations having their seat in Germany. That leaves questions with regard to the enforcement of arbitral interim relief orders made by an arbitration tribunal sitting abroad or measures which need enforcement abroad. It has been concluded by some scholars that the enforcement system established by Sect. 1041 applies only to interim measures which have been issued by an arbitral tribunal sitting in Germany and which are to be enforced by the German courts in Germany;[100] and by others that it has yet to be seen whether the new law allows the enforcement of interim measures granted by an arbitration tribunal sitting abroad.[101] It has also been concluded that the assistance of the German courts in accordance with Sect. 1041 cannot be invoked unless the arbitration tribunal is based in Germany because of a conclusion e contrario from the fact that this provision is not contained in the catalogue of exceptions outlined in Sect. 1025(2)-(4) which provide (inter alia) that Sect. 1033 will also be applicable when the seat of the arbitration is outside Germany.[102]

However, Sect. 1062(2) provides:

> If the place of arbitration in cases referred to in subsection 1 ... No. 3 [enforcement of an order for interim measures of protection by the arbitral tribunal] is not in Germany, the competence for decisions lies with the Court of Appeal in the area where the party opposing the application has its place of business or habitual residence, or where assets of that party or the property in dispute or affected by the measure are located. ...

Hence Sect. 1062(2) may provide for the competence of the German court to enforce an interim measure ordered by an arbitration tribunal where the seat of arbitration lies outside Germany, provided the parties chose German procedural law to apply to their arbitration.[103] Further, Sect. 1062(2) provides that Sect. 1033 also applies to cases where the arbitral seat lies abroad or has yet to be determined, suggesting that a party may then apply directly to the German court for interim measures. Nonetheless, the important questions regarding arbitration tribunals not applying German law as the lex arbitri and the enforcement of interim measures abroad remain unsolved. For these cases, German scholars have suggested the

---

[99] *Ibid.*

[100] *Ibid.*

[101] A. REINER, "*Les mesures provisoires et conservatoires et L'arbitrage international, notamment l'Arbitrage CCI*", 125 J.D.I, p. 853, et seq., at p. 870.

[102] S. BESSON, *op. cit.*, fn. 97, para. 505.

[103] See SCHAEFER, *op. cit.*, fn. 87, p. 22.

drafting of a new international convention for the enforcement of interim arbitral orders, beyond Art. 24 of the Brussels Convention.[104]

Although it appears doubtful, as discussed above, whether arbitral tribunals can grant ex parte relief, German law provides for enforcement proceedings which involve only one party. Sect. 1062(3) provides:

> The presiding judge of the civil court senate (*Zivilsenat*) may issue, without prior hearing of the party opposing the application, an order to the effect that, until a decision on the request has been reached, the applicant may pursue enforcement of the award or enforce the interim measure of protection of the arbitration court pursuant to Section 1041. In case of an award, enforcement may not go beyond measures of protection. The party opposing the application may prevent enforcement by providing as security an amount corresponding to the amount that may be enforced by the applicant.

This provision will help to prevent a party from frustrating an order made by a tribunal before it becomes effective. However, as the right to be heard needs to be given at least minimal acknowledgment, the unheard party is to be heard as soon as possible after the enforcing order has been issued. At that point the order can be confirmed, cancelled or varied by the court. Additionally, the court should always require security for claims for compensation arising in those circumstances.[105]

(4) Switzerland

(a) Interim relief and the power of the tribunal

Swiss law applicable to international arbitrations allows the arbitration tribunal broad authority with regard to the granting of interim measures of protection. Like German law, it falls into the first category outlined above of the various national arbitration laws. Art. 183(1) of the Swiss PIL[106] provides:

> Unless the parties have agreed otherwise, the arbitral tribunal may, at the request of a party, order provisional or protective measures.

Therefore, at least theoretically, the powers conferred are wider than those given by the UNCITRAL Model Law and hence also by German law, because Art. 183(1) omits the phrase "it considers necessary in respect of the subject matter of the dispute". This is probably not of great practical significance: it is assumed that

---

[104] BERGER, *op. cit.*, fn. 99, p. 12.
[105] LEW, MISTELIS and KRÖLL, *op. cit.*, fn. 72, p. 615.
[106] Unless stated otherwise, all articles referred to subsequently are those of the Swiss PIL.

THE NEED FOR CROSS-BORDER ENFORCEMENT 271

provisional measures are necessarily tied to the subject matter of the principal dispute.[107] Paras. 2 and 3 of Art. 183 also provide:

(2) If the addressee of such an order fails to comply therewith voluntarily, the arbitral tribunal may request the assistance of the competent court; the latter applies its own law.

(3) The arbitral tribunal or the state court can make the order of precautionary or conservatory measures contingent upon the furnishing of appropriate security.

A right to an interim measure exists if the order is necessary in order to prevent detriment to the applicant which would be very difficult to make good; and the jurisdiction of the arbitral tribunal may only be exercised when this criterion is fulfilled.[108]

Although there exists in Switzerland no court procedure comparable to the *référé-provision* in France, in certain situations monetary claims may be secured by way of a provisional attachment order. Attachment orders directed against foreign companies and persons residing outside Switzerland may be granted provided the plaintiff is able to show a reasonable probability that it has a claim against the other party and that its claim is due and payable. The plaintiff is not required to establish that the assets are in jeopardy of being removed or disposed of.[109] Only in exceptional circumstances, are attachment orders made by the Swiss court against Swiss residents or Swiss companies.[110] Before the Swiss court, in certain cases of particular urgency, the requirement of the opposing parties' right to be heard can be restricted and the order can be made by the court ex parte, without prior notice to that party. Then, however, the affected parties' right to be heard must be granted as promptly as possible.[111]

In contrast to Swiss court procedures, Art. 183 does not stipulate in which form interim measures have to be ordered by an arbitration tribunal. Normally, these measures will be issued in the form of an order. If the party fails to comply with the order made by the arbitration tribunal, the tribunal does not have the power to impose penal sanctions. Although Art. 292 of the Swiss Penal Code contains a provision allowing for a penalty for failing to comply with an official order, the arbitral tribunal does not make official orders in this sense.[112] Additionally, legal scholars consider that the arbitral tribunal cannot order a party to refrain from disposing of

---

[107] B. PETER, "Switzerland", in A. BÖSCH, ed., *Provisional Remedies in International Commercial Arbitration – A Practitioner Handbook* (Berlin/New York 1994) p. 697 with further references.

[108] S. BERTI, *International Arbitration in Switzerland – An introduction to and commentary on articles 176-194 of the Swiss Private International Law Statute* (Basel 2000) Art. 183, para. 7.

[109] H. FREIMÜLLER, "Attachments and other interim court remedies in support of arbitration", IBL (1984) p. 119 et seq. at p. 120.

[110] *Ibid.*

[111] BERTI, *op. cit.*, fn. 109, para. 8.

[112] *Ibid.*, para. 9.

272   ON ARBITRATION

particular assets.[113] However, Art. 183 speaks generally of conservatory measures, one form of which is the attachment of assets. Hence it has been argued that there is no reason why an arbitration tribunal in Switzerland could not order a party to refrain from disposing of specific assets.[114] Art. 183(3) gives both the arbitral tribunal and state court the competence to grant an interim measure dependent on appropriate security for a possible claim for damages should the order subsequently prove to have been unwarranted.[115] According to many scholars, Art. 183, especially with para. 2, is not limited to interim measures granted by an arbitration tribunal based in Switzerland. It allows equally a tribunal outside Switzerland to order interim measures which will then be enforced with the assistance of the Swiss court, as provided by Art. 183(2).[116]

(b) The competence of the state courts

It is accepted that state courts have the competence to act before an arbitral tribunal is established.[117] Although not specifically enshrined in the Swiss legislation on international arbitration, the majority opinion agrees that the competence of the courts exists side by side with the one of the arbitral tribunal, when formed.[118] The competence of the court is not subsidiary, but equal and concurrent to the competence given to the arbitration tribunal, so that the Swiss court can be requested directly to grant interim relief in support of the arbitral tribunal.[119] Nevertheless, another opinion exists which denies this possibility by virtue of Art. 183(2) and argues that the arbitration tribunal has exclusive competence starting from the moment when the arbitration tribunal is established.[120] The competence of the Swiss court in cases when the arbitral tribunal is seated abroad is derived from Art. 10.[121] It states that Swiss judicial or administrative authorities may enter provisional orders even if they do not have jurisdiction on the merits, a provision consistent with Art. 24 of the Lugano Convention.

---

[113] *Ibid.*, para. 12 with reference to, inter alia, G. WALTER/W. BOSCH/J. BRÖNNIMANN *Internationale Schiedsgerichtsbarkeit in der Schweiz* (Berne 1991) p. 130 et seq.

[114] *Ibid.* with reference to T. RÜEDE/R. HADENFELDT, *Schweizerisches Schiedsgeichtsrecht*, 2nd ed. (Zurich 1993) p. 253.

[115] *Ibid.*, para. 14.

[116] A. REINER, *op. cit.*, fn. 102, p. 868 with further references; but see contra FREIMÜLLER, *op. cit.*, fn. 110, p. 123.

[117] BESSON, *op. cit.*, fn. 97, para. 231.

[118] *Ibid.* with further references, inter alia, WALTER/BOSCH/BRÖNNIMANN, *op. cit.*, fn. 114, p. 143; CRAIG, PARK and PAULSSON, *International Chamber of Commerce Arbitration*, 3rd ed. (New York 2000), p. 579, para. 33.03.

[119] BESSON, *op. cit.*, fn. 97, para. 310 with further references, inter alia, WALTER/BOSCH/ BRONNIMANN, *op. cit.*, fn. 114, p. 146 and W. WENGER, *Die Internationale Schiedsgerichtsbarkeit*, (RJB 1989) p. 337 et seq. at p. 350.

[120] BESSON, *op. cit.*, fn. 97, with further references, inter alia, RÜEDE/HADENFELDT, *op. cit.*, fn. 115, p. 252.

[121] *Ibid.* with further references, inter alia, P. KARRER, "*Les rapports entre le tribunal arbitral, les tribunaux étatiques et l'institution arbitrate*", RDAI (1989) p. 761 et seq. at pp. 768-769.

(c) The enforcement of interim measures

Although the provisional measure ordered by an arbitral tribunal is binding on the respondent party, the tribunal has no sanctions to secure its enforcement. Therefore, Art. 183(2) provides that the tribunal may request the assistance of the competent Swiss court, which applies its own procedural law. The wording of this provision excludes an application by the parties themselves. However, the rights of the parties are not endangered due to the existing concurrent power of judges and arbitrators, described above. In case the tribunal refuses to require the assistance of the court, the party seeking to have the order enforced may require the necessary support from the competent court which will then act in accordance with its local law for interim measures independently from the legal regime set for international arbitration.[122] The competent Swiss court will be the court at the place where the order is to be enforced, which is not necessarily the seat of the arbitral tribunal.[123] When assisting the tribunal, the court should confine itself summarily to establish that a valid arbitration agreement existed and that the order was made by a tribunal which was validly constituted.[124] Although the law does not restrain the arbitration tribunal with regard to the content of the order it grants, the court will be confined to the methods of enforcement which its own law provides.[125] However, the court has no power to examine the substance of the order except from the point of view of Swiss public policy.[126] Swiss law does not contain a provision on the enforcement of provisional measures in Switzerland ordered by a foreign state court, save for Art. 24 of the Lugano Convention.[127]

(5) France

(a) Interim relief and the power of the tribunal

French law does not contain an express provision allowing the arbitral tribunal to grant interim relief; and hence it falls into the third category, French law nonetheless recognizing the conferral of powers on the tribunal by the parties.[128] It has long been accepted that the arbitral tribunal can grant interim measures, as long as the arbitration clause or arbitration rules incorporated contain words to that effect; and that this can be done in the form of a partial award[129] or procedural order.[130]

---

[122] BESSON, *op. cit.*, fn. 97, para. 511.
[123] BERTI, *op. cit.*, fn. 109, para. 17.
[124] *Ibid.*, para. 18 with reference to WALTER/BOSCH/BRÖNNIMANN, *op. cit.*, fn. 114, p. 149.
[125] BERTI, *op. cit.*, fn. 109, para. 18 with reference to Sect. 306 et seq. ZPO ZH.
[126] *Ibid.*
[127] PETER, *op. cit.*, fn. 108, p. 709. Peter states that this is also the case when provisional measures ordered by a foreign tribunal are to be enforced in Switzerland.
[128] LEW, MISTELIS and KRÖLL, *op. cit.*, fn. 72, p. 591.
[129] REINER, *op. cit.*, fn. 102, p. 866.
[130] BUCHMAN, "France" in A. BÖSCH, ed., *op. cit.*, fn. 108, p. 264.

274 ON ARBITRATION

In practice, only the French court can order urgent measures which are immediately enforceable; and given the court's concurrent jurisdiction with a tribunal, such urgent measures are usually ordered by the court before the formation of the tribunal.

The types of provisional remedies generally available from the court under French law are (a) attachments (*saisies conservatoires*), (b) judicially granted guarantees (*sûretés judiciaires*) such as provisional judicial mortgages (*hypothèques judiciaires provisoires*) or judicial pledges (*nantissements judiciaires*) and (c) injunctions and temporary restraining orders (*ordonnances de référé*). Although under French law (a) and (b) are theoretically available by an ex parte procedure while measures in accordance with (c) are granted only after both sides have been heard, any arbitration tribunal will be extremely reluctant to grant interim relief on the basis of an ex parte application as failure to hear both sides might expose the arbitrator to an accusation of bias.[131] Furthermore, arbitrators are not empowered to order a judicially granted guarantee[132] or an attachment, as attachments are seen to be part of the enforcement process, which falls within the jurisdiction of the state courts.[133] Nevertheless, as in Belgium, the arbitral tribunal is entitled to impose a fine (*astreinte*) if the opposing party does not comply with the relief granted.[134] This remedy is in practice infrequently ordered and still more rarely enforced.

(b) The competence of the state courts

As the competence of the arbitrators to grant interim relief is not written into French law, a strong assumption is made that French courts maintain jurisdiction even when faced with the existence of an arbitration clause. Indeed, in domestic arbitration, the French courts consistently decide that "where a state of urgency has been duly established, the existence of an arbitration agreement cannot prevent the exercise of the powers of the courts to grant interim relief".[135] That approach is viewed to be equally applicable to international arbitration, as the courts are the only authorities capable of taking urgent measures which are immediately enforceable, regardless of whether or not a tribunal is constituted.[136] Thus, the Paris *Cour d'appel* held that due to the urgency in the case it was able to order the escrow of disputed shares pending a decision by the arbitrators on the substance of the dispute and to prohibit a company from issuing new shares intended for the directors in breach of a shareholders' agreement.[137] Hence, the state courts remain competent side by side with the arbitral tribunal; and in cases which do not involve the

---

[131] *Ibid.*, p. 260.

[132] *Ibid.*

[133] *Ibid.*; LEW, MISTELIS, and KRÖLL, *op. cit.*, fn. 72, p. 599, *Fouchard/Gaillard/Goldman, op. cit.*, fn. 93, para. 1334 et seq.

[134] BUCHMAN, *op. cit.*, fn. 131, p. 258.

[135] See, e.g., Cass. 3e civ., 3 June 1979, *Société d'exploitation du cinema REX v. Rex*, 1979 Bull. Civ. III, No. 122; Rev. arb. (1980) p.78.

[136] *Fouchard Gaillard Goldman, op. cit.*, fn. 93, para. 1328

[137] *Ibid.*, with reference to CA Paris, 12 Dec. 1990, *Terex v. Banexi*, 1991 Bull. Joly 595.

référé-provision, this jurisdiction is concurrent and not subsidiary.[138] It is accepted, however, that the parties can explicitly or impliedly agree not to apply to the courts for interim relief during the arbitration proceedings.[139]

French law also provides for the *référé-provision*. It enables a creditor to benefit from emergency procedures to have its rights enforced, fully or in part.[140] In a case where the existence of the obligation is not seriously in dispute,[141] a party can require a summary order for interim payment of a debt or damages from the defendant. Due to the hybrid nature of this measure, the issue of whether a party which has agreed to be bound by an arbitration agreement can nevertheless seek a *référé-provision* is a delicate matter. In order to determine whether a *référé-provision* should be granted, the French court must examine the substantive claims of the party alleging that it is the creditor since the issue whether the creditor's claim is "seriously disputable" or not, is a substantive issue. Therefore, when ruling on this issue, the court is liable to infringe the arbitrators' jurisdiction over the merits of the parties' dispute.[142] On the other hand, the decision taken by the court will have a provisional nature and does not bind the arbitral tribunal or other court which has jurisdiction over the merits. The possible infringement of the arbitrators' authority is therefore intended to be temporary only. Nevertheless, it can have considerable impact since the party whose claim has been satisfied (even if only temporarily) no longer has the burden of maintaining legal or arbitral proceedings; and it is no longer, as a paid creditor, at the same risk of its co-contractor becoming insolvent.[143]

The option of applying to the court for a *référé-provision* remains open where the claim on which the application is founded is a substantive issue covered by the jurisdiction of an arbitral tribunal, but only under certain conditions. These conditions are, first, that the arbitral tribunal is not constituted; and, second, that the party requesting the relief proves urgency.[144] This will limit the infringement of the arbitral tribunal's jurisdiction over the merits of the dispute and takes into account that in the absence of urgency, the requesting party could simply promote the constitution of the arbitral tribunal and ask the arbitrators to rule on its claim.[145]

---

[138] BESSON, *op. cit.*, fn. 97, para. 413.

[139] *Fouchard Gaillard Goldman, op. cit.*, fn. 93, para. 1319 with reference to Cass., 1e civ., 18 Nov. 1986 *Atlantic Triton*.

[140] For the possibility of obtaining the full payment of a debt by an emergency hearing in France: see CA Paris, 20 Jan. 1988, *V.S.K. Electronics v. Sainrapt et Brice International S.B.I.*, Rev. arb. (1990) p. 651.

[141] See Arts. 809(2) and 873(2) of the French Code of Civil Procedure.

[142] *Fouchard Gaillard Goldman, op. cit.*, fn. 93, para. 1340. See also DERAINS and SCHWARTZ, *op. cit.*, fn. 81, at pp. 277-279 re the *Eurodisney* Case, Rev arb. (1966) pp. 191-233.

[143] *Ibid.*

[144] *Cour de cassation*, 1ère Ch. civ., 29 Nov. 1989, *Société Balenciaga v. Société Allieri et Giovanozzi*, and *Cour de cassation*, 1ère Ch. civ., 6 March 1990, *Société Horera v. Société Sitas*, Rev. arb. 1990 p. 633; *Fouchard Gaillard Goldman, op. cit.*, fn. 93, paras. 1343-1345; CRAIG/PARK/PAULSSON, *op. cit.*, fn. 119, p. 556, para. 31.03.

[145] *Fouchard Gaillard Goldman, op. cit.*, fn. 93, para. 1345.

276   ON ARBITRATION

Hence, the jurisdiction of the *référé-provision* as compared to the powers of the arbitral tribunal is considered subsidiary. As with "ordinary" court assistance related to interim relief during arbitration proceedings, the court's jurisdiction to order a *référé-provision* can be excluded by the parties, either directly or by reference to arbitration rules.[146] Equally, the parties may agree their own form of *référé provision*, such as the ICC's pre-arbitral referee procedure; and the French court will not treat the referee as an arbitrator, nor subject his decision to an action to set it aside as an arbitral award.[147]

(c) The enforcement of interim measures

The enforcement of interim measures in France is made by the state courts. To make an interim measure more effective with regard to its enforceability, the requesting party can ask the arbitration tribunal to state in the award that it shall be provisionally enforceable against the losing party.[148] The award will be subject to exequatur by the French courts. The French courts will not enforce foreign protective measures originating from a foreign arbitrator or a foreign national court, unless an exequatur has been granted.[149]

D. Conclusion

There is no great overall crisis in regard to interim measures; and yet there is useful work still to be done for transnational trade. Within arbitration tribunals and the state courts at the arbitral seat, national regimes for interim measures appear to work satisfactorily, albeit differently, in the several jurisdictions surveyed above. Under these national laws, the system needs no urgent or wholesale amendment.[150] The problem is the cross-border enforcement of an interim measure made by an arbitration tribunal or state court against a party situated in a different jurisdiction: the lack of a universal regime for cross-border enforcement is a curious gap in the modern system of international commercial arbitration. Within the European Union and other countries subject to the Brussels and Lugano Conventions, a partial solution exists, after the *Van Uden* case, for the cross-border enforcement of interim measures ordered by a state court in support of the arbitral process; and it would of course be possible to create like solutions on a regional or bilateral basis. This would be a pity. It would be far better to create a uniform solution on a broader basis, consistent with these Conventions and the 1958 New York

---

[146] *Ibid.*, para. 1342.
[147] GAILLARD and PINSOLLE, "The ICC Pre-Arbitral Referee: First Practical Experiences", Arb Int (2004) p. 13.
[148] BUCHMAN, *op. cit.*, fn. 131, p. 267.
[149] *Ibid.*, p. 268.
[150] REDFERN, "Interim Measures" in *The Leading Arbitrators' Guide to International Arbitration* (NY 2004) p. 217 at p. 242.

Convention, where cross-border enforcement of both court and arbitral orders for interim measures was possible in certain circumstances, subject to safeguards. For practical purposes, the former reform regarding court-ordered interim measures is more significant, given that an arbitral tribunal can only be formed after the outbreak of the parties' dispute.

The principal barriers to reform are four-fold. First, the subject matter is juridically complicated, technical and controversial, as shown by the difficulties, past and present, arising from Art. 24 of the Brussels and Lugano Conventions and the limited progress so far made at the UNCITRAL Working Group on Arbitration. Second, the cross-border enforcement of certain interim measures made by a court (or arbitration tribunal), particularly an interim order for payment, requires strict safeguards to avoid the risk of forum-shopping, oppression and injustice; and certain other measures should perhaps not qualify for cross-border enforcement at all, particularly interim measures by a state court made ex parte, without any prior notice to the defendant (and still more so by an arbitration tribunal). Third, it would be wrong to limit the enforcement of measures to cases of urgency: there are many interim measures which are useful, if not essential to the arbitral process, without always being urgent; and yet, as soon as urgency is dispensed with, the non-nuclear family of non-urgent interim measures will inevitably attract controversy.

The last difficulty is not the least: without an international court imposing a uniform interpretation (such as the European Court of Justice interpreting Art. 24 of the Brussels Convention),[151] it is imperative that the drafting of any supplementary treaty or non-legislative text be right and be seen to be right by contracting states and users of international commercial arbitration. This debate cannot therefore be resolved within the community of international arbitration specialists: many others now have too much at stake in the debate's outcome. In particular, rightly or wrongly, there is a growing lack of confidence in the even-handedness of the international arbitral process; and there are now too many fears, in Felix Frankfurter's words, of "legal maladjustment" in regard to interim measures. To this end, the UNCITRAL project on interim measures and the Hague Conference (or its successor) may have to work closely together. It will also involve others; and it may take time, much longer than was first thought. Otherwise, all the work that has been done and remains to be done may remain a purely bureaucratic exercise. Moreover, given that what is here required is the best but not the most urgent solution, even the merely good, still more the less than good, remains paradoxically "the enemy of the best".

---

[151] The hopeful dreams expressed by Judges Schwebel and Holtzmann (for the Creation and Operation of an International Court of Arbitral Awards and for the Enforceability of Awards) remain dreams: see HUNTER, MARRIOTT and VEEDER, eds., *The Internationalisation of International Arbitration* (1995) pp. 109 and 115.

15

The Transparency of International Arbitration

Process and Substance

A. Introduction: Arbitral Confidentiality in Related Court Proceedings

Much has been written about the confidentiality and privacy of arbitration proceedings from *Esso* (1995)[1] via *Bulbank* (2000)[2] to *Aegis* (2003);[3] but, until recently, almost nothing has been said about the secrecy of court proceedings relating to a confidential arbitration or confidential award.

Whereas by their arbitration agreements parties may expressly agree to differing degrees of secrecy in relation to their own arbitration, no similar agreement is usually made in relation to court proceedings ancillary to that arbitration; no institutional or other arbitration rules, to my knowledge, currently provide expressly for the secrecy of such court proceedings, still less the express waiver of any legal right to a public court hearing otherwise enjoyed by a party;[4] and of course, in any event, such court proceedings are rarely consensual. In non-arbitration proceedings in court, subject only to specific exceptions, state courts do not usually sit in secret, delivering secret judgments and making secret orders.

---

[1] *Esso Australia Resources Ltd and others v. The Hon Sidney James Plowman, The Minister for Energy and Minerals and others*, 10 Commonwealth Law Reports 183 (1995). See also expert reports by Bond, Boyd, Lew and Smit in 11 *Arb Int* 231 (1995).

[2] Supreme Court, 27 October 2000, *Bulgarian Foreign Trade Bank Ltd v. AI Trade Finance Inc*, 15(11) Mealey's IAR B 1 (2000), 13(1) WTAM 147 (2001).

[3] *Associated Electric & Gas Insurance Services Ltd v. European Reinsurance of Zurich* [2003] UKPC 11, [2003] 1 WLR 1041.

[4] For example, Article 25(4) of the UNCITRAL Arbitration Rules provides that the arbitration hearings shall be held "in camera"; and by Article 32(5), the award "may be made public only with the consent of both parties". The broadest institutional rules on the confidentiality of arbitration, Article 30 of the LCIA Rules and Articles 7376 of the WIPO Arbitration Rules, are either silent on the confidentiality

---

On Arbitration. Edited by: Sam Wordsworth KC and Marie Veeder, Oxford University Press. © Oxford University Press 2023. DOI: 10.1093/oso/9780192869135.003.0015

THE TRANSPARENCY OF INTERNATIONAL ARBITRATION 279

Such secrecy is the historical hallmark of absolute tyranny; and its despotic attractions remain self-evident. Hence Article 6(1) of the European Convention on Human Rights is designed to protect the citizen from secret justice by requiring "a fair and public hearing".

A quarter of a century ago, in its report on the *Axen* case (1981), the European Commission on Human Rights explained the rationale for Article 6:

> [...] the public nature of the proceedings helps to ensure a fair trial by protecting the litigant against arbitrary decisions and enabling society to control the administration of justice ... Combined with the public pronouncement of the judgment, the public nature of hearings serves to ensure that the public is duly informed, notably by the press, and that the legal process is publicly observable. It should consequently contribute to ensuring confidence in the administration of justice.[5]

That rationale has since been applied time and time again by the European Court of Human Rights, most authoritatively in *Werner v. Austria* (1997) where the Court described the visible and public administration of justice as the guarantee of a fair trial "which is one of the fundamental principles of any democratic society".[6] This publicity is even more important for the court judgment than for the court hearing itself.

In a legal system based on judicial precedent, the rationale can be extended to the need to develop the law by judicial reasoning and to allow legal practitioners to practise their profession with access to published law reports. In English legal proceedings, the English judge takes the law from the practitioners in the case; and he has no law clerk nor even sufficient time to conduct any significant legal research by himself. As Lord Justice Denning said in one of his early judgments: it was

> unfortunate that the principle I have enunciated was not drawn to the attention of the court in [an earlier judgment of the Court of Appeal], but that was my fault because I was counsel in the case.[7]

---

of legal proceedings ancillary to the arbitration or merely limit disclosure to the extent necessary in connection with court proceedings on the award.

[5] Commission Report of 14 December 1981, B.57 (1982-1983).

[6] *Werner v. Austria* (1997) 26 EHHR 310.

[7] *Cassidy v. Minister of Health* [1951] 2 KB 343, 363, referring to *Gold's Case* [1942] 2 KB 293 (cited in Pannick, *Judges* (1987), p 209).

280   ON ARBITRATION

Without publicly reported reasoned judgments available to practitioners, the English legal system could not work as it does, the common law and statutory interpretation could not develop as it has; no useful textbooks could be written; and law schools would eventually fall silent, even Queen Mary College.

B. Established Confidentiality

Until recently, only three jurisdictions had addressed expressly the confidentiality of the arbitral process in court proceedings ancillary to the arbitration. The first was France, in *Aita v. Oijeh* (1986).[8] The losing party to an English arbitration there challenged the award, which had been made by Lord Wilberforce in London, before the Paris Cour d'appel. The French Court rejected the challenge because it was legally hopeless to try to set aside under the new 1981 Decree an award made outside France; but more significantly, the Court ordered the applicant to pay significant costs (200,000 FFrs) for having in bad faith caused in court a public debate on matters which should have remained confidential between the parties. Where applications to set aside an award are made without bad faith or abuse of process, the court judgment and award in France become public documents, as Dr Crépin's archival work has demonstrated.[9]

The second was Bermuda. In enacting the UNCITRAL Model Law in the Bermuda International Conciliation and Arbitration Act 1993, the Bermudan legislator added two important provisions: Section 45 provided that, subject to the Bermuda Constitution, proceedings in any Bermudan court under the 1993 Act shall be heard otherwise than in open court on the application of any party to the proceedings; and Section 46 contained a detailed code imposing restrictions on the reporting of court proceedings not so heard in open court. Under this statutory scheme, there is no judicial discretion to hold a hearing in open court; and only a limited discretion to direct that any information from a private hearing can be published. There is, however, a judicial discretion to permit the publication of a judgment "of major legal interest" in law reports and professional publications, subject (on a party's application) to the removal of names and other details of the case and a delay in publication, not to exceed ten years.

---

[8] *Aita v. Oijeh*, Cour d'appel de Paris, 18 February 1986, *Dalloz Jur* 1987, 339 and *Rev Arb* 1986, 583, note Flécheux, *Dalloz Jur* 1987, 339 and note Gaillard, *Dalloz Chron* 197.153, 155. (Professor Emmanuel Gaillard was Counsel for the successful respondent in this case).

[9] Sophie Crépin, *Les sentences arbitrales devant le juge français: pratique de l'exécution et du contrôle judiciaire depuis les réformes de 1980-1981* (Paris, 1995).

One of the factors which led to this legislation was the enforcement in Bermuda of a Soviet award made "in camera" by the Foreign Trade Arbitration Commission in *SNE v. Joc Oil* (1984). Under earlier legislation enacting the 1958 New York Arbitration Convention, the Bermuda court proceedings were held in public; and the court file, including the Russian original text of the confidential award, remained publicly available in the archives of the Bermuda Supreme Court. This led directly to its publication (*inter alia*) in the *ICCA Yearbook*.[10] What was thereby lost in confidentiality was subsequently gained by English jurisprudence: the Bermuda Court of Appeal's judgment and the FTAC award led significantly to the English Court of Appeal's decision in *Harbour v. Kansa*, re-stating the modern English rule on the separability of the arbitration clause, which is now codified in Section 7 of the English Arbitration Act 1996.[11]

The third was a case in New Zealand. In *TV New Zealand* (2000)[12] a confidential award made in New Zealand was subjected to court proceedings in New Zealand. The award dealt, apparently, with the private life of a well-known public figure in highly embarrassing personal detail (although his company was the successful party in the arbitration). The award was challenged by the losing party under New Zealand's arbitration legislation apparently in good faith, without any abuse of process. Of course, the press were eagerly awaiting the public unveiling of this award in these court proceedings. However, the public figure did not wish his private life to be publicly unveiled; and the New Zealand Court had therefore to weigh the award's confidential status under Section 14 of the New Zealand Arbitration Act 1996[13] with New Zealand's constitutional requirement for a public court hearing. Balancing these two conflicting texts, the learned Judge decided in favour of a public hearing; and the confidential award then became publicly available to the press. Curiously, the challenging party then discontinued its court application.

---

[10] *Sojuznefteexport (SNE) v. Joc Oil Ltd*, (1990) XV YBCA 384 (Bermuda Court of Appeal, 7 July 1989); (1993) XVIII YBCA 92 (FTAC Award in English translation; 1984. The original Russian text remains unpublished).

[11] *Harbour Assurance Co Ltd v. Kansa General International Insurance Co Ltd* [1993] 1 Lloyd's Rep 455, [1993] QB 701, per Hoffmann LJ at p. 723F.

[12] *Television New Zealand Ltd v. Langley Productions Ltd* [2000] 2 NZLR 250; note D. Williams (2000) NZLR 61.

[13] Section 14 [entitled: Disclosure of Information Relating to Arbitral Proceedings and Awards Prohibited] provides:

(1) Subject to subsection (2), an arbitration agreement, unless otherwise agreed by the parties, is deemed to provide that the parties shall not publish, disclose, or communicate any information relating to arbitral proceedings under the agreement or to an award made in those proceedings.

(2) Nothing in subsection (1) prevents the publication, disclosure, or communication of information referred to in that subsection-

(a) If the publication, disclosure, or communication is contemplated by this Act; or

(b) To a professional or other adviser of any of the parties.

282 ON ARBITRATION

These French and New Zealand cases illustrate different aspects of the same problem, without offering any effective solution approaching the Bermudan legislation.

C. Confidentiality and English Law

To these three jurisdictions addressing the issue a fourth has recently been added. In *Bankers Trust (2005)*,[14] relating to an award made in London by a Swedish sole arbitrator, the English Court of Appeal had to consider the question whether and, if so, to what extent English court proceedings challenging the award were secret. The leading judgment was delivered by Lord Justice Mance (as he then was), who before his appointment to the English bench was a prominent arbitration practitioner and commercial arbitrator; and, thankfully, this important judgment was not delivered in secret. It merits the widest attention, together with the judgment of the Commercial Court (Mr Justice Cooke), which was upheld on significantly different grounds.

The case concerned a contractual dispute between two entities of the City of Moscow and two commercial bankers, under Russian substantive law. The arbitration took place by express agreement under the UNCITRAL Rules; and accordingly the arbitration hearings were held "in camera"; and in the absence of all parties' consent otherwise, the award remained confidential and unpublished. The bankers then challenged the award under Section 68 of the English Arbitration Act 1996 in the English Court, on the basis that the arbitrator had committed a "serious procedural irregularity" affecting the award. It was alleged that the arbitrator had failed to act fairly and impartially in accordance with the mandatory requirements of Section 33 of the 1996, to comply with the requirements as to the form of the award and to decide all issues put to him, thereby frustrating the object of the arbitration (namely the fair resolution of the parties' dispute). It was accepted that the bankers made their challenge to the award in good faith; and their applications were heard by the Commercial Court "in private". The arbitrator was a nominal party to those proceedings but not present or there legally represented. In March 2003 after a hearing lasting five days, Mr Justice Cooke in a reasoned judgment dismissed the applications. The issue then arose as to whether this first judgment was public or secret.

The bankers wanted this judgment to be secret, limited only to the disputing parties. The City of Moscow wanted the judgment to be public. As recorded in the later judgments, its "expressed reason" for wishing publication was a desire to demonstrate to the international financial markets or investment community generally

---

[14] *Department of Economics, Policy & Development of the City of Moscow & another v. Bankers Trust and another* [2005] QB 207, on appeal from the Commercial Court [2003] 1 WLR 2885 (Cooke J).

that the arbitration award, deciding that the City of Moscow had not committed any financial default, had been the subject of a detailed and careful scrutiny by the English Commercial Court which had rejected all attacks upon the award.[15] Its *unexpressed* reason was possibly to achieve indirectly what it could not achieve directly, namely the public dissemination of the award's reasons which may have been quoted, extensively, in Mr Justice Cooke's first judgment.[16] It seems unlikely that Moscow's tax-payers would be equally interested in the interpretation of Section 68 of the English Arbitration Act 1996 on "serious procedural irregularity". It also appears that the City of Moscow's desire for publicity post-dated the first judgment: it had not earlier requested the court hearing to be held in public; it had made no earlier application that this first judgment should be delivered in public, even in an edited form; and it had even sought a specific order from the arbitrator confirming the confidentiality of the arbitration, given that the arbitration raised "highly sensitive political issues so far as Moscow itself was concerned".[17] Mr Justice Cooke concluded that the City of Moscow had provided no good reason for requiring publication of his first judgment.[18] If hard cases make bad law, bad cases can make for interesting law.

This dispute over secrecy was fully argued by the parties at a later court hearing, also held in private; and in June 2003, Mr Justice Cooke delivered a second reasoned judgment that his first judgment was secret. This second judgment, however, was public and not secret. He decided that the privacy of an English arbitration and the confidential status of an English award did not automatically transfer to an English court hearing on a challenge to that award under the 1996 Act; but nonetheless, applying his judicial discretion under the relevant English Civil Procedural Rules (CPR r 62.10),[19] he decided that his first judgment should be known only to the disputing parties. He also decided that the result of the first judgment as formally recorded in the Court's order, "like the result of the arbitration" could be published by any party. The Court's order is therefore publicly known; but the

---

[15] As described by the Lord Justice Mance, see paragraph 6 at page 214C of the law report.

[16] See Cooke J's second judgment, paragraph 44 at p 2897 of the law report.

[17] See Cooke J's second judgment, paragraphs 27 & 28 at p 2893 of the law report. In sensitive commercial litigation, the English Court can readily "edit" its public judgment: for example, see the remarkable judgment of Mustill J in *Spinneys v. Royal Insurance* [1980] 1 Lloyd's Rep 406, a case involving Lebanon's civil strife, where on the parties' request the learned judge refrained from citing the names of the many witnesses whose lives could be endangered from undue publicity (although this trial took place in public). Using its powers to hear cases in camera, the Commercial Court and Court of Appeal have heard appeals from awards stated in the form of a special case (where lives were at risk from publicity); and more recently, part of the *AEGIS* appeal in the Privy Council, supra note 3, was heard under non-reporting restrictions, given that the issue was whether or not the award was confidential (see also reference below).

[18] See Cooke J's second judgment, paragraph 45, at p 2898 of the law report.

[19] CPR r. 62.10 (for full citation, see footnote 31 below):

> (1) The Court may order that an arbitration claim be heard either in public or private ... (3) Subject to any order made under paragraph (1) ... (b) all other arbitration claims will be heard in private.

284   ON ARBITRATION

reasoned first judgment itself remains unavailable to the public; and, perhaps surprisingly, for a long time its terms were not even made available to the arbitrator whose conduct of the arbitration and award had been so thoroughly vindicated by Mr Justice Cooke.[20] Less surprisingly, given the powers of the English Court for contempt of its orders, this first judgment has not become available in *samizdat*, not even in *Mealey's* published in the USA; and it remains tantalizingly secret still. In the Court of Appeal, Lord Justice Mance identified a "spectrum" of confidentiality. At one end was the confidential arbitration; in the middle was the court hearing on the arbitration application under Section 68 of the 1996 Act; and at the other end was the Court's formal order following its reasoned judgment. A formal order could be public: its bare recital that an application had been granted or dismissed (with costs) could disclose little or nothing. A reasoned judgment might well disclose much about a confidential award or arbitration; but, in the learned Judge's words:

> there could be no question of withholding publication of reasoned judgments on a blanket basis out of a generalised, and in my view, unfounded, concern that their publication would upset the confidence of the business community in English arbitration.[21]

The decision to permit or withhold publication of a judgment would therefore depend upon the discretion of the Court, fitted to the particular case-at-hand; and as regards CPR 62.10, the learned Judge significantly referred to the rule as a "starting-point" only, and expressly not as a "presumption".[22]

In the end, Lord Justice Mance decided against publication of the first judgment, concluding:

> Here the parties agreed contractually on a confidential alternative to litigation. The Arbitration Act 1996 and the CPR allow access to the court in the public interest, in order to support fundamental principles of fairness governing arbitration. It cannot be a breach of UNCITRAL Rules to invoke the court's supervisory jurisdiction. It could serve as an inappropriate deterrent to such access if the making of such an application were to dispose a court to order, at the instance

---

[20] By accident, however, certain members of the public attended part of the court hearing; and by another accident the Commercial Court made this first judgment publicly available as a result of which the full text was published in good faith on Lawtel's web-site (the judgment was not itself marked "private"), with a separate summary issued to its 15,000 or so subscribers. (Lawtel is an electronic on-line library for legal practitioners). The latter error was soon corrected upon Bankers Trust's urgent protest; but Lawtel's brief summary was allowed to remain in circulation by the Court of Appeal (from which it appears that this first judgment may be of general importance to the interpretation and application of Section 68 of the English 1996 Act, including the scope of an arbitrator's duty to give "reasons" in his award).

[21] Supra note 14, at para 41.

[22] *Ibid*, at para 42.

of a party, a public hearing or judgment in circumstances when the sensitivity and confidentiality of the subject matter would otherwise point in an opposite direction.[23]

In his concurring judgment, Sir Andrew Morritt VC also referred to this same spectrum, concluding:

Plainly not all the arbitration claims referred to in CPR r 62.10(3)(b) need to be treated as confidential. And those that do will vary in the extent to which they should be treated and the method by which to do so.[24]

These appellate judgments repay quiet study; and there is time here only to select two points. The first arises from the change in English legal terminology from court hearings "in chambers" to court hearings "in private" under the CPR, which was effected in 2002 under Lord Woolf's reforms enacted by the Civil Procedure Act 1997. Under the old pre-Woolf rules, the phrase "in chambers" did not refer to a secret hearing "in camera", but rather to the practice that such chambers' hearings could be heard in the judge's room rather than a courtroom.[25] In the Commercial Court, however, arbitration hearings "in chambers" usually took place in the same court-room as a public hearing.

Under Lord Woolf's reforms to civil procedure, the use of all Latin tags being considered antiquated, the phrase "in camera" disappeared; and the new CPR introduced in 2002 the more limited concepts of a "public" hearing and a "private" hearing which was secret. Many commentators wrongly assumed that the new phrase "in private" in the CPR was to be equated with the old phrase "in chambers", without attracting the attributes of a secret hearing formerly "in camera". It is well settled, however, both before and after the CPR, that generally a judgment delivered in a court hearing in chambers or in private does not thereby automatically acquire a secret status; and even the exclusion of the public or the press at a private hearing does not generally amount to a ban on the later publication of what took place at that hearing. As Mr Justice Cooke decided, the general position, apart from arbitration, is that a court judgment "is open to the world unless the court should decide otherwise".[26] However, arbitration is placed in a special category under the CPR.

As recited by Lord Justice Mance's judgment, it was the practice before the 1996 Arbitration Act, under the old RSC Order 73, to hear applications challenging an award in public. As a result, the law reports contain many judgments on such

---

[23] *Ibid*, at para 47.

[24] *Ibid*, at para 56.

[25] *Hodgson v. Imperial Tobacco* [1998] 1 WLR 1056. For court hearings "in chambers", see *Scott v. Scott* [1913] AC 417, at pp 436–437, 443, 445–446, 453, 476–477.

[26] The second judgment, paragraph 15 at page 2889 of the law report.

arbitral challenges; and they still fill many footnotes in *Mustill & Boyd, Merkin* and *Russell*. Generally, even judgments delivered in chambers could be released by the judge into the public domain, notwithstanding the joint protests of the parties, if the judge thought the judgment raised a point of law of general public importance. There are many reported judgments under the old 1950-1979 Acts which fell into this category. In the days before Queen Mary's School of International Arbitration existed, when no law school taught the law and practice of English arbitration, that judicial practice was the way which allowed many of us to learn about English arbitration. Moreover, in the Commercial Court, every Friday morning, there would be crammed before the Commercial Judge a mass of Junior Counsel, Solicitors and Solicitors' Managing Clerks, all awaiting their turn to make their applications in chambers. In the meantime, each had to listen and learn from the earlier applications. It was there, whilst waiting, that we heard the young Mustills, Binghams, Savilles and the much-missed Brian Davenport argue the finer points of English arbitration law; and it was that same practice which allowed the Commercial Judge and practitioners to keep the pulse of London Arbitration. All this took place "in chambers"; it was far from secret; and it was a very good arbitration school.

The question is whether the regime under the 1996 Act was intended to be different from its statutory predecessors. When it was brought into effect in January 1997, the 1996 Act was accompanied by a new Order 73 of the Rules of the Supreme Court, the predecessor to the later CPR. This new Order 73 provided, in the language of the earlier rules, that court applications under the 1996 Act would ordinarily be heard "in chambers"; and in a formal statement by the Commercial Judge in January 1997, delivered in public, it was noted that special arrangements would be required to publicise court decisions on the 1996 Act amongst judges and practitioners to facilitate "consistency of approach".[27] The school of arbitration, in one form or another, would continue through publicity. As recited in Lord Justice Mance's judgment, however, the full implications of a court hearing "in chambers" remained relatively unexplored in 1997 (para. 18). The present CPR was introduced by the Rule Committee after consultations in 2001, including the Commercial Court Users' Committee. It was a very English form of consultation; and few can therefore remember being consulted; or if they were, whether the implications of the rule change were fully brought to their conscious understanding. There is always a danger for the user and practitioner in changing procedural rules; and the CPR changes very often. All this explains why many practitioners read Mr Justice Cooke's second judgment with surprise and dismay: it seemed to put off forever the third edition of *Mustill & Boyd* and make it increasingly difficult for practitioners to advise on the application of the 1996 Act if important judgments on the 1996 Act were now predominantly to be delivered in secret.

---

[27] Practice Note (Arbitration: New Procedure) [1997] 1 WLR 391, per Colman J.

THE TRANSPARENCY OF INTERNATIONAL ARBITRATION   287

It is fair to add that a careful reading of Lord Justice Mance's judgment can assuage many of these fears. But not all. How can the Rule Committee consider making such important substantive changes to the law and practice of English arbitration, without the same kind of genuine consultation which preceded the 1996 Act in regard to the confidentiality and privacy of the arbitral process? In the quotation from Bentham cited by Lord Justice Mance,[28] taken from Lord Shaw's speech in *Scott v. Scott* (1913):[29]

> Publicity is the very soul of justice ... it keeps the judge himself while trying under trial;

to which Lord Shaw wisely added:

> [...] there is no greater danger of usurpation than that which proceeds little by little, under cover of rules of procedure, and at the instance of judges themselves.

It cannot be assumed that English legal practitioners are sufficiently astute or informed to detect always the effects of minor changes in the wording of the CPR; and it ought not to take Lord Justice Mance to rescue London Arbitration from such effects.

The second point is whether English arbitration proceedings and awards are implicitly so confidential under English law; and, if so, whether they should be. Lord Justice Mance started his judgment with a statement of broad principle:

> Among features long assumed to be implicit in the parties' choice to arbitrate in England are privacy and confidentiality.

This generalisation was irrelevant to the case, given the parties' express agreement to the UNCITRAL Rules; and it is somewhat controversial as an unqualified statement of English law. The first hint that an arbitration hearing was generally "confidential" under English law, as opposed to being merely "private", came with Mr Justice Leggatt's judgment in *The Eastern Saga* (1984), twenty years ago; and the recent decision of the Privy Council in *Aegis* (2003) suggests there may exist an important distinction between confidentiality and privacy, with only the latter providing the general principle implicit under English law.[30] There may also be an important distinction between the privacy of the arbitration hearing (including the arbitral deliberations) and the status of the arbitration award.

---

[28] Paragraph 15 at pp 217-218 of the law report.
[29] [1913] AC 417.
[30] *Oxford Shipping Company Limited v. Nippon Yusen Kaisha (The Eastern Saga)* [1984] 2 Lloyd's Rep 373; *Associated Electric & Gas Insurance Services Ltd (AEGIS) v. European Reinsurance of Zurich* [2003] UKPC 11, [2003] 1 WLR 1041 (PC), per Lord Hobhouse.

288   ON ARBITRATION

As a result of this attribution of confidentiality, confirmed by the CPR, both Mr Justice Cooke and the Court of Appeal treated arbitration applications as a special hybrid category. Under the CPR, court applications under Section 68 fall to one side; and court judgments under Section 69 of the 1996 Act, on appeals from an award on questions of English substantive law, fall to the other side of this category: CPR Rule 62.10(3)[31] imports a different rule that such hearings will be heard "in public", subject to an order otherwise. Both are only "starting points" and not fixed rules or even a presumption. The most important aspect of Lord Justice Mance's judgment, therefore, is that all these questions eventually turn not upon any absolute rule applicable to a uniform special category applicable to all arbitrations but upon a judicial discretion whether or not to apply the rule or its exception in any particular case, depending upon its own individual circumstances. Moreover, the recent practice of the Commercial Court confirms that the *Bankers' Trust* case, contrary to initial fears, has not led to a judicial reaction against publicity for important judgments on the law and practice of arbitration. English arbitration has not become a state secret.

A pragmatic balance has to be struck; but publicity, or transparency, remains essential to the working of the 1996 Act and more generally to the public acceptance of arbitration.

At one extreme, arbitration is sometimes seen as so private, so unaccountable, so suspicious to third parties, practitioners, regulators and other state agencies, that only full publicity can demonstrate how it really works. But with full publicity, other parties may turn away from arbitration completely; or at least from those jurisdictions which do not respect a reasonable amount of privacy agreed by the parties. At the other extreme, the lack of all confidentiality in court may lead certain commercial parties to establish a private and confidential appellate process, separate from state courts. But strict privacy at this appellate level could lead increasingly to the atrophy of arbitration law. In the middle lies the compromise suggested by the Bermudan legislation and so carefully analysed by Lord Justice Mance. It is reflected elsewhere by the practice of "anonymisation" in Germany and

---

[31] This rule provides:

    (1) The court may order that an arbitration claim be heard either in public or in private.

    (2) Rule 39.2 does not apply.

    (3) Subject to any order made under paragraph (1) –

        (a) the determination of –

            (i) a preliminary point of law under section 45 of the 1996 Act; or

            (ii) an appeal under section 69 of the 1996 Act on a question of law arising out of an award, will be heard in public; and

        (b) all other arbitration claims will be heard in private.

    (4) Paragraph (3)(a) does not apply to –

        (a) the preliminary question of whether the court is satisfied of the matters set out in section 45(2)(b); or

        (b) an application for permission to appeal under section 69(2)(b).

Switzerland, whereby reported judgments have names and identifying details removed from the law report of the court proceedings on an arbitration award[32]; and both in Norway and more recently in New Zealand, legislative proposals have been made to strike a new balance between public justice and private confidentiality for arbitration parties.[33]

D. Conclusion

In conclusion, we do need a new "spectrum" which is sufficiently flexible to cater for all horses for all courses. For some arbitrations, even the existence of the dispute will be strictly confidential. For others, the full award can be a public document. Whilst a successful party should not have its confidential secrets disclosed in court proceedings, it is also essential that arbitration law develops publicly with legal reasoning by state judges, for the ultimate benefit of all arbitration users themselves. The world of arbitration would be much the poorer, for example, without *Tobler v. Blaser*,[34] *Gosset*[35] and the *BGH Decision of 27 February 1970*[36] from Switzerland, France and Germany on the legal autonomy of the arbitration clause from the substantive contract in which it is embedded; and without the public judgments in *Bankers Trust*, so too would English law. If the position were ever to change significantly in the future, the next anniversaries of the School of International Arbitration would probably, of necessity, be much less interesting and much, much shorter.

---

[32] An excellent analysis on the "anonymisation" of German judgments may be found at: http://www.jurpc.de/aufsatz/20040073.htm.

[33] See Clause 14F et seq of the New Zealand Law Commission's proposed Arbitration Amendment Bill 2004, whereby the Court may derogate from the general principle of public court proceedings on the application of any party and only if the Court is satisfied that the public interest in having the proceedings conducted in public is outweighed by the interests of any party to the proceedings in having the whole or any part of the proceedings conducted in private.

[34] Swiss Federal Supreme Court, *Tobler v. Blaser*, BGE 59 I 177 (on separability).

[35] Cour de cassation, 7 May 1963, *Ets Raymond Gosset v. Carapelli*, 91 Clunet 82 (1964), Dalloz (1963) p. 545, with note J. Robert (on separability).

[36] BGH Decision of 27.2.1970 – VII ZR 68/68(2) OLG Cologne, translation in English (1990) 6 *Arb Int* 79, with notes by Schlosser and Boyd.

16

Free Spirits—the Search for "International" Arbitration

As a philosophical question of seemingly high importance for the modern state of international commercial arbitration, the question is frequently asked by many: which came first – the arbitral egg or the arbitral chicken? The egg-loving tribe proclaim the Great Egg as the exclusive source of all that is good in arbitration. Conversely, the chicken-loving tribe contend that the Big Chicken laid the first arbitral egg. Other arbitral tribes disagree with both.

These tribes cannot all be right; but perhaps none need be completely wrong. As a matter of biology, an avian egg had necessarily to be fertilised, laid and hatched before the world saw its first arbitral chick; but that does not necessarily mean that this was an arbitral egg or that the arbitral chick's ancestors were necessarily arbitral chickens. The process of arbitral evolution, or alternatively intelligent design, suggests that such parents could have been ducks or swans (or both). There was obviously a slow transition from the primeval slime of the pre-arbitral world, not limited to one egg or one chicken; and that transition is only part of a continuous rainbow, even now stretching towards a distant golden horizon.

In the modern arbitral world, whilst there is much room for philosophical debate as to the origins of the arbitral species and its current effects, there is equally room for wise figures of moderation, even of immoderate moderation, in actual practice. These are required to interpret the rainbow's different colours and to work with different historical traditions; in other words, the free spirits of practical common sense of whom Me Serge Lazareff is an outstanding example both in Paris and elsewhere, as an international commercial arbitrator and arbitral statesman.

Before turning to arbitral philosophy, it is first necessary to acknowledge the enormous significance of France to the development of international commercial arbitration. It has been rightly said by several scholars (none French) that the modern practice of arbitration owes a disproportionately large debt to the conceptual advances of French scholars, judges and arbitrators in Paris and Dijon[1].

---

[1] For example, see Arthur von Mehren, "International Commercial Arbitration: The Contribution of the French Jurisprudence" (1986) Louisiana Law Review; and Jan Paulsson, "Arbitration in Three Dimensions" (2010) LSE, p. 15.

On Arbitration. Edited by: Sam Wordsworth KC and Marie Veeder, Oxford University Press. © Oxford University Press 2023. DOI: 10.1093/oso/9780192869135.003.0016

FREE SPIRITS—THE SEARCH FOR "INTERNATIONAL" ARBITRATION   291

The ICC Court was formed in Paris almost a century ago; and its symbiotic relations with the Cour d'appel de Paris has benefited international commercial arbitration everywhere, not limited to ICC arbitration or the law and practice of French arbitration. Together with the long tradition of French teachers of arbitration, from Professor David to Professor Fouchard, students of French arbitral traditions have long spread their influence around the world. Long may it continue.

It is equally necessary to acknowledge the serious philosophical nature of this French contribution, most recently by Mr Gaillard's book entitled, originally in the French version (here translated): "The philosophical aspects of the law of international arbitration"[2]. It is perhaps no surprise that the book's English title, subsequently published, has dropped the word "philosophical"; although the substitute word, "theory", is scarcely an improvement to most English arbitration specialists[3]. In England, we do not often do 'philosophy' or even 'theory' in arbitration. Like Molière's Monsieur Jourdain, we barely do arbitral prose and certainly not arbitral poetry; and it suffices for us if the thing works in practice, without necessarily working in theory. And so, as with many texts by French scholars, we receive these philosophical treatises much as English heathens received St Augustine at Canterbury.

Has the time now come for English arbitration to try serious French philosophy? The English Arbitration Act 1996 was a wonderful thing in 1996, a seemingly whole conceptual loaf and not the feared 'half a loaf'. It was then often said (particularly by its authors) that the 1996 Act was not only the best thing since sliced bread but also the best thing before that thing (whatever it was) was bettered by sliced bread. But the 1996 Act today, more than a decade later, particularly after the *West Tankers* case, appears significantly deficient; and the 1996 Act's partial codification of English law, albeit significantly incomplete, has erected a high wall against possible judicial reforms at common law. What is broke now needs to be fixed, by judge or legislator; and serious philosophical theories go down well with both; or at least better than no serious theories at all.

English arbitration has hitherto been essentially pragmatic, historical and fragmented. It is not based upon a single coherent theory. Apart from a few notable exceptions, notably Francis Mann, Michael Mustill, Stewart Boyd and Roy Goode, no English arbitration scholar has attempted in recent times to tackle the legal theory of English arbitration, as opposed to describing it. Until fairly recently, arbitration was not taught at any English universities: outside international law, it was not regarded as an academic subject. It is now, as demonstrated by the hundreds of students of arbitration attending Queen Mary College, King's College and the LSE (taking London University as only one of several academic institutions in the United Kingdom). Each of these arbitration courses necessarily addresses the law and practice of French arbitration.

---

[2] Emmanuel Gaillard, "Aspects philosophiques du droit de l'arbitrage international" (Livres de Poche de l'Académie de droit international de La Haye; 2008, Nijhoff).

[3] Emmanuel Gaillard, "Legal Theory of International Arbitration" (2010, Nijhoff).

The French thesis espouses the concept of a truly autonomous legal order for international arbitration, independent of any single national legal system, rooted in the parties' will and their freedom of choice. Such an arbitration is not legally tied to the law of the place of the arbitration, or the law applicable to the parties' contractual or other relationship, or any of their personal laws; the parties and the tribunal are not constrained by law to apply any national law to their arbitration agreement or their dispute; and the legal result, the award, is supranational and not the creature of any national legal system. Accordingly, amongst its many consequences, that autonomous legal order will permit an arbitrator to complete his or her arbitral mission without necessary regard for territorial laws, court orders or other national and regional legal impediments, such as an anti-arbitration injunction or the Brussels Regulation. It will also allow a French court to enforce an award which has been annulled by the courts of a foreign friendly state, such as Switzerland or England in the *Hilmarton* and *Putrabali* cases, under Article VII of the New York Convention.

International arbitration, under French legal theory, is thus not the private sector of a particular state's dispute resolution process; nor is an arbitrator a subordinate tribunal operating as a junior court to any state's superior courts. It is quite remarkable that France, with the top-down traditions of Louis XIV and Napoleon has achieved this result without significant legislation or government decree. Is this French theory, however, a sufficiently complete theory for international arbitration in England? Is it in fact simply a rule of French law and not an autonomous doctrine at all? As Mr Gaillard himself acknowledges in his work, who frees the slave, but the slave-master? And why is it that French law distinguishes so greatly between domestic awards made in France and international awards? There remains much to be understood, apparently, even in France.

This is not a civil-common law divide. The French thesis is bluntly rejected in the work of Jean-Francois Poudret and Sébastien Besson, francophone scholars in Switzerland in another haven for international arbitration[4]. Most recently, it has been specifically attacked by Jan Paulsson in his recent LSE lecture, in favour of a more three-dimensional pluralistic legal theory of arbitration, albeit replacing the awkward concept of "a delocalised award" with, perhaps, the still more awkward " pluralocalised award"[5]. Yet Mr Paulsson's antithesis may be more helpful to the future of transnational arbitration, particularly within the European Union. These different approaches all raise important questions; the current philosophical debate is illuminating; and it must surely inure eventually to the benefit of all; but the final answers, if any, cannot yet be surveyed. As someone once said, there may be a Third Way; or at least, a quicker way in England to justify necessary reforms to the 1996 Act.

---

[4] Poudret & Besson, *Comparative Law of International Arbitration* (2007; Sweet & Maxwell).
[5] Jan Paulsson "Arbitration in Three Dimensions" (2010; LSE).

FREE SPIRITS—THE SEARCH FOR "INTERNATIONAL" ARBITRATION   293

A particular English obstacle derives from a fundamental principle of English law, most forcibly expressed in *Doleman v Osset* (1912) and since restated many times[6], that the English Court always has jurisdiction over any arbitration seated in England. A contractual provision purporting to exclude a party's right to sue in the English Court will not be recognized by the Court[7]. As a result, the English enactment of the 1923 Geneva Protocol and the 1958 New York Convention requires the English Court only to "stay" an action brought by a party in breach of an arbitration agreement; and an arbitration agreement does not operate in England as a defence to a claim or a bar to the Court's jurisdiction, as opposed to barring the Court's exercise of jurisdiction. This might be thought in practice to be a distinction of little importance; but it remains a fundamental English principle, now enshrined in the 1996 Act. As a result, Section 1(c) of the 1996 Act distorts Article 5 of the UNCITRAL Model Law: the latter provides, in mandatory language: "In matters governed by this Law, no court shall intervene except where so provided in this Law"; whereas the former provides, in discretionary language only: "In matters governed by this Part, the Court *should* not intervene except as provided by this Part" (emphasis supplied).

This approach precludes in English law the negative effect of Kompetenz-Kompetenz, as espoused under French law. That doctrine's absence fed the English Court's need for anti-suit injunctions to protect English arbitrations, now proscribed by the European Court of Justice in *West Tankers*. It seems unlikely that the Brussels Regulation will be amended to feed the English Minotaur; hence the need to modify English law. Given the role of English judges, the common law and the bottom-up libertarian traditions of arbitration in England since the 17th century, it would not seem impossible for England to achieve a necessary reform – but for the straightjacket now imposed by the 1996 Act. It has always been very difficult to amend English arbitration statutes, as demonstrated by the 19th Century failures of Lord Brougham's statutory reforms in 1853 and Baron Bramwell's draft arbitration code of 1884-1889, before the Arbitration Act 1889.

After 1889, there were green shoots of internationalism in England. It was the United Kingdom which prompted the 1923 Geneva Protocol; and it was an English judge, Sir Francis Mackinnon, who largely drafted its text as the chairman of the expert group advising the League of Nations. France was then a rural backwater in trans-border arbitration. Unfortunately, this green shoot soon died. By 1927, the United Kingdom had lost active interest in trans-border arbitration, albeit ratifying the 1927 Geneva Convention. For that drafting committee, working in French, the Board of Trade had even appointed a non-specialist barrister who did not speak French. Then the United Kingdom opposed, with unfortunate success, Professor David's UNIDROIT Model Law of Arbitration in 1932-1936; it took the

---

[6] *Doleman v Ossett* [1912] 23 KB 257.
[7] See Mustill & Boyd, Commercial Arbitration (2nd ed), p. 57.

United Kingdom 17 years to enact the New York Convention with the Arbitration Act 1975; and more than 10 years were required to reflect the UNCITRAL Model Law in the 1996 Act.

There were other green shoots raised by several of our greatest English figures in arbitration. First, Lord Wilberforce, the judge, in 1970: In *James Miller v Whitworth Street Estates* [8], the House of Lords decided that the right of a party to ask for a case to be stated under Section 21 of the Arbitration Act 1950 was essentially a matter of procedure. Lord Wilberforce, after argument from counsel (which included a young Lord Hope), expressly left open whether that rule applied to an ICC arbitration taking place in England. His actual words were: "It is a matter of experience that numerous arbitrations are conducted by English arbitrators in England on matters governed by contracts whose proper law is or may be that of another country, and I should be surprised if it had ever been held that such arbitrations were not governed by the English Arbitration Act in procedural matters, including the right to apply for case stated. (*I leave aside as a special case arbitrations conducted under the rules of the International Chamber of Commerce, though even these may be governed by the law of the place of arbitration.*)" [emphasis supplied]. We should note well the cautionary phrase "may be"; and we should also note also that it was a very gratuitous obiter dictum. That particular green shoot withered with the *Kuwait Prison Case* in 1972[9] in the Commercial Court and, later, with the Arbitration Act 1979.

Next, Lord Wilberforce, the legislator, said this in the House of Lords on the second reading of the bill that became the 1996 Act: "Nobody can say that this Bill does not give maximum effect, in spite of a few mandatory provisions, to the will of the parties .... I would like to dwell for a moment on one point to which I personally attach some importance. That is the relation between arbitration and the courts. I have never taken the view that arbitration is a kind of annex, appendix or poor relation to court proceedings. I have *always* wished to see arbitration, as far as possible, and subject to statutory guidelines no doubt, regarded as a free-standing system, free to settle its own procedure and free to develop its own substantive law – yes, its own substantive law. I have *always* hoped to see arbitration law moving in that direction. That is not the position generally which has been taken by English law, which adopts a broadly supervisory attitude giving substantial powers to the court of correction or otherwise, and not really defining with any exactitude the relative positions of the arbitrators and the courts...."[10] [emphasis supplied].

---

[8] *James Miller v Whitworth Street Estates (Manchester) Ltd* [1970] AC 583. (This was a decade before the decision of the Paris Cour d'appel in *General National Maritime Transport Co v Götaverken*, 1980 *Rev arb* 107).

[9] *The Ministry of Public Works of the Government of Kuwait v Gruppo International Contracting Company (Cooke J; 17 May 1971, unreported)*. However, the arbitration agreement there expressly subjected the ICC arbitration to English procedural law, to be held in England.

[10] Hansard, col 778, 18 January 1996.

FREE SPIRITS—THE SEARCH FOR "INTERNATIONAL" ARBITRATION   295

We should note the "always" – both of them; and the importance attributed, as in French law, to "the will of the parties". With these words, Lord Wilberforce welcomed the Bill (later, the 1996 Act), although, on the whole, he said that he did not find that it went as far as he would have liked personally. Apart from the reference to statutory guidelines, his speech could have been written in Dijon or Paris. Later, Lord Wilberforce's views as a legislator received strong judicial approval in Lord Steyn's judgment in the House of Lords' decision in *Lesotho v Impregilo* (2005)[11].

There were other early signs. Mr Justice Megaw in *Orion v Belfort* (1962) recognised the possibility, under English law, that private parties could agree that a part or the whole of their legal relations should be decided by an arbitration tribunal on the basis of principles of international law[12]. Under the influence of Dr Mann's scholarly writings, this became English law and was later codified in Section 46 of the 1996 Act. Another green shoot was *Bremer Vulkan*[13], with the speech of Lord Diplock abjuring any general supervision by the English Court of English arbitration tribunals. The Court of Appeal, for the conjoined sister-case *Gregg v Raytheon*[14], had the benefit of the expert evidence of Dr Frédéric Eisemann, the former Secretary-General of the ICC Court; it rejected that evidence but, in substance, his approach was accepted by the House of Lords in *Bremer Vulkan*, in reversing the decision of the Court of Appeal[15]. That approach is now reflected in the 1996 Act.

There is therefore no need for the reform of English law to start with a blank piece of paper. There is still less any need for aspirants to the new age of arbitration to over-simply if Francis Mann's approach or Michael Kerr's skills as a caricaturist of 'free-floating arbitration'. It is certainly not possible to dismiss Dr Mann's many scholarly writings, particularly his famous essay "Lex Facit Arbitrum"[16], as an example of one-dimensional arbitration or "dogmatic territorialism"[17]. Dr Mann's rigorous approach subjects every commercial arbitration to the *lex fori* or, rather, *lex loci arbitri* as the law of the arbitral seat applying to that arbitration. That law is different from the substantive law of the parties' contract and even the law applicable to the parties' arbitration agreement[18]. As was later decided by the English Court of Appeal, citing Dr Mann's work, the parties' agreement to English arbitration permitted the English Court to support that arbitration by appointing an arbitrator even where there was a jurisdiction clause in favour of a foreign court[19].

---

[11] *Lesotho v Impregilo* [2006] AC 221 (HL).
[12] *Orion v Belfort* [1962] 2 Lloyd's Rep 257, 264.
[13] *Bremer Vulkan* [1981] AC 909 (HL).
[14] *Gregg v Raytheon* [1980] 1 Lloyd's Rep 255 (Court of Appeal).
[15] *Ibid*, see Lord Denning MR (at p. 274) and Roskill LJ (at p. 279).
[16] F.A. Mann, "Lex Facit Arbitrum", first published in *International Arbitration, Liber Amicorum for Martin Domke* (1967) and re-published in (1986) *Arbitration International* 241.
[17] Jan Paulsson's LSE Lecture, p. 2.
[18] Dr Mann's scholarly writings on the *lex arbitri* and applicable law are analysed by Lord Collins in his contribution on Dr Mann, in *Jurists Uprooted* (2004), at pp. 428–429.
[19] *Naviera Amazonica Peruana SA v Cia Int. de Seguros del Peru* [1988] 1 Lloyd's Rep 116.

296   ON ARBITRATION

Until the Brussels Regulation and *West Tankers*, this English approach seemed to work well in practice. There is only now an apparent problem.

Professor Goode concluded his comparative survey on the *lex loci arbitri*: "The objections to concept of the stateless award are overwhelming and should now be universally accepted. None of the arguments in favour of the stateless award has explained why, apart from *force majeure*, the courts of the enforcement state [i.e. France under the 1958 New York Convention] should be considered to have a prerogative denied to others. If, which is not suggested, there is to be a single court the judgments of which are in principle to have effect *erga omnes*, it should be the court of the seat."[20]. This was hardly dogmatic territorialism; but it reflects the practical importance of the courts at the arbitral seat. Before the 1996 Act, as Lord Wilberforce noted, the English theory of arbitration rested on the legal relationship between the arbitration seated in England and the English Court. Under the 1996 Act, as indicated above, the Court still retains, in theory, a permanent jurisdiction over English arbitrations and English arbitration agreements, which cannot be ousted by the will of the parties. Hence, the English Court, as codified in the 1996 Act, cannot recognise the negative effect of "Kompetenz-Kompetenz" (as in France).

This approach was best illustrated in the introductory words to the first edition of Mustill & Boyd's *Commercial Arbitration* (published in 1982): "The law of private arbitration is concerned with the relationship between the courts and the arbitral process". Neither author was then a friend of the French thesis, as stated in the foreword: "... What is quite clear is that the concept of the trans-national arbitration has found no place in the law and practice of England." Yet the second edition of Mustill & Boyd (published in 1989) contains a long explanatory footnote to this passage; and the authors' *Companion* on the 1996 Act (published in 2001) strikes a markedly different approach – as Lord Steyn noted in *Lesotho*. It would seem that, indirectly, the 1996 Act has significantly influenced the orthodox approach to English arbitration. English doctrinal writings remain short on theory and subtle, if not opaque; and the subject-matter is always dependent on the viewer's perspective of arbitration. In particular, it would seem that now, more than a decade after the 1996 Act, the most significant relationship with English arbitration lies not with the English courts but with the regulators in London and Brussels. These regulators need a coherent legal theory of English arbitration. Let me list two examples:

First, Section 46 of the 1996 Act permits parties to agree that their arbitration tribunal, unlike the English Court, can apply a non-national law or rules of law, including Jewish law and the Sharia. This was no accident: the use by religious tribunals of the English arbitral process, subject to consent, arbitrability and enforcement by the English Court was specifically considered by the Departmental

---

[20] Sir Roy Goode, "The Lex Loci Arbitri in International Commercial Arbitration" in *Lex Mercatoria: Essays on International Commercial Law in Honour of Francis Reynolds* (2000) 245, 267.

Advisory Committee (DAC) and Department of Trade and Industry (DTI) in the drafting of this new provision. In 2008, over a decade later, several national newspapers, both tabloid and non-tabloid, began a malign campaign against so-called "Islamic courts" in London and four other English cities, which had apparently decided 100 cases in 2007 as arbitrations under Section 46 of the Act.

There were and remain legitimate queries as to what exactly was taking place in these Islamic tribunals, albeit limited to civil disputes referred by consent; but the critical tone was set by the Daily Mirror. Its headline read: "Secret Sharia Law Courts already used in UK Cases". And it continued: "The Muslim Tribunals are exploiting a loophole in the Arbitration Act 1996 which allows sharia courts to be classified as arbitration courts, with their rulings binding in law". The Sun's headline was unusually muted: "Sharia Law gets OK in Britain"; and it continued: "Islamic law has been ushered into Britain by the back door", quoting the Shadow Home Secretary as saying: "If these tribunals are passing binding decisions I would consider such action unlawful." Perhaps this shadow minister, now the Attorney-General, was misquoted; but it would certainly be wrong to criticise the then Labour Government for a statute passed by an earlier Conservative administration and also to rebuke any arbitration tribunal from sitting in private or to consider its awards, if validly made, as legally binding on the consenting parties.

The point here is not the populist or political reaction to arbitration, but the silence from the responsible Minister nominally responsible for the 1996 Act, a well-known senior politician not known for his shyness. Why that silence? He was not a lawyer; and he was new to arbitration. Worse, like many laymen, we must suspect that he could not understand it. In the absence of a coherent theory, we should accept that such non-comprehension is shared by many as regards both domestic and international arbitration. In fact, we must doubt whether more than a few thousand persons in England understand anything about arbitration; and that is our fault. As English scholars and practitioners, we do not explain English arbitration, as in France; and in England it will remain difficult for us to explain English arbitration to non-specialists without some coherent legal theory.

The second example is the European Commission, following the Heidelberg Report and the decision of the European Court of Justice in *West Tankers*. We may see, probably next year, new draft regulations from Brussels regarding the Arbitration Exception to the Brussels Regulation. France doubtless remains ready to impose her 'de facto' veto, armed with her own powerful legal theory of international arbitration. Other states will point to the subordinate role of mediation within the European legal space, as expressed in the Mediation Directive. The choice currently appears to lie between two extremes: (i) nothing: and (ii) a form of Arbitration Directive. The latter would be catastrophic for the New York Convention and for arbitration generally in the European Union. The former, even if garlanded with comforting words to assuage the United Kingdom, would leave untouched the problems for English arbitration caused by the *West Tankers* case.

In conclusion, what can we now do in England to meet the inevitable demands of the regulators in Brussels and Whitehall for a legal theory of English arbitration from England's judges and legislature? This task will not be easy. We can, however, learn much from the French school of arbitral philosophy, befriending both arbitral eggs and arbitral chickens; but we can also learn from the free spirits of international arbitration, such as Me Lazareff.

17

The Role of Users

A. Introduction

The user of arbitration is an important economic, legal and necessary fact. Economically, because it is not the ICC Court of Arbitration that pays the fees and expenses of the arbitrators but the users of international arbitration, and it is also the users who pay the administrative fees of the ICC. And who pays the lawyers as the parties' legal representatives in the arbitration? It is again the users or, increasingly the users' insurers and funding agents. Legally, because without users as disputing parties there could be no dispute referable to arbitration. Finally, if users settled their disputes amicably, there could be no arbitration or award. In short, users are a necessary fact to every international arbitration: it is their arbitration.

Accordingly, in practice and theory, users and lawyers should share substantially the same interests, because the latter's clients lie at the heart of the arbitration. To a material extent, at least objectively, many of these identical interests are shared by arbitrators and arbitral institutions. In reality, as we all know, this is not quite so.

Increasingly, most one-off users agree to international arbitration unwittingly or with less than fully informed consent. With the emergence of a dispute, users may appear fleetingly at the origin of the arbitration, and they may then attend the first procedural meeting, if held in person, to sign the terms of reference and influence, marginally, the timetable for the arbitration. Thereafter, users generally disappear behind their lawyers into an arbitral form of Siberian exile. It is not that users, in the field of international arbitration, are treated as customers who are always wrong or less than right. It is more a case of the vanishing user, leading to an assumption that users' interests are exactly the same as lawyers' interests. It need not be so—and it used not to be so.

B. The Sewage Farm Case

My first arbitration, about a sewage farm in the desert many decades ago, took place in a country in the Persian (or Arabian) Gulf. It was a building dispute

On Arbitration. Edited by: Sam Wordsworth KC and Marie Veeder, Oxford University Press. © Oxford University Press 2023. DOI: 10.1093/oso/9780192869135.003.0017

300 ON ARBITRATION

between the contractor, a well-known local construction company, and the employer, the Ministry of Public Works of that country. There were no factual witnesses, because the two individuals most familiar with and mainly responsible for both the building project and the dispute had been appointed as the two arbitrators for the contractor and the employer, namely the contractor's chief executive officer and the Ministry's chief engineer. The hearing was commendably short, and the arbitration quickly concluded with an award, which unsurprisingly was not unanimous. It seemed to reflect the decision of the third arbitrator, an electrical engineer, who no doubt thought it useful to hear privately, firsthand, from those most knowledgeable about the project and the parties' dispute. The award was fair; and the arbitration was regarded as a success by both users. Because this was my first arbitration, I assumed that this was how most international arbitrations could be conducted: by the users, for the users and, of course, with the informed consent of the users. I soon learnt that this was a very unusual form of arbitration, viewed with horror by most other lawyers who knew of it. Such an arbitration, even by consent of the users, could probably not be held even under existing arbitration rules. Even if it could survive the application of the new ICC Rules, it could not survive the English Arbitration Act 1996, nor French law.[1] And so, over the years, I learnt that international arbitration has surprisingly little to do with users, beginning with the drafting of arbitration agreements long before any dispute. Again, that was not always so.

C. The Brunel Case

There is an early 19th century case in the English courts about the great Anglo-French architect and engineer, Isambard Kingdom Brunel (1806-1889), the celebrated builder of steamships, bridges, tunnels and railways. He was also a great entrepreneur and businessman, and as the employer (of which he was at least a shareholder), he regularly drafted an early form (almost) of the FIDIC Conditions of Contract. For his grand projects, the agreement between the employer and the contractor appointed in advance as arbitrator of all disputes the engineer nominated by the employer who best knew the employer's mind, namely Brunel. The law reports record a challenge by the contractor against the employer engineer on the basis that the engineer (Brunel) was necessarily

---

[1] See, for example, the recent decision of the Cour d'appel de Reims of 2 November 2011 in *Avax v. Tecnimont*.

dependent upon and partial towards the interests of the employer. That challenge was rejected by the House of Lords, notably because the contractor had agreed to the engineer in advance in the contractual documentation. Given that agreement between the two users and Brunel's undoubted reputation as a true gentleman and a great engineer, the English court was content to leave him to decide all disputes under the agreement.[2] At the time, the idea of appointing the two users as co-arbitrators, let alone one user as sole arbitrator, worked successfully with the users' consent. We probably cannot re-introduce today the practices of those good old days. Form has overtaken substance in many parts of our lives, and arbitration is much more adversarial and is now played for much higher stakes. In a more recent case, we see a different situation where interference in the separate relationships between the users, the lawyers and the arbitrators can prove fatal to an arbitration.

D. The Turner Case

In the *Turner* case, there was a dispute—well known at the time but since happily resolved—about the right of foreign lawyers to represent a foreign party in a Singapore arbitration, without the risk of arrest, injunction or deportation by the Singapore authorities.[3] In that case, the sole arbitrator was also removed for misconduct by the Singapore court. He was an experienced arbitrator (not a lawyer) and a former president of the Chartered Institute of Arbitrators. There were several grounds for a disgruntled party to challenge him, one of which was his attempt to go over the heads of the apparently bickering lawyers and their seemingly interminable procedural wrangles by writing directly to their clients, the users. For that conduct, treated as misconduct but readily understandable in other contexts, this sole arbitrator was admonished and removed from office by the Singapore Court. It seems that the interests of the users in that arbitration were not universally shared by all their lawyers, and that the interests of certain of these lawyers were treated with greater deference by the Singapore Court. It remains a puzzling decision and a cautionary tale: it suggests that an arbitrator should not second-guess the interests of users as represented by their lawyers during the arbitration.

---

[2] *Ranger v. Great Western Railway Co.* (1854) 5 HL Cas 72, 10 ER 824 (HL).

[3] *In the Matter of an Arbitration between Builders Federal (Hong Kong) Limited and Joseph Gartner & Co. v. Turner (East Asia) Pte Ltd* (1988); see also Michael Polkinghorne, 'The Right of Representation in a Foreign Venue' *Arbitration International* 4 (1988) p. 333.

302   ON ARBITRATION

E. Arbitration Agreements

As far as drafting agreements is concerned, we know from practical experience that at the conclusion of successful commercial negotiations, users often pay little attention to the drafting of a specially tailored provision for the best resolution of any future dispute relating to their transaction. Understandably, the parties appear to take legal advice late, and then those lawyers choose a standard system of dispute resolution, readily available and easily known to them as arbitration rules, the ICC, LCIA, IRDC, SCC, SIAC or, increasingly, UNCITRAL. This significantly reduces the risk of pathological arbitration clauses; but it has also removed the influence of users on the drafting of their own arbitration clauses in favour of standard form arbitration rules that have traditionally been drafted by lawyers, not users.

In recent times there have been several attempts to involve users, most notably by those responsible for drafting the new ICC Rules.[4] What is surprising is that when users are consulted on the drafting of arbitration rules, they seem to be conservative and cautious. In recent rule reforms, users have significantly not insisted upon or even proposed radical changes to arbitration rules. For example, let us look at the factors that affect users most in any arbitration: the heavy costs, efforts, disruption and delays of wide-ranging document production (or "discovery"). Why do none of the most used arbitration rules provide for arbitration without any form of document production? Why is it that before a dispute users still seem more concerned to have in existence a rule-based right to document production rather than specially tailored procedural rules more appropriate to their particular transaction, trade or future dispute? We know that this point was raised in the reform of the new ICC Rules, but users, when consulted, preferred the safety of familiar habits. Or is this, again, a case of users consulting their own lawyers and identifying their views and interests with theirs out of an abundance of caution?

F. Oral Hearings

Under many domestic arbitration rules, small claims procedures preclude oral hearings and/or oral witnesses and require the dispute to be decided on written submissions only, by consent of the users expressed in advance of their dispute.

---

[4] The high-water mark among modern arbitration rules was contained in the LCIA's 1985 Rules: "The parties may agree on the conduct of their arbitral proceedings and they are encouraged to do so ... " (now Article 14.1 of the LCIA's 1998 Rules).

In London, the LMAA Small Claims Procedure has proved successful with both domestic and international users of maritime arbitration in London. This is obviously not a procedure for large claims—nor indeed for complex small claims—but why is it assumed by users to be inapplicable to all other international disputes? Given the high costs of hearings in international arbitrations, why is it so rare to see an arbitration conducted without hearings or at least without any oral witnesses? Hearings add massively to the costs of an arbitration, and it is a sad fact of life that many lawyers will advise a client not to pursue a claim by means of international arbitration if the amount is less than a certain figure. In London, 10 years ago, we inquired of several City firms what this figure was for ICC and LCIA arbitrations. It ranged between USD 3 and USD 5 million then; and it must be higher now. If so, this is regrettable. It does not seem right for claimants to be disenfranchised from making relatively small claims by means of international arbitration, and it seems more than regrettable that a possible cure, an adjusted procedure, could not be developed to make international arbitration possible even for very small claims. Something seems to be wrong. If the most ambitious solutions cannot prevail, let us start with a relatively small reform.

G. Capped Costs

For many users, the new imperative is to win their arbitration at almost any cost. The allocation of costs against the losing party by the tribunal is therefore an important weapon in the arbitral armoury that few users would wish to abandon (the so-called ABBA principle: "the winner takes it all"). However, as regards costs incurred from the first procedural meeting to the award, we again see the absence of users' direct input in the arbitration process. This is even more surprising given that every international arbitration conducted between users and lawyers of different background is itself an exercise in comparative procedure, requiring flexibility, compromise and a methodology best suited to that particular arbitration. There should therefore be an important role for all users as regards costs: not only the costs of the arbitrators and the arbitral institution but also the far greater legal costs and expenses payable to the users' own lawyers, experts and witnesses, all compounded twice over by the application of the loser-pays-costs rule.

Why not, therefore, place a user-agreed cap on the total legal costs of the arbitration at the outset of the arbitration? This cap could work in two ways. For large claims, it would at least prepare both sides at the outset (i.e., the actual users as distinct from their lawyers) for what could be a significantly high bill for legal

304   ON ARBITRATION

costs (compounded twice over). The mutual of that potential liability could persuade parties to come to an amicable settlement. In more modest cases, where the quantum of the claim is relatively low, it would be important for the users to decide at the outset, by agreement with the tribunal, to keep legal costs at a level proportionate to the amount of the claim. It is notorious that, for a relatively modest claim raising no fundamental principles, users can spend a far greater sum in legal costs to recover the lesser sum in dispute.

Such cost-capping was introduced in England under sections 63 and 65 of the Arbitration Act 1996. Under section 63, parties are free to agree what costs of the arbitration are recoverable as between themselves; and under section 65, unless otherwise agreed by the parties, the tribunal may direct that the recoverable costs of the arbitration (or any part of such costs) shall be limited to a specified amount.[5] The first provision depends upon the parties' consent, but the second depends on the tribunal only, with no need for the parties' consent. There was no counterpart to these provisions in the 1985 UNCITRAL Model Law, and the Department Advisory Committee (DAC) on the Law of Arbitration recorded its legislative intentions, as follows:

> *"We consider that such a power, properly used, could prove to be extremely valuable as an aid to reducing unnecessary expenditure. It also represents a facet of the duty of the tribunal as set out in Clause 33 [i.e., the tribunal's mandatory duty 'to adopt procedures suitable to the circumstances of the particular case avoiding unnecessary delay or expense ... ']. This power enables the tribunal to put a ceiling on costs, so that while a party can continue to spend as much as it likes on an arbitration it will not be able to recover more than the ceiling limit from the other party. This will have the added virtue of discouraging those who wish to use their financial muscle to intimidate their opponents into giving up through fear that by going on they might be subject to a costs order which they could not sustain."[6]*

This provision in section 65 has been used surprisingly little by English tribunals. The same applies to the use of section 63 by parties, but in recent difficult economic times there was renewed interest in its application.[7]

---

[5] Section 65 states simply: "Unless otherwise agreed by the parties, the tribunal may direct that the recoverable costs of the arbitration, or any part of the arbitral proceedings, shall be limited to a specified amount. Any direction may be made or varied at any stage, but it must be done sufficiently in advance of the incurring of costs to which it relates, or the taking of any steps in the proceedings which may be affected by it, for the limit to be taken into account."

[6] See the DAC's First Report (January 1996) para. 272; Mustill & Boyd: Commercial Arbitration: 2001 Companion Volume (2001) p. 439.

[7] It has attracted attention even outside England. See Daniel Wehrli, 'Zum Höhe und Umfang erstattungsfähiger Parteikosten', *DIS-Materialen X* (2005) pp. 77-78.

In 2009, the London Maritime Arbitrators Association (LMAA) in its new Intermediate Claims Procedure (ICP) for LMAA arbitration disputes addressing claims between USD 50,000 and USD 400,000. This procedure provides for a specific cap on legal costs: "The parties' recoverable costs are to be capped so that neither party shall be entitled to recover more than the sum equivalent to 30% of the claimant's monetary claims as advanced plus the amount of a counterclaim, if any." If there is an oral hearing, the percentage increases from 30% to 50%. This new provision concludes: "These percentages are maximum figures, and the tribunal may at any time in its absolute discretion cap the parties' future costs so that the total cap amounts to some lesser percentage than is here stated." Could similar cost-capping work for international arbitrations? It could certainly provide an element of confidence for users who are nervous about the allocation of legal costs according to the loser-pays principle or about the disproportionate amount of legal costs. For ICC arbitrations, the initiative would have to start by consent with tribunals and parties at the first procedural meeting in clearly appropriate cases. However, if it did work in practice, it could be considered in the future as a possible change to the new ICC Rules and other arbitration rules currently being revised by other institutions.

H. Conclusion

But could this really work in practice? Can any major reform ever be introduced by users of international arbitration? The likely fate of the LMAA's ICP rules may provide a salutary lesson: they are about to be abolished as a result of opposition by maritime users. This is the place where, it seems, the interests of users and lawyers do diverge, not for reasons of self-interest or financial greed, but because users are essentially even more cautious and even more uncomfortable than lawyers with what is unknown, unfamiliar and as yet unproven—all traits that bend towards orthodoxy rather than radicalism. As St Augustine, here the patron saint of arbitral users (almost) said: "Grant me innovation and reform in the new ICC Rules, only not yet."

18

From Florence to London via Moscow and New Delhi

How and Why Arbitral Ideas Migrate

V.V. Veeder*

In olden times, ideas were often spread by individual pilgrims travelling on foot or by mule across vast inhospitable distances. In recent times, the spread of ideas, good and bad, has become paradoxically both easier and more difficult for international arbitration. This article examines the spread of a bad idea migrating from London to India and Pakistan (on the exercise of extra-territorial jurisdiction over foreign awards), culminating in the recent decision of the Indian Supreme Court in *Bharat Aluminium* (2012); and of a good idea migrating from Moscow eventually to London (on the broad principle of the separability of an arbitration clause), culminating in Section 7 of the English Arbitration Act 1996.

A. Introduction

International arbitration has long been a highly flexible system for both the prevention and the resolution of many categories of disputes. Its capacity for evolutionary change is also immense, not only over the ages but, still more so, in modern times for very different transactions, institutions and traditions. It could not have evolved without the introduction of new ideas; but it has also had to survive ideas that have harmed arbitration. On many occasions, it has been 'citius, altius, fortius';

---

* Essex Court Chambers, London, Visiting Professor on Investment Arbitration, King's College, University of London. E-mail: vvveeder@londonarbitrators.net. This was a lecture delivered at MIDS in Geneva on 26 September 2012 for the beginning of the academic year and graduation ceremony (albeit here without accompanying photographs). While all errors and responsibility for views here expressed remain his alone, the author expresses his thanks to the following persons for their generous help and guidance in conducting research for different parts of this lecture: Professor Hans van Houtte, Professor Loukas Mistelis; Professor Alexander Komarov; Makdoom Ali Khan SC; TT Landau QC; C Melnikova-Raich; and B Dye.

On Arbitration. Edited by: Sam Wordsworth KC and Marie Veeder, Oxford University Press. © Oxford University Press 2023.
DOI: 10.1093/oso/9780192869135.003.0018

B. Maxim The Greek

In the early spring of 1553, at a time when Edward VI ruled England, Henri II ruled France and more than 200 years after the death of William Tell, the Russian Tsar, Ivan IV, also known as Ivan the Terrible, left Moscow on a pilgrimage to northern Russia. Near Moscow, the Tsar and his family stopped at the Monastery of the Holy Trinity to receive the blessing of Maximos the Greek (or 'Maxim' in Russian), a pious Orthodox monk living in deliberate poverty who was now well over 80 years old. Maxim was already renowned in Russia as a writer, theologian, philosopher and scholar of great ability, with an immense knowledge of ancient Greek, Roman and other secular literature, including Aristotle, Plato and Cicero. Maxim was also familiar with ideas and events in Western Europe. It was he who first told Russians of Columbus' voyage to the New World; and as well as Greek, Latin and Russian (including Slavonic), Maxim spoke Serbian, Bulgarian, Italian and most probably Turkish. Maxim was also an arbitrator.

Originally from the Vatopedi Monastery on Mount Athos in northern Greece, Maxim had come to Russia 35 years earlier in March 1518, at the direction of the Orthodox Patriarch in Constantinople (by now under Ottoman rule). The Patriarch was responding to a request from the Russian Grand Prince at that time, Basil III (Ivan IV's father) for a Greek scholar and skilled translator to work in the royal libraries in Moscow, where Greek was no longer known, not even to him (the son of one of the last Byzantine princesses). Shortly after his arrival in Moscow, Maxim was asked by the Grand Prince to decide a religious and political dispute within the Russian Orthodox Church, between the so-called 'possessors' and the so-called 'non-possessors'.[1] This important dispute had divided the Russian Church from the late 15th century, long before Maxim's arrival in Moscow. The possessors believed that the Russian Church could possess secular property and exercise political power in order to fulfil its religious mission. The non-possessors believed that the Church should not aspire to political power or to accumulate worldly possessions, particularly the ownership and commercial exploitation of whole villages and peasants. Under Mongol rule, the Orthodox Church had been exempt from taxes; it had grown rich; and by now it controlled almost one third of Russian lands.

The dispute turned in significant part on Russian translations of Greek holy texts, suspected by both sides to have been heretically mistranslated. Maxim, as

---

[1] The possessors were also known as the Josephians (or by their enemies, the 'greedy ones') and the non-possessors were also known as the Judaizers (or, by themselves, the 'non-greedy ones'). In Russian, 'styazhateli' and 'nestyazhateli'.

a Greek scholar, was therefore asked to arbitrate between these different views with new authoritative translations. He worked on his translations for almost two years. He decided that the Greek texts permitted Orthodox monasteries to own 'ploughed fields and vineyards'; but not, as the possessors argued, 'villages with resident peasants', still less the Russian Church's massive accumulation of worldly riches, the exercise of state powers and the commercial exploitation of the peasantry. This led Maxim to denounce, in his alliterative Russian, 'love of sweets, love of praise and love of silver' and to utter a strong warning against the possessors' 'devious rules', rather than 'just rules' for both Church and State.[2] From the arbitral perspective, we can see here, of course, the early work of a sole neutral arbitrator deciding an existing dispute under an ad hoc non-institutional form of arbitration. That is not, however, the point of the story. It derives from this extraordinary traveller: a rational humanist, a religious moralist and a cosmopolitan historian with ideas originating far beyond Mount Athos.

Maxim's arbitral career was cut brutally short, following political changes in both palace and cathedral. The non-possessors lost royal favour; and the possessors took over the Russian Church, with a determination to punish both the non-possessors and also those who had supported them. In 1525, Daniel, the new Russian primate, had Maxim tried and condemned on charges of heresy, sorcery and sedition. Found guilty, Maxim was re-tried again in 1531 for not freely acknowledging his guilt. As punishment, he was confined to solitary darkness in a monastic prison, forbidden to read or write. He was later transferred to other prisons where he was able to resume his scholarly writings. Maxim was eventually released in 1548, when Ivan IV pardoned him after successive appeals from the Orthodox Patriarchs in Constantinople and Alexandria. Maxim was still refused permission to leave Russia in order to return home to Mount Athos, from fear, it was said, that Maxim might report unfavourably on his treatment in Russia (as well he might). Maxim died in 1556, two years after Ivan IV's visit to his monastery.

Over the centuries which followed, Russian scholars speculated as to the origins of Maxim the Greek. Still much renowned as a theologian and philosopher who brought to Russia new ideas which helped later to make Russia a European country, questions persisted as to how he had learned what he taught to his many Russian followers. Who was he, exactly? How did a poor Greek monk from Mount Athos, not even ordained as a priest, acquire such knowledge and ideas? In particular, why was his way of thinking so strikingly new for the Orthodox Church and so rooted in non-Orthodox, secular and classical literature? For almost 400 years, these questions went unanswered. In 1943, during the German occupation of Belgium, there was published an enlarged doctoral thesis at the University at Louvain, by a Russian scholar in exile, Elie Denissoff.[3] It was the result of a decade's meticulous archival

---

[2] In Russian: 'slastoliubie, slavoliubie, srebroliubie'; and 'krivila' rather than 'pravila'.

[3] Elie Denissoff, *Maxime le Grec et l'Occident: Contribution à l'Histoire de la Pensée Religieuse et Philosophique de Michel Trivolis* (Desclée de Brouwer 1943).

research in Western Europe, all the more remarkable given the war and given also that the author was not granted access to any archives in the Soviet Union.

Elie Denissoff's work showed, through the extensive use of manuscripts in Italy, Greece, Germany and England, accompanied by great detective work, that Maxim's original name was Michael Trifolis. Born in 1480 in Arta in Northern Greece under Ottoman rule, at 10-years old Michael moved with his family to Corfu, then under Venetian rule; and from 1492 until 1506 he spent his formative years studying in Florence, Bologna, Padua and at the Aldine printing press in Venice. In Florence, Michael attended Girolamo Savonarola's sermons and, after Savonarola's execution by the Inquisition in 1498, he became a Catholic, a Dominican monk attached to Savonarola's former monastery in Florence, San Marco. This was a time when the Inquisition was still persecuting Savonarola's followers amongst the Dominican order and, possibly as a result, Michael left Florence for Mount Athos in 1506, there to become Maximos, an Orthodox monk working in the Library of the Vatopedi Monastery. Since Elie Denissoff's publication, Russian and Western scholars have written further on the origins of Maxim's ideas in the Cinquecento, the Renaissance and the early Reformation, the moral fervour and polemical style of Savonarola's sermons, and the teachings of the Dominican brothers in Florence, so actively opposed to the moral corruption and venalities of the Catholic Church in Rome.[4] This literature is now extensive in Russia, England, the United States and also Geneva. In English, it includes the works of James Billington, Sir Dimitri Obolensky and Professor Richard Pipes.[5]

For present purposes, Maxim's example provides a simple lesson. In the 16th century, when travel and communications were more than difficult, one man, a foreigner armed only with ideas from Northern Italy, influenced the course of history in Russia and, hence, Europe. And this so discreetly, that it took another scholar working in the worst of times in the 20th Century to discover the

---

[4] Elie Denissoff's own life is also an extraordinary story: Born in 1893 in St Petersburg into a Don Cossack family, he was educated in France and Germany, later working in 1916 as private secretary to the Czarist Prime Minister (BV Stürmer). After the October 1917 Revolution, he was one the few members of his family to survive, eventually arriving in Paris six years later. He there married a young Belgian, Maria Haot; and in Belgium, they managed several hotels in the Ardennes and elsewhere (including the Grand Hotel Majestic in Durbuy). His thesis was first prepared for the Institut Catholique in Paris but later transferred as a doctoral thesis to the Institute of Philosophy at Louvain. After the Second World War, Elie Denissoff and his family emigrated to the United States, where he was Professor of Philosophy at Notre Dame University, Indiana (1948–57) and Head of the Philosophy Department at St. Procopius College in Lisle, Illinois (1957–67). He was ordained a Greek Catholic priest in 1962 and died in Chicago in 1971. See Hugh Olmsted, Two Exiles: The Roots and Fortunes of Elie Denissoff, in *The New Muscovite Cultural History*, eds Valerie Kivelson and others (Slavica 2009).

[5] James H Billington, *The Icon and the Axe: An Interpretive History of Russian Culture* (Alfred A Knopf 1966); Dimitri Obolensky, *Six Byzantine Portraits* (OUP 1988); and Richard Pipes, *Russian Conservatism and its Critics: A Study in Political Culture* (Yale University Press 2005); see also William K Medlin and Christos G Patrinelis, *Renaissance Influences and Religious Reforms in Russia* (Librairie Droz 1971); Jack V Haney, *From Italy to Muscovy: The Life and Works of Maxim the Greek* (W Fink 1973); and John Meyendorf, *Rome Constantinople Moscow Historical and Theological Studies* (St. Vladimir's Seminary Press 1996).

310 ON ARBITRATION

unimaginable, the direct link of these ideas between Florence and Moscow. If we turn to the history of arbitration, we can see also the same powerful effect of a mere idea, born in one place and migrating to another distant place. We here address two arbitral ideas: first, a bad idea born in London in colonial times migrating to New Delhi with malign long-term results for both India and Pakistan; and, secondly, a good idea with many parents, including (particularly) Switzerland, but eventually migrating from Moscow to London, with benign effects for international arbitration everywhere.

C. The English 1930 Act

In 1930, England enacted the 1927 Geneva Convention on Arbitral Awards, the second of the two multi-party international treaties on arbitration negotiated at the League of Nations in Geneva, the first being the Geneva Protocol on Arbitration Clauses of 1923. In that 1930 enactment, unwittingly, the UK Parliament committed an error with far-reaching consequences: it added a provision not found in the 1927 Convention: 'Section 6(b)'. Section 6(b) of the 1930 Act provided that nothing in Part I of the Act on the recognition and enforcement of (Geneva) Convention awards shall: 'apply to any award made on an arbitration agreement governed by the law of England.' This ostensibly modest phrase indirectly introduced into English law a new idea that the English Courts could exercise an extra-territorial jurisdiction over an arbitration held outside England when the arbitration agreement was governed by English law (as its applicable law), notwithstanding the arbitration's foreign seat and *lex loci arbitri*. This idea was all the more pernicious because English law generally assumed, at that time, that an arbitration clause was subject to the same law applying to the substantive contract, without regard to the foreign seat of the arbitration or other factors. Hence, a contract of sale expressly or impliedly subject to English law would, under English conflict rules, subject the arbitration clause in that contract also to English law, even if the arbitration were to be held in Geneva.[6] This provision was later re-enacted as Section

---

[6] In *Hamlyn v Talisker* [1894] AC 201, the House of Lords had decided that, as a general rule, an arbitration clause would be governed by the same law as the law applying to the contract in which that clause was contained. This orthodox approach prevailed under the English 1950 and 1975 Acts: for example, see Mustill and Boyd, *Commercial Arbitration* (1st ed, 1989) 62–63; and Redfern & Hunter, *Arbitration* (1st ed, 1986) 113: 'Where the agreement to arbitrate is contained in an arbitration clause which itself forms part of a wider contract, the arbitration clause is normally governed by the same law as the rest of the contract'. Under the English 1996 Act, the English Court of Appeal has decided otherwise, with the parties' choice of the arbitral seat now a more significant factor: *Sulamérica Cis Nacional de Seguros SA v Enesa Engenharia SA* [2012] EWCA Civ 638; [2012] 1 Lloyd's Rep 671. The new 15th edition of Dicey, Morris and Collins, *The Conflict of Laws* (2012), confirms that, in the absence of any express or implied choice by the parties otherwise, the applicable law governing the material validity, scope and interpretation of an arbitration agreement will be, in general, 'the law of the seat of the arbitration': Rule 64(2), vol 1, 829.

40(b) in Part II of the Arbitration Act 1950; but its extra-territorial approach was abandoned as regards New York Convention awards, by the English Arbitration Act 1975[7]; and it does not exist under the English Arbitration Act 1996.

Between 1930 and 1975, in practice, this provision was not significant in England. Perhaps parties agreeing English law for their substantive contract tended almost always also to arbitrate their disputes in London. As was noted by Michael Mustill (in 1975) in regard to London arbitrations, conflicts of law issues 'rarely arise in England, even in arbitrations with significant foreign contacts'.[8] We may also recall the sharp (albeit accurate) observation from a distinguished professor in Geneva that, in those times, an 'international' arbitration in London was invariably an arbitration in English, before English arbitrators, by English Counsel and English Solicitors, on an English standard form of contract under English substantive and procedural laws. In 1936, the young Quintin Hogg, later Lord Hailsham and the first Lord Chancellor appointed by Mrs Thatcher as Prime Minister, did not think it even necessary to make even a single reference to Section 6(b) of the 1930 Act in his work on arbitration, apart from reciting its text.[9] The 1957 edition of Russell on Arbitration likewise contains no commentary on Section 40(b) of the English 1950 Act.[10] In 1961, the Lord Chancellor's Law Reform Committee did not consider this statutory provision 'a matter of great practical importance'.[11] There is indeed no reported English case turning on this awkward provision in the 1930 and 1950 Acts. Unfortunately, this was not true of other jurisdictions. In 1937, Section 6(b) of the English 1930 Act found its way from London to New Delhi in the form of Indian colonial legislation also enacting the 1927 Geneva Convention, as Section 9(b) of the Arbitration (Protocol and Convention) Act 1937.[12] Unfortunately, Section 9(b) remained in effect in Pakistan and India after their independence in 1947.

How could this error have occurred in London in 1930? While not a public document at the time, the Notes on Clauses prepared within the British Government for the Parliamentary debates on the proposed legislation were later made public in

---

[7] Section 2 of the English 1975 Act preserved the position under English law as regards awards under the 1927 Geneva Convention (Part II of the English 1950 Act); but with Pakistan's accession to and first enactment (by successive ordinances) of the New York Convention in 2005, this provision became otiose: see Article VII(2) of the New York Convention (Pakistan was the last State party to the 1923 Geneva Protocol and 1927 Geneva Convention still to accede to the 1958 New York Convention).

[8] MJ Mustill QC (later Lord Mustill), as cited in Smedresman, 'Conflict of Laws in International Commercial Arbitration: A Survey of Recent Developments' (1977) 263 Calif W Int LJ, 291.

[9] Quintin McGarel Hogg, *The Law of Arbitration* (1936) 329.

[10] Russell, *Law of Arbitration* (eds TA Blanco White and A Walton; 1957) 361.

[11] Fifth Report (Recognition and Enforcement of Foreign Arbitral Awards), Private International Law Committee (1961 *HMSO* Cmnd 1515) 22.

[12] For the text of the Indian 1937 Act, see Justice RS Bachawat's, *Law of Arbitration & Conciliation* (5th ed, 2010), Vol 2 at 2826, 2829. The effect of Section 9(b) of the Indian Act 1937 is to be considered with the Indian Act 1940, the colonial enactment of the English 1889–1934 Arbitration Acts providing for judicial controls over domestic arbitrations, arbitrators and awards, including the case stated. For the text of the Indian 1940, as later amended, see OP Malhotra and Indu Malhotra's *Law and Practice of Arbitration and Conciliation* (2nd ed; 2006) 1662.

archives at the Public Record Office. It appears from these Notes that the Ministry responsible for Section 6(b) was inspired by a decision of the Privy Council in 1902, *Spurrier v La Cloche* [1902] AC 446.[13] In that case, the insured had secured a court judgment in Jersey, a legal space juridically foreign to England, disregarding the parties' arbitration agreement providing for London arbitration under the English Arbitration Act 1889 as a condition precedent to any claim against the insurer under the insurance policy, ie the standard form *Scott v Avery* clause. The Privy Council's judgment seems uncontroversial, then as now: it decided only that the Jersey Court was required to give due effect to the arbitration clause in the policy and could not give judgment on the merits to the insured, ignoring that arbitration clause and its condition precedent. Yet, this case was interpreted by the Ministry to mean that a submission to arbitration, 'like any other Contract', must be construed by the law which governs it; and that an arbitration clause would be governed by English law, if English law governed the contract, wherever the arbitral seat (be it in England or abroad). Hence, so the Ministry's Notes continued, an arbitration held abroad, under an arbitration agreement governed by English law, might lead to an award made abroad being enforced in England inconsistent with its applicable law, namely English law. In those circumstances, the Ministry concluded, in its words: '... such a submission ought to have all the consequences of a submission within the meaning of the Arbitration Act [1889]; and an award on such a submission ought to be enforced like any other award made under the Arbitration Act', ie as a domestic award made in England and not as a Convention award under the 1927 Geneva Convention. Obviously, the Ministry considered that foreign courts could not be trusted to handle 'English' arbitration awards: hence, the need for Section 6(b) of the 1930 English Act qualifying the 1927 Geneva Convention.

There was, it seems, no understanding at that time that the English 1889 Act was subject to a territorial limitation and could not apply to an award made in an arbitration held outside England, at a foreign arbitral seat, even if English law governed the arbitration agreement. Nor was there any understanding that the law applicable to an arbitration clause could be different from the law applicable to the substantive contract: *depeçage* was not then an English arbitral word. Nor was there yet any inkling that an arbitration clause was to be treated as a self-contained agreement juridically different and separate from the substantive contract in which the clause was physically, but not legally, embedded. As Sir Michael Kerr noted in an article written in 1997, the Ministry's interpretation of the Privy Council's decision was erroneous under English law and, with this error, the migration of Section 6(b) of the English 1930 Act to India and Pakistan as Section 9(b) of the Indian 1937 Act was, in his words (born of personal experience), 'something of a disaster'.[14] In the recent judgment of the Indian Supreme Court delivered earlier this month

---

[13] Notes on Clauses, English Arbitration Act 1930, (PRO, Kew) LC02/1040. See 16.
[14] Michael Kerr, 'Concord and Conflict in International Arbitration' (1997) 13 Arb Int 212.

(to which we shall return), the subsequent abuse of this provision in India was described as 'disastrous', without any qualification.[15]

When applied in combination with legislation applying to domestic arbitrations in India, this English idea meant that foreign awards made outside India, including Convention awards under the 1927 Geneva Convention and later the 1958 New York Convention, could be judicially reviewed as domestic awards by the Indian Courts, as if made in India. Accordingly, an international contract subject to Indian law providing for arbitration in London, with London as the seat expressly chosen by the Parties and an award made in London under English law as the *lex loci arbitri*, would be treated by the Indian Courts as a domestic arbitration, with the award as a domestic award subject to full review by the Indian Court without regard to the Geneva or New York Conventions—because, as there expressly stated, the Indian legislation enacting these conventions 'shall not apply to any award made on an arbitration agreement governed by the law of India'.

In England, this problem was first identified by the Lord Chancellor's Private International Law Committee in its Fifth Report of 1961 on the possible enactment of the 1958 New York Convention into English law. Its members included well-known arbitration specialists, such as Mr Justice Wilberforce (later Lord Wilberforce), Mr Justice Megaw (later Lord Justice Megaw), Dr Francis Mann and Professor Wortley (the latter having been the UK's delegate for the New York Convention).[16] The Committee analysed the drafting history of Article I of the Convention, applying to all awards made in the territory of a State other than the State where the award's recognition and enforcement was sought. The Committee advised that Section 6(b) of the English 1930 Act was inconsistent with a Contracting State's international obligations under the New York Convention: a State could not 'exclude awards made in the territory of other Contracting States on the ground that they are regarded as "domestic" under its own law'.[17] As a result of the 1961 Committee's recommendation, the English Arbitration Act 1975, enacting the New York Convention, abandoned Section 6(b) as regards New York Convention Awards. That remains the position, as already indicated, under the English Arbitration Act 1996. In India and Pakistan, however, the

---

[15] *Bharat Aluminium*, Indian Supreme Court, 6 September 2012 (unreported as yet; infra) 37.

[16] The Law Reform Committee was chaired by Mr Justice Cross (later Lord Cross of Chelsea); and its distinguished members included DW Dobson, Asst Permanent Secretary to the Lord Chancellor (later Sir Denys Dobson QC); WAH Druitt, Treasury Solicitor (later Sir Harvey Druitt); JH Gibson, Legal Secretary and First Parliamentary Draftsman for Scotland (later Sir John Gibson QC); Robert Speed, Counsel to the Speaker of the House of Commons and previously Solicitor to the Board of Trade (later Sir Robert Speed QC); FA Vallat, Legal Adviser to the Foreign Office (later Professor Sir Francis Vallat QC); and JC McFadyean (a senior London City Solicitor and a partner of Messrs Slaughter & May). Sir Robert ('Bobby') Speed is still remembered as a scratch golfer, winning the Bar Golf tournament in 1938 and reaching the final in 1939: see N Hague, *Wigs on the Links – A Centenary History of the Bar Golfing Society 1903–2002*, (2003), 38, 49 & 65.

[17] *Fifth Report* (ibid), 21–23.

314 ON ARBITRATION

problem remained in regard to arbitration awards under the Geneva Convention and the New York Convention, respectively.

D. Pakistan

In *Rupali*, decided in 1994, the Pakistani Supreme Court treated two awards made in London as domestic awards, subject to review under Pakistani law and not as foreign awards under the 1927 Geneva Convention.[18] The named defendants included the three arbitrators, none of whom were resident in Pakistan and of whom one was Sir Michael Kerr—hence his later article (cited above). The dispute between the parties concerned a contract for a plant in Pakistan; the contract was signed in Pakistan; and it was expressly governed by the law of Pakistan. The arbitration clause provided for ICC arbitration, in London if the claimant was the Pakistani party and in Karachi if the claimant was the foreign party. (The claimant in the arbitration was the Pakistani party, hence the London seat). The Pakistani Supreme Court's approach was simple: the arbitration clause was part of the contract; the contract was governed by Pakistani law; and therefore the arbitration agreement was also governed by Pakistani law as its applicable law. The Court held: 'if no express choice of proper law of arbitration agreement is made, it will be the same as proper law of contract if arbitration agreement is embedded and contained in the main contract itself especially when the parties have, as in the present case, expressly given their choice about law applicable to the contract'. The Supreme Court also decided that the arbitral seat in London could give concurrent jurisdiction to the English Courts; but that this factor would not deprive the Pakistani Courts of jurisdiction over the arbitration, including the removal of the arbitrators for alleged misconduct and challenges to their awards as domestic awards under Pakistani law. The Court recorded that, given these factors, the respondent had rightly conceded that the awards could not be foreign awards under the 1927 Geneva Convention. It was a concession made because the contrary was plainly regarded as unarguable in Pakistan given the effect of Section 9(b) of the Indian (now Pakistani) 1937 Act, corresponding to Section 6(b) of the English 1930 Act.

In 2000, in *Hubco v WAPDA*,[19] the Pakistani Supreme Court, by a majority, refused to recognize an arbitration agreement providing for ICC arbitration in London on the ground that allegations raised by the respondent state entity were unarbitrable under Pakistani law and that the Pakistani Courts, therefore, had exclusive jurisdiction to decide the whole of the parties' dispute, including the claimant's contractual claims under the power purchase agreement (where the

---

[18] *Hitachi v Mitsui, Rupali & Ors* PLD 1998 SCMR 1618; (2000) XXV *ICCA Yearbook* 443 (The three respondent-arbitrators were Dr Nael Bunni, Professor John Uff, QC, and Sir Michael Kerr).
[19] *Hubco v WAPDA*, reported in [2000] 19 Arb Int 439, ann. Nudrat Majeed (431).

applicable law was expressly agreed to be English law). The respondent state entity, WAPDA, had initially accepted the validity of the arbitration clause; but the Supreme Court decided, as a matter of Pakistani law, that WAPDA's mere allegation of corruption against the claimant sufficed to displace both the arbitration clause and the application of the 1923 Geneva Protocol and 1927 Geneva Convention (to which Pakistan was a party). It is difficult to understand the reasoning of the Supreme Court's majority, being contained in two short paragraphs. It cannot be overlooked that, between these few lines, the Supreme Court treated this international dispute as a domestic dispute and, somehow, the London arbitration clause as a domestic arbitration agreement subject to the full control of the Pakistani courts under Pakistani law. Section 9(b) of the 1937 Act cast a long shadow. Other similar decisions by Pakistani courts brought Pakistan into disrepute as regards international arbitration, compounded by its failure to enact the New York Convention and also the ICSID Convention.

In 2011, however, Pakistan enacted the New York Convention in the form of the Recognition and Enforcement (Arbitration Agreements and Foreign Arbitral Awards) Act 2011. It has several corrective features. First, Section 9(b) of the 1937 Act disappeared, following the example set by the English 1975 Act. Second, Section 7 of the 2011 Act provides: 'The recognition and enforcement of a foreign arbitral award shall not be refused except in accordance with Article V of the Convention'. Any implicit reference to domestic arbitral legislation and case-law in Pakistan is thereby intended to be excluded. Third, Section 8 of the 2011 Act provides, unusually: 'In the event of any inconsistency between this Act and the Convention, the Convention shall prevail to the extent of the inconsistency'. Hence the text of the New York Convention is intended to have supremacy over other provisions of the 2011 Act. (The reverse is more usual in common law enactments of international conventions, including English statutes). Thus was an English colonial error in 1937 eventually corrected by Pakistan in 2011. Do Pakistani leopards change their spots, particularly with a Pakistani judiciary often so hostile to international arbitration? We can at least hope so with the 2011 Act, as also the 2011 Pakistani legislation enacting the ICSID Convention. If hopes are disappointed, however, it would now be the fault of a Pakistani leopard and not a bad English colonial idea migrating from London 75 years ago.[20]

---

[20] The omens may be ominous: In regard to an ICC award made in Singapore, the Lahore High Court applied the *Rupali* judgment in permitting a challenge under the Pakistani 1940 Act applying to domestic awards, notwithstanding the Pakistani 2011 Act: *Taisei Corporation v A.M. Construction* (27 April 2012). Moreover, the Pakistani Supreme Court's order of 7 February 2012 directed at both ICSID and ICC arbitrations in *Balochistan, BHP & Tethyan* may likewise be troubling for international arbitration: although rejecting the petitioners' applications to initiate contempt of court proceedings, the Pakistani Supreme Court directed the Governments of Balochistan and Pakistan, notwithstanding both 2011 Acts, 'to make a request to the ICC and ICSID Washington DC not to take any further steps and extend the period for nomination of the Arbitrator [to be nominated by Balochistan], so that in the meantime this Court, which is already seized of the matter since the year 2007 and is hearing the

E. India

In India, Section 9(b) of the Indian 1937 Act was re-enacted as Section 9(b) of the Indian (Foreign Awards Recognition and Enforcement) Act 1961 enacting the 1958 New York Convention, to which India had become a party as an independent state.[21] Its application meant that arbitrations held outside India, say in London, Paris or Singapore, could be the subject of injunctions from the Indian Courts preventing the arbitration, directed not only at a non-Indian party but also at foreign arbitrators personally; and, as in Pakistan, that an award made abroad could be set aside and refused enforcement by the Indian Courts under domestic legislation on grounds exceeding anything in the New York Convention. It also meant that foreign arbitrations were subjected to significant delays inherent in the Indian legal system.

For example, in *ONGC v Western*, an ICC tribunal made an award in London, where the substantive contract was subject to Indian law.[22] The losing Indian party applied to set aside the award in India. In 1987, the Indian Supreme Court decided that the Indian Courts had jurisdiction to decide the application because the New York Convention could not apply to an arbitration agreement governed by the law of India, under Section 9(b) of the 1961 Act. Moreover, with such jurisdiction, the Indian Court also had the power to injunct the successful foreign party from enforcing the ICC award under the New York Convention in the United States until the Indian legal proceedings were finally concluded, a period ordinarily measured in years. Another example was *National Thermal Power Corporation v Singer*, decided by the Indian Supreme Court in 1992.[23] An ICC award made in London as an English and New York Convention award was treated as a domestic Indian award, because Indian law was the law applicable to the substantive contract and, hence, also that contract's arbitration clause. Applying Indian law on domestic awards, the ICC award was set aside by the Indian Courts and not recognized or enforced under the New York Convention.

In 1996, it appeared that Section 9(b) of the 1961 Act had been effectively repealed by the Indian Arbitration and Conciliation 1996 Act, which enacted (with significant modifications) the 1985 UNCITRAL Model Law. These modifications include two provisions in Part 1 of the Indian 1996 Act. Section 2(7) provides: 'An arbitral award made under this Part [i.e. Part 1] shall be considered as a domestic

petitions filed subsequently on the same subject under Constitutional provisions, may dispose of the same finally'.

[21] For the text of the Indian 1961 Act, see Justice RS Bachawat's, *Law of Arbitration & Conciliation* (ibid), Vol 2, 2837, 2839.

[22] *Oil and Natural Gas Commission v Western Company of North America*, A.I.R 1987 S.C. 674; (1988) XIII *ICCA Yearbook* 473.

[23] *National Thermal Power Corporation v Singer*, A.I.R 1993 S.C. 998; (1993) XVIII *ICCA Yearbook* 403.

award.' Section 2(2) provides: 'This Part [i.e. Part 1] shall apply where the place of arbitration is India.' However, this second provision does not say that Part 1 shall *not* apply where the place of arbitration is outside India. There is an old story of the lawyer caught smoking a cigarette in a library under a large sign reading 'No Smoking Allowed'. When apprehended, this lawyer defends himself: 'The sign gives me a choice – it says only that no smoking is allowed; and it does not say that smoking is not allowed.' Likewise, this omission in Section 2(2) was interpreted by the Indian Courts to mean that an arbitration with a foreign seat subject to a foreign *lex loci arbitri* could still be subject to Part 1 of the Indian 1996 Act. Read together, these two provisions in the 1996 Act were thus interpreted judicially as an effective re-enactment of Section 9(b) of the Indian 1961 Act. Hence, the Indian courts decided that, even where the arbitration had a foreign seat, the Indian Court had jurisdiction under Part 1 of the Indian 1996 Act to set aside a foreign award when the contract and hence the arbitration clause were governed by Indian law, because any resulting award was to be treated as a domestic Indian award not subject to the New York Convention.

The high water mark of this jurisprudence under the Indian 1996 Act came with the decisions of the Indian Supreme Court in *Bhatia International*, decided in 2004, and in *Venture Global*, decided in 2008.[24] In his introduction to Bachawat's Law of Arbitration & Conciliation (5th ed, 2010), Arvind P Datar described the first decision as being subject to 'substantial criticism' and 'at the time contrary to the decisions of the majority of High Courts in the country'; and OP Malhotra and Indu Malhotra doubted the correctness of the same decision 'because it purports to replace the clear and unambiguous language from s 2(2) with court-coined language, which is tantamount to judicial legislation – an area beyond the jurisdiction of the court.'[25] These two cases (with others) produced the 'disaster' for international arbitration involving India, which has adversely affected foreign investment in India and the full development of a modern industrial economy, particularly in the electricity sector. The reasons for last summer's power shortages in Northern India, involving massive blackouts for hundreds of millions of electricity users, are doubtless complex; but one of them may well include India's legal system. However, this is an Indian story that could end as happily as in Pakistan.

On 6 September 2012, the Indian Supreme Court decided eight consolidated appeals in an important judgment known as *Bharat Aluminium*.[26] In a unanimous

[24] *Bhatia International v Bulk Trading* (2002) 4 SCC 105, (2002) XXVII *ICCA Yearbook* 234; *Venture Global v Satyam Computer Services* (2008) 4 SCC 190, (2008) XXXIII *ICCA Yearbook* 239. For later cases, *see Indtel Technical Services v WS Atkins Plc* (2008) 10 SCC 308; and *Citation Infowares Ltd v Equinox Corp* (2009) 5 UJ 2066 (SC).

[25] Justice RS Bachawat's *Law of Arbitration & Conciliation*, Vol 1, 117ff; and OP Malhotra and Indu Malhotra's *Law and Practice of Arbitration and Conciliation* (2006) 143–4.

[26] One of these appeals was *White Industries v Coal India*, where the delays under Indian law for enforcing an ICC award made in Paris in 2002 had already led an UNCITRAL tribunal to hold India liable to the investor under India's bilateral investment treaty with Australia. In its award of 20 November 2011 (made in Singapore), this UNCITRAL tribunal decided that a delay of 9 years was

318 ON ARBITRATION

and powerfully reasoned judgment, the Supreme Court asserted the general principle of territoriality of domestic Indian arbitration legislation, rejected the application of Part 1 of the Indian 1996 Act to New York Convention arbitration agreements and awards outside India, even where the substantive contract and arbitration agreement were governed by Indian law; and overruled the Supreme Court's earlier decisions to the contrary in *Bhatia* and *Venture Global*. It is an important decision; it merits careful study; and it is to be welcomed without reservation as a major development for international arbitration, except for one unfortunate factor. For reasons not recorded in the judgment, the Indian Supreme Court decided 'in order to do complete justice', in the penultimate paragraph of its judgment, to limit the effect of its decision to arbitration agreements executed *after* the date of its judgment.[27] Hence, the old law may continue to apply to all arbitrations taking place and all awards made under arbitration agreements executed before 6 September 2012. In other words, not much may soon change in India despite this judgment; and for all the parties to these conjoined appeals, the judgment changes nothing at all. It is not clear how India can square this prospective ruling with its existing obligations in the New York Convention under international law, as suggested by the Private International Law Committee's Fifth Report (supra). We shall doubtless hear much more of this penultimate paragraph, if it remains Indian law, particularly in the field of investment arbitration.[28] An Indian leopard can change most of its spots; but, apparently it can still retain the largest spot of all. It should not be the English, however, who should criticize the Indian judiciary and legislature. The original cause of this problem was and remains the bad idea migrating from London to New Delhi in 1937, in colonial times, before Indian independence.

F. Section 7 of the English 1996 Act

We now turn to the second idea, eventually migrating to London. Here, we need to work backwards from the present to the past, beginning with Section 7 of the

---

a breach of India's international obligation under the treaty to ensure to the investor 'effective means of asserting claims and enforcing rights' under the ICC award and the New York Convention: see the UNCITRAL Final Award dated 30 November 2011 (J William Rowley, chairman; Charles Brower; and Christopher Lau).

[27] Paragraph 201 of the Supreme Court's judgment.

[28] The scope of this limitation may depend upon the relevant arbitration agreement: is it, for this purpose, the agreement to refer future disputes to arbitration or the later reference thereunder of an existing dispute to arbitration? Under English law, both may be considered as arbitration agreements, the first as the 'continuous' arbitration agreement and the second, later in time, as the 'individual' arbitration agreement: see the English legal materials cited by the author in 'Towards a Possible Solution: Limitation, Interest and Assignment in Paris and London', *ICCA Congress Series No 7 – Vienna* (1996) 267, 276.

English 1996 Act, stating under English law the general principle of separability of an arbitration clause in a substantive contract, actual or putative:

> Unless otherwise agreed by the parties, an arbitration agreement which forms or was intended to form part of another agreement (whether or not in writing) shall not be regarded as invalid, non-existent or ineffective because that other agreement is invalid, or did not come into existence or has become ineffective; and it shall for that purpose be treated as a distinct agreement.

This is unique statutory language in English law; and it addresses both the initial invalidity and the non-existence of the substantive contract. It is not the language of Article 16(1) of the UNCITRAL Model Law, which otherwise strongly influenced the English 1996 Act. Section 7 was the product of the UK's Departmental Advisory Committee (the DAC) responsible for researching and developing the 1996 Act for the UK Government, a difficult and lengthy exercise described by one informed critic as a period of 'elephantine gestation'.

Before the English 1996 Act, English law on separability was somewhat less than an arbitral butterfly (as in Switzerland and France) and more of a chrysalis, particularly where the substantive contract was alleged to be initially invalid or initially non-existent. Until the DAC's work, the English principle had several characteristic features: first, it was a creation of the common law made by English judges, forming part of the private law of contract, and not statute; secondly, it had emerged haphazardly over many years, including the House of Lords' decision in *Heyman v Darwins* (1942);[29] thirdly, it had become muddled (as elsewhere) with the power of an arbitration tribunal to address its own jurisdiction ('compétence de la compétence'); fourthly, it had become intertwined with the different question of the scope (or interpretation) of an arbitration agreement and the reference to arbitration under such an agreement; fifthly, this process of legal reasoning consisted of judicial decisions, *dicta* of the highest authority and scholarly writings, but these materials were difficult to reconcile (particularly the different speeches in *Heyman v Darwins*); and sixthly, its judicial development remained incomplete at English common law.[30] Significantly, it was said by one distinguished commentator (writing in 1984), Johan Steyn, that 'the concept of the separability of the arbitration clause has not been fully worked out by the English courts, but it is thought that one may be witnessing the gradual evolution of such a concept'.[31]

---

[29] *Heyman v Darwins* [1942] AC 356.
[30] See generally, Mustill and Boyd, *Commercial Arbitration* (2nd ed; London, 1989) 105–21.
[31] 'ICCA National Report on England', in *International Handbook on Commercial Arbitration* (1984), revised from (1983) VIII *ICCA Yearbook* 3. Johan Steyn, originally a senior practising lawyer in South Africa, was called to the English Bar in 1973, took silk in 1979 and was appointed a High Court Judge in 1985, a Lord Justice of Appeal in 1992 and a Law Lord in 1995.

320 ON ARBITRATION

We must now return to Moscow, to an 1984 arbitration award made (in camera) by the Foreign Trade Arbitration Commission (FTAC), comprised of three Russian arbitrators who decided a dispute between a foreign buyer (Joc Oil of Bermuda) and the Soviet foreign trade organization responsible for exporting oil from the USSR, V/O Soyusnefteexport (SNE).[32] The president of the Moscow tribunal was Professor SN Bratus, one of the principal draftsmen of and commentators on the 1964 Russian Civil Code; the second arbitrator was Professor VN Pozdniakov, the president of FTAC; and the third arbitrator was Professor RL Naryshkina, a specialist in comparative and private international law. The issues in the arbitration raised (amongst many others) a simple question: under Russian law (being the law applicable to the ostensible contract of sale, its arbitration clause and also the arbitration with its seat in Moscow),[33] did this arbitration tribunal have jurisdiction to award non-contractual compensation under the Russian Civil Code in circumstances where the sale contract was initially invalid ('ab initio') and, arguably, initially non-existent (also 'ab initio')? The factual circumstances were unusual: for reasons undisclosed during the arbitration, SNE's president had signed alone for SNE, in Paris, the ostensible sale contract agreed with Joc Oil, which included amongst its terms a standard form arbitration clause providing for FTAC arbitration in Moscow. Under Russian law (as SNE's personal law) and also under its corporate statute, SNE had no contractual capacity to agree a sale contract in the form of a foreign trade transaction with less than two signatories representing SNE, for which the express sanction under Russian law included the nullity of the ostensible contract. That limitation, however, did not directly apply to an arbitration agreement, where it sufficed for the one signatory to bind SNE under both its statute and Russian law (incorporating the New York Convention), with no penal sanction.

Faced with these several factors, after 33 days of hearing, the Moscow tribunal decided that SNE's claim for the contractual price must fail, as also Joc Oil's contractual counterclaim; that the initial invalidity of the sale contract could not infect the arbitration clause as an otherwise valid separate arbitration agreement; that the tribunal had jurisdiction to award compensation for SNE's alternative non-contractual claim under the Russian Civil Code; and that such compensation should be ordered in restitution and for unjust enrichment. It was a result reached by these three arbitrators largely as a matter of legal logic, without citing any specific provision regarding separability in the Russian legal codes (because there was none). It was also, let it be said, a result that caused no offence to common-sense in East or West: Soviet oil worth over US$ 100 million had been shipped by SNE to Joc Oil for which Joc Oil had paid nothing. However, other parts of the award,

[32] The Moscow award dated 9 July 1984 was published, in English translation from the original Russian, in (1993) XVIII *ICCA Yearbook* 92. It was later published, in Russian, in *MKA* (April–June) 2007, 135ff.

[33] For ease of reference, the laws of the USSR and the RSFSR are here collectively described as 'Russian law'.

concerning compensation for unjust enrichment (in addition to monetary compensation in restitution) and the non-assignment/re-assignment of SNE's claim were and remain controversial under Russian law; but these other factors need not concern us here.[34] Of relevance for present purposes is the fact that Joc Oil was advised in the arbitration by a legion of international arbitration experts and advisers, deploying a mass of international and comparative materials on the separability of an arbitration clause, including Swiss law, French law, German law and English law. One of these legal advisers was Johan Steyn. It was thus, we can surmise, that he became increasingly aware of the arguments made outside England as regards the separability of an arbitration clause.

The Moscow award was then successfully enforced in Bermuda against Joc Oil; and, after the majority decision of the Bermudan Court of Appeal in 1989 (while an appeal was pending to the Privy Council in London),[35] Joc Oil amicably settled the case with a substantial payment to SNE. The Court of Appeal unequivocally recognized the doctrine of separability under Russian law, ensuring that the FTAC arbitration clause, as a self-contained separate arbitration agreement, was not affected by the initial invalidity or non-existence of the sale contract.[36] During the legal proceedings before the Bermudan Court of Appeal, Joc Oil was represented by Sydney Kentridge, who, like Johan Steyn many years earlier, had found it necessary to live and work in England, outside South Africa.[37] During these legal proceedings, both parties were now being advised by other legal experts, two of whom gave lengthy expert evidence on separability under the laws of France, Switzerland, Germany,

[34] See the recent memoirs of Professor AA Kostin, SNE's counsel in the FTAC arbitration (now the President of the ICAC in Moscow, FTAC's successor): 'Brief Memoirs of Long Arbitration Proceedings' *MKA* 2007 (April–May) 130, in Russian. As to its award of pecuniary compensation for unjust enrichment (equivalent to commercial interest), Professor Kostin expresses doubts as to the correctness of the Moscow tribunal's reliance on Article 473 of the 1964 Russian Civil Code, as opposed to restitution under Article 48 of the Civil Code only.

[35] The judgment of the Bermuda Court of Appeal is published in (1990) XV *ICCA Yearbook* 384. The leading judgment was delivered by Sir Denys Roberts (the former Chief Justice of Hong Kong) for the majority (with H. da Costa). The President, Sir Alistair Blair-Kerr, dissented on the principal basis that the arbitration clause was non-existent, as was the sale contract: '... It is quite ridiculous to suggest that the arbitration clause which formed part of that "non-existent" contract would nevertheless, somehow, be deemed to have come into existence' (434).

[36] In denying the existence under Russian law of any doctrine of separability, Joc Oil's expert witnesses contended that only the limited Russian legal rule on partial nullity (of an otherwise indivisible transaction) could apply, namely Section 60 of the 1964 Russian Civil Code. However, Section 60 re-enacted the same provision in Article 37 of the 1922 Russian Civil Code which, being drafted by former Czarist law professors within a short deadline imposed by the Soviet regime, was derived from Article 89 of the draft 1903 Russian Civil Code which was itself based on Article 139 of the German Civil Code with, so it seems, Article 20 of the Swiss Federal Code of Obligations. Since the similar legal rule on partial nullity in Germany and Switzerland had played no part in the development of the separability doctrine in either of these two legal systems, SNE's expert witnesses contended that the Russian legal rule on partial nullity was no bar to the existence of such a doctrine under Russian law.

[37] In South Africa, Sydney Kentridge had appeared for Nelson Mandela at the Rivonia treason trial in 1963; and he had also appeared for Steve Biko's family at the 1977 inquest into Steve Biko's death in the custody of the South African police. In England, he was called to the Bar in 1977, took silk in 1984 and was knighted in 1999.

322   ON ARBITRATION

Sweden, the United States[38] and other countries. For Joc Oil, the expert witness was Dr Broches, the former General Counsel to the World Bank, the draftsman of the 1965 ICSID Convention and ICSID's first secretary-general. For SNE, the expert witness was Professor Berthold Goldman, of the Dijon school of arbitration and now best known as the co-author of that great work on international commercial arbitration, Fouchard, Goldman & Gaillard. As a result of these legal proceedings in Bermuda, the Moscow award became public; and both the Moscow award and the Court of Appeal's judgment became known in England, together with foreign legal materials cited by the experts during their testimony.[39]

As a further result, many of these legal materials were cited in England to the Commercial Court and later the Court of Appeal in *Harbour v Kansa* in 1992.[40] The claimant was there seeking to enforce the arbitration clause in an insurance policy and to obtain a stay of English litigation under Article II of the New York Convention (enacted as Section 1 of the English 1975 Act). The respondent (the plaintiff in the litigation) maintained that the arbitration clause was invalid because the policy was illegal from the outset under English law. The claimant was represented by Sydney Kentridge; and the judge in the Commercial Court was (as you have already guessed) Mr Justice Steyn. He was already a member of the DAC (then chaired by Lord Justice Mustill); and later, as Lord Justice Steyn, he became the second of the DAC's three chairmen, without whom the project for the 1996 Act would have foundered long before its eventual arrival as a baby elephant.

The issue squarely raised in this English case was whether, under a principle of separability under English law, an arbitration clause could confer jurisdiction on an arbitration tribunal in London where the substantive contract was illegal from the outset and therefore initially invalid under English law, although that illegality did not affect the validity of arbitration clause directly. As the Court of Appeal later noted, the orthodox English view was that if the contract was invalid 'ab initio', then so too any arbitration clause contained in that contract: it had been said, simplistically: 'nothing can come of nothing; ex nihil nil fit'.[41] Latin, as almost always,

---

[38] In the United States, the doctrine of separability (or 'severability') was established in the decision of the US Supreme Court in *Prima Paint v Flood & Conklin* 388 US 395 (1967), after its recognition in Switzerland and France. Its rationale may also derive from a different legal policy, namely the contractual freedom to arbitrate any justiciable issue, including fraud inducing the substantive contact: see Gerald Aksen (then AAA's Counsel), 'Prima Paint v Flood & Conklin – What does it mean?' (1968) XLIII St John's L Rev 1.

[39] These materials included the *Bundesgerightsthof Decision of 27 February* 1970 JZ 1970, 730 (Germany), translated into English with its contemporary case-note by Professor Dr Schlosser and an accompanying article by Stewart Boyd QC, 'Arbitration under A Still-Born Contract: The BGH Decision of 27 February 1970' (1989) 5 Arb Int 75, 79, 86.

[40] *Harbour Assurance v Kansa* [1993] 1 Lloyd's Rep 455 (CA) and [1992] 1 Loyd's Rep 81 (Steyn J), contra *David Taylor v Barnett Trading* [1953] 1 Lloyd's Rep 181.

[41] Ibid, 457. These orthodox views were well-settled amongst English arbitration practitioners: see, for example, Alan Redfern and Martin Hunter (eds), *Law and Practice of International Commercial Arbitration*, (1st ed, Sweet & Maxwell, 1986) 216: 'If the main contract was valid when made but became invalid because (for example) of supervening illegality, the arbitration clause may indeed survive .... However, if the main contract was invalid ab initio, then the arbitration clause could not survive'.

obfuscates all. In the Commercial Court, Mr Justice Steyn held reluctantly that he was bound by judicial precedent of the Court of Appeal to uphold this orthodox view. However, he did so after laying out powerful arguments why, but for such precedent, the English principle of separability should recognize the validity of an arbitration agreement where it was only indirectly impeached by the invalidity of the substantive contract, even where that contract was initially invalid.

The English Court of Appeal had little difficulty in distinguishing its own judicial precedent; and in three persuasive judgments, the Court allowed the appeal and enforced the arbitration agreement. (There was no appeal to the House of Lords). One of these appellate judges was Lord Justice Hoffmann, another jurist with South African origins. He cited the judgment of the Bermudan Court of Appeal, enforcing the SNE award, concluding significantly: 'The decision was reached under Soviet law, but I think that the answer in English law would have been the same'; and 'In every case it seems to me that the logical question is not whether the issue goes to the validity of the contract but whether it goes to the validity of the arbitration clause.'[42] He also invoked the German *BGH Decision of 27 February 1970*[43] as a 'landmark decision', as cited in the Bermudan judgment, on the presumed intention of parties favouring the resolution of their dispute by the same arbitration tribunal and not two different tribunals, a state court and, depending on the answer, an arbitration tribunal (or vice-versa). This learned Judge then developed a phrase which became famous in English arbitration law: 'the practical advantages of one-stop adjudication'.[44] That is the same principle of legal logic evident in the Moscow award: it made no practical sense for that tribunal to decline jurisdiction, having decided that the sale contract was a nullity, and then to leave the parties to continue their non-contractual dispute before a state court of uncertain jurisdiction, whether in Moscow, Bermuda or nowhere at all. It made logical sense for the same tribunal, within the same arbitration, to decide upon both the invalidity of the sale contract and the claimant's non-contractual claim consequent upon such nullity, in an award under a valid, existing arbitration agreement conforming to Russian law and the New York Convention.

From here, it was a small step for the DAC to propose what eventually became Section 7 of the English 1996 Act. In 1994, the DAC advised that the doctrine of separability was to be regarded as essential to the practice of international arbitration: 'Whatever degree of legal fiction underlying the doctrine, it is not generally considered possible for international arbitration to operate effectively in jurisdictions where the doctrine is precluded.'[45] From there, it was an even smaller step

---

[42] Ibid, 469.

[43] See fn 39 above.

[44] Mr Hoffmann was called to the English Bar in 1964, took silk in 1977 and was appointed a High Court Judge in 1985, a Lord Justice of Appeal in 1992 and a Law Lord in 1995. He now acts (*inter alia*) as an arbitrator.

[45] As to the DAC's proposal, see the DAC Consultation Document of 3 February 1994 on the widespread acceptance of the separability of an arbitration clause [1994] 10 *Arb Int* 189, 226 at

324 ON ARBITRATION

to compose Section 7 of the 1996 Act.[46] Accordingly, triggered by this idea from Moscow (via Bermuda), the English chrysalis became a butterfly. The new statutory doctrine received its flying colours with the subsequent decision of the House of Lords in *Fiona Trust v Privalov* (2007) in a dispute originating, of course, from Moscow.[47] The leading judgment was given by Lord Hoffmann (who else); and we can do no better than here read part of his conclusion:

> 17. The principle of separability enacted in section 7 means that the invalidity or rescission of the main contract does not necessarily entail the invalidity or rescission of the arbitration agreement ... Of course there may be cases in which the ground upon which the main agreement is invalid is identical with the ground upon which the arbitration agreement is invalid ... But the ground of attack is not that the main agreement is invalid.

> 18 Even if the allegation is that there was no concluded agreement (for example, the terms of the main agreement remained to be agreed) that is not necessarily an attack on the arbitration agreement. If the arbitration clause has been agreed, the parties will be presumed to have intended the question of whether there was a concluded main agreement to be decided by arbitration.

227: '... historically, that international consensus on autonomy has now grown very broad: see *Tobler v. Blaser* 59 I 177 1933 (Switzerland); AB Nörrkopings NJA 1936 521 (Sweden); *Gosset v. Carapelli* Cass. Civ., Dalloz 1963, 545; *Navimpex v. Wiking Trader* J.D.I. 1990.134 (France); *Prima Paint v. Flood & Conklin* 388 US 395 (1967) (USA); The BGH 27 February 1970 Case JZ 1970, 730 and in English translation [1990] Arb. Int 79 (Federal Republic of Germany); and *SNE v Joc Oil* (1984) (USSR), a FTAC award enforced under the 1958 New York Arbitration Convention by the Bermudian Court of Appeal (1990) XV ICCA Yearbook 384; (1993) XVIII ICCA Yearbook 92; and generally Judge Schwebel, International Arbitration: Three Salient Problems, particularly at pages 58-59. English law now fits firmly into the mainstream of this international consensus: *Heyman v. Darwins* [1942] AC 356, as applied in *Kansa v. Harbour Assurance* [1993] QB 701.'

[46] As to the DAC's drafts prepared by Parliamentary Counsel, see Clause 3(2) the 1994 draft bill [1994] 10 *Arb Int* 194: 'An arbitration agreement which forms part of another agreement ("the primary agreement") shall in all cases be regarded as constituting (and as having [been] constituted since it was made) an agreement which is separate from the primary agreement and, accordingly, an arbitration agreement shall not be void, voidable, unenforceable or otherwise ineffective by reason only that the primary agreement is void, voidable, unenforceable or otherwise ineffective'; and as to Clause 7 of the subsequent 1995 Bill leading to Section 7 of the English 1996 Act, see the DAC Report of February 1996, paras 43–47 and the DAC Report of January 1997, para 20 (Both DAC Reports are published as appendices to Mustill & Boyd's *Commercial Arbitration: 2001 Companion* (2001) 404ff and 465; see also 135ff).

[47] *Fiona Trust v Privalov* [2007] UKHL 40 [2008] 1 Lloyd's Rep 254. The passages cited from Lord Hoffman's judgment are taken from 257–8. This judgment was later followed by Mr Justice Gross (now Lord Justice Gross) in *U.R. Power v Kuok Oils* [2009] EWHC 1940 (Comm). In a case concerning an arbitration clause in a contract alleged never to have been legally binding, this learned English Judge decided (para 40): '... to my mind, the wording of s.7 of the [English 1996] Act makes it plain that even though the underlying contract never came into existence, the arbitration agreement may still be binding' (As Peter Gross QC, also of South African origins, he was one of Joc Oil's Counsel in its Bermudan legal proceedings, before his appointment as an English High Court Judge).

The words are English, spoken in London by an English judge as regards English law; but the legal logic comes from the idea underlying the Moscow award.

G. Conclusion

Maxim the Greek was eventually canonized by the Russian Orthodox Church in 1988. He is the only known arbitrator to be a saint, or more appropriately perhaps, the only saint known to have been an arbitrator. In 1997, the Russian Orthodox Church returned part of his earthly remains to the Vatopedi Monastery on Mount Athos, making his wish to return home come true, albeit more than 450 years too late. His ideas live on, both in Russian philosophy and for the Orthodox Church in Russia and Greece.[48]

As for the migration of arbitral ideas, our world is shrinking ever further and more swiftly, as ideas cross frontiers with an ease even greater than that with which Maxim brought news to Moscow of Columbus, Plato and Florence in the 16th century. As for bad ideas, princes and princely institutions still threaten the practice of international arbitration, as in 1930 and 1937. Yet, good ideas still migrate, empirically, from the myriad participants working in arbitration, be they practitioners, scholars, arbitrators or judges. It is the arbitral triumph over institutions and ministries by individuals from all over the world, from whatever legal, cultural or national background.

It was therefore no accident that Professor Bratus and Professor Pozdniakov were early members of ICCA and were no strangers to that informed community of international arbitrators; it was no coincidence that the Russian Civil Codes were influenced by law professors personally familiar with legal codes in Germany and Switzerland; nor that Dr Broches and Professor Goldman were eminent scholars in the different fields of public and private international law; nor that Lord Steyn, Lord Hoffmann and Sir Sydney Kentridge QC are familiar not only with English law, but also with Roman-Dutch and other civilian legal thinking; nor, of course, that students here at MIDS come from all four corners of this earth. As Lord Mustill (the DAC's first chairman) once wrote, 'Cross-fertilization between legal systems has been a powerful instrument for more than two centuries in the elaboration and the refinement of national laws.'[49] It has also been a very necessary instrument. It was such cross-fertilization that produced separability as a national and international doctrine. Perhaps, not much has changed from Maxim's time: ideas still matter; and borders are no obstacle to their migration.

---

[48] See G Speake and Metropolitan Kallistos Ware (eds), *Mount Athos: Microcosm of the Christian East* (Peter Lang 2009) 143ff.

[49] MJ Mustill, 'The New Lex Mercatoria' in *Liber Amicorum for Lord Wilberforce*, eds. M. Bos & I. Brownlie (ILA 1987), 149.

326   ON ARBITRATION

Finally, tribute must be paid to whom and where this good idea started as regards the separability of an arbitration clause: both here in Switzerland with the early *Tobler* decision of the Swiss Federal Tribunal (1933),[50] but also in Florence, without whom there would have been no Michael the Dominican in San Marco, no Maximos on Mount Athos and no Maxim the Greek in Moscow; and without Maxim's followers, Russia might have become another country; and hence, amongst other effects, is it just possible that there could have been no Section 7 of the English 1996 Act? In any event, without the continuous migration of good ideas and individual travellers, there would be much less 'fortius ...' and far more 'infirmius ...' for the world-wide practice of international arbitration.[51]

[50] *Tobler v Blaser* 59 1 177 1933, cited in the 1994 DAC Consultation Document (supra); see also Adam Samuel, *Jurisdictional Problems in International Commercial Arbitration: A Study of Belgian Dutch, English, French, Swedish, Swiss, U.S. and West German Law* (Institut suisse de droit comparé 1999) 162.

[51] The author is not Orthodox; nor South African. He was a member of the DAC; one of SNE's Counsel in its Bermudan legal proceedings; and the president of an arbitration tribunal which, many years ago, made an award in Singapore in a case lately one of the eight appeals in *Bharat Aluminium*.

19

Jurisdiction, Admissibility, and Choice of Law in International Arbitration

'Quixotic Limitations on Party Autonomy under the United Kingdom's Arbitration Act 1996'

A. Introduction[*]

There are surprising limitations on party autonomy under the United Kingdom's Arbitration Act 1996 for international arbitrations between commercial parties. The starting-point is London (or elsewhere in England and Wales or Northern Ireland) being designated or determined as the juridical seat of the parties' arbitration within the broad meaning of Section 3(a) of the 1996 Act. That designation can be made by the parties themselves, an arbitral institution (such as the ICC Court) and the arbitration tribunal (under the UNCITRAL, SIAC or LCIA Rules), or otherwise determined, in the absence of any such designation, by the English Court.[1] Hence, by virtue of such an English seat and Section 2(1) of the 1996 Act, Part I of the 1996 Act applies to the parties' arbitration taking place under their arbitration agreement.[2] But for that seat, the parties, their dispute and their arbitration could have nothing to do with English law, whether as part of the applicable substantive law, the *lex arbitri*, the 1996 Act or otherwise.

---

[*] I am much indebted to Toby Landau QC for his original comments on Section 4(5) of the Arbitration Act 1996. All errors and opinions are, however, mine alone.

[1] Section 3 of the 1996 Act provides: 'In this Part "the seat of the arbitration" means the juridical seat of the arbitration designated – (a) by the parties to the arbitration agreement, or (b) by any arbitral or other institution or person vested by the parties with powers in that regard, or (c) by the arbitral tribunal if so authorised by the parties, - or determined, in the absence of any such designation, having regard to the parties' agreement and all the relevant circumstances.' Under Section 5 of the 1996 Act, the arbitration agreement, designating the arbitral seat (whether directly or indirectly, expressly or impliedly) must be 'in writing' as there defined.

[2] Section 2(1) of the 1996 Act provides: 'The provisions of this Part [Part 1] apply where the seat of the arbitration is in England and Wales or Northern Ireland.'

On Arbitration. Edited by: Sam Wordsworth KC and Marie Veeder, Oxford University Press. © Oxford University Press 2023.
DOI: 10.1093/oso/9780192869135.003.0019

328   ON ARBITRATION

This contribution examines two quixotic features of the 1996 Act impinging upon party autonomy exercised by international commercial parties in regard to: (i) pre-dispute agreements on costs in their arbitration agreement; and (ii) the absence of any express provision in their arbitration or other agreement for pre-award interest. The former is a real problem; but the second, it is suggested, is a myth.

(1)   Costs

Under Section 60 of the 1996 Act, any agreement between the parties to an arbitration with an English seat which has the effect that a party is to pay the whole or part of the costs of the arbitration 'in any event' is only valid if made after the dispute in question has arisen.[3] This is a 'mandatory' provision from which the parties may not derogate, as a matter of English public policy.[4] The costs of the arbitration here include the parties' legal costs, as well as the costs of the arbitrators and any arbitral institution.[5] As to timing, the parties may agree in writing at any time *after* their dispute has arisen that costs should be paid by one party 'in any event' (up to the making of the award), but not *before* their dispute has arisen; e.g., in a standard or printed form of contract such as the early Bermuda forms of excess liability insurance.[6]

This statutory provision was not new to the 1996 Act. It re-enacted Section 18(3) of the Arbitration Act 1950, which itself re-enacted Section 12(1) of the Arbitration Act 1934.[7] The latter provision resulted from the recommendations

---

[3] Section 60 of the 1996 Act provides: 'An agreement which has the effect that a party is to pay the whole or part of the costs of the arbitration in any event is only valid if made after the dispute in question has arisen.'

[4] Section 4(1) and Schedule 1 to the 1996 Act.

[5] Section 59 of the 1996 Act.

[6] The Bermuda standard forms for excess liability insurance provided (prior to the Bermuda standard form XL004) that the costs of the arbitration 'shall be borne equally by the parties to such arbitration'. *See also* R. Jacobs, L.S. Masters and P. Stanley, *Liability Insurance in International Arbitration – The Bermuda Form* (2011; 2nd ed), paras 11.61 and 17.32. Since the mid-1980s, the Bermuda forms have been the principal wording on which high value excess insurance for legal liability is written for US-based insureds. The forms' common feature is a hybrid arbitration agreement providing for London Arbitration and the application to the merits of New York substantive law by the arbitration tribunal.

[7] Section 12(1) of the 1934 Act provided: 'Any provision in an arbitration agreement to the effect that the parties or any party thereto shall in any event pay their or his own costs of the reference or award or any part thereof shall be void; and the principal Act [the 1889 Act] shall in the case of an arbitration agreement containing any such provision have effect as if that provision were not contained therein: Provided that nothing herein shall invalidate such a provision when it is part of an agreement

JURISDICTION, ADMISSIBILITY, AND CHOICE OF LAW IN ARBITRATION 329

of the 1927 MacKinnon Report on Arbitration.[8] The MacKinnon Committee had heard evidence that older insurance policies provided that each side should bear its own costs, although (so it found) new policies generally did not. The Committee was nevertheless concerned that such a term could drive an insured (as the financially weaker party) to compromise with its insurer (as the stronger party), rather than continue the proof of items of its claim at its own irrecoverable expense. The Committee concluded that, as a matter of public policy, a term 'in a common form of arbitration clause that each side shall pay his own costs shall be void, and that the arbitrator or umpire, notwithstanding such [term], shall have full power to order either party to pay the costs'.[9] By 'common form', the Committee meant arbitration clauses in printed forms of contract, i.e. contracts of adhesion drafted and imposed by the stronger commercial party. However, for the 1934 Act, the United Kingdom Parliament decided to make the provision of general application, not limited to printed forms or contacts of adhesion.[10] It also decided, as advised by the McKinnon Committee, not to limit its application to contracts of insurance, from which the original mischief had apparently originated. Nor did the 1934 Act distinguish between consumer and commercial disputes or limit its application to domestic arbitrations or contracts subject to English substantive law.

This issue of public policy was reconsidered by the Departmental Advisory Committee on the Law of Arbitration responsible for drafting the arbitration bill which was submitted to Parliament and enacted as the 1996 Act (the 'DAC'). The DAC baldly concluded 'that public policy continues to dictate that such a provision should remain'.[11] This succinct recommendation addressed a non-existent problem in practice that was barely evident to the MacKinnon Committee in 1927, some seventy years earlier. It did not derive from the 1985 UNCITRAL Model Law: to the contrary, it conflicted with Articles 19 and 28 of the Model Law.

---

to submit to arbitration a dispute which has arisen before the making of such agreement.' As noted by Quintin Hogg (later Lord Hailsham LC), this provision did not apply to oral arbitration agreements: *see The Law of Arbitration* (1936), p. 175. Similarly, the 1996 Act (Part 1) does not apply to such agreements, but in practice these are exceedingly rare.

[8] The Report of Committee on the Law of Arbitration, March 1927, p. 14 (Cmnd 2817). The MacKinnon Committee was chaired by Mr Justice MacKinnon, who had earlier chaired the experts' committee at the League of Nations responsible for the 1923 Geneva Protocol on Arbitration Clauses. Its members included Sir Thomas Chitty (late Senior Master), Sir James Martin (President of the London Chamber of Commerce), F.B. Merriman KC MP (later Solicitor-General) and W. Raeburn KC.

[9] The 1927 MacKinnon Report, *ibid.*, p. 14.

[10] Notes on Clauses to the Arbitration Bill 1934, regarding 'Clause 13 – Provisions as to Costs', p. 50 (PRO: LCO 2/1789 XL 25358).

[11] DAC Report of February 1996, para. 267 (*See* Mustill and Boyd's *Commercial Arbitration, 2001 Companion*, pp. 345 & 439, here cited as '*M&B Companion*'). To the best of my knowledge, the DAC had received no written submissions from users regarding the re-enactment of Section 18(3) of the 1950 Act.

330   ON ARBITRATION

As with several other re-enacted provisions, Section 60 of the 1996 Act smacks of legislative compromise. Moreover, it was inserted in Part I of the 1996 Act applicable to international arbitration and not Part II applicable to domestic arbitration.[12] Not unreasonably, this infringement of the principle of party autonomy in Part I of the 1996 Act has been attacked by many international commentators and international users of London Arbitration.[13] It remains a problem for party autonomy, unlikely to be remedied within the foreseeable future by any amendment to the 1996 Act. In the meantime, doubts must exist as to the enforceability outside England of a costs award subjected to Section 60, for the failure of the arbitral procedure to accord with the agreement of the parties under Article V(1)(d) of the New York Convention or Article 36(1) (a)(iv) of the Amended UNCITRAL Model Law.

The simplest solution is for international users of London Arbitration to draft their arbitration agreements differently, in conformity with Section 60 of the 1996 Act. Thus, the current Bermuda forms simply provide that any order as to the costs of the arbitration shall be in the sole discretion of the arbitration tribunal.[14] This forced solution does not accord with party autonomy; and for present purposes, it can be discarded as providing no solution at all. A partial solution to Section 60, consistent with party autonomy, is however, possible in practice. Early in the arbitration, particularly at the first procedural meeting (whether held in person or by telephone), the arbitration tribunal can record in a written consent order, made with the authority of the parties, that the parties agree to confirm the offending provision in or incorporated into their arbitration agreement.[15] At that time, taking place *after* the parties' dispute has arisen, both sides usually retain a common interest in doing so. Alternatively, if one or more parties intend (as the likely prevailing party in the arbitration) to receive an award recovering their costs, the effect of Section 60 can be explained by the arbitration tribunal to the parties at the outset of the arbitration, without the risk of any later unpleasant surprise.[16] There have been such surprises: unfortunately not a few arbitrators have overlooked (with the parties) the effect of Section 60, with damning results for their award under Section 67 or 68 of the 1996 Act in the English Commercial

---

[12] Sections 85-87 of Part II on domestic arbitration agreements have never been brought into force, owing to the effect of EU law as decided by the English Courts in *Philip Alexander v. Bamberger* [1996] CLC 1757; *see* the DAC Report of January 1997, paras 47ff and *M&B Companion*, pp. 470-471 and 377-378. After 'Brexit' in or after 2019, it is possible that these provisions in Part II may be brought into force by the United Kingdom Parliament.

[13] For example, *see* W.W. Park, 'Arbitration in the Autumn' (2011) 2:2 *Journal of Int Dispute Settlement* 1, at pp. 20-21.

[14] D. Scorey, R. Geddes and C. Harris, *The Bermuda Form* (2011), paras 16.11 and 22.35ff (in regard to Bermuda Form XL004); *see also* R. Jacobs et al, *ibid.*, para. 11.60.

[15] Under Section 5(4) of the 1996 Act, there is an agreement if 'recorded by a third party with the authority of the parties to the agreement'; i.e., by the arbitration tribunal in a written consent order.

[16] Article VI.N (Arbitration) and VI.O (Law of Construction and Interpretation); *see* R. Jacobs et al, *ibid.*, para. 15.21.

Court.[17] Whilst this incomplete solution may often work in practice, it does not of course work in theory.

Accordingly, as Professor W.W. Park has fairly concluded: 'The provision casts a wide net, catching even reasonable arrangements among sophisticated business managers to split arbitrator compensation on a 50/50 basis, and/or to require each side to cover its own legal expenses. In such an instance, what is to be done by a conscientious arbitrator?'[18] In the absence of further agreement by the parties, that arbitrator's choice lies between making a costs award invalid under English law or, alternatively, unenforceable under the New York Convention and Amended Model Law. Section 60 is therefore a regrettable quixotism on the 1996 Act's escutcheon.

(2) Interest

The issue of pre-award interest is different. It results from an unfortunate misunderstanding of a judgment of the House of Lords on the 1996 Act: *Impregilo v. Lesotho*.[19] This misunderstanding is widely shared and has made legal commentators more than cautious.[20] The *Lesotho* case concerned an ICC arbitration (with an English seat) between parties to a major construction dispute in the Kingdom of Lesotho, where the arbitration tribunal had awarded to the contractors pre-award interest under Section 49 of the 1996 Act on compensation awarded in foreign currencies under Section 48 of the 1996 Act. The employer contended that both pre-award interest and compensation should have been addressed under the parties' chosen applicable law, namely the law of Lesotho (with very different results highly favourable to the employer) and not under Sections 49 and 48 of the 1996 Act. The employer challenged the award before the English Courts under Section 68 of the 1996 Act on the ground of serious irregularities. After judgments to different effect by the Commercial Court and the Court of Appeal, the House of Lords dismissed the employer's challenge by a majority. (For reasons of space, this contribution addresses only the issue of pre-award interest and not also the issue of currency; but both issues raise similar points on party autonomy under the 1996 Act).

This issue of pre-award interest arises where the parties have expressly agreed that the arbitration tribunal must apply a non-English substantive law to the merits

---

[17] These cases have not been reported publicly.

[18] W.W. Park (2011), *ibid.*, p. 20.

[19] *Lesotho Highlands Development Authority v. Impregilo Spa & Ors* [[2005] UKHL 43, 2006] 1 AC 221, reversing the Court Appeal [2003] EWCA Civ 1159, affirming the Commercial Court on different grounds [2002] EWHC (Com) 2435 (Morison J); *see also*, for a French translation, *Rev arb* 2006.1011 (with case-note by this author and S. Moollan QC). The judgment of the House of Lords is here cited as 'Lesotho'. *See also* A. Crivellaro, 'All's Well That Ends Well ... ' [2005] *ICLR* 480; A. Sheppard 'Currency of Awards and Interest' (2003) *International Arbitration Law Review* 54; and W.W. Park, 'The Nature of Arbitral Authority: A Comment on Lesotho Highlands' (2003) *Arb Int* 483.

[20] For example, *see* R. Jacobs et al., *ibid.*, para. 17.12-17.16.

of their dispute (e.g., Lesotho law as in *Lesotho* or, more commonly, New York law as in the Bermuda forms). That agreement is in writing within the meaning of Section 5 of the 1996 Act.[21] The parties have not agreed to the application of any other applicable substantive law. As with most contractual references to a substantive law, it is a succinct reference to that law without spelling out in the arbitration agreement expressly the full contents of that law, e.g., its specific provisions on pre-award interest.

Hence (in the case of New York law), by virtue of Section 46(1)(a) and 46(2) of the 1996 Act,[22] the arbitration tribunal is required, by contract and statute, to apply New York law as the substantive law chosen by the parties for the determination of their dispute. The question then is whether the tribunal may also exercise the power to order pre-award interest under Section 49(3) of the 1996 Act as a default 'non-mandatory' provision, notwithstanding the parties' agreement on the application of New York substantive law and its provisions on pre-award interest.[23]

The starting-point is Section 4(5) of the 1996 Act. It provides: 'The choice of a law other than the law of England and Wales or Northern Ireland as the applicable law in respect of a matter provided for in a non-mandatory provision of this Part [i.e., Part I] is equivalent to an agreement making provision about that matter. For this purpose an applicable law determined in accordance with the parties' agreement, or which is objectively determined in the absence of any express or implied choice, shall be treated as chosen by the parties.' This was a new statutory provision for the law of arbitration in England; but it was not new to English law as the *lex loci arbitri*. It was explained as follows by the DAC in its Report of February 1996 'Sub-section 5: Although we believe that the choice of a foreign law would anyway have the effect set out in this provision, it seemed for the sake of clarity to be useful to state this expressly, so as to remind all concerned that a choice of a foreign law does amount to an agreement of the parties to which due regard should be paid.'[24]

Next, it is necessary to consider Section 49 of the 1996 Act as regards interest. Section 49 is not a 'mandatory' but a 'non-mandatory' provision.[25] Under Section 4(2) of the 1996 Act, non-mandatory provisions 'allow the parties to make their own arrangements by agreement but provide rules which apply in the absence of such agreement'. Consistent with Section 4(5), Section 49(1) provides: 'The parties are free to agree on the powers of the tribunal as regards the award of interest.' Only

---

[21] For Section 5 of the 1996 Act, *see* footnote 1 *supra*.

[22] Section 46(1)(a) and 46(2) of the 1996 Act provide that the arbitral tribunal 'shall decide the dispute in accordance with the law chosen by the parties as applicable to the substance of the dispute' and, for that purpose, 'the choice of the laws of a country shall be understood to refer to the substantive laws of that country and not its conflict of laws rules'.

[23] Under New York law, Section 5001(a) CPLR provides that interest 'shall be recovered upon a sum awarded because of a breach of performance of a contract'; and Sections 5001(b)-5004 address the commencement dates, computation and rates of such interest. (It is assumed, for present purposes, that these provisions are to be characterised as forming part of New York's substantive law.)

[24] DAC Report of February 1996, para. 29 (*M&B Companion*, p. 401).

[25] Section 4 and Schedule 1 of the 1996 Act.

JURISDICTION, ADMISSIBILITY, AND CHOICE OF LAW IN ARBITRATION   333

in the absence of such agreement (the provision uses the phrase 'unless otherwise agreed'), do the default provisions apply under Sections 49(2)–(6), including Section 49(3) on pre-award interest.[26]

In the DAC Report of February 1996, it explained the intention underlying what became Section 4 of the 1996 Act as regards 'mandatory' and 'non-mandatory' provisions, such as Section 49: 'This provision is intended to make clear that the [Arbitration] Bill has certain provisions that cannot be overridden by the parties, and for ease of reference these are listed in Schedule 1 to the Bill. The Clause also makes clear that the other provisions of this Part can be changed or substituted by the parties, and exist as 'fall-back' rules that will apply if the parties do not make any such change or substitution, or do not provide for the particular matter in question. In this way, in the absence of other contrary agreement, gaps in an arbitration agreement will be filled.[27]

Why, then, is it said that Section 49(3) of the 1996 Act nonetheless applies in such a case? To the contrary, the parties' express written agreement on New York substantive law is a choice of law 'other than the law of England and Wales or Northern Ireland' within Sections 5 and 46; New York substantive law under the CPLR is applicable 'in respect of a matter [i.e., pre-award interest] provided for by a non-mandatory provision', namely Section 49(3); and accordingly, under Section 4(5), the choice of New York law 'is equivalent to an agreement making provision about that matter'. Hence, so it would seem from reading the unambiguous language of Sections 4(5) and 49 of the 1996 Act, as also confirmed by the DAC, that Section 49(3) should be *inapplicable* to the parties' dispute over pre-award interest. Accordingly, so it would seem also, nothing could be clearer as regards the DAC's intention and the wording of the 1996 Act: the parties' choice of a foreign law, in writing and providing for the particular matter in question, is to be treated as a change or substitution making inapplicable the statutory 'fall-back' or default rule in a 'non-mandatory' provision of the 1996 Act. There is then no 'gap' for the 1996 Act to fill; and party autonomy would be respected in full.

However, the answer is said not to lie in the statutory language of the 1996 Act, but, rather, passages in the speech of Lord Steyn in *Lesotho*. The case is more often cited for other purposes in regard to Section 68 of the 1996 Act; but Lord Steyn did address the powers of the ICC tribunal in that case to order pre-award interest under Section 49(3) of the 1996 Act as a subsidiary issue: *see* paragraphs 35–40 of his speech. The critical passage in his conclusion reads as follows: 'Counsel [for the

---

[26] Section 49(3) of the 1996 Act provides: 'The Tribunal may award simple or compound interest from such dates, at such rates and with such rests as it considers meets the justice of the case on any amount awarded by the tribunal.' These provisions give broader powers to arbitration tribunals to award interest than those exercised by the English High Court under English law.

[27] DAC Report of February 1996, para. 28 (*M&B Companion*, p. 401); *see also* Dicey, Morris & Collins, *The Conflict of Laws* (15th ed), Vol. 1, para. 16-038 and 16-044. (The next para. 29 of the DAC's Report addressed what is now Section 4(5) of the 1996 Act: *see* footnote 24 *supra*).

respondent employer] submitted that the law to be applied to the entitlement of the contractors was the law of Lesotho. This submission founders on two separate grounds. The law of Lesotho cannot be an agreement to the contrary under section 49(2). The power to award simple or compound interest as the 'tribunal considers meets the justice of the case' was therefore available to the tribunal [under Section 49(3) of the 1996 Act] ... ' (Lord Steyn's second ground related to Section 68 and is not here relevant).[28] Lord Steyn's full speech repays careful reading; but it is unnecessary to set out its full wording here. Lord Steyn was a remarkable judge, held in the highest regard, who used his words carefully. What is more significant is what was not in his speech and what was missing from the employer's case on the appeal as argued before the House of Lords.

Lord Steyn did not refer in his speech to Section 4(5) of the 1996 Act, seemingly for two reasons. First, 'Counsel for the employer submitted that the arbitrators exceeded their power pursuant to section 49(3). But counsel advanced his challenge in respect of pre-award interest in an almost apologetic way. He said this aspect was parasitic on the currency point ... ' (paragraph 35);[29] and later, 'Rightly counsel for the employer found himself unable to support the reasoning of the Court of Appeal ... ' which had held Section 49(3) inapplicable, in Lord Steyn's words, 'for reasons which are difficult to follow' (paragraph 39).

Accordingly, whilst the ICC tribunal's powers under Section 49 were an issue before the House of Lords and Lord Steyn's statements (with which the majority of his judicial brethren agreed) are not therefore to be regarded as mere *obiter dicta*, it was not the most important and still less the decisive issue on the appeal; and, clearly, it was not subject to the most exhaustive argument by Counsel. Hence, it is fair to conclude that Lord Steyn's succinct reasoning assumed a familiarity with the provisions of the 1996 Act, including Section 4(5). It is out of the question that Lord Steyn could have overlooked Section 4(5) or that his decision was made *per incuriam*: Lord Steyn was the second of the DAC's three chairmen responsible for the 1996 Act; and as an experienced arbitration practitioner and, later, highly respected judge in the field of arbitration, it has to be assumed that he had Section 4(5) well in mind, even if he did not think it necessary to cite the provision expressly in his speech.

The appellate record in *Lesotho* confirms this. In the parties' joint statement of facts and issues filed for the appeal before the House of Lords, Counsel for the parties had agreed on their joint interpretation of Section 4(5) of the 1996 Act as follows: ' ... Arbitrators also have the power to grant pre-award interest unless the parties have agreed to the contrary: s. 49 of the Act. The formalities of any agreement to the contrary are set out in s. 5 of the Act. Section 4(5) of the Act provides that the choice of a law other than that of England and Wales or Northern Ireland

---

[28] *Lesotho*, para. 39.
[29] Lord Steyn also did not cite Section 4(5) on the currency point.

JURISDICTION, ADMISSIBILITY, AND CHOICE OF LAW IN ARBITRATION   335

as the applicable law in respect of a matter provided for by a non-mandatory provision of Part 1 of the Act (including sections 48 and 49) is equivalent to an agreement making provision about that matter.'[30] In addition, the employer's written case for the House of Lords made several submissions on Section 4(5). Accordingly whatever the scope of the issue regarding Section 49 before the House of Lords, it is clear that no issue arose on the appeal from the interpretation and application of Section 4(5) of the 1996 Act. The parties' argument lay elsewhere. Again, therefore, it cannot be assumed that Lord Steyn was unaware of or overlooked Section 4(5).

It is also confirmed by the manner in which the Court of Appeal subsequently understood Lord Steyn's speech. In *C v. D*, the Court rejected the insurer's argument that the 1996 Act allowed parties to a London Arbitration under a Bermuda form to contract out of the Act's 'non-mandatory' provisions in favour of a challenge to the award before the US Federal Courts. Its reasons included the following passage:[31]

> The fact, however, that the 1996 Act allows parties to contract out of its non-mandatory provisions does not mean that the proper law of a contract to refer disputes to arbitration can constitute an 'agreement to the contrary' and thus import a method of challenge to the award not permitted by the seat of the arbitration. For example section 49 of the 1996 Act gives an arbitration tribunal power to award interest. That provision is one of the non-mandatory provisions of the Act. It was argued in Lesotho Highlands Development Authority v Impregilo SpA [2006] 1 AC 221 that, if the proper law of the underlying contract did not permit an award of interest, the choice of that proper law amounted to an agreement to the contrary so as to preclude the Tribunal from awarding interest. Lord Steyn (with whom the majority of the House agreed) pointed out (para. 37) that by reason of section 5 of the Act only an agreement in writing as defined by the 1996 Act could qualify as an 'agreement to the contrary' and that a choice of proper law clause was not such an agreement. That is reinforced by the terms of section 4(5) of the Act which refers not to a choice of law clause generally but to a choice of law as 'the applicable law in respect of a matter provided for by a non-mandatory provision of this part' of the Act. In other words there has to be a choice of law with regard to the specific provision of the Act which the parties agree is not to apply.

The Court of Appeal thus readily identified the application of Section 4(5) with Sections 5 and 49 of the 1996 Act. Moreover, the Court identified the necessity under Section 4(5) of a relevant link between the choice of the foreign law and the specific provision of the 1996 Act as regards interest. It did not suffice for the

---

[30] Paragraph 13 of the parties' joint statement of facts and issues, *Lesotho*.
[31] *C v. D* [2007] EWCA Civ 1282; [2008] 1 Lloyd's Rep 239, at [19].

336   ON ARBITRATION

respondent employer to assert that the mere choice of Lesotho law, by itself alone, qualified as an 'agreement to the contrary'.

Second, it will be recalled that Section 5 of the 1996 Act requires the parties' written agreement. Although the statutory definition is broad, there must still be a relevant written agreement proven by the applicant. As the DAC had explained, there should be a requirement for a written agreement (*inter alia*): 'to help reduce disputes as to whether or not an arbitration agreement was made and as to its terms'.[32] A non-written agreement is legally ineffective under Section 5 of the 1996 Act. From two passages in Lord Steyn's speech, it is apparent that he considered that the respondent employer had failed to discharge its burden of proving a relevant written agreement within Sections 5 and 49 of the 1996 Act:

> The only other possibility [on the employer's argument] is to have regard to the law of Lesotho so far as it governs the substance of the dispute between the parties. There is however no finding about the law of Lesotho in the judgments of either Morison J or the Court of Appeal. Counsel [for the employer] observed that it must have been assumed that there was a substantial injustice. This is not good enough. The burden is squarely on the applicant, who invokes the exceptional remedy under Section 68, to secure (if he can) findings of fact which establish the precondition of substantial injustice. The employer did not satisfy this requirement. *[Paragraph 35]; and*
>
> Morison J appeared to take the view that the law of Lesotho, as the law applicable to the construction contract, may be relevant. This presumably is on the basis that it constitutes an agreement to the contrary under section 49. Ignoring for the moment the fact that one does not know what the law of Lesotho is, this view comes up against the difficulty that only an agreement in writing as defined in the Act can qualify as an agreement to the contrary under Section 49: section 5(1). This is no mere technicality. In the words of the DAC, at p. 14, para 35: 'By introducing some formality with respect to all agreements, the possibility of subsequent disputes (eg at the enforcement stage) is greatly diminished.' The law of Lesotho is not an agreement in writing. *[Paragraph 37].*

The appellate record in *Lesotho* confirms this. It contains no evidence of the substantive law of Lesotho on pre-award interest. In the parties' joint statement of facts and issues, Counsel agreed the issue of pre-award interest as follows: 'In relation to pre-award interest, the Respondent relies upon the choice by the parties of Lesotho law as the substantive law of the Contract. The Respondent says that Lesotho law does not give the arbitrators power to make the award of pre-Award interest which they made.'[33] This plea (repeated at greater length by the respondent employer in

---

[32] DAC Report of February 1996, para. 33 (*M&B Companion*, p. 402).
[33] Paragraph 15 of the parties' joint statement of facts and issues, *Lesotho*.

its written case) fell far short of proving the substantive law of Lesotho relevant to pre-award interest required by Sections 4(5), 5 and 49 of the 1996 Act.

Accordingly, although Lord Steyn accepted that the parties had there agreed in writing that their contract was governed by the law of Lesotho (paragraph 4 of his speech), there was in his view no evidence before the House of Lords as to what that substantive law provided as regards pre-award interest and, hence, there was nothing regarding pre-award interest qualifying as a relevant written agreement under the 1996 Act. As Lord Steyn held, the employer had therefore failed to prove its case under the 1996 Act (the law of Lesotho, as a foreign law pleaded before the English Courts, required positive proof by the employer).

The alternative interpretation of Lord Steyn's speech is, I suggest, mistaken. It asserts, necessarily, that a written agreement by disputing parties as to New York substantive law that includes a relevant law as to pre-award interest, falling within the formalities required by Sections 4(5), 5 and 46 of the 1996 Act, is somehow not an 'agreement' within Section 49(1) and 49(2) of the 1996 Act because the parties' agreement must *expressly* (in writing) address the matter of pre-award interest under New York law within their arbitration agreement. That interpretation cannot be found within the 1996 Act, the DAC Reports, or the speech of Lord Steyn in *Lesotho*.

It would also make a practical nonsense of the 1996 Act. The Act contains at least 35 'non-mandatory' provisions. Like Section 49(3), each of these default provisions takes effect 'unless otherwise agreed by the parties' (or subject to a variant of this phrase). Accordingly, notwithstanding the plain language of Section 4(5) of the 1996 Act, this interpretation would require parties in choosing a foreign law also to record, expressly and in writing, each specific part of that foreign law which provided for the matter otherwise applied by these 'non-mandatory' provisions. In other words, it would not suffice for an arbitration tribunal to apply a foreign law regarding specific performance of a contract unless the parties had specifically agreed in writing, in addition to agreeing that foreign law, that particular remedy also within their arbitration agreement. If not, so it must be inferred, Section 48(5) (b) of the 1996 Act applies notwithstanding Section 48(1). That is not the way commercial contracts are drafted by laymen or lawyers. Nor could they be, at least not without appending to the parties' contract or arbitration agreement the foreign law equivalents of the multi-volume Chitty on Contracts or Halsbury's Laws of England. In practice, therefore, a 'non-mandatory' provision would operate as a 'mandatory' provision under the 1996 Act.

This interpretation would also throw doubt on the efficacy of parties agreeing to apply institutional rules of arbitration, notwithstanding the express liberty to do so in Section 4(3) of the 1996 Act.[34] Such arbitration rules are invariably incorporated by reference under a short form of model wording. Thus, the LCIA recommended

---

[34] Section 4(3) of the 1996 Act provides: 'The parties may make such arrangements by agreeing to the application of institutional rules or providing any other means by which a matter may be decided.'

model arbitration clause provides: 'Any dispute arising out of or in connection with this contract including any question regarding its existence, validity or termination, shall be referred to and finally resolved by arbitration under the LCIA Rules, which Rules are deemed to be incorporated by reference into this clause .... The governing law of the contract shall be the substantive law of [...].' The LCIA Rules contain specific provisions on pre-award interest (Article 26.4); but, as can be seen, these are not specifically set out in the standard form of LCIA arbitration clause. Accordingly, is it to be said that the LCIA Rules' specific provisions on pre-award interest are inapplicable to an LCIA Arbitration with an English seat?

The absurd consequences resulting from such an interpretation speak for themselves. At the very least, such an interpretation must necessarily assume that Lord Steyn intended to rewrite the statutory language of Sections 4(5) and 49 of the 1996 Act, with the former *sub silentio*. That is not the function or habit of a senior appellate English judge, such as Lord Steyn or other members of the House of Lords. Moreover, even if Homer can nod, it seems highly improbable that Lords Hoffmann, Scott and Rodger could have nodded simultaneously. It is also wrong in principle to parse Lord Steyn's speech as if it were an exhaustive English statutory code, interpreting words out of context and inconsistently with the express terms of the 1996 Act.

There is a last, but not least, important factor. One of the four general principles, or 'pillars', on which the 1996 Act is founded and to be interpreted is party autonomy or, in the language of Section 1(b) of the 1996 Act: '... the parties should be free to agree how their disputes are resolved, subject only to such safeguards as are necessary in the public interest'. This issue of pre-award interest in regard to an international commercial dispute unconnected with English law (save as to the *lex loci arbitri*) raises no overriding public interest and requires no necessary safeguard. What matters here is what the parties have agreed as regards the substantive law applicable to their dispute: it is their dispute, their arbitration agreement and their arbitration.

In particular, where non-English parties, in good faith and for good reason, have agreed in writing upon a non-English substantive law and that law specifically provides how their dispute should be resolved, it seems regrettable that it can then be said that there is an 'absence' of any agreement, not because their agreement is non-existent, invalid or fails to meet the formal requirements of the 1996 Act as the *lex loci arbitri*, but rather because of isolated passages in a judgment of the House of Lords. That result does not pay 'due regard' to the parties' agreement. To the contrary, it wrongly usurps the parties' arbitration agreement; and it therefore violates the fundamental principle of party autonomy in arbitration. It also works a grave disservice to the legal predictabilities and procedural certainties required for international commercial arbitration in London. Worse, it is not only a quixotic interpretation, it is simply wrong.

PART III

KEY QUESTIONS FOR ALL USERS OF INTERNATIONAL ARBITRATION

Introduction to Part III[*]

In my own view, the demise of arbitration, domestic and international, is far from inevitable, provided that we bear in mind certain fundamental matters.

The quote above comes from the Alexander Lecture 2015, 'What Matters—about Arbitration' (Chapter 28), a topic that, with its overt grand scale, few other than Johnny Veeder would have had the skill, knowledge, or authority to address. The same can be said for most of the issues covered in the essays and lectures collected in this final part, which read like a roll call of challenges and critical questions for arbitration in the twenty-first century, including: 'Who ultimately controls the arbitral process?', 'Is there a need for a generally applicable code of ethics?', 'Should it be taken for granted that deliberations are entirely confidential?', 'Is the New York Convention up to the task?', the same question for the International Centre for Settlement of Investment Disputes (ICSID), 'What more can be done to address unconscious discrimination in the selection of arbitrators?', 'What is the appropriate means of responding to potential claims against arbitrators and/or arbitral institutions by a disappointed party to an arbitration?'.

It is typical of Johnny Veeder that, although he was unusually well qualified to address the bigger questions, the thoughts that he conveys are based in a modest appreciation of what can and cannot be achieved through arbitration. As he points out in his Alexander Lecture, 'If we ask too much of arbitration, we breed not only disappointment, but also disillusion and, eventually, derision.' At the same time, however, Veeder asks that much more be achieved to address pressing problems within the world of arbitration. Thus, for example, in his 2015 paper, 'Who Are the

---

[*] By Sam Wordsworth.

340 ON ARBITRATION

Arbitrators?' (Chapter 26), Johnny Veeder highlights the unacceptable problem of discrimination within a system that professes to be based on reason and equality:

> inadvertent discrimination based on gender and race damages arbitration, because it assumes, unthinkingly, that a class of persons have always the relevant qualities and that another class always do not, thereby wasting the human resources available to arbitration. Such discrimination is also grossly irrational in a process otherwise founded upon rationality: the choice of an arbitrator should not be exercised arbitrarily; and if a distinction is to be drawn between arbitral candidates, it should have a rational basis related to the particular requirements of the parties for their arbitration. Lastly, but not least, such discrimination is wrong; and, if allowed to continue, it will bring arbitration into disrepute.

Inaction is not an option. The same urgency can be seen in the earlier piece, 'Why Bother and Why It Matters?' (Chapter 23) concerning threats to the good functioning of ICSID, and also in 'Arbitrators and Arbitral Institutions: Legal Risks for Product Liability?' (Chapter 27), where Johnny invites arbitrators, institutions, and users to 'do better than lemmings' in the face of the potential exposure to claims from a dissatisfied party to an arbitration, including because 'an arbitrator is increasingly likely to be made a party to a legal proceeding brought in bad faith by a disappointed party as a collateral attack on an award'.

It is extraordinary that Johnny Veeder found the time to speak and write on such a range of important issues. He was, after all, horribly busy with his day job— sitting on a large number of arbitral tribunals, hearing and deliberating on some of the most difficult and complicated cases of the past two decades: for example, *Methanex v. USA*, which concerned environmental protection measures by the state and generated multiple important orders and awards, including on the transparency of arbitration; the *Achmea (Eureko) v. Slovakia* and *Electrabel v. Hungary* cases, which have so frequently been followed by other arbitral tribunals when it comes to jurisdiction over intra-European Union investment treaty cases; *Chevron v. Ecuador (II)*, which, with its unique complexities, by the time of Johnny Veeder's retirement due to ill health had required more than fifty procedural orders and the division of the issues into various 'tracks', leading, in 2018, to the important determinations on liability (including denial of justice) in the Second Partial Award on Track II.[1]

Nonetheless, time was found and the required thought and research was put in (by Johnny himself, not by an underlying army of research assistants), although

---

[1] Excerpts from some of the awards made by tribunals chaired by Johnny Veeder are to be found in Appendix I.

KEY QUESTIONS FOR ALL USERS OF INTERNATIONAL ARBITRATION   341

those who knew Johnny well saw that denial and organized last-minute chaos also played key roles. The passage that follows has its origins in Johnny Veeder's role as Editor and then General Editor of *Arbitration International* but without doubt applied more generally to the never-ending deadlines that Johnny had to meet:

> It was said by the great English anthologist, John Julius Norwich, that W.S. Gilbert began his letter of complaint to the station-master at London's Baker Street: 'Dear Sir, Saturday morning, although recurring at regular and well-defined foreseen intervals, always seems to take this railway by surprise'. Like that old railway time-table on the Metropolitan line, with the journal's quarterly issues over 20 years' publication, that has meant print deadlines at 80 well-defined foreseen intervals. Almost without exception, each took the journal's general editors and editors by surprise.[2]

---

[2] From V. V. Veeder, 'A Personal Editorial', *Arbitration International* (2005), Volume 21, Issue 4.

With his beloved daughter, Anne, 2001

At Château de Millemont, France, 2009

Relaxing at his summer home in Manchester-by-the-Sea, 2013

20

Whose Arbitration Is It Anyway—The Parties' or the Arbitration Tribunal's?

A. Introduction

To many arbitrators, this debate is sterile in almost every practical sense. To the simple question, whether the arbitration tribunal or the parties are the masters now, there can be only one answer. It is the parties' dispute; and the parties can settle their dispute at any time, in whatever manner, and on whatever terms of their own choosing. It is therefore the parties' arbitration; and subject to reasonable payment for its services, the arbitration tribunal exists subject always to the parties' collective will; and still more so, an arbitral institution administering the arbitration.[1] There is no room for arbitral dictators; no arbitration tribunal functions by divine right; and in any consensual arbitration an arbitrator's primary qualification derives only from his or her appointment, directly or indirectly, by the disputant parties. Without that, an arbitrator is nothing; and in their creation, arbitrators necessarily acknowledge as their creator the disputant parties. And yet, the perennial nature of the debate suggests that this apparently simple question is much more complicated. How can this be?

B. Three Complications

The first complication arises from the fact that the debate thrives on anecdotes which concern not the parties but the parties' legal representatives. There is a natural tendency, particularly where the arbitration tribunal is comprised of non-lawyers (or even lawyers not or not recently in practice) for a commercial arbitrator to second-guess the parties' legal representatives in the belief that an arbitrator

---

[1] In a recent ICC arbitration, having appointed three arbitrators but before signing the Terms of Reference, the parties then decided to discontinue the ICC proceedings and start new ad hoc proceedings before a sole arbitrator who was the chairman of the ICC tribunal nominated by his two arbitral colleagues, now dispensed with. From the deposit, the ICC paid the two ex-arbitrators for their redundant services; but there was of course no challenge to the parties' legal right to so conduct the resolution of their dispute.

On Arbitration. Edited by: Sam Wordsworth KC and Marie Veeder, Oxford University Press. © Oxford University Press 2023. DOI: 10.1093/oso/9780192869135.003.0020

346   ON ARBITRATION

better understands the parties' true interests than their own rapacious lawyers, particularly in matters of arbitral procedure. It is not always easy for arbitrators to remember that an advocate's task is usually more difficult than the arbitrator's function and, moreover, that in any major international arbitration the role of the parties' advocates is no less essential to the arbitral process than that of the arbitration tribunal. Nonetheless, sometimes the arbitrator may be right; an advocate can be foolish or unskilled or parochial; but even then the thesis is proven: the arbitrator is asserting the parties' true interests and not his own independent status separate from the parties. The debate is therefore not advanced by tales of warfare between lawyer and arbitrator: both are asserting different applications of the same principle: it remains the parties' dispute and the parties' arbitration.

The second complication is that an international arbitration tribunal is not a state court. A court has public duties beyond the disputant parties; and in his own person, a state judge maintains an independent status and dignity. In practice, the state of the judge's list has repercussions on other parties awaiting public justice: undue delay in trying the disputant parties' dispute will usually inflict delay on other parties awaiting trial in the same court. Moreover, in England and other common law countries, the Court is a public law-maker; and its decisions are needed, for the contemporary development of the law, unlike the individual awards of commercial arbitrators, often unpublished and not infrequently confidential. Lord Devlin successfully argued long ago in supporting the repeal of the English Special Case (permitting appeals on law from arbitrators to the English Court), that there should be no "annual tribute of disputants to feed the minotaur;"[2] but there has never been a like campaign to restrict all judicial appeals within the English legal system, from the Commercial Court to the House of Lords. With his public duties and status, a state judge is more easily a procedural dictator (albeit subject to appeal), overriding the joint wishes of the parties; and accordingly the position of a state court is materially different from an arbitration tribunal. It therefore serves no purpose to import into the debate the draconian powers and practices of state judges. It is pointless to compare apples to oranges.

The third complication derives from the debate's highly theoretical nature, divorced from actual practice. There is however no doubt that theory is fun; and many hours, if not days, can be spent on the theoretical tension (say) between Sections 33, 34 and 40 of the English Arbitration Act 1996. In olden times, it was doubtless equally fun for philosophers to dispute the number of angels capable of sitting on a pin. For a practical craft like arbitration, such theoretical discussions contribute little.[3] Unlike philosophy, a particular arbitrator in a particular arbitration addressing a particular dispute between particular parties (with their

---

[2] Lord Devlin, *The Judge* (1979), p. 106.

[3] For the further reason, as Professor Park has famously remarked in his 2002 Freshfields Lecture, that there are in theory three kinds of arbitrator: (i) those who can count and (ii) those who cannot.

particular advocates) is faced with concrete problems requiring practical solutions. And this emphasis on practice, rather than theory, supplies the first part of the answer. It is rare that parties issue an agreed procedural ultimatum to an arbitration tribunal. Rather, the parties may present joint proposals, which fall short (under English law) of the procedural written agreement required by Section 5 of the 1996 Act.[4] These are only proposals for the arbitrators to consider, qualify or reject at their discretion. It is indeed far more usual to find disputant parties disputing each other than making a common procedural front against their arbitration tribunal.

C. The Ship's Captain

Thirty years ago, this debate would have seemed incomprehensible to most arbitrators. In London maritime arbitrations, for example; the senior arbitrators were drawn from a small group of "commercial men" and experienced commercial lawyers who were chosen because their judgement was respected and trusted by all concerned with London Arbitration. They were men of affairs, as likely to be counselors as arbitrators. It was as if two medieval villagers had approached the parish priest; and his word was law as regards both demurrage and off-hire. In the hands of such arbitrators, to whom so much had been entrusted on the substance of the parties' dispute (albeit subject to the Special Case), it would not have occurred to many parties to challenge their judgement on procedural matters. There were of course exceptions, as the law reports demonstrate with their record of judgments on arbitral misconduct; but these relatively few exceptions prove the rule. With these senior arbitrators, much was achieved by agreement or tacit consent. For example, as sole arbitrator, the late Cedric Barclay would conduct arbitrations with a minimum of formality and procedural rulings. There was an ambiance of collegiality, particularly in evening arbitrations at his house near Sloane Square, which made it impossible to develop strident adversarial procedures such as exist today. There was no false reverence or undue deference: his judgement was trusted; and what he proposed was accepted because it was usually a wise proposal. He thereby imposed his will on the parties because he was invited to do so, but not as an arbitral despot. The better analogy is the master of a vessel in dangerous waters, with the owners aboard. It is their vessel; the voyage is their venture; it is their cargo at risk; and the master is their salaried employee liable to dismissal by them; but none are quite equal to him in years, experience and skill as a seaman and navigator--which is why they chose him. As the cliffs

---

[4] In addition to the parties' arbitration agreement, Section 5(1) of the 1996 Act provides that "any other agreement between the parties as to any matter is effective ... only if in writing." In other words, the parties' joint proposal made orally at a procedural hearing does *not* qualify as an agreement under Section 34(1) of the 1996 Act.

348 ON ARBITRATION

loom in the dark and the sound of breaking surf drowns the blasts of other vessels' fog-horns, the owners will follow the master's decisions. Likewise, thirty or more years ago, if an arbitrator was in practice the master of the arbitration, he was never the parties' master.

D. The English 1996 Act

In England, this position requires reassessment under the new arbitration legislation. The Arbitration Act 1996; begins by reciting three general principles on which Part 1 is founded (Section 1). The first states that the object of arbitration is to obtain the fair resolution of disputes by an impartial tribunal without unnecessary delay or expense; the second recognises party autonomy in the choice of procedure, subject only to such safeguards as are necessary in the public interest; and the third enjoins the English Court not to intervene in the arbitral process except as the 1996 Act presides. The first principle is also contained in Section 33, a "mandatory" provision imposing on the arbitration tribunal a general duty to act fairly, impartially and efficiently, and Section 40, also a "mandatory" provision imposing a general duty on the parties to ensure the proper and expeditious conduct of the arbitration proceedings. As the third principle illustrates (being derived from its Article 5), the philosophy of the 1985 UNCITRAL Model Law pervades the 1996 Act even where the Model Law's language is missing or modified. It is however the second principle which is relevant to the present debate, enshrining party autonomy over the arbitral procedure. This second principle is also expressed in Section 34(l), taken almost directly from Article 19(1) of the UNCITRAL Model Law, being the Magna Carta for party autonomy in all modern laws on international commercial arbitration.[5] It is only where no such procedural agreement exists between the parties that the arbitration tribunal has a discretion over the arbitration's procedure: Article 19(2) of the Model Law.

The 1996 Act's restrictions on party autonomy are expressly listed as "mandatory" provisions in Section 4(1) and Schedule 1.[6] Of these, only four can be regarded as true restrictions on the will of the parties,[7] the remainder being intended to protect the substantive rights of arbitrators, arbitral institutions and

---

[5] Article 19(1) provides: "Subject to the provisions of this Law, the parties are free to agree on the procedure to be followed by the arbitral tribunal in conducting the proceedings." Section 34(1) of the 1996 provides: "It shall be for the tribunal to decide all procedural and evidential matters subject to the right of the parties to agree any matter." The order is reversed; but does it matter?

[6] These mandatory provisions are contained in Sections 9-11, 12-13, 24, 26(1), 28-29, 31-33, 37(2), 40, 43, 56, 60, 66-68, 70- 71 (part) and 72-75 of the 1996 Act.

[7] Section 13 (Application of Limitation Acts 1980-1984); Section 40 (general duty of parties), Section 60 (certain agreements on costs), and Section 73 (loss of right to object). If the parties were to choose a foreign seat, albeit holding hearings in England for geographical convenience only, even these "mandatory" provisions would not be applicable under the 1996 Act.

other third persons and to entrench certain legal remedies for an aggrieved party; Apart from these "mandatory" provisions, the "non-mandatory" provisions of the 1996 Act are effectively only default procedures where the parties have not chosen their own procedure. Indeed, almost all "non-mandatory" provisions in Part I of the 1996 Act are prefaced by the phrase *"unless otherwise agreed by the parties."* Section 4(3) specifically provides for the parties' choice of institutional rules such as the arbitration rules of the ICC, LCIA, AAA or UNG1TRAL (or other rules such as the IBA Rules of Evidence); and where those rules apply to the matter in issue, the English Court has either no power to intervene at all or (in the case even of certain "mandatory" provisions such as the removal of an arbitrator under Section 24), or no power to intervene unless the aggrieved party has first exhausted its remedy under the rules. Moreover Section 4(4) generally provides that the parties' choice of a foreign law as the law applicable in respect of any matter; covered by a "non-mandatory" provision is equivalent to an agreement not to apply the 1996 Act's default provision. In this way, English commercial arbitration is formally liberated from rigid adherence to the procedures of the English Court in favour of a consensual procedure chosen by the parties for their particular arbitration and dispute, set within a broad statutory framework intended only to guarantee fundamental principles of fair treatment, impartiality and efficiency. The spirit of this approach was long ago captured by Article 5.1 of the 1985 LCIA Rules: "The parties may agree on the arbitral procedure, and are encouraged to do so."

E. Lord Wilberforce

With such legislative provisions in the Model Law and the English 1996 Act, the debate should cease: the arbitration is, as it always was, the parties' arbitration; and subject to the parties' collective will, the arbitrator is the master of the arbitration but not the parties' master. Nothing has changed juridically. And yet the 1996 Act has exposed a different and more significant part of the debate, with far-reaching implications. In his extra-judicial speech welcoming the Arbitration Bill during its second reading in the House of Lords, Lord Wilberforce said:[8]

> I have never taken the view that arbitration is a kind of annex, appendix or poor relation to court proceedings. I have always wished to see arbitration, as far as possible, and subject to statutory guidelines no doubt, regarded as a free-standing system, free to settle its own procedure and free to develop its own substantive law ...

---

[8] *Hansard*, col. 778, 18th January 1996.

I was present in the House of Lords as Lord Wilberforce spoke these words; and until I checked Hansard, I thought I had misheard him. When I did check Hansard, I suspected a stenographic mistake; but having checked with the speaker, it was not. Of course, it has long been assumed that arbitration was becoming a free-standing system with its own *procedure*; and indeed many of Lord Woolf's reforms of English civil court procedure could be traced via the English Commercial Court to the best practices of international commercial arbitration. But what did Lord Wilberforce mean by emphasising, in his carefully chosen words, the free development of arbitration's *own substantive law*? And development by whom? As to the latter question, the answer can only be the arbitration tribunal; it cannot be the parties. As to the former question, here lies the answer to the more significant part of the debate: the arbitrator is the master of the award; his unique power derives from the award; and by their awards, commercial arbitrators have gradually developed substantive rules of law, incorporating into commercial law the reasonable expectations and practices of disputant parties. This part of the debate is far from sterile; it has become increasingly important to international commercial arbitration; and a useful historical illustration lies in the development of an English arbitrator's power to award interest, both simple and compound.

F. Interest

In all international commercial arbitrations where a claim for the payment of money is advanced, whether debt or damages, it is highly probable that the claimant has also suffered financial loss resulting from late payment of the principal amount. That loss can amount to a significant proportion of the total claim; and in certain cases, it can exceed the principal amount. In a modern arbitration regime, it is unthinkable that a claimant should not have the right to recover that loss in the form of interest. It is surprising that any difficulties can lie in the path of such a claim; but traditionally, such difficulties were Legion.[9] The explanation lies in history; and for convenience, what follows is limited to European history because historical issues elsewhere raise different religious and cultural issues. Aristotle maintained that all interest was unlawful because money could not breed money; and St Luke recorded the divine injunction: "Lend, hoping for nothing again; and your reward shall be great." In Europe, this classical and biblical tradition was maintained up to medieval times, where canon law and civil law proscribed interest as a sin and a crime. By the 15th century, however, the growth of trade had demonstrated that borrowed money could facilitate trade and that between merchants moneylending with interest could be mutually advantageous to lender and borrower. Then, as

---

[9] See Wetter, *Int financial Lam Review*, December 1986; and Hunter & Triebel, [1989] *Journal of Int Arb* 7; see also *ICCA Congress Series* No 7 (1996) 268, at pp. 280-283.

WHOSE ARBITRATION IS IT ANYWAY? 351

now, the exigencies of trade forced changes in the law; and those changes were developed still further in the practice of commercial arbitration.

In 1685, Malynes, the English merchant and early recorder of the lex mercatoria, still railed against the practices of bankers which were not to be suffered in any well ordered commonwealth: "The French King Lewis the Ninth, and Philip the Fake, did with great cause confiscate the Bankers' goods, and for discovery of their Debts, ordered their Subjects to pay only the principal money into their Treasuries. Philip de Valoys did the like, and indicted them as cozners[10] of the Common-wealth; for it is found that in a short time, with 24 thousand sterling, they had accumulated and gotten above two millions four hundred thousand pounds."[11] In medieval times, princes were generally bad risks and their loans carried high rates of interest, with corresponding resentment. In 1297, the English King Edward I borrowed money from the Lombards, fully secured on his jewels and gold plate, at a rate of 18.3% per annum; and his grandson Edward III pledged his crown for loans carrying interest at 35% and 42%.[12] Significantly, this class of interest formed no part of any commercial transaction: for both prince and pauper, these were usurious personal loans advanced at times of immediate crisis or for wasteful extravagance, likely to ensnare the borrower into ever deeper indebtedness with no hope of repayment.

Commercial interest fell into a different class: for merchants' money had a productive character, like a ship or a horse. In 1271 the Lombard canon lawyer, Henry of Susa, distinguished mere moneylending from the advance of money characterised by *lucrum cessans*: "If some merchant, who is accustomed to pursue trade, and the commerce of the fairs, and there profit much, has ... lent [me] money with which he would have done business, I remain obliged from this to his *interesse*, to recompense him for the profit he would have made had he engaged in the business himself."[13] In Italy, the growth of trade and private wealth eventually confirmed this distinction between personal and commercial interest-bearing loans; and for the latter, commercial rates fell to the enormous advantage of Italian merchants competing against other European traders. By the 17th century, English law also distinguished between the payment of interest for the use of money (being unlawful) and payment where the lender risked the loss of his money if the commercial venture foundered or where the borrower compensated the lender's proven loss in the borrower's not repaying a "gratuitous" loan (both lawful). This distinction between lawful and unlawful interest plainly rested on the exigencies of trade––as illustrated by Malynes' own explanation: " ... if I do lend Mony to him that hath need, and can afterwards prove that for want of that Mony I have sustained great loss, or if my debtor do break day with me when I look to have it at the time

---

[10] A "cozner" was a cheat or fraudster.
[11] Malynes, *Lex Mercatoria*, (1685), Chapter IX.
[12] Spufford, *Power and Profit: The Merchant in Medieval Europe* (2002), p.45.
[13] Cited in Spufford, *ibid*, p. 44.

352 ON ARBITRATION

appointed, and so am endangered to my neighbour for my necessary payments, it is great reason that my debtor bear my loss, rather than I should sustain harm or danger for my good will... In like manner, if a shop-keeper lend Mony freely to this neighbour till such day, having then occasion to use it at some Fair, to lay it out in Wares, if he break touch, the shop-keeper may in justice take the benefit for his Mony, losing the profit which he should have had by the wares which he was hindred to buy, and this is taken for lucro cessante: But in neither of these was an intention to deliver Mony at Interest."[14] It was the practical needs of trade that forced this approach, which, it seems, had already been reflected in the practice of commercial arbitration.[15] Nonetheless, there was to be, as Malynes also recorded, no compound interest, or "interest upon interest."

(i) The English Court

For the next three hundred years, English law as applied in the English courts evidenced an ambivalent attitude towards interest. On the one hand, the English Parliament recognised interest at a just rate. Even in Malynes' time, in 1651, Cromwell's Commonwealth had set the legal rate of simple interest at six per cent; and after the Restoration in 1660, the English Parliament under Charles II confirmed this same rate of six per cent. On the other hand, the English Court lacked for a long time any general power to award pre-judgment interest; and it still lacks today any general power to award compound interest. The historical development of the Court's power to award interest was only consistent in its inconsistency: In *De Havilland v. Bomerbank* (1808),[16] where Lord Ellenborough greatly limited the Court's power to award simple interest, the law reporter wistfully commented: "It would fortunately be a very difficult matter to fix upon another point of English law on which the authorities are so little in harmony with each other;" and more recently as regards compound interest, in *Westdeutsche Landesbank Girozentrale v. Islington Borough Council* (1996),[17] Lord Goff identified, as a historical problem, the fact that "our law of interest has developed in a fragmentary and unsatisfactory manner, and in consequence insufficient attention has been given to the jurisdiction [of the Court] to award compound interest."

---

[14] Malynes, *ibid*, Chapter XI.

[15] See Derek Roebuck, "L'arbitrage en droit anglais avant 1558" *Rev arb* 2002.535, 561 where in a case decided in 1313, the English Court rejected an argument to the effect that a bond of 40 l. securing an arbitration agreement relating to a debt of 20 l. was usurious and made the arbitration agreement unlawful.

[16] (1808) 1 Camp. 50; 170 ER 872. Lord Ellenborough decided; inter alia, that if the party lost the use of his money before the demand for payment, "it was his own fault in not suing for it." The law reporter was John Campbell (1779–1861), later Chief Justice of the King's Bench and Chancellor.

[17] *The Swaps Case* [1996] AC 669, 682 (restitutionary claim in equity for compound interest relating to an ultra vires swap agreement).

For the English Court, the present position as regards both simple and compound interest, in equity and common law remains extremely complicated.[18] Where proceedings are brought before the English Court for debt or damages, the Court has a statutory discretion under Section 35A of the Supreme Court Act 1981 to award simple interest from the date on which the cause of action arose until judgment (or until payment in the case of any amount paid after the commencement of the action but before judgment). The Court has a limited statutory power to award simple interest at a legal rate on unpaid commercial debts owed to defined small business suppliers under the Late Payment of Commercial Debts (Interest) Act 1998. By contract, the Court can order simple or compound interest pursuant to the parties' agreement; and it has qualified powers, in very limited circumstances, to order such interest under its equitable and admiralty jurisdictions. Lastly, it can award damages at common law for breach of contract, measured by simple or compound interest, under the second limb of *Hadley v. Baxendale*.[19] As regards post-judgment interest, the judgment debt will carry simple interest from the date of judgment until payment under the Judgments Act 1838; and since that judgment debt may include pre-judgment interest, it follows that the statute has long provided, to that limited extent, for post-judgment interest upon interest, or compound interest.

G. The English Arbitrator

It is however quite different for an English arbitration tribunal, for both simple and compound interest. Section 49 of the 1996 Act, a non-mandatory provision, provides:

(1) The parties are free to agree on the powers of the tribunal as regards the award of interest.[20]
(2) Unless otherwise agreed the following provisions apply.

---

[18] From *London, Chatham and Dover Railway Co v. South Eastern Railway Co* [1893] AC 429 to *President of India v. La Pintada Cia Navigacion SA ("La Pintada")* [1985] AC 104; and see generally *McGregor on Damages* (1997), Chapt 14 (pp 418-466); the Law Commission's Consultation Paper, cited below; and *KAC v. KIC (No.3)* [2000] Lloyd's IR Rep 678.

[19] *Wadsworth v. Lydall* [1981] 1 WLR 588; and see Boyd [1985] 1 *Arbitration International* 153, at p. 157.

[20] For example, Article 26.2 of the LCIA Rules provides: *"... the Arbitral Tribunal may order that simple or compound interest shall be paid by any party on any sum awarded at such rates as the Arbitral Tribunal determines to be appropriate, without being bound by legal rates of interest imposed by any state court, in respect of any period ... "* Article 16.5 of the 1999 Scottish Arbitration Code, a non-statutory document, provides more broadly for: *"power to order that simple or compound interest shall be paid by any party on any sum awarded at such rate or rates as the Arbitrator determines to be appropriate without being bound by legal rates of interest imposed by any state court or any agreement between the parties in respect of any period which the Arbitrator determines to be appropriate including a date prior to the appointment of the Arbitrator and ending not later than the date upon which the award is complied with."*

354 ON ARBITRATION

(3) The tribunal may award simple or compound interest from such dates, at such rates and with such rests as it considers meets the justice of the case –
  (a) on the whole or part of any amount awarded by the tribunal, in respect of any period up to the date of the award;
  (b) on the whole or part of any amount claimed in the arbitration and outstanding at the commencement of the arbitral proceeding but paid before the award was made, in respect of any period up to the date of payment.
(4) The tribunal may award simple or compound interest from the date of the award (or any later date) until payment, at such rates and with such rests as it considers meets the justice of the case, on the outstanding amount of any award (including any award of interest under subsection (3) and any award as to cost.
(5) References in this section to an amount awarded by the tribunal include an amount payable in consequence of a declaratory award by the tribunal.
(6) The above provisions do not affect any other power of the tribunal to award interest.[21]

The wording is starkly simple, conferring much wider powers on English arbitrators than on the English Court; and compound interest is self-evidently intended as an efficacious and reasonable remedy.[22]

The award of compound interest has recently been re-considered by the Law Commission of England & Wales. Its Consultation Paper[23] identifies as an apparent anomaly under English law the power to award compound interest in arbitration proceedings under Section 49(3) of the 1996 Act, cited above. The Law Commission notes an argument in favour of conferring a like power on the English Courts that, as the function of arbitrators is to act as a substitute for a court, it is curious that arbitrators should have wider powers than the English Court. It invites evidence on the way in which the power to award compound interest is currently exercised by arbitrators in England and abroad, together with any juridical justification for such practice. Such materials might provide guidance for how an English Court might act if it had the same general power as an

---

[21] It thereby remains possible to claim interest in contract or under the applicable substantive law, e.g. a claim under Swiss substantive law (which classifies interest as substantive and not procedural).

[22] See the DAC's Report on the Arbitration Bill, paras. 235-237: "235. The responses we received demonstrated to us that there was general desire to give arbitral tribunals a general power to award compound interest." This response from English and foreign users was numerous and almost unanimously in favour of the suggested power to award compound interest. As to fears of arbitral abuse, the DAC concluded; "237. ... We do not share those fears. To our minds any competent arbitrator seeking to fulfil the duties laid on him by the Bill will have no more difficulty in making decisions about compound interest than he will in deciding in any other context what fairness and justice require ...": cited in Merkin, *Arbitration Act 1996* (2nd ed; 1990), at p. 278.

[23] Law Commission Consultation Paper No. 167 of September 2002, available at http: www.lawcom. gov.uk.

arbitration tribunal. The response to the Law Commission and the eventual legislative result may prove interesting; but how did the law and practice of English arbitration reach a different result long before the English Court? It began long before Section 49 of the 1996 Act.

In *re Badger* (1819),[24] the Court decided that an arbitrator was not bound by a rule of practice adopted by Courts for general convenience; and therefore the Court refused to set aside the award on the ground that the arbitrator had allowed interest when it would not be allowed by a Court of Law or Equity. Abott C.J. held: "If an arbitrator acts contrary to a general rule of law it is undoubtedly the duty of the Court to set aside his determination. But there is a material distinction between those rules which are found on the immutable principles of justice, from which neither the Court nor an arbitrator can be allowed to depart, and those which depend on the practice of the Court: from the latter, indeed, the Court will not depart, because it is of great importance in Courts of Justice to adhere to them even though it may operate to the prejudice of some particular case. For by abiding by general rules we avoid that uncertainty which would be productive of very great inconvenience to the suitors of the Court. But an arbitrator, to whom a particular cause is referred, is not placed in this situation; he is not, as it seems to me, bound by those rules of practice which are adopted by the Court, for those reasons which I have stated. And as this rule of not allowing interest on unliquidated accounts is a rule of practice, I think that the arbitrators in this case were not bound by it. Then the question arises, whether they were excluded from allowing interest by the terms of this submission. I think they were not. The submission is of a suit in Chancery, and all other matters in difference. That gave them an authority to adjust the account between the parties; and an authority to do that carries with it an implied authority to allow interest unless expressly excluded by the terms of the submission." Holroyd J also distinguished between the powers of the court and arbitration tribunal: "... But this reason does not apply to a case before an arbitrator whose duty it is to do justice, according to the circumstances of the particular case, and no mischief can arise from his not abiding by a general rule. I think that this is a case in which the arbitrators might allow interest." Best J held: "... It does not appear that the arbitrators here have violated any general rule of law, but they have only not complied with the practice of the Court. It is this very circumstance which, in many cases, makes a decision by an arbitrator preferable to that of the Court; viz. that the former is not bound by the strict rules of practice, but may do full justice according to the particular circumstances of the individual case." The sense of the judgment indicates that the English Court was here recognising an established power exercised by London arbitrators, doubtless influenced by the practices of merchants in the City of London. It is perhaps significant

---

[24] *In re Badger (1819)* 2 B & Ald 691; 106 E.R. 517. Charles Abbott, Chief Justice of the King's Bench and later Lord Tenderden (1762-1832) had first set out to become a clergyman before turning to the law.

356   ON ARBITRATION

that in Scotland, absent like commercial pressures, the Scots arbitrator's powers to award interest were circumscribed and remain today reduced below the powers of the Scots Court.[25]

This old English approach, as regards simple interest, was followed in London Arbitration at least up to 1889. There exists a copy of an old award made by T. Scrutton as Sole Arbitrator[26] on 27th October 1883 in conjoined arbitrations between the shipowners of the vessel "Parthenia," Messrs Houlder Bros and Co and the Executors of the late Ralph Firbank Esq. The award is in the arbitrator's handwriting and unmotivated; but it clearly records his decision that "the Executors of the late Ralph Firbank Esq do pay to Messrs Houlder Bros & Co the sum of £260 with Interest at 5% per annum [from] 5th December 1882 to date of payment;" i.e. pre-award and post-award interest. If further evidence of this ancient arbitral power was required, it came in 1889. In that year, Lord Bramwell's Arbitration (No. 2) Bill, albeit eventually defeated by Lord Halsbury in the House of Lords and replaced by a lesser Bill which became the Arbitration Act 1889, proposed a simple provision in Clause 90 to codify the arbitral power to award interest under English law. It stated: "an arbitrator may in his awards direct that interest at the current rate be paid on the sum awarded."[27] In the Bramwell Bill's notation citing the principle so codified, Lord Bramwell cited as authority *In re Badger*. Although there was nothing similar in the 1889 Act or the 1934 Act,[28] Quintin Hogg (later Lord Hailsham), cited the same authority in his extra-judicial work (1936) that: "... an arbitrator ordinarily has power to award interest up to the date of the award, even though a Court of law in a like case could not have done so."[29] This was a reference to pre-award interest; by then the power of an arbitrator to award post-award interest was already enacted by Section 11 of the 1934 Act (re-enacted as Section 20 of the 1950 Act).

More recently, Lord Denning MR sought to revive the traditional arbitral power to award interest in *The Finix*[30] (1978): "For years now it has been the practice in

---

[25] Under Scots law, an arbitrator must be granted by the parties an express power to order pre-award interest: see F. Davidson, *Arbitration* (2000), p. 325. (Unlike Section 31 of the Bermuda International Conciliation and Arbitration Act 1993, the Scots enactment of the UNCITRAL Model Law contains no express provision on interest).

[26] It was not T.E. Scrutton, later Lord Justice Scrutton of the Court of Appeal. Indeed, the Sole Arbitrator was a commercial man and not a lawyer, the award showing expenses of 6 shillings and 8 pence (US$ 50 cents), incurred by the arbitrator for a legal opinion. The arbitrator charged 6 guineas (US$ 10).

[27] See [1992] *Arbitration International* 353, at p. 376.

[28] The 1934 Act did not include a general provision on the award of interest by arbitrators because it was regarded by the sponsoring Government Department as a *"major issue"* and a general provision for the English Court had just been deleted from the Administration of Justice Bill because it would have raised *"a very controversial question and would overload the Bill"* (Notes on Clauses, "Memorandum", at p. 48; Public Record Office, Kew; LCO 2/1789).

[29] Hogg, *Arbitration* (1936), at p.129; but already views had been expressed to the contrary: see the 1927 MacKinnon Report, at fn. 35 below.

[30] [1978] 1 Lloyd's Rep 16, 19.

commercial arbitrations, certainly in the City of London, for the arbitrators to award interest on the amounts found to be due without restriction. They have a complete discretion as to the amount of interest and as to the period of time. That practice goes back at least to the year 1819. See *In re Badger*, (1819) 2 B. & A. 691. This is so well understood that we need not inquire into its origin. It is to be taken as read into all commercial arbitrations in the City of London. To my mind there is no possible doubt of the jurisdiction of the umpire here to award interest on the amount which was eventually found to be due, the sum of £22,982.40." In this case Lord Denning was a dissenting minority because the law on interest had become muddled: an arbitrator's implied powers on pre-award interest were now treated as subsidiary and dependent upon the statutory powers of the English Court. For London Arbitration, this was not satisfactory and indeed historically inaccurate. Accordingly, in 1982 a new provision was introduced into the Arbitration Act 1950: Section 19A provided that every arbitration agreement, subject to the parties' contrary agreement, shall be deemed to contain a provision that the arbitrator may award simple interest in certain circumstances up to the date of the award.[31] This amendment was drafted and enacted by Parliament with surprising ease, prompted also by a decision in 1979 of the Supreme Court in Victoria, Australia[32] which demonstrated that the leading English authority on the arbitrator's implied power to award interest, by analogy to the English Court's power, was fundamentally flawed in its reasoning.[33] Section 19A also enacted recommendations first made by the 1927 MacKinnon Committee on the Law of Arbitration.[34] From here the legislative step to Section 49 of the 1996 Act was relatively small, albeit extending to both simple and compound interest.

For English law, the current anomaly is not that arbitrators can award compound interest when English judges cannot; it is rather that English judges cannot do it. There is no logical impediment to compound interest if a power to award simple interest is accepted under the general law. As Lord Goff concluded in *Swaps*, "One would expect to find, in any developed system of law, a comprehensive and reasonably simple set of principles by virtue of which the courts have power to award interest. Since there are circumstances in which the interest awarded should take the form of compound interest, those principles should specify the circumstances

---

[31] The Administration of Justice Act 1982.

[32] *Barlin-Scott Air Conditioning v. Robert Salzer Constructions* (26th April 1979; Sir John Young CJ, McInerney & Fullagar JJ; unreported).

[33] *Chandris v. Isbrandsten-Moller* 84 Ll L 347; [1951] 1 KB 240, where the Court of Appeal (in an unreserved judgment) reversed Mr Justice Devlin and decided that an arbitrator had an implied power to award simple interest based on an analogy to the powers of a "court of record" under Section 3 of the Law Reform (Miscellaneous Provisions) Act 1934.

[34] See the 1927 MacKinnon Report, *ibid*, at, para. 29, where it considered that there was no English arbitral power to award pre-award interest. The same view was expressed by Devlin J, at first instance, in *Chandris v. Isbrandtsen-Moller* (1950) 83 Ll L 385 at p. 391, following the Divisional Court in *Podar Trading v. François Tagher* [1949] 2 KB 277 where *In re Badger* was summarily distinguished (see, p. 289, per Lord Goddard CJ).

358   ON ARBITRATION

in which compound interest, as well as simple interest, may be awarded; and the power to award compound interest should be available both at law and in equity. Nowadays; especially since it has been established (see *National Bank of Greece S.A. v. Pinios Shipping Co. No. 1* [1990] 1 A.C. 637) that banks may, by the custom of bankers, charge compound interest upon advances made by them to their customers, one would expect to find that the principal cases in which compound interest may be awarded would be commercial cases. Sadly, however, that is not the position in English law. Unfortunately, the power to award compound interest is not available at common law. The power is available in equity; but at present that power is, for historical reasons, exercised only in relation to certain specific classes of claim, in particular proceedings against trustees for an account. An important – I believe the most important – question in the present case is whether that jurisdiction should be developed to apply in a commercial context, as in the present case." For the English Court, the Law Commission's project may answer Lord Goff's inquiry; but for international commercial arbitration, that answer is already much advanced.[35]

In his great work, *A History of Money*,[36] the late Professor Davies described the centuries-long gavotte, from late medieval times to the 20th century, whereby the English Church and State allowed usury to be re-defined to allow indigenous developments in banking, divorcing traditional ethics from trade and marking new expectations driven by the exigencies of an expanding economic system. Whilst interest is still regulated for consumers and lenders are often themselves regulated, no-one would seriously consider today returning to the beginning of that strange dance for international commercial arbitrations in London or elsewhere. Outside England, for example in ICC award No 5514 (1990),[37] the arbitration tribunal in Geneva awarded compound interest on damages in a dispute between a state and a French company, based on the application of a trade usage under Article 13 of the ICC Rules. It had no difficulty in identifying and applying a trade usage providing for compound interest in a case where the company had been forced to borrow monies at compound interest as a result of the state's failure to honour its own financing obligations to the company. Based on the facts recorded in the award, any other approach would have flouted commercial common-sense and produced rank injustice. Nevertheless, in his contemporary commentary, the French jurist Me Yves Derains queried whether such a usage had yet reached the juridical status of a règle matérielle (owing partly to his own previously expressed reservations); and accordingly his approving case-note emphasised the facts of the particular case. In the subsequent decade, these qualifications have largely disappeared from the

---

[35] See the excellent account by Natasha Affolder "Awarding Compound Interest in International Arbitration" [2001- sic] 12/1 *Am Rev of Int Arb* 45.

[36] Glyn Davies, *A History of Money* (2002; 3rd ed; Cardiff) pp. 218-223.

[37] (1992) 110 *JDI* 1022; Arnaldez, Derains & Hascher (eds), *Collection of ICC Arbitral Awards 1991-1995* (1997), p. 459.

practice of international commercial arbitration: where compound interest would provide a fair and reasonable element of compensation to the innocent victim of a contract-breaker, it is increasingly awarded by international commercial arbitrators either as trade usage, règle matérielle de droit international or under an expressly agreed provision, e.g. Article 26.6 of the LCIA Rules. In Switzerland and England, as with other European countries hospitable to international arbitration, the award of such compound interest in commercial dealings is not contrary to public policy, ordre public or other mandatory law;[38] and as changes on the award of simple interest have taken place in many jurisdictions, the reasonable expectations of commercial parties engaged in transnational trade are producing like changes in regard to compound interest.

H. Conclusion

How was this achieved by international commercial arbitrators, without any international convention or model law or national legislation? Historically, the answer is simple. It is the same answer provided by the emerging powers of commercial arbitrators to award arbitration costs or to express their awards in a foreign currency without technical court rules so productive of injustice in transnational trade.[39] As Lord Wilberforce noted, arbitration can and does develop its own substantive rules of law; and from Malynes to the little-known T. Scrutton, commercial arbitration has done so gradually by the successive awards of commercial arbitrators reflecting the practices and exigencies of the parties' trade; and by those awards, it is the *arbitrators* who are the true masters of the arbitral process.

---

[38] See the references in Berger, *The Creeping Codification of the Lex Mercatoria* (1999; Kluwer), p. 308.
[39] In England, neither were first achieved by statute. As regards foreign currency, for England see Mustill & Boyd, *Commercial Arbitration* (2nd ed, 1989) at p. 389, fn 14; and for the USA, see Hans Smit, "Elements of International Arbitration in the United States," 1 *Amer Rev of Int Arb* 64, at pp. 72-74 (April 1990); and also Hans Smit, "Managing an International Arbitration: An Arbitrator's View," 5 *Amer Rev of Int Arb* 129, at p. 138 (1994).

21

Is There Any Need for a Code of Ethics for International Commercial Arbitrators?

Is there a need for any new, comprehensive code of ethics for international commercial arbitrators? And if so, what should that code contain? And what juridical status should it have? None of these questions is now theoretical; and current proposals for reform deserve the utmost scrutiny from the perspectives of arbitrators, arbitral practitioners and arbitration users. If such improvements are required to adjust arbitral ethics, a common solution may be required for both arbitrators and arbitral practitioners as the parties' legal representatives. An international arbitration requires the active co-operation of arbitrators and practitioners; and it is, after all, the parties' dispute and their arbitration. However, any analysis of contemporary practice requires arbitrators and practitioners to be considered separately.

For international arbitrators, modern practice has raised surprisingly few ethical problems, beyond the increasingly awkward requirement of disclosure on appointment and arbitral challenges. There has been an almost total absence of corruption amongst international arbitrators; and even the national problem of the partisan arbitrator is largely missing amongst international arbitration tribunals. It is only recently that arbitral deliberations have emerged as an area where ethical rules may be required, beyond the established convention that such deliberations should be secret. Almost twenty years ago, the IBA published its Code of Ethics for Arbitrators (1987) as a mild and useful guide, codifying best practice in limited areas; and there were many who thought the document was unnecessary, as merely stating the obvious. Even to its supporters, it was neither a legislative code nor comprehensive in its treatment of arbitral conduct. Until recently, therefore, there was no evidence that any formal code of conduct was required to regulate the ethics of international arbitrators generally.

However, as challenges to arbitrators have multiplied, particularly tactical challenges, the situation may be changing, particularly with the IBA Guidelines on Conflicts of Interest (2004). Its broad "orange" category and its drafting style introduce uncertainty for both arbitrators and parties where procedural certainty is highly desirable; and it may significantly increase the risk of default by an honest

---

On Arbitration. Edited by: Sam Wordsworth KC and Marie Veeder, Oxford University Press. © Oxford University Press 2023.
DOI: 10.1093/oso/9780192869135.003.0021

arbitrator making an honest mistake. These concerns are becoming increasingly felt; and the first concern is triggered by the very idea of arbitral "guidelines". There is an inevitable difficulty in drafting general legal principles as an apparently exhaustive code with illustrative examples which are by definition incomplete; and there is a practical problem of turning the orange categories into red categories at the time of the claimant's nomination of its arbitrator. At that time, early in the arbitration, the claimant is necessarily wary of a recalcitrant challenge by a respondent; and to avoid any delay to its claim, it can safely only choose an arbitrator squarely within the green category, thereby significantly excluding a large number of candidate arbitrators for any particular case. Thus, the pool of available qualified arbitrators becomes ever smaller, a feature decried by many arbitration users and every informed commentator; and the practical problems for practitioners in conducting an international arbitration are thereby materially increased.

The IBA Guidelines demonstrate several other dangers posed by any ethical code for international arbitrators. First, how can any private body, like the IBA, usurp the role of a legal rule-maker for all international arbitrators (whether lawyers or not); and in particular, how can a private body replace different national mandatory rules on the impartiality and independence of arbitrators, almost everywhere treated as a matter of public policy? Second, is there a danger in a code adding to those mandatory rules, without replacing them? The IBA Guidelines' first arbitral casualty, in an ad hoc arbitration, took place recently in the Dutch courts[1]; and it appears that the IBA Guidelines may have played a part in a challenge recently decided in an ICC Arbitration, albeit to a less malign extent[2]. In the Dutch case, it was alleged that the arbitrator appointed by the investor lacked impartiality or independence because he had acquired two roles, the first acting as arbitrator in that particular case and the second acting as counsel in a quite different case between different parties but allegedly (albeit not self-evidently) raising a similar issue in the annulment proceedings pending before an ICSID ad hoc committee. Inevitably, the challenging party cited extensively from the IBA Guidelines. The Dutch court decided to allow the challenge unless the arbitrator immediately withdrew as counsel from the other case. The arbitrator having done so, a further challenge was made but the second court rejected this challenge on the basis that the arbitrator was no longer exercising a dual role.

The lesson from these recent cases is twofold, neither of which establishes the need for an ethical code. First, appointing authorities like the PCA and arbitral institutions such as the ICC Court should give reasoned decisions for accepting

---

[1] *TMB v Ghana, ASA Bulletin* 2005.186ff (This was a BIT investment arbitration held under the UNCITRAL arbitration rules with its seat at The Hague and the Permanent Court of Arbitration as the appointing authority, which had rejected the challenge without giving any reasons).
[2] HWANG, "Arbitrators and Barristers in the Same Chambers - An Unsuccessful Challenge" (2005) *BLI* 235.

or rejecting arbitral challenges; and these decisions should be made public. Each arbitral challenge is usually fact specific; and whereas general principles are difficult to apply in a useful manner, a growing body of actual examples by respected arbitral institutions could overcome the difficulties inherent in a document such as the IBA Guidelines. It is regrettable that the IBA took most of its examples from national court decisions (as it had to), without the benefit of institutional decisions from those most qualified and experienced in deciding challenges. Second, an arbitrator must have professional indemnity insurance cover, if only as regards the legal expenses incidental to defending a challenge to his or her appointment or professional reputation. An arbitrator forced to resign or removed from appointment may incur legal liability in damages to one or both parties for the wasted costs of the arbitration; and these costs can measure millions or tens of millions of US dollars. An arbitrator can be equally ruined in legal costs if drawn into legal proceedings to which he or she may have only adjectival relevance. This is an accident now waiting to happen: a minor misjudgement by an arbitrator, whether merely alleged or even in fact, should not lead to ruinous financial penalties.

The controversy over the IBA Guidelines will doubtless continue; but it would be wrong to blame the messengers for the message. The document's epitaph has perhaps already been written by Professor Thomas Clay: "These guidelines are undoubtedly useful and innovative which should be well received because they could provoke debate. But that is without doubt all they are good for because if they were really used to provide guidance, they would risk creating more problems than they would solve."[3] The debate must of course continue to the benefit of international arbitration; but it is already clear that the IBA Guidelines do nothing to foster the proposal for an ethical code for arbitrators.

For arbitration practitioners, there may be a more significant problem over different professional practices deriving from different legal cultures, particularly over written witness statements, witness preparation and document production[4]. The harmonising effect of Articles 3 and 4 of the IBA Rules of Evidence (1999) has helped considerably; but important differences remain in the conduct of international arbitrations. For example, the practice of "shadow" or moot arbitrations by one party to prepare witnesses before the actual hearing is growing in certain jurisdictions; and albeit elegantly described by a distinguished US practitioner, this could be the future for international arbitration: "...the critical element of preparing a witness is to stage a moot cross-examination, making it as realistic as possible. Ideally, the lawyer in charge of the direct examination will ask another lawyer to prepare and conduct a very thorough moot cross- examination. Having another

---

[3] Thomas CLAY, *Rev. arb.* 2005.991, at p.995 (Translation by the present author).
[4] LEVY & VEEDER (ed), *Dossiers: Arbitration and Oral Evidence* (2005, ICC Institute); see also DERAINS, "La pratique de l'administration de la preuve dans l'arbitrage commercial international", *Rev arb* 2005.781.

IS THERE ANY NEED FOR A CODE OF ETHICS? 363

lawyer do this adds to the realism of the exercise, leaves lead counsel free to play the role he will play at the evidentiary hearing, and helps lead counsel preserve a cordial relationship with the witness not withstanding the roughness with which the moot cross-examination might be conducted. Most important, however, this leaves lead counsel free to watch how his witness bears up under cross and free to interject advice when he sees difficulty. If this process is carried out with real thoroughness, one hopes that the witness will have been confronted with every possible difficulty he should experience at the hearing..."[5].

Cultural neutrality amongst international arbitrators is not always mirrored amongst the parties' different legal representatives; and as the use of international arbitration increases exponentially, a cultural gap exists between new practitioners not from their different nationalities but from their different practices in state courts on the one hand and international arbitration on the other. There is also a growing difficulty over the non-transparency of success fees by which a party pays its legal representative, in the absence of any external control or discipline. In a quite different field, prompted in part by the treatment of fees, it is significant that the International Criminal Tribunal for the former Yugoslavia at The Hague now has an international code of conduct for defence counsel: the ICTY-ADC Code of Conduct[6].

There is still no international code of conduct for legal representatives practising in international commercial arbitration. The regional scope of the CCBE Code of Conduct for Lawyers in the European Union is of course limited to Europe. It is currently under revision, provoked by the European Commission's Draft Directive on Services in the Internal Market of 2004 (Articles 39 and 40). The current CCBE Code originates in the Perugia Declaration of 1977; it was first promulgated in 1988 as a code and has twice been amended in 1998 and 2002. It currently affects over 600,000 lawyers in the EU and EEA. It is not in the words of the CCBE an "an omni-comprehensive and universal code"; nor will it become so even with this third proposed revision. Significantly the CCBE code barely touches arbitration. Article 4.2 deals with a lawyer's general duty of fair conduct towards a court or arbitration tribunal; Article 4.3 deals with a lawyer's duty of respect and courtesy towards a court or arbitration tribunal; and Article 4.4 precludes a lawyer knowingly giving false or misleading information towards a court or arbitration tribunal. None of these three provisions, so it appears, will be revised in the proposed new version of the CCBE Code. As regards international arbitration in Europe, it is in practice a code-free zone.

The position is remarkably different in the code-rich USA. It is ironic that the principal force for ethical codes for lawyers has come from the USA. There is

[5] Robert RIFKIND, *Dossiers (ibid)*, p.61.
[6] ICTY Constitution of the Association of Defence Counsel (2002) Archbold *International Criminal Courts*, 2003, pp. 955 ff.

364   ON ARBITRATION

probably no country in the world in which the general population holds the legal profession in lower respect with a mass of antilawyer jokes, as often tasteless as cruel. Could it be worse without the USA's ethical codes for lawyers, mediators and arbitrators? It must be assumed so. It is therefore no coincidence that the current proposals for an ethical code for international arbitration derives from the work of US scholars, most notably Professor Catherine Rogers. Professor Rogers has written two extensive articles on ethical regulations for international commercial arbitration. Both are essential reading on this topic, if only to understand fully the deep waters into which this debate may lead us. Her thesis begins with an assumed crisis, which merits citing at length: "Even if international arbitration is a resilient institution, the absence of ethical consensus or regulation is increasingly disrupting arbitral proceedings. For example, a party may discover half way through proceedings that contrary to its own practices the other party has been engaging in ex parte communications with its party-appointed arbitrator (even about such matters as case strategy) [footnote omitted] or in pre-testimonial communications with witnesses (a practise forbidden in most civil law jurisdictions) [footnote omitted]. Compounding these problems, arbitrators who are unaware of party's disparate ethical traditions may unfairly discredit one party's presentation of its case based on perceived misconduct... Alternatively, those arbitrators who might attempt to resolve the ethical collisions on an ad hoc basis risk disrupting the parties' settled expectation, if not their nationally established procedural rights"[7].

The scope of Professor Rogers' assumptions may be questioned in the practise of international arbitration, but her solution is well-argued, thoroughly researched and deserves attention. She suggests that arbitration rules, forming part of the parties' arbitration agreement, should include an extensive code of ethical conduct to be enforced by arbitrators and arbitral institutions. Thus, the revised ICC Rules would contain a new appendix, as would the LCIA, UNCITRAL and other rules. If not expressed in arbitration rules, she suggests that the code form part of the Terms of Reference or the first procedural order agreed by the parties. In order to make this appended ethical code legally binding on the parties' legal representatives, Professor Rogers proposes that as a condition of representing a party in an arbitration, the lawyer must personally and contractually agree to be bound by the ethical code. It could be done, she suggests, as part of the statement of case or statement of defence served by the party's lawyer or by a like-signed agreement also forming part of the Terms of Reference or first procedural order. Any breach of these ethical rules by a lawyer would be actionable in damages or punishable by a fine at the instance of the arbitration tribunal; and the tribunal's decision, which Professor

---

[7] Catherine A. ROGERS, "Fit and Function in Legal Ethics: Developing a Code of Conduct for International Arbitration", 23 *Mich. J. Int'l L* 341 (2002). See also Catherine A. ROGERS, "Context and Institutional Structure in Attorney Regulation: Constructing an Enforcement Regime for International Arbitration", 39 *Stan. J. Int'l* 1 (2003).

Rogers calls a "sanction award", should be enforceable against the defaulting lawyer by the courts of the arbitral seat or a foreign court under the 1958 UN New York Arbitration Convention. The sanction award would also be published to form a body of persuasive authority, although the name of the lawyer could in certain cases be expunged. Professor Roger's work is obviously based on experience in the USA; and by "experience", it must be based on bad experience. It clearly does not take full account of experience elsewhere. In particular, it bears little relevance to the realities of international arbitration in the established centres of arbitration in Europe. Nevertheless, her methodology deserves serious consideration and serious answers.

My answer, for the time being at least, is to do nothing. Faced with such a massive proposal with potentially enormous consequences for international arbitration, "benign neglect" is often the best policy, even if King George III was unlucky in its application to the early American Revolution. There is still too much to be said against the increasing introduction of new guidelines, codes, notes and rules, particularly from a jurisdiction where these regulations are not renowned for securing widespread compliance. It may nonetheless be the course which the rest of the world will in the future have to adopt and apply. Today, however, this regulatory fury should be resisted. There is no greater system of international arbitration more worthy of universal respect than ICSID arbitration; and it cannot be wholly coincidental that ICSID has so far not only forsworn any ethical code for arbitrators and legal practitioners in ICSID arbitration but also that Articles 21 and 22 of the 1965 ICSID Convention expressly provide for blanket immunity for all arbitrators and all practitioners, subject only to a waiver of the President of the World Bank, which has never been done. In short, if it ain't broke, don't fix it; and so please, unlike Oliver Twist, no more ethical porridge.

22

Still More On Arbitral Deliberations

An English Perspective

A. Introduction

How does an international arbitration tribunal comprised of three multi-national arbitrators decide a dispute, as a matter of form? A reasoned award will usually inform the parties why a decision has been reached on the substance of the dispute; but the same award will rarely relate by what formal process that decision has been reached by the arbitrators. An award may therefore describe in lengthy procedural detail the hearings, the pleadings, the evidence and the arguments presented by the parties to the tribunal; but it will not similarly describe the procedures taken by the arbitrators for their internal deliberations, listing their own meetings, written exchanges or voting arrangements. No major arbitration rules prescribe any particular procedure for their arbitrators' deliberations; most national laws are equally silent, including the UNCITRAL Model Law; and historically, in most scholarly works on arbitral procedure, there has been surprisingly little to describe how a multinational tribunal actually organises its own internal decision-making process. Although the confidentiality of arbitral deliberations may preclude public discussion of their substantive content, no such rule cloaks with secrecy the form of arbitral deliberations. Yet, international arbitrators must inevitably employ such processes (whatever these may be); and no less obviously, such procedures cannot mirror national court or domestic arbitral procedures, precisely or at all.

In past years, specific aspects resulting indirectly from arbitral deliberations have been addressed, for example majority awards, dissenting opinions, recalcitrant arbitrators and truncated tribunals; but only recently has the spotlight fallen on the more general subject of how arbitrators actually reach their decisions. In Switzerland and France, the topic has been addressed most recently in Bredin's magisterial essay (2004)[1]; and following the Svea Court of Appeal's decision in the *CME* case, Heuman (2003) contributed a detailed study in his work on Swedish Arbitration[2]. Elsewhere, however, the general topic has been largely ignored, as

---

[1] JEAN-DENIS BREDIN, "Retour au délibéré arbitral", in *Liber Amicorum Claude Reymond* (2004), p. 43.
[2] LARS HEUMAN, *Arbitration Law of Sweden: Practice and Procedure* (2003), pp. 484 ff.

On Arbitration. Edited by: Sam Wordsworth KC and Marie Veeder, Oxford University Press. © Oxford University Press 2023.
DOI: 10.1093/oso/9780192869135.003.0022

if the process were either unimportant or best kept secretly mysterious either to preserve its full majesty or possibly to conceal its most dangerous deficiencies. Nowhere has this been more true than England, with even Mustill & Boyd (1989) devoting only one short paragraph[3]; and for English arbitrators taking part for the first time in deliberations with Swiss and French arbitrators, in particular, it is sometimes like Aladdin finding a second genie emerging from his lamp. That was certainly my fortunate experience on first meeting François Knoepfler as president of an international tribunal. His skill and diplomacy in handling deliberations was remarkable; it was apparently effortless and seemingly unplanned; and even in a particularly difficult arbitration with more than one awkward moment, his approach tempered complete fairness with rigorous efficiency. It was a salutary experience: it can be humiliating not to understand something that a master so obviously knows; but it is made worse when you did not even know that this something existed. Thus began a personal odyssey in waters almost completely uncharted, watching other master mariners navigate the shoals of arbitral deliberations to arrive safely at the award. How is it done?

In England, it is not difficult to see how an English judge decides a case (without a jury) because at trial the judge usually conducts a lively debate with both advocates in turn, at the end of which the judge traditionally delivers judgment orally. In this sense, the judge's deliberations are public. Even where judgment is reserved to a later date, it is not difficult to guess the result, if not always its full reasons; and of course the single judge can only deliberate and debate these reasons with himself. The English "adversarial" process in court thus more easily describes the process between the judge and the parties' advocates than between those advocates themselves. In the Anglo-Saxon appellate process where judges sit in benches of two or more, appellate judges still work more as individuals than as a cohesive judicial group. In Karl Llewellyn's famous research in the USA[4], an appellate court is more likely to produce a "net view" with a wider perspective and fewer extremes than a single judge; unrecorded doubts or observations which a single judge could later easily overlook are more likely to be recalled and revived by a member of an appellate group; and the need for written, reasoned decisions tends to produce stabilisation between one judicial member intent upon the past and another upon the future. Beyond these features, however, the results of his research into the appellate process do not depend upon any group decision. For example, the figures for New York appellate cases over 45 years showed a range of dissenting opinions running at between one in four to one in seven cases, a proportion not mirrored for international arbitration cases. International arbitration tribunals achieve a much

---

[3] MUSTILL & BOYD, *Commercial Arbitration* (1989), p. 361. This is no criticism of the greatest work on English arbitration; and much the same could be said of the relatively short passage in Sanders' exhaustive inquiry, "Arbitration" in Vol XIV, Civil Procedure, *International Encyclopaedia of Comparative Law* (1996), # 12.183.

[4] KARL LLEWELLYN, *The Common Law Tradition: Deciding Appeals* (1960), pp. 31 & 463.

368   ON ARBITRATION

higher degree of uniformity for their decisions, which is not explained by certain traditions precluding dissenting opinions (but not dissenting votes).

In London Arbitration, at least before the Arbitration Act 1979, the practice of the traditional arbitration tribunal was usually different from the English Court; but it provided no useful guidance on the subject here discussed. With two arbitrators plus an "umpire", there were usually few public or private "deliberations", for several reasons. First, if the two arbitrators disagreed on the result, the matter would usually be passed immediately to the umpire to decide as sole arbitrator. Second, prior to such disagreement, the tribunal could sit silently during the hearing with only an occasional remark from one or other of the party-appointed arbitrators directed at the parties; but these were unilateral sallies not to be assumed as representing the views of the whole tribunal, still less the umpire. These exchanges did not mirror the English judge's inquisition. By the end of the arbitration, therefore, it could be difficult to guess at its result; and the explanation was perhaps economic. In those days, London arbitrators rarely ordered during the arbitration interim deposits from the parties in order to secure payment of their fees and expenses, relying instead on their ability to exercise a lien on the award requiring payment as a prior condition to releasing the award to the parties. If, however, the arbitrators revealed during the hearing that the claimant's claim would fail, neither the respondent nor the claimant would have any interest in procuring the award's release; and there are tales of some awards still gathering dust under ancient liens made by arbitration tribunals too uneconomic and untimely with the truth. Third, before 1979, an English arbitration tribunal was not then as concerned with producing reasons for their award; it was not usually required for commercial arbitrators to give any formal reasons; and where "informal reasons" were given, not forming part of the award, the reasons were succinct and usually drafted by the most diligent member of the tribunal with little or no contribution from other arbitrators. Accordingly, none of this national experience prepared an English arbitrator for an international commercial arbitration.

The logical starting-point is to distinguish an arbitrator from a judge, a sole arbitrator from a tribunal comprised of three arbitrators and a domestic arbitration tribunal from a multi-cultural international arbitration tribunal. For international arbitration, a sole arbitrator's inner mental process cannot be merely replicated three times over when the tribunal is comprised of three arbitrators; and there must necessarily exist a collegiate decision-making process for making their award. Indeed, the general principle of collegiate deliberations between members of an arbitration tribunal has long been generally recognised. The classic approach was noted by Professor René David in 1985: "It is unanimously admitted that, if there is more than one arbitrator, the award must be made after a deliberation in which all the arbitrators have taken part."[5] In 1994, Professor Claude Reymond remarked

---

[5] DAVID, *Arbitration in International Trade* (1985), p. 315. The original French version contains a similar passage: *L'arbitrage dans le commerce international* (1982), p. 436.

in his paper on "The President of the Arbitral Tribunal"[6]: "No matter what form proceedings take, it is essential that the deliberations be organized in such a way that all arbitrators can participate. It is up to the president to arrange this, although the choice of method of deliberation may be an internal procedural decision to be made by the tribunal and, in case of any disagreement, by the majority." This general principle operates even where the collegiate approach is not explicit in national legislation or institutional rules of arbitration. Today, the general principle of collegiate deliberations today is well described in Fouchard, Gaillard & Goldman (1999)[7]: "The role of the arbitrators is to resolve all of the disputed issues by one or more decisions, and to express those decisions in a document which is subject to certain formal requirements and which is known as the arbitral award. The process which enables the arbitrators to reach such a decision is referred to as the deliberations." In Poudret & Besson (2002)[8], there is the fullest and most recent discussion, beginning with a similar statement of the general principle: "Dès lors que le tribunal arbitral est composé de plusieurs arbitres et constitue une juridiction collégiale, le délibéré est une opération essentielle qui doit avoir lieu même s'il n'est pas prévu expressément par la loi. Il s'agit à la fois d'un droit des parties, découlant selon plusieurs auteurs du droit d'être entendu, et d'un droit et devoir de chacun des arbitres. Malgré son importance, il n'est que rarement réglementé et même mentionné dans les lois d'arbitrage." The general principle of collegial deliberations itself cannot therefore be doubted for international commercial arbitration tribunals; but what is its legal source; and in practice, how does it apply?

B. Legal Theory

As already noted, there is no express legislation or arbitration rule prescribing the particular form of an international arbitration tribunal's deliberations. The doctrine of equality of arms is often cited as the implied source of an arbitrator's legal duty to deliberate collegially. The argument runs that equality of arms is a cornerstone of arbitration; equality of arms governs both the arbitration procedure and the composition of the arbitral tribunal, as confirmed by the *Dutco* decision in France; equality of arms also extends to arbitral deliberations where each party has nominated one arbitrator; equality of arms in the context of deliberations means that each arbitrator must be treated equally (e.g. all must receive the same

---

[6] CLAUDE REYMOND, "The President of the Tribunal", 9 *ICSID Review - Foreign Investment Law Journal* 1, 12 (1994); republished from the original French in *Etudes offertes à Pierre Bellet* (1991).

[7] FOUCHARD, GAILLARD & GOLDMAN, *International Commercial Arbitration* (1999; ed Gaillard & Savage), Section II – "The Making of the Award", pp. 746–753. (This edition is the English version of the second edition of this work, first published in French in 1996 – where the equivalent passage appears at pp. 759–764).

[8] POUDRET & BESSON, *Droit comparé de l'arbitrage international* (2002; Geneva), p. 689 ff.

materials and have an equal opportunity to participate in the deliberations); and unequal treatment of one arbitrator is therefore equivalent to unequal treatment of the party nominating that arbitrator. However, this argument necessarily treats an independent and impartial arbitrator as the agent of the party nominating that arbitrator, an unacceptable and even dangerous assumption for international commercial arbitration. Even more, it assumes that the nominating party is always the victim of another's misfeasance during deliberations whereas practical experience shows this not to be invariably so, with a party quite capable of attacking its own nominated arbitrator[9]; and it wholly ignores the situation where a party has not nominated any arbitrator. It is well settled, at least outside the USA, that an arbitrator, albeit nominated by one party, is not the agent or advocate of that party; and once appointed, the arbitrator must perform his function impartially between the disputing parties. In other words, whether or not nominated by one or other party, an arbitrator is the arbitrator for both parties and owes the same duties to both parties. (In England, this has been settled law for at least 200 years[10], and so too in other countries – all long before the modern doctrine of equality of arms and Article 6 of the European Convention on Human Rights). It must be doubted, therefore, whether a disputing party's procedural right to equality of arms can be the source of the general principle governing arbitral deliberations.

Nonetheless, there is no doubt that parties have a procedural legal right to collegiate deliberations and that a legal duty exists requiring an arbitrator to deliberate collegiately with this arbitral colleagues, with a reciprocal legal right to be consulted by them collegiately; and that a breach of these legal obligations may render a decision or award invalid. Certain scholars maintain that each arbitrator's personal status, mandate or contract with the parties creates this duty[11]. Others see the mutual obligation originating from due process extending from the hearing into the deliberations or as a rule of international procedural public policy, including Fouchard, Gaillard & Goldman; and still others as arising from each of these, including Poudret & Besson.Yet other scholars ignore the source of the legal duty, including Heuman; and they are perhaps right to do so. Whilst the precise source of the legal duty can provoke interesting academic debate, it has for the time being little practical importance. Whatever its source, a breach of the general principle may affect the award's validity, both at the arbitral seat and before the enforcement court under the 1958 New York Convention; and even before any award or

---

[9] *Himpurnia California Energy v Republic of Indonesia* (2000) *ICCA Yearbook* 111 (where one party "kidnapped" its own appointed arbitrator in the Netherlands, on his way to the Peace Palace at the Hague).

[10] A statement to this effect, based on cases decided since 1790, was approved by Erle J in *Oswald v Earl Grey* (1855) 23 LJQB 69, 72.

[11] From England, Lord Mustill has long been the principal critic of the contractual theory, in favour of an arbitrator's *sui generis* status: see most recently MUSTILL, "Is it a Bird", in *Liber Amicorum Claude Reymond* (2004), p. 205.

decision, it may lead to a challenge to one or more arbitrators. It is therefore not unimportant to ascertain what can, in practice, amount to a breach.

C. Arbitral Practice

At this point, the topic becomes surprisingly diffuse; but at the outset, it is still possible to identify four practical features of this general principle. First, collegiate deliberations are not formalistic: deliberations between international arbitrators are essentially pragmatic fitted to the particular case and the particular tribunal and do not follow a pre-ordained ritual or fixed procedure, particularly with the use of modern methods of communication between arbitrators working at great geographical distances from each other and in different time-zones. Second, the objective is to give each arbitrator a fair opportunity to take part in deliberations; and if that arbitrator omits to take up that opportunity, there is no automatic malfeasance by the tribunal. As the old saying goes, you can lead a horse to water but you cannot make it drink; and a recalcitrant arbitrator cannot completely frustrate the work of a truncated tribunal. Third, a dissenting arbitrator has no essential role in deliberating the reasons for a majority award, after taking part in arbitral deliberations, expressing his dissent and the majority having decided upon a different result. Fourth, in all this, the arbitration tribunal remains the master of its own procedure, as it did with the procedure directly involving the parties; and the majority of the tribunal remains usually empowered to make majority decisions, notwithstanding the dissent or deliberate non-participation of one co-arbitrator.

These pragmatic features have gradually emerged from the practice of English arbitration, as elsewhere. Historically, however, the principle of arbitral collegiality under English law was unduly strict. Until 1934, it was considered at common law that the office of arbitrator being joint, if one co-arbitrator refused or failed to act at any stage, there could be no valid award made by the other arbitrator or arbitrators at all. An arbitrator could not delegate the making of an award to another person; and accordingly a co-arbitrator could not delegate any part of his functions to his fellow-arbitrators, including the making of an award. In practice, this meant that arbitrators had to act unanimously – unless the parties agreed otherwise. For obvious reasons, many did so by incorporating into their arbitration agreements a provision that the award could be made by a majority. The Arbitration Act 1934 (Section 4) codified this practice; it was restated in the Arbitration Act 1950 (Section 9(1)); and provisions to the same effect are now contained in Sections 20(3) and 22 of the Arbitration Act 1996, reflecting Article 29 of the UNCITRAL Model Law. The rigours of the old common law rule were thereby significantly relaxed in the face of modern needs and new forms of communications.

There remained, however, a degree of strict formalism in the making of an award under English law, even where one arbitrator dissented from the result. To such an

372 ON ARBITRATION

extent that, until 1982, one of the leading textbooks on English law stated that in the case of an award made by more than one arbitrator, "all the arbitrators making the award should execute it at the same time and in the presence of each other"[12]. In *European Grain v Johnston*[13], the Court of Appeal decided that the old English rule was no longer applicable in modern conditions; but that it was still not acceptable that one arbitrator should sign the award form in blank and depart for Australia without *any* deliberations, leaving the decision entirely to his co-arbitrators (as happened in that case). As was stated by Kerr LJ: "I have myself been party to cases [i.e. as an international commercial arbitrator before his judicial appointment] where the arbitrators were in different countries and took many important decisions by correspondence or by telephone. This would be in the interests of all parties in saving costs. Therefore, like Lord Denning MR and Oliver LJ, I do not regard the coincidence in time and place for the purely formal purposes of signing the award as something which is essential, unless it is prescribed by rules which govern the arbitration." (p. 528). That is certainly the modern practice today in London Arbitration in making an award, where full use is made of email, fax, telephone and courier in communications between co-arbitrators. It can extend, however, to all aspects of deliberations before the award, without any strict formalities[14].

As intimated by Kerr LJ, there remained difficulties in English arbitrations where institutional rules of arbitration expressly derogate from these legal presumptions. In *Cargill v Soc Iberica de Moltnracion SA* (1998) [15], the GAFTA arbitration rules required all three arbitrators to sign the reasoned award, apparently reintroducing the old common law rule of unanimity. The dissenting arbitrator wanted his own dissenting reasons incorporated into the majority's award as a condition of his signing the award. The Court of Appeal decided that it was for the majority of the tribunal to decide whether and to what extent their dissentient colleague's demand should be accommodated; and if they refused his demand (as they did), he had no right to insist. His consequent refusal to sign the award, albeit as a dissenter, would therefore justify his removal as arbitrator. This approach is also interesting for another reason: it reflects the difference between the result and the reasons for that

---

[12] *Russell on Arbitration,* 20th ed (1982), p. 301.

[13] *European Grain v Johnston* [1983] 1 QB 520 (Court of Appeal), affmg [1982] 1 Lloyd's Rep 414 (Parker J).

[14] The UNCITRAL "Notes on Organising Arbitral Proceedings" provide a useful guide to the modern practice regarding communications in arbitral proceedings. Note 8 states: "The consultations, whether they involve only the arbitrators or also the parties, can be held in one or more meetings, or can be carried out by correspondence or tele-communications such as tele-fax or conference telephone calls or other electronic means. Meetings may be held at the venue of arbitration or at some other appropriate location." This applies as much to deliberations as it does to the organisation of the arbitral hearings with the parties. (Let no-one, however, propose that UNCITRAL now prepare "Guidelines on Arbitral Deliberations").

[15] *Cargill v Soc Iberica de Molturacion SA* [1998] 1 Lloyd's Rep 489 (Court of Appeal), regarding an arbitration before three commercial arbitrators of the Grain and Feed Trade Association in the City of London (GAFTA).

result: having disagreed with the result, the dissenting arbitrator had no necessary role in regard to the majority's reasons for that result.

Under the 1950–1979 Acts, shorn of its strictest formalities, the collegiate principle for deliberations remained at English law. In *Bank Mellat v GAA Development* (1988)[16], in relation to an ICC arbitration held in London, the majority had not included the dissenting arbitrator in their deliberations on the final version of the award, finalised after receipt of his dissenting opinion. On a challenge to the award, the majority were charged with misconduct under the 1950 Act. In a factually complicated case, the Court decided: "In my judgment there are several answers to the charge of misconduct. The first question is whether there was any duty, owed by the majority to [the dissenting arbitrator] or to the parties, to consult with [the dissenting arbitrator] about the revision of the majority award. This question cannot be viewed in the abstract. It has not been suggested at any time that any of the observations of the ICC court, or amendments to the reasons for the award, involved anything that had not been canvassed at the hearings, and discussed at meetings between the arbitrators. And it is not in every international commercial arbitration of the scale and scope of this arbitration that the opportunity exists for such extensive oral deliberations as took place in the present case. Moreover, it would be fanciful to suggest that a further meeting or consultation would have afforded [the dissenting arbitrator] an opportunity to convert the majority to this point of view. The sole purpose of a further meeting or consultation would have been to enable [the dissenting arbitrator] to discuss with the majority the redrafting of the reasons of their majority award. [The dissenting arbitrator] disagreed fundamentally and comprehensively with the majority award and its reasons, and it is difficult to conceive of the utility, at that late stage, of a discussion with him of a drafting exercise which was intended to strengthen those reasons. No doubt courtesy between colleagues required a further reference to him, but in my view the governing principle, which I have stated, did not require it as a matter of law. On this ground alone the application must fail ..." This statement from an experienced former arbitrator, now a senior English judge (Lord Steyn in the House of Lords), represents the modern practice of international arbitrators in commercial arbitrations taking place in England. Under the English 1996 Act, unless the parties' arbitration agreement provides otherwise, an award is formally valid even if not signed by a dissenting arbitrator: Section 52(3) provides that the award shall be signed by all the arbitrators *or* all those assenting to the award; and where a dissenting arbitrator has indicated that he dissents from the result of a draft award, it is not considered legally necessary to consult that arbitrator as to the majority's reasons for that result. Without any cross-reference to comparative developments, English law seems to have arrived at the same starting-point reached in other countries.

---

[16] *Bank Mellat v GAA Development* [1988] 2 Lloyd's Rep 44, 50–51 (Steyn J).

374 ON ARBITRATION

In France, the old domestic rule requiring meetings of the arbitrators in person was likewise held inapplicable to the making of an international arbitration award. In *Industrija Motora Rakovita v Lynx Machinery* (1978)[17], which was an ICC arbitration subjected to French procedural law between Indian and Yugoslav companies, one of three arbitrators had refused to sign the award; and it was contended by the party challenging the award in the Paris Cour d'appel that by virtue of article 1028(3) of the old code of civil procedure, the award was null. It was held by the Court that article 1028(3) was inapplicable to international arbitration, so long as the award recited the third arbitrator's refusal to sign the award. By that recitation, it was necessarily demonstrated that some deliberations had taken place between all three arbitrators sufficient for the third arbitrator to declare his dissent. The Court did not prescribe any particular procedure for such deliberations, given the difficulties of organising meetings between arbitrators residing in different countries: i.e. these could take place by letter or telephone-call between one or more arbitrators without an actual meeting of all three arbitrators together. This decision was upheld by the Cour de cassation (1981)[18]; and it states still the position in French law today[19]. However, the subsidiary complaint was the absence of collegiate deliberations on the final version of the award, as to which there had been no deliberations involving the third arbitrator. This raised the question whether collegiate deliberations were directed only at the result of the award, or "dispositif", or whether such deliberations extended also to the drafting of the reasons for that result even where one arbitrator had indicated his dissent from that result. The Court's decision suggests that what is important is the former; namely deliberations towards the result; and that once an arbitrator has dissented on the result, his or her further involvement on drafting the reasons for that result is unnecessary. This is largely common-sense: what can the dissident arbitrator usefully contribute to the reasoning of a result from which he or she disagrees?

In Switzerland, article 31(1) of the old 1969 Concordat provided that all the arbitrators must participate in all the deliberations and decisions of the arbitral tribunal ("Tous les arbitres doivent participer à chaque délibération et décision du tribunal arbitral"). This provision required a two-stage process: first collegiate deliberations and second a vote. The Swiss Federal Tribunal decided in *Séfri v Komgrap* (1985)[20], an ICC arbitration held in Geneva, that such deliberations and vote did not require a meeting between the members of the arbitration tribunal. These could take place by correspondence; and there were no special formal requirements for arbitral deliberations. The Swiss Private International Law Act of 1987 contains no similar

---

[17] *Industrija Motora Rakovita v Lynx Machinery*, Rev. arb. 1979.266, ann. VIATTE.

[18] *Rev. arb.* 1982.425, ann. FOUCHARD.

[19] BREDIN, *supra*; see also DE BOISSÉSSON, *Le droit français de l'arbitrage* (1990), p. 801; and HASCHER, "Principes et Pratique de Procédure dans l'arbitrage commercial international", *Recueil des cours* 279 (1999) p. 157.

[20] *Séfri SA v Komgrap* ATF 111 Ia 336; (198) *Bull. ASA* 77; XIV *ICCA Yearbook* 232.

two-stage process; and although a combination of articles 189 and 190 requires collegiate deliberations, the arbitration tribunal is free to decide the form of those deliberations (subject to any special agreement of the parties binding upon the tribunal). In an unreported decision of 31st March 1999, the Swiss Federal Tribunal has confirmed the position, excluding formalisms and permitting deliberations by writing only[21].

In Sweden, the recent decision by the Svea Court of Appeal in the *CME* case (2003)[22] took a similarly pragmatic approach. The losing party under a partial award on liability made by a majority of the arbitration tribunal (X and Y) under the UNCITRAL Arbitration Rules challenged that award's validity under Swedish law, as the law of the arbitral seat, on the ground that its nominated arbitrator (Z) had been unlawfully excluded by X and Y from the arbitral deliberations. All three arbitrators testified orally before the Court, with X disclosing all or almost all the papers comprising the private written record of the deliberations. By any standards, it was an unusual and important case; the facts are not here relevant; but the Court's legal reasons for rejecting the challenge are worth citing: "To begin with, it may be noted that the [Swedish] Arbitration Act contains no formal requirements as to the manner in which the arbitrators' deliberations shall be conducted. Clearly, a general reason why the procedure is not governed in detail has been to allow for the possibility smoothly and expeditiously to adapt the various stages in the proceedings to the circumstances of the particular case, thereby promoting the public interest of promptness and flexibility in arbitration proceedings. Certain guidelines as to the manner in which proceedings are to be conducted are provided in Sections 21 and 30 of the Arbitration Act. Section 30, first paragraph, provides that where an arbitrator fails to participate in the arbitrators' assessment of an issue without valid cause, that factor shall not prevent the other arbitrators from determining the issue ... the conclusion may be drawn that the main rule under Section 30 is that all arbitrators shall participate in the deliberations. Section 21, first sentence, provides that the arbitrators shall handle the dispute impartially, expeditiously, and promptly. This must also include the deliberations. The requirement of impartiality thus means that the arbitrators shall be treated equally and be provided the same possibilities to participate in the deliberations and attempt to influence the other arbitrators though substantive arguments.The requirement of expeditiousness means that the deliberations shall be conducted in a cost-efficient and flexible manner. As a consequence of the lack of formal rules, the deliberations may be oral or written, a timetable for the deliberations may but need not be established, and deadlines may be set within which the arbitrators must express their

---

[21] POUDRET & BESSON (*supra*), pp. 691–692; LALIVE, POUDRET & REYMOND, *Le droit de l'arbitrage interne et international en Suisse* (1989), pp. 166 & 411.
[22] *CME v Czech Republic* (15th May 2003: President Ulla Erlandsson, Judges Per Eklund and Måns Edling), reported in (2003:2) *Stockholm Arbitration Report* 167, ann. RUBINS.

opinions. However, the deadlines may also be changed as required. The lack of formal rules also means that there is no obligation on the chairman to arrange a formal vote when it becomes clear that two arbitrators are in agreement regarding an outcome of the dispute which the third arbitrator cannot support. Against the requirement of promptness, due process aspects must of course be guaranteed. The parties have legitimate interests in the arbitrated dispute being adjudicated in detail and with due care. However, the requirement of promptness and the provisions of section 30 entails that when two arbitrators have agreed upon the outcome of the dispute, the third arbitrator cannot prolong the deliberations by demanding continued discussions in an attempt to persuade the others as to the correctness of his opinion. The dissenting arbitrator is thus not afforded any opportunity to delay the writing of the award. On the other hand, the deliberations should not be deemed concluded before the arbitral award is signed. The dissenting arbitrator should, therefore, be afforded an opportunity to submit comments on the proposed award. Better conditions are thereby created for a substantively correct award ...." Whatever the result on the facts of that case and its reliance on Swedish legislation (albeit not materially different from the Model Law), it would be hard to quarrel with this general approach applying to the deliberations of all international arbitrators anywhere.

From England and the more established arbitral seats, it seems therefore that old domestic rules requiring each arbitrator's joint participation at every stage of the arbitral deliberations, including the making and signing of the award, do not now govern the practice of arbitrators sitting on international arbitration tribunals. It is the substance of collegiate deliberations which matter, whereas mere ritualism does not, demonstrating the pragmatic function of the decision-making process. There is no fixed process for such deliberations, provided that each arbitrator has enjoyed a fair opportunity to take part. If one arbitrator ignores or abuses that opportunity, there is no automatic malfeasance by the other members of the tribunal. At the point of dissent in a tribunal's deliberations, the minority arbitrator has no further necessary role on the reasons for the majority's result, save that which courtesy or common-sense might suggest; and a dissenting arbitrator, whether or not willing to sign the award, cannot impede or prevent the making of the majority award, or the majority's reasons for that award, in a timely and efficient manner. But having discarded formalism, what is a "fair" opportunity to take part in arbitral deliberations?

It must first depend on the form of the arbitral deliberations. Generally, their form is decided by the arbitration tribunal; and if there were a dispute between the arbitrators about form, it would be decided by the chairman or, possibly, the majority of the arbitrators. As to recommended forms of deliberations, there is clearly no single version, nor should there be. Given the diversity of legal cultures and traditions, even disregarding the diversity amongst individual arbitrators, the form of deliberations will differ from tribunal to tribunal and arbitration to arbitration.

It must all be dependent on the exigencies of the particular case. For most arbitrations, the deliberations will at least include meetings between the arbitrators; but in others, such meetings may be impractical. For example, the Formula One FIA/ FISA Contract Recognition Board in Geneva has never met for deliberations, being required to publish its awards within three days of a hearing which until recently has never exceeded one day and which must itself, in principle, take place within five days of the dispute between the driver and the rival teams[23]. For the arbitrators in three different jurisdictions, there is simply no sufficient time after the hearing to meet for a "conferenza personale": everything must be resolved subsequently by fax and telephone. At the other end of the scale, in a very complex and sensitive dispute, there have been meetings after meetings of the arbitrators, with deliberations exceeding in days and overall time even the oral hearings with the parties. In the middle, there are procedures ranging from an informal list of issues handwritten on the back of a restaurant menu to sophisticated written questionnaires, such as was used by the tribunal's chairman in the *CME* case. Written questionnaires requiring written answers with no meeting can bring their own problems, forcing a premature dissent when further, open-minded oral discussion could foster unanimity; and what if an arbitrator fails or refuses to answer the written questions? In Lalive, Poudret & Reymond (1989)[24], it is suggested that the chairman of an international arbitration tribunal in Switzerland can prepare a written questionnaire for his co-arbitrators requiring answers within a stipulated time, failure to answer timeously being treated as a dissent, being a procedure implicitly approved by the Swiss Federal Tribunal in *Séfri v Komgrap* (1985)[25]. In France, a similar procedure was recommended in a commentary on ICC Arbitration Case No 5082 by the ICC International Court of Arbitration's then General Counsel[26]. In that ICC arbitration, the chairman of the tribunal had prepared a questionnaire of 28 questions in regard to two contracts under separate headings for liability and quantum, together with two more general questions. His coarbitrators were required to answer before a stipulated deadline; and unlike the proposed Swiss questionnaire, as regards one important question the chairman indicated that he would consider "absence of answer as equivalent to the affirmative".

In England, such questionnaires are very rare; and it is not difficult to imagine possible abuse by the majority of the arbitrators and consequent unfairness to the other arbitrator. Often, answers can depend too much on the questions, particularly questions formulated too early in the arbitration. For an English arbitrator used to relying on the parties' counsel to elucidate the decisive issues, it seems

---

[23] KAUFMANN-KOHLER & PETER, "Formula 1 Racing and Arbitration: The FIA Tailor-Made System for Fast Track Dispute Resolution", (2001) 17 *Arbitration International* 173.

[24] LALIVE, POUDRET & REYMOND, (*supra*), p. 411; see also REYMOND (*supra*).

[25] *Séfri SA v Komgrap* ATF 111 Ia 336; XIV *ICCA Yearbook* 232.

[26] HASCHER, *Collection of Procedural Decisions in ICC Arbitration 1993–1996* (1997), 70, reprinted from 121 *JDI (Clunet)* 1081 (1994).

wrong in principle to conclude any part of the deliberations before the closing of all submissions, including the parties' post-hearing briefs. In the *Alabama Claims Arbitration*, the English arbitrator was deeply offended by the Swiss arbitrator's declaration of his conclusions before even the first hearing; and it may have helped provoke his subsequent dissent. Even now, undue or even unexplained haste in deliberations will raise the suspicion of unfairness and improper motive. In all cases, however, the arbitration tribunal is required to *decide* the result; and in commercial disputes, time is money; and delay can work injustice, even if mitigated by the award of interest. There is a danger in three arbitrators chasing unanimity endlessly towards an infinite horizon or engaging in drafting exercises so elaborate as to make "the best the enemy of the good". As required by arbitration rules or national laws, the tribunal may be required to state the reasons upon which the award is based; but it is not required to state "reasons for reasons" or to address different reasons on which the award is *not* based. An arbitration award is not a doctoral thesis: it need state only the legal and factual reasons for the decision by arbitrators who have conscientiously applied legal principle to their factual determinations. Those reasons inform each party why one has lost and the other has won, of which the former purpose is by far the more important. Is it possible to ask for more?

D. Conclusion

In his famously humorous book on the English judiciary[27], David Pannick quoted from Kafka's Trial where it was observed that "it had never occurred to the advocates that they should suggest or insist on any improvements in the system, while – and this was very characteristic – almost every accused man, even quite ordinary people amongst them, discovered from the earliest stages a passion for suggesting reforms." Could the same soon be said of deliberations in international commercial arbitration? So long as arbitrators preside in the tradition of François Knoepfler, this is unlikely; but the vast increase in the use of international commercial arbitration, with new faces and new traditions, means that demands for "reforms" are inevitable in the future. Moreover, unlike Kafka's advocates, new advocates are already seeking changes to international commercial arbitration: precluded from challenging an award directly on the merits, it is becoming increasingly frequent to attack arbitrators and their procedural conduct of the arbitration as an indirect means of attacking an award. There is no logical reason for such attacks to exclude the conduct of arbitral deliberations; and the prospect of arbitrators testifying on their deliberations may not be infrequent in years to come. Historically, it was

---

[27] DAVID PANNICK, *Judges* (1987), p. v. (This book accompanies the author's similar book on "Advocates"; and with his author's skill in describing the frailties, pretensions and ludicrous conduct of both, it is to be hoped that one day he will turn his attention to English arbitrators).

almost unprecedented for an arbitrator to disclose an arbitration tribunal's private deliberations. An attempt to use such material was made by Iran before Dr Moons, the President of the Netherlands' Supreme Court as the appointing authority at the Iran–US Claims Tribunal, in Iran's challenge to one presiding arbitrator; but the material was summarily rejected (1989)[28]. It was equally rare for an arbitrator personally to give oral evidence in court on the tribunal's deliberations: it was a practice criticised by the German Supreme Court in *AAW v W* (1930); and in the *FFM* case (1990) in the USA the challenge failed miserably[29]. In the recent *CME* case, the attempt also failed; but the precedent was there firmly established of three arbitrators being cross-examined under oath as to the form of their confidential deliberations; and given the gravity of the accusations against the majority of the arbitrators in that case (all eventually rejected by the Court), it would undoubtedly be followed in England under the 1996 Act. To those who maintain that arbitrators are a special profession beyond such attacks, the litigious fate of the medical profession in the USA and England is a salutary warning: doctors must now view their patients as potential claimants, knowing that any clinical decision can lead to litigation or professional misconduct proceedings instigated by the plaintiffs' bar[30]. It may be much worse for international arbitrators, with even larger sums at issue and a dissident co-arbitrator in the complainant's camp. Moreover, unlike doctors, many arbitrators required to defend themselves and their professional reputations will still not carry any professional insurance for legal expenses. For arbitration users generally, nothing will be gained by such "reforms"; but that is not now a sufficient reason to preclude change. In particular, it would be a terrible set-back if the result of fresh attacks on arbitral deliberations caused a retreat into impractical formalisms from which international commercial arbitration has so successfully escaped. Or is it now time for arbitrators in their awards to make the form of their deliberations more transparent? Whatever the answers, there is still much more to be written on arbitral deliberations from England – and elsewhere.

---

[28] *Documents relating to the Challenge*, 24 Iran-USCTR 309 (1990); also MAPP, *The Iran-United States Claims Tribunal – The First Ten Years 1981–1991* (1993), p. 49.

[29] *A-A Werke Gmbh v W* (1930) KG 2 129, 15 ff; and *FFM v Chemical Carriers*, 751 F. Supp. 467 (SDNY 1990); ann. REILLY "The Court's Power to Invade the Arbitrators' Deliberation Chamber" (1992) *Journal of Int Arb* 27.

[30] In England, for example, see MAKINA WHEELER (an English barrister), "Physician, steel thyself for litigation ahead", *Daily Telegraph* 30th December 2004.

23

Why Bother and Why It Matters?

Presented to the Institute for Transnational Arbitration – Dallas June 2006

Yogi Berra got it wrong.[1] The problem with *déjà vu* is not that you only understand the real message when you see it for the third or fourth time. The problem is that you cannot see *déjà vu* the first time. There are many problems in this world which could be avoided entirely if you could understand *déjà vu* before the second time, or the third. The fourth time may be far too late. If we can, we should try to understand something that is happening now for the first time and try to fix it before it is too late, so as to avoid saying, like Yogi Berra, in years to come, that we could and should have understood and done something now, the first time, before it became "*déjà vu* all over again."

This something that is happening now is the story of an arbitral institution under threat for more than one year, with no fix immediately in sight: the ICSID.

In London we know too well how legal institutions begin to crumble, at first imperceptively, and then, suddenly, with alarming speed. This happened to the English Commercial Court in the early 1960s. Those problems were fixed by their users provoked by Lord Devlin, one of our greatest commercial judges and later a distinguished international arbitrator. It also happened to the LCIA in the early 1990s. That institution was also fixed by its users motivated by Sir Michael Kerr and Bertie Vigrass, without whom the LCIA would not now exist at all.

The brutal fact is that it can take decades, or more, to build up an institution. Its founding fathers can be famous historical names. The institution then looms large and seemingly impregnable – but it is in fact very small and very brittle. It can weaken in a short time, to the point where its basic functions and even its existence are threatened.

We are all here, directly or indirectly, users of ICSID. ICSID is the best institution in its field, the best run, the best staffed, with the best rules and the best treaty. Yet it needs no compliments from us today. The question today is whether

---

[1] Lawrence Peter "Yogi" Berra is a former Major League Baseball player who played for the New York Yankees from the late 1940s to the mid 1960s. He is known to have said "It's déjà vu all over again."

On Arbitration. Edited by: Sam Wordsworth KC and Marie Veeder, Oxford University Press. © Oxford University Press 2023.
DOI: 10.1093/oso/9780192869135.003.0023

the ICSID we know and support will still exist in a few years from now? This question has begun to bother many of us and it matters to all of us.

Why does it matter at all? Let me take three illustrations drawn from Peru, Pakistan, and China.

A. La Brea y Pariñas

In 1908, the Peruvian Government granted a large oil concession, La Brea y Pariñas, to a British investor, William Keswick. He died and his heirs transferred the concession's benefit to a British company. In 1911, the Peruvian Government unilaterally subjected the concession to the general body of mining laws prevailing in Peru. The British investors protested, contending that their concession could not be subject to these general laws because it had a distinct legal status under the concession agreement. By 1921, the British Government, espousing its subjects' claim by diplomatic means, was in dispute with Peru. To resolve this dispute, in August 1921, Peru and Great Britain agreed to a one-off arbitration treaty, referring the single dispute over the concession agreement to an arbitration which was eventually held in Paris.

The arbitration took place in April 1922 before three arbitrators, one appointed by Peru, the second by Great Britain, and the third, the then President of the Swiss Federal Tribunal, was appointed by the two co-arbitrators. The tribunal made a consent award, formally recording the settlement reached by the disputing parties' legal representatives gathered in Paris for the arbitration hearing.

This award put an amicable end to a potentially grave investment and diplomatic dispute. This investment arbitration was quick; it was final; it was to all outward appearances fair. The arbitration reflected no public humiliation on either the state or the investors, and the consent award was respected by all parties. That is what investment arbitration can do. The same story can teach us what happens when there is no investment arbitration. This story resumes 50 years later, in 1963.

In that year, the Peruvian army returned to barracks, again, and democratic government was, again, restored in Peru. The new democratic president was Fernando Belaunde Terry. Early in the period of his government there were renewed political and economic difficulties over the concession. The concession was then owned by or leased to a Canadian company which was a subsidiary of the Standard Oil Company of New Jersey. Supported by the U.S. Government, this acrimonious dispute not only caused widespread anger within Peru at a political and social level, but it also created potentially grave diplomatic complications between Peru and the U.S.

There was, however, no mechanism to refer any part of this dispute to state/investor or state/state arbitration. The ICSID Convention of 1965 still lay in the future, and there was no possibility of a second one-off arbitration treaty between Peru and the U.S. or Canada. In this context, the Standard Oil Company considered, with the assistance of an eminent jurist in Cambridge, whether the UK could be persuaded to bring a claim against Peru before the ICJ. In 1963 this remedy could not be pursued by the investors.

The result in August 1968, after considerable diplomatic and commercial pressure, was an enforced settlement between the Peruvian Government and the Canadian subsidiary of Standard Oil. Its terms were publicly announced by the Government on Peruvian television.

The document produced by President Belaunde consisted of 10 pages. The document published by Standard Oil consisted of 11 pages. The missing last page 11 contained the secret undertaking by the Peruvian Government to pay compensation to the unpopular Yankee investor. In the 10 page copy published by the Government, the signatures had been removed from page 11 and squeezed in at the bottom of page 10, with the promise of compensation found in page 11 entirely removed.

This editorial exercise became an immediate scandal in Peru. The furor lead directly to the military coup of October 1968, to President Belaunde's exile, and to more than a decade of military rule. Democracy did not return to Peru until 1980. By then, the "Shining Path" guerrillas had begun their terrible campaign of intimidation and murder, with more than 70,000 civilians killed in this 20 year conflict. The economy of Peru lay in ruins, with massive unemployment. Politically there remained the gravest difficulties, with the rule of law and democracy seriously weakened. The next 20 years were difficult times for the people of Peru, from President Fujimori's election to last week's election, which we all hope will bring happier times to Peru.

But what has all this to do with investment arbitration? First, most political commentators today would attribute Peru's recent difficulties, directly or indirectly, to the military coup of October 1968. The army is never best qualified, neither in Peru nor elsewhere, to govern a country. Military rule inevitably brings corruption and it can have baleful and long-lasting consequences. Next, of those Peruvians who lived through the investment dispute over La Brea between 1963 and 1968, all would attribute, directly, the military coup of 1968 to the failure to properly and fairly resolve Peru's dispute with Standard Oil.

That is why, in short, investment arbitration matters and particularly why ICSID matters. If an arbitral remedy before ICSID existed in 1963, it is not impossible that Peru's present condition would be materially different, much for the better. If the ICSID Convention could then have operated – particularly its article 27 precluding diplomatic protection pending such arbitration – it is likewise not impossible that political relations between the U.S. and Peru could have remained more benign.

ICSID therefore matters to states and investors, but it can matter much more for the whole people. ICSID is not a mere arbitration service adjectival to a bank, even if that bank is the World Bank. ICSID matters more than that.

B. The Draft U.S.-Pakistan Bilateral Investment Treaty

The second illustration relates to Pakistan. During President Bush's brief visit to Pakistan earlier this year, he did not sign the much mooted draft U.S.-Pakistan BIT. This BIT was intended as a gift to Pakistan by the U.S., resulting from the analysis in the Report of the 9/11 Commission on the economic causes of terrorism historically rooted in West Asia.

It had long been widely rumored that Pakistan was unhappy with the small print of the proffered draft BIT. In fact, most BITs historically have been poorly drafted and perhaps also unhappily drafted from the perspective of the host state. What is now really needed, some suggest, is a new legal concept whereby a state can correct in one new BIT all the drafting errors made in earlier treaties and thereby strike a new balance between investor and host state. Taking advantage of all those advocates who require the broadest interpretation of all MFN clauses, it could be called the "least favored nation" clause. But that, perhaps, is another debate best left to another day.

The problems with the U.S.-Pakistan draft BIT go much deeper. There is an issue of tariffs for Pakistani exports to the U.S. There is an increasing problem of foreign contractors in major infrastructure projects side-stepping commercial arbitration agreements to recover contractual losses under BITs. Further, any BIT with the U.S. will more likely, in practice, favor U.S. investors in Pakistan than Pakistani investors in the U.S. These and other problems will, no doubt, be eventually resolved in further negotiations between the U.S. and Pakistani Governments, to the direct benefit of Pakistan's economy and, indirectly, to the struggle against terrorism.

But their resolution is, I suggest, greatly facilitated by the mere existence of ICSID and the ICSID Convention providing a neutral arbitral forum which functions so well in practice. Conversely, if ICSID and the ICSID Convention did not exist, then their resolution would be much more difficult, if not impossible. For the people of Pakistan, ICSID matters; and if it matters to them, it matters to us.

C. Dr. Wang Sheng Chang

The third and last illustration relates to China. Until recently, the Secretary-General of the China International Economic and Trade Arbitration Center (CIETAC) in Beijing was Dr. Wang Sheng Chang. He is a distinguished jurist and international arbitrator; personally known to many of us in this room.

In mid-March 2006, Dr. Wang was arrested by the Chinese authorities on charges of financial irregularities in CIETAC's affairs. He remains in detention.[2] It

---

[2] Since the time of this article, Dr. Wang Sheng Chang has been released and is practicing arbitration in Washington, D.C.

was reported in the press that these irregularities consisted of his payment of bonuses to CIETAC's staff. The criminal process in China is not always transparent and it is not easy to say anything about criminal charges which are, at present, not formulated and thus impossible for outsiders to understand. I shall therefore say nothing here about any allegations of financial impropriety.

However, it was also reported in the press that Dr. Wang was being criticized in China for disloyalty for his actions as an arbitrator in two international arbitrations held in Stockholm, involving Chinese interests. We know from public sources that Dr. Wang was indeed the signatory to two Swedish arbitration awards, as a co-arbitrator in arbitrations held under the rules of the Arbitration Institute of the Stockholm Chamber of Commerce (SCC).

The first was a Final Award of January 26, 2005; the second was a Final Award of July 7, 2005. These two awards were made in linked but separated disputes between PepsiCo and a PepsiCo subsidiary as claimants and Chinese entities in the Chengdu and Sichuan Provinces, as respondents. These awards were challenged by the Chinese parties before the Svea Court of Appeal (Stockholm) under the Swedish Arbitration Act 1999. Both appeals were eventually abandoned by these Chinese parties. The enforcement and recognition of these awards is now being resisted by the Chinese parties in China.

In these two arbitrations, PepsiCo had appointed Dr. Wang as its party appointed arbitrator. In both awards, Dr. Wang decided the dispute for PepsiCo and against the Chinese respondents. In the first award, the arbitrator appointed by the Chinese respondents refused to sign the award. So, Dr. Wang and the Swedish chairman signed as the majority of the tribunal. In the second award, the arbitrator appointed by the Chinese respondents signed the award, but dissented only on the order for the costs of the arbitration. So, for the most part there was unanimity between the two Chinese arbitrators and the Swedish president. These awards are long, in all over 350 pages, and the disputes appear both difficult and complicated. It is not obvious to an outsider, that either award is perverse or obviously wrong.

In any event, it would be shocking for a state to arrest and detain an arbitrator for disloyalty to his own state for the arbitrator's failure to side in the award with the state parties to that arbitration. An arbitrator is appointed as arbitrator for all parties and, for all parties, the arbitrator must be independent and impartial. It would therefore be more than disappointing if Dr. Wang were arrested and detained in prison for not deciding these two awards in favor of the Chinese parties. It would strike a malign blow to international arbitration everywhere.

If Dr. Wang is not released soon and if the criminal charges remain so untransparent, an independent commission of inquiry should be appointed to investigate what did, or rather what did not, happen in these two Swedish arbitrations. This matters to Dr. Wang personally, it matters to CIETAC and to China's hitherto strong reputation for international arbitration; but it also matters for international arbitration everywhere. This incident cannot be ignored as if it did not exist.

Yet this same incident also shows the unique strength of ICSID as an arbitral institution. ICSID has article 21 of the ICSID Convention, expressly providing for immunity from legal process of all ICSID arbitrators with respect to all acts performed by them as arbitrators. ICSID also has the authority of the World Bank to ensure a state's respect for this essential immunity from legal process. Private arbitration institutions and rules of arbitration confer no equivalent immunity. In short, it is hard enough to believe that Dr. Wang should be criticized at all for being an independent and impartial arbitrator in two SCC arbitrations. However, it would be impossible for us to believe that such criticisms could be acted upon by the Chinese authorities if these had been two ICSID arbitrations. China is, of course, a contracting state to the ICSID Convention.

In the near future, ICSID and the World Bank may thus have an important role to play in the case of Dr. Wang as an international arbitrator, with the SCC, and the International Federation for Commercial Arbitration Institutions (IFCAI). The World Bank's new General Counsel and ICSID's new Secretary-General, when eventually appointed, would be well-suited to undertake a commission of inquiry, if it were to be required.

In conclusion, I return to *déjà vu*.

ICSID has now lost its two most senior officers in the last 12 months. This may be both a catastrophe and a misfortune; but to lose another senior officer, to adopt Oscar Wilde, would look like carelessness. ICSID's new premises are appalling and by any standard unfit for their purpose. ICSID's budget, as we hear, is under continuous critical and downward review, as if ICSID had any influence on services which are necessarily demand-led by claimants initiating ICSID arbitrations. In the short term, these unexplained developments have troubled many of us. However, for the time being, perhaps, it is not ours to reason why.

In the long term, however, we know that, out there, there are many thousands of ICSID arbitration clauses contained in thousands of BITs and investment agreements. Over many years the World Bank has caused investors and states to expect that these clauses can be triggered, if and when required, efficaciously. In these circumstances, it is unthinkable, and legally wrong, for an arbitral institution to disappear or its services to degrade to the point where those legitimate expectations are disappointed, or completely frustrated. This long-term interest matters very much and it should bother us now. How then can we help ICSID before *déjà vu* comes around again, but too late?

The English Commercial Court was rescued in part by Lord Devlin's idea of a Users' Committee. For the last 40 years, it meets informally in London four times a year to discuss with the Commercial Judges current topics of concern and reform regarding the Court's services. This committee is purely advisory. It has no powers, it has no legal or constitutional basis, and its membership and attendance fluctuate widely. Its members are all professional users in the broadest sense from England and abroad: barristers, solicitors, foreign lawyers, and parties; and the commercial judges are drawn from all English courts – from the mercantile courts to the House of Lords.

Maybe ICSID should consider doing the same. ICSID has a fund of goodwill from its users, and its users have a wealth of ideas or responses to offer to ICSID based on practical experience (good and bad). Its users could also support ICSID in any difficulty, within and without the World Bank, affecting the future functions of ICSID and its services to disputing parties.

ICSID matters. It matters for people, states, investors and arbitrators everywhere; and ICSID's continuous existence and the quality of its services should bother us all now – before it is too late. After the first time, there may be no *déjà vu*, or a second, third, or fourth time.

24

The Importance of a Party Treating as Independent Its Independent Arbitrator

What can the United Kingdom contribute to this conference on the modern practice of investment arbitration in Asia? It would seem, at first sight, very little.

As to experience of investment arbitration, when the British Foreign Office was recently consulted in regard to possible reforms to investor-state arbitration under the UNCITRAL Arbitration Rules (currently under review in UNCITRAL), its legal advisers disclosed, sadly, that the United Kingdom had never been sued as a respondent state in any arbitration under any of the United Kingdom's many bilateral investment treaties.

Of course, private investors from the United Kingdom have often invoked investor-state protections against host states under BITs agreed between these host states with the United Kingdom, without the latter being a party to the investment arbitration. In the last twenty years, as publicly reported, United Kingdom investors have secured at least six arbitration awards based upon such United Kingdom BITs. Of these, two were awards against Asian host states; and the second as recently as last year was made by a sole arbitrator from Asia.[1]

However, in recent months a foreign investor from Asia has at last started arbitration proceedings against the United Kingdom under a BIT; and this slender historical first experience of investment arbitration apparently qualifies me to address you today from the perspective of the United Kingdom.

There is, however, a much older and universal lesson which the United Kingdom has learnt from ancient experience, long before the modern system of investment arbitration. It is the importance of the independent arbitrator and the still greater importance of treating such an arbitrator, as such.

Here, as almost everywhere, experience means bad experience; and for the United Kingdom's painful learning experience, it is necessary to go back in history, almost 150 years, to the Alabama Claims Arbitration of 1872 conducted in Geneva under the Treaty of Washington of 4th May 1871.

---

[1] These include: *Asian Agricultural Products v. Republic of Sri Lanka* (15 June 1990); *Wena Hotels Limited v. Arab Republic of Egypt* (8 December 2002); *Joy Mining Machinery Limited v. The Arab Republic of Egypt* (6 August 2004); *National Grid plc v. The Argentine Republic* (20 June 2006); *Suez et al v. The Argentine Republic* (3 August 2006); *Malaysian Historical Salvors SDN, BHD v. The Government of Malaysia* (17 May 2007).

On Arbitration. Edited by: Sam Wordsworth KC and Marie Veeder, Oxford University Press. © Oxford University Press 2023.
DOI: 10.1093/oso/9780192869135.003.0024

388 ON ARBITRATION

The British arbitrator, appointed by the United Kingdom, was Sir Alexander James Cockburn. It was a catastrophic appointment.

As a young man, Cockburn had been a great jury advocate, regarded by some commentators as second only to Erskine, perhaps one of the greatest advocates practising in England. At the time of the Alabama Claims Arbitration, Cockburn was Lord Chief Justice (1859-1880); and his reputation as a judge was mixed.

In the words of one historian: "His mind was perhaps too quick and susceptible to admit of the tenacity of grasp essential to the highest excellence in the formal exposition of legal doctrines"; and it was said that his knowledge of legal principles was derived only from sitting on the bench beside his great contemporary, Lord Blackburn[2]. In other words, to his contemporary critics in England, Sir Alexander Cockburn was arrogant, short-tempered, quick to prejudge an issue and an indifferent lawyer's lawyer.

In Lord Bingham's recent judgement, Cockburn "was not highly regarded as a judge and excited considerable controversy". Even as a young barrister, Coburn had escaped his debtors by climbing out of the window of the Court robing-room in Exeter, and there were still worse personal indiscretions.[3] None of these characteristics would appear to have qualified him as an arbitrator in any arbitration; and indeed all of them contributed to his scandalous behaviour as an arbitrator in the Alabama Claims Arbitration.

Much earlier, as an advocate and judge addressing to a jury, Cockburn had exhibited better qualities. His address to the jury in the Tichborne Case in 1873 merits citation today as to what any judge or jury or arbitrator should perceive as his or her public duty, particularly in a dispute of great public or state importance (including investment arbitrations):

"There is but one course to follow in the discharge of great public duties. No man should be insensible to public opinion who has to discharge a public trust... But there is a consideration far higher than that. It is the satisfaction of your own internal sense of duty, the satisfaction of your own conscience, the knowledge that you are following the promptings of that still, small voice which never, if we listen honestly to its dictates, misleads or deceives – that still, small voice whose approval upholds us even though men should condemn us, and whose approval is far more precious than the honour or applause we may derive, no matter from what source.... Listen to that, gentlemen, listen to that; do right, and care not for anything that may be thought or said or done without these walls. In this, the sacred temple of justice, such considerations as those to which I have referred ought to have and can have no place. You and I have only one thing to consider; that is, the duty we have to discharge before God and man according to the only manner we should desire to

---

[2] Judge Van Vechten Veeder, "A Century of English Judicature 1800-1900", in *Select Essays in Anglo-American Legal History*, Volume 1 (1907, 1968) 730, 767 & 769, revised from earlier publications in *The Green Bag* (1901-1902). (This author's grandfather).

[3] Lord Bingham, "The Alabama Claims Arbitration" (2005) 54 *ICLQ* 1.

THE IMPORTANCE OF A PARTY TREATING   389

discharge it, – honestly, truly and fearlessly, without regard to any consequences except the desire that this duty should be properly and entirely fulfilled."

There could be no clearer statement of an arbitrator's duty in any arbitration, requiring independence of mind, in thought and deed. Sadly, Cockburn did not live up to these ideals as an arbitrator in the Alabama Claims Arbitration.

It is impossible to exaggerate the gravity of the dispute between the United Kingdom and the United States which led to the Alabama Claims Arbitration. It was a time when the United States and the British Empire were on the brink of war, with the Union Army threatening to invade Canada, leading to its occupation and probable annexation by the United States.

The United States and its nationals were claiming massive reparations from the United Kingdom for permitting naval vessels to be built in England for the Confederacy during the American Civil War which had caused enormous damage to American shipping all over the world and probably extended the Civil War by several years. The total claim exceeded, in modern money, a trillion pounds sterling, enough to bankrupt the British Empire. The dispute was referred to arbitration in Geneva under the Washington Treaty, where the arbitration tribunal eventually decided that the United Kingdom had failed to use due diligence in the performance of its neutral obligations during the American Civil War in permitting the "Alabama" and other vessels to be built in England and delivered to the Confederacy; and as compensation the tribunal ordered the United Kingdom to pay the sum of US\$ 15.5 million in gold to the United States, equivalent, in modern money, to about £150 billion. This was a large sum by any standards; but it was, with hindsight at least, a small price to pay for avoiding a modern war between the United Kingdom and the USA.

The Geneva tribunal was truly international. The president was Count Sclopis, a minister from Italy, well over seventy, with M. Jacques Staempfli, a former president of Switzerland and Baron d'Itajuba of Brazil, a professor from Brazil. The American arbitrator was Charles Francis Adams, the son and grandson of US Presidents and at the time a potential presidential candidate in his own right.

The British arbitrator, Sir Alexander Cockburn, struck one observer in Geneva in these terms: He was "short of stature and ... somewhat ruddy. He had a head like a bullet and the eye of an eagle. Quick and nervous, his unceasing activity was in marked contrast to the almost rigid demeanour of Mr Adams."[4] This observer continued: "The Friends of Sir Alexander Cockburn have credited him with genius; and the claim, perhaps is not to be denied. A striking personage he was ... One saw at Geneva little in his bearing of the calm, judicial dignity which is commonly supposed to characterise the Lord Chief Justice of England. It is not uncharitable to say of him that, in discarding wig and gown, to become an Arbitrator Sir Alexander

---

[4] Hackett, F.W., *Reminiscenses of the Geneva Tribunal 1872* (1911, CUP), p. 214, and see also pp. 221-222, 281-282

seems to have laid aside also the greater part, if not all, of that self control, and chastening sense of responsibility, which marks the judge."

During the arbitration, Cockburn wrote privately to his friend in England, Lord Granville: "Things have gone badly with us here. I saw from our first sitting in July that they would. We could not have a worse man than Staempfli [the Swiss arbitrator] – or next to him than the president [the Italian arbitrator]. The first a furious Republican, hating monarchical government and ministries in which men of rank take part, ignorant as a horse, and obstinate as a mule. The second vapid and all anxiety to give a decision which shall produce an effect on the world, and to make speeches about civilisation "humanity", et cetera, in short, 'un vrai phrasier'. Baron d'Itajuba [the Brazilian arbitrator] is of a far better stamp, but not sufficiently informed and very indolent; and apt by reason of the latter defect to catch hold of some salient point without going to the bottom of things, with the further defect of clinging to an opinion once formed with extreme tenacity."

Sir Roundell Palmer, Counsel to the United Kingdom in Geneva and later, as Lord Chancellor, Lord Selbourne, politely recorded that Cockburn was "conscious of intellectual superiority" to his arbitral colleagues, "and at no pains to conceal what he felt". One American counsel wrote in a kindly manner to an English colleague in Geneva: "What is the matter with your arbitrator? ... He acts as if he were possessed. Last week he insulted the rest of us one at a time, but today he insulted us all in a bunch...". Another recorded: "I am not surprised at the violence of Sir Alexander Cockburn. I was prepared to expect such a display of pig-headed prejudice and temper from the conversation I had with him here, last winter. How much he must be helping us, unconsciously to himself, by such displays of anger and such insolent flings at his colleagues."

Towards the end of the arbitration, Cockburn did not attend the grand dinner given to all arbitrators and participants by the Canton of Geneva on the 7th September, over which the Swiss President presided. He also declined an invitation to visit the Swiss Federal Government in Bern, again missing the state dinner attended by the other arbitrators on the 11th September.

On the 14th September, the award was issued by the tribunal. Publicly, its secretary read the award in English in the banqueting chamber of Geneva's town hall (now the "Alabama Room") before a large gathering of the parties' counsel and other distinguished figures, following which the president and three of the arbitrators formally subscribed their names to the award. Having arrived late, Cockburn stood apart and refused to sign it. He handed to the secretary his dissenting opinion and left the hall.

In that dissenting opinion, Cockburn confirmed his peculiar view of the role required of him as a partisan advocate for the United Kingdom, in these words: "Sitting on this tribunal as in some sense a representative of Great Britain, I cannot allow these statements [in the argument of the United States] to go forth to the world without giving them the most positive and unqualified contradiction" [p 218]. Nor did he.

The dissenting opinion was colourful; and it took strong exception to many of the arguments advanced by the United States which had been accepted by the majority of the tribunal. It included the following condemnations of the United States' case at Geneva: "A stranger misrepresentation could scarcely have been penned"; "untrue"; "nothing of the kind"; "without the shadow of a foundation"; and best of all, "the imagination of the [American] writer must have been singularly lively, while his conscience must have slept who could venture to put on paper the following passages"; then quoting several extracts from the written argument of the United States, concluding: "There is in this extraordinary series of propositions the most singular confusion of ideas, misrepresentation of facts, and ignorance, both of law and history, which were perhaps ever crowded into the same space, and for my part I cannot help expressing my sense, not only of the gross injustice done to my country, but also of the affront offered to this Tribunal by such an attempt to practise on our supposed credulity or ignorance."

It all left an unpleasant impression of Cockburn as the British arbitrator. In the words of the senior American counsel, Mr Caleb Cushing: "To the universal expression of mutual courtesy and reciprocal good will there was but one exception, and that exception too conspicuous to pass without notice. The instant that Count Sclopis closed, and before the sound of his last words had died on the ear, Sir Alexander Cockburn snatched up his hat, and, without participating in the leave-takings around him, without a word or sign of courteous recognition for any of his colleagues, rushed to the door, and disappeared, in the manner of a criminal escaping from the dock, rather than of a judge separating, and that forever, from his colleagues of the Bench. It was one of those acts of discourtesy which shocks so much when they occur that we feel relieved by the disappearance of the perpetrator".

Cockburn had been born in 1802; and in 1814, his uncle, Admiral Cockburn of the Royal Navy, had taken part in the burning of the Capitol and the White House in Washington D.C. during that brief war between England and the United States. Cockburn was not, therefore, by inheritance or inclination, pro-American. Yet his behaviour stemmed rather from his lack of any independence as an arbitrator; and history has not judged him kindly. In the temperate judgement of Lord Bingham, Cockburn was "an ill-tempered partisan advocate [without] the even tempered objectivity of a judicial arbitrator".

Whatever the damage to Cockburn's reputation, the biggest loser from Cockburn's deficiencies was the party that appointed him as a partisan arbitrator, the United Kingdom. In contrast to Adams, Cockburn lost any collegiate influence with his arbitral colleagues, having successively alienated each in turn during the arbitration; and the British case thereby lost its best chance of any sympathetic understanding by the tribunal.

392   ON ARBITRATION

There have been many lessons learnt from the Alabama Claims Arbitration;[5] but the immediate lesson learnt in England was the importance of not appointing a partisan arbitrator out of basic self-interest by the appointing party. If the appointment is to have any beneficial purpose for the appointing party's case, the appointed arbitrator must be independent and treated as an independent arbitrator. This lesson applies both to state parties and to private parties; and it has never been forgotten in the United Kingdom.

As recorded by two English authors, Redfern and Hunter, in their current work on international commercial arbitration: "Experienced practitioners recognise that the appointment of a partisan arbitrator is counter-productive, because the presiding arbitrator will very soon perceive what is happening and the influence of the partisan arbitrator during the tribunal's deliberations will be diminished. It is a far better policy to appoint a person who may, by reason of culture or background, be broadly in sympathy with the case to be put forward, but who will be strictly impartial when it comes to assessing the facts and evaluating the arguments on fact and law."[6]

This passage states, however, only the first half of the lesson. The second is equally important. A party's appointment of an independent arbitrator carries with it an obligation to respect that arbitrator's independence. Independence means, in Cockburn's own phrase to the Tichborne jury, that "still small voice" which may lead to a decision by that arbitrator which is adverse to the appointing party. A party appointing an independent arbitrator is not appointing its advocate or delegate; and it is not buying a vote. That is what independence means.

It is here worth recalling the words of an eminent Swiss arbitrator (and editor), Jacques Werner, as regards party-appointed arbitrators generally: "Their purpose is to allow each party in the dispute to have someone on the arbitral tribunal whom it knows and trusts. Or, in other words, to have a friend, who must be independent enough to award against the party who appointed him should the merits of the case warrant it, but who will ensure that all the arguments of his party get a thorough and fair hearing. This distinctive feature of international arbitration ... is of great importance to ensure voluntary compliance with the awards, as the losing party will more readily accept the arbitral tribunal's decision if it knows that its contentions, if not finally followed, have at least been fully heard."[7] That says it all.

The practice in modern investment arbitration today is that host states almost invariably appoint independent arbitrators, including not infrequently arbitrators

---

[5] For example, see Wetter, *The International Arbitral Process*, Volume 1, pp. 13-173; and this author, V.V.Veeder, "Arbitral Lessons from the Private Correspondence of Queen Victoria ....", *Proceedings of the 98th Annual Meeting of ASIL*, March 31-April 3 2004.

[6] Redfern & Hunter, *Law and Practice of International Arbitration*, 4th Edit, p. 200. See also Fouchard, Gaillard & Goldman, *International Commercial Arbitration*, (ed. Gaillard & Savage) at # 1044ff, p. 573ff.

[7] Werner, Editorial: "The Independence of Party-Appointed Arbitrators: for a Rule of Reason", (1990) 7:2 *Journal Int. Arb.* 5.

who are not their own nationals. There are regrettable exceptions where partisan arbitrators are still appointed, just as there may be exceptions where states seek to treat independent arbitrators as if they were not independent; but these few exceptions prove the general rule. It serves an appointing party best if it appoints an independent arbitrator and treats that arbitrator as independent, with the paramount duty of deciding the dispute "honestly, truly and fearlessly, without regard to any consequences except the desire that this duty should be properly and entirely fulfilled."

And the final moral of this story? Returning to the United Kingdom's first experience of investment arbitration as a respondent, it may be worth noting the identity of the arbitrator recently appointed by the United Kingdom in these pending proceedings: that arbitrator is not only overtly independent and certain to be treated independently but he is also a citizen of the United States of America. After almost 150 years, the shadows cast by Sir Alexander Cockburn and the Alabama Claims Arbitration remain long.

25

Is there a Need to Revise the New York Convention?[*]

In a brave attempt to delay writing the second edition of his great work,[1] now almost 30 years old, my friend and name-sake Professor van den Berg, as we heard him both at and after the ICCA Congress 2008 in Dublin,[2] agitates with conviction for a thorough revision of the New York Convention, both within and without the UNCITRAL Working Group on Arbitration. His troops in Dublin were routed by Maréchal Gaillard,[3] but, like Napoleon, a new army is being assembled for the decisive battle. Will it be Austerlitz or Waterloo?

For some, encouraged by Dr van den Berg, the major criticism is that the New York Convention is far too short, incomplete and uncertain for a modern treaty on arbitration. It comprises only sixteen articles, of which only three are critically important: Articles II, V and VII.[4]

President Wilson's 14 points were all critically important during the First World War; but President Wilson failed as a statesman, as we know, because his points

---

[*] This article is adapted from a speech delivered in Dijon on 14 September 2008 on the occasion of a conference organized by Professor Emmanuel Gaillard and the International Arbitration Institute on 'The Review of International Arbitral Awards'. It was published in its original form in E Gaillard (ed.), *The Review of International Arbitral Awards* (2010) 183–194. It is reproduced here with kind permission of the book's editor.

[1] AJ van den Berg, *The New York Arbitration Convention of 1958 – Towards a Uniform Judicial Interpretation* (Deventer, Kluwer 1981).

[2] AJ van den Berg, 'Hypothetical Draft Convention on the International Enforcement of Arbitration Agreements and Awards: Explanatory Note' in *50 Years of the New York Convention – ICCA Congress Series No 14* (Alphen aan den Rijn, Kluwer 2009) 649.

[3] See Catherine Kessedjian, 'En revenant de Dublin: l'éventuelle réforme de la Convention de New York' (2008) 26 ASA Bull 644; Emmanuel Gaillard, 'The Urgency of Not Revising the New York Convention' in van den Berg (n 2) 689.

[4] Dr van den Berg, albeit one of the few numerate arbitrators, disputes this statistical observation. His word count of Arts I–VII(1) of the New York Convention (including the title) is 1025 words, whilst Articles 1 through 7 of the draft 'New' New York Convention (again including the title) comprise only 966 words, a significant downward change of 59 words. Moreover, Dr van den Berg's motto for change ('Yes We Can') has since been widely adopted and successfully applied elsewhere, apparently.

On Arbitration. Edited by: Sam Wordsworth KC and Marie Veeder, Oxford University Press. © Oxford University Press 2023. DOI: 10.1093/oso/9780192869135.003.0025

were too short. If only President Wilson had submitted more points, it is said, the First World War could have ended with a permanent and amicable peace; and the German Kaiser, the Russian Czar, the Habsburg Emperor and the Ottoman Sultan would have all kept their thrones, without any February or October Revolutions in Petrograd and with the result that today, amongst many other indirect consequences, Georgia would still be Russian with no opportunity for international conflict or illuminating decisions from the International Court of Justice. Accordingly, the historical lesson is, apparently, that the number of words matters: like Mozart's notes, the more the merrier.

Yet others say that long-winded drafting in international instruments, such as we have already seen within UNCITRAL as regards the modifications to the Model Law on Arbitration and the New UNCITRAL Arbitration Rules, does more harm than good. They point to the failures of the European Constitution and the Lisbon Treaty as recent examples. In these texts, they say, there were far too many words, most of them the wrong kind of words; and all of them insufficiently French, Dutch and Irish words. So, again, history teaches us that words and the number of words matter.

The controversial nature of our question requires us to look back for guidance to ancient history and other wording far beyond the Lisbon Treaty and President Wilson, because there is simply nothing in modern times to compare to the widespread success and importance of the New York Convention.

Apart from the founding treaties of the United Nations, the New York Convention is the most successful modern treaty measured by the number of its signatory States, 144 independent States. It may even have increased since these words were written and, unlike the ICSID Convention, no state is belligerently denouncing the New York Convention. The New York Convention is the lubricating super-oil for the complex machinery which has made the explosion of global trade possible over the past 50 years. It has been described in extravagant but accurate language by many distinguished commentators all over the world from very different legal cultures and disparate civilisations or none, including both English and Scottish arbitration specialists.

One English law lord is said to have said, extra-judicially, that the New York Convention is both the Best Thing since Sliced Bread and also whatever was the Best Thing before Sliced Bread replaced it as the Best Thing.[5] In short, the New York Convention affects directly the lives of billions of people around the world, every minute of every day, in both seen and still more unseen ways. It is therefore a

---

[5] This statement has since been perversely mis-applied to the Arbitration Act 1996 of England and Wales, in a vain attempt to shield its text from objective and informed criticism. There must be something about bread and conservatism; e.g. Marie-Antoinette.

396   ON ARBITRATION

secular, sacred text of the greatest practical significance to every inhabitant of the 21st century's global village.

With all this in mind, there is obviously only one practical comparison from ancient history: the wording of the Ten Commandments from the Bible's Old Testament.

As we know, Moses came down from Mount Sinai carrying two stone tablets bearing the Ten Commandments. These stones were a kind of supranational treaty independent of any national law, or at least *régles matérielles* free-floating in the firmament, a concept so beloved in certain circles in Paris and Dijon.[6] A pedant might comment that the Ten Commandments were not exactly a traditional multi-party treaty like the New York Convention; but this was long before the Vienna Convention and although the analogy may not be entirely precise, it is nonetheless helpful in addressing, objectively, the question before us in its full historical and linguistic perspective.

There are four particular reasons which make the Ten Commandments a potential model for reform like the New York Convention.

First, not many people know that Moses started his descent with three tablets, not two. The third large stone, much bigger than the other two, contained the explanatory memorandum and the *travaux préparatoires* explaining the object and purpose of each Commandment individually and collectively. We do know that Moses was not then a young man. According to the Bible, he was between 100 and 120 years old. Having climbed to the top of the mountain unaided, Moses had also undergone a religious experience which few human beings had then ever experienced. And so now, laden with three heavy stone tablets, physically tired and emotionally exhausted, Moses began his careful descent down Mount Sinai. But Moses was not careful enough. Juggling the one tablet and the other two from arm to arm as he balanced from rock to rock leaping downhill, Moses managed to drop the third stone, with the result that the Ten Commandments have never been illuminated by any contemporary *travaux* of any kind.[7]

That is effectively the same problem as the New York Convention. Notwithstanding the splendid efforts of Professor Gaja, the New York Convention is also un-illuminated by any of its *travaux*. On any point of any interest, these *travaux* are quite useless, irrelevant or wrong or a combination of all three. It would have been much better if its *travaux* had all been dumped in the East River. Like the Ten Commandments, we

---

[6] See for instance E Gaillard, *Legal Theory of International Arbitration* (Martinus Nijhoff, Leiden 2010).

[7] The renowned Biblical scholar, Professor Dr Mel Brooks, LLD suggests that this third stone contained the 11th to 15th commandments: see <http://www.youtube.com/watch?v=4TAtRCJIqnk>. He is probably incorrect; but he does rightly confirm that this third stone was accidentally dropped by Moses and forever destroyed. (I am most grateful to Klaus Reichert and Peter Leaver for this obscure archival reference).

are therefore left with only the language of the New York Convention, to be read, of course in good faith, in context and in its ordinary meaning or, in other words, with a reasonable degree of intelligence and common sense.

Second, there is a problem about the ordinary meaning of language when there is an issue about what language. The Ten Commandments were inscribed in Hebrew; but in what language were they originally conceived and drafted in the firmament? Outside France, few people still believe that God is a Frenchman; and many now wonder that, if God is not a Frenchman, then God must at least be an English-speaker, the *lingua franca* of mass communications. So, the question arises, which of these three distinct languages did God use to draft the Ten Commandments? And the further question then arises, inevitably, depending on the source language, whether God properly translated the Ten Commandments on the tablets of stone delivered to Moses.

This is equally true of the New York Convention, partly drafted by a Dutchman and translated into the five official languages of the United Nations at a time when the United Nations had no specialist translators for arbitration. So, Article II(2) of the New York Convention defines an 'agreement in writing' as including an arbitral clause in a contract or an arbitration agreement signed by the parties or contained in an exchange of letters or telegrams. That is the English version. It is also the Russian version (in Russian). However the French and Spanish versions are different and do not use the broad term 'include', apparently limiting an arbitration agreement to a special written form.

The tie-breaker amongst the five official languages should be the Chinese version. However, in 1958, Taiwan sat in the Chinese seat at the United Nations; and its translator was apparently an elderly mandarin scholar, not an arbitration specialist, writing an old form of Mandarin that few if any understand today, certainly not any of the Chinese friends and restauranteurs whom we had to consult in London during the work of the Departmental Advisory Committee on the Law of Arbitration (responsible for the English 1996 Act). It is arguable that the Chinese text can mean 'include'; but, on the other hand, it can be argued equally that it cannot. It all depends. And so the British Government, in re-enacting Article II of the New York Convention in the 1996 Arbitration Act was constrained to rely heavily on the English and Russian texts as trumping the French and Spanish versions, in order to produce the peculiar English version of a written agreement made orally in Section 6 of the 1996 Act.

Again, language played its crucial part with the Queen's printer unused to Russian wording in Cyrillic script. If you look in the official DAC report accompanying the 1996 Act, you will see instead of the Russian word for 'include' in Cyrillic, the Russian word for 'clavicle' or collar-bone.[8] It is a sad commentary on

---

[8] The Report on the Arbitration Bill of February 1996, para 34, of the Departmental Advisory Committee on Arbitration Law of the United Kingdom Government's Department of Trade and Industry (now 'BIS').

the reduced state of the Russian intelligence service in the United Kingdom that no one has ever noticed this curious error. Or maybe they have; and maybe that is why, having taken deep offence at such linguistic licence, Anglo-Russian diplomatic relations have been so poor of late. So language matters; foreign language matters; and translations also matter.

Thirdly, there is a problem with the ordinary language of both texts, in whatever language. Let us take, as an example, the Fifth Commandment. The Fifth Commandment would cause us to honour our father and mother. This doubtless made good sense thousands of years ago; but does it make sufficient sense today? Is it an injunction to honour both your father and your mother; or can the word 'and' be read disjunctively? And does it require simultaneous 'honouring' or can parental 'honouring' be discharged consecutively or even alternatively at the will of the honourer? This matters in an age of single-parent families; and it will matter with certain adoptive parents and civil unions where there may be two fathers or two mothers. And what of grandmothers and grandfathers: why is 'honouring' so limited? Read literally, without intelligence or common sense, this Fifth Commandment is clearly inapposite to the 21st century; and some would say that it requires urgent amendment.

There are many other likely candidates for re-drafting in the Ten Commandments; and there are many other missing commandments which could be included. For example, where does one find in the interstices of the Sixth Commandment the Bush Doctrine or the need for Second Resolutions of the United Nations' Security Council? And where is the Commandment to vote or to pay taxes or to avoid, whenever possible, printing out email messages?

It is therefore possible to suggest many reforms; but it would be manifestly absurd actually to re-draft the Fifth and Sixth Commandments and still more absurd to start adding further Commandments.

Exactly the same difficulties arise under the New York Convention. In Article V(2)(b), a State court may refuse recognition or enforcement of an award if it would be contrary to the public policy of that country. It has long been very difficult to define such public policy. Many have tried, including the International Law Association. Whatever other defects a national legal system may have, it is clearly impossible for our national judges to define and apply public policy as a uniform principle to be applied by all State courts, including certain States which it would be invidious to name, few in number but present in Central & Eastern Europe, Asia, the Middle East, Sub-Saharan Africa, Latin America and elsewhere. This is a large geographical area with a large proportion of the world's trade and, more significantly, State judges deciding cases under the New York Convention.

We know that certain of these States invoke public policy as a pretext and not as a true reason not to enforce an award under the New York Convention. Any re-draft of this Article V(2)(b) could therefore achieve nothing: another pretext would be found by these States to the same effect. We may be seeing this already, where the national courts of certain States are now careful to avoid using public policy too openly even as a pretext so as to pre-empt criticism from abroad. In these countries, it is said that judges are covertly instructed to use in their public judgments, if possible, a pretext other than public policy under the New York Convention to refuse enforcement of foreign awards. As with the Ten Commandments, it would therefore serve no purpose to re-draft the public policy exception in the New York Convention.

Fourthly, the human race is not stupid. Most, if not all, of the apparent difficulties regarding both the Ten Commandments and the New York Convention can be and are resolved by intelligent and reasonable interpretation made in good faith by members of the human race, including judges. Dr van den Berg's proposals are well-considered and admirably formulated;[9] but they condemn themselves: all of them are essentially capable of resolution by treaty and legislative interpretation without requiring any actual change of wording in the text of the New York Convention. Moreover, this rational approach could most easily be established by Dr van den Berg finishing his belated and much needed second edition;[10] and one practical proposal would be to raise a special fund to persuade him and his assistants to do so as soon as possible on a remote island, free of any other distractions, like Bali—or even England despite recurring problems in the Channel Tunnel.

But all this is not enough to dissuade those extreme activists who want to change the New York Convention, to add words for the sake of more words and to reform for the sake only of reform. For them, the only answer is to show them how the UNCITRAL Working Group actually works in practice. In saying this, I make no criticism of the UNCITRAL Secretariat or the presidents of the Working Group. Despite their best efforts, for many years, the UNCITRAL Working Group on Arbitration is now the classic example of an institution where the inmates have taken over the lunatic asylum. If it can do something in a day today, it will be done tomorrow in two and then, like Sisyphus or Groundhog Day, again and again. If UNCITRAL had been in charge of building Rome, it would still be, after 3000 years, a small rustic village.

It is equally possible to imagine what would happen if the Ten Commandments were subject to reform and amendment by the assembled churchmen and women of the world. They cannot agree on transubstantiation, married priests, women

---

[9] See AJ van den Berg, 'The "New" New York Convention – Preliminary Draft Convention on the International Enforcement of Arbitration Agreements and Awards' <http://www.newyorkconvention. org/draft--convention> accessed 15 July 2010.
[10] See n 1, above.

400 ON ARBITRATION

priests and bishops and many, many other matters, including God. No-one has, in fact, dared to propose such an assembly of believers, where the Pope and his cardinals would sit with the Chief Rabbis, the Religious Right with the Russian Orthodox, the Scottish Wee Frees with the Uniates, and the Maronites with the Copts. I have not even mentioned Dr Paisley of Northern Ireland, 50% of whose vocabulary has always been 'no'. The mind boggles at the idea of such a convocation to re-draft the Ten Commandments. It could never lead to anything good or useful or, indeed, anything.

The fate of the New York Convention would be no different at UNCITRAL. All other work on arbitration would stop. The UNCITRAL meetings would, however, never cease. Its delegates' tendencies would veer from homicide to suicide, even more than now. The new draft would jump from 16 to an infinite number of articles, with the mantra that 'more words are best and reform is good for the sake only of reform'. But there would be much worse: certain well-known States and every insane NGO, often a pleonasm at UNCITRAL, would add its own mad ideas and hare-brained schemes. And the end-product, if there were ever to be an end-product, could only lead to a two-tiered New York Convention, dividing the world's States into sheep and goats; and a great treaty, which had worked so well for so many decades, would have been smashed beyond repair.

There is a final reason against reforming the New York Convention. Article VII(1) of the New York Convention permits a State court to recognize and enforce an arbitration award under the higher standards of its own laws. It is this provision which has allowed French jurists, both judges and scholars, to advance many of the important legal innovations which underpin the modern system of international arbitration and which have been adopted, in whole or in part, over the last thirty years in other State courts, national laws and arbitral institutions.

These achievements must be allowed to continue and develop further. It is, in particular, scholars from Dijon which have led these intellectual achievements; and I mention here only those from the past: René David, Berthold Goldman, Henri Motulsky and the much missed Philippe Fouchard. Without Article VII(1), their ideas would have been much more difficult to assimilate, even in France. We should not therefore take Article VII for granted; and yet, above all other articles in the New York Convention, it now faces the threat of reform amounting to extinction.

With the Heidelberg Report on reforms to the EU's Brussels Regulation (and implicitly the Lugano Convention) and with the exclusive competence of the European Union under the Lisbon Treaty to negotiate and sign any 'New' New York Convention for the European Union's Member States, we can be fairly certain that this part of Article VII(1) would disappear from any revised New York Convention. And with it the great French contribution to international arbitration would be reduced to the lowest common denominator in the European Union. That would be more than a catastrophe. It would be, I suggest, a mistake.

In conclusion, even if the New York Convention were broke, which it isn't, the likely 'cure' would be far worse than any imagined malady. It would turn a healthy workhorse into a lame old nag, if not actual cat-food. So thank you, Dr van den Berg—but no thank you and please now return to your writing-desk...[11]

---

[11] Since this text was originally written, this story has acquired a happy ending: the second edition of Professor van den Berg's book is currently being written by Professor van den Berg and Marike Paulsson.

26

Who Are the Arbitrators?

A. Introduction

If the proverbial green creature from Mars arrived on this planet to study diversity in the practice of international arbitration, it would find a complicated situation where not all is what it seems. No arbitrator is green; and neither Kermit nor Ms. Piggy has ever been appointed an arbitrator. Despite eccentric exceptions in ancient times, the world's modern arbitrators are limited to the human species, discriminating against all other forms of intelligent life.

As the creature learnt English, it would soon find discrimination in the language of arbitration between human left-handers and right-handers. Thus, a good arbitrator is "adroit" and "dexterous", but a bad arbitrator is "maladroit", "gauche", "cack-handed" and even "sinister". Yet this Martian creature would soon learn that linguistic discrimination against lefties amongst the human species (50 percent of the world's population and comprising, so it is said, the best of the world's arbitrators) counts for nothing within the arbitration community, no more than the absence of green and porcine animals.[1] Yet, our Martian friend would eventually discover other forms of discrimination as regards gender and race, which, in his view, threatened to tarnish the legitimacy of international arbitration.

As regards gender, the creature would find in four different continents Meg Kinnear at the International Centre for Settlement of Investment Disputes (ICSID) in Washington DC, Teresa Cheng at the Hong Kong International Arbitration Centre in China, Annette Magnusson at the Stockholm Chamber of Commerce and Bernadette Uwicyeza at the Kigali International Arbitration Centre in Rwanda. Had the creature arrived a decade ago, it would have found Anne Marie Whitesell and earlier still Tila Maria de Hancock at the ICC International Court of Arbitration in Paris; and also Rosalyn Higgins at The Hague as the President of the International Court of Justice, only temporarily interrupting her even more illustrious career as an international arbitrator. If it delayed its arrival for only a few months hence, it would find Jackie van Hof at the LCIA in London. This Martian creature might therefore at first conclude that

---

[1] It should be disclosed that this author is left-handed, as also Leonardo da Vinci, Joan of Arc, Napoleon Bonaparte, Julius Caesar, Greta Garbo, King George VI, Jimmy Connors, John McEnroe, Shirley MacLaine, Harpo Marx, Marilyn Monroe and Pablo Picasso.

gender discrimination by users of arbitration and arbitral institutions plays no significant role in the appointment of arbitrators, just as with left-handers and right-handers.

However, having studied Latin on Mars, the creature would be troubled at the masculine form of "arbitrator", for which there seems to be no feminine equivalent. Next, it would study the available statistics. Women make up half (if not more than half) of the entrants to the legal profession in developed economies; but after entry, something happens. In the field of international commercial and investment arbitration, one commentator has calculated that of the top ten international teams listed by Global Arbitration Review, only 11% of their members are women and that of all arbitrators appointed in, respectively, ICSID arbitrations and commercial arbitrations, only 5% and 6% are women.[2] Many ICCA members have recently completed a questionnaire for the European Commission for arbitration users, practitioners and arbitrators in Europe: only 11.6% of such responses came from women; and only 0.5% were from Afro-Caribbean men and women.[3] These figures cannot of course be precise; but to the discerning Martian, these statistics would suffice to show that something is wrong with diversity in the practice of arbitration as regards both gender and race.

The situation for international arbitration is of course complicated, given its global reach amongst different participants from disparate cultures and jurisdictions. Here, as in many respects, arbitration is not always for the best, but also not always for the worst. Yet, it is surprising that the practice of arbitration does not reflect the broad diversity available to the arbitral community; and that the collective attention of many in that community has still not succeeded in removing the unfairness and sheer waste of discrimination based on grounds of gender and race. It is equally surprising how little reliable research has been done, outside the United States.

This is not an indictment. Few in the arbitral community actually intend to practice discrimination on grounds of gender and race. It is more a matter of habit and unconscious or institutionalized discrimination. Moreover, in a relatively short time, diversity in arbitration has already come a long away. In England, women lawyers and judges are relatively new. In the United Kingdom's archives, there is an extraordinary exchange in 1922 between the Czechoslovak *Chargé d'Affaires* in London (the Czech Republic then being a newly independent state establishing its own legal system) and the British Government:[4]

---

[2] C. TEVENDALE, Kluwer Arbitration Blog of 28 September 2012.
[3] This survey was being conducted by Brunel University (London) on the Law and Practice of Arbitration in the European Union.
[4] PRO Archives, Kew (London): LCO2/604 XC 25358; L 560/560/405.

404 ON ARBITRATION

"The Czechoslovak Chargé d'Affaires would esteem it a favour if his Lordship [Lord Curzon of the British Foreign Office] could cause him to be informed about the following questions: (1) Are women permitted to act as professional judges, and are they admitted to the preparatory practice necessary for an appointment as judge to the same extent as men?; (2) If so, have they the same rights and duties as men? Also as regards salary and pension?; (3) Are women judges allowed to marry unconditionally, or does their marriage affect their service relation and their claims and duties?; (4) If so, what are the consequences of pregnancy and childbirth upon their official positions, and in particular, what amount of leave is granted them in this case?; and (5) Has the employment of women judges proved satisfactory in general?"

The Lord Chancellor replied as follows:

"As regards Question 1: "Judges in England, of whatever status, are appointed only from amongst members of the Bar ('*avocats*'). The statutes regulating the qualifications which must be possessed by persons appointed to these offices require in each case that a specified period of time should have elapsed since entry into the profession before a barrister can be appointed to a judicial office. Until the 23rd December, 1919, when the Sex Disqualification (Removal) Act, 1919 (9 and 10, Geo. V, c. 71), passed into law, women could not be admitted to the English Bar. In order to be admitted to the English Bar it is necessary that a candidate for admission should have passed a certain defined period as a student and have passed certain specified examinations. As until 1919 women could not be called to the Bar, it followed that women were not admitted as students. As a consequence, although some women have lately passed through the period of studentship and been admitted to the Bar, no woman has yet fulfilled the conditions relating to length of service which are requisite to qualify the candidate for appointment to any judicial position. No legal decision has as yet been given upon the interpretation of the Act of 1919 so far as it concerns the holding by a woman of a judicial office. It is, however, apprehended that, since the passing of that Act, any woman who fulfils the other statutory condition would be eligible for appointment to a judgeship."

As regards Questions 2 to 5:

"No occasion has arisen for considering the questions asked in paragraphs 2, 3, 4 and 5 in the memorandum from the Czechoslovak Legation. It is, however, apprehended that if and when any woman becomes in fact eligible for appointment as a judge, and if the appointing authority should then see fit to appoint her, she would hold office upon the same conditions as would a man. So far as question 4 is concerned [i.e. maternity leave], judges in England are seldom appointed until they have reached an age which renders the conditions described in the question unlikely to arise."

This was written in 1922. Yet, the first woman High Court Judge was only appointed in 1974, more than fifty years later: Mrs. Justice Heilbron who was born in 1919, called to the English Bar in 1939 and appointed one of Her Majesty's Counsel in 1949, at the young age of thirty-four.[5] In England, woman lawyers began to appear as arbitrators in the 1970s, but not in significant numbers.[6]

B. Gender, Race and Nationality

In South Africa, notwithstanding its extraordinary first President, Nelson Mandela, race still plays, so it is said, a significant part in the practice of domestic arbitration, with the business community (predominantly white), preferring white arbitrators to black judges and arbitrators. There are, however, no reliable statistics. In the United States, Professor Benjamin Davis has conducted two most interesting studies. The figures are striking; and it is probable that the figures would be similar in England.

In his survey of 2013,[7] Professor Davis, a former officer of the ICC Court for many years, examined US diversity in international arbitration across a target population comprising minorities, women, those with disabilities and LGBTQ (Lesbian, Gay, Bisexual, Transgender, Queer or Questioning) lawyers. (These four groups are the target population described in the American Bar Association's Goal III: Eliminate Bias and Enhance Diversity). In addition to sending a survey to 413 international arbitration practitioners, he approached a diverse group of international arbitral institutions around the world. He concluded:

"It appears safe to conclude that as of today there are a significant number of American women (most likely white) in international arbitration in all phases

---

[5] See H. HEILBRON, *Rose Heilbron* (2012). This wonderful biography is written by the subject's daughter, herself a Queen's Counsel and arbitrator. In 1949, Rose Heilbron had taken silk with Helena Normanton (of 4 Essex Court) as the first women to be granted silk in English legal history. (In England and most common law countries, senior judges are appointed from senior trial lawyers of a mature age – hence it is pointless to compare judicial statistics under civilian and socialist systems with career-judges appointed at an early age).

[6] Margaret Rutherford QC was one of the first women arbitrators in England, a remarkable lawyer who proudly confessed that her favourite bedtime reading included the English Arbitration Act 1996. Elsewhere, others included Professor Bastid, Mme Simone Rozés and Judge Birgitta Blom.

[7] Benjamin G. Davis, "American Diversity in International Arbitration 2003-2013", available at <http://papers.ssrn.com/sol3/papers.cfm?abstract_id=2364967>. (This survey updates Professor Davis' earlier work: "The Color Line in International Commercial Arbitration: An American Perspective", 14 American Review of International Arbitration (2004) p. 461; "International Commercial Online and Offline Dispute Resolution: Addressing Primacism and Universalism", 4 Journal of American Arbitration (2005) p. 79 and 20 ABA Dispute Resolution Magazine (2014, no. 1).

406 ON ARBITRATION

of being counsel but not so many as arbitrators. To a much lesser extent than American women, while recognizing there may be double-counting, it appears safe to conclude that as of today there are a few American minorities active in international arbitration but even less as arbitrators. To a much lesser extent than American women and minorities (and given the paucity double-counting here is unlikely), there are an infinitesimal number of American LGBTQ lawyers in international arbitration. For me, the bright aspect in this picture as compared to when I worked in the field in the 1980s and 1990s is best captured in the paraphrase of an old Negro spiritual: there are not as many as there ought to be, but it is slightly better than it was."[8]

It is indeed better; but it is most certainly not for the best. What can be done? We must begin necessarily with party autonomy and legal restrictions on such autonomy. In no legal system worthy of the name can a party appoint a corrupt or partial arbitrator. Equally, parties cannot jointly agree under most arbitration rules the appointment of unsuitable arbitrators, with non-waivable impediments as regards independence, conflicts of interest and availability.

Such limitations on party autonomy were raised in a London ad hoc arbitration in a case under English law and the laws of the European Union. Under EU law, there are several legislative texts intended to promote diversity in many forms, proscribing discrimination on grounds of gender and race. In the Charter of Fundamental Rights of the European Union (2000), Art. 21 prohibits discrimination based on the ground of gender, race, colour, ethnic or social origin, genetic features, language, religion or belief, political or any other opinion, membership of a national minority, property, birth, disability, age or sexual orientation. The EU's Race Directive 2000/43/EC also provides that the principle of equal treatment means that there shall be no direct or indirect discrimination based on racial or ethnic origin. The Race Directive excludes nationality discrimination from its scope (Art. 3(2)); but that is prohibited generally under Art. 12 of the EC Treaty. Art. 10 of the Treaty on the Functioning of the European Union (TFEU) provides that, in defining and implementing its policies and activities, the European Union shall aim to combat discrimination based on sex, racial or ethnic origin, religion or belief, disability, age or sexual orientation.[9]

The EU Directive 2000/78/CE of 27 November 2000 also provides a general framework under EU law for combating discrimination on the grounds of religion or belief, disability, age or sexual orientation as regards "employment and occupation". For religion and belief, this 2000 Directive was first enacted in the United Kingdom by the Employment Equality (Religion or Belief) Regulations 2003 (now superseded, in like terms, by the United Kingdom's Equality Act 2010 and its Regulations). These texts gave rise in the curious case of *Jivraj v. Hashwani*,

---

[8] *Ibid.*, p. 10.
[9] Arts. 18 and 19 TFEU [Art 23 with Art 6 of EC Treaty].

raising a legal issue regarding discrimination in appointing an arbitrator based on religious grounds, with many considering that similar issues (requiring similar answers) would arise from discrimination based on nationality and, possibly, gender and race.

C. Jivraj v. Hashwani

This case arose under the 2003 Regulations and the 2000 Directive. It illustrates the tension between party autonomy and legal rules precluding discrimination. The case has special facts, but the decision of the UK Supreme Court (2011) has been understood to establish that parties and arbitral institutions can lawfully discriminate against the appointment of an arbitrator on the grounds of religion and nationality, under English and EU law.

Under the 2003 Regulations, the UK Supreme Court decided, in robust terms, that an arbitrator was not an "employee"; that accordingly discrimination in the appointment of an arbitrator on religious grounds was not impermissible under the parties' arbitration agreement; and that, even if prima facie impermissible, it was nonetheless made permissible under a legislative exception for "genuine occupational requirement" (also known as "GOR"). The UK Supreme Court thereby reversed the decision of the Court of Appeal (2010), which had unanimously reversed the decision of the Commercial Court (2009),[10] to widespread acclamation from many users of arbitration in the European Union (including the ICC and the LCIA which had intervened in the appeal as amici curiae). The unusual facts of the case are not directly material to this paper and can, for present purposes, be left aside.[11]

Unfortunately, even with the final decision of the UK Supreme Court, the controversy remains far from over. Implicitly, the effects of the decision are not limited to discrimination in the appointment of arbitrators by users and arbitral institutions on grounds of religion, but extend to other forms of discrimination, particularly those based on nationality (the latter being expressed, albeit in different terms, in almost all rules of international arbitration institutions).[12]

---

[10] *Jivraj v. Hashwani* [2011] UKSC 40; [2011] 1 WLR 1872, also reported in ICCA *Yearbook Commercial Arbitration* XXXVI (2011) p. 611; and Revue de l'arbitrage (2011) p. 1007. For the decision of the Court of Appeal, see [2010] EWCA Civ 712; [2010] ICR 1435; and for that of the Commercial Court (Steel J), see EWHC 1364.

[11] For those interested, see the author's article on the decision of the Court of Appeal: "Arbitral Discrimination Under English and EU Law" in Yves Derains and Laurent Levy, eds., *Is Arbitration Only as Good as the Arbitrator? Status, Powers and Role of the Arbitrator*, Dossier VIII, ICC Institute of World Busines Law (2011) p. 91.

[12] This paper does not address nationality discrimination under international law in state-state or investor-state arbitrations. Given the terms of so many bilateral investment treaties and the ICSID Convention, discrimination on the ground of nationality is there firmly entrenched as the universal badge of neutrality recognized by states. That need not be so as regards international commercial arbitration; nor is it in the European Court of Justice.

408 ON ARBITRATION

After the UK Supreme Court's decision, Mr. Hashwani complained to the European Commission that the Supreme Court had improperly failed to apply EU law (in the form of the 2000 Directive) and had also declined wrongly, with its Nelsonian view of "acte clair", to refer the case to the Court of Justice of the European Union (CJEU) in Luxembourg under Art. 267 TFEU, as formally requested by Mr. Hashwani. Far from dismissing this complaint summarily, the European Commission recorded the complaint under Art. 258 TFEU and, in December 2013, ordered the United Kingdom to respond in writing to Mr. Hashwani's complaint. There has been, as yet, no such response. Depending on such response and the Commission's resulting opinion, the European Commission may bring infraction proceedings against the United Kingdom (being responsible for the UK Supreme Court) under Art. 260 TFEU; and, if so, the CJEU may direct the United Kingdom to take necessary measures, i.e. for the UK Supreme Court to reconsider its decision leading to a different result.

It is therefore necessary to see what that result might be, starting with the decision of the Court of Appeal which was reversed by the UK Supreme Court. The Court of Appeal decided that this non-discrimination provision encompassed an arbitrator under a contract personally to do any work, being a form of words long used by the UK Parliament to cover those working under both a contract of service (i.e. an employee) and a contract for services (i.e. not an employee):[13]

> "The paradigm case of appointing an arbitrator involves obtaining the services of a particular person to determine a dispute in accordance with the agreement of the parties and the rules of law, including those to be found in the legislation governing arbitration. In that respect it is no different from instructing a solicitor to deal with a particular piece of legal business, such as drafting a will, consulting a doctor about a particular ailment or an accountant about a tax return. Since an arbitrator (or any professional person) contracts to do work personally, the provision of his [sic] services falls within the definition of 'employment', and it follows that his appointor must be an 'employer' within the meaning of Regulation 6(1) [of the 2003 Regulations]" (para. 16).

As Professor Racine rightly notes in his case-note, apart from its special technical meaning under the 2003 Regulations (with the Directive), the Court of Appeal did not decide that an arbitrator was in fact an employee of the disputing

---

[13] It appears to have been first used in the UK's Equal Pay Act 1970; and it now forms part of the Equality Act 2010 (Sect. 83). At least two decisions of the House of Lords supported a broad interpretation of this wording: *Kelly v. NIHE* [1999] 1 AC 428 and *Percy v. Church of Scotland* [2006] 2 AC 28 (now, *sed quaere*).

parties, it therefore being necessary to dismiss such simplistic criticism as a "caricature".[14]

The UK Supreme Court, in reversing the decision of the Court of Appeal, decided that the distinctive feature was an "employment" relationship, whether in form the person was employed or self-employed and that a difference should be drawn (as also reflected in EU law) between a person who was, in substance, "employed" and a person who was an independent provider of services not in a relationship of subordination with the person(s) receiving those services. Accordingly, so the Supreme Court decided, the role of an arbitrator "is not one of employment under a contract personally to do work" (para. 40), despite the receipt of contractual fees from and the provision of non-delegable services to the disputing parties.[15] As already indicated above, the UK Supreme Court also recognized and applied an exception for "genuine occupational requirement". This exception had been applied by the Commercial Court (Mr. Justice Steel); but not by the Court of Appeal, which interpreted this exception more restrictively. Even broadly interpreted, it can only apply in a rational and proportionate manner. It cannot therefore apply by way of general application to all cases.

Even after the Supreme Court's decision, it would be incorrect to assume that party autonomy is unlimited. Under English and EU laws, It would not be permissible for parties to agree always that only men (or only women) could be appointed as arbitrators; or that only WASPs but no Afro-Caribbeans were ever qualified as arbitrators; but it would be permissible for parties to stipulate that only persons religiously qualified or qualified by nationality could be appointed if religious or nationality factors were sufficiently relevant so as to justify such appointments in particular cases, such as (as regards religion) the *Beth Din* or certain Shari'a tribunals (including Ismaili tribunals), applying Jewish law and the Shari'a respectively. It is difficult to imagine any factors which could rationally justify discrimination based on gender and race. As Professor Racine points out, party autonomy regarding arbitration is circumscribed by the European Convention on Human Rights (Art. 14 and Protocol 12, ECHR) and rules of both national and

---

[14] Jean-Baptiste RACINE, "Much Ado About Nothing", Revue de l'arbitrage (2011) p. 1026 at p. 1031.

[15] For commentaries on the decision of the UK Supreme Court, see (inter alia) *ibid.*: where the second footnote lists the significant number of commentaries already then in existence, in the blogosphere and elsewhere; see now also C. STYLE and P. CLEOBURY, "*Jivraj v. Hashwani*: Public Interest and Party Autonomy", Arb Int (2011) p. 563; C. MCCRUDDEN, "Two Views of Subordination: The Personal Scope of Employment Discrimination Law in '*Jivraj v. Hashwani*'", 41 Industrial Law Journal (2013) p. 30; A.K. HOFFMANN, "Selection and Appointment of Arbitrators" (Chapter 13) in M. ARROYO, ed., *Arbitration In Switzerland: The Practitioner's Guide* (2013); U.A. OSENI and H.A. KADOUF, "The Discrimination Conundrum in the Appointment of Arbitrators in International Arbitration", 29 Journal of Int Arb (2012, no. 5) pp. 519-544; For an unusual and critical commentary, see Sir Richard BUXTON, "Discrimination in Employment: The Supreme Court Draws a Line", LQR (2012) p. 128. (This author was a member of the Court of Appeal in *Jivraj v. Hashwani*.)

410   ON ARBITRATION

international public policy, of which the French *Dutco* decision (1992) is only one example.[16]

Regrettably, Art. 11(1) of the 1985 UNCITRAL Model Law on International Commercial Arbitration does not restrict party autonomy in regard to discrimination based on gender and race. In regard to nationality, it provides: "No person shall be precluded by reason of his nationality from acting as an arbitrator, unless otherwise agreed by the parties." This provision, expressly respecting the principle of party autonomy, was intended only to remove restrictions in national laws preventing the appointment of foreigners as arbitrators.[17] The UNCITRAL Analytical Note A/CN/.9/264 (25 March 1985) records that there was no intention to preclude parties, arbitral institutions and trade associations "from specifying that nationals of certain States may, or may not, be appointed as arbitrators". This reference to national laws has its roots, amongst others, in the infamous amendment to Art. 1032(2) of Germany's ZPO of 7 April 1933, disqualifying all "non-Aryan" persons from appointment as arbitrators in arbitrations and, as originally intended, invoked against non-German arbitrators.

Accordingly, however uncertain in scope, there are clearly legal limits to party autonomy in the selection and appointment of arbitrators, whether directly by each party or indirectly on their behalf by an arbitral institution. The *Jivraj* case, albeit still unfinished business, demonstrates that international arbitration is not independent from national and international rules of law, but that it is part of the main, within England and Wales, the European Union and elsewhere.

D.   Conclusion

What can be done? The answer lies primarily with major users and arbitral institutions. It does not lie in more laws, legal rules and regulations. The objective is indisputable: inadvertent discrimination based on gender and race damages arbitration, because it assumes, unthinkingly, that a class of persons have always the relevant qualities and that another class always do not, thereby wasting the human resources available to arbitration. Such discrimination is also grossly irrational in a process otherwise founded upon rationality: the choice of an arbitrator should not be exercised arbitrarily; and if a distinction is to be drawn between arbitral candidates, it should have a rational basis related to the particular requirements of the parties for their arbitration. Lastly, but not least, such discrimination is wrong; and, if allowed to continue, it will bring arbitration into

---

[16] J.-B. RACINE, *op. cit.*, fn. 14, "*la discrimination serait tout aussi automatique et évidente .... que le critère soit tiré de la race ou de l'ethnie, du handicap, de l'orientation sexuelle, de l'âge, etc*", p. 1037.

[17] See H.M. HOLTZMANN and J.E. NEUHAUS, *A Guide to the UNCITRAL Model Law* (1989) at pp. 359 and 381.

disrepute. Hence, let us support the idea of a voluntary "pledge" by parties, appointing authorities and arbitral institutions, consciously, before appointing an arbitrator, to consider the broadest spectrum of suitable candidates, without unconscious discrimination based on gender and race. It could work, as have like pledges in favour of ADR (before litigation) promoted by the International Institute for Conflict Prevention and Resolution (CPR) for almost thirty years.[18] It would also have the advantage of being the right thing to do. And it might even work on Mars.

---

[18] More than 4,000 companies and 1,500 law firms have signed the CPR Pledge, committing the signatory to consider, before litigation, ADR in the form of appropriate negotiation, mediation and other ADR processes (see <www.cpradr.org>; last visited 20 May 2014).

27
Arbitrators and Arbitral Institutions
Legal Risks for Product Liability?

A. Introduction

Let us imagine a brown ginger beer bottle produced by a well-known global institution for your personal use. The bottle's label proudly proclaims that in addition to reaching regions of the world that other natural beverages cannot reach, its ginger beer is the best beverage that is better than any municipal water: not even "probably" so, like mere Danish beers, but indisputably so. This ginger beer is said to be more cost-effective, more efficient, and quicker at quenching your thirst than any other kind of beverage. The bottle's label contains no advisory, health information, or other warning whatsoever. So, this green, eco-friendly ginger beer is proclaimed as effectively "the only drink in town."

Now, let us also imagine that this global institution knows for certain that at least fifty percent of those of us who drink its ginger beer are likely to be greatly dissatisfied with this experience. In the ginger beer trade, the fifty percent of dissatisfied consumers are known as "losers" while the satisfied consumers are called "winners." Let us imagine further that those of us who would like to be winners find, once the bottle is opened, that our particular bottle contains not only a decomposed snail, which can make the drinking experience less than satisfactory, but worse, that the bottle contains no ginger beer at all. In the ginger beer trade, technically that is called "annulled ginger beer."

There are two additional details. First, there is a legally binding contract between the institution and the imbibers. This case is not an elderly case from an old casebook on torts or delicts. It is not exactly clear what the contract's applicable law might be or what court might have jurisdiction over any dispute between the imbibers and the institution. However, it is manifestly clear that the institution has assumed significant contractual obligations toward the imbibers of its ginger beer bottles. Furthermore, there may be certain non-contractual legal obligations on the institution as a promoter, manufacturer, and supplier of ginger beer, depending on the applicable law and the judicial forum. Second, the cost of a ginger beer bottle is not a modest five U.S. dollars or so. Taking into account

---

On Arbitration. Edited by: Sam Wordsworth KC and Marie Veeder, Oxford University Press. © Oxford University Press 2023.
DOI: 10.1093/oso/9780192869135.003.0027

all costs, the total can amount to millions, even tens of millions of U.S. dollars. However, that price will remain unfixed at the time a user purchases the bottle because it will usually be determined later by the institution itself. While this ginger beer bottle may be cost-effective, its price will not be cheap or fixed at the point of sale.

Now, on these facts, if we found the bottle empty or polluted, caused by the negligent act or omission of the institution, would we be surprised to learn that we had no legal claim against the institution? Would we also be surprised to learn that both the institution and its workers had legal immunity for any negligent act or omission on the ground of public policy? That, because ginger beer is so important to the national and global economy, ginger beer institutions and workers should not be held accountable because it might adversely affect their work? A lay person would likely be surprised because he or she would expect the contrary and so too would most regulators and legislatures. As a general principle, it is usually accepted that every institution should be legally accountable for its legal wrongs, including negligence, especially when the product sold is professionally produced, heavily promoted, and significantly expensive.[1] If we are not surprised, then we are almost certainly an arbitration user or an arbitration specialist because, traditionally, arbitration users have often been told that there was no possible legal claim against arbitrators and arbitral institutions apart from fraud, corruption, criminal activity and intentional wrongs. Other than these exceptions, there is no reported case in England of any arbitrator or arbitral institution being held liable to any arbitration user in the long-recorded history of English arbitration. The same was also true in France, a country with a legal system and a judiciary that is even more favorable to arbitration than England. However, this is no longer the case.

First, regarding English law, the House of Lords decided two cases concerning "quasi-arbitrators" (but not arbitrators as such), *Sutcliffe v Thackrah* (1975) and *Arenson v Arenson* (1977) that the immunity for arbitrators traditionally assumed by commentators might be ill-founded at common law.[2] As a result of this new judicial approach, the position of arbitrators at English law became unclear; the Arbitration Act 1950 stated nothing about arbitral immunity. It was even more doubtful that arbitral institutions enjoyed any legal immunity at common law. In the first edition of Mustill & Boyd's *Commercial Arbitration*, the authors analyzed the different directions that English law might take in the future.[3] Their third possible direction concluded, "[a]rbitrators are not immune from suit. There is no reason of public policy to exempt them from liability."[4] They rejected that

---

[1] There is here no exact analogy with the famous case where there was a decomposed snail from Paisley in the ginger beer bottle. *See Donaghue v Stevenson* [1932] AC 362 (holding Mrs Donaghue had no contract with the manufacturer or the tea-shop supplying the ginger beer.)

[2] *See Arenson v Arenson* [1977] AC 405; *Sutcliffe v Thackrah* [1974] AC 727.

[3] *See* Sir Michael J. Mustill & Stewart C. Boyd, COMMERCIAL ARBITRATION (Butterworth, 1982).

[4] *See id.*

414   ON ARBITRATION

proposition on the grounds of the long tradition of arbitration in England, but also of public policy so as to avoid "the worst of all worlds."[5] There was, however, no comfort for arbitral institutions. Whereas an arbitrator might still claim a special status at common law, an arbitral institution's relations with the parties was based on contract, not status, with no room for immunity influenced by public policy at common law.

Second, more recently in France in the *FFIRC* case (2010), the claimant recovered substantial damages in contract from an arbitral institution under French law.[6] The institution was a specialist trade association that organized an arbitration service for its members under its own arbitration rules. There was a dispute between a French company and a Spanish company that was referred to the institution under the parties' arbitration clause in their contracts. In due course, the sole arbitrator made an award in France ordering the Spanish company to pay substantial damages to the French company. That award was judicially challenged by the Spanish company, resulting in a judgment of Cour d'appel de Paris that annulled the award for failure to respect the rights of the defense. The following is what had gone wrong: the sole arbitrator made his award without an oral hearing on the basis of documentary materials sent to him by the institution. However, under the arbitration rules, the institution was solely responsible for the onward transmission of all evidentiary materials to the sole arbitrator and the parties. One document that the institution received from the French company was duly forwarded to the sole arbitrator, but by innocent mistake, it was not sent by the institution to the Spanish company. Inevitably, of course, the sole arbitrator based his award against the Spanish company on the very document that the Spanish company did not receive, depriving it of any opportunity to comment in its defense to the French company's claim. Based on these circumstances, the Cour d'appel had no difficulty in annulling the award under French law on the ground of due process ("le principe de la contradiction"), leaving the French company with a worthless, albeit expensive, piece of paper – in other words, an annulled ginger beer bottle.

In olden times, the limitation period not having expired, the French company would simply have begun new arbitration proceedings and having won once, it could reasonably anticipate winning again before a new arbitration tribunal. But, these are more aggressive times in the Twenty-First Century. Instead, the French company sued the institution for damages before the Tribunal de Grande Instance of Nanterre. That court decided that the institution was contractually liable in damages to the French company for having failed in its legal responsibility to

---

[5] *See id.* at 192, 194–95; *see also* SIR MICHAEL J. MUSTILL & STEWART C. BOYD, COMMERCIAL ARBITRATION 11,224-32 (2d ed., Lexis Law Pub, 1989).

[6] *See* Société Filature Française de Mohair v Fédération Françaises des Industries Lainières et Cotonnières, (1 ère Chambre 2010) JCP(G) No 51, 20 Dec 2010, ann. Ortscheidt, Dalloz 2011.3023, ann T. Clay; *see also* Charles Price, *Liability of Arbitral Institutions in International Arbitration, in* THE PRACTICE OF ARBITRATION: ESSAYS IN HONOUR OF HANS VAN HOUTTE 187–93 (2012).

organize the arbitration in accordance with its arbitration rules. The court awarded the French company its legal costs incurred in the annulment proceeding (some 10,000 euros) and also part of its costs of the court proceedings (some 3,500 euros). However, the court rejected the claim for the face value of the annulled award on the ground of causation given that the French company could start a new arbitration against the Spanish company and recover the same substantial damages with no apparent time bar for such claim. The court also rejected the claim for moral damages, albeit finding that there was no immunity for the institution under French law.

Why is this case of any interest to us? It is a decision by a relatively minor court and the case is not even reported in the "Revue de l'arbitrage." While it has attracted a number of legal commentaries elsewhere, the only substantive article was written by Charles Price for a foreign audience.[7] Mr. Price's article confirms that an arbitral institution can be liable in contract to its disappointed users for substantial damages under French law. Like any institution comprised of human beings, an arbitral institution can make a relatively small, innocent mistake with grave consequences for a disputing party resulting in a significant liability for the institution itself. If the applicable limitation period had time-barred the French company's renewed claim, it seems clear that the amount of the award could have been claimed as damages against the institution. The *FFIRC* dispute concerned a relatively small amount, producing a modest award with insignificant costs compared to a large international arbitration. What if such a dispute had concerned millions or billions of U.S. dollars?

The *FFIRC* case, to which we shall return later, also shows that attempts by an arbitral institution to protect itself in advance against liability are limited. In an earlier French case decided in 2009, *SNF S.A.S. v. International Chamber of Commerce (ICC)*,[8] the court declared invalid under French law the "ICC's" contractual attempt to exclude liability for itself (and its arbitrators) under Article 34 of the 1998 ICC Rules.[9] The ICC had optimistically (but mistakenly) intended that new provision to operate as an absolute immunity against all legal liability to users of ICC arbitration everywhere. In contrast to French law, English law sought to protect arbitral institutions with a limited form of statutory immunity under Section 74 of the English Arbitration Act 1996.[10] Unfortunately, such statutory

---

[7] *See* Price, *supra* note 6; *see also* Y. Derains & L. Kiffer, *France, Int Handbook Comm. Arb.* 41, n. 147 (Kluwer; 2011).

[8] SNF v ICC, JDI 2009.617, ann T. Clay; JIA 2009.579, ann. L. Kiffer.

[9] International Chamber of Commerce Arbitration Rules art. 34 (1998) [hereinafter "1998 ICC Rules"] ("Neither the arbitrators, nor the Court and its members, nor the ICC and its employees, nor the ICC National Committees shall be liable to any person for any act or omission in connection with the arbitration."). Following the *SNF* case, this wording was changed in Article 40 of the 2012 ICC Rules, by adding at the end: "except to the extent such limitation of liability is prohibited by applicable law."

[10] Arbitration Act 1996 § 74 (United Kingdom) [hereinafter "English Arbitration Act 1996"] ("(1) An arbitral or other institution or person designated or requested by the parties to appoint or nominate an arbitrator is not liable for anything done or omitted in the discharge or purported discharge of that function unless the act or omission is shown to have been in bad faith. (2) An arbitral or other

416 ON ARBITRATION

immunity is confined to the institution's appointment or nomination of arbitrators unless the institution's acts or omissions are shown to have been in bad faith. Moreover, this statutory immunity only applies if the seat of the arbitration is in England and Wales; how the immunity could apply to a suit against an arbitral institution outside England under an applicable law other than English law is far from clear. Today, given the increasingly aggressive tactics deployed by one-off users of international arbitration with no interest in the arbitral system beyond winning (or not losing) their case, there is clearly a growing problem with regard to the potential legal liability of an arbitral institution for its product, namely impartial arbitrators deciding a dispute with a valid award.

There is also a growing problem for international arbitrators. Increasingly, arbitrators are the collateral victims of attacks by a party on the award and the arbitration itself. These collateral attacks often take the form of a challenge to the arbitrator's impartiality and independence. In some jurisdictions, a successful challenge against one of three arbitrators may invalidate an award, even for unanimous decisions. A pending challenge may influence the adverse party toward an otherwise unfavorable settlement. In other jurisdictions, a pending challenge may automatically stay the arbitration until it is resolved by a state court, preventing the tribunal from proceeding with a partial award on liability to a final award on quantum for an indefinite period of time.[11] Recently, state courts have called an unprecedented parade of international arbitrators to account, and required several arbitrators personally to give evidence on oath before a state court (usually at their own expense). These actions have taken place in London, Stockholm, and most recently in New York and France – hardly exotic venues hostile to international arbitration. In short, functional immunity is no longer working for arbitration.

B. The Practical Problems

With this background, let us look more closely and advance a possible solution for the current practical problems facing arbitral institutions and arbitrators regarding potential legal liability to disappointed users. I can do so only in regard to English and French law because the subject is vast and varied. Over the years, well-known treatises and articles have been published including the work edited

---

institution or person by whom an arbitrator is appointed or nominated is not liable, by reason of having appointed or nominated him, for anything done or omitted by the arbitrator (or his employees or agents) in the discharge or purported discharge of his functions as arbitrator. (3) The above provisions apply to an employee or agent of an arbitral or other institution or person as they apply to the institution or person himself.").

[11] *See, e.g.,* International Centre for Settlement of Investment Disputes Arbitration Rules (2003) [hereinafter "ICSID Arbitration Rules"]. A challenge, however unmeritorious, will also suspend ICSID arbitration under ICSID Arbitration Rule 9(10).

by Julian Lew in 1990, Susan Frank's comparative survey in 2000, and Martin Meissner's more recent study.[12] I shall also say nothing at all about the laws and practices of this jurisdiction. I understand too little about the USA's different arbitral traditions. However, my common premise is simply stated at the outset: today, in the field of international arbitration everywhere, there are too many of us who are washing our hands like Pontius Pilate in the face of increasing legal risks to both arbitral institutions and arbitrators. As already described, England and France have taken two different paths, but regrettably, the result is materially the same. There is simply too much legal uncertainty and too much risk for individual arbitrators and arbitral institutions to bear alone. A great accident is bound to happen soon that may lead to the forced insolvency of an old arbitral institution or the involuntary bankruptcy of a much respected arbitrator. In particular, (1) individual arbitrators are not corporations; (2) an arbitrator cannot easily limit his or her legal liability (like a law firm); (3) there is no legal cap on damages against an arbitrator or an arbitral institution (like shipowners, airlines, or the medical profession); and (4) arbitral institutions themselves, even large ones, are almost invariably non-profit organizations usually with little or no capital assets. On that future day of reckoning, we may knowingly nod to each other that we sadly saw it coming. We may also greatly regret that our laws, judges, and legal systems can be so treacherous to innocent victims unless we collectively do something. But, what can be done?

(1) England and Wales

In English law, as with most common law systems, a professional person usually operates under an obligation to exercise a duty of care and skill: the breach of which may result in liability under both tort and contract law. A new bridge does not usually collapse without someone's negligent fault, probably by the engineer or the building contractor. If a new building suddenly falls down, the architect will invariably be blamed. No engineer, contractor, or architect will be entitled to immunity from suit. Therefore, expectations are high for professional products and services, particularly if that product or service is expensive. The professional person may have contractual limitations or exclusions on liability, but municipal laws and public policy will often regulate the scope of such contractual immunity.

---

[12] See Julian D. M. Lew, IMMUNITY OF ARBITRATORS (London Press Ltd, 1990), reviewed J. Paulsson (1991) 107 LQR 688; Susan Franck, The Liability of International Arbitrators: A Comparative Analysis and Proposal for Qualified Immunity, 20 N.Y.L. SCH. J. INT'L & COMP. L. 1, 15 (2000); Martin Maisner, Liability and Independence of the Arbitrator, in CZECH (& CENTRAL EUROPEAN) YEARBOOK OF ARBITRATION – 2012: PARTY AUTONOMY VERSUS AUTONOMY OF ARBITRATORS 149 (2012); see also Alan Redfern, The Immunity of Arbitrators, in THE STATUS OF THE ARBITRATOR (ICC, 1995).

418   ON ARBITRATION

Other than death or personal injury, a professional person can usually contractually exclude a liability which he or she would otherwise attract in tort or contract to the customer, save where that person is guilty of deliberate wrongdoing (although the deliberate wrongdoing by an employee for whom the professional is vicariously liable can usually be contractually excluded).[13] Under English law, there are statutory and regulatory restrictions on the legal effect of such contractual exclusions, notably under the Unfair Contract Terms Act 1977 and, regarding consumers, the Unfair Terms in Consumer Contracts Regulations 1999 (enacting the EU Council Directive 93/13). At the present time, English courts have yet to decide on these restrictions regarding arbitrators and arbitral institution.

Until the decisions of the House of Lords, in the two English cases in 1974 and 1977 mentioned above, for at least 250 years it was firmly assumed that an English arbitrator could not be sued in English law for damages.[14] There were many judicial obiter dicta to such effect in the law reports, but none of the reported cases actually concerned arbitrators (as distinct from quasi-arbitrators). Nonetheless, these dicta consistently suggested that English law was clear, beyond all doubt, as stated and restated in authoritative textbooks on arbitration.[15] The first stone cast in this still pond was *Sutcliffe v Thackrah*.[16] It concerned an architect who, acting as a certifier, allegedly issued negligent certificates for defective building work. The plaintiff-owner then paid the contractor, but he became insolvent and was unable to effect the necessary repairs. The trial judge found the architect liable for negligence and awarded damages for the cost of the repairs with no right to immunity from suit. The architect appealed. The House of Lords, dismissing the appeal, decided that a certifier was not a quasi-arbitrator and that there could be no analogy to the immunity of an arbitrator. This case was not a case about arbitral immunity, but there were important obiter dicta with four of the five judges expressing views that there was arbitral immunity under English law. Yet, the question had been raised.

The second case came before the House of Lords some two years later in *Aronson v Aronson*.[17] It concerned an auditor valuing shares in a company between the plaintiff seller and a buyer, where the sale contract provided that the auditor's valuation would be final as regards the price to be paid to the seller. The seller alleged that the valuation made by the auditor had been negligently made and was too low. Following its earlier decision in *Sutcliffe v Thackrah*, the House of Lords decided that the auditor could be liable for negligence because he was not a quasi-arbitrator.

---

[13]   CLERK & LINDSELL ON TORTS ¶¶ 10–17 (21st ed., Sweet & Maxwell, 2014).

[14]   *See supra* note 3.

[15]   Until Mustill & Boyd's first edition, *see supra* note 3, in 1991, the specialist works (including *Halsbury*, *Russell*, and *Hogg*), if they thought it necessary to address the matter at all, re-stated the same position: arbitrators could not be sued in damages (apart from fraud).

[16]   *See Sutcliffe v Thackrah* [1974] AC 727.

[17]   *See Arenson v Arenson* [1977] AC 405.

Again, it was not a decision about arbitral immunity as such; and three of the five judges concurred in stating, obiter, that there was arbitral immunity because an arbitrator, like a judge, was not liable in negligence at common law. In this case, there were important dicta from two other judges who said there should be no arbitral immunity. Lord Kilbrandon and Lord Fraser, both Scottish law lords, suggested that an arbitrator was no different from a valuer and that, like a valuer, an arbitrator had no immunity from suit at common law. It may be significant that these were Scottish and not English judges; under Scots law, the legal principles underlying judicial immunity are different from English law, making them inapplicable to a private arbitrator.[18]

These important dicta from the two senior appellate judges caused considerable concern within the English arbitral community. The Institute of Arbitrators instructed Michael Mustill QC to advise its members whether English law still conferred any immunity for damages on an arbitrator alleged by one party to have been guilty of negligence. From anecdotal evidence, it is possible that these instructions were also provoked by legal proceedings brought against the Institute of Arbitrators for allegedly appointing a wholly incompetent arbitrator without taking reasonable care to ensure his competency, ending in catastrophic results for one party. That case is not publicly reported. It may have been settled before judgment, but it is clear that the issue at the time extended beyond arbitral immunity to the position of an arbitral institution or appointing authority in nominating or appointing an arbitrator. In 1977, in a long and scholarly opinion, Michael Mustill QC advised that a degree of risk now existed that arbitrators could be held liable in tort under English law.[19] It is impossible to exaggerate the influence of Michael Mustill on the development of English arbitration over the last fifty years. He was always the House of Lords "Mark Two," even as Counsel at the English Bar, long before he began his distinguished judicial career. The result of his legal opinion, amongst others, was the first attempt by the London Court of International Arbitration (the "LCIA," then still part of the Institute of Arbitrators) to exclude liability for arbitrators and the LCIA as an arbitral institution in the LCIA's 1981 Rules.[20] Further, as explained below, Sections 29 and 78 of the later English Arbitration Act 1996 were enacted as mandatory provisions from which disputing parties cannot derogate in an English arbitration – that is an arbitration with an English seat.[21]

---

[18] *See generally* Abimbola A. Olowofoyeku, SUING JUDGES: A STUDY OF JUDICIAL IMMUNITY (Clarendon Press, 1994).

[19] This legal opinion is not published. Yet, over the years, it has entered the public domain.

[20] *See* English Arbitration Act 1996 § 29 ("(1) An arbitrator is not liable for anything done or omitted in the discharge or purported discharge of his functions as arbitrator unless the act or omission is shown to have been in bad faith. (2) Subjection (1) applies to an employee or agent of an arbitrator as it applies to the arbitrator himself. (3) This section does not affect any liability incurred by an arbitrator by reason of his resigning." *But see id.* § 25 ("Section 25 addresses the position of an arbitrator who has resigned in regard to personal liability, fees and expenses, as to which the Court may (not must) grant him relief.").

[21] *See* English Arbitration Act 1996 §§ 29, 78.

420   ON ARBITRATION

Statutory immunity for arbitrators was considered extensively by the Departmental Advisory Committee on the Law of Arbitration ("DAC") which was responsible for the content of the English Arbitration Act 1996, first chaired by (as he had become) Lord Justice Mustill. The DAC's published reports on this issue confirmed the doubts and concerns caused by the House of Lords' decision in *Aronson v Aronson*. In the DAC 1996 Report,[22] the DAC considered that at common law, there was "some arbitral immunity" because the reasons for such immunity were the same as those applying to judicial immunity under English law. The DAC added,

> It is generally considered that an immunity is necessary to enable an impartial third party properly to perform an impartial decision-making function .... We feel strongly that unless a degree of immunity is afforded, the finality of the arbitral process could well be undermined. The prospect of a losing party attempting to re-arbitrate the issues on the basis that a competent arbitrator would have decided them in favour of their party is one that we would view with dismay.[23]

That qualified phrase "some immunity" and the reasoning ostensibly limited to arbitral "decision-making" raised questions as to the full scope of such intended arbitral immunity. For example, was it intended by Parliament to exculpate an arbitrator who, by his own negligence or his own alleged negligence, failed to perform a sufficiently thorough conflict check prior to or after his appointment, as a result of which, he or she is successfully challenged by a party and the award set aside? That would not appear to form part of an arbitrator's decision-making process regarding issues comprising the party's dispute, particularly if he or she is not yet an arbitrator at the relevant time. This situation may suggest that an arbitrator's liability may not be fully exculpated by this statutory immunity. Despite Michael Mustill's valiant attempts over the years, as both a scholar and a judge, to maintain the arbitrator as having a distinct legal status under English law (such status more easily supporting a functional immunity at common law rather than a mere contractual relationship), the English courts have now recognized that even with an extra-contractual legal status, an arbitrator becomes a contractual party to a multilateral contract made with the disputing parties, and if relevant, also the arbitral institution. With such a contract for personal services, the arbitrator necessarily risks contractual liability, subject to considerations of public policy for arbitral decision-making.

Public policy at English common law, as the DAC had reported, was based on the assumption that English arbitrators were like English judges. However, that is manifestly not the case. First, international arbitrators are not English judges. No

---

[22] *See* Report, Departmental Advisory Committee on the Law of Arbitration, Report on Arbitration Bill 1996 (Feb. 1996) [hereinafter "DAC 1996 Report"].

[23] *See* DAC 1996 Report, *supra* note 22, at ¶ 132; Sir Michael J. Mustill & Stewart C. Boyd, COMMERCIAL ARBITRATION: 2001 COMPANION VOLUME 417ff (Butterworth, 2001).

English judge makes a contract with litigants nor is an English judge paid by any litigant. There is no accurate analogy between a state judge with imperium and an international arbitrator with none. Moreover, England's senior judges enjoy absolute immunity under English law, but that is not so of junior judges. There is no obvious reason to equate English arbitrators, the majority of whom are not lawyers, with senior members of the English judiciary. Moreover, in other jurisdictions, we know that senior judges do not enjoy absolute immunity, such as Austria.

Most importantly, immunity under English law has significantly receded in other related areas. In *Rondel v Worsley*, the House of Lords held that a trial lawyer enjoyed immunity from suit for negligence in the conduct of criminal proceedings.[24] However, in *Hall v Simons*, the House of Lords reversed itself, deciding that a trial lawyer enjoyed no immunity in both civil and criminal proceedings.[25] It is an important case on immunity by virtue of its new treatment of public policy considerations; the decision has been followed in New Zealand and, regarding civil proceedings, in Scotland.[26] Given that judges will decide upon immunities enjoyed by arbitrators and arbitral institutions, this decision provides no comfort in assuming that the traditional arguments for such immunity under public policy will prevail. Those arguments include, namely, that it allows disappointed parties indirectly to attack the final decision of a tribunal, that it bypasses the many procedural rules for impugning such a decision, and that the risk of personal liability unreasonably interferes with the independence and professionalism of the targeted defendant. All these arguments, as applied to trial lawyers, were examined anew by the House of Lords and firmly rejected. The result at common law is that arbitral immunity is more questionable than ever. There should be no reason to believe with any confidence that an arbitrator, still less an arbitral institution, enjoys any functional immunity at common law in England, in tort and, still less, in contract.

There is still the English Arbitration Act 1996 for arbitrations with an English seat, and as already indicated, Section 74 of that Act provides a limited immunity to arbitral institutions for wrongful failures in the appointment of arbitrators unless that wrong is shown to have been in bad faith. Does this suffice for the 21st Century? In its 1996 Report, the DAC provided two reasons for this statutory immunity.[27] The first, as with arbitral immunity, was the concern that the threat of litigation against the institution could be used to reopen matters finally decided by an award. The second was, in its words, of great importance:

Many organisations that provide arbitration services, including Trade Associations as well as bodies whose sole function is to provide arbitration

---

[24] *See Rondel v Worsley* [1967] 1 AC 191.

[25] *See Hall v Simons* [2002] 1 AC 615.

[26] *See Chamberlain v Lai* [2005] SC 19/2005 (NZ); *Wright v Paton Farrell* [2006] 2006 SC 404 (Scotland).

[27] *See* DAC 1996 Report, *supra* note 22.

422   ON ARBITRATION

services, do not in the nature of things have deep pockets. Indeed much of the work is done by volunteers simply in order to promote and help this form of dispute resolution. Such organisations could find it difficult, if not impossible, to finance the cost of defending legal proceedings or even the cost of insurance against such costs. In our view, the benefits which these organizations and indeed individuals have in arbitration generally, fully justified giving them a measure of protection so that their good work can continue.[28]

As a matter of legal logic, this rationale should have justified a larger measure of statutory immunity for arbitral institutions. Work at the more interventionist institutions like the ICC covers the organization of an arbitration from beginning to end, far beyond the composition of the original tribunal. It may include the prima facie assessment of jurisdiction, the removal of an arbitrator, the grant of extensions of time for the award and intermediate procedural steps, the arrangement of advance payments by the parties on account of arbitration costs, the suspension of those payments in a deposit account, the determination of the final amount of arbitral fees and expenses, the scrutiny of the draft award, and the issuance of the award to the parties. This process certainly consists of far more than merely appointing ICC arbitrators. I have already described how the scope of Section 74 is also limited to an arbitration with an English seat. In short, the limited scope and application of Section 74 is no longer fit for purpose, if it ever was.[29]

As for international conventions, the International Centre for Settlement of Investment Disputes ("ICSID") Convention of 1965 was enacted into English law in 1966, whereby ICSID as an arbitral institution and ICSID arbitrators enjoy statutory immunity.[30] But, the ICSID Convention is a solitary exception amongst arbitral conventions. There is nothing about immunity in the 1958 New York Convention.[31] There is also nothing in the 1985 United Nations Commission on International Trade Law ("UNCITRAL") Model Law on Arbitration.[32] This omission was addressed by UNCITRAL's former Secretary, Gerald Hermann, in his 1998 Freshfields Lecture.[33] There, he explained that, at UNCITRAL, the national delegations abstained from touching the issue of arbitral immunity, preferring "to

---

[28] DAC 1996 Report, *supra* note 22, at ¶ 301; Report, Departmental Advisory Committee on the Law of Arbitration, Supplementary Report on English Arbitration Act 1996, at ¶ 38 (1997); *see also* Mustill & Boyd, *supra* note 23, at 444, 469.

[29] In 1995, the DAC had been ready to consider recommending to the UK Government a broader form of statutory immunity, but the arbitral institutions did not consider it important – at that time.

[30] *See* ICSID Convention, Art. 21 (Apr. 2006) [hereinafter "ICSID Convention"].

[31] *See generally* New York 1958 Convention on the Recognition and Enforcement of Foreign Arbitral Awards, (UNCITRAL).

[32] *See generally* Model Law on International Commercial Arbitration, UNCITRAL (1985) [hereinafter "UNCITRAL Model Law"].

[33] *See* Gerold Herrmann, *Does the World Need Additional Uniform Legislation on Arbitration?*, 15 ARB. INT'L 211 (1999). As a consequence, several Commonwealth jurisdictions enacting the

let sleeping dogs lie" for the Model Law. The trouble with sleeping dogs is that they eventually wake up. Soon, as a tactical measure, arbitrators were threatened personally with challenges and claims against them. Accordingly, twenty-five years after the Model Law, UNCITRAL reconsidered arbitral immunity when drafting its new UNCITRAL Arbitration Rules 2010.[34] It was a long and troubled debate.

That debate started with the working paper prepared for the UNCITRAL Working Group on Arbitration.[35] This unofficial working paper recommended a provision, which by contract would form part of an arbitration agreement under the new UNCITRAL rules. It was to the effect that no arbitrator (including his or her employees or assistants), secretary, or expert to the Tribunal, "shall be liable to any party for any act or omission in connection with the performance of his or her tasks under these Rules except if that act or omission was manifestly in bad faith." It was intended that "bad faith" would be included in this exception, as also a deliberate violation of the arbitration agreement and the UNCITRAL Rules. It was also suggested that UNCITRAL might consider extending this contractual immunity to persons or institutions performing the function of an appointing authority under the UNCITRAL Rules although the Permanent Court of Arbitration ("PCA") itself, as an appointing authority under the UNCITRAL Rules, was legally immune from suit. During the elephantine gestation of the 2010 Rules, the new Article 16 eventually emerged: "[s]ave for intentional wrongdoing, the parties waive to the fullest extent permitted under the applicable law any claim against the arbitrators, the appointing authority, and any person appointed by the arbitral tribunal based on any act or omission in connection with the arbitration."[36] As the accompanying UNCITRAL commentary makes clear, the rationale for this contractual exclusion was, "to ensure that arbitrators were protected from the threat of potentially large claims by parties dissatisfied with an arbitral tribunal's rulings or rewards who might claim that such rulings or rewards arose from the negligence or thought of an arbitrator."[37] This immunity is intended to protect the arbitrator's decision-making process in an UNCITRAL arbitration. However, the UNCITRAL Rules do nothing to protect an arbitral institution acting other than as an appointing authority under the UNCITRAL Rules.[38]

UNCITRAL Model Law added their own statutory provision on arbitral immunity (for example, Bermuda).

[34] *See* UNCITRAL Arbitration Rules, UNCITRAL (rev. 2010) [hereinafter "2010 UNCITRAL Arbitration Rules"].
[35] *See generally* Working Paper, Suggested Changes to the ICSID Rules and Regulations (May 12, 2005) [hereinafter "Suggested Changes to ICSID Rules"].
[36] *See* 2010 UNCITRAL Arbitration Rules, *supra* note 34 art. 16.
[37] *See* Report, UNCITRAL Working Group II, (Arbitration and Conciliation) on the work of its fifty-second session ealand (A/CN.9/688) ¶ 46 (2010).
[38] If the arbitral institution is the PCA, it will enjoy a broader immunity under its founding treaties. It is not clear whether such a broader immunity would benefit arbitrators appointed by the PCA under the UNCITRAL Rules, outside the Netherlands (where the PCA has its headquarters).

424   ON ARBITRATION

From an English perspective, international conventions, model laws, and rules of arbitration provide little actual guidance. We are left only with the limited statutory provisions in the English Arbitration Act 1996 and multifarious, untested contractual exclusion clauses, such as Article 31 of the 1998 LCIA Rules (as since modified by Articles 31.1 and 31.2 of the 2014 LCIA Rules).[39] Regarding immunities in the LCIA Rules, as indicated, their history began with the 1981 LCIA Rules following Michael Mustill QC's influential legal opinion in 1977. Article 14(1) of the 1981 LCIA Rules excluded liability for the LCIA Court and LCIA arbitrators for any act or omission in connection with the arbitration, but with regard to LCIA arbitrators (albeit not the LCIA Court), it excluded "the consequences of any conscious and deliberate wrongdoing" on the arbitrator's own part from this immunity. Article 19.1 of the 1985 Rules repeated this provision. It was revised in Article 31 of the 1998 LCIA rules to allow also for the liability of the LCIA Court in the case of its own conscious and deliberate wrongdoing. Article 31 of the 1998 Rules also reversed the burden of proof requiring the claimant to prove wrongdoing by the LCIA Court or LCIA arbitrator, rather than impose a negative obligation on the LCIA Court or LCIA arbitrator to disprove such wrongdoing in order to qualify for contractual immunity. To my knowledge, none of these provisions has yet been tested in litigation in England or abroad.

It is not surprising to see a provision for the immunity of the LCIA as an arbitral institution because, like the ICC, its functions extend far beyond the appointment of arbitrators and are not simply administrative under the LCIA Rules. Although, unlike the ICC, the LCIA does not actively control the conduct of the arbitration or vet draft awards (thereby taking responsibility for both), the LCIA decides challenges to arbitrators, provides written reasons to the parties for such challenges, acts as a deposit-holder for the parties, and fixes the final amount of arbitral fees and expenses under the LCIA Rules. None of these functions are unusual for many arbitral institutions around the world. Would its contractual exclusion work in practice if tested for LCIA arbitrators and the LCIA both in English and particularly in non-English litigation? For that analysis, we need to go back to France.

(2)   France

Under French law, as in English law, there is a bilateral legal agreement between the contracting parties to an arbitration clause. But, even before that agreement,

---

[39] *See* LCIA Arbitration Rules § 31 (1998); now LCIA Arbitration Rules § 31.1 and 31.2 (2014). Apart from liability in tort or under the LCIA Rules, there is no reason why an arbitrator could not be liable in contract under English law. *See* M. Smith, *Contractual Obligations Owred by and to Arbitrators: Model Terms of Appointment*, 8 ARB INT 17 (1992).

there is a standing offer made by the arbitration institution recommending to the world, including these contracting parties, that the institution is ready, willing, and able to administer an arbitration resulting from the parties' arbitration agreement. Once the arbitration has commenced, under French law there is a multilateral legal relationship between the parties and the institution where the arbitrators become parties upon their respective appointments.[40] This means that, unlike a French judge, an arbitrator and an arbitral institution can be sued in contract at French law. Regarding arbitrators, this position was confirmed in the 2008 decision by the Cour d'appel de Paris in legal proceedings brought by a disappointed party against three arbitrators.[41] The French courts have recognized that an arbitrator could be liable in contract under French law, holding that a French arbitrator is charged with a "mission" or task, which that arbitrator must complete in good conscience, independence, and impartiality. Although an arbitrator enjoys a functional legal immunity under French law, the French cases establish that immunity does not exclude liability for fraud, denial of justice, and gross negligence ("équivalente au dol, constitutive d'une fraude, d'une faute lourde ou d'un deni de justice"). Applied to an arbitral institution, the Paris Cour de Cassation confirmed in the 2001 *Cubic* case that an arbitral institution could be held liable in contract to a disputing party under French law.[42]

An arbitral institution is not an arbitrator; therefore, it is not required to respect the rights of the defense or to provide its decisions in the form of an award subject to judicial review. However, as analyzed at length by Professor Philippe Fouchard in his 1987 article: "[t]he French cases established that an arbitral institution is contractually obliged to respect its own arbitration rules, and it may also be obliged to ensure a fair procedure for the arbitration" ("un procès équitable").[43] In his article, Professor Fouchard concluded that it would be inconceivable that an arbitral institution, paid for its services, could benefit from any legal immunity under French law.[44]

It was against this legal background that the ICC introduced Article 34 of its 1998 ICC Rules,[45] ostensibly granting an absolute immunity for ICC arbitrators, the ICC Court, and the ICC without any exception. The drafting of this new article provoked considerable controversy within the ICC. However, the ICC Council decided at its meeting in Shanghai in 1997 upon the absolute form of contractual immunity,

---

[40] *See* Philippe Fouchard, *Les institutions permanentes d'arbitrage devant le juge étatique (á propos d'une jurisprudence récente,* REVUE DE L'ARBITRAGE 225 (1987).

[41] *Charasse c/D* REVUE DE L'ARBITRAGE 376 (2009), ann. P. Leboulanger.

[42] *See Société Cubic Defense Systems Inc v Chambre de Commerce international,* Cour de cassation 1ère ch civ: 20 (Feb. 2001); *see also* T. Clay note in *Rev arb 2001.511;* P. Lalive, *Rev arb 1999.103;* P. Lalive, "Sur l'irresponsibilité arbitrale", *Etudes de procédure et d'arbitrage en l'honneur de Jean-François Poudret* (1999); and Philippe Fouchard ET. AL, FOUCHARD GAILLARD GOLDMAN ON INTERNATIONAL COMMERCIAL ARBITRATION ¶¶ 1153–1155 (Savage and Gaillard eds., 1999).

[43] *See* Fouchard, *supra* note 40.

[44] *See* Fouchard, *supra* note 40, at 225, 251.

[45] *See* 1998 ICC Rules, *supra* note 9 art. 34.

426   ON ARBITRATION

which became part of the 1998 ICC Rules.[46] Many legal scholars predicted that this broad wording, without any exceptions for fraud, corruption, or deliberate wrong-doing, could never survive judicial scrutiny in a state court. These critics included, famously, Professor Pierre Lalive and the ICC National Committees from France, Italy, and the United Kingdom. They were soon proven right.

In the *SNF* case (2009), the French courts had to consider the validity of Article 34 of the 1998 ICC Rules in legal proceedings brought by a disappointed party against the ICC as an arbitral institution.[47] This litigation was part of a larger battle between two commercial parties arising from two ICC awards made in Brussels that raged in the French and Belgian courts (where the ICC was not a party). SNF's claim against the ICC in France alleged that the ICC had effectively conspired with the arbitrators to evade illegally the European Union's mandatory competition rules contrary to French law and international public policy. During these pro-ceedings, the Cour d'appel of Paris required the ICC to disclose its confidential pa-pers relating to the work of the ICC Court in approving the two draft awards under the ICC rules. It further publicly criticized the ICC in its judgment for being reluc-tant to provide the essential papers to the Court. This criticism was without prece-dent in the ICC's long experience as a litigant in France. It was a bad omen. Having examined the confidential papers, the court rejected any liability of the ICC. It then went out of its way to declare that Article 34 was invalid under French law, its abso-lute terms purporting to excuse the ICC wrongly for performing its essential con-tractual obligation as an arbitral institution towards the parties.

There were, of course, a number of "I told you so's." But, "I told you" is never a solution. The solution chosen by the ICC for its new 2012 ICC Rules is the limited language of the new exclusion in Article 40. Article 40 seeks to exclude liability for a large number of people, including ICC arbitrators, the ICC Court, and the ICC it-self, "for any act or omission in connection with the arbitration except to the extent that such limitation of liability is prohibited by applicable law." Will this exclusion work any better than the old wording? Only time will tell. It will not be a benevo-lent arbitrator who will so decide, but a state court and not necessarily a court in France. In the meantime, little comfort is provided by the ICC Secretariat's Guide to ICC arbitration as recently published. The rationale provided there for this con-tractual immunity is based on the suggestion, "such bodies and individuals [were] exposed to liability"; "this could hinder their work making it difficult for them to provide the required level of service."[48] That simplistic rationale is not applied to other professions, such as engineers, architects, building contractors, trial lawyers,

---

[46] *See* W. Laurence Craig ET. AL, ANNOTATED GUIDE TO THE 1998 ICC ARBITRATION RULES: WITH COMMENTARY 183–84 (1988).

[47] *See* SNF SAS v Chambre de commerce international, Cour d'appel of Paris (2009), ann C. Jarosson *Rev arb* 2010.314; *see also Rev arb* 2007.847 and R. Dupeyre, 32:2 ASA Bulletin 265.

[48] *See* Jason Fry ET AL., *The Secretariat's Guide to ICC Arbitration*, ICC at 421ff (2012).

C. A Practical Solution

In a little box at the very end of the ICC Guide, "Note to Arbitrators and Experts – Liability Insurance," the following words appear: "[a]rbitrators and experts are advised to obtain insurance that adequately covers their work in arbitration matters so as to minimize the risk associated with any potential liability." Where contractual and statutory immunities are insufficient under English and French law, could such legal liability insurance be the Holy Grail as the only safe and certain solution for arbitrators and arbitral institutions? It seems to me that we are only left with professional indemnity insurance as the most effective practical solution to the potential liabilities of arbitrators and arbitral institutions.

For arbitrators who do not practice as arbitrators as a separate profession, there is usually adjectival cover for acting as an arbitrator that forms part of the professional liability insurance required by their regulator or professional body. For example, a practicing member of the English Bar has cover for arbitral liability as part of the professional liability cover required to practice as a barrister (as do avocats at the Paris Bar). However, many full-time arbitrators do not exercise a separate profession, particularly if they have retired from professional practice or from a judicial career or have chosen to pursue an academic career from the outset. Many of these arbitrators, including some of the best-known international arbitrators, may carry no professional indemnity insurance at all. Even for those arbitrators that have insurance, the geographical scope of the cover may be limited given the insurance market's traditional divisions between North American and non-North American risks. It is also difficult for an individual arbitrator personally to negotiate insurance cover: (1) the legal risks are too uncertain for underwriters; (2) they are complicated to explain satisfactorily; (3) insurers prefer high volumes and not singletons as insureds; and (3) as a result, even if cover is available, insurance premiums for individual cover can be very expensive.

If cover is to be obtained, it could be more easily done for a large group under a master policy that is agreed with one insurer, possibly even a captive operating with its own reinsurance programme. It could be done with little or no controversy, particularly because the ICC has set an important example that could be adopted and supported by other arbitral institutions, independently, or with a group cover collectively negotiated by IFCAI or ICCA. Today, the ICC carries professional indemnity cover, not only for itself and the ICC Court, but also for ICC arbitrators. This fact has only recently become publicly known, although the terms of such cover remain discretely veiled for good reason. It means that a small part of the administrative fees payable by the disputing parties to the ICC Court constitutes an insurance premium covering legal liability for both the ICC and ICC arbitrators. Is that not the basis for a practical solution to the problem?

Insurance cover, at least for arbitrators, does not need to be for a significant insured sum. An honest arbitrator is unlikely to be held liable in negligence for substantial damages measured in tens or hundreds of millions of dollars for making a wrong award as part of the decision-making process. Yet, an arbitrator is increasingly likely to be made a party to a legal proceeding brought in bad faith by a disappointed party as a collateral attack on an award. For example, this can be done not only by challenging the arbitrator's impartiality or independence, but also by instituting disciplinary proceedings before his or her professional body, or by threatening other legal proceedings directly against him, whether for alleged contempt of court, alleged defamation, or alleged criminal conduct. What an arbitrator then needs is not so much an indemnity against legal liability for damages, but rather immediate defense cover from an insurer so as to defend against such malign proceedings. These defense costs for an individual arbitrator can be expensive and in some cases, have run into six figures (USD). It seems wrong for an individual, uninsured arbitrator to bear such costs and expenses alone, particularly when the proceedings against him or her fail or are abandoned, having exhausted their collateral purpose. It does not seem right, as we saw in the USA (regarding legal proceedings brought against three arbitrators acting in a Geneva arbitration), to rely on local arbitration specialists giving so generously of their time to defend the impugned arbitrators pro bono. The same arguments apply equally to big and small arbitral institutions. This relatively modest cover for defense costs, with a relatively small sum insured for any legal liability, ought to be possible to place in current market conditions if sufficient numbers of arbitrators and institutions were willing to subscribe to such group insurance. It is now needed, but will it be done?

D. Conclusion

Let me conclude with a story about Norwegian lemmings. As you may well know, a lemming is a small, furry, brown rodent living in large numbers in the arctic tundra. From the beginning of time, every four years the lemming population plummets to near-extinction. For reasons never fully understood and also much disputed by scientists, migrating lemmings commit mass suicide by jumping into the ocean and swimming collectively to their watery deaths. At school many years ago, I became a minor expert on Norwegian lemmings because a friend and I were applying for a travel scholarship to northern Norway to observe the lemming migration. However, our scholarly application, of which we were mistakenly proud, was summarily rejected by the scholarship committee because we had chosen the wrong year. It was an off-year of non-migration with no mass suicides by lemmings, and we were not allowed to resubmit a more timely application. Like Norwegian lemmings, we may continue our lives as arbitrators and arbitral institutions for the next several off-years. I may be wrong again about the exact time, but unless we do something soon, we can be morally certain that one day a calamity will befall the international arbitral community. We should at least attempt a solution soon. If we tried together (arbitral institutions, arbitrators, and arbitration users), we could certainly do better than lemmings.

28
The Alexander Lecture 2015, London
26 November 2015

'What Matters—about Arbitration'

I am delighted to be invited to deliver this year's Alexander Lecture. I met Mr Alexander during my first meetings at the Chartered Institute long ago. He was then a senior member of its Council and later President; and I was a mere arbitral fledgling practitioner on the Institute's international committee. He was an engaging, friendly figure with a wealth of good stories. Once, when our committee was discussing possible conflicts of interest between arbitrators and counsel, he told the story about his own conflict as sole arbitrator in a large arbitration where his son appeared on the first day of the hearing, acting as counsel for one of the many parties. "Ladies and Gentlemen", so he told the parties, "this is a clear case of conflict requiring immediate recusal." And then turning to his son, he said: "Boy, get out!" The trouble with such stories is that you repeat them once too often, as I did much later to the son. He denied all knowledge of the incident. That was hardly surprising. There were two Mr Alexander's at this Institute; and I was addressing the wrong son.[1] Yet it remains an old parable from the past, perhaps even more true now than at the time.

For arbitration, the past is never another country. At sea, we watch the waves behind to know the waves that come ahead: and so too, with the history of arbitration. Over the last fifty years, we have watched the growing strength of arbitration as an effective method of resolving an increasing variety of disputes, both national and international, widely used and strongly supported by users around the world. Whether it be for trade, construction, investment, sport, employment or religious communities, arbitration has been not only well-regarded in contrast to many state courts and other non-consensual tribunals, but arbitration is often the only "game in town", particularly for transnational disputes.

---

[1] The Alexander lectures are held in honour of Mr J.R.W. Alexander (1897–1985), an early member of the Institute and partly responsible for the Arbitration Act 1934, who served for 40 years as a member of its Council and as its President for 1952–1955. I knew only Mr Leslie Alexander, who joined the Institute in the 1960s and was its President for 1973–74. (See Nigel Watson, *A History of the Chartered Institute of Arbitrators*, 2015).

On Arbitration. Edited by: Sam Wordsworth KC and Marie Veeder, Oxford University Press. © Oxford University Press 2023. DOI: 10.1093/oso/9780192869135.003.0028

'WHAT MATTERS—ABOUT ARBITRATION' 431

The world-wide success of the United Nations' New York Convention of 1958 speaks for itself, with 156 Contracting States: so too, the World Bank's 1965 ICSID Convention, still with 151 Contracting States. So also, the arbitration provisions for investor-state disputes, or ISDS, agreed by some 180 States in more than 3,000 bilateral investment treaties, of which almost half have been made by EU Member States (including 110 signed by the United Kingdom). The 1985 UNCITRAL Model Law of Arbitration has exercised a direct and indirect influence on the national legislation of very many countries with quite different legal traditions over the last 30 years. Not least of these, in England and Wales, influenced by the Model Law, we have the Arbitration Act 1996, a "near-perfect statute" for both domestic and international arbitration. We can never forget the wonderful tribute to the 1996 Act made by Margaret Rutherford and John Sims, both former Presidents of this Institute.[2] In the foreword to their work on the 1996 Act, they wrote of their "unashamed enthusiasm"; and, borrowing from Captain Kirk: "The Arbitration Act is an exciting vehicle to take us boldly into the third millennium."[3] The Act was so exciting, said Margaret Rutherford on another occasion, that she kept a copy by her bedside so as to read it every night, again and again. As Mark Saville used to say, in praise of the Parliamentary Counsel who so elegantly crafted that legislation: "The Act is the best thing since whatever was the best thing before sliced bread."

So, today, life in this 21st Century should be good for arbitration. Yet, there are several who feel that this Panglossian world cannot now long continue; that, like Icarus, arbitration may be flying ever closer to the sun, before plunging into the sea; that the arbitral gods may be taking offence at our collective self-confidence; and that hubris is coming, if it is not already upon us, with increasingly malign results. In my own view, the demise of arbitration, domestic and international, is far from inevitable, provided that we bear in mind certain fundamental matters. The first is that arbitration cannot do everything. It is a private, pragmatic, flexible and consensual creature. It has no imperium, no tipstaffs and no armies. It can exist only with the real consent and active support of its users. Arbitration should not therefore be stretched to encompass disputes that it cannot successfully address, often with minimal consent and negative public support. The result provokes disappointment and, eventually, opposition. However, the fault lies not with the concept of arbitration itself, but with its over-ambitious promoters. If users consent and use arbitration, so be it. To that end, as arbitrators, practitioners and arbitral institutions, we can welcome and add to their suggested reforms. However, if others have no use for arbitration, we should leave them alone.

Second, in this country at least, arbitration is a movement from the bottom-up. It is not imposed from above, by the State or the Prince. Historically, the initiatives

---

[2] Margaret Rutherford QC is a Fellow of the Chartered Institute and was its first woman President in 1992. John Sims is a Fellow of the Chartered Institute and was its President in 1994.
[3] Rutherford and Sims, *Arbitration Act 1996: A Practical Guide* (1996), p.xi.

432   ON ARBITRATION

leading to English arbitration statutes have come from private users, private in-
stitutions, practitioners, arbitrators and judges acting as individuals, not from
Government. This was true of Lord Bramwell's Arbitration Code in the 19th
Century (which led ultimately to the 1889 Act) and, still more so, the League of
Nations' 1923 Geneva Protocol on Arbitration Clauses (the first multilateral treaty
on arbitration). This was particularly true of the curious events leading to the 1996
Act. That statute would never have existed without the private initiatives led by
Arthur Marriott and Mark Littman, each a Fellow of this Institute both of whom
sadly died earlier this year. We shall always remember their pioneering work. We
shall remember another pivotal individual, a former President of this Institute, who
was behind all the reforms to arbitration leading to the 1996 Act, Michael Mustill,
also sadly no longer with us. He brought an intellectual brilliance to the subject,
with the first edition of his book in 1982 (with Stewart Boyd) and his contributions
at the many UNCITRAL meetings on the UNCITRAL Model law. Without him
and the Delphic paragraph 108 in the DAC's Report of 1989 (which he chaired),
there could have been no 1996 Act at all. These were all giants in the recent development of arbitration in England and Wales; and they acted as individuals, motivated by their own knowledge and practical experience of arbitration—not as
mandated representatives of the State.

Third, in order better to defend and explain arbitration to others, we need more
reliable statistical data for what users, arbitrators and courts actually do in regard
to arbitration, particularly users. The DAC had a small statistical sub-committee.
Its research was successfully used by the DAC to justify the abolition of the Special
Categories under the 1979 Act, as it did with its Special Report of 1993. After the
1996 Act, we have seen further attempts to collate statistical data, principally from
the Commercial Court, by the Mance Committee and, most, recently, by Bernard
Eder. These are all useful and interesting; but none are comprehensive or sufficiently user-based; and they clearly do not suffice to explain the practice of arbitration to our critics. For that, we need larger, specialist and more professional
exercises, such as was performed by Professor Hazel Genn for the civil justice reforms introduced by Lord Woolf.

With these three matters in mind, what then can we learn of arbitration's past
for its present and future years? On Sunday, 22 June 1941, a force of three million Germans and their allies, with massed tanks, artillery and aircraft, invaded
the Soviet Union, in the largest land invasion in military history. It was an unprecedented attack without any prior warning, without any justification under international law and in direct violation of the two countries' Non-Aggression Treaty
of 23 August 1939, the so-called Hitler-Stalin Pact, intended (ostensibly) to last at
least ten years, with a further option of five more years. We can be sure that none
of this mattered to Hitler and his colleagues in Berlin. Yet, we can be equally sure
that there was one man in Berlin who felt that the arbitral gods had spoken: that his
professional life, dedicated to arbitration as a peaceful form of resolving disputes,

'WHAT MATTERS—ABOUT ARBITRATION' 433

had come to a complete end. This man's name was Dr Friedrich Gaus. Today we know Dr Gaus only as a shadowy figure standing behind Ribbentrop, Molotov and Stalin, in the photograph of them toasting the success of their negotiations in the Kremlin on the Hitler-Stalin Pact. We also know his name as both a defence and prosecution witness in the Nuremberg War Crimes Trials which began 70 years ago, as from last week.

In 1941, Dr Gaus was the head of the Legal Department in the German Ministry of Foreign Affairs, a post he had held for almost twenty years. He was not and never became a member of the Nazi Party. His wife was Jewish under Nazi laws. He had worked in the Ministry since 1907, successively under the Kaiser, the Weimar Republic and the Third Reich. In that post, Dr Gaus had been responsible for helping to negotiate and draft Germany's arbitration and other treaties, including the Brest-Litovsk treaties of March and August 1918, the Rapallo Treaties of April and December 1921, the innovative German-Swiss arbitration treaty of 1922, the 1925 arbitration treaty with the USSR, the Locarno treaties; and Germany's participation in both the 1919 Versailles Treaty and the Kellogg-Briand Pact of 1928 for the Renunciation of War as an Instrument of National Policy. But, not least of all, he had taken part in drafting the Non-Aggression Treaty of 23 August 1939 between Nazi Germany and the Soviet Union.[4]

That Treaty, with its secret additional protocol, triggered Germany's invasion of Poland and the Second World War; and it still poisons Europe today. Yet the Treaty contained a dispute resolution clause, providing for a form of arbitration in the event of any dispute between Nazi Germany and the Soviet Union. This dispute resolution clause was drafted, at least in part, by Dr Gaus. It bears his handwritten correction to the final German version, made in Moscow, where he had accompanied Ribbentrop (the German Foreign Minister) for the urgent final negotiations with Stalin and the Soviet Foreign Minister, Molotov, on which Germany's imminent invasion of Poland depended. The dispute resolution clause was Article 5 of the Treaty.[5] It provided, in English translation: "Should disputes or conflicts arise between the High Contracting Parties over problems of one kind or another, both Parties shall settle these disputes or conflicts exclusively through friendly exchange of opinions or, if necessary, through the establishment of arbitration commissions."[6] Of course, Article 5 of the Treaty could not prevent Germany's

---

[4] See Gerhard Stuby, *Vom 'Kronjuristen' zum 'Kronzeugen' - Friedrich Wilhelm Gaus: ein Leben im Auswärtigen Amt der Wilhelmstrasse* (2008, Hamburg).

[5] In the original German: "Falls Streitigkeiten order Konflikte zwischen den Vertagschliessenden Teilen über Fragen dieser oder jener Art entstehen sollten, werden beide Teile diese Streitigkeiten oder Konflikte auschliesslich auf dem Wege freundschaftlichen Meinungsaustausches oder nötigenfalls durch Einsetzung von Schlichtungskommissionen bereinigen."

[6] This English translation is taken from the Avalon Project, Nazi-Soviet Relations, Yale: accessible at: avalon.law.yale.edu (last accessed: 8 November 2015). An earlier Soviet draft in similar wording (as article 3) had been handed by Molotov (the Soviet Foreign Minister) to Schulenburg (the German Ambassador in Moscow): see Schulenburg's telegrams to Berlin Nos 187, 189 and 190, all of 19 August 1939: ibid. From other public materials, it seems likely that the treaty's arbitration provision originated

434 ON ARBITRATION

invasion of the Soviet Union, less than two years later. Arbitration, whether state-state, or investor-state, or any other known form of arbitration cannot prevent or solve every conceivable dispute. As the massed German armies advanced towards Moscow, Leningrad and the Caucasus along a 2,000 mile front on that dreadful Sunday morning, it seems highly unlikely that Stalin or Molotov would have given the slightest thought to invoking the Treaty's dispute resolution clause. If we ask too much of arbitration, we breed not only disappointment, but also disillusion and, eventually, derision.

In September 2015, in the name of the European Union for its negotiations with the USA on their proposed trade treaty, the Transatlantic Trade and Investment Partnership, or "TTIP", the European Trade Commissioner, Dr Cecilia Malmström, finally rejected arbitration (ISDS), as an acceptable method of resolving invest-ment disputes under the TTIP's proposed investment chapter between foreign in-vestors and EU Member States, including the European Union itself.[7] On the basis of supposed surveys, consultations and demands from the European Parliament, the Swedish Commissioner concluded that arbitration was a flawed model. In her words: "there is a fundamental and widespread lack of trust by the public in the fairness and impartiality of the old ISDS model. This has significantly affected the public's acceptance of ISDS and of companies bringing such cases." As recently in-terpreted by one visiting professor of trade law at the LSE, arbitrators, arbitration practitioners and companies bringing claims against host States are now, in the eyes of the Commission, to be regarded as a "dodgy" lot.[8] Commentaries in the Press and by NGO's have been even less flattering.[9]

In place of "dodgy" arbitration, the European Commission now proposes for TTIP a new, international investment court, with a court of appeal, to be estab-lished by the European Union. There would be 15 first instance judges and 6 ap-pellate judges. These judges would be appointed for short limited fixed terms, by the European Union and the USA. None would be appointed by investors. In Dr

---

with the Soviet Government, taken from its existing treaties; and that this early draft was later modi-fied by Dr Gaus in Moscow: see J. Degras (ed), *Soviet Documents on Foreign Policy 1933–1941* (1978, New York), pp. 358–360 (Soviet draft of 19 August 1939).

[7] The European Commission published its proposals on 16 September 2015, with its proposed draft text of the TTIP's investment chapter.

[8] I am indebted for the use of this word to Professor Robert Howse (NYU), taken from his address to the BIICL Investment Treaty Forum on 18 September 2015.

[9] For example, the Economist (11.10.2014): ISDS provisions "give foreign firms a special right to apply to a secretive tribunal of highly paid corporate lawyers for compensation whenever a govern-ment passes a law to, say, discourage smoking, protect the environment or prevent a nuclear catas-trophe;" and the Guardian (06.11.14): "Millions of pounds, dollars and euros have been paid to private companies when a secret panel of arbitrators decides the government has overstepped the mark by legislating, say, to make generic drugs more widely available or to stop tobacco companies aggressively marketing to children ... The mechanism is a scandal." As for NGOs, see J.Hilary "TTIP — An End to Democracy", in Chapter 8, *A Charter for Deregulation, an Attack on Jobs* (2014; War on Want/Rosa Luxemburg Stiftung).

Malmström's words, "It will be judges, not arbitrators, who sit on these cases. They must have qualifications comparable to those found in national domestic courts, or in international courts such as the International Court of Justice or the WTO Appellate Body." She continued: "And like in courts, you won't be able to choose which judges hear your case. Furthermore, we will guarantee there is no conflict of interest. Again, like domestic and international courts, the judges won't be able to continue any activities which might interfere with their judicial functions." Hence, it seems that such judges, if working part-time (like members of the WTO Appellate Body), could not work as arbitrators, practitioners, experts, or, possibly, even law professors teaching investment protection or investor-state arbitration.[10]

The Commission's proposals, since further developed, invite several responses, of which only a few can be addressed here.[11] First, the attack on arbitration in the form of an "old" ISDS is odd. ISDS in its current form dates only from the 1965 ICSID Convention and arguably only from 1990; and its spectacular growth began less than 20 years ago.[12] I was a translator in the first ICSID arbitration in the mid-1970s. Apart from the English counsel in that case, no one else I knew in England had ever heard of ICSID or the ICSID Convention. For the history of arbitration, ISDS is therefore scarcely "old". That ISDS has accumulated in such a relatively short time such a massive body of arbitral experience and jurisprudence with multiple users from around the world is, therefore, all the more impressive.[13] Arbitration has become entrenched in the practice of states for disputes involving foreign investors, including, particularly, the USA. It has made over 50 bilateral investment treaties with a provision for investor-state arbitration, together with its multilateral treaties, such as NAFTA, CAFTA and, most recently, the TPP, the Trans-Pacific Partnership agreed with 12 States from the Pacific Rim.[14] There is therefore, little chance that the USA will accept the Commission's proposal for the TTIP to abandon arbitration in favour of a new and untried international investment court to be established unilaterally by the European Union. That would affect not only the TPIP, but also, adversely, the USA's still more desired future trade agreement with China. More likely, at best, the Commission's proposal may form

---

[10] Article 11(1) expressly prohibits any judge from "acting as counsel in any pending or new investment protection dispute under this or any other agreement or domestic law." There is no express rule regarding arbitral or professorial activities.

[11] The European Commission published its further proposals on 12 November 2015. It has since published the agreed text of the EU-Vietnam Free Trade Agreement (of January 2016), with proposals for a similar international tribunal and appellate tribunal (Ch.8) and the amended text of CETA on 29 February 2016 (see below).

[12] The first BIT between Germany and Pakistan in 1959 contained no provision for ISDS; and ICSID's first BIT arbitration was *AAPL v Sri Lanka* (Award 27 June 1990) ICSID Case No. ARB/87/3; 4 ICSID Rep 250.

[13] Its substantive achievements can be seen from ICSID's recent publication: Kinnear et al (eds), *Building International Investment Law: The First 50 Years of ICSID* (Wolters Kluwer. 2016).

[14] The TTP contains a provision for ISDS: see Chapter 9 (Investment), Section B, Articles 9.18ff with a choice of the ICSID Convention, the ICSID Additional Facility Rules, the UNCITRAL Rules or (if the disputing parties agree) any other arbitral institution or any other arbitration rules.

436 ON ARBITRATION

part of an inchoate annex in the TTIP with a general commitment to replace its orthodox ISDS provision if and when other States can be persuaded to subscribe to the new court, so as to make it a truly international investment court. That is what the CAFTA States agreed in regard to a possible appellate arbitration tribunal. However, no agreement has yet been reached between the CAFTA States or with any other States; and this appeal tribunal remains an inchoate proposal. That same fate may await the Commission's proposal, if there is to be any TTIP with an investment chapter at all. At times, it does seem that ISDS has become an easy target for those opposed to TTIP as a whole or to any form of treaty-based globalisation of transnational trade and services.

How could the European Commission establish this new investment court? If the political will was there, it could of course be done. The Nuremberg War Crimes Tribunal was established within six months of the London Conference; but that was a military tribunal established by common consent of the four Allies. The Commission's proposal would be much more difficult and take much longer to achieve with 28 EU Member States, likely to be measured in years or even decades. As to expense, we know from our own new UK Supreme Court how expensive was its modest conversion from a Parliamentary Committee in the House of Lords to a new specialist building, both as regards capital costs and operating costs. Quite apart from the costs of refurbishing and maintaining its new building, the UK Supreme Court's operating costs have jumped from £1.1 million to over £13 million. A new international investment court, with a permanent registry and associated library, properly housed and staffed, will probably cost several hundred million Euros to set up, together with substantial annual operating costs. The EU's Luxembourg Courts have annual operating costs of about 415 million Euros (equivalent to about US\$ 440 million). The WTO's total annual budget is almost 200 million Swiss Francs, equivalent to US\$ 195 million. (That, of course, includes more than the WTO Appellate Body). The current system of arbitration seems to be significantly less expensive (being also largely cost-free for most States, including the UK). For example, ICSID covers most of its operating costs with fees from users, with in-house contributions from the World Bank limited this year to US\$ 8.5 million. Expense, time and delay may not, of course, discourage the European Commission.[15] As to likely case-load, the proposed 21 judges are either too many or too few. Too many because it may take years before the first cases reach the court; and too few because, if successful, subsequent numbers may swamp the court, just as investment cases now flood ICSID, the PCA, the Stockholm Chamber (SCC), the ICC, the LCIA and ad hoc arbitration.

---

[15] The money will not, apparently, be spent on paying the judges' salaries: the first instance judges are to be paid a monthly retainer of about 2,000 Euros; and the appellate judges are to receive a monthly retainer of 7,000 Euros.

'WHAT MATTERS—ABOUT ARBITRATION' 437

How would the European Union choose its judges? Agreeing a closed list of EU judges will not be easy with 28 EU member states. Nor will it be easy for the participating States to agree the list of neutral judges. For example, it has proven impossible for the three NAFTA States to agree their proposed roster of tribunal presidents for Chapter 11 arbitrations, even after more than a decade in the attempt.[16] Why should a much more ambitious exercise be easer for the European Commission? And where will the Court be established? It must be, of course, a neutral place. Having put aside party autonomy, we should not expect the Commission to abandon the traditional principle of a neutral venue for the new investment court. So the court's venue cannot lie within the European Union, such as Luxembourg or The Hague or even European countries closely associated with the EU, such as Switzerland and Norway. Subject to the result of our own EU referendum, that may leave only Russia, but that European venue would have its detractors. So, if we exclude Europe and also the USA and Canada as parties to the new EU treaties (TTIP and CETA[17]), it probably only leaves Iceland. That could be an ideal place, geographically convenient for, or at least relatively proximate to the EU and USA. However, if the court is to become a truly international investment court for multiple participating States, the venue should perhaps be located in Asia or Africa, say Singapore, Hong Kong, Mauritius or Kigali. Last, but not least, how will the judgments of this investment court be recognised and enforced? It cannot be the New York or ICSID Conventions. Doubtless, as always, the Commission may have an undisclosed cunning plan, but could it ever work on a world-wide legal basis outside the European Union?

Let us, however, leave aside all these practical matters. The question is what we should do now with the Commission's proposals: Arbitrators, arbitration practitioners and, dare I say it, even arbitral institutions, are not the most persuasive advocates for arbitration. We are, of course, thoroughly objective and fair-minded people; but what we say in defence of arbitration can often seem to others as self-interested. Rather like Ms Rice-Davies famously during the Profumo Inquiry, "they would say that, wouldn't they". There have been notable exceptions. In particular,

---

[16] Article 1124(4) required the three NAFTA States, in 1994: "to establish, and thereafter maintain, a roster of 45 presiding arbitrators meeting the qualifications of the [ICSID] Convention and rules referred to in Article 1120 and experienced in international law and investment matters. The roster members shall be appointed by consensus and without regard to nationality." The EU has had, however, little difficulty to date in nominating "judges" for inter-state trade disputes, most recently with Korea and Singapore. Such trade disputes do not include private claims for damages, the hallmark for an ISDS provision.

[17] The original text of CETA, the Comprehensive Economic and Trade Agreement between Canada and the EU, contains a provision for ISDS: see Ch.10, s.6 (26 September 2014). The subsequent text of 29 February 2016 contains no ISDS provision. It provides for an international tribunal with an appeal tribunal, comprised of members (not "arbitrators") appointed by the two States: see Ch.8. Most significantly, it is there agreed that, eventually, this bilateral system will be replaced with a multilateral system agreed with other States. (This text is much developed beyond the text agreed for the EU–Vietnam Free Trade Agreement of January 2016.)

438   ON ARBITRATION

Peter Goldsmith has led the defence of ISDS in this country, much to his credit. It would have been less difficult if more users of ISDS had taken up that burden, with the active support of BIS. For some reason, that has not happened. It is perhaps not hard to see why. Either the significant users will bring their influence to bear on the US side of the TTIP negotiations, with an executive branch far more receptive to the needs of foreign investors; or, if ISDS disappears from the TTIP, these users will resort to concession agreements or procure foreign investment laws with arbitration provisions, each providing for consensual and, doubtless also, confidential forms of arbitration. We shall then return, perversely, to the days when non-transparency ruled investor-state arbitration.

We have also had to deal with several highly damaging events, affecting perceptions for both domestic and international arbitration. The worst of these events is the continuing Tapie case in France. This was a domestic arbitration between the businessman M. Bernard Tapie and the French State, as the legal successor to M. Tapie's creditor bank, the Crédit Lyonnais. At first, M. Tapie brought legal proceedings against the French State in the French courts, to little avail after series of minor victories and defeats on procedural issues lasting more than ten years. Then, to cut these procedural wrangles short, the disputant parties agreed to refer the merits of their dispute to arbitration in France, under an ad hoc arbitration submission before three senior and distinguished French jurists. The first was Me Jean-Denis Bredin, a member of the académie française; the second, who acted as the tribunal's president, was Me Pierre Mazeaud, a former president of the constitutional council; and the third was M. Pierre Estoup, a retired professional judge and former president of the Versailles Court of Appeal. A unanimous award was made by these three arbitrators on 7 July 2008. Together with three further consequential awards, the tribunal ordered the French State to pay 403 million Euros to Mr Tapie. Their award included 45 million Euros as moral damages. These sums were duly paid to M. Tapie. Then all hell broke loose.

First, there was a strong public reaction to the French State having even agreed to arbitration, as opposed to litigation in its own courts and, worse, having to pay anything under an arbitration award made by three private individuals. There was particular outrage at the award of moral damages to a man who had served time in prison and who was regarded by many as having no morals to be damaged. In vain, Me Serge Lazareff, then the president of the arbitration commission of the French committee of the ICC; and Me Yves Derains, as the president of the French committee of arbitration, wrote a public letter on 31 July 2008 defending the French system of consensual arbitration, including arbitration by States. Then, as a result of criminal investigations in Paris, it appeared that M. Estoup, the arbitrator appointed by M. Tapie, had undisclosed close links with both M. Tapie himself and, in particular, M. Tapie's lawyer in the arbitration. From documents seized from the three arbitrators during police raids at their homes and offices, it also appeared that the award had been substantially drafted by M. Estoup alone. It was also suggested that M. Estoup was party to a criminal conspiracy to fix the result of the arbitration, without the knowledge of his two co-arbitrators. It also began to appear that, from the outset, the arbitration submission had been secretly agreed at several private meetings between M. Tapie and President Sarkozy. It was in effect, so it was suggested, a disguised form of settlement with a pre-determined result, improperly motivated by political reasons.

On 17 February 2015, the Paris Court of Appeal annulled the awards on the ground of fraud in the arbitration. It also adjudged the arbitration as a domestic arbitration under French law, reserving to itself a further judgment where it would decide upon the merits, or demerits, of the parties' dispute. That second civil judgment is currently awaited; and this scandal rumbles on.[18] It may be years before the criminal proceedings are concluded. In the meantime, however it all ends, the Tapie case has badly scarred the traditional confidence and respect which arbitration has generally enjoyed in France. That may change in time. What may not change soon is the attitude to arbitration of French judges and administrators to arbitration. It may no longer be seen as the pristine activity of a respected elite, operating above national laws. The French courts have traditionally been gentle with awards, particularly international awards. That may now no longer be true. It is already clear that the Commission's proposals for a new investment court, in place of arbitration, are now strongly supported by France.

This was not a good year for arbitration elsewhere, particularly the Philip Morris cases attacking national legislations on plain paper packaging for tobacco. We could also consider the Yukos ECT cases with the unprecedented attack on the arbitration tribunal and its assistant secretary; the investment arbitrations and court proceedings brought by the Swedish investor, Vattenfall, and its operators against Germany, seeking compensation for over US$ 5 billion; the Micula case under the Sweden-Romania BIT of 2002 where the European Commission has intervened to thwart the host State's performance of its international obligations under the ICSID Convention; and also the recent distressing events in the PCA arbitration between Slovenia and Croatia at The Hague.

Time, however, allows us to consider only the Philip Morris cases. As to the first case brought by Philip Morris against Uruguay under the Switzerland-Uruguay BIT of 1988, we are now awaiting from the arbitration tribunal an award on the merits after the recent hearing at ICSID, following that tribunal's decision of 2 July 2013 rejecting the host State's jurisdictional objections. As to the second case brought against Australia under the Hong Kong-Australia BIT of 1993, we expect soon the UNCITRAL arbitration tribunal's decision on Australia's jurisdictional

---

[18] The second judgment of the Paris Court of Appeal has since been issued on 3 December 2015. It decided that the French state bore no liability to Mr Tapie, who was ordered to repay the sums paid under the annulled awards. There may still be appeals to the Cour de cassation.

440 ON ARBITRATION

objections.[19] If either result is adverse to the host State, we can expect new outrage from the European Parliament, the European Commission and others condemning arbitration, including France and Germany. There will then be still further support for an international investment court with state-appointed judges (policed by an appellate court) who could be relied upon to decide such cases very differently. If, however, these two cases are decided against Philip Morris, we shall probably hear little. The hostility towards NAFTA and TPP in the USA, including the criticisms made by Senator Warren, is not in the least diminished by the fact that the USA has never yet lost any NAFTA arbitration. Indeed, Senator Warren (as Professor Warren from Harvard) was a legal expert witness for the USA in its successful defence against the first NAFTA claimants in the Loewen arbitration. She knows as an experienced jurist how arbitration works, which makes her political criticisms of ISDS all the more disturbing.

In conclusion, I return to Dr Gaus and Icarus. As arbitration specialists, we cannot now realistically hope to defeat, by ourselves, the European Commission in its proposals for an international investment court. The major European users of ISDS have not persuaded the Commission otherwise, so how can we succeed in their place with much less standing and presumed self-interest? There will therefore be some amongst us who will be tempted to give the Commission's proposals a guarded welcome and support. There is some idea that investment arbitration, with an existing registry, can somehow be morphed with an international investment court, so as to produce the best of all possible worlds. This would, I suggest, be a grave mistake. Consensual arbitration and court proceedings are two very different creatures. Arbitration in the form of ISDS can co-exist separately with an international investment court, just as it does with state courts and other tribunals. If users want arbitration, arbitration will continue, as it has always. Arbitration, including investment arbitration, should not depend for its existence upon the European Commission and European Parliament. As private individuals and institutions, we could still do much, by ourselves, to meet the demands of users and to improve arbitration generally. In England and Wales, we could even upgrade the 1996 Act from a near-perfect statute to a perfect statute, suitable as bedtime reading for all.[20]

As to all that, I shall finish where I began in regard to our need for more comprehensive statistical data on arbitration. Many years ago, in 1997, Lord Peston delivered the Bernstein Lecture in the Middle Temple Hall. As the Labour front-bench

---

[19] This award was issued 17 December 2015, upholding Australia's jurisdictional objections. (It is not yet publicly available).

[20] As for permanent "Sharia courts" operating as arbitration tribunals under the 1996 Act (said to number between 30 to 85 in the UK), the Home office has begun an inquiry following concerns that they operate a parallel system of justice that discriminates against Muslim women and children: see the "Times" of 22 December 2015 (pp. 2d & 33b). This follows Baroness Cox's several attempts in the House of Lords to amend the 1996 Act with her Arbitration and Mediation Services (Equality) Bill.

spokesman in the House of Lords on the Arbitration Bill, Lord Peston had led his party's support for the Bill in 1995 introduced by the Conservative government. As an economist (like his broadcaster son), he had had to learn quickly about the law and practice of arbitration. Increasingly, Lord Peston had become, in one word, appalled. A year after the Arbitration Act 1996, he told me privately that if he had known then all that he learnt later, he would have opposed the Arbitration Bill. This is what he said publicly in his Bernstein lecture in 1997:[21] "I would like to see some continuing monitoring and research on arbitration under the new law. To emphasise my concern, let me list some of the questions I have asked myself in preparation for this lecture which I am unable to answer" He then listed ten specific questions. Almost 20 years later, there are still no adequate statistical answers to his questions. What he, as an economist, needed, he said, was facts, not anecdotes or theories; and he concluded with these words: "Ways must be found of placing more information about what happens in practice in the hands of first class researchers. Their work might well lead to improvements in how arbitrations operate. Although these are early days, and a later generation will have the responsibility, we must recognise that some time in the future there will be a new arbitration act, and I for one would like to see it research based, and evolving from the monitoring of the 1996 Act." We are now that later generation. Arbitration, always flexible, has indeed evolved since the 1996 Act, as has ISDS. Too late, we have clearly failed sufficiently to research and report the statistical facts for investment arbitration; and we can now see the baleful result in the European Commission's proposals.[22] Let not the same be said of arbitration itself, particularly in this country with its long tradition and rich experience of arbitration over the centuries. We all need to know whether, as Isaiah Berlin would put it, arbitration is to be a fox or a hedgehog. Of all things, perhaps, that is now what matters most about arbitration.

[21] Peston, "The 1997 Bernstein Colloquium: Arbitration — An Economist's View" (1998) 64 *Arbitration* 19.
[22] A notable, albeit recent, exception would include Dr Lauge Poulsen, *Bounded Rationality and Economic Diplomacy* (2015, Cambridge).

29

Lessons for the Future from the Past

Individual Hedgehogs and Institutional Foxes
(Tenth Kaplan Lecture, 23 November 2016)

A. Introduction

In preparing for this lecture, searching for a topic relating to Hong Kong and China, I was shown an article by Neil Kaplan on 'The History and Development of Arbitration in Hong Kong', published in 1996 – twenty years ago.[1] As you would expect from the author, it is a fascinating article on the origins of modern arbitration in Hong Kong, beginning with the arrival in 1841 of Hong Kong's first senior colonial officer, Governor Pottinger, who introduced an Arbitration Ordinance in 1844. The ordinance was subsequently disallowed by the Colonial Office in London for spurious reasons; but it is clear that the idea of arbitration did not come from Governor Pottinger alone, but also from others dealing with commercial disputes at a time where there was no Supreme Court in Hong Kong. Who were these others, influenced by English and Chinese users seeking the resolution of their disputes by arbitration? It made me think of others largely unknown in other countries, who were also not governors, but who played a crucial part, as individuals, in the history and development of international commercial arbitration.

It is a fact that most armies, in practice, usually succeed or fail on the work not of their generals and staff but, rather of their captains and ordinary soldiers. The generals, as with governors, are rarely forgotten, with statues to their name. In the field of arbitration, who are the equivalent of these captains working with its ordinary users? Their names may be well known to some in their own life-time; and in their life-time, each may be much respected within their own community. As time passes, their names and contributions are forgotten, even though, indirectly, their influence may continue to be felt far beyond the community in which they worked. This is the story of four such individuals, each of whom, I suggest, made a significant contribution in the long term to the current system of international commercial arbitration. Each acted, in the delphic phrase made famous by Sir Isaiah Berlin, as hedgehogs

---

[1] Y.B. *Int'l Fin. & Econ. L.* 203 (1996). I am grateful to Ms Maria-Krystyna Duval for bringing this material to my attention.

On Arbitration. Edited by: Sam Wordsworth KC and Marie Veeder, Oxford University Press. © Oxford University Press 2023. DOI: 10.1093/oso/9780192869135.003.0029

LESSONS FOR THE FUTURE FROM THE PAST   443

who knew one big thing and not as foxes who knew many things.[2] Without initiatives from such individuals, international arbitration could not have developed as a pragmatic system of dispute resolution responsive to its users, mostly unlimited by geography and largely in disregard for political and economic differences.

B. Pavel Mincs

This story starts in the birthplace of Isaiah Berlin, the town of Riga in the Russian province of Livonia, now the capital of Latvia. Latvia was the birthplace of Pavel Mincs, a figure now almost unknown even in Latvia. Mincs was born in 1868, some forty years before Isaiah Berlin, but from the same Jewish community in this mixed province dominated by Russian and German-speaking traders and merchants, exporting lumber and other goods to Western Europe. Mincs attended secondary school in Riga, graduated from the law school in St. Petersburg and received his post-graduate degree from Tartu University in Livonia. He first worked as a professional lawyer in Riga; and then, as a 'dozent' or law professor at Moscow University in Czarist Russia.

For many years before 1917, Czarist Russia had favoured the amicable settlement of certain disputes by means of international arbitration. For disputes between States, it was a Czarist initiative that led to the Hague Peace Conferences in 1899 and 1907 and the establishment of the Permanent Court of Arbitration (the 'PCA'). In particular, it was the intellectual energy of the Russian legal representative at the First Hague Conference, F.F. Martens, who was largely responsible for this remarkable achievement.[3] Of course, most unfairly, it is the large portrait of Czar Nicholas II, as the general, which has dominated the Small Arbitration Room in the Peace Palace at The Hague – and not the arbitration captain Martens. As for Russian domestic arbitration between private persons, Russian law in Czarist times was primitive, even for disputes between commercial parties. Following the end of Czarist rule in February 1917, there was a new Minister of Justice under the Provisional Government, the non-marxist socialist, Kerensky. In his ministry, a young law professor was put in charge of arbitration law reform. He was Professor Pavel Mincs.

---

[2] The phrase came from a poem by the ancient Greek poet, Archilochus. It remains unclear (at least to me) quite what Sir Isaiah Berlin meant by this phrase in *The Hedgehog and the Fox: An Essay on Tolstoy's View of History* (1953). Ronald Dworkin used the same phrase to propagate the idea that ethical and moral values depend upon one another, in *Justice for Hedgehogs* (2001). Here, it is used to contrast an individual's pursuit of a particular objective for the common good with an institution pursuing multiple competing ambitions for itself.

[3] V.V. Pustogarov, *Our Martens: F.F. Martens: International Lawyer and Architect of Peace* (translated W.E. Butler, 2000); *see also* W.E. Butler, *Russia and the Law of Nations in Historical Perspective* (2009), pp. 264ff. F.F. Martens (1845–1909), who also called himself Friedrich Fromholz von Martens, was born in Livonia (now Latvia). His bust is now displayed, very belatedly, in the Small Arbitration Room at the Peace Palace.

444   ON ARBITRATION

In the chaos of an incomplete revolution, a desperate war with the Central Powers and the invasion by German troops deep into Russian territory, Professor Mincs drafted a new Russian arbitration law, with an historical commentary drawing on Roman, French and German laws.[4] There was a precedent in the years following the French Revolution, where, as with Czarist Russia, there was profound mistrust of the old regime's state courts. The early revolutionary laws in France (1790–1793) guaranteed a citizen's right to have recourse to arbitration, which was advocated for users as the most rational method of resolving private disputes.[5]

This draft Russian law, taking the form of amendments to the old Czarist laws, was never enacted by the Russian legislature. As we know too well, there was a second revolution, or coup d'état, in October 1917; and arbitration under the new Soviet regime took a different direction. There was still to be a limited form of domestic arbitration between private persons enacted under the Soviet Civil Procedure Code of 1923; but after the end of the New Economic Policy in the late 1920s, that was made ineffective. In the 1920s, international commercial arbitration was frequently agreed between Soviet Russia and foreign traders and concessionaires; but after 1930, with the final demise of foreign concessions, that form of ad hoc international arbitration was abandoned by the USSR. However, the restructuring of Soviet foreign trade in the early 1930s ensured that international commercial arbitration revived with the foundation in Moscow of the Maritime Arbitration Commission in 1930 and of the Foreign Trade Arbitration Commission in 1932 (itself much later the model in China after its revolution in 1949 for FTAC, later renamed FETAC and CIETAC). Both Soviet arbitral institutions still exist in the Russian Federation, with the later re-formed and now called the International Commercial Arbitration Court. For a marxist-socialist country, with a centrally planned economy, it is perhaps hard to understand why the USSR continued to be interested in international commercial arbitration, whilst so hostile to international courts generally and, ostensibly, to its own legal history. It shows that foreign trade has its own apolitical imperatives; and, as with foreign trade, so too international commercial arbitration. It is a hard lesson for some to learn and re-learn; but, as some say, international arbitration remains 'the only game in town', with every available alternative worse.

Thus, in June 1946, Soviet arbitration specialists attended the first conference convened by the ICC in Paris, with a view to agreeing a uniform procedural law

---

[4] The Mincz article and draft law were published in the Ministry of Justice's Journal of May-June 1917, Issues Nos 5–6, pp. 154ff. In 2005, these materials were re-published in 'Treteiskii Sud' (Nos. 1, 2, 3 and 4) of 2005.

[5] R. David, *L'arbitrage dans le Commerce International* (1981), pp. 126ff. As with Soviet Russia, private arbitration soon waned as the French Revolution developed into the Directorate and the Empire: *see* J-J Clère, 'L'Arbitrage Révolutionaire: Apogée et Déclin d'une Institution' (1790–1806) 1981 *Rev.arb* 3.

for international arbitration and improving upon the system of enforcing arbitration agreements and awards under the League of Nations' Geneva Protocol of 1923 and the Geneva Convention of 1927. An earlier attempt to do so by Professor René David, then of UNIDROIT, had failed in 1936. The so-called UNIDROIT draft model law had then been successfully opposed by the United Kingdom and its Dominions, for reasons which now seem at least obscure, if not mistaken. Neither the USSR nor the USA, for different reasons, had acceded to the arbitration treaties of the League of Nations. Now, in 1946 with the Cold War already begun, arbitration specialists from many countries met for three days at the ICC's headquarters in Paris to plan what eventually became the ICC's draft treaty of 1952/1953 leading to the United Nations' 1958 New York Arbitration Convention. It is significant that these specialists did not represent States, but attended as members of 'the emerging community of arbitration practitioners itself'.[6]

The names in the ICC's minutes of this meeting of June 1946 are familiar.[7] They include Dr Pieter Sanders, then still the secretary to the Dutch Prime Minister; René David, now a Professor in Paris, and also from France, Jean Robert and René Arnaud; and from the ICC itself, Fréderic Eisemann. There were other specialists from many international institutions: the International Law Association, the Inter-American Commercial Arbitration Commission and the Canadian-American Commercial Arbitration Commission, and others. The British specialists were few, reflecting the United Kingdom's then indifference to the ICC: Sir Kenneth Lee, a banker, and Mr J.G. Allanby, the Registrar of the London Court of Arbitration (now the 'LCIA'). The Soviet specialists came from the Maritime Arbitration and Foreign Trade Arbitration Commissions, including Professor Dimitri Ramzaitsev. He was a senior law professor and a legal specialist in foreign trade and international commercial arbitration. The USSR was not indifferent to the development of international commercial arbitration. It was to be one of the first Contracting States to accede to the 1958 New York Arbitration Convention; and its arbitration specialists (including Professor Ramzaitsev) were early supporters of ICCA, hosting the fourth ICCA conference in Moscow in 1972. (These also included the late Professor Lebedev, the chairman of the Maritime Arbitration Commission for many years and a strong supporter of the 1958 New York Convention and the 1985 UNCITRAL Model Law.)

The lesson is two-fold. The movement towards a new regime for international commercial arbitration was no longer comprised of States. It had been so with the League of Nations and UNIDROIT; but now it now came from a community of

---

[6] T. Hale, *Between Interests and Law: The Politics of Transnational Commercial Disputes* (2015), pp. 129ff.
[7] I am grateful to Professor Jérôme Sgard for sending me a copy of these ICC minutes which he found in the archives of Columbia University, NY. *See also* his chapter 'A Tale of Three Cities' in *Contractual Knowledge, A Hundred Years of Legal Experimentation in Global Markets* (2017).

arbitration specialists and users. There were no States attending this ICC conference in 1946; and, without these specialists, there would have been no ICC draft or New York Convention. Second, the Mincs draft of 1917 remained unknown to foreign scholars as a public document until 2005, when it was published in a Russian arbitration journal long after the end of Soviet rule.[8] Yet its text and commentary cannot have been unknown to those Soviet jurists who worked on the text of the 1923 Soviet Civil Procedural Code, the foreign trade reforms of the early 1930s and from 1946 onwards the attempts at the ICC and the United Nations to promote international commercial arbitration, culminating in the 1958 New York Convention. This is a period of only forty years, less than a working lifetime. After October 1917, the old legal institutions from Czarist times and from the Provisional Government disappeared and their laws proscribed, but the individual jurists remained the same individuals. Many of the new professors had been the same old professors.

For example, the Soviet Russian Civil Code of 1922 was drafted within four months, largely in response to foreign criticisms before and during the 1922 Genoa Economic Conference (influenced by the British Prime Minister, David Lloyd George) that Soviet Russia had no system of law sufficient to support any inward foreign investment in the form of concession agreements. This drafting exercise was a formidable achievement in such a short time; but it was of course impossible to draft such a code from scratch. In fact, there was no blank piece of paper. The new so-called first socialist civil code was drafted with the active support of individual jurists who had been Czarist professors working for many years on a new draft Czarist civil code dating way back to 1903 and much influenced by the civil codes of Germany, France and Switzerland, none marxist-socialist legal systems. For political reasons, that intellectual inheritance could never be acknowledged publicly at the time or later by Soviet commentators; but privately it was generally known. After the end of Soviet rule, it has at last been acknowledged. For example, in a recent translation of the current Russian Civil Code, it is said in the preface co-written by a senior Russian jurist: 'In the early years of the twentieth century, a Russian government commission published an excellent civil law codification in draft form, along with extensive commentary. War and revolution prevented this draft from becoming law, but the drafters of the Civil Code of 1922 drew on it – along with foreign sources – in a hasty but successful effort to provide a legislative basis for the emerging free market under the New Economic Policy of the early 1920s.'[9] It is unfortunate that political imperatives

---

[8] *See* footnote 5 above.

[9] *See* O.M. Kozyr, P. B. Maggs & A.N Zhiltsov, Introduction, *Civil Code of the Russian Federation – First Part*, (2016); *see also* W.E. Butler, *Russian Law*, (2003, 2nd ed.) p. 359.

seek to wipe clean the historical contribution of such individual draftsmen, along with their texts.

Hence, it is right that we should look more closely at the life of Professor Mincs. Pavel Mincs was his Latvian name. His Jewish name was Shmuel Favel Mintz. He emigrated from Russia in 1918 during the Civil War; and from 1921 he worked as a law professor at the University of Latvia, now an independent state and a member of the League of Nations. He became a Latvian politician, eventually the leader of the Latvian Jewish National-Democratic Party. He co-authored the Latvian constitution and was a Senator, a State Controller and a member of the Latvian Cabinet as Minister of Labour. Later, he acted as the interim president of the Latvian Supreme Court. From his legal bibliography, it does seem, regrettably, that after 1917 his legal interests lay in the field of criminal law and not arbitration. His younger brother was Dr Vladimir Mintz. He had also studied at Tartu University and from 1897 worked as a surgeon in Czarist Russia. After the Bolshevik Revolution, he became one of Lenin's personal doctors. Upon treating Lenin, successfully, after the failed assassination by Fanny Kaplan in 1918 he asked Lenin to allow him to return to Riga; and, in gratitude for his medical skills, he was granted permission to emigrate from Soviet Russia.

In August 1941, following the German invasion of the USSR, Dr Mintz was arrested by the Nazis and died in Buchenwald concentration camp in 1945. His brother, Professor Pavel Mincs, was already dead. He had been arrested in Latvia in 1940 by its earlier invaders, the USSR, following the USSR's annexation of Latvia under the Soviet-Nazi Pact of August 1939. Pavel Mincs was deported from Latvia (with his family); and he died in a prison at Taishet in early 1941, on his way to the Siberian camps. With his brother's death four years later, it is a tragic and European story. We know little more than this of Professor Pavel Mincs, the arbitration captain; and yet there must be much more to his life and work still to be found in Latvian and Russian archives. From what little we do know, what is the lesson for us today? From a small step, in terrible times, a draft law during the short-lived Provisional Government caused a seed to be sown in Russian legal minds favourable to arbitration. It was not the only seed; but, with others in and outside Russia, it grew in time into the great oak-tree we now know as international commercial arbitration, which, with the New York Convention and the Amended UNCITRAL Model Law, overshadows revolutions, political differences and economic changes.

C. Dr Gaus

From Riga, we go to Berlin. Before 1933, Germany, particularly Berlin, was the world centre of international arbitration. The names of many of its captains

448   ON ARBITRATION

remain well known: Martin Domke, Arthur Nussbaum, E.J. Cohn, Otto Kahn-Freund, Francis Mann and Heinrich Freund. The names of certain of its other captains are less well-known, including Dr Friedrich Gaus. Dr Gaus was the head of the legal department of the German Foreign Office from 1922 to 1943 (the Auswärtiges Amt or 'AA'). He was a specialist in international law and arbitration, having drafted several arbitration treaties for Weimar Germany, including the 1925 Treaty of Arbitration between Germany and the USSR. He had also attended the Versailles Peace Conference in 1919 and the Genoa and Hague Conferences in 1922; and he later took part in the drafting in Moscow of the 1939 Nazi-Soviet Pact.

In 1933, there were several international commercial arbitrations taking place in Germany, under consensual arbitration clauses falling under the 1925 German-Soviet Treaty of Arbitration. One of these arbitrations in Hamburg concerned a dispute between a private German company and a Soviet state trading company, each of whom had appointed a German and Soviet arbitrator respectively in accordance with their arbitration clause. The third arbitrator, a German, was appointed by the German Court, as provided by the parties' arbitration clause. However, there was in January 1933 a well-known political change in Germany, as also in April 1933 to its laws relating to arbitrators. There thus came a challenge by the German company to the Soviet arbitrator on the ground that he was disqualified to be an arbitrator under the new Nazi laws against non-Aryans. Under Article 1032(3) of the new 1933 Nazi Code of Civil Procedure (ZPO), non-Aryans could not be arbitrators. The leading German textbook on civil procedure confirmed this general prohibition.[10] The German Court upheld the challenge and removed the Soviet arbitrator under the Nazi ZPO.

In Moscow, that decision was the subject of a highly critical article in *Izvestia* on 18 August 1933 by Professor A.G. Goikhbarg of the USSR Ministry of Foreign Trade's Legal Department.[11] He deplored the malign political influence of Nazi ministers on German judges and suggested that Soviet-German commercial disputes should be arbitrated not in Germany but 'at some neutral location',

---

[10] Article 1032(3) ZPO 1933, on persons legally incompetent to act as arbitrators, provided: '... *Abgelehnt werden können ferner Nichtarier im Sinne des gesetzes zur Wiederherstellung des Berufsbeamtentums vom 7. April 1933 (Reichsgesetzbl. I, S. 175) und der dazu ergangenen Durchfuöhrungsverordnungen.'* See Jonas, ed., Kommentar zur Zivilprozessordnung, (1939, 16th ed). Dr M.R. Jonas, as an officer in the German Ministry of Justice, appears to have been involved in the drafting of this provision in the Nazi ZPO. *See also* Adolf Schönke, *Die Schiedsgerichtsbarkeit*, Vol. 1 (1944), pp. 107 & 86. The cited Nazi law of 7 April 1933 'for the restoration of the professional civil service' excluded non-Aryans from German public service, including the German judiciary: *see* http:// www.documentarchiv.de/ns/beamtenges.html. For Nazi laws racially discriminating against German lawyers and judges generally, *see* J. Beatson and R. Zimmerman, eds., *Jurists Uprooted: German Speaking Emigré Lawyers in Twentieth-Century Britain* (2004).

[11] Doc 1, 370, 371 (Pol Archiv des AA R94759). Professor A.G. Goikhbarg had been one of the draftsmen for the 1922 Soviet Civil Code and its earlier Czarist drafts before 1917: *see* Butler (*ibid*) p. 359.

LESSONS FOR THE FUTURE FROM THE PAST   449

thereby questioning the continuing efficacy of the 1925 Treaty. That in turn led to diplomatic exchanges between the USSR and Nazi Germany. Internally, the German Foreign Office in Berlin decided to seek the legal opinion of its own legal department as to the effect of the new Nazi ZPO on the 1925 Treaty. The German archives do not identify those who issued the legal opinion; but, as the most senior legal adviser in the AA and as a co-draftsman of the 1925 Treaty, that opinion almost certainly would have been prepared or approved by Dr Gaus.[12]

The AA's legal opinion dated 15 January 1934 explained that such an international arbitration in Germany was materially different from a domestic German arbitration.[13] In addition to the parties' arbitration clause, the 1925 Treaty provided for international arbitration in either Germany or the USSR, with the right of the Soviet party to appoint any national of the USSR. There were few non-Aryans in the USSR as defined by Nazi laws; and such a limitation on qualified nationals would therefore subvert the object and purpose of the 1925 Treaty, effectively requiring the Soviet Party to appoint an Aryan *German* arbitrator and not a Soviet arbitrator at all. As explained in the opinion: 'In actual fact it cannot be dismissed that the interests of the USSR may be negatively affected by the carrying out of the new German law ... For the Russians, there would therefore be a significant restriction to the group of persons whom they may appoint as arbitrators in Germany.' The legal opinion concluded that the prohibition on non-Aryan arbitrators in the Nazi ZPO referred only to such persons 'who can also be considered in Germany as officials ["Beamte"], i.e., only German members of the Reich.' It did not apply to Soviet nationals appointed as arbitrators in an international arbitration tribunal. From a sense of caution, this opinion was subject to confirmation by the Ministry of Justice. The German Ministry of Justice confirmed the AA's opinion.[14]

Thus, the objection to non-Aryan Soviet arbitrators appointed by a Soviet party to an arbitration in Germany was rejected by the German Government's own arbitration specialists. Given the political times, this was a somewhat unusual and brave decision. Yet, its reasoning makes complete sense to us, quite apart from the rejection of the infamous Nazi ZPO. Domestic arbitration is different in principle from international commercial arbitration; and that distinction remains an important factor under many national laws on arbitration. With hindsight, this was

---

[12] The opinion was issued by the AA's Russian Department IVA and sent (*inter alios*) to Dr M.R. Jonas at the Ministry of Justice under cover of a letter dated 18 January 1934 (signed by Dr Hey).

[13] Doc I.372, *ibid.*

[14] The Ministry of Justice supported the AA's opinion, concluding: '... bei einem Schiedsgerichtsverfahren mit einem [Aus]lander für die Ablehnung eines von dem Ausländer # 1032 Abs. 3 Satz 2 kein Raum ist.' (signed by Dr Volkmar).

450   ON ARBITRATION

another small but significant seed, albeit sown in the most terrible of times. So who was the sower of this seed?

Dr Gaus was not and never became a Nazi, one of the very few senior figures in the German Foreign Office who were not to join the National Socialist Party (voluntarily or otherwise). He was technically an Aryan under Nazi laws; but his wife was not. She was considered Jewish and therefore at great risk of arrest, deportation and worse. They somehow survived Nazi rule and the Second World War, apparently under the personal protection of successive German Foreign Ministers, including the Nazi minister, Ribbentrop, with whom Gaus worked closely as a 'Greek slave'. After 1945, Dr Gaus was attacked for his anti-Nazi evidence for prosecutors during the Nuremberg War Crimes Trials (where he also refused to testify in Ribbentrop's defence); but, by non-Nazis, he was also attacked for having worked at such a senior level with the Nazi regime, with personal knowledge of its gravest crimes.[15] His reputation is still mixed, perhaps undeservedly so.[16] Yet, as regards international commercial arbitration, he can be remembered as a hedgehog, associated with an idea that today forms an important part of the arbitral oak-tree.

D. Brian Davenport

From Berlin, we move to London. Specifically, we move to a sub-basement lecture-room of King's College, London University, on a Friday in July 1994. It was the venue for a large conference of English arbitration specialists to discuss a draft bill and commentary on the new Arbitration Act proposed by the DAC, the Departmental Advisory Committee on the Law Arbitration. It was a critical meeting, with a massively important decision to be made by the Department of Trade and Industry (DTI), the Government ministry sponsoring (with increasing reluctance) the reforms of the United Kingdom's Arbitrations Acts 1950–1979.

The DTI had to choose between the minimalist arbitration bill drafted for the Government by Parliamentary Counsel hostile to the UNCITRAL Model Law and the less orthodox approach in the DAC's commentary largely influenced by users

---

[15] One such critic was Ernst von Weizäcker, the former administrative head of the AA, who had faced (but escaped) the death penalty in the last of the Nuremberg War Crimes Trial (the 'Wilhemstrasse' trial). In his biography, he contrasts the role played by Gaus in support of the Allied prosecutors, in contrast to Gaus' servile role working in 'Ribbentrop's ante-chamber': E. von Weizäcker, *Memoirs* (1951), p. 308.

[16] M. Bloch, *Ribbentrop* (1992) pp. 209 & 246; *see also* Eckart Conze, Norbert Frei, Peter Hayes, Moshe Zimmerman & ors, *Das Amt and die Vergangenheit* (2010); and Johannes Hürter, 'The German Foreign Office', *Bulletin of the GHI*, 49 (2011) 81, part translation of the latter's 'Das Auswärtige Amt', *Vierteljahreshefte für Zeitgeschichte* 59 (2011) 167. 59.

and the UNCITRAL Model Law.[17] As commentators had rightly noted, the draft bill and the commentary bore little relationship to one another; and one clearly had to go. There were many arbitration captains in the lecture-room: Lord Mustill, the first DAC chairman; Lord Justice Steyn, the then-DAC chairman, Lord Ackner; and, as I recall, Lord Wilberforce, Martin Hunter and Neil Kaplan. It was a well-attended large meeting; and the list of attendees goes on and on. As did, unfortunately, the speakers. One after the other, spreading darkness where there had been light, sowing confusion where there had been certainty; and all of them leaving the gloomy DTI none the wiser, albeit better informed that arbitral lunatics had indeed taken over the asylum. There then spoke a figure well known and much respected, whose contribution proved to be decisive. His name was Brian Davenport QC. He argued bluntly that there should be no compromise with the timid draft bill. What arbitration users needed should prevail; there was no point in accepting minimalist legislation; and it was far better for the DAC to refuse this mere half loaf. It should be the full loaf or nothing.

What followed is history. The DAC insisted upon the full loaf; the DTI eventually accepted the DAC's approach; and, later, under Lord Justice Saville as the third and last DAC chairman, the end product was the Arbitration Act 1996. The 1996 Act may not be perfect; no legislation with so many compromises could ever satisfy everyone; but it is manifestly *not* half a loaf. Without Brian Davenport's pugnacious contribution that Friday, I do not believe we could have seen the 1996 Act. The Government would have imposed a minimalist statute, mostly consolidating earlier legislation without reference to the UNCITRAL Model Law, to the disappointment of many users of London Arbitration.

Brian Davenport was called to the English Bar in 1960; from 1974 to 1980 he was Junior Counsel to the Board of Inland Revenue; he took silk in 1980; and he became a Law Commissioner in 1982, later working as a consultant with Norton Rose in London. He died in 2002, from a terrible illness (multiple sclerosis), with physical symptoms having badly affected his career. Lord Goff in his obituary for Gray's Inn wrote that Brian Davenport was one of the most distinguished lawyers of his generation; and that he would have been a great judge, probably destined for the House of Lords.[18] He was certainly a very powerful advocate and, in the best sense, a lawyer's lawyer. Lord Goff also recalled meeting the Lord Chancellor, then Lord Hailsham, to resolve an apparent objection to Brian Davenport's appointment as a Law Commissioner, on the ground that, with his illness, he was no more than a 'lame duck'. As Lord Goff recalled, Lord Hailsham retorted: 'I do not regard Davenport as a lame duck. I regard him as a ram caught in a thicket.' His illness and premature death are remembered by his contemporaries as a great loss

---

[17] These two documents are published in (1994) *Arbitration International* 189.
[18] Lord Goff, *Graya*, No. 113, p. 105.

452   ON ARBITRATION

to the English legal system; but as arbitration specialists, we remember him best for his timely speech at King's College. It was again at the time a small seed; but it worked in making possible the 1996 Act. Brian Davenport was both a ram and a hedgehog.

E. Bertie Vigrass

Finally, we now move from London to Yorkshire, where he still lives in quiet retirement, well-known and much respected to many of us present here tonight. Bertie Vigrass was the Secretary, later the Secretary-General and Director General of the Institute of Arbitrators, from 1972 to 1986; and he then became the Director-General of the independent LCIA until his retirement many years later.[19] Before joining the Institute, Bertie Vigrass had been the executive director of the British Institute of Management; but he was no bureaucrat, still less a lawyer or, originally, an arbitration specialist at all.

He had been an engineering student at Loughborough University at the beginning of the Second World War. He volunteered in 1940 as a pilot in the Royal Navy's Fleet Air Arm. He flew solo after six hours' training in Tiger Moths, a remarkable achievement until you consider that, with the press of war, ten hours was the maximum period allowed for all students to fly solo. As Bertie says, 'it concentrated the mind.' After further training in Canada, Greenwich and Scotland, in January 1942 as a pilot officer, he joined 8209 Squadron on the aircraft-carrier HMS 'Illustrious', flying single-engined Fairey Albacore torpedo-bomber bi-planes. He took part in the liberation of Madagascar, which was thought to be used by Japanese submarines attacking Allied shipping in the Indian Ocean. He was then the youngest carrier pilot in the Fleet Air Arm. It is said that carrier pilots have to be young before their sense of invincibility fades away; but Bertie's stories make you feel that even invincibility might not suffice.

The LCIA, despite its origins in the nineteenth century, remained a fledgling institution for international arbitration until its new rules in 1980. Its growth since that date, particularly since its independence from the Institute, now the Chartered Institute of Arbitrators, has been as remarkable as it is surprising to those who knew it in the 1980s. That could not have happened without Sir Michael Kerr, the LCIA's President. However, as he was the first to say, it *would* not have happened without Bertie Vigrass. His superlative administrative and imaginative fund-raising skills defy definition; they were somewhat unique and unorthodox; but they worked. There were of course awkward and impecunious times, best now forgotten. However, I do remember one discussion at

---

[19] N. Watson, *A History of the Chartered Institute of Arbitrators* (2015), pp. 48ff.

an LCIA board meeting as to the difference under English law between fraudulent trading and wrongful trading, with no third option under consideration. I also remember Dr Wetter, the Swedish arbitration scholar, complaining again at the LCIA's lack of reliable statistics, perennially blamed by Bertie on the IRA bombing which had destroyed the LCIA's offices and archives in the Baltic Exchange, in the City of London. But, as Dr Wetter complained, how could that incident preclude reliable statistics for periods *after* the bombing? And when the Lord Chancellor asked Bertie Vigrass for the financial statistics to support the bill which became the Arbitration Act 1979, the eventual figure cited to him as relevant to the UK's balance of payments was mistakenly enhanced by some 1,000%, with no fault attributable to Bertie – or at least not ostensibly so.[20] Bertie Vigrass acted always in a good cause, to good effect. Without him, the LCIA and London Arbitration would be much diminished. With a 'concentrated mind' from his flying days, he was another hedgehog in keeping the LCIA afloat in challenging circumstances.

F. Conclusion

In conclusion, why are any of these individuals important? We should recall the difference between hedgehogs and foxes. Curling up into an impregnable ball of sharp bristles in self-defence is certainly a big thing for a hedgehog; but that may not get it very far compared to what an institutional fox can do in the field of arbitration. We see today large numbers of arbitral bodies, law firms and barristers' chambers competing with each other as rival businesses, seeking near-monopolies, promoting themselves with few restraints and meeting ambitious financial targets as absolute priorities. We cannot really complain at this, still less turn the clock back. It is a direct result of the enormous growth and success of arbitration over the last thirty years, from which we have all benefited as arbitration specialists. Yet, all these institutions are staffed by individuals. Many of the younger individuals, the new generation of arbitration specialists, are more knowledgeable and better trained than any in the past, whether acting as juniors to their principals, working in arbitration secretariats, as secretaries to tribunals or as teachers in law schools. They are the future of arbitration; and it is what they do as individuals for arbitration that will determine what that future will be. If they each act as an individual hedgehog and not as an indivisible part of an institutional fox, that future is good despite apparent difficulties – with one important caveat. This arbitral oak-tree has deep historical roots. In reforming and re-legitimising arbitration, there are ways

---

[20] *See* Lord Elwyn-Jones, on the Arbitration Bill's second reading, *Hansard*, 12 December 1978, p. 436, col 1 and p. 441, col 1.

454 ON ARBITRATION

to apply lessons from the past, without having to plant a new sapling every time or to re-invent an existing wheel. That is why, I suggest, these four and many other individuals from the past should remain important for us. Unlike most institutions, they each kept their minds as individuals on one big thing, without even knowing that it was to become so big.

Postscript

Johnny Veeder as Teacher, Mentor, Colleague, and Friend

As teacher (by Sam Wordsworth)

While most of the readers of this book will have got to know Johnny Veeder either as arbitrator or, in his earlier days, as counsel, others will have been inspired by his teaching, which also became very important in the last two decades of his life. Quite how Johnny found the time for teaching is a mystery, but at 5.30 p.m. each Thursday in the spring term, Johnny and I would meet for some variation of coffee and a ham sandwich near King's College London to check that we knew who was going to be leading on which subject during the two-hour lecture to LLM students that was about to follow. Not that this was last-minute planning—Johnny had several files of investment arbitration notes, case extracts, and (this being Johnny) photos for each lecture; rather, Johnny really enjoyed teaching, but teaching following a coffee and catch-up was even better.

Note for Johnny, lecture 1—here is the International Centre for Settlement of Investment Disputes (ICSID) Convention. Instead, lecture 1—who can name an arbitrator that was a saint? A photograph of Maxim the Greek would then appear on the screen (with an equivocal bonus point awarded to any student who named Pope John Paul II for his role in the *Beagle Channel* dispute). Then—who can name an arbitral appointee who was a Nobel Prize winner? A short delay and a photo of Albert Einstein would appear, followed by an explanation as to how the default position of arbitrating parties is unfortunately to say 'No' to a proposal from the other side, even when someone as manifestly exceptional as Einstein is proposed (by the USSR in the *Lena Goldfields* case). Then, and with a much more developed focus—should a State like Bhutan become a party to the ICSID Convention? The answer ultimately given was 'No', although communicated by Johnny with reference to St Augustine as 'grant me this particular aspect of attractiveness to investors, but not yet'.

And thus, from the very first moment, Johnny's lectures gave an exceptional depth and meaning to investment arbitration. If students arrived at the first lecture anticipating some dry introduction, they soon learnt that Johnny's lectures located international arbitration as something that matters, that the foundational cases helped to avoid wars or involved household names like Lenin and Stalin. And so the students would be introduced to the *Alabama* case, to the Hague Peace

---

On Arbitration. Edited by: Sam Wordsworth KC and Marie Veeder, Oxford University Press. © Oxford University Press 2023. DOI: 10.1093/oso/9780192869135.003.0030

456 ON ARBITRATION

Conferences, to *Lena Goldfields*, and then to the alternatives to investment arbitration as illustrated by the history of the La Brea concession and the sharp contrast between the successful arbitration of 1922 and the enforced settlement of 1968, which Johnny depicted as leading to the military coup in Peru and to decades of insurgency, terror, and violence.

So, with Johnny, even the driest issues—like what constitutes an investment—would take on a wholly unexpected colour and depth because they formed part of a broader picture, an evolving story, as to which Johnny would always insist that he could only teach the questions to ask but never the answers as we (including Johnny) were all learning all the time. It was truly worth focusing—because it mattered to real pensioners who had lost their investments and to real States who had to meet their budget commitments—on whether, for example, the purchase of entitlements to bonds on the secondary market could correctly be considered as an investment, with all the multiple issues of interpretation of international law that this entailed. One had to learn how to approach and interpret the given treaty or other instrument but also to understand who the participants were, including the names of the arbitrators who wrote the most persuasive awards,[1] and the names and functioning of the institutions that had shaped investment arbitration (ICSID, the Permanent Court of Arbitration (PCA) and others) or that were now unpicking it (e.g. the European Commission). One also had to recognize the systemic failings, including discrimination and the under-representation of women and people of colour in the pool of arbitrators. The students learned about a system that was full of flaws that had to be addressed without delay, but that appeared essential and more likely to succeed than any alternative.

We all learned so much from Johnny in these lectures—not only on the law but also on the different ways of looking at a given topic, how to see the complexities, and even how to teach and to entertain. It is not possible to capture Johnny's extraordinary combination of warmth, generosity, and prodigious intellect and his strong sense of fairness and justice. Although the course continues, I approach each lecture with a deep sense of loss, and there is an ever-powerful absence at the lectern, from where Johnny would captivate and enthral.

As mentor (by Toby Landau)

Johnny was one of the most brilliant, visionary, and respected counsel, arbitrators, and scholars in the field of international dispute resolution and international

---

[1] Johnny never spoke of his own role as arbitrator or focused on cases where he had been sitting. One lecture on the King's College London investment arbitration course, now devoted to the extraordinary contribution that Johnny made, focuses on key awards to which he contributed, including the awards in *Methanex*, *Achmea*, *Electrabel*, and *Chevron v. Ecuador (II)*. He would not approve.

law: truly an original thinker and truly an inspiration. He had an astonishing knowledge of diverse areas of law over diverse historical periods and was able to see connections and perspectives that nobody else had ever thought of. But his was a genius set apart from that of others because it was infused with an extraordinary and utterly profound humility, warmth, kindness, and generosity. He shied away from compliments and was allergic to any form of vanity or puffery. Rather than focus on himself, he was forever concerned with the youngest person in the room; the least confident; the most neglected. And this changed lives. In the course of submissions before the House of Lords in one case, he went out of his way to credit a struggling pupil by name for locating an authority—a gesture that that pupil credits to this day as the motivation for his whole career. When the guest of honour at an international conference, Johnny disappeared from the top table at dinner and was later found at the other end of the hall sitting next to a lone student who had nobody to talk to. The instances are endless.

And along with the humility, generosity, and kindness, there were demanding professional values. He believed in absolute honesty and candour as counsel. He maintained the highest professional courtesy to everyone, whether judge, arbitrator, opponent, court clerk, shorthand writer, doorman, or cleaner. Child of cleaner. By reason of his steadfast standards, he commanded the attention of courts and tribunals worldwide because he was universally trusted. And it was these professional values that, later in his career, caused him to become increasingly disenchanted with modern lawyering. He hated the increasing focus on money. He complained of the aggression. He was appalled by the self-promotion and self-congratulation. Most of all, he hated professional directories and regularly cautioned us that you should never take a professional directory seriously, 'unless you are listed in it'. And he hated Chambers' brochures. For many years, Chambers thought that our brochures were extremely popular, not knowing that when passing through Chambers' reception Johnny would routinely scoop up the entire pile of brochures and hide them all. In years to come, someone will unearth the many hundreds that remain concealed to this day.

And then, there was the humour—a humour that permeated everything he did, that was infectious and completely disarming. However tense or solemn the situation, he had an extraordinary ability to generate laughter, and with it, mutual goodwill. For Johnny, nothing was to be taken too seriously, and his charm and wit would carry everyone with him. Usually from the first encounter. On my first day as a pupil in Chambers, at the difficult time of Chambers' controversial move from Middle Temple to Lincoln's Inn Fields, he instructed me to go to the clerks' room at 4 Essex Court and put up a large sign which read: 'Closing Down: Pollock Half-Price'.[2]

---

[2] A reference to Gordon Pollock, the close friend of Johnny Veeder and former Head of Chambers of Essex Court Chambers for many years, who sadly died in April 2019.

458 ON ARBITRATION

And it was Johnny's room in the newly located Chambers in Lincoln's Inn Fields that encapsulated much that was Johnny—a centre of instruction, inspiration, gossip, and laughter, as well as complex operations to implement practical jokes on others. It was a room in which time behaved differently. People would pass by and then spend all day. From this centre of operations, there was frequent and urgent telephone summoning of other members of Chambers, normally with the words 'Disaster' or 'Nightmare'. Typically, it would be the morning of a Court or tribunal hearing. I would rush down to his room, only to find that the panic had nothing to do with the impending hearing but rather some difficulty completing a fake fax he was sending to a colleague—inviting them to speak at a non-existent conference on 'Recent Developments in the Latvian Law of Demurrage'.

This was the room in which, twenty-five years ago, an impoverished intern from Pakistan whom he had only just met was told by Johnny that she should attend an arbitration conference. On realizing that she could not afford it, in an unflinching instant, motivated by nothing other than pure kindness, he wrote her a cheque (in his hallmark indecipherable black ink) to cover the substantial cost. And so she attended the conference. And so we met. And so we married—all under Johnny's warm, nurturing, and irreplaceable watch.

But these are just glimpses of an extraordinary man and an extraordinary life. They sit in an ocean of remembrances of the countless people for whom Johnny did something, or said something, that left an indelible mark. The world has not just lost a man, scholar, mentor, friend, confidante. The world has lost the grace of a great soul. Some religions say that until we reach a state of human completion on our deaths, we will keep coming back. Of Johnny, we can safely say—he will not be coming back. But then, in so many hearts and minds across the world, Johnny never left. The depth of the imprint he made continues to guide, shape, and inspire us. And though the pain of his physical absence persists, it is softened by laughter from the sky.

As colleague (by Albert Jan van den Berg)

I met Johnny for the first time during the enforcement proceedings in 1986 on Bermuda where his client, the Soviet State-owned enterprise Sojuznefteexport (SNE), sought enforcement of an award made in Moscow against Joc Oil. I was part of the team defending Joc Oil led by Ken Rokinson. From my vantage point in the venerable court room in Hamilton, I saw a distinguished QC who was regularly interrupted by receiving notes from his junior who I thought had a striking resemblance to the Soldier of Orange. When I found out his name, it confirmed my suspicion of Dutch roots: Van Vechten and Veeder are Dutch names.[3] Later,

---

[3] Later on, as I have 'Van' in my last name as well, Johnny referred to us as the 'Van Family'.

Johnny told me that he had to stay in a rented house with his clients under a restraining order not to fraternize with our side. When he was allowed to take some fresh air by having a stroll in the harbour, he saw our team having a great time on the schooner of our client. Johnny recalled the bitter complaint of his Soviet clients: 'There sails our money.'

During the years after Bermuda, I met Johnny frequently in various settings, notably the revision of the English Arbitration Act 1975, his seminal (at the time outsized) National Report on England for the Inns of Court College of Advocacy's (ICCA's) International Handbook and at numerous ICCA meetings. We also regularly sat together on panels at conferences. I admired his speeches both in content and in delivery. One that I remember vividly is our joint session in Singapore in 2012, where we had to quiz five Supreme Court judges from various jurisdictions on their approach to arbitration. We were anxious about this event. We had a fair amount of experience in 'counsel control' in arbitration. But 'judge control' at a conference? For both of us, this was new. His impressive introductory speech alleviated all my fears. Thanks to Johnny, it is one of the best panel sessions I have ever participated in at an ICCA congress.

Johnny was an extraordinary arbitrator. His views were very balanced. His approach to parties was very gracious but firm. He waited until deliberations after the hearing to make up his mind and share his views with his colleagues on the tribunal. His award drafting was usually in episodes: each chapter was a separate document—checking and integration into one single document were no easy task.

We were together in the *Plama v. Bulgaria* case. The respondent had argued that the claimant had misrepresented claimant's true ownership to the Bulgarian authorities. In the Decision on Jurisdiction, we essentially rejected that jurisdictional defence as having been belatedly introduced in the jurisdictional phase of the proceedings. In the merits phase, on the other hand, having received further evidence, we accepted the respondent's allegation of misrepresentation and found it to constitute deliberate fraud. A sentence dear to Johnny's heart was: 'the ECT [Energy Charter Treaty] should be interpreted in a manner consistent with the aim of encouraging respect for the rule of law'. We concluded that the substantive protections of the ECT cannot apply to investments that are made contrary to domestic law and applicable principles of international law. This is quintessentially Johnny: he had a strong aversion to illegality and deceptive behaviour. Actually, his moral compass was superb: he had zero tolerance for corruption.

Another case in which we sat together was *Achmea v. Slovak Republic*. The case involved a Dutch company that had invested in the health-care business in the Slovak Republic, with the respondent asserting an intra-EU jurisdictional objection. Reviewing the email exchange today, it struck me how gender-neutral Johnny was. In an email in autumn 2009, he wrote: 'I am content with the draft letter, save for the jarring franglais "Dear Mesdames, Dear Sirs". There must be a better form of address, perhaps in Dutch or certainly with the more usual gender-neutral "Dear

460   ON ARBITRATION

Colleagues". In another email, Johnny convincingly concluded: 'if we say nothing, then nothing will come from nothing'.

We rejected the intra-EU jurisdictional objection for the reasons set out in the Award of 26 October 2010. The European Court of Justice (ECJ) disagreed with us in its judgment of 6 March 2018. The Award in *Achmea* resonates with Johnny's particular interest in the status of EU law vis-à-vis international law and domestic law, as is evident from the Award of 25 November 2015 in *Electrabel v. Hungary*. It came to Johnny as a surprise when attending a public lecture at King's College in London on 21 March 2019 that Professor Koen Lenaerts, who presided over the ECJ in the *Achmea* case, declared that 'Achmea has nothing to do with arbitration.'

Until the very end, Johnny was fully committed as arbitrator. In the case of *Strabag v. Poland*, Johnny was chairperson, and Karl-Heinz Böckstiegel and I were co-arbitrators. With the benefit of Johnny's leadership, we completed the draft of the Partial Award in February 2020. On 4 March 2020, the day that the Partial Award was notified to the parties, I wrote to his wife, Marie: 'Also on behalf of Karl-Heinz (who is travelling), please give our very best wishes to Johnny. Tell him that we miss him dearly both personally and professionally—his humour, kindness and perspicacity are irreplaceable.' Those words remain true today more than ever.

As friend: A personal tribute (by Marie Veeder)

Johnny Veeder was a faithful steward to so many causes, both within the legal world and without. Although this book is a tribute to his professional and academic achievements, those who knew him know that this was only one aspect of this remarkable man. He also helped dissidents and supported human rights organizations that opposed harsh regimes. He assisted musicians and gave generously to bring music and performance into schools and prisons. He supported various writers and artists and he gave generously of his time to all. He even helped to build an opera house. Today, he is fêted as one of the great names in the world of international arbitration. But why and how did he become the man he was?

A dual UK and US citizen by birth, Johnny was a true international citizen. Though born in a London hospital in 1948, Johnny's family lived in France on the rue Casimir Pinel in Neuilly-sur-Seine near the Bois de Boulogne. He attended a French primary school and, as his parents travelled often, he and his two younger sisters spoke French at home. His father, John Van Vechten Veeder, an American, had established the European headquarters of Tidewater Petroleum in Paris after the war. His Scottish mother, Helen Letham Townley, had met her future husband in 1946 onboard the Queen Mary when both were travelling to England after the

Second World War. She had served as an officer in the Women's Royal Air Force with a specialty in aerial photographic reconnaissance and had been seconded to the US Pentagon after VE Day to assist the Americans with the Pacific war. Johnny's father had been a major in the US Marine Corps and had survived terrible fighting all across the Pacific.

At the age of eight, Johnny was sent to England to be educated at Clifton College, Bristol under the tutelage of his uncle, Nick Hammond, who was headmaster there. Hammond was a notable scholar of Ancient Greece and had been a special operations executive (SOE) operative in Greece during the war. Johnny excelled at his studies and at sport. He played rugby for Clifton and was named in the All England Schoolboys team. He also rowed for Clifton, as his father had for Phillips Exeter Academy and then Harvard University. After Clifton, Johnny attended Jesus College, Cambridge. Although Johnny played rugby for Cambridge, he avoided rowing there by hiding in his rooms for two days while they searched for the new intake. He was a fine linguist (French and German) and initially read Modern Languages before switching to Law after his first year.

Johnny spent school holidays in France and Belgium even after his family moved to England in 1958. His parents favoured a hotel in the South of France at Le Lavandou, while his godparents maintained a villa near Cannes. Johnny was particularly close to his Belgian godparents, Jean ('John') and Yvonne de Prelle de la Nieppe. Johnny received his nickname, 'Johnny', from this association. Sadly, Jean died in 1965, but Johnny was a faithful and loving godson to Yvonne for the rest of her life. In her lovely hotel-de-ville in Ixelles, Brussels, model airplanes and other evidence of his youthful visits featured in the main guest bedroom. Yvonne de Prelle, as she was known, took over the oil business that her husband had run and was an extremely competent businesswoman. Johnny learned much from her quiet competence. After his parents' divorce a few years after their return to England, Yvonne remained close to Johnny's mother and provided much support to both of them until her death in 1992.

Prior to joining Essex Court Chambers (originally 4 Essex Court in the Middle Temple), Johnny had a brief stop at Freshfields, where he worked under the tutelage of Alan Redfern and Martin Hunter. While assisting them on a Middle Eastern case, Mark Saville QC (now Baron Saville of Newdigate) was brought in to lead the team. It was Mark who introduced Johnny to 4 Essex Court and became his pupil master. Surrounded by so many excellent legal minds, his career prospered and he remained at Essex Court Chambers for the whole of his life. The very first time I visited Johnny in Chambers, I was introduced to John Thomas (now the former Lord Chief Justice, Lord Thomas of Cwmgiedd), who had the room next door. A lifelong friend, John would kindly and discreetly warn me when Johnny was overworking even more than normally. So many of his Chambers' colleagues became his (and my) most treasured friends.

462   ON ARBITRATION

I first met Johnny in 1985. He was living in a small flat in the Barbican in the City of London and I was, unknowingly, his next-door neighbour. He rang my doorbell in desperation one day after finding that he had locked himself out of his flat when attempting to welcome several guests for Sunday lunch. It was imperative for him to find an immediate re-entry as a substantial lunch was cooking in the oven. Safe passage for him and his guests through our communal garden allowed a successful return to his flat. This marked the beginning of an incredible thirty-five-year odyssey.

I was fascinated by his hardworking, sensitive, and humble nature. He was interested in so many different things: history, human rights, theatre, politics, music, languages—and restaurants. To me, he appeared to be an expert in so many areas. The breadth of his knowledge was incredible and there seemed to be no end to his ability to store away facts that would be brought out at a moment's notice—but never in a show-off manner. He was as good a listener as he was a raconteur. He was always courteous.

Perhaps as a way to prevent him from working every single minute of the day, I somehow persuaded Johnny to aspire to becoming a keen sailor in his late thirties. As with everything else, he wanted to make sure he knew everything about the subject. We enlisted in Royal Yachting Association courses, progressing through both classroom and sea-based levels to becoming Royal Yachting Association (RYA) Yachtmasters in the early 1990s. For some reason, we even thought it was a good idea to buy a fifty-year-old wooden Concordia yacht called *Hurricane* and keep it in my home town in the United States. Though much restoration was required, Johnny was delighted by life aboard, particularly as the original owner was also very tall and had built extremely long bunks, with equally long bookshelves above. When he called out to me that he was 'going below to check the chart', I knew it was a euphemism for returning to his bunk with one of the stack of books he hauled onboard each year before we set off for the Maine coast. I was quite happy to tend the sails and the course while he read and dozed and rebuilt his strength for another year's work. I believe he did a lot of his best thinking onboard.

He also loved working and writing at our summer home in Manchester-by-the-Sea, Massachusetts. His office window looked out over the head of the harbour and the lobstermen's dock. He, too, became a lobsterman and maintained around five lobster pots for our own use. After several years, it became clear that he liked the lobstering more than the eating, and there was more than one occasion where the 'catch' were ceremonially set free back into the harbour.

He was fascinated with new technology that was surfacing to assist weather forecasting and navigation. Our closets were littered with each season's new unsuccessful gadgets that never quite fulfilled their early promise. Not content with computer navigation, Johnny also made several attempts to learn celestial navigation, though I made sure the courses we steered were not completely dependent on these calculations. It was only during the summer when our daughter, Anne, turned two that a clever Garmin navigation system allowed one person to sail the boat while the other could make sure that Anne was safe and content. She always was, of course, and she treasured her summers onboard. There were so many firsts—first lobster meal, first sighting of a humpback whale, first ice cream cone when ashore in a Maine harbour.

The last article Johnny wrote was not a legal treatise. Rather, it was an article about our Concordia sailboat, *Hurricane*. It was written for, and published in, the autumn 2019 edition of *The Concordian* magazine, edited by our dear friend, Jay Panetta of Manchester-by-the-Sea, MA. It ends with the following paragraph. Much of it was written during the month we spent onboard in August 2019. Memories of that last summer cruise will stay with me forever.

> We have owned Hurricane for 30 years. During that time, the two of us have spent many summers sailing in Maine, eventually joined by our daughter—until she discovered the paramount joys of horses. We were then limited to daysailing for a time, which is no hardship from Manchester-by-the-Sea, our summer home. Nothing in the world, however, compares to sailing in Maine. In Summer and Fall, it provides one of the most interesting, safe, and friendly cruising grounds in the world. And nothing in boating can compare to sailing a traditional wooden boat like Hurricane. She is still greeted by many as an old friend, and we continue to encounter crew and shipwrights who have sailed aboard or worked on her in the past. Even the seagulls take note, seeing her as an oversized lobster boat and approaching her with hopes of oversized bait. During our ownership there have been many changes: from Loran to a GPS chartplotter, from a simple VHF radio to an AIS receiver, and from 'potato navigation' to radar. We can pass over quickly the list of our trials and tribulations: her old mainsail tearing at the seams at a most inopportune moment, her old engine perversely refusing to start in remote anchorages, the storm during which that cranky engine failed, requiring us to sail reefed and upwind for 36 hours back to Manchester, and the near loss of her mast in the aftermath of Hurricane Andrew. The list goes on, but these tests are now best forgotten. Whatever the pain, she has repaid it all in delight, with interest. We remain more than content to have become Hurricane's owners, extending her life span into the 21st century. Yet these old wooden boats are perhaps never actually owned. As Hurricane's many devoted keepers have proved over the past 80 years, her stewards are mere trustees, of a tradition which one hopes will never die.

The lymphoma that struck Johnny back in 1982 fundamentally damaged his health and contributed to his early death at the age of seventy-one. He would have liked to continue teaching and writing, to continue to shape minds and foster understanding, and to continue to be a good *steward* to those causes that mattered most to him. Just as he was a good shepherd that fostered the next generation, so, too, did he benefit from the kindness and stewardship of the generation that oversaw his development. They all helped to create a most wonderful and honourable man. Johnny left an incredible mark on those who knew him. I was always aware of how special Johnny was and how incredibly lucky I was to accompany him through the last decades of his life. There was no line between his private and public life: he was completely and everlastingly kind, good, and just.

APPENDIX I

Selected Extracts from Certain Key Arbitral Awards (in Cases Where Johnny Veeder Was the Presiding Arbitrator)

As noted in the introduction to this volume, Johnny Veeder's contribution to the field of investor–State arbitration was immense, including through his participation as arbitrator in many of the most important cases of the past twenty-five years. This appendix seeks to illustrate that contribution through a number of short extracts from arbitral decisions or awards of particular interest or significance in terms of the development of law. The reader is referred to the relevant awards for the full reasoning.[1]

Methanex Corporation v. United States of America, UNCITRAL, Partial Award of 7 August 2002: on the meaning of 'relating to', and Cleopatra's nose

This was the first North American Free Trade Agreement (NAFTA) case chaired by Johnny Veeder. It is an important case for many reasons, including as to the Tribunal's treatment of procedural issues (including transparency), jurisdiction, and the content of the substantive protections under NAFTA (including the scope of indirect expropriation and permitted regulatory activity by the State). The extract below concerns Article 1101 NAFTA, pursuant to which Chapter 11 'applies to measures adopted or maintained by a Party relating to: (a) investors of another Party [or] (b) investments of investors of another Party in the territory of a Party'. The issue concerned the meaning to be given to the deceptively simple words 'relating to', in circumstances where the relevant measure targeted the sale of a petroleum additive, MTBE, of which the product supplied by the claimant (methanol) is a constituent. Neither methanol nor the claimant, Methanex, was directly targeted by the measure. The particular facts demonstrated how essential it is to identify the correct legal meaning of formulae such as 'relating to', including at a jurisdictional phase.

127. [...] There is no dispute as to the existence of 'measures' falling within Article 1101(1): i.e. the California Executive Order and the California Regulations (US Memorial on Jurisdiction, pages 48-49; Methanex Rejoinder of 25th May 2001, page 70). Similarly, there is no dispute that Methanex falls within the rubric of 'investors of another Party'.

128. The issue that divides the Disputing Parties is whether these US measures, on the assumed facts, 'relate to' Methanex because, as recited above, neither measure was

---

[1] Of course, in each case, the award reflects the deliberations and contains the reasoning and decision-making of all members of the tribunal concerned. In each case, the permission of the co-arbitrators to publication of the excerpts has been sought and has been given.

466   APPENDIX I

expressly directed at methanol, methanol producers or Methanex. Applying the approach described in the previous chapter, it is necessary first to interpret definitively this phrase; and second to determine on the basis of the assumed facts, whether or not any of these measures relate to Methanex and its investments.

The meaning of the phrase: 'relating to':

129. It is a short phrase; and it might be thought, as with many issues of linguistic interpretation, that the answer was a matter of first impression. In order not to lengthen an already long document, we shall again refrain from dealing here with every submission on the issue made by the Disputing Parties and the NAFTA Parties, Canada and Mexico. We have nonetheless considered all those submissions; and in deciding here that the matter can properly be decided on a more limited basis, we intend no discourtesy to any person.

The ordinary meaning:

135. These rival interpretations can each be advanced in good faith; and under Article 31(1) of the Vienna Convention, the first issue turns on the ordinary meaning of the phrase 'relating to'. Methanex relies on definitions of 'relate' and 'related' contained in three English language dictionaries: American Heritage Dictionary ('related' defined as 'connected, associated'), the Oxford English Dictionary ('related' defined as 'having relation to, or relationship with, something else'), and Funk & Wagnalls New Comprehensive International Dictionary of the English Language ('related' defined as 'standing in relation; connected'). In each case, the word 'relate' has an associated definition.

136. In the Tribunal's view, none of these dictionary definitions decide the issue. To a limited extent, they support the USA's reliance on the requirement of a 'connection'. These definitions imply a connection beyond a mere impact, which is all that the term 'affecting' involves on Methanex's interpretation. Nevertheless, we do not consider that this issue can be decided on a purely semantic basis; and there is a difference between a literal meaning and the ordinary meaning of a legal phrase. It is also necessary to consider the ordinary meaning of the term in its context and in the light of the object and purpose of NAFTA and, in particular, Chapter 11 (as required by Article 31(1) of the Vienna Convention).

Context, object, and purpose:

137. For Methanex, the phrase 'relating to' should be interpreted in the context of a treaty chapter concerned with the protection of investors; and hence, a broad interpretation is appropriate. Because of its simple application, it is an attractive interpretation; but it is also a brave submission. If the threshold provided by Article 1101(1) were merely one of 'affecting', as Methanex contends, it would be satisfied wherever any economic impact was felt by an investor or an investment. For example, in this case, the test could be met by suppliers to Methanex who suffered as a result of Methanex's alleged losses, suppliers to those suppliers and so on, towards infinity. As such, Article 1101(1) would provide no significant threshold to a NAFTA arbitration. A threshold which could be surmounted by an indeterminate class of investors making a claim alleging loss is no threshold at all; and the attractive simplicity of Methanex's interpretation derives from the fact that it imposes no practical limit. It may be true, to adapt Pascal's statement, that the history of the world would have been much affected if

APPENDIX I   467

Cleopatra's nose had been different, but by itself that cannot mean that we are all related to the royal nose. The Chaos theory provides no guide to the interpretation of this important phrase; and a strong dose of practical common-sense is required.

138. In a legal instrument such as NAFTA, Methanex's interpretation would produce a surprising, if not an absurd, result. The possible consequences of human conduct are infinite, especially when comprising acts of governmental agencies; but common sense does not require that line to run unbroken towards an endless horizon. In a traditional legal context, somewhere the line is broken; and whether as a matter of logic, social policy or other value judgment, a limit is necessarily imposed restricting the consequences for which that conduct is to be held accountable. For example, in the law of tort, there must be a reasonable connection between the defendant, the complainant, the defendant's conduct and the harm suffered by the complainant; and limits are imposed by legal rules on duty, causation and remoteness of damage well-known in the laws of both the United States and Canada. Likewise, in the law of contract, the contract-breaker is not generally liable for all the consequences of its breach even towards the innocent party, still less to persons not privy to that contract. It is of course possible, by contract or statute, to enlarge towards infinity the legal consequences of human conduct; but against this traditional legal background, it would require clear and explicit language to achieve this result.

139. The approach here can be no different. Methanex's interpretation imposes no practical limitation; and an interpretation imposing a limit is required to give effect to the object and purpose of Chapter 11. The alternative interpretation advanced by the USA does impose a reasonable limitation: there must a legally significant connection between the measure and the investor or the investment. With such an interpretation, it is perhaps not easy to define the exact dividing line, just as it is not easy in twilight to see the divide between night and day. Nonetheless, whilst the exact line may remain undrawn, it should still be possible to determine on which side of the divide a particular claim must lie.

140. *UN New York Convention*: This interpretation is supported by the reference to the UN 1958 New York Convention in Article 1222 NAFTA, whereby the consent of the NAFTA Party to arbitration under Article 1122(1) is to be treated as satisfying the requirement of Article II of the New York Convention. Article II(1) of the New York Convention limits the recognition of written agreements to arbitrate differences that may arise 'in respect of a defined legal relationship':

> Each Contracting State shall recognize an agreement in writing under which the parties undertake to submit to arbitration all or any differences which have arisen or which may arise between them in respect of a defined legal relationship [fn. The equivalent phrase in the French and Spanish texts are: '*au sujet d'un rapport de droit déterminé*' and '*respecto a una determinada relación jurídica*'], whether contractual or not, concerning a subject matter capable of settlement by arbitration.

It is therefore not sufficient for the purpose of Article II(1) that there be a limitless agreement to arbitrate any future disputes that may ever arise between the parties. More is required for a valid arbitration agreement: the dispute must arise in respect of 'a defined legal relationship' [fn. See van den Berg, The New York Arbitration Convention of 1958 (1st edn), p. 149].

468 APPENDIX I

Pac Rim Cayman LLC v. Republic of El Salvador, ICSID, Decision on the Respondent's Jurisdictional Objections of 1 June 2012: on abuse of process

In *Pac Rim*, the Tribunal had to consider how and where to draw the line between corporate restructuring so as to acquire, for general purposes, the benefit of investment treaty protection (not problematic) and corporate restructuring to gain the benefit of investment treaty protection with respect to a specific dispute (potentially abusive). The passage below identifies how it is the claimant that has the benefit of being able, to a large extent, to shape the claim and when it is brought, while the dividing line between what is and is not abusive is highly fact dependent, and 'will rarely be a thin red line, but will include a significant grey area'.

2.96. Abuse of Process: The Tribunal first considers the point in time when a change of nationality can become an abuse of process. Several different answers were suggested by the Parties as the crucial dividing-line: (i) where facts at the root of a later dispute have already taken place and that future dispute is foreseen or reasonably foreseeable; (ii) where facts have taken place giving rise to an actual dispute; and (iii) where facts have taken place giving rise to an actual dispute referable under the parties' relevant arbitration agreement.

2.97. The Tribunal starts with the last of these three suggested answers, as submitted by the Claimant during the Hearing: '... the temporal determination for abuse of process purposes must be made on the basis of evaluating what concrete acts were taken by the Party asserting jurisdiction to invoke the instrument on which it intends to base its consent and under which it intends to assert its claims'.

2.98. The Respondent contested this dividing-line as far too late and also as an absurd logical impossibility: 'As El Salvador indicated at the hearing, under this standard there could never be abuse of process for change of nationality because the jurisdictional instrument relied on by a claimant committing an abuse cannot be invoked until after the putative claimant changes nationality. This guarantees that the moment of the temporal determination "would always be after the change of nationality and the change could thus never be abusive"'.

2.99. The Tribunal accepts the force of the Respondent's submission; and it therefore rejects this third suggested answer. As far as the two other suggested answers are concerned, the Tribunal considers that they can be examined together for the purpose of this case. In the Tribunal's view, the dividing-line occurs when the relevant party can see an actual dispute or can foresee a specific future dispute as a very high probability and not merely as a possible controversy. In the Tribunal's view, before that dividing-line is reached, there will be ordinarily no abuse of process; but after that dividing-line is passed, there ordinarily will be. The answer in each case will, however, depend upon its particular facts and circumstances, as in this case. As already indicated above, the Tribunal is here more concerned with substance than semantics; and it recognises that, as a matter of practical reality, this dividing-line will rarely be a thin red line, but will include a significant grey area.

2.100. To this extent, the Tribunal accepts the Respondent's general submission that: '... it is clearly an abuse for an investor to manipulate the nationality of a shell company subsidiary to gain jurisdiction under an international treaty at a time when the investor is aware that events have occurred that negatively affect its investment and may lead to arbitration'. In particular, abuse of process must preclude unacceptable

APPENDIX I   469

manipulations by a claimant acting in bad faith and fully aware of an existing or future dispute, as also submitted by the Respondent: '... In addition, the investor has substantial control over the stages of the development of the dispute [as described in Maffezini]. Because it is the investor who must express disagreement with a government action or omission and the investor who must formulate legal claims, the investor may delay the development of the dispute into these later stages until it has completed the manipulative change of nationality. Relying on this test would permit an investor that is fully aware of a dispute to create access to jurisdiction under a treaty to which it was not entitled at the time of the actions affecting the investment, and at the same time provide no protection to the State from this abusive behaviour.'

Electrabel SA v. Republic of Hungary, ICSID, Decision on Jurisdiction, Applicable Law and Liability of 12 November 2012: on the relationship between the Energy Charter Treaty and EU law, on the degree of deprivation required for an indirect expropriation, and on attribution

Electrabel has a particular importance as one of the early cases considering, and rejecting, jurisdictional objections by a European Union (EU) Member State based on an alleged incompatibility between an investment treaty and EU law (Johnny Veeder was also a member of the Tribunal that made the Award on Jurisdiction, Arbitrability and Suspension of 26 October 2010 in *Eureko B.V. v. The Slovak Republic*, i.e. the case that ended up before the CJEU as Case C-284/16, *Slowakische Republik v. Achmea BV*). The reasoning in the *Electrabel* Decision is extensive, and the excerpt below concerns the contention (supported by the European Commission) that the existence of arbitral tribunals interpreting EU law could jeopardize its uniform application and hence rendered the agreement to arbitrate invalid. The Tribunal, and multiple arbitral tribunals since, have rejected that contention (although cf. the judgment of the Court of Justice of the European Union (CJEU) in the *Achmea* case). *Electrabel* is also often referred to for its consideration of what is required for an indirect expropriation, including the Tribunal's rejection of the so-called 'salami slicing' of an investment and also for its discussion of the international law rules on attribution. The relevant passages from the Decision of 12 November 2012 are also excerpted below.

On the need for harmonious interpretation (between the Energy Charter Treaty (ECT) and EU law):

4.146. In the Tribunal's view, there is no need to harmonise the ECT's provisions for the settlement of investor–state disputes by international arbitration with EU law because there is no inconsistency. The Tribunal understands that the main concern of the European Commission is to protect the ECJ's [European Court of Justice's] monopoly over the interpretation of EU law, operating as its ultimate guardian and also its gate-keeper. With this concern, so it is said, there must be a unique EU court entrusted with the final word on what EU law means, whereas the existence of arbitral tribunals interpreting EU law could jeopardise its uniform application.

4.147. The ECJ's monopoly is said to derive from Article 292 EC (now Article 344 TFEU [Treaty on the Functioning of the European Union]) which grants to the ECJ exclusive jurisdiction to decide disputes amongst EU Member States on the application of EU law. Article 292 states: 'Member States undertake not to submit a dispute concerning the interpretation or application of the Treaties to any method of settlement other than those provided for therein.' However, as is well known and recognised by the

470   APPENDIX I

ECJ, such an exclusive jurisdiction does not prevent numerous other courts and arbitral tribunals from applying EU law, both within and without the European Union [fn. omitted]. Given the widespread relevance and importance of EU law to international trade, it could not be otherwise.

4.148. First, as far as the courts and tribunals of EU Member States are concerned (but not private arbitration tribunals), a certain uniformity of interpretation is made possible by their capacity (by any such court or tribunal) and their obligation (by a court or tribunal against whose decisions there is no judicial remedy under national law) to refer preliminary questions of interpretation of EU law to the ECJ under Article 234 EC (now Article 267 TFEU) [fn. omitted]. The Tribunal notes the fact that EU national courts retain a certain degree of discretion in their decision to refer a question of interpretation to the ECJ and that the courts of last resort may use the legal theory of *acte clair* to retain also a further element of discretion. In other words, there is no automatic reference to or seizure by the ECJ, as soon as any question of EU law arises in a dispute before an EU national court. This factor leaves open the possibility, if not even probability, of divergent interpretations or applications of EU law to similar disputes by courts and tribunals within the European Union.

4.149. Second, as far as the courts and tribunals of non-EU Member States are concerned, there is no possibility for them to refer to the ECJ any question of interpretation of EU law. In other words, to take only one example, a Japanese court deciding a dispute between an EU company and a Japanese company might have to interpret and apply a mandatory rule of EU law relevant to the parties' transaction: in such a case, this exercise cannot be controlled by the ECJ if there is no later enforcement of the Japanese judgment within the European Union. Only if there were such enforcement proceedings before the national court of an EU Member State could the possibility arise of a reference to the ECJ, but the same discretions would then apply as described above, meaning that control by the ECJ would remain only a possibility and not a certainty. This factor leaves open the further probability of divergent interpretations or applications of EU law to similar disputes by courts and tribunals outside the European Union.

4.150. Third, as far as arbitration is concerned, Article 234 EC (now Article 267 TFEU) prevents arbitration between EU Member States. This was ostensibly decided in the *Mox Plant* case between the United Kingdom and the Republic of Ireland [fn. omitted], where the ECJ held that EU Member States are prevented from submitting their disputes to 'any other method of dispute settlement' than the method provided by EU law; and that, as a result, the ECJ has exclusive jurisdiction to resolve any dispute between two EU Member States that at least partially raises an issue of EU law. It is however doubtful whether this decision of the ECJ would prevent, for example, the International Court of Justice (ICJ) from deciding any issue of EU law, if raised in a dispute involving two or more EU Member States. It is not however necessary to interpret any further the ECJ's decision in the *Mox Plant* case, given that the Parties' dispute does not here involve two EU Member States.

4.151. Fourth, as regards an international or national arbitration tribunal in a dispute not involving two or more EU Member States as parties, there is no provision equivalent to Article 292 EC (now Article 344 TFEU) dealing with arbitration between two or more private parties, nationals of Member States, or with mixed disputes settlement mechanisms such as investor–state arbitration between individuals, nationals of EU Member States and an EU Member State under the ICSID [International Centre for Settlement of Investment Disputes] Convention or other international instruments. Article 292 EC is not applicable to these arbitration tribunals. If the submissions made

APPENDIX I   471

by the European Commission were correct, this would seem to be an extraordinary omission.

4.152. As regards arbitrations between private parties, it has long been recognised by the ECJ that such arbitrations are frequently held within the EU, interpreting and applying EU law, and do not thereby infringe the monopoly of interpretation of EU law by the ECJ, as illustrated (for example) by the *Eco Swiss* case. [The *Eco Swiss* case is then considered.]

4.153. However, the Tribunal recognises that one reason why the ECJ did not find such an arbitration objectionable under EU law in the *Eco Swiss* case was because the award made in that arbitration (with its arbitral seat in the Netherlands) remained subject to the control of the Dutch national courts; and these Dutch courts could seek an interpretation of EU law from the ECJ under Article 234 EC. The ECJ long ago decided that a private arbitration tribunal is not a national court or tribunal under Article 234 EC, with no capacity itself to refer any question of EU law to the ECJ [fn. omitted]. This recognition necessarily extends not only to arbitration tribunals seated within the European Union but also to tribunals seated outside the European Union. The present case concerns an international arbitration between a private party—a national of an EU Member State—and an EU Member State, held outside the EU. It also concerns an arbitration subject to the ICSID Convention, as incorporated in Hungary and in the laws of almost all EU Member States. In the Tribunal's view, this arbitration does not come under Article 292 EC and cannot therefore infringe EU law. There is indeed no rule in EU law that provides, expressly or impliedly, that such an international arbitration is inconsistent with EU law. Again, if the submissions made by the European Commission were correct, this would also seem to be an extraordinary omission.

4.154. The Tribunal's conclusion is confirmed by the Opinion 1/09 of the ECJ (Full Court) of 8 March 2011, delivered pursuant to Article 218(11) TFEU [then considered]. [...]

4.157. Moreover, as explained by the Tribunal elsewhere in this Decision, this case does not turn on the interpretation of the EC Treaties or the validity of decisions made by EU institutions. It has already been stated above that the Parties' dispute is about alleged violations of the ECT by the Respondent; it does not include any attack by the Claimant on the legal validity of any decision by the European Commission (including its Final Decision of 4 June 2008); and it does not concern any alleged violations of EU law by the Respondent or the European Union.

4.158. Moreover, the Tribunal notes the important legal fact that the European Commission itself, in signing the ECT, accepted the possibility of international arbitrations under the ECT, both between a non-EU investor and an EU Member State or between an EU investor and a non-EU Member State, without any distinction or reservation. This factor reinforces the Tribunal's conclusion. It is also noteworthy that this acceptance applied to both ICSID and non-ICSID arbitrations, in other words (i) non-ICSID arbitration awards whose recognition or enforcement within the European Union could entail possible control by EU national courts (under the lex loci arbitri or the New York Convention) with a possible reference to the ECJ, and (ii) ICSID arbitration awards equivalent under the ICSID Convention to judgments of national courts which are not equally susceptible to like control by EU national courts, if enforced within the EU.

4.159. The apparent absence of control by the EU national courts over ICSID awards may lie behind the concerns of the European Commission expressed in this ICSID arbitration as regards applicable law and therefore jurisdiction. The Tribunal considers that such concerns lack any juridical basis under EU law because there remains the possibility to ensure a uniform application of EU law by the ECJ in proceedings involving an EU Member State, regardless of any arbitration or award under the ICSID Convention.

4.160. This possibility was explained by Professor Thomas Eilmansberger in his scholarly article: 'If the fallacious application of EC law by the arbitral tribunal, or its failure to apply EC law at all, however, results in EC law being rendered ineffective in a given case, again nothing prevents the Commission from initiating proceedings against a Member State which, in execution of the award, would be acting in violation of EC law (e.g. by paying out an illegal subsidy promised to the investor).'

4.161. It is useful to cite here Article 226 EC (now Article 258 TFEU) and Article 228 EC (now Article 260 TFEU) [...]

4.162. In other words, even when disputes raising issues of EU law are decided by international arbitration, if the resulting award is honoured voluntarily by the EU Member State or enforced judicially within the European Union against that Member State, the ECJ retains the possibility, through different mechanisms for both ICSID and non-ICSID awards under the EU Treaties, to exercise its traditional role as the ultimate guardian of EU law.

4.163. The Tribunal notes the still more important fact that the European Union also accepted in signing the ECT to submit itself to international arbitration, thereby accepting the possibility of an arbitration between the European Union and private parties, whether nationals of EU or Non-EU Member States and whether held within or without the EU. This acceptance did not and could not include ICSID arbitrations, given the inability of the European Union (not being a State) to sign the ICSID Convention and its reservation to such effect. There is however no reason to infer that, if the European Union had been able to accede to the ICSID Convention, its acceptance of international arbitration would not have extended to arbitrations under the ICSID Convention.

4.164. In the Tribunal's view, if the European Union has itself accepted to submit to arbitration a dispute with a private investor concerning the application of the ECT (as it did), it cannot properly argue that such an arbitration is not similarly available to the same private investor advancing a claim under the ECT against an EU Member State, including an arbitration under the ICSID Convention.

On indirect expropriation:

6.57 [...] If it were possible so easily to parse an investment into several constituent parts each forming a separate investment (as Electrabel here contends), it would render meaningless that [*Tecmed*] tribunal's approach to indirect expropriation based on 'radical deprivation' and 'deprivation of any real substance' as being similar in effect to a direct expropriation or nationalisation. It would also mean, absurdly, that an investor could always meet the test for indirect expropriation by slicing its investment as finely as the particular circumstances required, without that investment as a whole ever meeting that same test. The Tribunal also notes that the wording in the *Metalclad* award as to 'significant part' qualifies the required gravity of deprivation and not the investment; and it interprets that phrase as describing in different terms the same approach later described by the *Tecmed* tribunal.

APPENDIX I   473

6.58 In this Tribunal's view, it is clear that both in applying the wording of Article 13(1) ECT and under international law, the test for expropriation is applied to the relevant investment as a whole, even if different parts may separately qualify as investments for jurisdictional purposes. Here the investment held by Electrabel as a whole was its aggregate collection of interests in Dunamenti; it was thus one integral investment; and in the context of expropriation it was not a series of separate, individual investments with Dunamenti's PPA [power purchase agreement] as an autonomous investment set apart from Electrabel's other interests in Dunamenti. In the Tribunal's view, Electrabel's investment was manifestly not confined to the PPA; and the PPA formed an intrinsic and inseparable part of Electrabel's investment as a whole.

6.59 Electrabel also cited several awards made by the Iran-US Claims Tribunal, including *Starrett, Tippetts* and *Phillips Petroleum* [fn. omitted]. Electrabel contends that these decisions and other legal materials dispense with the need for the investor to establish for indirect expropriation any substantial deprivation equivalent to a direct expropriation; and Electrabel also contends that a sovereign's termination by force of law of a contract between two private parties (such as the PPA's termination) should be treated, without more, as an expropriation.

6.60 The Tribunal does not accept that these decisions and other materials cited by Electrabel reflect, under the ECT or international law, a different standard for direct and indirect expropriation. In *Starrett,* the tribunal stated the test under international law as requiring an interference with property rights 'to such an extent that these rights are rendered so useless that they must be deemed to have been expropriated, even though the state does not purport to have expropriated them and the legal title to the property formally remains with the legal owner' (at paragraph 154). In *Tippetts,* the tribunal preferred the word 'deprivation' to the more orthodox term 'taking', not because a different test was there being proposed but because this wording was considered 'largely synonymous' seen from the investor's perspective; and the tribunal also emphasised the need under international law for the deprivation of the investor's 'fundamental rights of ownership' (at paragraph 225).

6.61 The Tribunal notes that 'taking' had been defined by the American Law Institute (in its Second Restatement of the Foreign Relations Law of the United States of America, published in 1965) as conduct which (inter alia) effectively deprived an alien 'of substantially all benefit of his interest in property ... even though the state does not deprive him of his entire legal interest in the property'. This restatement reflected the relevant definition under international law at the time of the decision in *Starrett* (1983) and *Tippetts* (1984).

6.62 In short, the Tribunal considers that the accumulated mass of international legal materials, comprising both arbitral decisions and doctrinal writings, describe for both direct and indirect expropriation, consistently albeit in different terms, the requirement under international law for the investor to establish the substantial, radical, severe, devastating or fundamental deprivation of its rights or the virtual annihilation, effective neutralisation or factual destruction of its investment, its value or enjoyment. In addition to *Metalclad* and *Tecmed* (above), arbitral decisions and awards to such effect include *Pope & Talbot* (2000), paragraphs 102–104; *S.D. Myers* (2000), paragraphs 282–285; *Lauder* (2001); paragraphs 200–201; *CME* (2001), paragraphs 603–604; *GAMI* (2004), paragraphs 123–126; *Telenor* (2006), paragraphs 63–67; *Sempra* (2007), paragraphs 284–285; and *Parkerings-Compagniet* (2007), paragraph 455. Conversely, arbitral tribunals have rejected claims for expropriation under international law where the investor has failed to meet this test for 'substantial' deprivation, including: *CMS* (2005), paragraphs 260–264; and *Azurix* (2006), paragraph 321. It is unnecessary to

474   APPENDIX I

add to these citations here, given their consistent approach to the juridical point here at issue.

On attribution:

7.58 (ii) General Approach: In order to constitute a violation of the ECT, an act has to be both attributable to the State and a violation of an international obligation under the ECT. The Tribunal must therefore first examine the question of attribution. If an act is considered attributable to Hungary, the Tribunal must then determine whether such an act entails its international responsibility under the ECT. If the Tribunal were to find that an act is not attributable to Hungary, this should ordinarily be the end of the matter. This case is, however, somewhat different. Considering the Parties' extensive and detailed submissions on different (alleged) violations of the ECT, the Tribunal considers it appropriate to address both attribution and alleged ECT violations, whatever its decision on attribution.

7.59 This is the same approach as that taken in *Plama*, where the Tribunal helpfully explained why it had decided to proceed in this way:

> The Parties have extensively documented their allegations; numerous exhibits, witness statements and expert reports have been submitted by both Parties. The factual and legal arguments have been discussed in detail during the Final Hearing, in which a number of witnesses and experts were also examined by the Parties and the arbitrators. The Tribunal has therefore decided that, in acknowledgement of the Parties' efforts, it will consider their further allegations on the merits.

7.60 (iii) Attribution: The Tribunal decides the issue of attribution under international law as required by the ECT; and it refers as a codification of customary international law to the Articles on State Responsibility adopted on second reading in 2001 by the International Law Commission and commended to the attention of Governments by the UN General Assembly in Resolution 56/83 of 12 December 2001 (the 'ILC Articles').

7.61 The question of 'attribution' does not, by itself, dictate whether there has been a violation of international law. Rather, it is only a means to ascertain whether the State is involved. As such, the question of attribution looks more like a jurisdictional question. But in many instances, questions of attribution and questions of legality are closely intermingled; and it is then difficult to deal with the question of attribution without a full enquiry into the merits. This is the reason why, as mentioned earlier, the Parties and the Tribunal decided to deal with this issue at the merits stage.

7.62 Electrabel's complaint refers to the conduct of the Parliament, the Ministry of the Economy, HEO and MVM, the latter as a private company under Hungarian law owned by the Hungarian State and allegedly acting under the instruction or direction and control of the Hungarian Government. It is common ground between the Parties that the acts of the Hungarian Government, including HEO, are attributable to Hungary under Article 4 of the ILC Articles. The Parties disagree, however, as to whether the conduct of MVM can be attributed to Hungary. As for MVM's conduct in 2005–2006 and 2008, Electrabel contends that it is attributable to Hungary; and for its part, Hungary denies this allegation and has submitted, as already noted, an objection to the Tribunal's jurisdiction concerning the commercial acts of MVM (now joined to the merits).

7.63 Electrabel invokes Article 8 of the ILC Articles, which provides as follows:

The conduct of a person or group of persons shall be considered an act of a State under international law if the person or group of persons is in fact acting on the instructions of, or under the direction or control of, that State in carrying out the conduct.

7.64 According to the Commentary to the ILC Articles (the 'ILC Commentary'), attribution may occur where there exists a special factual relationship between the person or entity engaging in the conduct and the State, regardless of whether the acts or issue are commercial or contractual (CA-6, p. 110). Article 8 ILC sets out two alternative situations that give rise to such 'special factual relationship': (i) first, where a non-State entity acts 'under the instructions of' the State, and (ii) second, where it acts 'under the direction or control of' the State.

7.65 Electrabel submits that MVM was acting both (i) 'under the instructions' and (ii) 'under the direction or control' of Hungary when MVM unilaterally reduced the price that it paid under the PPA to Dunamenti in 2006 and 2008. For Hungary, the actions of MVM and MVM Trade do not result, either de jure or de facto, from (i) its instructions or (ii) its direction or control.

7.66 The ILC Commentary explains that the role of the State differs for each of these two alternatives. Referring to the first alternative ('acting under the instruction of'), the ILC Commentary states:

In such cases it does not matter that the person or persons involved are private individuals nor whether their conduct involves 'governmental activity'. Most commonly, cases of this kind will arise where State organs supplement their own action by recruiting or instigating private persons or groups who act as 'auxiliaries' while remaining outside the official structure of the State.

7.67 These 'auxiliaries', although not part of the State's organisation, act under its authorisations and instructions.

7.68 Referring to the second alternative ('acting under the direction or control of'), the ILC Commentary states:

More complex issues arise in determining whether conduct was carried out 'under the direction or control' of a State. Such conduct will be attributable to the State only if it directed or controlled the specific operation and the conduct complained of was an integral part of that operation. The principle does not extend to conduct which was only incidentally or peripherally associated with an operation and which escaped from the State's direction or control.

7.69 The degree of control necessary and sufficient for purposes of attribution is a very demanding one, as was stated for example in *Jan de Nul* in the following terms:

International jurisprudence is very demanding in order to attribute the act of a person or entity to a State, as it requires both a general control of the State over the person or entity and a specific control of the State over the act the attribution of which is at stake; this is known as the 'effective control' test.

7.70 A showing that the requirement of either alternative for attribution is fulfilled will result in attribution of the acts in question to the State.

7.71 Although the conduct of private persons or entities is not attributable to the State under international law as a general principle, factual circumstances could establish a special relationship between the person engaging in the conduct and the State. In consequence, the Tribunal is required to assess for each alleged treaty breach, the possible

476   APPENDIX I

direction or control of Hungary over the conduct of MVM in the context of events un-
folding during 2005–2006 and 2008 in connection with PPA pricing and the existence
of any instruction to MVM from Hungary regarding such events. [See later passages of
the award for this assessment.]

Apotex Holdings Inc. and Apotex Inc. v. United States of America, ICSID, Award of 25 August 2014: on *res judicata* and issue estoppel

One key issue in the *Apotex* case concerned whether the Respondent could invoke the doctrine of *res judicata* by reference to an earlier award (the Apotex I & II Award) made between
Apotex Inc. and the Respondent. Apotex Holdings was not a named party to the earlier
Award or the arbitration in which that Award was made, while the *dispositif* of the earlier
award did not in terms address the issue of whether there was an investment that arose
in the second case (in particular whether ANDAs—abbreviated new drug applications—
constituted investments). The question of whether or how the concepts of *res judicata* and
issue estoppel apply in investor–State arbitration are of ever-increasing significance, and the
discussion from which excerpts are taken below stands as a very important contribution in
this respect (footnotes are omitted).

Res Judicata in international law:

7.10. The Parties agree that the Tribunal, under NAFTA Article 1131, 'shall decide the
issues in dispute in accordance with this Agreement [NAFTA] and applicable rules of
international law'.

7.11. In the Tribunal's view, the doctrine of *res judicata* is a general principle of law and
is thus an applicable rule of international law within the meaning of NAFTA Article
1131. In its Advisory Opinion of 13 July 1954, the ICJ affirmed that '[a]ccording to a
well-established and generally recognized principle of law, a judgment rendered by … a
judicial body [such as the U.N. Administrative Tribunal] is *res judicata* and has binding
force between the parties to the dispute' …

7.15. Whilst the triple identity test is often referred to in describing the requirements
for *res judicata* to operate, certain international tribunals and scholars have questioned
its division between *petitum* and *causa petendi*; and many cases have used a simpler
analysis. The British–US Claims Arbitral Tribunal saw the doctrine as involving only
two elements: 'res judicata applies only where there is identity of the parties and of
the question at issue'. The *Pious Fund* tribunal (applying *res judicata* in the Permanent
Court of Arbitration's first case and viewed as '[t]he leading early case') also applied a
two-part test, emphasising that 'there are not only the same parties to the suit, but also
the same subject-matter that was judged' in a prior arbitral award.

7.16. Professor Cheng questions the division between *petitum* and *causa petendi*,
observing that 'an examination of international decisions … throws some doubt about
the accuracy of this sub-division, especially in border-line cases'. Professors Schreuer
and Reinisch point out that '[i]international tribunals have … been aware of the risk
that if they use too restrictive criteria of "object" and "grounds", the doctrine of *res judicata* would rarely apply: if only an exactly identical relief sought (object) based on
exactly the same legal arguments (grounds) in a second case would be precluded as
a result of *res judicata*, then litigants could easily evade this by slightly modifying either the relief requested or the grounds relied upon'. Professor Dodge voices a similar

APPENDIX I   477

concern, although he indicates (as do Professors Schreuer and Reinisch) that tribunals have not allowed 'claim splitting' by claimants seeking to avoid the preclusive effect of earlier awards.

7.17. The Claimants and the Respondent disagree on the scope of *res judicata*'s effect in international law. The Parties agree that the provisions of the *dispositif*, or operative part, of a prior judgment or award have *res judicata* effect. They disagree whether *res judicata* in international law includes the broader concept of or akin to issue estoppel, the principle that a party in subsequent proceedings cannot contradict an issue of fact or law not reflected in the *dispositif* if it has already been distinctly raised and finally decided in earlier proceedings between the same parties (or their privies). The Claimants submit it does not; whereas the Respondent says it does.

7.18. It is clear that past international tribunals have applied forms of issue estoppel, without necessarily using the term. Umpire Plumley's award in *Orinoco Steamship* found that 'every matter and point distinctly in issue ... and which was directly passed upon and determined in said decree, and which was its ground and basis, is confirmed by said judgment, and the claimants ... are forever estopped from asserting any right or claim based in any part upon any fact actually and directly involved in the said decree'. In Professor Lowe's opinion, the tribunal in the resubmitted *Amco* case 'clearly applied the principle of issue estoppel to the determination of specific facts and of the legal characterisations of facts by the previous tribunal'. Most recently, the ICSID tribunal in *Grynberg v. Grenada* applied issue estoppel (albeit describing it as 'collateral estoppel') to foreclose the claimants' efforts to re-open issues decided in an award made in a prior ICSID arbitration.

[The *Grynberg* award is then considered.]

7.21. The Claimants denied the relevance of the *Grynberg* award to the present case, contending that the parties there had agreed to the application of collateral estoppel (issue estoppel) under the governing law. In the Tribunal's view, this submission is incorrect. The parties strongly disputed its application to their case; but, significantly, there was no dispute as its requirements as a general principle of international law.

7.22. The Claimants also contend that *Orinoco Steamship* (and presumably other like authorities) do not correctly reflect *res judicata* under international law. In their submission, the case reflected Umpire Plumley's common law orientation, as evidenced by his reliance on a decision of the US Supreme Court decision as legal authority for the cited principle. The Claimants contend that notions of issue estoppel found in common law systems are not found in civil law systems, which typically (so the Claimants submit) limit *res judicata* effects to matters addressed in the *dispositif* of an award or judgment. Given this significant difference in approach between two major systems of law, the Claimants contend that issue estoppel cannot be said to be an aspect of *res judicata* as a general principle of law 'recognised by civilized nations'.

7.23. The Tribunal recognises that historical differences as to issue estoppel have existed and, to a lesser extent, still exist in national laws between certain common law and certain civil law systems. As the ILA Interim Report makes clear, however, there is no sharp divide between these two legal systems. It is also clear that international courts and tribunals have regularly examined under international law a prior tribunal's reasoning, and the arguments it considered, in determining the scope, and thus the preclusive effect, of the prior award's operative part. The first international tribunal's analysis and reasoning thus often play a significant role before the second international tribunal in determining the *res judicata* effect of the earlier award.

478   APPENDIX I

7.24. This is illustrated in the *Pious Fund* arbitration, where the tribunal held that an umpire's award in a prior mixed claims commission proceeding had *res judicata* effect, and obliged Mexico to pay certain annuities to the USA on behalf of the Archbishop of San Francisco and the Bishop of Monterey. The tribunal rejected Mexico's contention that only the amount specified in the prior award had *res judicata* effect, instead considering that it must consider the earlier award in its entirety to determine the *res judicata* effect of its *dispositif*: 'Considering that all the parts of a judgment or a decree concerning the points debated in the dispute enlighten and mutually supplement each other, and that they all serve to render precise the meaning and bearing of the *dispositif* (the decisory part of the judgment), to determine the points upon which there is *res judicata* and which therefore cannot be put in question.'

7.25. The Permanent Court of International Justice was of like mind in *Advisory Opinion No. 11*: 'It is perfectly true that all the parts of a judgment concerning the points in dispute explain and complete each other and are to be taken into account in order to determine the precise meaning and scope of the operative portion. This is clearly stated in the award of the Permanent Court of Arbitration of October 14th, 1902, concerning the Pious Fund of the Californias ... The Court agrees with this statement.'

7.26. In his dissent in *Chorzów Factory*, Judge Anzilotti was of the view that 'the binding effect attaches only to the operative part of the judgment and not to the statement of reasons'. However, he added: '[w]hen I say that only the terms of a judgment are binding, I do not mean that only what is actually written in the operative part constitutes the Court's decision. On the contrary, it is certain that it is almost always necessary to refer to the statement of reasons to understand clearly the operative part and above all to ascertain the *causa petendi*.'

7.28. The International Court of Justice also looks to the parties' arguments and submissions to determine the legal effect of prior judgments. As Professor Rosenne observes, '[t]he relevance of whether a question was argued between the parties might arise ... if it is necessary to determine the scope of the *res judicata* ... In the *Asylum* case ... the problem was ... of the scope of the binding force of the decision. The *res judicata* does not derive from the operative clause of the judgment, which confined itself to stating which submissions of the parties were rejected or accepted and to what extent, but from the reasons in point of law given by the Court.' Accordingly, cases such as *Asylum* and *Corfu Channel* 'bring into sharp relief the delayed-action effect attaching to the written and oral pleadings. In the last analysis the scope of *res judicata* can only be determined by reference to the pleadings in general, and to the parties' submissions in particular.'

7.29. The jurisprudence of the European Court of Justice (ECJ) is to like effect. For the ECJ (applying the laws of the European Union and international law), the legal effect of a decision by the ECJ and other EU institutions is not to be limited to the wording of the operative part. In *Asteris & Greece v. Commission*, the ECJ noted that the EU institution was required to have regard not only to the operative part of the decision but also to the *motifs* which led to that decision in order to determine the former's exact meaning. In *Commission v. BASF*, the ECJ noted that: 'the operative part of such a decision can be understood, and its full effect ascertained, only in the light of the statement of reasons'; and that a decision's *dispositif* and *motifs* constituted 'an indivisible whole'. In *Deggendorf v. Commission*, the ECJ held that: 'the operative part of an act is indissociably linked to the statement of reasons for it, so that, when it has to be interpreted, account must be taken of the reasons which led to its adoption.'

7.30. Thus, where there is a question regarding the extent of a prior decision or award's *res judicata* effect, international tribunals regularly look to the prior tribunal's reasons and indeed also to the parties' arguments, in order to determine the scope of what was finally decided in that earlier proceeding.

Summary as to the *res judicata* doctrine:

7.37. Applying NAFTA Article 1131(1), the rules of international law and the UNCITRAL [United Nations Commission on International Trade Law] Arbitration Rules, the Tribunal concludes that the Apotex I & II Award, with its relevant reasons, operates in this arbitration as *res judicata* as regards both named parties to that arbitration, namely Apotex Inc. and the Respondent. It remains to be considered in what manner it operates in regard to the specific claims made by Apotex Inc. in this arbitration.

7.38. As regards Apotex-Holdings, the Claimants agreed at the Hearing that Apotex-Holdings, for the purpose of *res judicata*, should be identified as a 'privy' to the Apotex I and II Award: '... having reviewed the RSM versus Grenada decision, the second one, Apotex would agree that privies are bound to the same extent as the Party with which they stand in privity. So we would accept that Apotex Holdings could not bring the claim asserted and decided in the Apotex [I and] II case ...' In other words, the two named Claimants in this arbitration stand in similar shoes, as regards the effect of *res judicata* resulting from the Apotex I and II Award, notwithstanding the fact that only one of them was a named party to the Apotex I and II Award.

7.39. However, Apotex-Holding's shoes are only similar and not the same. As the Claimants made clear towards the end of the Hearing, in answer to the Tribunal's Question A2: '... there is a distinction between derivative claims made on behalf of a company and claims made directly by a shareholder on its own behalf. In this arbitration, Apotex Holdings brings a claim in its own right and in its own name. It is different from the claim made by Apotex-Canada [Apotex Inc.]. Apotex Holdings is bound by the Apotex I and II Award only to the extent that it addresses Apotex-Canada as the investor and holder of the two tentatively approved ANDAs at issue.'

7.40. In the Tribunal's view, independently from the concession (rightly) made by Apotex-Holdings at the Hearing, Apotex-Holdings is a 'privy' with Apotex-US, albeit not a named party in the Apotex I & II arbitration. Its relevant claims in this arbitration, albeit made in its own right and in its own name, depend upon Apotex Inc.'s ANDAs as investments under NAFTA Articles 1116 and 1139; and if these are not investments, Apotex-Holdings cannot bring such claims before this Tribunal as a matter of jurisdiction.

The application of *res judicata*:

7.41. It is self-evident that the 'Operative Order' in Paragraph 358 of the Apotex I & II Award (pages 118–119) does not, read strictly in isolation by itself, address the Claimants' specific claims in this arbitration. That operative part merely records, in Paragraph 358(a), that Apotex Inc. 'does not qualify as an "investor", who has made an "investment" in the U.S., for the purposes of NAFTA Articles 1116 and 1139, and accordingly both the Sertraline and Pravastatin Claims are hereby dismissed in their entirety, on the basis that the Tribunal lacks jurisdiction in relation thereto'. The Claimants in this arbitration make no similar claims regarding Sertraline and Pravastatin.

480 APPENDIX I

7.42. However, in this Tribunal's view, that operative part as a '*dispositif*' can and should be read with the relevant '*motifs*' or reasons for that operative part, as decided above. Hence, the Tribunal concludes, for the purpose of *res judicata*, that Paragraph 358(a) of the operative part is to be applied together with the reasons applicable to that paragraph, namely the relevant passages in Paragraphs 177 to 246 of the Apotex I & II Award (pages 55 to 78).

[There is now detailed consideration of the earlier Award and whether/how *res judicata* applies.]

7.57. Shorn of all semantic technicalities, it is worth asking the simple question after reading the relevant passages from the Apotex I & II Award in the Annex to this Part VII: how would that tribunal respond to the specific claims made by Apotex Inc. in this arbitration under NAFTA Article 1139? In this Tribunal's view, that question admits of only one answer: the Apotex I & II tribunal would say that it had already decided the essential issues relating to these claims in its award; and, applying the same two lines of its operative part with its same supporting reasons, that these claims failed to meet the requirements of NAFTA Article 1139 for jurisdiction under NAFTA's Chapter Eleven.

7.58. In the Tribunal's view, it is impossible to dismiss those reasons as mere 'obiter dicta' or to read one passage in isolation from those reasons as a whole. Those reasons under both NAFTA Articles 1139(g) and 1139(h) were essential to the operative part and thereby distinctly determined matters distinctly in issue in the Apotex I & II arbitration. It is also impermissible to parse the two sets of claims in the two arbitrations, so as artificially to distinguish one case from the other. The purpose of the *res judicata* doctrine under international law is to put an end to litigation; and it would thwart that purpose if a party could so easily escape the doctrine by 'claim-splitting' in successive proceedings.

7.59. Thus, the Claimants did not argue (nor could they) that simply because the Apotex I & II Award addressed specific claims relating to Sertraline and Pravastatin, the Claimants could still bring the same claims relating to other drug products. Similarly, in the Tribunal's view, the Claimants cannot now distinguish tentatively approved ANDAs from finally approved ANDAs so as to frustrate the application of *res judicata* to issues decided in the Apotex I & II Award. That is an impermissible attempt to re-argue and overturn the final and binding decisions in the Apotex I & II Award. The Tribunal notes that, in *Grynberg v. Grenada*, that tribunal likewise rejected an analogous attempt based upon a new allegation of corruption. Indeed, were it so easy to side-step the application of *res judicata*, the doctrine would be largely meaningless under international law, a risk recognised by several scholars, including Professors Dodge, Schreuer and Reinisch in the works cited earlier in this Part. The costs and time required for investor–state arbitrations, already not inconsiderable, would be multiplied several times over if unsuccessful claimants could persuade later tribunals to restrict the effect of earlier awards by simply reformulating their claims and arguments. As already described, there is a strong interest, both public and private, in bringing an end to a dispute by one final and binding arbitration award.

7.60. In regard to Apotex-Holdings, the Tribunal decides that same result must follow, albeit for additional reasons. Given that Apotex Inc.'s ANDAs are not 'investments' under NAFTA Article 1139, it follows that Apotex-Holdings cannot make any claim in respect of its indirect interest in such ANDAs because Apotex-Holdings is not, for that purpose, an investor with a relevant 'investment' under NAFTA Article 1139.

APPENDIX I   481

Chevron Corporation and Texaco Petroleum Corporation v. Ecuador (II), UNCITRAL, Second Partial Award on Track II, dated 30 August 2018: on denial of justice

Chevron (II) is a case of remarkable procedural complexity concerning at its core very serious allegations of denial of justice, including corruption of the judiciary. Absent the allegations of denial of justice, the approach of the Tribunal to the findings of the domestic courts would have been as stated in the important passage in the Decision on Track 1B of 12 March 2015, at paragraph 140 (footnotes omitted):

> whilst not strictly bound to follow their result or reasoning as a matter of international law, this Tribunal would have wished to be guided, as regards any relevant issue of Ecuadorian law, by the decisions of the Lago Agrio Court, the Appellate Court of Lago Agrio and the Cassation Court. Such an approach would extend beyond courtesy, comity and due respect for the Respondent's judicial branch. As a practical matter, without more, the considered judgments of any municipal court applying its own municipal law, especially an appellate court, are (absent special circumstances) the best evidence of the content and application of that law to the same or similar situations. Further, the publicly stated reasons of a municipal court would ordinarily carry far more weight than the submissions of disputing parties. This orthodox approach appears to be common ground between the Parties, based on the well-known decision of the International Court of Justice in *Diallo*.

However, as the Tribunal then explained, the allegations of denial of justice precluded such an approach. Those allegations were then decided in the Second Partial Award on Track II, dated 30 August 2018. An extract from the consideration of the relevant legal principles follows (footnotes omitted), dealing inter alia with burden of proof and containing the critically important observation that there have been many shocks and surprises caused by court judgments in legal history, but without much more, such do not amount to a denial of justice.

8.35 As to the doctrine of denial justice under international law, the Tribunal has been guided generally by four awards cited by the Parties: *Azinian v Mexico* (1999), *Mondev v USA* (2002), *Loewen v USA* (2003) and *Oostergetel v Slovakia* (2012).

8.36 In *Oostergetel*, it was decided that the standard for denial of justice (as part of the FET standard) was 'a demanding one. To meet the applicable test, it will not be enough to claim that municipal law has been breached, that the decision of a national court is erroneous, that a judicial procedure was incompetently conducted, or that the actions of the judge in question were probably motivated by corruption. A denial of justice implies the failure of a national system as a whole to satisfy minimum standards.'

8.37 The Tribunal has also borne in mind, as these legal materials confirm, that the doctrine of denial of justice essentially addresses procedural unfairness and not (by itself) an error of fact or applicable national law, although both may equally defeat the complainant's substantive rights. An international tribunal, such as this Tribunal, cannot act as a court of appeal. As a former ICJ judge once wrote: '... if all that a judge does is to make a mistake, i.e. to arrive at a wrong conclusion of law or fact, the State is not responsible ... the only thing that can establish a denial of justice so far as a judgment is concerned is an affirmative answer, duly supported by evidence, to some such question as "Was the court guilty of bias, fraud, dishonesty, lack of impartiality, or gross incompetence?" ... *bona fide* error does not entail responsibility.'

482 APPENDIX I

8.38 As to the threshold required for denial of justice, the Tribunal adopts the approach taken by the NAFTA tribunal in *Mondev v USA* (2002), citing the judgment of the International Court of Justice in *ELSI* (1989), that the impugned judgment must be clearly improper and discreditable (with footnotes here omitted):

127. In the ELSI case, a Chamber of the Court described as arbitrary conduct that which displays 'a wilful disregard of due process of law, ... which shocks, or at least surprises, a sense of judicial propriety'. It is true that the question there was whether certain administrative conduct was 'arbitrary', contrary to the provisions of an FCN treaty. Nonetheless (and without otherwise commenting on the soundness of the decision itself) the Tribunal regards the Chamber's criterion as useful also in the context of denial of justice, and it has been applied in that context, as the Claimant pointed out. The Tribunal would stress that the word 'surprises' does not occur in isolation. The test is not whether a particular result is surprising, but whether the shock or surprise occasioned to an impartial tribunal leads, on reflection, to justified concerns as to the judicial propriety of the outcome, bearing in mind on the one hand that international tribunals are not courts of appeal, and on the other hand that Chapter 11 of NAFTA (like other treaties for the protection of investments) is intended to provide a real measure of protection. In the end the question is whether, at an international level and having regard to generally accepted standards of the administration of justice, a tribunal can conclude in the light of all the available facts that the impugned decision was clearly improper and discreditable, with the result that the investment has been subjected to unfair and inequitable treatment. This is admittedly a somewhat open-ended standard, but it may be that in practice no more precise formula can be offered to cover the range of possibilities.

8.39 The approach in this passage has been followed subsequently by other international tribunals, including *GEA v Ukraine* (2011), *Arif* (2013) and *Mamidoil* (2015).

8.40 The Tribunal emphasises that the legal test for denial of justice requires the claimant to prove objectively that the impugned judgment was 'clearly improper and discreditable', with the failure by the 'national system as a whole to satisfy minimum standards'. There have been many shocks and surprises caused by court judgments in legal history, but without much more, amounting to discreditable improprieties and the failure of the whole national system, such judgments do not amount to a denial of justice.

8.41 A claimant's legal burden of proof is therefore not lightly discharged, given that a national legal system will benefit from the general evidential principle known by the Latin maxim as *omnia praesumuntur rite et solemniter esse acta donec probetur in contrarium*. It presumes (subject to rebuttal) that the court or courts have acted properly. This general principle was described by Professor O'Connell as follows, as cited to the NAFTA tribunal in *Loewen* (with footnotes there and here omitted):

When one comes to examine failure of the courts themselves 'palpable deviation' from the accepted standards of judicial practice are not so readily ascertained. For one thing, there is a presumption in favour of the judicial process. For another, defects in procedure may be of significance only internally, and not work an international injustice. For a third, wide discretion must be allowed a court in the reception and rejection of evidence, in adjournment, and in admission of documents, and it cannot be said that deviations even from the municipal law rules of evidence are deviations from an international standard. The first thing that must be ascertained is whether as a result of court manoeuvrings substantial injustice has been done to the claimant; the second is whether these manoeuvrings really amount to obstruction of the judicial process, and are extrinsic to the merits of his claim. Bad faith and not judicial error seems to be the heart of the matter, and bad faith may be indicated by an unreasonable departure from the rules of evidence and procedure.

8.42 This general principle subsumes a second principle, namely that a court is permitted a margin of appreciation before the threshold of a denial of justice can be met. Nonetheless, the balance of probabilities remains the standard of proof, with the claimant bearing the overall legal burden of proof.

APPENDIX II

Excerpts from Lectures given by Johnny Veeder to LLM Students at King's College London (in the Period 2017–2019)

These notes were taken from the lectures given as part of the LLM course, International Investment Arbitration. Johnny taught on this course for almost twenty years.

Introduction—on questions, not answers [from lecture 1]

Now we say this at the beginning of each year. We're here to teach you the questions and when you leave here we'd like you to remember to keep asking the questions because unfortunately the answers may change. But the questions don't. So very often you'll see that we'll disagree or we'll ask you something and there may not be a right answer, there may be several, but as long as you remember just to ask the question you'll still be doing the right thing. But it's quite possible in this field to arrive at different answers to the same question.

So, what do the questions centre around? The three attributes of arbitration generally are:

Consent: both for investor state and for commercial arbitration, the first thing you've got to look for is consent. Did the disputing parties consent to arbitration? And if the answer is no you stop there. This goes back a long time, in fact at least to the first Hague Peace Conference in 1899. Russia proposed at the First Hague Peace Conference to have compulsory arbitration. States would permanently agree to resolve their disputes by arbitration, before the dispute, and that was rejected in particular by Germany, although strongly supported by Russia, Great Britain and the United States of America. If the Russians had won the argument in 1899, would the First World War have taken place? You'd at least have to ask yourself that. I suspect the answer is yes, of course it would, they wouldn't have cared less about arbitration; but it is possible it might not have done. And, ever since 1899, this failure of Russia through its particular specialist, a man called FF Martens, means that states only arbitrate where they have specifically agreed and where the other party has agreed as well. So, consent is absolutely critical.

The next thing is finality. In arbitration you want something that results in something that ends, so finality is absolutely crucial to arbitration. That's why in most arbitral systems, certainly investor state arbitration, there is no appeal. We'll come onto that later.

And the last thing, unless you want a piece of paper to plaster on your wall, the award has got to be enforceable, and this is really problematic in investor state arbitration because you're dealing with a sovereign state and a sovereign state can always plead sovereign immunity subject to exceptions.

486 APPENDIX II

So, it's consent, finality, enforceability that provide the litmus paper test for any system of investor state arbitration, just as they are for international commercial arbitration.

On life before ICSID/the BIT, Bhutan and ICSID arbitration [from lecture 2]

As to consent, you've seen how important it is, and the trouble is if you're used to consent in the contractual field whether it's common law or civilian systems, that is simple compared to consent in the field of investor state arbitration. Most books spend about a third of their pages dealing with consent and jurisdiction. It's incredibly complicated and people think that we've got into an area now where we are talking about fictitious consent. See what you think at the end of this class. But it's a very hot topic in many fields.

And it is useful to start with consent in the world before investor state arbitration as we know it today. The story is a rather sad one. This is the Lena Goldfields case, and this is a picture [on the screen] of the Soviet arbitrator and he had also been the Soviet arbitrator in the Harriman arbitrations, a man called Dr S.B. Chlenov. He was an international lawyer, he'd studied in Germany, he'd lived in Berlin, he lived for many, many years in Paris, he spoke fluent French and he was without doubt the major expert throughout the 1920s, up until 1937, in the Soviet Union for International arbitration. We know very little about him. We have this photograph, why isn't he wearing a tie? [Student: 'At the time they didn't have ties?' VVV: 'They did.' Another audience member: 'It's a mug shot?'] It is a mug shot. This is the evening of his arrest. So he's been arrested. He lived in central Moscow and he's been arrested, he's been taken, probably, to Lubyanka and these are the photographs that still exist in an organisation called Memorial. After that he disappeared. He was supposed to stand trial, at a show trial, but I think maybe he didn't cooperate, or he was very brave, and he was shot and tried in secret. Probably in the reverse order, tried in secret and then shot. This story is interesting also because of the arbitration clause. Lena Goldfields was an English company, very sophisticated, they'd operated these same mines before the revolution, they'd been expropriated, they wanted to go back, and they knew how to get them back and working, and at that time USSR was desperate for gold. Gold was the one way they could buy equipment and food from Western Europe, because gold was better than dollars, in fact gold was dollars.

Now the clause, again, is a very long clause. It starts off, as with Harriman: 'All disputes and misunderstandings ...' blah, blah, '... shall be examined and settled by an arbitration court' so that's standard. There's then an even longer and more sophisticated series of provisions to deal with default situations in setting up the tribunal. I'll skip past those quite quickly because there's one very important provision. It's sub-clause (F). So basically, you've got the tribunal up and running, the parties are submitting their pleadings, and you're going to have a hearing: 'If, upon receipt of the summons from the super-arbitrator ...'—and this is a mis-translation from the German obmann, so the German influence here is even felt when people use the English language. You also have that same term also in Scotland, haven't you, super-arbitrator. But all it means is the president of the tribunal—'the date and place of the first session'—and this was to be in Berlin—'one of the parties, in the absence of insuperable obstacles, fails to send its arbitrator ...'—this is a bit old fashioned, looking as though you have one arbitrator who is your arbitrator, whereas the tradition now, if not a legal requirement, is that an arbitrator is an arbitrator for both parties—'... fails to send its arbitrator to the arbitration court, or the arbitrator avoids participating in the arbitration court, then the matter in dispute shall, at the request of the other party, be settled by the super-arbitrator and the other member of the court …'—that is the other co-arbitrator appointed by the other party—'… such settlement to be valid only if unanimous'.

And this is the problem with the truncated tribunal. It still exists today in commercial arbitration. We've all had to revise our national laws, introduce provisions into arbitration rules, but this existed way back in the days of Lena Goldfields in 1925. The truncated tribunal is when the party feels it's going to lose, it yanks out its arbitrator, thinking that can sabotage the arbitration. Or, if the hearing is over, it yanks out its arbitrator during the deliberations and tells him or her to refuse to sign the award hoping that that will, again, thwart the arbitral process. Now, Lena Goldfields thought about this in 1925 and they were very wise to do so, because that was the award. What's wrong with this award? You have two signatories. You have the super-arbitrator, Dr Stutzer, who was a Professor of mining from Freiburg and the other was appointed by the English party, Lena Goldfields, Sir Leslie Scott, who was the former Solicitor General and later Lord Justice of Appeal. But Dr Chlenov had been told not to go to the hearing by his government and he didn't go; but they went ahead, they made the award in draft, he refused to sign it. This award, nonetheless, was a valid award and eventually, a very, very, very, very long time later, the USSR paid part of this award. When I say later, I am talking about 1964, so 34 years later, and they did it because the UK lent them the money. Not a happy story.

So basically, if you're trying to think what would you do in the private sector by yourselves, without the benefit of treaties or conventions or laws, you really have to recreate what the Lena Goldfields and the Harriman arbitration clauses do, which doesn't really work.

So, to BITs [bilateral investment treaties] and ICSID [International Centre for Settlement of Investment Disputes]. The world is now much better for investors, and we will be spending a lot of time exploring the protections that may now be available, but it is important to note up front that there may be huge dangers in states signing BITs. Now the question is 'why should they sign?' We don't have that much research but we now have a lot of criticism and this is an area we're going to look at as to why a state signs a BIT referring a dispute to ICSID arbitration. The example I want to give tonight is such a state, which is Bhutan. Has anyone been to Bhutan? Nobody is from Bhutan? Well, Bhutan, as you know, is a very small state in the Himalayas sandwiched between India and China. If there's a Third World War it could start in or near Bhutan. We had an incident a year ago, Indian troops and Chinese troops struggled, thankfully without shooting, on Bhutanese soil in the high Himalayas. So, it's a small country, very vulnerable to its neighbours. But it's a developing country which is being developed very successfully.

And the question I want you to think about is would you advise Bhutan to sign a BIT and the ISCID Convention? The figures are actually quite simple. Bhutan is a developing country, it has a very high growth rate, it's a recent democracy, a very unusual democracy because the old king said, 'I don't want to be an absolute monarch anymore, I want you to be a democracy and I want to be a representative figure without political power.' And the people said 'no, no we don't want that' and he said, 'well that's my point, you are the people, and you will have democracy whether you like it or not.' And they had two elections. They had a practise election where there was, I think, a yellow team against a blue team, and then they had a real election and a party came into power, slightly surprising as it wasn't the king's brother it was somebody else, and

488 APPENDIX II

then after a certain number of years there was another election he was tossed out and the opposition became the government. So basically, it looks as though it's a flourishing democracy, which is always good for investors. The population is very small, 800,000, the government is very poor—US$407 million a year, their budget, which is heavily subsidised by India. The average annual income is US$7,641. Principal foreign earnings are very limited: tourism, Indian subsidies and the Tala Dam. I should explain that the subsidies date back to the British days of the Raj because Bhutan was the only army in India that defeated the British army. That's why they never formed part of India. The British very wisely thought, rather than defeat them, we'll pay them to be peaceful and so they were given subsidies not to attack British India and those subsidies have been continued by India today. But basically it's the Tala Dam which is important. This is a huge hydro-electric project, heavy investment, where the electricity is sold to India. So foreign direct and indirect investment in the shape of electricity, roads, hotels, social developments, schools, universities are extremely important. They don't have the capital themselves, they need to attract foreign capital from overseas, and attracting foreign capital you think could be done by foreign aid—it can't be—for every dollar in foreign aid developing countries receive nine in private foreign direct investment. So FDI [foreign direct investment] is extremely important for developing countries.

So, should Bhutan accede to the ICSID Convention? I think not, no, and it gels with what I said at the time in Bhutan, which is: not now, there's no immediate advantage. There could be an advantage in the future, but that is a decision for the future and although legally there is this double requirement of consent, we're going to come onto that later tonight, once you are known to have signed and ratified the ICSID Convention, the difficulty is that a foreign investor may put immense pressure upon you to agree a concession contract with an ICSID arbitration clause. So, in a sense, although legally you can say no, commercially and politically you may have to say yes, and that would not be a good thing at the moment. But the other factor that we mentioned, namely India—India controls Bhutan's foreign affairs, and Bhutan was happy for the New York Convention because India is a signatory and has ratified the New York Convention, but I think there are real problems with India permitting Bhutan to sign a convention which India has declined to sign. So it's all very interesting, but like St. Augustine, not now.

On arbitrators [from lecture 3]

This is a quiz. First of all, can you name a Nobel Prize winner who was nominated in one of the most important arbitrations in the 20th century? If you don't, you're in big, big trouble. It means you didn't pay attention in school at all. We'll give you a clue. Albert Einstein. He was nominated by the USSR in the *Lena Goldfields* case. He was going to be chairman of the tribunal. Again, not a lawyer, isn't that interesting? There was a mining engineer who was eventually appointed to replace him, but the British said: 'Oh my God, Einstein, if the Russians want Einstein it must be because it's good for them and bad for us. So, we might have proposed Einstein because it was good for us and bad for them, the fact that they did it shows that it's a bad thing so we'll veto it.' And so they vetoed it. It's a great pity, isn't it?

Ok, next question: An arbitrator who was a saint? You probably won't know this because I didn't know this myself until a few years ago. [Audience: the pope.] Actually, you probably are right, the popes used to be arbitrators, although they never did the work themselves, they delegated it to a cardinal, but are there any popes that are saints?

APPENDIX II   489

Very few of them are saintly, but perhaps yes. Anyway, for this one, you've got to go back a very long way, he was called Maxim the Greek and he was sent in the late 15th century from Mount Athos, where he was a monk, to Moscow by the Patriarch of what is now Istanbul, to Moscow to act as an arbitrator because there was a division in the Russian Orthodox church, which was causing a lot of trouble, and the Tsar, who was the father of Ivan the Terrible, wanted to have a Greek religious translator to settle the text, to decide who was right and who was wrong. So he went out there and for two years he laboured over these texts and then produced an award that was very for one side and against the other. Unfortunately, by that time the other side was in power, so they put him in prison for about twenty years and when he got out he said he wanted to go home to Mount Athos and they said 'no you can't because you might say bad things about us', so he died in Russia. But he was a very famous philosopher and if you speak to Russian historians or philosophers they will know about Maxim the Greek but they won't know about him being an arbitrator.

Ok, now name 15 ICSID arbitrators. Who can name 15? You can name some from what you've heard tonight, but we want 15. [...] Well done, you're quite right, you are the first class that has ever done this, well done. Next year I'm going to put it up to 25 because this was too easy. But it's interesting, when you look at awards you've got to look at the names and you recognise them very quickly because they give you the flavour of the decision. So if you look at a Gabrielle Kaufmann-Kohler award or a Crawford award, obviously they have been very carefully thought through, it's likely to be a very good and influential award. There are some awards, I won't mention any names, where you don't feel quite the same confidence. It's very important that you pick up on the names.

Now, ten non-lawyer ICSID arbitrators? Can you name one? I used to have the answer at my fingertips, but I've forgotten what it is, I can think of one but I've forgotten his name! In one important case, which we'll come on to later in this term, the tribunal had a former Greek Cypriot diplomat. But he was a lawyer, so that doesn't really count. The basic problem is there aren't any non-lawyer ICSID Arbitrators, for something that was set up to have bankers, financial experts, it's amazing how the lawyers have taken over. And that has not been a good thing.

Name ten women ICSID arbitrators. We've heard Gabrielle Kaufmann-Kohler, Brigitte Stern and Rosalyn Higgins from you, and she is retired now. The problem is, it's still very few. ISCID will say we've had 15% appointments this year with women and you say yes, but apart from Kaufmann-Kohler and Brigitte Stern, oh well it's only 1%. So you've got to look rather carefully as to who the women are when people talk about women ICSID arbitrators. But those two are the pre-eminent figures. And the truth is the system appears to be massively weighted in favour of Western European and American males, there doesn't seem to be a great diverse system, and this is why this next thing is so important.

Young ICSID arbitrators. We have got to get the next generation into the field as arbitrators. You can't do that without being counsel, a specialist in the field, an academic, a writer and so forth. But if we're going to get rid of double-hatting and there are conflicts that prevent certain people from becoming arbitrators, this group, the young ICSID arbitrators are going to dry up. And so, it is going to get worse not better.

ICSID does have a list system, we'll come on to that, these are lists produced by some Member States and on that list, if you're listed on a Member State, you are then qualified to be appointed by ICSID as the president of an arbitration tribunal, or as a member of the ad hoc committees. The trouble is that a lot of countries don't bother with their lists, including the UK, our list is now, what, 20 years old, and I think some of the people

490 APPENDIX II

have died actually! And basically, what you can do if you're that way inclined, you go to a friendly country, even if it is not your country of nationality, and you persuade them to appoint you. I mean this is all a bit artificial, I mean we think it's all very funny, but in fact the list system isn't working at ICSID. ICSID have to make appointments as president by consent of the parties. There was a NAFTA [North American Free Trade Agreement] List, NAFTA thought we're going to do great things we Mexicans, Americans and Canadians, we're going to have a list of independent presidents of tribunals so we don't have to muck around. We'll draw up a list, 15 names, five each, and then we won't have to waste time trying to choose people. And NAFTA was 20 years ago? It's even longer isn't it? How many people do you think are on this list? The NAFTA List? They can't even agree. That's why when the EU [European Union] says we're going to have this list for our multilateral court system you get a bit cynical because the five to be appointed by the European Union will have to come from 28, possibly 27, member states, how are they going to choose them? How are they going to do just their own?

Now the arbitrators, I have to say the good ones, are very, very good—such as the Kaufmann-Kohlers, the Greenwoods, the Crawfords, the Don McRaes. It's not a long list, but the good ones are really very, very good, and their awards are public and you can see what they do even in procedural orders, which are made public, and they're all on the ICSID website and they're accessible to other arbitrators, to professionals, to users. And so what you get, although you don't have a sort of *res judicata* system of precedent, you do get what is called *jurisprudence constante*. Now, in England you always use a foreign language, usually Latin, if you don't really want people to understand what you're saying. So, who speaks French here as their first language? *Jurisprudence constante c'est quoi*? It is not a precedent? Well, the thing is, it is *jurisprudence et constante*. The thing is it's influential in the sense that if you're counsel you would cite it to a tribunal for example, as you heard from Sam, he cited *Pac Rim* to the *Philip Morris* Tribunal. Now what the *Philip Morris* Tribunal do straight away is look at who the arbitrators are and they might have then said, 'ok shut up and we'll move on', but one of them was Brigitte Stern so they would have said 'oh that's interesting'. But it's not binding on them in a way that they're bound to follow it. It's sort of an interesting development the way you might read a very relevant article by a distinguished academic, they've dealt with the problem, they've thought about it, they're trying to write it down in words, for public use as well as for use by the disputing parties, does it help us? It may have helped. The difficulty is that as arbitrators you decide the case. I never think it's right to decide a general principle, you apply a general principle to *that* case and you don't decide other cases and that's a very important discipline. You're an arbitrator, you're not a judge making law, you're applying the law as you determine it to be. But there are others of my colleagues, as you will hear in a minute, who go much further.

Ok, those are some of the arbitrators. Would you appoint this man (Arsene Wenger) as an arbitrator? You might actually, you might, he is quite bright isn't he? Depends what the dispute was. What about this guy? (Jose Mourinho) I'm afraid in real life it is very personal, you would never appoint this guy? No, exactly. More seriously, how about this person? (Sir Anthony Mason.) Do you know who he is? He is one of the most distinguished Australian judges, he presided over the Australian High Court, a very respected jurist, retired, who came over to do investor state, as a very senior common law judge, hardworking, distinguished, thorough. He was the president of the *Loewen* Tribunal, the first NAFTA case bought by a Canadian investor in this company against the USA and this award is still controversial. People still get upset about it. I don't get upset about him because he's an absolutely first rate jurist, but he never worked again in this field. He just felt, forget it. So, even very famous, respected jurists from another field, don't always make it across to investor state. Who is this one? Not difficult if you can read! As it says, it is Gabrielle Kaufmann-Kohler, I think it's a wonderful picture. Who is that? Very famous. We were doing a case together and the World Bank had these expositions in the foyer and you could go into this booth to see what it felt like to be in a hurricane in the Caribbean, so we all took it in turns to go into the booth and be photographed, and so this is Brigitte Stern in the middle of a hurricane in the World Bank.

How about this photograph? This is how, when you arrive at the World Bank, you may get handed a piece of paper by protestors. This is a fairly typical example. This was a fairly early hearing, when *Pac Rim* was being heard and do you see you always get this phrase 'fat cats'. I think they're a bit sensitive, but that's the tribunal and it's a kangaroo court and there are various insults on the basis that the tribunal can undermine democracy. This is the Canadian operated Pacific Rim seeking to open a gold mine that could poison a river supply in half of El Salvador's drinking water, but they're never knowingly undersold in their propaganda. But this was perfectly innocent. This was quite a friendly demonstration, and those were the days when it was quite easy. It is not now. Now we have very high security, there have been threats, lawyers have been threatened, even within the World Bank now we have security. So we have security to get into the World Bank, we have security now on the door of the arbitration hearing room and this is why it's getting slightly nasty. It is not now quite so friendly and people have to be a little bit careful. So, it's getting a little bit more awkward and maybe that's a compliment, maybe arbitration is important when before it wasn't.

On the Magnificent Seven, bonds and raptors [from lecture 4]

Now, this is someone who you should know. Who is that? Come on, someone must know, this is terrible, he's incredibly famous. [Student: John Wayne?] Completely wrong. I'll give you a clue, he was born in Vladivostok. Okay, the Magnificent Seven: does that film mean anything to you? The Magnificent Seven? Do you know Kurosawa's film about the Samurai? The Seven Samurai? Culturally you are very deficient, this is terrible, these are the two most important films ever made. Well, the Seven Samurai was about the Samurai protecting a small village in Japan and of course they are sacrificed, they protect the village successfully, the villagers are saved from the bandits, but they die. And this film was remade as the Magnificent Seven in Hollywood and this guy, Yul Brynner, was the leader of the Magnificent Seven who protects the villagers and saves them from very bad people.

Now what is interesting for us, is not because we're into cowboys in this class, is that his father was a Swiss-German, as was his grandfather, in Vladivostok, and they had enormous wealth—several mines, a shipping company and other interests—in Korea. They lost it all in 1930 and he was taken as a young boy first to Shanghai then to Paris, then to America, where he became a very famous actor. He's wearing a hat because he was folically challenged, he was completely bald, that's how you recognise him. Anyway, his father was party to what is called the *Tetiuhe* arbitration, again this is an ad hoc arbitration between the USSR, a Swiss, British, Irish company. In Russian he was called Bryner. It's a Swiss name and you may know a very famous Swiss arbitrator who died only a few years ago named Robert Briner, he was President of the ICC for a long time. Well, they were cousins, but when Yul's family went to America they pronounced it Brinner and they had to add an extra 'n' to his name. That's another pub quiz on which you can make a lot of money!

492   APPENDIX II

Enough of that. We are going to move on to bonds as investments. Usually these bonds are packaged in New York, they are subject to terms as to their issue, which are subject to New York law, usually New York court jurisdiction and there is a right on the bond holder, just as I have a five pound note I can go to the Bank of England, and they have to give me five pounds, it's not often done but you could do it in theory. Now in this case these bond holders obviously had rights against the bank who dealt with them in Italy, they sold them, they may have been subject to a duty of care, or because they were consumers they had special statutory rights, but they weren't asserting rights against the bank that sold them on the secondary market, these bonds, and they weren't asserting contractual rights against Argentina because that would have taken them to New York. But they were asserting that they had made an investment and therefore had the protection of the BIT, and they were asserting their rights under the BIT. I think people don't realise that there are three separate routes available to them, this is only one of them.

[...] Do you remember that last part of the definition of investment includes, and this is why the tribunal looked at the word, 'obligation', you remember the definition of investment 'includes without limitation ... obligations, private or public titles and any other right to performances', because *Abaclat* did look at this, and again they played the language trick by saying what does obligation mean, because when you read it in English it doesn't sound right, you realise there's some conceptual mistranslation, that's why I said it's not a question of translation, it's legal translation from one legal system to another legal system. And what the tribunal said is obligation is actually the French term *obligation* and they looked to it, they say in Spanish and Italian that it in fact means a bond.

[...] Can I explain why this is devastating to the system is that if you remember if you make an ICSID claim you end up with an ICSID award if you win on jurisdiction, liability, quantum, and then you can go around the world and enforce your award as an ICSID Convention award. If you have to go to New York and you get a judgment you are subject to the Paris club, this is an informal but very powerful group of states that ensures that when an insolvent state gets into difficulties, they're not taken to the cleaners by private law claimants, usually banks or, more likely now, third party funders or people who buy claims. And that's why this is a dangerous precedent because it bypasses the protection of insolvent states, like Argentina, like Greece, and they need protection because an individual can go bankrupt, a company can become insolvent and there are rules about what happens about the pro rata share of the remaining assets of the bankrupt or the insolvent company—and ultimately if you have a capitalist system, it's geared on the basis that you can go bankrupt and start again, look at Mr Trump.

States can't do that, they're stuck, basically. If you could make any number of ICSID claims, ICSID awards, against Argentina, there's no discounting, you can just keep enforcing these, and some, some, I don't want to be rude, but I call them 'raptors' but you shouldn't use that language, should you, they're called what, they're called something else. [Audience member: vulture funds.] Vulture funds, they don't like being called vulture funds either actually, but that's what I mean, these guys do not compromise, we'll come to a case later this term, where they go to Zambia and say 'we'll take 90% of what you owe', and Zambia says, 'but you only paid 1%, you bought the debt off somebody else because we can't afford to pay', 'we don't care, we want 90%', 'but that's our health budget for one year', 'we don't care'. Now this system drives a coach and horses through that, now this country introduced legislation to prevent that, and we'll come on to that later this term. We asked other countries in the EU to do the same, we asked other countries in the rest of the world to protect the poorest states from claims

APPENDIX II   493

like this and no one else has followed the example given by this country. So this is actually a problem for the future, if you can bring an ICSID claim leading to an ICSID award on a Sovereign bond you will find impecunious states have no remedy, they're going to be exposed to financial blackmail by vulture funds. That's the end of my political speech.

On the lack of certainty in ISDS (in the context of 'investment') [from lecture 5]

Now we're going to talk about what I think is a most interesting case, and that is *Poštová*. This is ICSID and it is an award on jurisdictional objections, not a decision. So, that was bad news for the Claimant because the tribunal dismissed the case for want of jurisdiction. I'm going to read the first question 'Whether the first claimant has an investment protected under the Cyprus–Greece BIT.' And the Claimants say yes they do because they have an indirect investment through Bonds, through Poštová Bank and that investment is protected under the BIT, so it's the old argument, we've got this, *'every kind of asset'*, we've got this thing and it's expressly an investment under the BIT and so it must satisfy Article 25(1); and what this tribunal says is 'wait a minute', it's the point that when you look at 'every kind of asset' it's in the context of it being an investment, it colours that definition, it doesn't mean just any kind of asset. It means any kind of asset within the umbrella, some people call it a chapeau, of investment.

Let me show you the Slovakia–Greece BIT, you see on the face of it this looks very good doesn't it: 'Investments means every kind of asset and in particular', not exhaustive, though not exclusive, includes these things 'shares in and stock and debentures of the company and any other form of participation in a company ... loans claims to money or to any performance under contract having a financial value'. These are very broad terms, but do they apply to bonds, and it is said they don't. This is quite an important paragraph: '287 However, the tribunal is not persuaded that a broad definition necessarily means that any and all categories, of any nature whatsoever, may qualify as an "investment", nor that the only manner which a category may be excluded as an investment, under a broad asset based concept, is by express exclusion in the given treaty.' Then they go on to the VCLT [Vienna Convention on the Law of Treaties], Article 31.

Then the tribunal turns to *Abaclat*, and they obviously state this to disagree with it, that ' "obligations" and "public securities" were wide enough to encompass the bonds ...'. Then they deal with *Ambiente*, which they consider in detail, but of course they're dealing with their own BIT, and this is really important when you think of the structure of the World Bank. The World Bank covers direct and indirect foreign investment, the IMF [International Monetary Fund] does bonds. ICSID is to do with the World Bank, it is not the IMF, so there is a kind of functional difference between the World Bank and the IMF and this is obviously something that got home to this tribunal. Look at paragraph 328: 'Bonds issued by a Sovereign are subject to ratings by rating agencies and to a continuous monitoring of the State's credit rating (which in turn varies depending on a number of factors ...).' Then at paragraph 329: 'The requirements, characteristics and tradability of the GGBs [Greek government bonds] are amply documented in the record ... [they] are sovereign debt, in the form of securities, in general, and bonds, in particular, that are subject to strict requirements in their issuance. These securities are heavily regulated not only by the issuing State but also in the markets where they are traded, including measures by banking regulators . . .' etc. etc. And then the question they pose themselves is 'whether the wide list of investments provided for under the

494 APPENDIX II

BIT includes sovereign debt'. And they say it does not. Basically they go through the requirements of the BIT and they say 'is there a claim to money under a contract having a financial value?' And they say—no, with sovereign debt there is not, and therefore the claimants don't satisfy the BIT in the Slovakia–Greece wording or in the Cyprus–Greece wording either. So no *ratione materiae* jurisdiction under the BITs. They then deal very quickly with Article 25, but they come to the same view. The decision is no jurisdiction over the dispute, bear the costs in equal shares. On that different point, this was a total defeat for the Claimants. The Respondent State spent a lot of money, we're talking about serious experts and very serious counsel, why should the costs be borne in equal shares? I mean, the tax payer is paying for this, and if they've won and the Claimant has lost, why should the costs be equal? Just remember that. There's an unhealthy practice of saying 'let's do 50/50 because it looks nice', but actually this was one sided, it was like Arsenal last night, it was a total defeat. And there are consequences. Now, that's the award.

Then, there is the annulment. We've got all these cases, which don't say the same thing, we've got *Abaclat* at one extreme, we've got *Ambiente* that rows back a little bit, we've got *Alemanni* which also qualifies things, but they are all saying jurisdiction sort of, and then we've now got *Poštová* saying 'no, no jurisdiction', so we've got an incredible diversity of views, plus we've got the dissenting opinions. It goes to the ad hoc Committee, and what do you think the ad hoc Committee should do? What does an appellant court do? When you go to the supreme court? What's the function of a supreme court? It tries to solve the problem, because they may be right, they may be wrong, these different decisions, but you need one answer to be applied in practice, by practitioners and by lower courts. So, two requirements of any supreme court: they've got to resolve differences by other courts and secondly they've got to do it in a very clear way so that people can apply what they say, it's not an academic article, so that they can apply it in practice for future cases, because certainty and predictability are essential to the rule of law. It's no good going to a lawyer and spinning out your story and he or she says 'well it all depends, if the judge has red hair then we're going to win, but if the judge has blue eyes then we're going to lose', that's not a system of law that works, you've got to have somebody saying 'you're right, we're going to win' and then the other side is advising the other party, 'no you're wrong, we're going to lose this case, we've got to settle it'. So that's why, if the law is clear and certain, 99% of all disputes don't get to arbitration or litigation. But as soon as you have these different decisions, well you say 'it all depends'.

But annulment is not appeal, and the ad hoc committee in *Poštová* carries through its limited mandate and finds that there is no basis for annulment. This is crying out for somebody to say 'yes, mass claims, yes, investment', or 'no mass claims, no investment', and then we move on. But at the moment, what do you do? This was a decision that cost a lot of money, this ad hoc decision, and what is the status now of the award in *Poštová Bank* by these three distinguished people? I think it probably has quite a high status but if you try and run that argument through an arbitration you'll be met with *Ambiente*, *Abaclat* and *Alemanni* and I guarantee nobody will predict the answer. Whoever the arbitrators are might help you guess, but that won't tell you the answer. Have a look at this award, because when we started several weeks ago with consent it sounded like such a simple thing didn't it? Did we consent to arbitrate? Did we consent in writing? You can now see how difficult it is because the consent of a state is conditioned by the terms of the BIT, and then, are those conditions truly conditions of jurisdiction? Are they conditions to admissibility (assuming jurisdiction)?

APPENDIX II   495

On the *Achmea* case [from lecture 6]

The story starts in 1991 when the Netherlands made a BIT with Czechoslovakia. At that time Czechoslovakia is not a member of the EU and it's being encouraged to bring its so-called socialist economy into line with the liberal free Western democracy. Now, one of the things it's being encouraged to do is to sign BITs with EU Member States, there are many, many of these. Poland signed them, Romanian signed them, Bulgaria signed them. This was interesting because when the Slovaks and the Czechs split, the Slovaks succeeded to this 1991 BIT and when it became a member of the EU it maintained that treaty with the Netherlands. So that's the treaty background. It had an ISDS provision, it had substantive protections. There was then a dispute and an award on 7 December 2012 in a dispute between a Dutch investor in Slovakia and the Slovakian state.[1] That was immediately challenged by the Slovakian party because the Tribunal had chosen Frankfurt, Germany as its seat.

So this is unusual, this is an intra-EU BIT sitting within the EU. So it's quite different from ICSID, which doesn't have a seat, or a BIT with a seat outside the EU. If any case was going to be upheld by the ECJ [European Court of Justice] it was this case. So this went through the German system and the German Supreme Court, the Bundesgerichtshof, referred certain questions, as they were bound to, to the European Court of Justice. Quite normal procedure, some countries don't do it. France doesn't do this in arbitration, it's never referred an arbitration case to Luxembourg. We've done it several times, so have the Dutch and so have the Germans. So, so far everything works, and what they asked was—is this compatible with Article 344 and Article 267 of the TFEU [Treaty on the Functioning of the European Union]. Article 344 prevents two EU Member States from privately arbitrating their disputes. In a case called *Mox*, a dispute between the Republic of Ireland and the United Kingdom and they tried to arbitrate that and they were told 'no they couldn't', EU member states have to resolve their disputes before the ECJ in Luxembourg.[2] So, the whole case went off to Luxembourg and the arbitration was stayed, and so we all looked at Article 344 and thought, yes, that's right, that's what it means, two Member States can't privately resolve their disputes, they have to go to the ECJ because that is the paramount umpire of disputes between EU Member States.

It was then argued by the Commission in a series of cases that that applied to private arbitrations as well, so when there was a private person, an investor say, and a state, that also could not be arbitrated. Why that's very important is that what they were suggesting is you could bring a claim in Luxembourg, well you can if you're a direct investor but not if you're an indirect investor. Now all this came up in a series of cases. One of them was *Achmea*, the other was *Electrabel*, and there have been other cases which have looked at Article 344 and really tried their best to work out what it means and they all said it can't cover a private investor and a state because Article 344 is dealing with the relationship between two states. Now if Article 344 applied, Article 267 also applies because that's a duty of loyalty to solve your dispute in accordance with EU law with ultimate reference to the ECJ. But of course, private arbitration tribunals like this one, the *Achmea* tribunal, can't refer any question to Luxembourg, only an EU Member State can do that, or very rarely in certain designated state to state tribunals. So basically Article 344 and Article 267 did not seem to provide the answer that the Commission wanted, that's why these cases all said it doesn't apply, it's only state to state

---

[1] *Achmea B.V. v. The Slovak Republic*, UNCITRAL, PCA Case No. 2008-13 (formerly *Eureko B.V. v. The Slovak Republic*). Johnny Veeder was one of the arbitrators in this important case.

[2] Case C-459/03, *Commission v. Ireland*, Judgment of the Court (Grand Chamber) of 30 May 2006.

496   APPENDIX II

and it doesn't cover investor state arbitrations. Well this case, as I said, was referred to Luxembourg and there's a very interesting opinion by Advocate General Wathelet. He basically says 'absolutely no, of course you can have ISDS [investor–State dispute settlements]', and in a way his opinion is almost too strong the other way.

So then we had the judgment of the 6 March 2018[3] and why this is extremely interesting is that they confirmed *Eco Swiss*.[4] *Eco Swiss* was a very important case arising from a private arbitration, two parties, not states, where a question of EU law had arisen and the Dutch court referred that to Luxembourg saying 'is this ok? because they are going to deal with EU law, these private arbitrators are going to interpret and apply EU law, is that ok?' And in *Eco Swiss* the ECJ decided yes that was fine, that's not against EU public policy. So basically this judgment says *Eco Swiss* is ok, so private international arbitration between private parties is not caught by Article 344. But, they say, ISDS is different. You want to look at that passage, at para. 55: it's very short, they say that ISDS is not, they imply, truly consensual, which is incorrect; they focus on this being a treaty derogating from court jurisdiction, whereas a national court could make a reference of the question to the ECJ. Now, the trouble is, that's what arbitrators do in the private sector too, an arbitration agreement is a derogation agreement from national courts, so we don't really understand how they can say on the one hand *Eco Swiss* is ok but on the other hand ISDS is different. But one of the concerns some of us had is that this is the beginning of an attack on private international commercial arbitration in the EU. It's encroached upon it in the past, it got defeated, *Eco Swiss* is a good example, and we don't really understand now why, if ISDS is different, why the same considerations shouldn't apply to *Eco Swiss*. So that's the first question. The second question is, although they say that intra-EU BITs don't confer jurisdiction upon their chosen tribunals, so *Achmea* awards would be annulled eventually, they say the position of the EU is different, it's a bit tentative, but what I'm sure they had in mind is what they're going to have to consider the *CETA [Comprehensive Economic and Trade Agreement]* case. We're going to look at *CETA* very carefully, that's pending, the Belgian reference will be heard soon.[5]

But there's another important treaty, which is the Energy Charter Treaty. Now the Energy Charter Treaty was signed by the European Union, not as a state because it's not a state, and a lot of the cases which are pending are Energy Charter Treaty cases. So does *Achmea* apply to them, and we're talking of dozens of cases, or not? We don't know.[6] Now, this was a German arbitration, with a German arbitration award, subject to review by the German courts, as the courts of the seat, not as the courts of enforcement, and it was always understood that the German courts could make a reference to Luxembourg. So this was, if you like, a very good test case, but it failed and now watch *Achmea*, because I don't think it's given the green light to the Multilateral Investment Court, I think it's given either a red light or a blinking light, because the Multilateral Investment Court is going to sit outside the EU, we're talking about a multilateral court, it may sit in Geneva, it may sit in Singapore, we don't know. Now that is a foreign court for the ECJ, they will be reviewing awards, interpreting and applying EU law, now we know from *Achmea* that is an anathema to the ECJ. So unless the Multilateral

---

[3] Case C-284/16, *Slovak Republic v. Achmea*, Judgment of the Court (Grand Chamber) of 6 March 2018.

[4] Case C-126/97, *Eco Swiss China Time Ltd v. Benetton International NV*, Judgment of the Court, 1 June 1999.

[5] See now Opinion 1/17 of 30 April 2019.

[6] See now Case C-741/19, *Republic of Moldavia v. Komstroy*, Judgment of the Court (Grand Chamber) of 2 September 2021.

Investment Court is implanted in the EU subject to EU law, with a right of reference and a duty to refer to Luxembourg, I don't see this court approving the Multilateral Investment Court.

Now a lot can happen politically, this is a very political decision, the membership of the court can change, there wasn't a British judge on the court and in fact the UK didn't even turn up for the argument, there were 17 Member States, but the UK was not one of them. So, just keep an eye on *Achmea*, because it's going to have very dramatic repercussions. We criticise President Trump for his protection programme, but this is a kind of legal protectionism, this is saying that EU law is more important than international law. And so I think we're heading into a crisis because nothing in this decision would give you any other impression than that EU law is paramount. International law doesn't play a part in this, the law of treaties didn't play a part in this. So there we go. And I'm sorry to be rude about the EU, because I actually am a federalist, but not in this respect.

[...] you can see their problem, they've got an EU law system, which they do not want to subcontract to international arbitration tribunals, not even with very senior ICJ retired judges like Chris Greenwood, and the ECJ is adamant that only *it* can decide issues of EU law and its decisions are binding throughout the European Union and they have to be respected by every EU Member State and every EU Member State's court. Now if you were to say that about China to a big investor they may think 'well that's rather silly, you know, how can China behave like that, how can they expect us as an international investor under international law to go to China and build a multi-billion dollar factory and when there's a dispute with China we have to go to a Chinese international investment court, in China, applying Chinese law as a supreme paramount law, over and above international law'. But that's what we're facing. Or am I being very unfair?

On arbitral seats and the Nazi invasion of Russia
[from lecture 7]

So, what we're going to look at now is what happens when you do have a seat, you do have a legal seat. Now there are many scholars, particularly from France, who think that you can have a free-floating arbitration. Well, if you look why French lawyers say that, it's because there's a French seat. That is, the law of the seat, or the law attributed to arbitration under French law, means that it doesn't have a seat, but it nonetheless has a legal link with French law. So essentially, when you're looking at a non-ICSID situation, UNCITRAL [United Nations Commission on International Trade Law], Stockholm Chamber, Vienna, Singapore, Beijing arbitration, CIETAC [China International Economic and Trade Arbitration Commission], you've got to bear in mind that it's not ICSID, it has a seat, it has a legal place. And here are the LCIA [London Court of International Arbitration] Rules 'The parties may agree in writing the seat (or legal place) of their arbitration', so they can certainly agree to Paris, they can agree to Tokyo, but 'Failing such a choice the seat of arbitration shall be London unless and until the LCIA Court determine in view of all the circumstances, and after having given the parties an opportunity to make written comment, that another seat is more appropriate.' Now this is a default seat, it can be changed, but basically once you have an arbitration under LCIA Rules, the 1998 Rules, there was a default seat of London, although it could be changed. Now why do you think that was?

Well, you may have problems before you get to the arbitral institution, for example, you may have a time bar. Now, the English court has power to extend the time bar for

498 APPENDIX II

starting an arbitration. But you can't go to the English court unless it's the seat. So do you see the catch 22 situation? It's also appointing an arbitrator by default, maybe the rules don't provide for that to be made by the institution, you can go to an English court to appoint the missing arbitrator, so a respondent can't sabotage the arbitration by refusing to appoint. So that was the default situation. Now that led to huge criticisms of the LCIA, that basically they were English biased, or London biased, and that by having a default seat it meant that it remained the seat, nobody changed it, it was too powerful and because it was the default seat the institution and the parties always appointed English arbitrators. So things had to be changed.

Now, years and years ago I helped draft the Bermuda Arbitration Act. We were very excited because it's a Commonwealth country, it was a model law, we put it in, with conciliation, it had knobs and whistles to cope with common law countries. It was a wonderful common law UNCITRAL model law system. And we thought Bermuda would take off as a seat of arbitration because it's near America, it's a stable legal system with a right of appeal to the Privy Council in London. And why did it fail? Basically, I'm a general counsel, you're my chairman, you finish this massive contract and I say, 'we've got to have a good arbitration clause' and you say, 'ok what do you recommend?', and I recommend Bermuda. 'Tell me more' and I show him or her this photograph of a beach paradise, what are they going to do? 'Pull the other one', they're going to say, 'don't you ever mention Bermuda again.' 'I bet there's a golf course there' they'll say, and of course there is, and a bit of sunshine, a lot of beaches. The Bermuda factor is a problem because once you try and sell a forum, you can say it's got the best laws in the world, but when it has beaches, it doesn't help. You are supposed to suffer pain when you arbitrate, not get a sunburn. That is a problem for Mauritius too,

Now, we're going to jump completely to a different age now as it is important that you know a little bit about Dr Friedrich Gaus. He's not very well known but he was an incredibly experienced German Foreign Office lawyer, he served the Kaiser, the Weimar Republic and unfortunately Hitler too. So basically he was there from about 1909 to 1945. He had a very difficult time during the war because his wife was Jewish and he protected her because he was in turn protected by Ribbentrop who was the Foreign Minister who had Hitler's ear until the end. He was, you might say, the European expert on Arbitration and these are some of the treaties that he drafted. It was called the Gaus System and it was, if you like, an early form of obligatory arbitration from the 1920s onwards. He certainly attended the Versailles Treaty, which he didn't like, he didn't draft that, but after that there was the Swiss–German Treaty of 1921, the Locarno–German treaties and then there were other treaties with Belgium, France, Poland and Czechoslovakia, which is all Weimar Republic, and then one with Turkey, still Weimar Republic, so this was the good period. The bad period started with the Brest–Litovsk Treaty, one of a series of Soviet or Russian treaties, and the one he ended up with was the really horrible one, the Nazi–Soviet Pact of August 1939, which led to the Second World War in September and then Hitler broke that treaty by invading the USSR in June 1941.

This 1939 photograph shows a meeting in Moscow where Gaus was called in very late in the day, he wasn't involved in the political ramifications of the treaty, that was done by Ribbentrop, a thoroughly loathsome figure, and next to him you'll recognise Stalin and the Soviet Foreign Minister, Molotov, and then there is Gaus, who played a role in drafting the arbitration clause. It's Article 5 of this extremely important treaty where the USSR and Nazi Germany carved up Central and Eastern Europe: 'Should disputes or conflicts arise between the High Contracting Parties over problems of one kind or another, both parties shall settle these disputes or conflicts exclusively through friendly

APPENDIX II   499

exchange of opinion or, if necessary, through the establishment of arbitration commissions.' Now, who thinks that's a good arbitration clause? It's obviously a political treaty with a political arbitration clause. It started with a draft from the Soviet side and you can see Gaus has managed to put in changes, which are no more than corrections to that draft, which was in Russian and German, this is an English translation. Who thinks that's a good clause? It's actually meaningless isn't it? Totally useless 'both parties shall settle these disputes or conflicts exclusively through friendly exchange of opinion' well yes, of course, 'or, if necessary, through the establishment of arbitration commissions' commissions was the Soviet phrase for tribunals, so that's ok, but it's an agreement to agree isn't it? So when in June 1941, when I think it was two or three million German troops and their allies invaded the Soviet Union, I can guarantee that Stalin didn't turn to the arbitration clause: it was completely irrelevant. One of the problems is no machinery, no seat, no rules. There is nothing which did not depend upon the mutual further agreement of the parties.

Now, we're going to move now to the present day. I haven't got the completely up to date figures, but what you're going to see in all these figures is a huge uplift in the caseloads of arbitral institutions. And you will see that in all the arbitral rules published by these institutions, there is provision for establishing the seat of the arbitration, as well as all the other matters that are absent in Article 5 of this disastrous treaty.

On quantum expertise [from lecture 8]

The quantum phase can be a real, real problem. The experts are often pretty much acting for one side or the other and I have trouble with that being even a question of expert evidence. Why don't they sit alongside the lawyer because what they are doing is often expert advocacy, they are advocates. They are forcing you into a shoe size which doesn't fit as so-called independent experts. I guarantee when you have the quantum phase, assuming you're going to get the case past jurisdiction, admissibility, liability, you then get the quantum experts and lo and behold the claimants have a figure up here of several hundred million, if not billions, and lo and behold the defendant's expert says nothing or some derisory sum, or less, a minus figure; it does happen actually, a minus figure. In American baseball arbitration they have a very simple solution, the arbitrators can only choose one figure or the other, and what happens? The experts become reasonable, they bring their figures together. If you come up with a too low figure, there's a great risk that the tribunal will have to choose the higher figure. If you choose too high a figure, there's a great risk the tribunal will choose the lesser figure. So baseball arbitration is one pretty crude solution to this, but unfortunately that isn't happening and what you now often get is a fudge, very short reasons, as indeed David Caron says in the *Glamis* award, when it comes to quantum.[7] And the parties don't help.

On appeals to arbitration (or not), via the 1899 Hague Conference [from lecture 9]

Okay, if you know the answer to this, don't say! Who was the first to give women the vote in Europe? Russia. After the 1905 revolution the Tsar had a streak of liberal thought and gave Finnish women the vote, they were the first in Europe to have the vote. He had

---

[7] *Glamis Gold, Ltd v. United States of America*, Award of 8 June 2009, fn. 5.

500 APPENDIX II

another streak of genius and that was in 1907. He thought let's have a peace conference because we're all spending a fortune on armaments because we're going to fight each other to the death, that's rather silly because actually we're going to go bankrupt before we can fight each other, so let's have a big peace conference and he delegated the work to an incredibly distinguished jurist, he was a Baltic German, although he was obviously living in Tsarist Russia, called Martens. I've only discovered him quite recently and the reason is, although he was very distinguished at the time in 1907, he became a pariah because he was a Tsarist jurist, so the Soviets and even to the present day most Russian lawyers have never heard of him. Outside of Russia, because he was Russian, everybody forgot about him and it's only very recently that we have rediscovered what he contributed.

Martens was the soul of many ideas at the Hague Conference, one of which was arbitration between states. So, he introduced the idea that you could arbitrate between states and also within a treaty you could make it an obligation to arbitrate before any dispute. Before there was a dispute first and then you agreed to arbitrate if you wanted to, depending on the dispute. What he introduced was the idea 'no, no, no, that makes it too difficult to dispute, if you must agree after the dispute. You need an obligation *before* the dispute in a treaty, and then obviously if that happens you go off to arbitrate.' So the origins of state–state arbitration leading to investor state arbitration have a lot to do with Martens. So basically everyone got very excited about this, but the Americans think it's their idea, the British think it's their idea, the French think it's their idea. The only people who don't think it's their idea are the Germans because they've effectively vetoed it.

But, at the first Hague Conference the Americans 'proposed a right of appeal from an adverse award, exercisable within three months, for a substantial error of fact or law'. Again, look at the weasel word 'substantial', not <u>any</u> error of fact or law, but a substantial fact or law and nobody would really understand what substantive was until too late. Now the Dutch, and this was T.M.C. Asser, who was a great Dutch jurist, he said no, that goes too far, we'll have revision for an award, that is enough. Certainly a clerical error, or maybe even so far as excessive jurisdiction, but certainly not an appeal, so this was very limited. This is what Martens said:

'In what does the importance of this question consist? Is it true that a rehearing of a judicial award based upon error or upon consideration not sufficiently founded as revision is not desirable, ought we not, on the contrary, to wish to have an error corrected by new documents or new facts which may be discovered after the close of the arbitration? No gentlemen, it would be most unsatisfactory and unfortunate to have an arbitral award, duly pronounced by an international tribunal, subject to a reversal by a new judgment. It would be profoundly regrettable if the arbitral award did not terminate, finally and forever, the dispute between litigating nations, but should provoke new discussions, inflame the passions anew, and menace once more the peace of the world. A rehearing of the arbitral award as provided for in Article 55'—that was the American proposal—'must necessarily have a disastrous effect. There should not be left the slightest doubt on this point.'

So, Martens was absolutely opposed to this proposal for an appeal, and why this is important is that this is still the debate that is going on today, and you're going to have to understand the scope of that debate. His argument was accepted, and the Conference accepted only the revision proposal of T.M.C. Asser.

APPENDIX II   501

On set offs and equity [from lecture 10]

We've talked about counterclaims and I want to talk about something called a crossclaim, and a crossclaim is important because it's not necessarily a counterclaim. Now, we have crossclaims as counterclaims in concession contracts, you've heard that referred to already, so basically a basic private law contract between the state and a concessionaire can lead to claims and counterclaims and off they go to arbitration. If it's ICSID, no problem, as you've seen from the provisions of the Convention, also in investment law, depending on the wording of the host state's investment law you can have a claim by a state, a crossclaim in the form of a counterclaim by a state, as well as a claim by the investors. But the problem at the moment is limited to the old form, or existing form of BITs. As I said, it's not going to apply to the future form of free trade agreements, which are much more elaborate exercises by states. And the question is, could a crossclaim operate as a defence to a claim under a BIT where the BIT does not permit a counterclaim?

So, we're talking about a crossclaim as a defence. Now, the guidance here is English law and English law is never the applicable law of an international law ICSID arbitration. But it's an old form of justice and as you probably know our legal system here was divided into two, common law, which was quite rigid, and then the Courts of Equity, which were very flexible. We now have a system which merges the two systems together, so common law and equity. Now, we have three basic kinds of set-off, we have the legal set-off, which is irrelevant for our purposes because they're mutual debts arising essentially from the same contract between the same parties and that's a very limited form of relief at common law, please forget about legal set-off. Insolvency set-off is when the claimant is insolvent and there can be, under insolvency legislation, a set-off because the so-called debtor is in fact a creditor of the claimant to the same or a greater sum. So, in mutual dealings there is then a statutory set-off. But I want to talk about equitable set-off. There is a judicial tradition that goes back, in this jurisdiction, several hundred years, when equity regards the crossclaim as entitling the respondent, who is making the crossclaim by way of defence, to protection against the claimant's claim.

Let me give you a very simple, basic example. When I started my practice at the English Bar the only practice you inherit are applications for summary judgment in front of the Masters of the High Court. So, you walk in there and you've got ten minutes and you've got to show the judge you have an arguable defence if you're acting for the respondent. This was a case where a long-term employee of Hertz, in England, had been dismissed, I think he'd been there thirty years, he'd been dismissed wrongly and in those days there was no protection except a month's pay, there was no unfair dismissal. So, with that money he took his wife to Holland and they hired a car from Hertz and they drove it around and then they returned it at the airport and refused to pay. When he came back to England Hertz sued him for the price of renting the car in Holland for a month. And when he came to me, he said 'well, I think that's unfair because they sacked me after thirty years and they gave me a month's pay and I think they should have paid me a lot more money'. So, I went to the Master and I said: 'Hertz have behaved badly, they've fired this man and he has a substantial crossclaim by way of defence, we have set-off, therefore he shouldn't have to pay the rent for the rental car in Holland, it's not fair.' And of course, Hertz said 'well hang on a second, Hertz UK has nothing whatever to do with Hertz Netherlands, they're different legal persons, even though the headline on the bills were Hertz, Hertz and Hertz'. And the judge agreed, he said 'that's totally unfair, I give you leave to defend'.

502 APPENDIX II

Now what I would like to suggest is that we ought to look at this a bit more carefully and in the context of international law because Professor Reisman hinted at it in the passage that you've just seen, set-off, crossclaim by way of set-off, *not* counterclaim, and that would not face the bar that was faced by the tribunal in the other limited BIT cases.[8] The principle in English law was cited by the Court of Appeal years ago in a case called *Hanak v Green*, now I'm not suggesting you go off and read that, but if you want to look at the reference there it is.[9] This is how it's applied in practice, this is a more recent case in the Court of Appeal 'claims to equitable set-off ultimately depend upon the judge's assessment of the result that justice requires'.[10] Now, translated into international law you are talking, maybe, of 'good faith', you're talking of 'clean hands', and that's why I'm just wondering, whether if you face this situation again, where you have a solid crossclaim that you want to apply as a defence to an investor's claim, don't plead it as a counterclaim because, as you'll see, you'll get into trouble, unless the BIT is broadly phrased, but plead it on the basis that it's just fundamentally unfair that the investment gets a free ride.

Let me give you a good example. Claim for denial of justice by a claimant against a host state. He had a claim for, let's say, a hundred million dollars but was defeated by the misconduct of the judiciary in that host state. So, he starts an ICSID arbitration, limited BIT wording, and he says—'denial of justice, and my damages are a hundred million because that was my claim and I recovered nothing'. The state comes along and says—'wait a minute, you may have had a claim for a hundred million, but actually, you so polluted the water table in the area of the concession that you are liable to individuals and to the state for two hundred million dollars. How can you recover a hundred million without taking account of the damage you did operating the concession? Now, we're not making any counterclaim, because we can't, but we're just saying there ought to be a set-off, and the set-off in your case means you get nothing because two hundred million is more than one hundred million.'

So, why can't the arbitration tribunal do that? It could be said that it does have jurisdiction because you're allowed to raise a defence. As you've seen, if you use the terrible word counterclaim, you immediately get jurisdictional trouble. That's why Professor Reisman uses that phrase 'set-off procedures'. That's a much easier avenue for a state to defend itself. I'm not saying that every crossclaim would succeed, if it had nothing to do with the investment, if you hadn't paid your taxes on your bicycles in regard to a different concession, that obviously wouldn't be very helpful. But if it's to the point where, in this phrase, 'the result that justice requires', I mean how can you take with one and then ignore what the other hand has been doing.

[...] I agree too, if it's unrelated, but I think you put your finger on it, what is meant here by obligation? Is it a qualified obligation, and depending on the obligation, for example the FET [fair and equitable treatment] standard, you're right in there with a chance of saying this is unjust, I have this cross-complaint in the form of a set-off and therefore I don't want more money, but you can't give an award in favour of the claimant. But this has not yet been explored.

---

[8] Referring to *Spyridon Roussalis v. Romania*, Declaration, 28 November 2011.

[9] *Hanak v. Green* [1978] 2 QB 927 (Morris LJ), pp. 23ff.

[10] Per Thorpe LJ in *Esso Petroleum Co. v. Milton* [1997] 1 WLR 938, p. 953.

Onboard *Hurricane*, 2012

First Publication List

The essays and lectures in this volume were first published as described below. The editors extend their sincere thanks for the permissions that have been received.

1. The Historical Keystone to International Arbitration: The Party-Appointed Arbitrator—from Miami to Geneva, *Proceedings of the ASIL Annual Meeting, Volume 107*, Cambridge University Press, 2013.
2. Investor–State Disputes and the Development of International Law: Arbitral Lessons from the Private Correspondence of Queen Victoria and Lenin, *Proceedings of the ASIL Annual Meeting 98*, Cambridge University Press, 2004.
3. Inter-State Arbitration, *Oxford Handbook on International Arbitration*, eds. Schultz and Ortino, Oxford Publishing Ltd, 2020.
4. 1922: The Birth of the ICC Arbitration Clause and the Demise of the Anglo- Soviet Urquhart Concession, *Commerce and Dispute Resolution: Liber Amicorum in Honour of Robert Briner*, ed. Aksen, Bockstiegel, Mustill, Patocchi and Whitesell, ICC Publication 693.
5. The 1921–1923 North Sakhalin Concession Agreement: The 1925 Court Decisions between the US Company Sinclair Exploration and the Soviet Government, *Arbitration International*, Volume 18, Issue 2, Oxford University Press, 2014.
6. Lloyd George, Lenin and Cannibals: The Harriman Arbitration, The 1999 Freshfields Lecture,
   Arbitration Insights: Twenty Years of the Annual Lecture of the School of International Arbitration, eds. Lew and Mistelis 96, Sponsored by Freshfields Bruckhaus Deringer, International Arbitration Law Library Volume 16, Kluwer Law International, 2007.
7. The Lena Goldfields Arbitration: The Historical Roots of Three Ideas, *International and Comparative Law Quarterly*, Volume 47, Issue 4, Cambridge University Press, 2008.
8. The Tetiuhe Mining Concession 1924– 1932: A Swiss– Russian Story (Where the Arbitral Dog Did Not Bark), *Liber Amicorum. Mélanges Offerts à Claude Reymond— Autour de l'Arbitrage*, LexisNexis Litec, 2004.
9. Two Arbitral Butterflies: Bramwell and David, *The Internationalisation of International Arbitration: The LCIA Centenary Conference*, eds. Hunter, Marriott and Veeder, Graham & Trotman/Martinus Nijhoff, 1995.
10. The 'Y2K Problem' and Arbitration: The Answer to the Myth, *Arbitration International*, Volume 16, Issue 1, Oxford University Press, 2014.
11. The Lawyer's Duty to Arbitrate in Good Faith, *Arbitration and Oral Evidence*, ed. Lévy and Veeder, ICC Institute of Business Law Dossier, 204.
12. The Natural Limits to the Truncated Tribunal: The German Case of the Soviet Eggs and the Dutch Abduction of the Indonesian Arbitrator, *Law of International Business and Dispute Settlement in the 21st Century: Liber Amicorum Karl- Heinz Böckstiegel*, Wolters Kluwer Deutschland GmbH (Carl Heymanns Verlag), 2001.
13. Issue Estoppel, Reasons for Awards and Transnational Arbitration, *Complex Arbitrations* (ICC Pub. No. 688E 2005) 238.

506 FIRST PUBLICATION LIST

14. The Need for Cross- border Enforcement of Interim Measures Ordered by a State Court in Support of the International Arbitral Process, *New Horizons in International Commercial Arbitration and Beyond*, ed. Van den Berg, ICCA Congress Series No. 18, Kluwer, 2005.

15. The Transparency of International Arbitration: Process and Substance, *Pervasive Problems in International Arbitration*, ed. Mistelis and Lew, Kluwer, 2006.

16. Free Spirits – the Search for "International" Arbitration, *Liber Amicorum en l'honneur de Serge Lazareff*, eds. Lévy and Derains, Pedone, 2011.

17. The Role of Users, *Players Interaction in International Arbitration*, ed. Hanotiau and Mourre, ICC Institute Dossier IX, 2012.

18. From Florence to London via Moscow and New Delhi: How and Why Arbitral Ideas Migrate, *Journal of International Dispute Settlement*, Volume 4, Issue 1, Oxford University Press, 2013.

19. Jurisdiction, Admissibility and Choice of Law in International Arbitration, *Jurisdiction, Admissibility and Choice of Law in International Arbitration: Liber Amicorum Michael Pryles*, eds. Kaplan and Moser, Kluwer, 2018.

20. Whose Arbitration Is It Anyway — The Parties' or the Arbitration Tribunal's?, *The Leading Arbitrators' Guide to International Arbitration*, ed. Newman and Hill, JurisNet, 2014.

21. Is There Any Need for a Code of Ethics for International Commercial Arbitrators?, *Les Arbitres Internationaux, Colloque du 4 février 2005*, Société de Législation Comparée, 2005.

22. Still More on Arbitral Deliberations: An English Perspective, *Mélanges en l'honneur de François Knoepfler*, Helbing Lichtenhahn, 2005.

23. Why Bother and Why It Matters?, *World Arbitration & Mediation Review*, Volume 7, No. 1, Institute for Transnational Arbitration, JurisNet, 2013.

24. The Importance of a Party Treating as Independent Its Independent Arbitrator, Hong Kong International Arbitration Centre, Special Publication Series 1, *Investor-State Arbitration - Lessons for Asia*, eds. Moser, JurisNet, 2008.

25. Is there a Need to Revise the New York Convention?, *Journal of International Dispute Settlement*, Volume 1, Issue 2, Oxford University Press, 2010.

26. Who Are the Arbitrators?, *Legitimacy: Myths, Realities, Challenges*, ed. Van den Berg, ICCA Congress Series No. 18, Kluwer, 2015.

27. Arbitrators and Arbitral Institutions: Legal Risks for Product Liability?, *American University Business Law Review*, Volume 5, Issue 3, 2018. Digital Commons, Available at: http//digitalcommons.wcl.american.edu/aublr/vol5/iss3/7.

28. "What Matters— about Arbitration", *Arbitration: The International Journal of Arbitration, Mediation and Dispute Management*, ed. O'Reilly, Volume 82, Issue 2, Chartered Institute of Arbitrators, 2016. This essay is based on the Alexander Lecture 2015 delivered for the Chartered Institute of Arbitrators.

29. Lessons for the Future from the Past: Individual Hedgehogs and Institutional Foxes (Tenth Kaplan Lecture, 23 November 2016), *International Arbitration: Issues, Perspectives and Practice: Liber Amicorum Neil Kaplan*, HKIAC (ed), Kluwer, 2019.

Index

For the benefit of digital users, indexed terms that span two pages (e.g., 52–53) may, on occasion, appear on only one of those pages.

Abbreviations used in the index
1996 Act (Arbitration Act 1996 (England [and Wales]))
AA (UK Arbitration Act 1996 [England and Wales])
AAA (American Arbitration Association)
CCBE (Council of Bars and Law Societies of Europe)
CETA (EU-Canada Comprehensive Economic and Trade Agreement)
CFR (EU Charter of Fundamental Rights (2000))
DAC (UK Departmental Advisory Committee)
ECHR (European Convention on Human Rights (1950))
ECT (Energy Charter Treaty (1994))
FTAC (Foreign Trade Arbitration Commission)
Geneva Protocol (Geneva Protocol on Arbitration Clauses (1923))
HRA (UK Human Rights Act 1998)
IBA (International Bar Association)
ICC (International Chamber of Commerce)
ICJ (International Court of Justice)
ICSID (International Centre for Settlement of Investment Disputes)
ICTY-ADC (ICTY Constitution of the Association of Defence Counsel)
ICTY-ADC (International Criminal Tribunal for the former Yugoslavia)
ILC(SR) (International Law Commission's Articles on State Responsibility)
LCIA (London Court of International Arbitration)
LMAA (London Maritime Arbitrators Association)
MAC (Maritime Arbitration Commission)
MFA (Ministry of Foreign Affairs)
NAFTA (North Atlantic Free Trade Agreement)
New York Convention (New York Convention on the Recognition and Enforcement of Foreign Arbitral Awards (1958))
NYC (New York Convention (1958))
PCA (Permanent Court of Arbitration)

PCIJ (Permanent Court of International Justice)
RSFSR (Russian Soviet Federated Socialist Republic)
RYA (Royal Yachting Association)
TEC (Treaty Establishing the European Community)
TFEU (Treaty on the Functioning of the European Union (2007))
TTIP (Transatlantic Trade and Investment Partnership)
WIPO (World Intellectual Property Organization)
WTO AB (World Trade Organization Appellate Body)
WTO (World Trade Organization)

Achmea 340, 459–60, 469, 495–97
Adams, Charles Francis (US-appointed Alabama Claims arbitrator)
  diplomatic skills 18, 37–38, 391
    brokering the indirect claims compromise xxxvii, 18–30, 36–37
  family background/career 14–15, 18, 389
  language skills 14–15, 18
  personality 18
    a cold fish 18, 23, 389–90
    obituary 18
  role in establishment of Tribunal 15
Aegis case (issue estoppel)
  applicability to English arbitration and court proceedings 240–41
  confidentiality of original award 243, 278, 283n.17, 287
  definition 243
  summary xliv–xlv, 242–43
Alabama Claims Arbitration (1872) 13–30
  see also Washington Treaty (1871)
  alternatives to arbitration considered 15–17
  appointing authorities 14–15, 17
  award 13–14, 34–35
    dissenting opinion (Sir Alexander Cockburn) 29–30, 34–35, 390–91

508 INDEX

Alabama Claims Arbitration (1872) (*cont.*)
  composition of tribunal 14–15, 34–35
    avoidance of truncation 36
    linguistic competence 14–15
    proposal for a sole arbitrator, rejection 15–17,
      30–31
    quality of 389
  importance of xxxvi, 14, 30–32, 37, 40
  indirect claims jurisdiction
    brokering a compromise xxxvii, 18–30, 36–37
    Washington Treaty ambiguity/parties'
      disagreement over inclusion of
      indirect claims in the Tribunal's
      mandate xxxvii, 23, 35–36
  lessons from (Veeder) xxxv–xxxvii, 30–32
  party-appointed arbitrators *see also* Adams,
      Charles Francis (US-appointed
      Alabama Claims arbitrator);
      Cockburn, Sir Alexander (British-
      appointed Alabama Claims arbitrator)
    introduction of the principle 14–15, 17,
      30–31, 34–35
    as key to successful resolution of the
      dispute 14–15
  Queen Victoria's views on 33–34, 35–36, 38
  a truncated tribunal?, 36
American Arbitration Association xxxviii
Anglo-Iranian Oil Company case
  applicable law (PCIJ 38) 144
  Concession Agreement (1933), Idelson's
      responsibility for/Lena arbitration as
      basis xl–xli, 126, 144
  Kompetenz–Kompetenz doctrine 127–28
  separability principle xlvi, 127–28
  sole arbitrator 144n.64
Apotex (res judicata/issue estoppel), 476–80
  see also issue estoppel; res judicata
  overview 476
  issue estoppel 477
  res judicata
    application to the case 479–80
    as a general principle of international law 476
    reasons, relevance 478–79, 480
    requirements (same subject matter, same
      legal bases and same parties), 476–77
arbitral awards
  confidentiality
    Aegis 243, 278, 283n.17, 287
    issue estoppel and 243
  finality/appeal *see* finality of award/appeal/
      revision; issue estoppel
  reasons for
    as contribution to finality of award 238–39
    purpose 238–39

arbitral confidentiality *see* confidentiality of
      arbitration proceedings in related
      court proceedings
arbitral deliberation
  collegiate decision-making *see also* truncated
      tribunals
    applicability regardless of inclusion in the
      arbitration rules 368–69
    arbitrator's legal duty to deliberate
      collegiately 229
    arbitrator's right to a fair opportunity to
      participate 371, 375–78
    breach, potential consequences 370–71
    dissent or deliberate non-participation of
      one co-arbitrator, effect *see* truncated
      tribunals
    dissenting arbitrator's role in deliberating
      reasons for a majority award 371,
      372–73, 374
    equality of arms principle,
      relevance 369–70
    as long-established general
      principle 368–69
    parties' procedural legal right to 370–78
    pragmatic approach to 371, 376–77
    theoretical basis for obligation, scholarly
      disagreement on 370–71
    tribunal's control of procedure 368–69, 374–75
    written questionnaires 376–78
  commentaries on
    Bredin (Retour au délibéré' arbitral
      (2004)) 366–67, 374
    David (Arbitration in International Trade
      (1985)) 368–69
    Fouchard, Gaillard & Goldman (International
      Commercial Arbitration (1999)) 368–69,
      370–71
    Heuman (Arbitration Law of Sweden
      (2003)) 366–67, 370–71
    Lalive, Poudret & Reymond (Le droit de
      l'arbitrage interne et international en
      Suisse (1989)) 374–75, 376–77
    Poudret & Besson (Droit comparé' de
      l'arbitrage international (2002)) 368–
      69, 370–71, 374–75
    Reymond ('The President of the Arbitral
      Tribunal' (1994)) 368–69
  disclosure of
    examples 378–79
    Loewen 9–13
    a new phenomenon 378–79
  a largely closed book
    absence of rules relating to/academic
      discussion 366–67

INDEX 509

irrelevance of English/US judicial
 practice 367–68
irrelevance of London Arbitration pre-1979
 Arbitration Act 368
learning on the job 367–68
UNCITRAL Notes on Organising Arbitral
 Proceedings (1996/2016) 371–72
arbitral tribunals, composition
 five-member tribunal
  advantages 31–32
  inter-State arbitration practice 31–32
  treaty provision for 31–32
 sole arbitrator
  Alabama Claims Arbitration 15–17,
   30–31
  Anglo-Iranian Oil Company case 144n.64
  Bankers Trust (2005) 282
  Brunel 300–1
  Cedric Barclay as 347–48
  Costa Rica Packet Arbitration 41n.5
  dislike of 31
  FFIRC (2010) 414
  J.R.W. Alexander as 430
  Maxim the Greek as 307–8
  Parthenia arbitration 356
  parties' right to opt for 7n.1
  presiding arbitrator acting as 237, 368
Arbitration Act 1996
 drafting history, key contributions to 431–32,
  450–52
 Lord Peston's criticism of 440–41
 Lord Wilberforce on 146, 294–95, 349–50
 making it perfect 440
 praise for 431
  but 'significantly deficient', 291
 a straightjacket/West Tankers 291, 293, 296
  adoption of Doleman v Osset
   principle 293
arbitration treaties and similar international
  instruments (multilateral) see EU
  instruments; Geneva Protocol (1923)/
  Geneva Convention (1927); Hague
  Conventions; New York Convention
  (1958); UNIDROIT model law (1936
  Rome Draft)
arbitration treaties/clauses (bilateral)
 see also Harriman arbitration clause; Lena
  Goldfields Arbitration; Tetiuhe
  Concession; Urquhart Concession
  Agreement
 an agreement to agree 498–99
 change of practice (1899-1914) 47–48
 Franco-Danish Treaty (1911) 47–48
 French opposition to 190

Nazi–Stalin Pact (23 August 1939), 432–34,
 447–48, 498–99
Weizäcker on 450
arbitrators
 discrimination in choice of see discrimination
  (judicial/arbitral appointments)
 ethics code see an ethics code for international
  commercial arbitration practitioners?
 ICSID see ICSID, arbitrators
 Idelson, V.R. see Idelson, V.R.
 increasing tendency to attack 360–61, 378–79,
  416–27, 439–40, see also international
  commercial arbitration, hostility
  towards/risk to
 arbitrator's potential legal liability/insurance
  against 361–62, 416–28
 non-appearance see truncated tribunals
 party-appointed see party-appointed
  arbitrators
 sole arbitrator see arbitral tribunals,
  composition, sole arbitrator
 super-arbitrator (Lena arbitration
  clause) 133n.32, 134n.35, 148n.70,
  149, 185n.38
arbitrators of note
 Adams, C.F. see Adams, Charles Francis (US-
  appointed Alabama Claims arbitrator)
 Alexander, J.R.W., 430n.1
 Alexander, Leslie 430n.1
 Barclay, Cedric 347–48
 Bingham, Lord (on Cockburn) 13, 388, 391
 Bramwell, Lord see Bramwell Arbitration Code
  (1883)
 Chlenov, S.B. see Chlenov, S.B. (Lena
  Goldfields arbitrator)
 Cockburn, Alexander see Cockburn, Sir
  Alexander (British-appointed
  Alabama Claims arbitrator)
 Davenport, Brian see Davenport, Brian
 David, René see David, René
 Devlin, Lord 128n.14, 346, 356nn.33, 34,
  380
 Gaillard, Emmanuel (philosophical
  writings) 291, 292, 396
 Gaus, Friedrich see Gaus, Friedrich (Head of
  German MFA Legal Department)
 Goode, Roy 213, 291, 296
 Holtzmann, Judge 192, 276n.150
 Kerr, Michael 52–53, 295–96, 312–13, 314,
  380, 452–53
 Knoepfler, François 366–67, 378–79
 Lazareff, Serge 290, 298, 438–39
 Mann, Francis see Mann, Francis
 Martens, F.F. see Martens, F.F.

510 INDEX

arbitrators of note (*cont.*)
  Mincs, Pavel *see* Mincs, Pavel
  Mustill, Lord *see* Mustill, Lord
  Paulsson, J, 7–11, 206
  Rutherford, Margaret 405
  Schwebel, Judge *see* Schwebel, Judge
  Sims, John 431
  van den Berg, A.J. *see* van den Berg, A.J.
  Vigrass, Bertie *see* Vigrass, Bertie
  Wang Sheng Chang 383–85
  Wilberforce, Lord *see* Wilberforce, Lord
autonomy *see* party autonomy

Balch, Thomas (Alabama Claims
    Arbitration) 15–16, 17
Bermuda
  costs of arbitration (Bermuda forms of excess
    liability insurance) 328, 330n.14,
    331–32, 335
  International Conciliation and Arbitration
    Act 1993
    arbitral immunity 422–23
    confidentiality of arbitration proceedings
      in related court proceedings 280–81,
      282, 288–89
    issue estoppel (Aegis) 240n.9, 242–43
    Veeder's role 498
Bhutan, as potential ICRIS signatory 455,
    486–88
BITs (bilateral investment treaties) xxxviii
  arguments against signing 487–88
  draft US–Pakistan BIT 383
  drafting issues 383
  ICSID role, importance xxxviii, 385–86
  intra-EU BITs *see* EU (intra-EU BITS)
  'investment', interpretation problems
    Abaclat/Ambiente/Alemanni 492–94
    Poštová 493–94
  potential abuse of, 198, 240–41, 246, *see also*
    issue estoppel
  statistics 435–36
  UK experience of 387
Bramwell Arbitration Code (1883) 186–89
  adoption 186
  an example of private initiative 431–32
  Arbitration Act 1889 and xli–xlii, 431–32
  key features
    consensual nature of commercial
      arbitration xli, 187
    internationalization of arbitration xli–xlii,
      187–89
  Lord Halsbury's disapproval of/replacement
    by the Arbitration Act 1889, xli,
    186–87

re-emergence (Mustill & Boyd's Commercial
    Arbitration (1982)) 186–87, 431–32
Brussels Convention (1968) *see* interim measures
    (Brussels Convention (1968), Art. 24,
    issues)

cause of action estoppel
  applicability as an alternative to issue
    estoppel 245–46, *see also* issue
    estoppel
  definition 240–41
CCBE Code of Conduct for Lawyers in the EU
    (1998)
  adoption and scope 205, 211
  relevance to international arbitration 205–6
Chevron v. Ecuador (II) (denial of justice) xxxv,
    481–83
  overview 481
  jurisprudence considered
    Azinian 481
    ELSI 482
    GEA 482
    Loewen 481, 482–83
    Mondev 481, 482
    Oostergetel 481
  standard/burden of proof 481–83
    balance of probabilities 483
    bias, fraud, dishonesty, lack of impartiality,
      or gross incompetence 481
    clearly improper and discreditable 482
    failure by the national system as a whole to
      satisfy minimum standards 481, 482
    presumption against impropriety 482–83
    procedural unfairness vs error of fact or
      national law 481
    standard of appreciation 482–83
Chlenov, S.B. (Lena Goldfields arbitrator) 10,
    116, 117n.50, 118, 139–40, 147–56, 487
CME (issue estoppel)
  lessons learnt 246
  potential abuse of BIT 34
  'privies', limitation to 243–44, 245–46
  reasons for rejecting the challenge 375–76
  res judicata/lis pendens 245
  summary CPP 29, 243–44, 375–76
  timing of award xxv
Cockburn, Sir Alexander (British-appointed
    Alabama Claims arbitrator)
  see also Tenderden, Lord (Alabama Claims
    (British agent))
  career 19–20
    climbing the legal ladder 19–20
    failure to make the peerage 20
    McNaughton 19–20

a master of difficult cases 19–20
a mixed reputation 388–89
Tichborne Case 388–89, 392
diplomatic skills (or lack thereof)
'a catastrophic appointment', xlviii, 388, 389
brokering the indirect claims
compromise 28–29
clear distaste for the Washington Treaty 26
colleagues' attempt to exclude from
participation in discussion of the
indirect claims 26
colleagues'/fellow arbitrators' dislike of 26,
389–91
dissenting opinion, unwisdom of 29–30,
34–35, 390–91
language/cultural skills 14–15, 19
a long shadow 393
evaluation
Alabama Tribunal arbitrators/members
of the American and British
delegations 19–20, 389–91
Hackett, F.W. (member of American
delegation) 389–90
Lord Bingham 13, 388, 391
Van Vechten Veeder, Federal Judge 19–20, 388
family background 19, 391
personality
'a natural illiberal British chauvinist', 19–20
'ardent' temperament 19
'colourful', 31
a dark and morally troubled novel 20–23
hasty, arrogant and short-tempered 388,
389–91
irresponsible approach 389–90
a ladies' man 20
partisan and discourteous xlviii, 390–91
'warm-blooded', 23
compound interest *see* interest
(English practice)
confidentiality of arbitration proceedings in
related court proceedings 278–89
absence of rules or practice providing
for 278–79
arbitral confidentiality as norm
LCIA Rule 16, 278–79n.4
UNCITRAL Rules 25(4) and
32(5) 278–79n.4
WIPO Arbitration Rules 73-76, 278–79n.4
Lord Mance's 'spectrum' of
confidentiality 284–85
national recognition of
Bermuda (International Conciliation and
Arbitration Act 1993) 280–81, 282,
288–89

English law (Bankers Trust) 282–89
see also England [and Wales], confidentiality
of arbitration proceedings in related court
proceedings (Bankers Trust)
France (Aita v. Oijeh) 280
New Zealand (TV New Zealand) 281
open court hearings as the norm 278–79, *see
also* fair and public hearing (ECHR 6),
importance of
striking the balance 288–89
consent, need for 31, 55, 157–58, 431, 485, 486–35
see also party autonomy
confidentiality of proceedings/award 278–79, 282
cost-capping 304, 305
a minefield 486–88
religious tribunals (UK) 296–97
costs
see also quantum
arbitrator's potential liability for/insurance
against 361–62, 427–28
capping costs xlv, 303–5
1966 Act provisions 304, 328–31
see also costs, capping costs (Arbitration
Act 1996, s 60)
LMAA Intermediate Claims Procedure
(2009) 302–3, 305
LMAA Small Claims Procedure 302–3
UNCITRAL Model Law, absence of
comparable provision 304, 329–30
capping costs (Arbitration Act 1996,
s 60) 328–31
1834 and 1950 Acts as fore-runners 328–29
conflict with New York Convention
and amended UNCITRAL Model
Law 329–30, 331
'costs' for purposes of 328
enforceability outside England of award
subject to 329–31
MacKinnon Report on Arbitration
(1927) 328–29
mandatory nature 328, 348–49
party autonomy, impact on 329–31, 348–49
public policy as justification 328–30
text 328n.3
work-arounds 330–31
concerns about size of/disproportionate
amounts xlv, 305
contributory factors
discovery/alternatives to xxiii, 302
oral hearings xlv
right of challenge to an award 480
signature of award formalities 371–72
three or more arbitrator tribunals 31
witness hearings xlv

512 INDEX

costs (*cont.*)
  interim measures and (1996 Act) 262
  users and
    conservatism 305
    objection to LMAA procedure 305
    role in deciding 303–5
    'winner takes all' rule, reluctance to
      abandon 303, 493–94
crossclaims vs counterclaims 501–2

Davenport, Brian
  Arbitration Act 1996 and 450–52
  career 451–52
  health and early death 451–52
David, René
  collegiate decision-making 368–69
  as leading French teacher of arbitration 190,
    290–91, 400
  UNIDROIT Rome Draft (1936) and xlii,
    190–91, 194–95, 293–94, 444–45
Davis, Bancroft (Alabama Claims (US
  agent)) 24, 25–26
denial of justice *see* Chevron v. Ecuador (II)
  (denial of justice)
Denissoff, Elie
  life of 309n.4
  on Maxim the Greek 308–10
Descamps, Baron (Belgian delegate to the 1899
  Hague Conference) 44, 45–46
discovery
  costs and xlv, 302
  damaging effect on arbitration/
    unacceptability, 339–40, 410–11
  of new facts 209–11
discrimination (judicial/arbitral appointments)
  addressing the problem 410–11
  discriminatory language
    'Dear Mesdames, Dear Sirs', 459–60
    left-handed/right-handed 402
    use of 'arbitrator', 403
  EU legislative provisions 406–7
  gender/race 402–6
    ICCA members as reflection of 403
    South Africa 405
    US 405–6
  ICSID arbitrators *see* ICSID, arbitrators
  LGBTQ 405–6
  making slow progress
    lack of research 403, 405
    Lord Chancellor's summary of the position
      (1922) 403–5
    some successful women 402–3,
      405, 489
    timeline (women judges/arbitrators) 405

  nationality 406–7, 409–10
    UNCITRAL Analytical Note (1985) 410
    UNCITRAL Model Law (1985) 410
  Nazi law (Article 1032(3) ZPO 193) excluding
    non-Aryans 410, 448–50
    text 448
  party autonomy and (Jivraj v.
    Hashwani) 407–10
  statistics
    'American Diversity in International
      Arbitration 2003-2013' (Davis) 405–6
    Brunel University study (C2015) 403
    Tevendale (Kluwer Arbitration Blog
      (2012)) 403
  a systemic failing 456
Doggerbank Incident (1904) 47–48

Eco Swiss case 471
  Achmea/Electrabel confirmation of 471, 496
Einstein, Albert (nomination as Lena arbitrator) xl,
    116n.49, 149, 151, 488
Electrabel (extract), 469–76
  overview 469–76
Electrabel (extract) (attribution), 474–76
  general approach 474
  applicable law (international law/
    ILC(SR)), 474
  ILC(SR) 8 (conduct directed or controlled by a
    State), 474–76
    'auxiliaries', 475
    establishment of necessary relationship
      between private person and the
      State 475–76
    Jan de Nul 475
    'under the direction or the control', 475
  as issue for jurisdiction and the merits 474
Electrabel (extract) (harmonious interpretation
    between ECT and EU law), 469–72
  Note: the argument hinges on the alleged
    threat posed by arbitration to ECJ's
    monopoly of the interpretation of EU
    law
  Commission's argument 469
  EU acceptance of possibility of arbitration
    absence of control over ICSID
      awards 471–23
    signature of ECT 471, 472–25
    'harmonious interpretation' as
      irrelevance 469, 471
  remedies open to EU in case of erroneous
    interpretation/application of EU
    law 471–24
  TEC 292 [TFEU 344] (ECJ's exclusive
    jurisdiction: exceptions), 469–71

INDEX 513

arbitration between a Member State
national and a Member State held
outside the EU 471
arbitrations between private parties (Eco
Swiss), 471
ECJ Opinion 1/09, 471
impossibility of non-Member States referral
to the ECJ 470
Member States' courts' discretion to refer
preliminary questions (TEC 234
[TFEU 267]), 470
Mox Plant 470
non-applicability of TEC 292 [TFEU 344]
to disputes involving non–Member
States 470–71
text 469–70
Electrabel (extract) (indirect
expropriation), 472–74
jurisprudence considered
Azurix 473–74
CME 473–74
CMS 473–74
GAMI 473–74
Lauder 473–74
Metalclad 472
Parkerings-Compagniet 473–74
Pope & Talbot 473–74
S.D. Myers 473–74
Sempra 473–74
Starrett 473
Tecmed 472
Telenor 473–74
Tippetts 473
salami-slicing, rejection 469, 472–73
substantial deprivation requirement 473–74
'taking', 473
enforcement see interim measures, cross-border
enforcement; Lena Goldfields
Arbitration, recognition/enforcement;
New York Convention (1958)
England [and Wales]
see also theories of international commercial
arbitration, French vs English approaches
Arbitration Act 1996 see Arbitration Act 1996
BITs litigation experience 380
confidentiality of arbitration proceedings in
related court proceedings (Bankers
Trust) 282–89
1996 Act, effect 286–89
court hearing in chambers/in private, relevance
to confidentiality of proceedings 285–87
Lord Mance's 'spectrum' of
confidentiality 284–89
striking the balance 288–89

Geneva Convention (1927)
half-hearted approach to 293–94
ratification 293–94
Geneva Convention (Arbitration (Foreign
Awards) Act 1930) (erroneous extra-
territorial provision) xlvi, 310–14
India/Pakistan adoption of CPP 31, 311
rectification (1975 Arbitration Act) xlvi
Geneva Protocol (1923)
1996 Act, conflict with 292–93
opposition to 188–89, 292–93
responsibility for 293–94
good faith (English law) 213, 216–17
interim measures see England [and Wales]
(interim measures)
issue estoppel see issue estoppel
Kompetenz–Kompetenz doctrine 293, 296
New York Convention (1958), enactment
(Arbitration Act 1975) 293–94,
313–14
publicly reported reasoned judgments,
importance 279–80
recognition of the USSR (1924) 114, 176–77
separability principle see England [and Wales]
(separability principle (1996 Act, s 7))
truncated tribunals see truncated tribunals
(England)
UNIDROIT model law (1936) see UNIDROIT
model law (1936 Rome Draft), UK
opposition to/grounds
unjust enrichment 126–27
England [and Wales] (interim measures)
arbitration tribunal
general powers (AA 38) 262
Kastner v. Jason 262–63
parties' agreement to greater powers (AA
39) 262–63
injunctions
acceptability as ex parte measures 247–48,
249–50, 259–60
Anton Piller order 247–48, 263–64
labour injunction (Gouriet) 249–50
Mareva injunction 247–48, 249–50,
252–53, 257–58, 263–64, 265
provisional payments 255–56
State court competence in respect of arbitral
proceedings (AA 44) 263–64
English arbitration and foreign arbitration
outside England, applicability to 264
powers/constraints 263–64
England [and Wales] (separability principle
(1996 Act, s 7)) 158–59, 281, 318–25
jurisprudence
Fiona Trust v. Privalov 323–25

514 INDEX

England [and Wales] (separability principle
(1996 Act, s 7)) (*cont.*)
Harbour v. Kansa 158–59, 281, 322–24
Heyman v. Darwins 159n.102, 319
SNE v. JocOil (1984), influence 281,
320–22, 323–24n.45
muddled state of the law pre-1996 Act 319
text 319
UNCITRAL Model Law distinguished 319
English Commercial Court
at risk/rescue from 380
jurisprudence 99–100, 216–17, 219
Aquarius Financial Enterprises (witness
statements) 219–21
as master of its own procedure 350
estoppel
see also cause of action estoppel; issue estoppel
as good faith/New York Convention
principle 213–14
an ethics code for international commercial
arbitration practitioners?
alternative approaches
moot arbitrations 362–63
Rogers' proposal for modification of
arbitration rules to include a code of
ethics 363–65
benign neglect the best approach
the dangers of regulatory fury 365
ICSID Convention's uninvoked blanket
immunity for arbitrators and
practitioners 365
ICSID rejection of a code 365
Rogers' failure to address the realities of
non-US arbitration 364–65
the pros
CCBE inadequacies 363
gap between practices in State courts and
international arbitration 363
ICTY-ADC Code of Conduct 363
problems arising from different legal
practices 362–63
an ethics code for international commercial
arbitrators (counterarguments)
alternatives to a code
professional indemnity insurance
cover 361–62, 416–28
reasoned decisions on arbitral
challenges 361–62
IBA Code of Ethics for Arbitrators (1987)
'a mild and useful guide', 360
no clear need for/use of 360
a statement of the obvious 360
IBA Guidelines on Conflicts of Interest (2004)
casualties of 361

impropriety of a private body assuming
'legislative' role 361
'orange list' problems 360–61
rarity of arbitrator corruption 360
EU instruments
see also CCBE Code of Conduct for Lawyers in
the EU (1998)
EU Directive 98/5/EC (1998) 205
EU (intra-EU BITs)
Achmea 340, 459–60, 469, 495–97
Eco Swiss 471, 496
Electrabel 340, 460, 469–76, 495–96
Moldavia v. Komstroy 496n.6
Mox Plant 470
EU proposal for an international investment
court xxxvi–xxxvii, 317, 434–39, 440,
496–97
Note: discussion is largely in relation to the
TTIP-related proposal with only
passing references to the proposal in
other contexts.
Commission criticism of arbitration/rejection
for free trade agreements 39n.1, 434–
35, *see also* Electrabel (extract)
counter-arguments 435–36
concerns xlviii
State appointment of judges/exclusion of party
choice xxxvi–xxxvii, 39n.1, 434–35
incompatibility of ISDS with 440
non-TTIP proposals
CETA (29 February 2016 version) 437
EU–Vietnam FTA proposal 435n.11,
437n.17
Opinion 1/17 (30 April 2019), 496
structure/organization
15 first instance judges/6 appellate
judges 434–35
judicial qualifications 434–35
prohibition of 'conflicting' activities 434–35
short, fixed terms 434–35
expert evidence (quantum) 499

fair and public hearing (ECHR 6), importance of
see also confidentiality of arbitration
proceedings in related court
proceedings
Axen 279
dependence on publicly reported reasoned
judgments 279–80
ex parte injunctions without notice
and 259–60
Werner 279
finality of award/appeal/revision
see also issue estoppel

appeal on legal or factual merits and
challenge on procedural grounds
distinguished 50–51
Hague Conference (1907) 48–50
Marten's views on appeal/revision 49–50
revision of award, agreement to 48–49,
50–51
US proposal for right of appeal/revision of
award 45, 48–49
ICSID 51
ILC Model Rules on Arbitral Procedure
(1958) 50–51
PCIJ as possible court of appeal 50–51
reasons for award as contribution to 238–39
Urquhart Concession Agreement 109
France
arbitration, opposition to 190, 438–40
collegiate deliberations 374, 376–77
confidentiality of arbitration proceedings in
related court proceedings
(Aita v. Oijeh) 280
equality of arms 369–70
French contribution to the development of
international commercial arbitration xlv,
290–91, *see also* theories of international
commercial arbitration, French vs
English approaches
interim measures *see* France (interim
measures)
issue estoppel 239–40
Kompetenz–Kompetenz doctrine 293, 296
separability principle 289, 323–24n.45
Tapie case 438–39
France (immunity/liability of arbitrators/arbitral
institutions) 424–27
arbitral institutions
contractual liability 424–25
Cubic 424–25
FFIRC 414–16
ICC Rules (1998) (absolute immunity)/
SNF 425–27
procedural fairness obligations 425–27
arbitrators
Charasse 424–25
contractual liability 424–25
potential legal liability/insurance
against 416–27
France (interim measures)
competence
State courts 274–76
tribunal (agreement of the parties) 273–74
enforcement 276
examples
freezing orders 247–48

référé provision 252–53, 254–56, 257, 274,
275–76
saisie conservatoire 257, 274
sûretés judiciaires 274
'specific assets ... located within the
territorial jurisdiction' limitation (Van
Uden) 256–57

Gaus, Friedrich (Head of German MFA Legal
Department) 447–50
a mixed reputation 450
Nazi law (Article 1032(3) ZPO 193) excluding
non-Aryans, legal opinion 409,
447–449
Nuremberg Tribunal and 432–33
Politics xxxvi, 433, 450
responsibility for key German treaties
(1987–39) xiv, 432–34, 447–48, 498
Nazi–Soviet Non-Aggression Pact
(1939), 432–34, 447–48, 498–99
General Act for the Pacific Settlement of
International Disputes (1928) 48
general principles of law
Lena xviii, 124, 126, 140–47, *see also* Lena
Goldfields Arbitration
Geneva Protocol (1923)/Geneva Convention
(1927) 99–100
a beginning for the internationalization of
arbitration 188
Bramwell Code and 187, 188, 431–32
conclusion 103n.17
diversity of laws, problems of 189–90
German–Soviet Treaties (1921/1925) and 227
ICC role 56, 189–90
Russia/Soviet Union and *see* Russia/Soviet
Union (arbitration), multilateral treaties
UK and *see* England [and Wales], Geneva
Protocol (1923)
US exclusion from 162, 191
Genoa/Hague Economic Conferences (1922) 56,
58, 101–2, 103, 109, 176, 446–47
Germany
see also Gaus, Friedrich (Head of German
MFA Legal Department)
interim measures
applicable law (UNCITRAL Model
Law/Code of Civil Procedure) 265–66
arbitration tribunal's competence 265–66
enforcement 268–70
ex parte relief/audiatur et altera
pars 266–67, 270
examples 255–56, 266
measure in respect of the subject matter of
the dispute, limitation to 266

516 INDEX

Germany (*cont.*)
    'real connecting link' requirement 257–58,
        269–70
    requirements (urgency, risk of substantial
        harm and a good arguable case on the
        merits) 266
    State courts' competence 267–68
  non-Aryans, exclusion as arbitrators (1933
    ZPO) 410, 448–50
  separability principle (Case JZ
    1970) 323–24n.45
Goff, Lord 204
good faith 213–14
  civil law approach to/pacta sunt servanda
    principle and 213
  English law 213, 216–17
  estoppel and 213–14
  in Hong Kong 213–14
  international arbitration, role 212, 213–14,
    223
  jurisprudence
    China Nanhai Oil v. Gee Tai
      Holdings 213–14
    Three Rivers DC 213
    Walford v. Miles 213
Goode, Roy 213, 291, 296

Hague Conferences (1899/1907), legacy
  see also Martens, F.F.; PCA (Permanent Court
    of Arbitration)
  arbitration requirements
    moral binding force 55
    neutral appointing or administering
      authority 55
    parties' consent 55
    party autonomy 55
    party involvement in appointment of
      tribunal 55
    settled procedure 55
  failure of plans for a third conference
    (1915) 47
  finality of award/rejection of appeal on the
    merits 48–50, *see also* finality of
    award/appeal/revision
  General Act for the Pacific Settlement of
    International Disputes (1928) 48
  'obligatory arbitration', 39n.2, 40–41
  PCIJ/ICJ compulsory jurisdiction option
    (PCIJ 36/ICJ 36(2)) 48
Hague Conference (1899) (Martens'
    draft convention on obligatory
    arbitration) 42–46
  British support for/as basis for draft
    articles 44–45

  emergence of the 1899 Hague Convention 45–46
  opposition to 44–46
Hague Conference (1899) (organization and
    purpose)
  agenda (Martens' memoranda) 41–42
  attendance 42–43
  as a peace conference/unresolved international
    conflicts 34
  a Russian initiative 41–55, 499–500
Hague Conference (1907) (achievements/
    disappointments)
  1907 Hague Convention for the Pacific
    Settlement of International
    Disputes 46–48
  confirmation of the role of inter-State
    arbitration 47
  failure to agree on exclusion of an appeal 500
  failure to agree on a permanent court/
    obligatory arbitration 46–47
  impact of inter-State rivalries 46–47
Hague Conference (1907) (organization and
    purpose)
  attendance 46–47
  Marten's pre-Conference consultations 46
  President Roosevelt's proposal for 46
  Russia/Netherlands as hosts 46
Hague Conventions
  1899 (Peaceful Settlement of International
    Disputes) 45–46, 50
  1907 (Pacific Settlement of International
    Disputes) 31–32, 46–48, 50, 52–53
Hailsham, Lord *see* Hogg, Douglas (later 1st Lord
    Hailsham); Hogg, Douglas (later 3rd
    Lord Hailsham); Hogg, Quinton (later
    2nd Lord Hailsham)
Hailsham, Lord 97, 188, 192–94, 311, 328–29n.7,
    356, 451–52
Hammer, Armand
  Armand's 'Cheka' arbitration clause 108
  business skills 107–8
  first American concessionaire in Soviet
    Russia 107
Hammer concession (1921) 107–8
  amical termination (C1924) 107–8
  dispute settlement provisions 108
  Lenin's approval 108
  a sham 108
Harriman Arbitration (1928)
  appointment of arbitrators 116
  confidentiality of proceedings 98–99
    release of US and Russian archives 98–99
  hostile background 100
  settlement agreement
    arbitration clause/invocation 118

compensation 117–18
  reasons for 109–10
  Soviet compliance 118
  terms 117
  US Government's concerns 117–18
  significance 98–99, 100
  truncated tribunal xxxix
Harriman arbitration clause
  composition of tribunal 112
  inclusion in the settlement agreement 118
  neutral presiding arbitrator xvii, 112–14
  neutral seat 113–14
  text 120–22
Harriman Concession Agreement
        (1925) 110–12
  grant (post-Bolshevik revolution) 97–98
  Harriman's difficulties in operating the
        concession 111–12, 114–16
    attempt to resolve (Trotsky
        negotiations) 114–16
  protracted negotiations 110–11
  termination/compensation 98–99
  terms of the agreement 111
Harriman, William Averell
  family and career 96–97
  a great diplomat and statesman 98
  Kruschev's views on 97–98
  Lord Hailsham's views on 97
  a realist 98
Hogg, Douglas (later 1st Lord Hailsham),
        opposition to the Geneva Protocol
        (1923) 188
Hogg, Douglas (later 3rd Lord Hailsham) 192n.12
Hogg, Quintin (later 2nd Lord Hailsham)
  Arbitration 311, 328–29n.7, 356, 418
  on Brian Davenport 451–52
  Harriman Concession and 97–98
  opposition to the Geneva Protocol (1923)/
        international arbitration 192–94
Hong Kong
  good faith 213–14
  origins of arbitration in 442

IBA Rules 214–15
  Code of Ethics (1986) 223
  historical overview 214
  Rules of Evidence (1999) 223–24
    document production 217
    expert reports 218
    theory and practice, divergence 214–15
    voluntary nature 223
ICC
  arbitration clause, importance of 56, 71
  establishment (1922) 56

a French institution 290–91
  truncated tribunals 236
ICJ
  compulsory jurisdiction (ICJ 36(2)) 48
  as court of appeal from challenged arbitral award
    Guinea-Bissau v. Senegal (1989) 51
    Honduras v. Nicaragua (1960) 51
    ICSID 64 provision for 51n.38
    ILC Model Rules (1958) 50–51
    limitation to disputing parties' express
        consent 51
    Special Rapporteur's rationale 51
    non-State actors 50–51
ICSID
  arbitrators
    competent vs incompetent 489, 490–91
    ineffective list system/shortage 37–38
    Nobel prize winners 488
    non-lawyers 489
    women 489
    young arbitrators 489
  at risk xlvii–xlviii, 380–86
    loss of senior staff xlvii–xlviii, 385
    tackling the problem 385–86
    threats to budget xlvii–xlviii, 385
  ethical code, rejection 365
  investor–state arbitration, development of 53
  Pakistan's record 314–15
  in praise of 365, 380–81, 385–86, 431
  why it matters
    BITs-based arbitration cases xvi, 53, 385
    immunity provisions (ICSID 21/ICSID
        22) xlvii–xlviii, 365
    La Brea y Pariñas concession disputes
        (1921/1963) xlvii–xlviii, 381–82
    US–Pakistan draft BIT 383
    Wang Sheng Chang 383–85
  why not to sign 455
ICSID Convention (1965) by article
  21 (immunity of ICSID officials, conciliators
        and arbitrators) xlvii–xlviii, 365
  22 (immunity of parties, representatives,
        witnesses and experts) xlvii–xlviii, 365
  26(1) (diplomatic protection) 53
  52 (grounds for annulment) 50–51
  64 (dispute on interpretation/applicability,
        referral to ICJ) 51n.38
Idelson, V.R.
  Anglo-Iranian Concession Agreement (1933)
        and xl–xli, 126, 144
  Lena arbitration and xviii, 129, 144, 145–48
    assessment of Lena's prospects 138–39
    views on reasons for Soviet withdrawal 151,
        154–55

518   INDEX

Idelson, V.R. (*cont.*)
  life/career xl, 129, 143–44
  Russian Gold 143
  The Rose Mary 144
ILC Model Rules on Arbitral Procedure (1958)
  by article
    35 (grounds for challenging an arbitral
      award) 50–51
    36(1) (challenge to arbitral award: ICJ
      competence) 51
immunity/liability of arbitral institutions
  English vs French law 415–16
  exclusion of public policy
    considerations 413–14
  ICC Rules 1998/2012, 415–16, 425–27
  jurisprudence
    FFIRC (210) 414–16
    SNF 415–16
immunity/liability of arbitrators/arbitral
    institutions
  see also immunity/liability of arbitral
    institutions
  setting the scene 412–16
    risks of liability/consequences 416–27
    scholarly studies 416–27
immunity/liability of arbitrators/arbitral
    institutions (England and
    Wales) 417–24
  AA 74 (functional immunity)
    limitations 415–16
    text 415–16n.10
  contractual exclusion of product liability/
    legislative restrictions on 417–18
  uncertainty of applicability to arbitrators/
    institutions 417–18
  product liability (Donoghue v.
    Stevenson) 412–13
  Scots law distinguished 418–19
  traditional assumption of immunity, sole
    grounds for liability 413
  traditional assumption of immunity, challenge
    to 413–16
    Arenson v. Arenson (1977) 413–14, 418–19
    growing challenge to arbitrators/impact on
      functional immunity 416
    public policy arguments 413–14
    Sutcliffe v. Thackrah (1975) 413–14,
      418–19
India, New York Convention (1958) and *see*
    Indian Arbitration and Conciliation
    Act 1996
Indian Arbitration and Conciliation Act 1996
  as enactment of the New York Convention
    (1958) 316

interpretation as re-enactment of s
    9(b) 316–17
  appeal (White Industries v Coal
    India) 317–18n.26
  Bhatia International 317
  reversal (Bharat Aluminium)/a caveat xxiv,
    306, 312–13, 317–18
  'something of a disaster', 312–13, 317
  Venture Global 317
  as modified enactment of the 1985
    UNCITRAL Model Law 316–17
  as repeal of 1961 Act 316–17
Indian (Foreign Awards Recognition and
    Enforcement) Act 1961, s 9(B)
  (erroneous territorial provision) xxiv,
    311, 312–13, 316–18
  effective repeal (Indian Arbitration and
    Conciliation Act 1996) 316–17
  Indian Arbitration Act 1940 and 311n.12, 313
  National Thermal Power Corporation v
    Singer 316
  ONGC v Western 316
interest (English practice)
  see also pre-award interest (1996 Act, s 49(3))
  arbitration (compound interest) xlvi–xlvii,
    354–58
    1996 Act, s 49, 353–54
    Badger 355–57
    court practice distinguished 354–59
    enthusiasm for 354
    exclusion (Malynes' Lex
      Mercatorio) 351–52
    Lena award and 129n.21
    Scottish practice distinguished 356
  arbitration (general)
    1889 Act 356
    1934/1950 Acts 129n.21
    1996 Act, s 49, C7P8 n.21, 353–54
  court practice (compound interest)
    at time of writing [2008], 353
    equity vs common law 352, 353, 357–58
    fragmentary and unsatisfactory
      development 129, 352–53
    general power to award compound interest,
      absence 352
    as laggards xxv, 354
    Law Commission Consultation Paper No.
      167 (2002) 354–55
    Swaps 352, 357–58
  historical background 350–52
    as example of arbitrators' control of the
      development of arbitration law 350
  international practice (compound
    interest) 358–59

compatibility with public policy, ordre public and other mandatory law 358–59
growing acceptance of 358–59
trade usage/règle matérielle, whether 358–59
interim measures *see* England [and Wales] (interim measures); France (interim measures); interim measures (Brussels Convention (1968), Art. 24, issues); interim measures (Brussels Convention (1968), Art. 25, jurisprudence); interim measures, cross-border enforcement
interim measures (Brussels Convention (1968), Art. 24, issues)
overview
'Brussels Convention', history and related instruments 251
contribution to the development of a workable solution 249–50
as protection against forum-shopping 256
text 251
applicability
arbitration proceedings (Arbitration Exception) 251–52
at a place different from the arbitral seat 252
enforcement against third party 252
enforcement not obtainable within the arbitration tribunal 252
EU State court jurisdiction 252
interim measures as parallel, non-ancillary, measures of support 252
measures not obtainable from the arbitration tribunal 252
proceedings already commenced 251–52
ex parte orders without notice 247–48, 249–50, 259–60, 270
pressure for change/resistance to 260, 277
State practice 260
functions
draft UNCITRAL Model Law Art. 17 [February 2004], 253–54
preservation of status quo pending final determination 253–54
securing of assets for final settlement 253–54
protective attachment/injunctive relief 249–50
Anton Piller order 247–48, 263–64
Mareva injunction 247–48, 249–50, 252–53, 257–58, 263–64, 265
saisie conservatoire 257, 274
Swiss provisional attachment orders 271–72

'provisional, including protective measures' cumulative nature 253–54
the pre-Van Uden debate 252–56
proposed definition, rejection 254–55
provisional payment orders 249–50, 252–57
challenge to 'provisional' status 253–59
ILA Principle 22, 255–56
kort geding 247–48, 251–53, 256
Leistungsverfügung 255–56
référé provision 252–53, 254–55, 257, 274, 275–76
'specific assets ... located within the territorial jurisdiction' limitation (Van Uden) 256–57
'real connecting link' requirement 257–58, 269–70
urgency/imminent harm requirement 254–56
interim measures (Brussels Convention (1968), Art. 24, jurisprudence)
Antonissen 256
Denilauler v. Couchet 253–54, 259–60
Marc Rich 251–52
Mietz 252, 259
Mulox v. Geels (Cour d'Appel, Chambéry) 254–55
Reichert and Kockler 252n.12
Reichert v. Dresdner Bank (No. 2) 253–54
Rucheret v. Karmann (Luxembourg Court of Appeal) 254–55
Van Uden 251–52, 253, 254–59, 254n.23, 276–77
opinion of AG Léger 252, 258–59
Virgin Atlantic 257–58
interim measures, cross-border enforcement 247–77
absence of a universal system for, reasons for 247–48
arbitrators' lack of authority 248–49
diversity of national approaches 247–48
timing of the formation of the tribunal 248–49
barriers to reform
conflicting texts/absence of an authoritative interpretation 277
doubtful fairness of certain measures 276–77
escaping the urgency constraint 277
forum-shopping concerns 277
juridically complicated, technical and controversial nature of the subject matter 277
flailing efforts to resolve the problem
draft Hague Convention on Jurisdiction and Foreign Judgments in Civil and Commercial Matters (1999) 249

520 INDEX

interim measures, cross-border enforcement (*cont.*)
  UNCITRAL Arbitration Rules (1976), evasions 249
  UNCITRAL Model Law (1985), evasions 249
  UNCITRAL's slow progress with project on interim measures 249, 277
  national practice, summary 261–62, *see also* England [and Wales]; Germany; Scotland (interim measures); Switzerland
  general effectiveness 276–77
international commercial arbitration
  evaluation
    arbitration as preferred model 99–100
    as catalyst for amicable resolution 167
    the dog that did not bark 167–85
    precariousness/threats to 99–100, 431
    statistics 53, 167–68
    a venerable history 40, 99–100
    why it matters 119–20
    world peace and 206–7
  hedgehog or fox (Isaiah Berlin) xxxv, 442–54
    meaning 443
  hostility towards/risk to 430–41
    EU *see* Electrabel (extract); EU proposal for an international investment court
    ICSID *see* ICSID, at risk
    Micula 439
    NGOs 434
    Philip Morris cases 439–40
    press criticism 434
    US 439–40
    Vattenfall 439
    Yukos ECT cases 439
  a passion for suggesting reform 378–79
  protective action
    realistic demands of arbitration, limitation to 431, 433–34
    statistical data, importance 432, 440–41
  'slow-track arbitration', 129
  Soviet approach to *see* Russia/Soviet Union (arbitration)
  State responsibility for breaches of investment contracts 40
  State trading and 40
  support for, ICSID success 435–36
international commercial arbitration ('a free-standing system') 349–50
  development of its own procedure 349, 431–32
  1996 Act and 348–49, 431–32
  see also party autonomy

arbitrator vs party's representative 345–46
Bramwell Arbitration Code (1883) 431–32
  see also Bramwell Arbitration Code (1883)
ICC role 445–46
master of the arbitration vs master of the parties 347–48
power to award interest 350–53
  see also interest (English practice); users, a vanishing species
practice over theory 346–47
role of a judge and arbitrator distinguished 346
setting the 1996 Act on the right track 450–52
development of substantive law 349
Lord Wilberforce on 146–47, 294–95, 349–50, 359
role of individuals C28 *see also* arbitrators of note
inter-State arbitration 39–55
  history C3 *see also* Hague Conferences (1899/ 1907), legacy; Hague Conventions
  Nazi–Soviet Non-Aggression Pact (1939), 432–34, 447–48, 498–99
  non-State actors and *see* ICSID; non-State actors, arbitral resolution of disputes involving a State
  participation of non-State actors, ICJ 50–51
  role (Hague Conventions) 47
investor–State treaty-based arbitration 52–55
  see also NAFTA Chapter XI (investment)
  'a significant and successful substitute for … gunboat diplomacy' (Schwebel) 54–55
  espousal of national's claim distinguished 53
  public international law, applicability 54–55
  statistics (UNCTAD (2015)) 53
  sui generis nature/characteristics 53–55
    Corn Products 54
    Loewen 53
    Mondev 54
    Occidental v. Ecuador (UK Court of Appeal) 54–55
investor–State treaty-based arbitration, jurisprudence, AAPL 53
Iran–US Claims Tribunal xxxvii–xxxviii, 53, 126–27, 165–66, 378–79
issue estoppel 238–46
  absence of a uniform concept, 198
  applicability to English arbitration and court proceedings 240–41
  in the absence of any decision and any reasons in the first award (Henderson) 240–41

failure to raise a material issue of fact or law in earlier proceeding 240–41
history (Sybray v. White) 239
applicability other than in England 239–40
confidentiality of original award, effect 243
definition 240–41
   abuse of process distinguished 240–41
   res judicata/cause of action estoppel distinguished 240–41
jurisprudence *see also* Aegis case (issue estoppel); CME (issue estoppel)
   Amco 477
   Apotex 477
   Arnold v. National Westminster Bank 241
   Grynberg 477
   Henderson rule 240–41
   Johnson v. Gore Wood 240–41
   Mills v. Cooper 241
   Orinoco Steamship 477
   Thoday 241n.14
   Thrasyvoulou 241n.14
'privies', limitation to 241–42, 245–46, *see also* 'privy', definition and applicability
requirements (same subject matter, same legal bases and same parties) 241n.15, 245–46
   res judicata/cause of action estoppel in case of failure to meet 245–46
as response to potential abuse of BITs 34
timing of awards, relevance xlvii

Japan, recognition of the USSR (1925) 75
Jay Treaty (1796) (joint/mixed commissions) 13n.21, 39–40
   ex post status 39–40
   Kompetenz–Kompetenz 128n.14
   limitation to parties' representatives 39–40
joint/mixed commissions
   Alabama Claims proposals for 15–17
   Alaskan Boundary Case 12n.17
   Jay Treaty provision for 13n.21, 39–40
   obligatory arbitration distinguished xxxvi, 39–40

Khrushchev, Nikita 96–97
Kompetenz–Kompetenz doctrine
   Anglo-Iranian Oil Company case 127–28
   France 293, 296
   importance of doctrine 160–61
   Jay Treaty (1796) 127–28
   Lena 124, 160–61
   relationship with separability principle 124
   separability principle 281, 320–22, 323–24n.45

SNE v. Joc Oil 160–61
Soviet Union 160–61
UK 293, 296
UNCITRAL Model Law/Arbitration Rules 160–61
Krasin, Leonid (Soviet Commissar for International Trade) xxxviii–xxxix, 57
see also Urquhart Concession Agreement
   business background 104–5
   death in London 110
   Lloyd George's relations with 101
   Luther v. Sagor 98–99n.6
Krassin, Leonid *see* Krasin, Leonid (Soviet Commissar for International Trade)

LCIA
   costs 302–3
   history 452–53
   LCIA under threat/rescue 380, 452–53, 497–98
LCIA Rules xvi
   applicable law 147
   arbitrator/arbitration institution immunity 419, 424
   confidentiality of arbitration 278–79
   interim relief 262
   issue estoppel, omission 238–39
   party autonomy 302, 327, 337–38, 348–49
   rules of conduct 205–6
   seat of arbitration 497
   tribunal's power to order payment of interest 353, 358–59
   truncated tribunals 113, 147–48, 236
Lena Goldfields Arbitration 123–66, 487
   overview 123–24
      factual background 132–33, 136–37
      increase in Soviet use of commercial arbitration following Lena 164
      source documents 130–37
      Soviet termination of all foreign concessions (25 February 1930) 139–40
      special features 129
      summary of the award 124–29
   applicable law, absence of reference to arbitration clause 126, 140–41
      Lena's notice of arbitration/statement of claim 140–41
      Lena's oblique references to 140–41
      Soviet correspondence during the proceedings 141
      Soviet counterclaim 139–40
   applicable law, parallel private and public law 145–46
   arbitration clause 134–36

522 INDEX

Lena Goldfields Arbitration (*cont.*)
  applicable law, absence from 140–41
  appointment of 'super-arbitrator', 133n.32,
    134–35, 134n.35, 148n.70, 149,
    185n.38
    status as concession agreement provision
      under Soviet law 134–36
    status under Soviet law 135–36
    text, P7, 164–66
    three-arbitrator tribunal 134–35
  arbitration proceedings
    Lena's institution of proceedings/
      appointment of arbitrator (12 February
      1930) 137–38
    Soviet counterclaim/appointment of
      arbitrator (25 February 1930) 139–40
  arbitrators
    Chlenov, S.B., 10, 116, 117n.50, 118,
      139–40, 147–56, 487
    Einstein, USSR nomination of 488
    Scott, Sir Leslie 137–38
  compensation
    discounted-cash flow method 126–27
    Iran–US Claims Tribunal's citation
      of 126–27
    for unjust enrichment xl, 124–29, 141–43
  concession agreement 133–36
    Litvinov's signature 133–36
    status under Soviet law 135–36
    terms of concession 133–36
  general principles of law, applicability xl, 124,
    126, 140–47
    absence of provision on applicable
      law 126
    Idelson's argument 145–47
    Lena's argument 141–42
    separability principle xl, 127–28, 156–61
    tribunal's position 142–43
    unjust enrichment as 141–43
  recognition/enforcement
    absence of mechanisms for
      enforcing 162
    dissolution of Lena (1976) 162–64
    settlement agreement (March 1935)/patchy
      compliance 162–64, 183
    Soviet attack on the award/Lena 60–61,
      123, 161–62
    UK's compensation of Lithuania,
      Estonia and Latvia for their
      missing gold, 162
    UK–Soviet Settlement Agreement
      (1968) 162–64
    ups and downs of UK–Soviet diplomatic
      relations 162–64, 183

scope of dispute
  definition of the scope 159
  Foreign Office legal advisers' views
    on 158–59
  limitation to terms of compromis/no new
    claims 156–59
  Shreter and Pergament on 157–58
status of arbitration
  as an 'English' award 125
  lex loci arbitri (English law) 125
  London as place of arbitration under the
    arbitration agreement 125
  as private arbitration 125
  public international law, theoretical
    exclusion/general presumption of
    applicability 125
termination of concession (Art. 86)
  absence from Lena's notice of arbitration
    (12 February 1930) 138–39
  absence from Soviet reply to Lena (25
    February 1930) 139–40
  dependence on decision of arbitration
    court 139–40
  text 138n.46
as truncated tribunal xviii, 127–28, 147–56
  arbitration clause provision 147–48
  'Lena show-trial', 149–50, 151
  Lena's 'abandonment' of concession 151–52
  procedural hearings 154–55
  'Stutzer problem', 149
  USSR withdrawal 152–54
Lenin, Vladimir
  illness 57, 59, 62, 66–67
  Queen Victoria and (or not) 33–34, 38
  Soviet concessions and xxxviii–xxxix, 56–59,
    62, 65–70, 102–5, 106, 107–8, 109–10
    Hammer concession 108
    Urquhart Concession Agreement xxxviii–
      xxxix, 57, 65–67, 68–70, 104–5, 109–10
Lincoln, Abraham
  Alabama Claims Arbitration (1872) 15–16
  establishment of the Federal District Court
    Eastern District New York, 1–2
lis pendens 245
Lloyd George, David, efforts to promote peace
    through trade 101–2
  1920 negotiations with Russian Trade
    Delegation 101
  1921 Anglo-Russian Trade Agreement/de
    facto recognition 101
  1921 Genoa/Hague Economic
    Conferences 101–2, 103, 131–32
  departure from office (October 1922) 102, 110
  opposition from France and own Cabinet 101

Russian Civil Code, influence on 103, 446–47
support for a system of law/arbitration 101, 103, 119
Loewen Arbitration (US arbitrator's public disclosure of pre-appointment interview) 9–13
alleged government pressure on arbitrator 10–11
erroneous allegation of arbitrator's commitment to appointing party 10–11
NAFTA award 9
Paulsson's criticisms 9–11
propriety of/justification for pre-appointment interviews 10–13
Lugano Convention (1988) 249–50, 251, 259–60, 261, 272, 276–77, 400–1
Luxembourg, interim measures 254–55

Mann, Francis
applicable law (Lena) 125
enactment of the New York Convention and 313–14
on Marshall v Grinbaum 177n.24
as theorist 291, 295–96
unjust enrichment 142n.60
Marshall, A.G.
Lena settlement and 162–64, 182
Russian Gold (Marshall v. Grinbaum) 143, 163n.113, 176–77, 177n.24, 178, 180–81, 182
Tetiuhe Concession and 176–77, 178, 180–81, 182
Martens, F.F.
biography 41and–42nn.5,7, 445–46, 499–500
death (1909) 47
Hague Peace Conferences, role xxxvi, 41–51, 52–53, 499–500
1899 Conference agenda 41–42
PCA, role xxxvi, 443
positions taken by
finality of award 500
obligatory arbitration 41–42, 52–53, 500
opposition to an international court binding upon States 41–42
Maxim the Greek, 199, 307–10
as arbitrator 307–8
disgrace, pardon and death 308
life and career, scholarly accounts 308–10
move to Russia/role 307
a saintly arbitrator 489
skills 307
Methanex ('relating to'), 465–67
overview 465–66
Cleopatra's nose 466–67
context, object, and purpose 466–67

ordinary meaning 466
Mincs, Pavel 443–47
biography 443, 447
draft Russian arbitration law with commentary (1917) 444
in limbo following the October Revolution 444
probable influence on Soviet legislation/arbitration policy 444–47
recovery of text (2005) 396
Mustill & Boyd (Commercial Arbitration) 293–94, 296, 310n.6, 319
Mustill, Lord
arbitral immunity 419, 420, 424
arbitrator's status 370–71
conflict of laws issues 311
cross-fertilization, importance of 325
DAC Chair 322, 325, 420, 431–32, 450–51
'precious little self-discipline, comradeship or community spirit', 215–21
proceedings in camera (Spinneys) 283n.17
'slow-track arbitration', 129
as theorist 291, 431–32

NAFTA Chapter XI (investment)
difficulties in agreeing on roster of tribunal presidents 437
sui generis nature/characteristics of investment arbitration 53–55
Nazi–Stalin Pact (23 August 1939), 432–34, 447–48, 498–99
negotiating techniques 56–57
a long spoon 102
Netherlands
cross-border enforcement of interim measures (kort geding) 247–48
interim measures, status of Kort geding 251–53, 256
neutral arbitration
difficulties in selecting arbitrators/judges
EU's proposed investment court 437
NAFTA 437
as essential pre-condition for foreign trade and investment 66, 119
essentials
acceptance of reality that there is no better alternative 71
confidence in fairness and justice for both sides 71, 119
Hague Conventions/PCA practice 55
history
Harriman Arbitration and xxxix, 112–14
ICC contribution 71
see also ICC
ICSID 383

524 INDEX

neutral arbitration (*cont.*)
  Lena 133
  Urquhart Concession Agreement
      and xvi–xvii, 58–68, 105–7, 109
  neutral appointing authority 7, 8, 55
  neutral presiding arbitrator xvii, 106, 109–10,
      112, 113, 116, 118, 119
    Soviet rejection of for Moscow arbitrations 164
  neutral seat of arbitration, importance 109,
      113–14, 119, 248–49, 437
  Paulsson/van den Berg, views on 7–9
  sole neutral arbitrator 307–8
New York Convention (1958)
  enforcement of an award annulled by a foreign
      friendly state (NYC VII(1)) 292
  good faith obligation 213–14
  India and 313
  interim awards 248–49, 265, 268
  Pakistan and xxiv, 311n.7, 315
  refusal of recognition/enforcement of award,
      grounds (NYC V)
    English courts' attitude towards 215–21
    public policy exception
        (NYC V(2)(b)) 215–21
  revision of *see* New York Convention (1958)
      (proposals for revision of)
  a success story 395–96, 431
New York Convention (1958) (proposals for
      revision of) xlviii
  counter-arguments
    likely negative approach of the EU 400–1
    likely outcome of a UNCITRAL drafting
        effort 399–400
    risk of losing advantages of NYC VII(1) 400
  justification ('too short, incomplete and
      uncertain') 394–96
    Lisbon Treaties (too long) 395
    President Wilson's 14 points (too
        short) 394–95
    UNCITRAL new Model Law/Arbitration
        Rules (too long) 395
  opponents
    Gaillard 394
    Kessedjian 394
  problems
    no travaux?, 396–97
    'public policy' (ICSID V(2)(b)),
        impossibility of definition 398–99
    translation issues 397–98
  problems, resolution of
    intelligent and reasonable
        interpretation 399
    second edition of van den Berg's magnum
        opus 399

proponents, van den Berg 394, 399, 401
  Ten Commandments as model 396–400
New Zealand
  confidentiality of arbitration proceedings in
      related court proceedings
    proposed Arbitration Amendment Bill
        2004, 289n.33
    TV New Zealand 281
Nolde, B.E. (Russian jurist/Paris-based
      émigré) 46, 118
non-State actors, arbitral resolution of disputes
      involving a State
  Hague Conference rejection of 48–49
  ICJ approach to 50–51
  ICSID *see* ICSID
  Martens' proposal for 52–53
  NAFTA *see* NAFTA Chapter XI
      (investment)
  PCA approach to 52–53, *see also* PCA
      (Permanent Court of Arbitration),
      non-state actors, evolution of
      approach to disputes
      involving
North Sakhalin Concession Agreement
      (1921–23) *see* Sinclair Case

obligatory arbitration, hostility towards
  examples
    Hague Conference (1899) 44–46
    US blocking of new WTO AB
        members 39n.1
  as treaty-based obligation 39, 44–46
obligatory arbitration (treaty-based)
  compromis distinguished 39
  growing acceptance of (PCA) 51–52
  Hague Conference (1899) 41–46, *see also*
      Hague Conference (1899) (Martens'
      draft convention on obligatory
      arbitration)
  'obligatory arbitration', introduction of
      term 39n.2, 40–41
  Hague Conference (1907), failure to agree
      on 46–47
  opposition to 39, 44–46
  PCIJ/ICJ compulsory jurisdiction option
      (PCIJ 36/ICJ 36(2)) 48

Pac Rim (abuse of process/dividing line for
      corporate restructuring), 468–69
  overview 468
  parties' arguments 468
  Tribunal's decision 468–69
    'rarely a thin red line but … a significant
        grey area', 468

Pakistan
  Arbitration (Protocol and Convention)
    Act 1937, s 9(b) (erroneous extra-
      territorial provision)
    correction (2011 Act enacting the New York
      Convention) xlvi, 311n.7, 315
  Hubco v. WAPD 314–15
  origin (English Geneva Convention Act
    1930) xlv, 311, 312–13
  reversion to Rupali 315
  Rupali, P1818 n.20, 314
  'something of a disaster', 312–13
party autonomy, 55, 198
  see also consent, need for; users, a vanishing
    species
  1996 Act
    adoption of lex arbitri principle and 125,
      293
    as endorsement of consensual procedure
      chosen by the parties 348–49
    s 4(1) (mandatory provisions) 348–49
    s 13 (Limitation Acts) 348–49
    s 34(1) (procedure: parties' right to agree
      any matter) 348
    s 40 (general duty of parties) 348–49
    s 46 (applicable law) 296–97
    s 49(3) (pre-award interest) 331–38
      see also pre-award interest (1996 Act, s 49(3))
    s 60 (cost-capping) 329–31, 348–49
      see also costs, capping costs (Arbitration
        Act 1996, s 60)
    s 73 (lost of right to object) 348–49
  discrimination and (Jivraj v.
    Hashwani) 407–10
  French approach to 292
  LCIA Rules (1985) and 348–49
  UNCITRAL Model Law 348
party-appointed arbitrators 7–32
  see also Adams, Charles Francis (US-
    appointed Alabama Claims arbitrator);
    Cockburn, Sir Alexander (British-
    appointed Alabama Claims arbitrator)
  criticism of the system see also Cockburn,
    Sir Alexander (British-appointed
    Alabama Claims arbitrator)
    dissenting opinions, apparent disposition
      to 7–8
    risk of pressure from appointing party/lack
      of independence 9–13
    special interest groups 9
  independence/impartiality of, importance
    appointing party's duty to respect xlviii
    equality of arms and 369–70
    as a long-standing principle 369–70

institution of (Alabama Claims) 14–15, 17,
  34–35
jurisprudence see Alabama Claims Arbitration
  (1872); Loewen Arbitration (US
  arbitrator's public disclosure of pre-
  appointment interview)
pre-appointment interviews, disclosure of
  disclosure to co-arbitrators/non-appointing
    party 11–12
  public disclosure 9–13
pre-appointment interviews, propriety
  Aksen Rules 10–11
  Chartered Institute of Arbitrators'
    Guidelines 10–11
  suggested alternatives to/restrictions on 8
  permanent international court/sole
    arbitrator 9
  suggested alternatives to/restrictions on,
    counter-arguments
    advantages of a five-party tribunal 31–32
    difficulty of reversing long-held right 8
    parties' lack of trust in tribunal
      appointments 8, 30–31
    parties' preference for ownership of the
      proceedings 31
    right to dissent as significant aspect of
      judicial/arbitral independence 8
    usefulness of dissents/colourful
      characters 31
  views of
    Paulsson 7–11
    van den Berg 7–9
Pauncefote, Sir Julian (British delegate to the
  1899 Hague Conference) 44–46
PCA (Permanent Court of Arbitration)
  history/evolution
    arbitrations (1899-1999) 51–52
    arbitrations (1902-14) 47–48
    arbitrations (1999-2016) 51–52
    commissions of inquiry (1902-14) 47–48
    establishment (Hague Conventions) 47–48
    hibernation xxxvii–xxxviii
    obligatory arbitration, growing acceptance
      of 51–52
    opposition to 44–46
  Iran–US Claims Tribunal and xxxvii–xxxviii, 53
  membership, increase in 51–52
  non-State actors, evolution of approach to
    disputes involving
    initial rejection 52–53
    PCA optional Rules (1993) 52–53
    PCA Rules (1982) 52–53
    Radio Corporation v. China (1935) 52–53
    Turiff Construction (1970) 52–53

526 INDEX

PCA (Permanent Court of Arbitration) (*cont.*)
status/choice of name xv–xvi, 45–46
  ICJ/PCA complementarity (Judge Shi
    Jiuyong) 55
PCA Rules
  1982 (Rules for Settlement of Investment
    Disputes between Two Parties of
    Which Only One is a State) 52–53
  1993 (Optional Rules for Arbitrating Disputes
    Between Two Parties of Which Only
    One Is a State) 52–53
  2012 (PCA Arbitration Rules
    (consolidation)) 52n.44
PCIJ
  compulsory jurisdiction (PCIJ 36) 48
  as possible court of appeal 50–51, 191
  principles of international law (PCIJ 38(1)(c)) 126
  sources of law (PCIJ 38) xviii
permanent international court, 1907 Hague
  Conference rejection 46–47
Pious Fund Arbitration (1902), 41n.5, 47–48,
  476, 478
Poštová , 493–94
pre-award interest (1996 Act, s 49(3)) 331–38
  see also interest (English practice)
  the issue
    circumstances giving rise to 331–32
    Lesotho 331
    the question 332
  interpretation of ss 49(3) and 49(5)
    Lord Steyn (Lesotho) 333–34
    non-applicability in case of express
      agreement on foreign law as applicable
      law (ss 4(5) and 49), 198–34, 333
    parties' joint statement of facts and
      issues 334–35
    post-Lesotho (C v. D) 335–36
    written agreement, need for (s 5) 336–38
  parties' autonomy, impact on, 198
    party autonomy as a pillar of the
      Act (s 1(B)) 338
    problem or myth?, xlvi, 328, 338
    section 49(3) as expression of 338
  relevant law (1996 Act)
    s 4 (mandatory and non–mandatory
      provisions) 333
    s 4(5) (choice of a foreign law in respect of
      non–mandatory provisions) 332
    s 49(1) (interest: parties' freedom to agree
      on tribunal's powers) 332–33
    s 49(2) (interest: rules in absence of parties'
      agreement o) 332–33
  relevant law (1996 Act), historical background
    Arbitration Act 1982, s 19A, 356–57

Barlin-Scott Air Conditioning v. Robert
  Salzer Constructions (1979) 356–57
MacKinnon Report (1927) 356–57
'privy', definition and applicability
  doctrine of mutuality 241
  English law 242
    practical approach to 244–45
  issue estoppel and 243–44, 245–46
  jurisprudence
    Ali Shipping Corporation v. Shipyard
      Trogir', 244–45
    Apotex 479
    Bain v. Cooper 244
    Carl Zeiss v. Rayner 242
    CME 243–44, 245–46
    Gleeson 244
    House of Spring Cardens 242
    Mox Plant 241n.15
    Salomon 244–45
procedural fairness *see* England [and Wales];
  good faith; IBA Rules; procedural
  fairness, overview; procedural
  fairness (international arbitration);
  professional conduct; USA, procedural
  fairness
procedural fairness, overview, 197–198, 204,
  206–9
  difficulties of definition 207–8
procedural fairness (English practice)
  document disclosure 216–17
  expert reports 214, 215, 217–18
  factors affecting
    finality of awards, importance 211–12
    legal, professional and cultural
      diversity 207, 211
  factual witness statements 214–15, 219,
    221–22
  jurisprudence
    Aquarius 219–21, 223–24
    CII 220–21n.30, 221–22
    Clough 218
    Naylor 218
    Odyssey Re London Limited v. OIR Run-
      Off Limited 220n.29
    Profilati Italia v. Paine Webber 216–17
    Refco Capital Markets 220–21n.30
    The Ikarian Reefer 218, 221–22
    Vernon v. Bosley (No 2) 209–10
    Whitehouse 217–18
  legislative provisions
    AA 1(a) (fair resolution of disputes) 208
    AA 68(2) ('serious irregularity' for purpose of
      remittal of award to tribunal) 211–12,
      215–21

AA 68(2)(g) (public policy
exception) 215–21
HRA 8 (fair hearing) 208
NYC provisions, attitude towards 215–21
rules and guidelines
Civil Procedure Rules (CPR) 220, 221–22
Commercial Court Guide/Appendix 10,
220, 221–23
Iolanthe (Gilbert and Sullivan) 224–25
Law Society's Guide to the Professional
Conduct of Solicitors 220–22
Woolf reforms 221–23
procedural fairness (international arbitration)
decline in professional courtesy/
standards 215–21
particular difficulties 214–15
finality of awards, importance 48–49,
211–12
legal, professional and cultural
diversity 211
parties' contractual obligation to arbitrate/
rules influencing their legal
representatives, linkage 212
transparency issues 212
see also transparency (international
arbitration)
a self-policing system 212, 215–21
procedural fairness (international arbitration),
suggestions for reform (Veeder)
contractual duty of good faith as legal
umbrella/limitations 212, 213–14, 223
IBA examples 223
national judicial approaches,
inappropriateness 211, 223
reform at the right pace, 199, 223
a supra-national solution for a supra-national
problem 223
professional conduct
see also procedural fairness
CCBE Code of Conduct (1998) 205–6
EU Directive 98/5/EC (1998) 205
international arbitration rules/guidelines 206
national rules, applicability in the
international arbitration process 204
provisional measures see interim measures,
cross-border enforcement

quantum
see also costs
effect of pending challenge/enforcement
difficulties on payment 416, 492
expert evidence and 492
PLN cases 233n.17
questionnaire as prelude 376

res judicata
see also issue estoppel
applicability as an alternative to issue
estoppel 245–46
definition
diversity of meaning 34
issue estoppel/cause of action estoppel
distinguished 240–41
jurisprudence constante compared 490
as a general principle of international law 476
jurisprudence
Ali Shipping Corporation v. Shipyard
Trogir', 244–45
Apotex 476–80
see also Apotex (res judicata/issue
estoppel)
Asteris 478
Asylum case 478
BASF 478
Chorzów Factory (Anzilotti J
dissenting), 478
CME 245
Corfu Channel case 478
Deggendorf 478
Effect of Awards of Compensation 476
Pious Fund 41n.5, 47–48, 476, 478
Polish Service in Danzig 478
requirements (same subject matter, same legal
bases and same parties), 240–41, 476–77
appropriateness of petitum/causa petendi
split 476–77
revision of arbitral award see finality of award/
appeal/revision
Russia/Soviet Union
see also Harriman Arbitration (1928);
Harriman Concession Agreement
(1925); Lena Goldfields Arbitration;
Lenin, Vladimir; Sinclair Case; Stalin,
Joseph; Trotsky, Leon; Urquhart
Concession Agreement
de jure recognition of USSR
Japan (1925) 75
UK (1924) 114, 176–77
US (1933) 118
Germany (1928) 226
judicial competence 76
Kompetenz–Kompetenz doctrine 160–61
New Economic Policy (1922)/consequences
of demise xlix, 9, 57, 76, 100, 102–3,
136–37, 227, 444, 446–47
Russia/Soviet Union (arbitration)
arbitral practice see also Mincs, Pavel
from scepticism to acceptance to
rejection 100

528 INDEX

Russia/Soviet Union (arbitration) (*cont.*)
  increase in use of commercial arbitration
    following Lena 164
  MAC/FTAC 74–75, 76, 160–61, 164,
    320–22, 444
  bilateral agreements
    Anglo-Soviet Trade Agreement (1921) 98–
      99n.6, 104–5, 143, 176, 177n.24
    German–Soviet treaties (1921 and
      1925) 98–99n.6
    Nazi–Soviet Non-Aggression Pact
      (1939), 432–34, 447–48, 498–99
  multilateral treaties and similar international
    instruments
    Geneva Convention (1927), accession
      (1962) 164
    Geneva Convention on International
      Commercial Arbitration (1961) 160–61
    Geneva Protocol (1923)/Geneva
      Convention (1927), exclusion
      from 103, 134–35, 162
    Helsinki Final Act (1975) 164
    New York Convention (1958) 164
    UNCITRAL Model Law/Rules 160–61, 164
Russia/Soviet Union (concessions policy) 102–3
  apparent failure (1923)/turning point
    (1924) 110–11
  approach to
    Lenin xxxviii–xxxix, 56–59, 62, 65–70,
      102–5, 106, 107–8, 109–10
    Lenin *see* Lenin, Vladimir, Soviet
      concessions and
    Stalin 115–16
  Rapallo Treaty (1922) and 176
  termination of all foreign concessions (25
    February 1930) 139–40
Russian Claim for Indemnities (1912) 47–48
Russian Federation, issue estoppel 239–40

Schwebel, Judge
  importance of arbitration 54–55
  on separability 126–27, 323–24n.45
  'The creation and operation of an international
    court of arbitral awards' (1995) 192,
    276n.150
  on truncated tribunals 127–28n.13, 237
  on Veeder's interest in the history of
    international arbitration, 1–3
Scotland
  arbitral immunity 418–19
  compound interest
    arbitrators' and court practice
      distinguished 355–56
    English practice distinguished 355–56

interim measures *see* Scotland (interim
  measures)
Scotland (interim measures)
  applicable law (UNCITRAL Model Law/Law
    Reform (Miscellaneous Provisions)
    (Scotland) Act 1990) 264
  competence of State courts 265
  enforcement
    compliance with ECHR 265
    ex parte decisions without notification to
      respondent 265
    Mareva injunction, non-applicability 247–
      48, 265
    provisional order status of decisions,
      impact 265
    treatment of decision as an award 265
  examples
    Model Law travaux 264
    Scottish Arbitration Code 264
    security payment 265
seat of arbitration
  icing the cake, a mistake 498
  neutral seat of arbitration, importance 109,
    113–14, 119, 248–49, 437
  practical implications of choice, 497–98
separability principle 318–25
  English law *see* England [and Wales]
    (separability principle (1996 Act, s 7))
  jurisprudence
    Anglo-Iranian Oil Company Case xlvi
    cases cited by the DAC 323–24n.45
    Elf Aquitaine 127–28
    Gosset 289, 323–24n.45
    Lena xviii, 127–28, 156–61
    SNE v. JocOil (1984) 281, 320–22,
      323–24n.45
    Tobler v. Blaser 289, 323–24n.45
    Topco 127–28
  relationship with Kompetenz–Kompetenz
    doctrine 124
  UNCITRAL Model Law 319
set-off 501–2
Sinclair Case xxxix, 74–95
  background in date order
    Japanese arrest and deportation of
      expedition's members (1923)., 75
    Sinclair–Far Eastern Republic Concession
      Agreement (7 January 1922) 74–75
    incorporation of Far Eastern Republic into
      the RSFSR (November 1922) 74–75
    novation of the concession agreement with
      the USSR/RSFSR 74–75
    Sinclair's expedition to concession's
      properties in North Sakhalin 74–75

INDEX 529

Soviet–Japanese Treaty (20 January 1925) 75
    cancellation of Sinclair concession (20
        January 1925) 75–76, 99n.7
    Moscow Guberniya Court's ruling on
        validity of concession (24 March
        1925) 75–76
    Japanese concessionaires' arrival in North
        Sakhalin 75–76
    RSFSR Supreme Court's dismissal of
        appeal 75–76
decision of the Moscow Guberniya Court (24
        March 1925)
    circumstances of the case 77–80
    Government's compliance with obligation
        to assist concessionaire 85–86
    Japanese occupation of Sakhalin as force
        majeure xvii, 83–85
    questions for resolution 80
    Sinclair's entitlement to postpone
        exploratory work 83–84
    Sinclair's obligations to carry out
        exploratory work between 7 January
        1923 and 7 January 1924, 81–83
    standing 81
    text 77
    US Treasury's right to retain 200, 000
        roubles performance bond 86–87
decision of the Supreme Court Civil Appeals
        Board (22 May 1925)
    appeal issues 88–89
    applicable law 91
    Board's conclusion 91
    Board's jurisdiction to hear the appeal 89
    Government's compliance with obligation
        to assist concessionaire 90–91
    Japanese occupation of Sakhalin as force
        majeure xvii, 90–91
    Sinclair's entitlement to postpone
        exploratory work 90
    standing of USSR/RSFSR 89–90
    text 88
    McCullough deposition 92
SNE v. Joc Oil
    Kompetenz–Kompetenz doctrine 160–61
    separability principle 281, 320–22,
        323–24n.45
    unjust enrichment 320–21
sole arbitrator *see* arbitral tribunals, composition,
        sole arbitrator
Stalin, Joseph
    concession cases, involvement with xvi
    concessions, opposition to 115–16
    economic policies, consequences xli, 70,
        124–29, 168–69, 179–80, 181–82

Harriman concession 97–98, 115–16
    Lena award and xl
    Main Concessions Committee, membership
        of 139–40
    Nazi–Soviet Pact (23 August 1939), 432–34,
        447–48, 498–99
    Urquhart Concession Agreement and *see*
        Urquhart Concession Agreement,
        Stalin's involvement with
Stockholm Chamber of Commerce xxxviii
super-arbitrator (Lena arbitration clause) 133n.32,
        134n.35, 148n.70, 149, 185n.38
Sweden
    see also CME (issue estoppel)
    Alabama Claims Arbitration (1872) and 17
    arbitration practice
        Arbitration Act 375–76
        CME 375–76
        collegiate deliberations 375–76
        Heuman 321–22, 366–67
    Brussels Convention (1968) 251
    Hague Conference (1899) 42–43
    Sweden–Romania BIT (2002)/Micula
        case 316
    UNIDROIT and 190–91
Switzerland
    collegiate deliberations 374–75
        Formula One FIA/FISA Contract
            Recognition Board practice 376–77
        Private International Law Act 1987, 374–75
        Séfri v. Komgrap 374–75, 376–77
        tribunal's freedom to decide
            procedure 374–75
    interim measures
        applicable law (UNCITRAL Model Law/
            PIL) 270–73
        competence of the State courts 272
        competence of the tribunal 270–73
        enforcement 273
        examples 255–56, 271–72
        provisional attachment orders 271–72
    issue estoppel 239–40
    separability principle (Tobler) 289, 323–
        24n.45, 326

Tenderden, Lord (Alabama Claims (British
        agent)) 24, 25–26, 28
Tetiuhe Concession 167–85
    arbitration clause
        limitation of applicability to foreign
            concessionaire 176–77
        role in final settlement 183–84
        super-arbitrator 185n.38
        text 185

530 INDEX

Tetiuhe Concession (*cont.*)
  chronology
    acquisition of the Tetiuhe Mine
      (1902) 170–71
    Russo-Japanese War (1904) 170, 171
    Russian Revolution (1905) 171
    Bryner–Hirsch financing agreement
      (1907) 171
    Bryner–Hirsch agreement to form Tetiuhe
      (20 March 1909) 171
    Tsarist approval of Tetiuhe's by-laws (3
      August 1909) 171
    Hirsch in control of Tetiuhe (May
      1914) 172–73
    WWI, impact on Tetiuhe (1914-18) 172–73
    Hunter/Suzuki has bid for Tetiuhe accepted
      in principle (October 1917) 172–73
    Bolshevik Revolution leaves Tetiuhe in
      limbo (October 2017) 172–73
    Jules Bryner resumes de facto control of
      Tetiuhe (1917) 172–73
    formation of White Government of
      Siberia/termination of Japanese and
      German involvement with Tetiuhe
      (1918-19) 173–74
    abandonment of Tetiuhe (1919) 172–73
    collapse of White regime/Japanese
      occupation of Vladivostok (November
      1919-October 1922) 174
    Anglo–Soviet Trade Agreement (March
      1921) 176
    Rapallo Treaty (1922) 176
    failure of Hirsch's hopes to regain control of
      Tetiuhe (1922) 176
    incorporation of Vladivostok into USSR
      (15 November 1922) 174
    decree allowing Bryner and Co to resume
      Tetiuhe mining activities (3 May
      1923) 176–77
    grant of concession to Bryner & Co (25 July
      1924) 169, 176–77
    transfer of Tetiuhe Concession to Beatty (18
      May 1925) 178
    formation of Tetiuhe Mining to take over
      the concession (28 May 1925) 169,
      178
    Soviet confirmation of transfer of
      concession (July 1925) and extension
      (August 1927) 178
    Tetiuhe Concession's problematic operation
      (1926-1931) 178–80
    decision to suspend mining operations/
      commence negotiations (March
      1931) 180–81

  final agreement and transfer of the
    concession to the Soviet Government
    (2 January 1932) 180–81
  Tetiuhe's story post-1932 termination of the
    Concession 184–85
  personalities involved
    Beatty, Sir Alfred Chester (1875-1968) 169,
      177–78, 179–82, 183
    Bryner, Boris Yulievich (1889-1948) 174–
      75, 182–83, 184–85
    Bryner, Jules Joseph (1849-1922) 169–70
    Brynner, Yul 169, 174–75, 184–85, 491
    Gulbenkian, Calouste 169, 178, 182
    Hirsch 171, 172–75, 176–77, 178–79,
      185n.38
    Marshall, A.G., 163n.113, 176–77, 178,
      180–81, 182
  settlement
    factors conducive to 181–83
    follow-up 181
    negotiation and terms 180–81
theories of international commercial arbitration,
      French vs English approaches 290–98
  England's green shoots of internationalism
    Lord Diplock (Bremer Vulkan) 295
    Lord Steyn (Lesotho v. Impregilo) 295
    Lord Wilberforce 294, 295
    MacKinnon's drafting of the 1923 Geneva
      Protocol 293–94
    Megaw J (Orion v Belfort) 295
    Wilberforce and Boyd (2nd edition/
      Companion to the 1996 Act) 296
  England's pragmatic approach 291
    absence of a single coherent theory/
      consequences 291
    belated recognition as an academic
      subject 291
    lex loci arbitri rule 293, 295–96, 497
    paying the price (Sharia Courts
      dispute) 296–97
    paying the price (West Tankers/Arbitration
      Exception) 297
    practice over theory 346–47
    time for a change?, 291
  France's philosophical approach 291
    autonomous legal order free of any national
      legal system 292
    learning from 298
    objections to 292, 296
  French contribution to the development
      of international commercial
      arbitration xxiii, 290–91
    ICC/relationship with the Cour d'appel de
      Paris 290–91

transparency (international arbitration)
clear rules, importance of 212
a self-policing system 212, 215–21
treaties, drafting challenges 37
treaties and comparable international instruments
relating to arbitration (in chronological
order)
see also EU instruments
German Reich–RSFSR Provisional Treaty
(6 May 1921) (1921 Treaty) 226
Germany–USSR Agreement Concerning
Courts of Arbitration (12 October
1925) (1925 Treaty) 226
UNCLOS III (1982) xxxviii
IBA Rules 214–15
Jay Treaty 13n.21, 39–40, 127–28
Trotsky, Leon
dismissal from government/exile 114
Harriman concession and 114–16, 155n.94
Lena Goldfields concession and 133
truncated tribunals
see also arbitral deliberation, collegiate
decision-making
examples
Alabama Claims Tribunal, avoidance
of 36
Chlebprodukt v. IWA xliii–xliv, 229–33
CME 375–76
Harriman Arbitration xxxix, 113
Lena xviii, 127–28, 147–56
see also Lena Goldfields Arbitration, as
truncated tribunal
Peace Treaties Case 127–28
PLN cases xliv, 233–37, 370–71
minimization of the effect of deliberate refusal
to act
AAA International Arbitration
Rules 236–37
ICC Rules (1998) 236
importance of arbitral clause provision
for 147–48
LCIA Rules (1998) 236
risks of 236–37
Schwebel on 237
Scottish Arbitration Rules (1999) 236–37
UNCITRAL'S rejection of proposal for
Convention 237
national practice *see* France, collegiate
deliberations; Sweden, arbitration
practice; Switzerland, collegiate
deliberations; truncated tribunals
(England)
'The Natural Limits to the Truncated Tribunal'
(Veeder) c12, xliii–xliv

truncated tribunals (England)
falling into line (Bank Mellat v. GAA
Development) 373
strict approach 371
mitigation (parties' agreement to a majority
decision) 371
relaxation (1934, 1950 and 1996 Acts) 371
strict approach, lingering traces
Cargill v. Soc Iberica de
Molturacion 372–73
European Grain v Johnston 371–72
institutional rules derogating from modern
practice 372–73
presence of all arbitrators at execution of
award requirement 371–72

UNIDROIT model law (1936 Rome Draft) xlii,
189–95
chronology
ICC proposal for the unification of national
arbitration law (1914) 189
ICC call for uniform rules of procedure
(June/July 1921) 189–90
establishment of ICC Court of Arbitration
and rules for conciliation and
arbitration (June 1923) 189–90
ICC support for draft Geneva Protocol and
better enforcement of awards (March
1923) 189–90
foundation of UNIDROIT (1928) 190
UNIDROIT calls for a report on arbitration
in comparative law (December
1929) 190
UNIDROIT's publication of Professor Ren'
David's report (December 1932) 190
UNIDROIT Special Committee's
deliberations on David report
(1934-36) 191
Special Committee's drafts (June and
September 1936) 191–92
ICC Congress's approval of final draft with
key abstentions leading to demise
(June/July 1937) xlii, 192, 194–95
UNIDROIT draft Uniform Law on
Arbitration (1954) 194
UNCITRAL Model Law (1985) xlii, 194–95
Special Committee (1933-36)
absence of US representative 181–82
David, role xlii
draft Uniform Law/report 191
English representatives lack of arbitral
experience 186–87
European/civil law bias 191
meetings 191

532 INDEX

Special Committee (1933–36) (*cont.*)
  membership 190–91
  PCIJ proposed jurisdiction on questions of
      interpretation 191
  UK opposition to/grounds 293–94
  opposition to 'conciliation', 192–94
  undesirability of uniformity in commercial
      arbitration procedure 192
  UNIDROIT draft Uniform Law (1954)
      attempt to resolve 'conciliation' issue 194
unjust enrichment
  English/Scots law 126–27
  as a general principle of law 141–43
  Lena xviii, 124–29, 141–43
  RSFSR Civil Code 142–43, 320–21
  SNE v. JocOil (1984) 320–21
Urquhart Concession Agreement c4, 104–7
  arbitration clause
    Berlin text/description of terms xxxviii–
        xxxix, 64–65, 71–72, 109
    finality of award/scope for challenge 109
    insistence on neutral arbitration as sticking
        point xxxviii–xxxix, 58–68, 105–7, 109
    Krassin's attempts to persuade Stalin/
        Politburo to accept Berlin text xvi,
        60–61, 62–64
    limitation of tribunal's jurisdiction to
        private law issues 63–65, 71
    Politburo commission's review of 61–62, 63
    seat of arbitration 109
  economic arguments for rejection 65–66, 68,
      69–70, 110
  Krassin's friendship with Urquhart 104–5
  Lenin's opposition/refusal to ratify
      agreement xvi–xvii, 57, 65–67, 68–70,
      109–10
    absence from Politburo meetings 66–67
    initial encouragement 104–5
    letters to Stalin (4/12 September 1922) 62,
        65–66
  Politburo's role 59–60, 61–64, 65–68
    'Kamenev' commission 66–67, 68
    'Krassin' commission 60
    Mikhailov commission report 59–60, 62,
        65–67, 68, 71, 109–10
    Rykov commission 61–62, 63
  signature (Urquhart/Krassin) (Berlin, 9
      September 1922) 57, 64–65, 109
    delay in receipt of pre-signature
        instructions 62, 63–64
    Krassin's concerns 64, 65, 66, 70, 110
    Urquhart's satisfaction 65
  the stakes
    benefits to Urquhart 65

  importance of reaching agreement to
      Russia 57, 58, 68–69, 70
  Stalin's involvement with 56–57, 67–68
    Commissar for Foreign Affairs' letter
        to 68–69
    Krassin's letter to (26 August 1926) xxxviii,
        60–61
    Lenin's letters to 62, 65–66
    message from supporters of ratification
        (26 September 1922) 69
    Politburo reports to 67–68
    refusal to replace Krassin 61
  Trotsky's opposition xvi–xvii, 59–60
Urquhart, Leslie (business background) 57–58, 104
  move to Australia 110
USA
  cross-border enforcement of interim
      measures, labour injunction 249–50
  hostility to arbitration 39n.1, 439–40
  issue estoppel 239–40
  procedural fairness
    Gideon 208–9
    witness depositions 220–21
  recognition of the USSR (1933) 118
  separability principle (Prima Paint v. Flood &
      Conklin) 322n.38, 323–24n.45
users, a vanishing species 299
  see also international commercial arbitration
      ('a free-standing system'); party
      autonomy
  arbitration agreements 302
    bias towards standard system of dispute
        resolution 302
    user caution/reluctance to engage with
        reforms in their interests 302, 305
  capping costs *see also* costs
    LMAA Small Claims Procedure, users' failure
        to *see* scope for extension 302–3,
    users' preference for the 'winner takes all'
        principle 303
  once upon a time
    Ranger v. Great Western Railway (Brunel
        case) 300–1
    sewage farm case 299–300
    Turner case 301
  parties and parties' representatives
      distinguished 345–46
  users as a sine qua non 299, 345
    dependence of arbitration on disputing
        parties 299
    as the paymasters 299

van den Berg, A.J.
  on issue-estoppel/good faith 213–14

INDEX 533

on the New York Convention 394, 399, 401
on party-appointed arbitrators 7–9
on Veeder 458–60
Veeder, Van Vechten (New York Federal Judge
and V.V. Veeder's grandfather), 1–2,
19–20
Veeder, V.V. (biography)
education 460–61
switch from modern languages to law, 1, 461
godparents 461
Hurricane 462–63
illness and death, 340, 463–64
life in Maine 462–63
as lobsterman 462
meeting his future wife 458, 462
parents 460–61
as RYA Yachtmaster 462
school holidays 461
sports 458
Veeder, V.V. (career)
see also Apotex (res judicata/issue estoppel);
Chevron v. Ecuador (II) (denial of
justice); Electrabel (extract); Methanex
('relating to'); Pac Rim (abuse of
process/dividing line for corporate
restructuring)
arbitral skills 459
centre of operations (Lincoln's Inn Fields) 458
as colleague 458–60
Achmea 459–60
Electrabel 460
ICCA congress (Singapore 2012) 459
Plama 459
SNE v. Joc Oil 458–59
Strabag 460
Essex Court Chambers 461
grandfather's role, 1–2
New York Eastern District 150th Anniversary
Celebrations, 1–2
as teacher 455–56
as tribunal president, xxxv, 465
Veeder, V.V. (personal and professional qualities)
brilliance and vision 456–57
charm 457
exceptional powers of exposition and
analysis xxxv
flair and wit xxxv, 457
as friend 460–64
gift for connections and perspectives 456–57
hard worker 462
hatred of modern 'lawyering', 457
honesty and candour 457
humility 456–57, 462
humour 457

impartiality xxxv
kindness to the young and shy 456–57, 458
as mentor 456–58
meticulous scholarship xxxvii–xxxviii
originality 456–57
practical jokes 458
prodigious intellect 456
professional courtesy 457
sensitivity to the public and international
interest xxxv
teaching methods, 2–3, 455–56
a towering figure xxxv
Visiting Professor on Investment Arbitration,
King's College, London, 3
warmth and generosity 456–57, 463–64
wide range of interests 462
Veeder, V.V. (themes and issues)
consent 485, 486–88
discrimination/diversity see discrimination
(judicial/arbitral appointments)
enforceability of award 485
finality of award 485, see also finality of
award/appeal/revision
importance of historical cases and institutional
developments, Part xxxv–xxxvi,
1–195, 456–57
issue estoppel, 198
justice, 197–198, 204
Latin tags 198, 246, 285, 322–23, 482, 490
party autonomy, 198
procedural fairness and justice, 197–98,
204, 456, see also procedural fairness
(international arbitration), suggestions
for reform (Veeder)
reform at the right pace, 199, 223
separability, 199
status of EU law vs international law 460
Venezuela Preferential Arbitration (1904) 47–48
Victoria, Queen
and the Alabama Claims Arbitration 33–34,
35–36, 38
and Sir Alexander Cockburn 20
Vigrass, Bertie xxxvi, 452–53
career 452
saviour of the LCIA 380, 384

Washington Treaty (1871)
see also Alabama Claims Arbitration (1872)
Alabama Claims arbitration provisions 15–
16, 17
ambiguity/parties' disagreement over
inclusion of indirect claims in the
Tribunal's mandate xxxvii, 23, 35–36
solving the problem xxxvii, 18–30, 36–37

534 INDEX

Washington Treaty (1871) (*cont.*)
　drafting challenges/obligations 37
　negotiating history xxxvii, 15–17
　　Johnson-Clarendon Treaty (1969) 16–17
　　Thomas Balch's role 15–16, 17
Watson, J (ICC president) 206–7
Wilberforce, Lord
　'a free-standing system', 146–47, 294–95,
　　349–50, 359
　Arbitration Act 1996 and 146, 294–95, 349–50
　green shoots 294, 295

Woolf reforms 221–23
World Bank, access to 491
WTO AB
　budget 436
　EU view of 434–35
　US blocking of new members 39n.1

'Y2K Problem', xlii, 35

Zorn, P (German delegate to the 1899 Hague
　Conference) 45–46